D0881087

THE LIFE AND WORK OF THOMAS HARDY

Also by Michael Millgate

WILLIAM FAULKNER

AMERICAN SOCIAL FICTION: JAMES TO COZZENS

THE ACHIEVEMENT OF WILLIAM FAULKNER

THOMAS HARDY: HIS CAREER AS A NOVELIST

THE COLLECTED LETTERS OF THOMAS HARDY
Volumes I IV (*co-editor with Richard L. Purdy*)

THOMAS HARDY: A BIOGRAPHY

THE LIFE AND WORK OF THOMAS HARDY

by

THOMAS HARDY

Edited by

Michael Millgate

An edition on new principles of the materials previously drawn upon for *The Early Life of Thomas Hardy 1840–1891* and *The Later Years of Thomas Hardy 1892–1928* published over the name of Florence Emily Hardy

THE UNIVERSITY OF GEORGIA PRESS
ATHENS

Introduction © Michael Millgate 1985
Editorial matter and remaining text © The Macmillan Press Ltd 1985

Published in 1985
in the United States of America by
THE UNIVERSITY OF GEORGIA PRESS
Athens, Georgia 30602

ISBN 0-8203-0752-1

Printed in Hong Kong

Library of Congress Cataloging in Publication Data
Hardy, Thomas, 1840–1928.
The life and work of Thomas Hardy.

"An edition on new principles of the materials
previously drawn upon for The early life of Thomas Hardy
1840–1891 and The later years of Thomas Hardy 1892–1928
published over the name of Florence Emily Hardy."
Bibliography: p.
Includes index.
1. Hardy, Thomas, 1840–1928.   2. Authors, English —19th
century—Biography.   I. Millgate, Michael.   II. Hardy,
Florence Emily, 1881–1937. Early life of Thomas Hardy,
1840–1891.   III. Hardy, Florence, Emily, 1881–1937. Later
years of Thomas Hardy, 1892–1928.   IV. Title.
PR4753.A28   1985   823'.8 [B]   84–16185
ISBN 0-8203-0752-1

Contents

List of Illustrations

Acknowledgements

I wish to thank the Trustees of the Estate of the late Miss E. A. Dugdale for permission to quote from the letters of Thomas Hardy and Florence Emily Hardy, the Estate of J. M. Barrie for permission to quote from Sir James Barrie's letters, Sir Christopher Cockerell for permission to quote from his father's letters and diaries, and the following private owners and public institutions for making manuscripts available to me: Mr Frederick B. Adams, Mr Richard L. Purdy, the British Library, Colby College Library, the National Library of Scotland, and the New York Public Library. I am especially grateful to the Curator and Trustees of the Dorset County Museum for granting access during many years to the rich Hardy materials over which they preside and to the Macmillan Press Ltd for allowing me to edit a work of which it owns the copyright. I am also happy to acknowledge, once again, the assistance received from the Social Sciences and Humanities Research Council of Canada, directly through minor research grants administered by the University of Toronto, indirectly through the Council's long-standing and generous support of my work as co-editor of *The Collected Letters of Thomas Hardy*.

My personal debts are also numerous: to Dr Marjorie Garson, Miss Lesley Mann, Mr Gari Harrington, and Mr Keith Lawson, for research assistance of various kinds; to Mrs Freda Gough, for her excellent typing; to Dr Richard H. Taylor, for the valuable ground-clearing work embodied in his edition of *The Personal Notebooks of Thomas Hardy*; and to friends and colleagues—notably Mr John Antell, Dr C. J. P. Beatty, Professor Michael Collie, the late Mr Francis Dalton, Professor Henry Gifford, Mr Robert Gittings, Mr Desmond Hawkins, Mr David Holmes, Professor Heather Jackson, Professor W. J. Keith, Mr Roger Peers, Mr Richard L. Purdy, Mr Michael Rabiger, Professor J. M. Robson, Mrs Lilian Swindall, and the late Mr Malcolm Tomkins—for much help and advice. I owe, as always, a unique debt, at once personal and professional, to my wife,

Jane Millgate, and I take pleasure in paying a special tribute to Mr and Mrs T. W. Jesty for their enthusiastic and extremely productive participation in the preparation of the biographical index to the present volume.

Toronto   M.M.

Introduction

On 30 November 1919 Florence Emily Hardy, Thomas Hardy's second wife, wrote to Sir Frederick Macmillan about a "manuscript" in three copies, one of which Sir Frederick had offered to keep in his safe. She explained that she was anxious to complete final revision of the work, since her health was poor and she feared that, should anything happen to her, the copies of the manuscript at Max Gate "might possibly be destroyed" and the labour of "nearly four years" irrecoverably lost.[1] It seems safe to assume that the manuscript in question was in fact the typescript of the work which the Macmillan firm subsequently published over Mrs Hardy's name as *The Early Life of Thomas Hardy 1840–1891* (London, 1928) and *The Later Years of Thomas Hardy 1892–1928* (London, 1930) and which has come to be generally referred to as the "Life". Presumably, too, this is the typescript of which three copies are still extant, in complete or fragmentary form, in the Dorset County Museum, Dorchester: any deposit in Sir Frederick's safe can only have been temporary. Describing this material in his *Thomas Hardy: A Bibliographical Study*, first published in 1954, Richard L. Purdy made it abundantly clear—as, indeed, he had already done in a paper delivered in 1940–that although the two volumes were published as the work of Florence Hardy they had been very largely written by Hardy himself.[2]

In the years since the revelation of the true circumstances surrounding the composition of the "Life" there has been an understandable interest in the question of just how extensive Florence Hardy's participation actually was. And that question has assumed a new importance with the growing tendency among Hardy critics and biographers to speak of the work as an autobiography—a straightforward, unmediated presentation of the image of himself and his work that Hardy wished to project into the future, on beyond the moment of his death. Obviously such an image is presented, but neither straightforwardly nor without mediation. If the "Life" is to be read as autobiography it begins to matter a great deal whether particular passages were written by Hardy or not; even anecdotes often told by him do not have full autobiographical status if they were not included by Hardy himself, or upon his express instructions. It is for these reasons that the present edition sets out to reconstruct, as nearly as is now possible, the text of what was then—and is now again—called *The Life and Work of Thomas Hardy* as it stood at the time of Hardy's death, after receiving its last reading and revision at his hands.

The roots of the "Life" can perhaps be traced back to the winter of 1912–13 and the mood of intense introspection into which Hardy was thrown by the death of his first wife, Emma Lavinia Hardy, and the discovery of the memoirs and diaries, often hostile to himself, which she had composed in secret during her last years. By August 1914 Hardy had asked his friend Sydney Cockerell to act as his literary executor and promised to send him "some dates, &c." which could be used to refute erroneous stories that might circulate after his death.[3] There seems little doubt, however, that it was in late 1915—the date implied in Florence Hardy's letter to Sir Frederick Macmillan—that the idea of writing about his own childhood first began to take practical shape. Hardy, at the age of seventy-five, was oppressed that winter by the sense of personal mortality aroused by the death of his sister Mary in November 1915, just three years after that of his first wife, by his brother's serious illness, and by distressing illnesses of his own which impaired his activity and kept him indoors for several weeks. He had recently been alarmed at the possibility that his friend Edward Clodd would write indiscreetly about him in a forthcoming volume of reminiscences, and he was still exercised over the publication in 1911 of F. A. Hedgcock's *Thomas Hardy: penseur et artiste*, a work whose biographical chapters had seemed to him both offensive and impertinent.[4] But the deciding factors seem clearly to have been pressure from Cockerell— who pleaded with Hardy "to write down something about yourself—& especially about that youthful figure whose photograph I have got, & of whom you told me that you could think with almost complete detachment"—and the availability of an enthusiastic and competent collaborator in the person of his second wife, who was thirty-nine years younger than her husband, an efficient typist, and an author and journalist in her own right. With Florence's help, Cockerell told Hardy in that same letter of 7 December 1915, it should be possible for him to leave, like Jean-Paul Richter, a rich account of his childhood experiences, "even if, as you have intended, only landmarks and special episodes of the later years are recorded".[5] Cockerell and Florence, indeed, seem to have been at one—perhaps in league—in this matter, and the Prefatory Note to *Early Life** may well have been correct in insisting that it was at Mrs Hardy's initiative and "strong request" that the entire work was first undertaken. If she saw it chiefly as a means of serving her husband and protecting his posthumous reputation, she also cherished the prospect of directing her own literary energies into an undertaking of such obvious importance and scope.

Among the books in Hardy's library was the *Memoir of Thomas Hardy*, an autobiographical account of the public life of a namesake of Hardy's who had figured largely in certain religious controversies at the beginning of the nineteenth century. The work is written in the third person, and in a Preface that earlier Thomas Hardy explains: "I have chosen to write in the third, rather than in the first person, merely, to obviate the necessity of calling the great *I* so repeatedly to my assistance."[6] The third-person autobiographical work is not, of course, an especially unusual phenomenon, but it is pleasant to think that this particular example, which came as a gift from Sydney Cockerell in 1913, might have had a special significance for Hardy. Given the circumstances in which the chronicle of his own life was written—above all the presence of a collaborator who had already written and published books of her own—it would have been an easy step from the idea of a third-person autobiography to that of an authorized biography written by the subject himself but intended for publication after his death over the collaborator's name.

The progress and gradual expansion of the project can be approximately traced through the extensive correspondence with Cockerell which Florence Hardy maintained throughout her husband's last years. "I have been taking notes," she wrote on 23 July 1917, "but find them very difficult to do without constantly appealing to T. H. for verification, and he is now almost at the end of his present job—revising his note-books (they are practically diaries)—and we are going to work together. At least that is what we propose doing. Man proposes—."[7] In the late summer of that

---

* See p. 3; subsequent numbers within parentheses refer to the pages of the present edition.

year there was an interval largely occupied by Hardy's correction of the proofs of *Moments of Vision*: "After this job is finished [Florence told Cockerell on 9 September 1917] he wants to go on giving me facts about his life. I have got as far as the time he started work in London, but a lot can be filled in. He seems quite enthusiastic now about the idea, and of course I love doing it." What had been accomplished by this date seems to be represented by the eighteen-page typescript (now in the Dorset County Museum) which is headed "NOTES OF THOMAS HARDY'S LIFE./ by Florence Hardy./ (taken down in conversation, etc.)" and roughly corresponds to pages 7–49 of the present edition, breaking off in the middle of some anecdotes about Hardy's experiences as an architectural assistant in London in the early 1860s. The phrase "taken down in conversation, etc." tends to suggest, as do some of Florence's comments to Cockerell, that these pages were typed up by her from notes she had jotted down by hand while Hardy talked, and such a procedure would certainly help to explain some of the typescript's curious errors— notably "Thomas Hardy, the third child" for "Thomas Hardy the Third".

By early 1918, however, it is clear that Hardy and his wife had adopted the methods which seem to have prevailed throughout the writing of the "Life" proper: "I am in the midst of reading Colvins 'Keats' to *Him*," Florence told Cockerell on 2 February, "& working hard at notes, which he corrects & adds to daily, as I go along". Hardy, in the privacy of his study, was now doing the writing himself, in longhand, accumulating day by day a manuscript that he was subsequently to destroy. As he wrote he passed the holograph pages on to Florence to be typed up in three copies—the ribbon or "top" copy, eventually destined for the printer; the first carbon, intended to serve as a file copy or "copy of record" for the Hardys themselves; and the second carbon, designated as the "rough" or working copy. Once the typing was done, the basic procedure was for Hardy to make his corrections, revisions, and additions on the rough copy and then pass it to his wife for her to transfer the changes into the file copy; when Hardy had considered the changes further and given them his final approval, it would again be Mrs Hardy who transferred them into the top copy. Sometimes, it appears, changes would be inscribed into the file copy in pencil, to be inked in or erased once Hardy's final decision had been made. Admirably systematic though the procedure was, and specifically designed to prevent any betraying trace of Hardy's holograph from appearing on the printer's copy, Hardy himself seems to have grown impatient with its restrictions, making numerous changes and additions to the file copy in an elaborately calligraphic (hence disguised) hand which he had learned in his architectural days and even allowing that same hand to appear on the top copy from time to time. Very occasionally an item seems to have been transferred directly from the rough copy to the top copy without being entered into the file copy at all and Hardy may even have made one or two insertions into the top copy only. Uncertainty in these matters is compounded by the intrusion of other hands into the typescripts and especially by Florence's customary use of calligraphic formations closely based on Hardy's own.

Work on "the notes", as Florence continued to call them in her letters to Cockerell, persisted throughout the spring and early summer of 1918. By 11 June the year 1895 had been reached; by 22 June Hardy was "busy revising the notes. It seems a great labour, more difficult than actually writing them. I almost wish he would not do it, but the thing is so nearly completed that it would be a pity to stop now." Five days later Florence reported that there had been a bonfire in the garden of Max Gate: "first draft of the notes—1840 to 1892. T. H. insisted." Much of 1918 and 1919, in fact, seems to have been taken up with the sorting out and, more often than not, the destruction of old letters, reviews, proofs, and newspaper cuttings: as Hardy told his friend Sir George Douglas in May 1919, he had been "mainly destroying papers of the last 30 or 40 years, & they raise ghosts".[8] Such housecleaning may in certain respects have constituted a necessary preparation for the continuation of the "Life" up to the date at which Hardy was now writing. A comment within the text itself (346) speaks of the increasing meagreness of Hardy's "memoranda" from the early years of the twentieth century onwards, and in searching through the documents of the past Hardy seized upon those most likely to provide him with at least a minimal narrative framework for those more recent years when his abandonment of fiction had involved a corresponding falling-off from his old habits of notetaking.

In seizing upon such sources, or indeed upon usable passages from his own notebooks and diaries, Hardy did not hesitate to "improve" upon them whenever it seemed necessary or desirable to do so. His references to public events and his datings of private events are for the most part accurate enough, the occasional errors seeming to be the results of carelessness rather than of any deliberate (and pointless) attempt to deceive: thus, two letters received in November 1885 are wrongly assigned to November 1884 (175); a letter said to have been written to Gosse at "about the same time" as a letter arrived from Leslie Stephen was in fact sent a year earlier (231); the death of "the Tranter" (94–5), roughly assigned to the closing months of 1872 or the early months of 1873, actually occurred in August 1870. And one of the rewards of compiling the biographical index for the present volume has been the identification of several—though by no means all—of the local people, often referred to only by their initials or their occupations, who figure in anecdotes originating with Hardy himself or with the gossip and tale-telling of his parents. Much that Hardy included in the "Life", however, simply cannot be verified. Indubitably his are the many extracts from notebooks and diaries ascribed to specific dates, but since the originals of those notebooks and diaries were destroyed[9] after they had been cannibalised in this way it has become impossible to check the accuracy either of the dates or of the transcriptions themselves—impossible to be confident that the proffered text of a note dated, say, 1885, corresponds at all precisely to what Hardy actually wrote in 1885.

It is self-evident that some of the notes must have been reworked, among them the "Life's" one (indirect) allusion to Tryphena Sparks:

In the train on the way to London. Wrote the first four or six lines of "Not a line of her writing have I". It was a curious instance of sympathetic telepathy. The woman whom I was thinking of—a cousin—was dying at the time, and I quite in ignorance of it. She died six days later. The remainder of the piece was not written till after her death. (234)

Although this entire passage is assigned to a single date, it is obvious that the last four or even five sentences cannot have been written on the same day as the first. Even some of the more public documents in the "Life" show signs of alteration: the text of Hardy's March 1902 letter to H. Rider Haggard (335–7) shows minor differences from both the version published in Haggard's *Rural England* (London, 1902) and Hardy's draft in the Dorset County Museum. It is true that some of the many discrepancies between the texts of Hardy's letters and the versions of those same letters that appear in the "Life" may be the consequence of his working from the drafts he had retained and hence failing to incorporate changes that appeared in the letters as actually sent, but he clearly had no compunction about revising notes or letters that no longer struck him as happily phrased or refurbishing diary entries in the light of subsequent events. Florence Hardy acknowledged as much (489n) once she had had pointed out to her the discrepancies between Hardy's letter of 2 February 1915 to Caleb Saleeby as included, on the basis of a transcript supplied by Saleeby himself, in the second Appendix to *Later Years* and the portion of that same letter, as revised by Hardy from the draft he had found in his files, printed earlier in the same volume (399–400)—although one or two of the discrepancies in fact derived from errors made in working from Saleeby's handwriting.

Richard H. Taylor has noted that such changes were sometimes made after the passages in question had been inserted into the "Life" typescripts,[10] and Florence's remark to Cockerell of 22 June 1918 already noted (xiv) does suggest a fairly systematic process of revision; often, however, the alteration seems to have occurred—in Hardy's head, as it were—at the actual moment of transferring the item from its original draft or notebook form to its new biographical context. One of the very few surviving leaves from Hardy's working notebooks happens to contain—heavily overscored, in his usual manner, to indicate that it had been used in some way—the original version of one of the earliest notes that he chose for transcription and, hence, preservation. Though the thought of the "Life" version does not differ, considerable verbal revision has taken place— "minute & microscopic vision required to trace out"[11] becoming "microscopic vision demanded for tracing" (56). It was, perhaps, on a similar basis of fidelity to essentials rather than to details that Hardy allowed himself to minimize in the "Life" the struggles and deprivations of his youth and early manhood and to pass over other important episodes—personal and professional, early and late—without a single word.

By the spring of 1919 work on the "Life" was again in full swing. Florence told Cockerell on 18 April and again on 27 April that she was working on "the notes" several hours a day and it was not until 14 September that she could report that she had been correcting them for what she hoped was the last time. By 30 November, the date of her letter to Sir Frederick Macmillan, the narrative had evidently been completed up to May 1918—that is, to the end of chapter 34 of the present edition. The file-copy typescript in the Dorset County

Museum originally ended at this point and it was here that Hardy inserted a slip in his own hand: "The MS. is in approximately printable condition to here (p. 545)". On 24 June 1920 Cockerell, visiting Max Gate, noted that Florence had showed him "the volume of biographical notes which she has compiled with T.H's assistance. It has been done and redone, and is now finished, a very good thing".[12] Since Cockerell speaks of "volume", in the singular, it was perhaps after this date that the typescripts were divided following the conclusion of chapter 19 and bound up (by Hardy and Florence themselves) into separate volumes that were eventually to correspond to *Early Life* and the first fifteen chapters of *Later Years*.

Although Hardy seems never to have composed a fully fleshed-out narrative for the years subsequent to 1918, he continued to supply his wife with the raw materials from which a continuation of the narrative, up to the time of his death, could eventually be written. A forty-one page typescript, "T.H./Memoranda & Notes towards completing/the remainder of Vol. II (to end of book)", provided an essentially documentary framework—a loose sequence of letters sent and received, succinct summaries of events, and, as the single most extended item, the speech which Hardy delivered at the opening of the "Mellstock Club"—for the period from May 1918 to the end of 1920; it was later repaginated to follow on from the end of the original "Life" typescript and was used almost verbatim in the preparation of *Later Years*. A note in Hardy's hand on the last page of the top copy of the "Memoranda & Notes" typescript—"Refer to Note-Book of Memoranda beginning 1921, for continu- ation"—points clearly to the importance and function of the second of the two "Memoranda" notebooks which have recently been edited by Richard H. Taylor in *The Personal Notebooks of Thomas Hardy*. Its entries, the first dated 1 January 1921, constitute a fragmentary diary for the years up to and including 1927, in- termixed with miscellaneous notes and newspaper cuttings.

It is clear, however, that the working notes and documents for the final stages of the "Life"—an assemblage which both Hardy and Florence came to refer to as the "Materials"—also included notes on separate sheets, drafts of letters that Hardy had picked out as being of particular interest or importance, and even segments of text fully prepared for inclusion. In the Dorset County Museum there survive a series of notes written by Hardy on odd scraps of paper grouped together under the general heading "*Insert in Materials*"; similarly marked for possible inclusion are one or two letter drafts and what is apparently a very late note, headed "(*Materials for Life of T.*)", in which Hardy suggests the possibility of adding a final chapter to the "Life" as a catch-all for anecdotes which seemed worth preserving but had not been fitted into the basic chronological scheme. In the Frederick B. Adams collection are a note on Hardy's attitude to life as compared with Browning's which is marked "For insertion in Life of T. H. if necessary" and pencilled drafts of two *Later Years* segments which also appear (as carbon typescript cut into strips) in "Memoranda II". Clearly Hardy continued to be active in supplying additional materials for the "Life" well beyond the original cut-off date of 1918.

He also went back again and again to those sections of the work that his wife had allowed herself to think of as finished and done with. There was talk of publishing the first part of the "Life" as early as July 1925—partly in response to the appearance in the United States of another unauthorized biography[13]—and in the following spring a suggestion that it should at least be set up in type (presumably to await Hardy's death) was opposed by Hardy himself on the grounds that "knowledge of [t]he contents would leak out, through the printers". In that same letter of 18 April 1926 to Maurice Macmillan Florence Hardy added that her husband was "going over the MS. & correcting it very carefully. This may be wise, or the reverse. However he is greatly interested." Since the "Life" had now been a major preoccupation of Hardy's for something like ten years, the hint of weariness in Florence's words is perhaps understandable. Later, on 14 July 1926, she wrote to Daniel Macmillan, Maurice's son, to explain that although she had hoped to be able to send the typescript, "my husband has found so many fresh notes that he wishes put in, & then most of them have to be taken out again, so there seems no prospect of the work being completed". It was Hardy's death, on 11 January 1928, which brought finally to an end the long process of revision and reconsideration: Florence spoke of her husband as "going through his biography with me a few days before he went to bed with this last illness".[14]

Florence's phrase, "his biography", incorporated a nice, though no doubt unintentional, ambiguity. The book she was shortly to publish was at once a biography of Hardy and a biography by Hardy, a life of himself. Her avoidance of the term "autobiography" was, of course, necessary if the fiction of her own authorship of the work was to be kept up, but it was at the same time an avoidance in which she had long been instructed. As early as 1918 she told

Cockerell that they must never use the word "autobiography" or Hardy, who had so often declared that he would never write such a work, would destroy all the "notes" that he had already completed.[15] The "Life" itself contains a reference to Hardy's "absolute refusal at all times to write his reminiscences" (346; see also 377) and the phrase "autobiographical recollections" that once stood in the typescript of the Prefatory Note (signed "F. E. H." but as much Hardy's own work, in fact, as any other part of the text) was subsequently revised to read "recollections" only (3). This was something more than mere disingenuousness on Hardy's part. He had voiced to Cockerell his belief that he could write objectively and dispassionately about his own younger self, and that conviction, taken together with the largely documentary character of the work he in fact produced, constitutes in itself a challenge to any assumption that the "Life" can or should be read, directly and without qualification, as an autobiography. And the two-volume text that made its appearance as *Early Life* and *Later Years* possesses a still more equivocal claim to be so categorized, not so much because of the practical assistance Hardy received from his wife throughout the process of composition as because of the many changes that she made, on her own initiative and on the advice of others, after her husband's death.

It is of course true that all such changes had been formally authorized by Hardy in advance. In an undated "Private Memorandum./Information for Mrs Hardy in the preparation of a biography" he had specifically declared that the facts to which his wife had had access "are not enjoined to be included every one in the volume, if any should seem to be indiscreet, belittling, monotonous, trivial, provocative, or in other ways unadvisable; neither are they enjoined to be exclusive of other details that may be deemed necessary".[16] Florence was thus empowered to make deletions from and additions to the text that her husband had left, and while it is not always possible to distinguish the changes she made on her own responsibility from those she made while her husband was still alive and in conformity with his directly expressed wishes, it is certainly clear that she exercised her mandate with some freedom, and in ways that combined unyielding devotion to Hardy's memory with frequent disregard of his authorial intentions.

During the weeks and months following Hardy's death his widow saw the publication of the "Life" as the most urgent of her many responsibilities. Before the end of January the entire typescript (presumably the ribbon copy) was sent up to Daniel Macmillan, who acknowledged its receipt on 31 January, read through it himself, and then passed it on a week later to Charles Whibley, part-scholar, part-journalist, who was one of the firm's most trusted readers of manuscripts.[17] Macmillan, returning the typescript to Max Gate on 21 February, seems to have suggested that Whibley might assist in making the book ready for publication, but Florence replied with some firmness that while she would be glad to receive advice she did not need a collaborator, as she could see for herself "a great deal that must be altered". The biography, she added, "is just as it left my husband's hands after a lengthy revision and correction. I should not like it to be pulled to pieces and rewritten, which is what he warned me would happen if I had a too-eminent literary man to help me."[18] In March it was decided to publish the book in two parts; shortly thereafter the typescript was returned to Florence with pencil markings by Whibley to indicate where deletions might be made.[19] As Macmillan reported to the firm's New York office on 3 April 1928, Whibley's main objections had been to the excessive use of Hardy's diaries and especially to the long catalogues of London social engagements.[20]

In her uncertainty and distress Florence had meanwhile been seeking advice from those men whose company and friendship Hardy himself had particularly valued during his last years. Siegfried Sassoon had had to be told of the existence of the "Life" some time previously, a publisher having suggested that he undertake a biography of Hardy himself; he and Florence quarrelled, however, almost immediately after Hardy's death and he seems not to have been involved in any of the book's final stages. T. E. Lawrence, too, had known something of the composition of the "Life" and was apparently approached by Florence early in 1926 with the request that he undertake to prepare the entire work for publication; he had declined the task then, however, and was now in India and simply unavailable for consultation. E. M. Forster, on the other hand, does appear to have read the "Life" through and to have given Florence a certain amount of help and advice: in a letter of 17 April 1928[21] she thanks him for taking trouble over the wheelbarrow episode in the *Graphic*'s serialization of *Tess of the d' Urbervilles*—perhaps an indication that Forster had looked up the relevant issue of the magazine and so assisted in the composition of the three paragraphs that were added to the final page of *Early Life*. Cockerell, too, had read through the "memoir", as he calls it in his diary, during the course of several visits made to Max Gate in February and March 1928 for the purpose of sorting and destroying papers, arranging books, and consulting with Florence about their responsibilities as Hardy's joint literary executors. On 21 March, when Florence was preparing the first volume for the printer, he went through it again, cutting out "some uninteresting passages"—including, no doubt, some of those lists of names whose value Whibley had already questioned.[22]

Far and away the most important of Florence's advisors, however, was Sir James Barrie, to whom she increasingly turned for both practical and emotional support: on 14 June 1928 she confided to Cockerell that it was "as good as settled" that she and Barrie would be married in the following year.[23] Barrie received a copy of the typescript in late January (at the same time as that other copy went off to Daniel Macmillan) and on 3 February he wrote to praise the book as a "remarkable achievement" but also to suggest that its excellence was marred by the "intrusion of so many names of people in society [Hardy] met in London" and by the impression it left "that any silly unimportant reviewer could disturb and make him angry".[24] Just as Florence was about to send off the first volume to Daniel Macmillan at the end of March, "after having made some important additions", she received Barrie's letter of 26 March with its long list of items for possible inclusion—among them, as she told Macmillan, several anecdotes that she had told him herself but subsequently forgotten. Since it seemed important that "the very early part should be as complete as possible", she was holding back the manuscript until the necessary insertions had been made.[25]

Barrie's fifteen numbered suggestions included "The story of the pennies & 'The Boys Own Book'", "That girl he never spoke to & her grave at Stinsford", "The gate in the field where he was sad about his prospects", and "The 'Tess' dairymaids wheeled thro' river in barrow in *Graphic*"; he also asked whether there were any letters surviving from Hardy's London years, 1862–7.[26] The importance of this letter of Barrie's is that it makes possible the identification of several additions to the "Life" typescripts as having been made no earlier than the end of March 1928. Absent from the main text of this present edition, therefore (though included in full in the list of post-Hardyan revisions), are the story of the young Hardy's using money gained by fiddling to purchase *The Boy's Own Book*, the familiar version of Hardy's relationship (or non-relationship) with Louisa Harding, the episode of his reading the *Spectator* review of

Desperate Remedies as he sat on the eweleaze stile, and those paragraphs about the *Graphic*'s serialization of *Tess* to which reference has already been made. In a letter written after he had read the proofs of *Early Life* Barrie supplied the final sentences of the already much-expanded Louisa Harding story as well as the phrase about Hardy's father lacking "the tradesman's soul"; he also suggested a few verbal changes and the correction of a couple of factual statements.[27]

One of the latter, involving the alteration of Hardy's phrase "There was no underground railway" to Barrie's (and *Early Life*'s) "The Underground Railway was just in its infancy", was occasioned by the introduction into the volume of Hardy's letter of 19 February 1862, one of five early letters to Mary Hardy which Florence, prompted by Barrie, eventually extracted from a reluctant Kate Hardy. Four of these letters were included in *Early Life*, Florence rejecting the one "about borrowing a dress-suit" (i.e. that dated 3 November 1862) on the grounds, as she told Cockerell, that Hardy would so much have disliked it.[28] The addition of these letters undoubtedly expanded and enhanced the image of Hardy's young manhood which emerged from the pages of *Early Life*, but it is clear that their presence was in no sense intended by Hardy—who may not even have known of their survival—and that any changes made in them prior to publication (for example, the deletion of Martha Sparks's name from the letter of 17 August 1862) must have been made not by Hardy himself, as has sometimes been assumed, but on his wife's authority and probably on his sister's initiative. Two of the letters to Mary Hardy seem to have been added to the proofs of *Early Life*, and it must also have been at a late stage that Florence inserted the extended descriptions of Max Gate and of Hardy himself that were to occupy the final two and a half pages of chapter 13—and that are here relegated, like the early letters, to the list of post-Hardyan revisions. It was not Hardy himself who wrote that his smile was "of exceptional sweetness", the "nobility of his brow . . . striking", and his "whole aspect . . . almost childlike in its sincerity and simplicity".[29]

Cockerell received and read a set of the proofs of *Early Life* and on 29 June 1928 he travelled down to Max Gate to go over them with Florence. When they sat down to their task that evening after dinner Florence displayed extreme displeasure upon learning that Cockerell had already discussed the proofs with Barrie earlier that same day:[30] doubtless she had her own reasons—personal and literary—for resenting their alliance and for resisting some of the changes they wanted her to make. She seems also to have been distressed by Cockerell's taking it upon himself to extract from Macmillan better terms for the publication of the "Life" than had originally been offered. Florence continued to meet and correspond with Cockerell, mostly on business matters, until the spring of 1929, but she grew more and more distrustful of her partner in the literary executorship and his last involvement with the revision and publication of any portion of the "Life" seems to have occurred on 20 August 1928, when he and Florence spent a morning examining corrections made by Macmillan's reader to the final proofs of the first volume.[31]

It had been agreed, apparently at Cockerell's instigation, that the first volume should not only appear ahead of the second but carry a title capable of standing independently of any possible successor—not *The Life and Work of Thomas Hardy*, Volume One, but *The Early Life of Thomas Hardy 1840–1891*. Florence had entrusted the A. P. Watt literary agency with the negotiation of serial rights to the book (the firm's sticker is still affixed to the front cover of the second copy of the typescript) and six extracts appeared in successive issues of *The Times*, 22–27 October 1928, immediately prior to volume publication by Macmillan (in an edition of 3000 copies) on 2 November 1928. An American edition, published by Macmillan of New York later that same month, was set and printed in the United States from the proofs of the English edition.

Both editions carried a subtitle that was, in all the circumstances, remarkably full and frank: "Compiled largely from contemporary notes, letters, diaries, and biographical memoranda, as well as from oral information in conversations extending over many years". This was, however, very close to what Hardy himself had written (1), and the Prefatory Note to *Early Life*, also his work, makes essentially the same point: "It may be added that in the book generally Mr Hardy's own reminiscent phrases have been used or approximated to whenever they could be remembered or were written down at the time of their expression *viva voce*. On this point great trouble has been taken to secure exactness." (3) Hardy's concern—shared by Florence and the house of Macmillan—was to affirm the absolute authenticity of the book, to establish it permanently and beyond all question as the only authoritative biography. But such phrases seem, in retrospect, dangerously revelatory of the truth of the book's composition and several of the first commentators did come close to identifying a directly autobiographical element: "The style is direct and unpretentious," wrote Desmond MacCarthy in the *Sunday Times* of 4 November 1928 "and we are often conscious as we read that we are listening to the quietly emphatic or quaintly sardonic phrases of Hardy himself, as he talked and remembered".

The reception of *Early Life*, though rarely enthusiastic, was always respectful, and certainly not of a kind to deter Florence from preparing the second volume for publication after an appropriate interval. In a sense, *The Later Years of Thomas Hardy 1892–1928* was much more her book than *Early Life* had been, and the difference was registered—upon the book's publication (again in an edition of 3000 copies) on 29 April 1930—by the absence of any explanatory sub-title: a note preceding the contents page simply stated that "The present volume forms the second and concluding part of a biography, the first part being *The Early Life of Thomas Hardy*, published in 1928". Since Hardy had certified the text as ready for publication only up to the end of 1918, it had remained for Florence to fill out the record of the nine subsequent years of her husband's life, and her reluctance to tackle the task seems to have delayed publication of the volume longer than had originally been anticipated. In practice, she followed very closely the outline Hardy had provided for the years 1919 and 1920, and even in the two chapters that were more specifically hers she made extensive use of the "Memoranda II" notebook and, evidently, of other materials that her husband had, so to speak, prefabricated for her. Near the end of the final chapter she drew for some four pages—often sharply changing both phrasing and tone in the process—upon a diary that she had herself begun to keep in September 1927.[32]

In putting together a complete text for *Later Years* Florence sought, and obtained, from Charles Morgan and Godfrey Elton independent accounts of Hardy's visits to Oxford in 1920 and 1923; she also got Harold Child (whose *Thomas Hardy* of 1916 had met with the approval of Hardy himself) to write a brief description of the three funeral services for Hardy which took place on 16 January 1928. She decided to use only one of the many letters from Hardy to Mrs Henniker that she had available to her—apparently thinking that they might one day make a separate volume—but included, as appendices, at the last moment small groups of Hardy's letters to Caleb Saleeby and to Edward Clodd. In her haste, however, she failed to notice that one letter from each group had already been used in the main body of the text: the letter to Saleeby of 2 February 1915 remains in Appendix II, accompanied by Florence's embarrassed footnote, but the letter to Clodd of 22 March 1904 was evidently removed from Appendix III at the very last minute—in the American edition, indeed, it still stands. In those first fifteen chapters of *Later Years* to which Hardy had explicitly given his *imprimatur* the main results of Florence's intervention are visible in the insertion of several letters (including at least one to herself) and in the excision of much of the social chronicling and hostility towards critics that Barrie had so strongly registered when he first read the manuscript right through. It is also clear that she deleted (as in *Early Life*) a number of references to her predecessor, Emma Lavinia Hardy, whose role in the overall narrative was in any case so much more prominent than her own.

There seems little doubt, however, that one of Hardy's chief motivations and satisfactions in writing the "Life" had consisted in the prospect of saying at last what had for so long remained unsaid—of attacking, covertly and from beyond the grave, those critics from whom he had so unreasonably and yet so genuinely suffered throughout his career.[33] And if it is easy enough to sympathize with Sir James Barrie's objections to the long lists of metropolitan notables it is also necessary to try to understand the reasons for their presence in Hardy's text.[34] In part they must have provided a means of filling out the record of years whose really significant events—the onset of middle-age, the final desolation of his first marriage, the abortive affairs of the heart with other women—were too private and painful for public revelation. In part they must have reflected Hardy's active enjoyment of a world which had at the very least a colour, a glamour, perhaps a quality of cooking, certainly an appreciation of his distinction as an author, which was pleasantly at odds with the drabness of his early years and, indeed, with the later stages of his first marriage. But it seems equally likely that such social details were supplied for the simple reason that Hardy thought people would be interested in them—interested in his having met Lord Salisbury or even "Mr Stephen (a director of the North-western Railway)" (276) rather than in Lord Salisbury's and Mr Stephen's having met Thomas Hardy.

The reason given in the Prefatory Note for Hardy's opposition to biographies is that he "had not sufficient admiration for himself"

(3), and in curious and complicated ways there is perhaps much truth in the statement. The very miscellaneity of the "Life" can be interpreted as an attempt to make entertaining what Hardy himself saw as rather ordinary, uneventful, and dull, and while the early exaggeration of his family's class and economic status and the later allusions to friendships with the rich and famous may seem at first glance the products of a somewhat simple-minded vanity they may conceivably reflect an unusual modesty, a sense on Hardy's part that he was in himself, as a man divorced from his writings, a profoundly uninteresting person who had lived an unexciting life and who therefore needed all the external support and social consequence he could muster in order to cut a sufficient figure in his own life story. He professed to take "no interest in himself as a personage" (408; see also 346), and it is almost as if the "Life" were being directed towards the creation of a self who might provide a fit subject for just such a biographical exercise.

Understandable as it is, then, that Mrs Hardy, committed to the defence of her husband's reputation, should have wished to obliterate the more bitter and unforgiving of Hardy's attacks on his critics and the more tedious of his social chronicles, there can be no doubt that the omission of such passages from *Early Life* and *Later Years* did substantially depart from Hardy's own intentions and present him in terms other than those in which he himself had (wisely or unwisely) chosen to appear. So, too, did her extensive insertions and, indeed, all the changes she made of her own accord or at the instigation of others, and it is essential to keep in mind that the voice which speaks through *Early Life* and *Later Years*, though always faithful to Hardy's memory, is not necessarily Hardy's own, that much of what he wanted said does not find a place in the final text, that several sections of that text either had been or would have been rejected by him, and that the part played by Florence in her various roles of compiler, editor, and part-author was at least sufficient to justify the appearance of her name on the title-pages, even if it ought properly to have been linked there with that of Thomas Hardy himself.

What the present edition therefore offers, for the first time, is a text that can be unequivocally read and accepted as an integral part of the Hardy canon. By recovering—with as much fidelity as the surviving evidence will allow—the wording that stood at the time of Hardy's death, and by recording (in the list of selected post-Hardyan revisions) the biographically significant changes made for

Early Life and *Later Years*, it becomes possible to see just what Hardy himself wrote and what his widow subsequently altered and to confront *The Life and Work of Thomas Hardy* as an entirely Hardyan text—as an autobiography, in short, though scarcely as a characteristic representative of that genre.

That Hardy himself emerges less attractively from the pages of this new edition than from the pages of *Early Life* and *Later Years* there can be little doubt. His writing is ungainly at times, his organization repetitious; he places what seems an excessive valuation on his *entrée* into fashionable London circles; he displays a consistent hostility, ranging from irritability to outright ferocity, in responding to the pronouncements of contemporary critics. But that is how Hardy was in his old age, and no useful purpose is now served by following Florence Hardy and Sir James Barrie in their well-meaning but ultimately misguided attempts to edit his text in the interests of presenting him as other than he really was. It is, after all, in Florence's section of the book that a wise comment is made on the composition and publication of the self-justifying "Apology" to *Late Lyrics and Earlier*:

> Some of his friends regretted this preface, thinking that it betrayed an oversensitiveness to criticism which it were better the world should not know. But sensitiveness was one of Hardy's chief characteristics, and without it his poems would never have been written, nor indeed, the greatest of his novels. He used to say that it was not so much the force of the blow that counted, as the nature of the material that received the blow. (448)

NOTES

1. All cited letters to members of the Macmillan firm are in the British Library (subsequently referred to as BL).
2. Purdy, *Thomas Hardy: A Bibliographical Study* (London, 1954), 266–7, 272–3; Edward Larocque Tinker, "New Editions, Fine and Otherwise", *New York Times Book Review*, 12 May 1940, 25. The pre-publication materials for the "Life" in the Dorset County Museum (subsequently DCM) are more fully listed in Richard H. Taylor (ed.) *The Personal Notebooks of Thomas Hardy* (London, 1978) 205–8.
3. TH to Cockerell, 28 August 1914, Colby College Library.
4. Clodd's *Memories* (London, 1916) in fact mentions TH only briefly; the

margins of TH's copy of Hedgcock's volume (Paris, 1911), now in DCM, carry numerous critical comments in his hand.

5. Cockerell to TH, 7 December 1915, DCM.
6. *Memoir of Thomas Hardy . . . Written by Himself* (London, 1832) viii; TH's copy is in DCM.
7. All cited letters from Florence Hardy (subsequently FEH) to Cockerell are in the collection of Richard L. Purdy.
8. TH to Douglas, 7 May 1919, National Library of Scotland; Mary Hardy's death had earlier prompted Douglas, like Cockerell, to ask if TH were going to write his reminiscences (Douglas to TH, 28 November 1915, DCM).
9. Some of them were destroyed by TH himself, others by Cockerell after TH's death.
10. *Personal Notebooks*, xiv–xv.
11. The fragment is in DCM, on the back of TH's sketch of the view from the window of 16 Westbourne Park Villas.
12. Cockerell diary, BL.
13. Ernest Brennecke, Jr, *The Life of Thomas Hardy* (New York, 1925); at TH's prompting the firm of Macmillan threatened an action for breach of copyright against any publisher or bookseller who introduced the book into England (*The Times*, 11 April 1925).
14. FEH to Daniel Macmillan, 19 January 1928.
15. FEH to Cockerell, 7 February 1918.
16. DCM.
17. FEH to D. Macmillan, 28 January 1928; D. Macmillan to FEH, 31 January 1928, copy in Macmillan letterbooks, BL; "Record of Manuscripts", Macmillan Papers, BL.
18. "Record of Manuscripts", BL; FEH to D. Macmillan, 22 February 1928. TH's "Private Memorandum"—of which Macmillan had perhaps seen a copy—in fact specified that "The whole book before printing should be put into correct literary form, by an experienced writer and scholar. Should Mrs Hardy wish that her name alone should stand on the title page, such a one might possibly be found for her who would do what was required if paid a reasonable fee." FEH was, of course, already obtaining advice from Barrie, Cockerell and others.
19. FEH to D. Macmillan, 18 and 23 March 1928; D. Macmillan to FEH, 29 March 1928 (letterbook copy), BL.
20. New York Public Library, Manuscripts Division; a copy of Whibley's report still accompanies this letter.
21. King's College, Cambridge.
22. Cockerell diary.
23. Cockerell diary.
24. Viola Meynell (ed.) *Letters of J. M. Barrie* (London, 1942) 152.
25. FEH to D. Macmillan, 28 March 1928.
26. Barrie to FEH, 26 March 1928, DCM.
27. Barrie to FEH, 24 June 1928, typed transcript, DCM.
28. FEH to Cockerell, 23 May 1928; the letter FEH omitted appears in Richard Little Purdy and Michael Millgate (eds) *The Collected Letters of Thomas Hardy*, I (Oxford 1978) 2–3.
29. *Early Life*, 227–8.

30. Cockerell diary.
31. Cockerell diary.
32. The diary, written in an exercise book, is in DCM; only brief fragments survive of the pocket diaries kept by FEH at earlier periods.
33. "The Unconquerable", an unpublished story by Florence Hardy, has a suspiciously Hardyan plot about a dead man who succeeds—partly by selecting his own biographer—in exercising a posthumous control over the lives of others. The MS (DCM) is typed but carries revisions in TH's hand.
34. That Hardy was himself a little embarrrassed by them is suggested by the comment (certainly his) on p. 210.

Editorial Procedures

This edition seeks to deal in a straightforward yet responsible manner with what is in fact an extremely complex editorial problem. The aim being pursued throughout is recovery of the text "intended" by Hardy himself, but there are many elements in the situation which render such an ambition impossible of ideal achievement. An editor, lacking that holograph manuscript Hardy himself destroyed, is forced to depend upon a typescript which the author did not prepare and whose spelling, punctuation, hyphenation and layout he seems never to have reviewed in any systematic fashion. That typescript, moreover, was prepared in three copies, a ribbon copy and two carbons (see Introduction, pp. xiii–xiv) and all these were subjected to extensive revision. Only the second copy (the first carbon) has survived in its entirety, so that evidence of the precise source and occasion of a particular textual change is often lacking; but in those sections for which, on the other hand, two or even all three versions have survived problems of another sort are posed by the existence of variant readings—often the result of inaccurate copying from one version to another or into two or more versions from a common external source (such as a notebook). Above all, there is the difficulty presented by the sheer density of the cancellations, erasures, revisions, and insertions, in different hands and of different dates, which have resulted from the repeated handling of all three copies by Hardy and his wife, and subsequently by others, and which it would be impossible for an edition such as this to reflect in any comprehensive way.

It would, of course, be feasible to regard the "Life" as a work of shared or at any rate successive authorship, the product of a collaboration between Thomas Hardy and Florence Emily Hardy. Viewed from such a standpoint, the already published texts of *Early Life* and *Later Years* could be said to be reasonably adequate, needing only minor correction here and there. They could also very truthfully be said to embody the kind of thoroughgoing copyediting that, in certain respects, the original typescript sorely needed. If a new edition were to be undertaken along these lines the top copy of the typescript would presumably constitute the editor's preferred copy-text—although it would in fact be available only for fragments of the whole. Numerous changes to both the published volumes must have been entered for the first time on the proofs, but no proofs appear to have survived.

When, however, the attempt is made, as now, to edit the "Life" as an essentially Hardyan work, the preferred copy-text for the greater part of the book becomes (in the absence of Hardy's own manuscript) that second copy of the typescript (TS2)—the first carbon—which served as a record of the revisions and insertions to which Hardy had given his approval. It needs to be made clear, however, that "copy-text" here refers to that *layer* of the heavily-corrected typescript which appears to embody Hardy's final decisions and intentions. Since Mrs Hardy's detailed interventions during her husband's lifetime cannot always be distinguished from those made after his death, identification of the "Hardyan" layer becomes at times a difficult and, indeed, impossible task. In these circumstances, and at the acknowledged cost of almost certainly incorporating a number of post-Hardyan readings, it is the policy of the present edition to follow the "standing" (i.e. uncancelled) readings of the copy-texts—even when those readings are in Florence Hardy's hand—unless there seem to be good and demonstrable reasons not to do so. Fortunately the more extensive of Mrs Hardy's independent additions and deletions can in general be identified with a greater degree of confidence. Many passages cancelled in the typescripts as they now stand—especially those struck through with a roughness and boldness which Hardy himself, with his neat working habits, would neither have practised nor countenanced—were clearly part of the text at the time of his death and have accordingly been reinstated in the copy-texts. It has, on the other hand, been possible to reject, as clearly or probably dating from after Hardy's death, not just passages substituted for such non-Hardyan cancellations but also those dealing with matters mentioned in Barrie's letters to Mrs Hardy. Extensive passages present in *Early Life* and *Later Years* are, of course, absent from the typescripts altogether.

Where application of these principles seems straightforward, they are followed without additional explanation, but passages whose copy-text status seems to require justification—or is, indeed, genuinely in doubt—are discussed in the Textual Notes. Scholars interested in pursuing such specifically editorial matters are referred especially to these notes and to the microfilms of the "Life" typescripts obtainable from EP Microform Limited, East Ardsley, Wakefield, WF3 2JN, and already available in a number of institutional libraries.

For the first nineteen chapters of the book (those originally published as *Early Life*) only the one complete typescript is in existence, so that TS2 is necessarily the copy-text for both substantives (the actual words of the text) and accidentals (punctuation, spelling, etc.)—except that substantive variants in Hardy's holograph appearing on the surviving leaves of the ribbon copy (TS1) are accepted into the present edition as representing later authorial revisions. For chapters 20–31 and part of chapter 32—up to "in the title, went for them" on p. 396—both TS2 and the "rough" copy (TS3) are extant, and there is some temptation to select the latter as copy-text simply because it was, as its cover insists, Hardy's working-copy and because it carries, as such, a higher incidence of insertions and corrections in his hand. It is clear, however, that TS2 must be regarded as superseding TS3: several leaves of TS2 (for example, fols. 337, 338, and 338A) were re-typed during Hardy's lifetime, incorporating in the process matter which had been added in holograph to the corresponding leaves of TS3, and Hardy subsequently made to the re-typed pages corrections which are not present anywhere in TS3. Since, too, TS2 was the copy with which Florence Hardy and her advisers seem chiefly to have worked, it shows more clearly than TS3 the processes of deletion and expansion to which the text was subjected after Hardy's death. But while TS2 remains copy-text, the availability of TS3 does permit a more confident identification of some of Hardy's own readings, and in the case of any discrepancy between the reading of a TS2 insertion in Florence Hardy's hand and the reading of the same insertion in Hardy's hand in TS3, the latter is followed—silently if only accidentals are involved.

TS2 thus remains copy-text not just for chapters 20–31 and the first part of chapter 32 but also for the latter part of 32 and the whole of chapters 33 and 34—right to the point, in fact, at which TS2 itself concludes. This situation is not affected by the survival of TS1 for most of chapter 32 and all of chapter 33, except in so far as TS1 substantive variants in Hardy's holograph continue to be accepted as later authorial readings. For chapters 35 and 36 copy-text becomes copy 3 (MN3) of "Memoranda & Notes towards completing the remainder of Vol. II". MN3 has been selected in the absence of copy 2 and preferred to the surviving ribbon copy (MN1) on the grounds that the latter seems not to have been much worked on during Hardy's lifetime (or afterwards) nor to have had transferred to it all of the late revisions he made to MN3. A fresh typescript (MNR) seems to have been prepared after Hardy's death to serve as printer's copy for the corresponding pages of *Later Years*; now incomplete, it has in any case no standing as a potential copy-text for the present edition.

The Hardyan text concludes with the final paragraph of chapter 36, but the present edition also contains, by way of supplementation, the two additional chapters, 37 and 38, which were written entirely by Florence Hardy—though incorporating much material her husband had left for just such a purpose. Since these chapters were Florence's work, and especially since none of the surviving drafts represents printer's copy, the published form of *Later Years* (chapters 18 and 19) has been taken as copy-text, though with some modification of details by reference to the drafts and to available texts of the contributions made directly by Godfrey Elton and Margaret Carter; substantive emendations are recorded in the list of Editorial Emendations. *Later Years* (again modified by reference to Mrs Hardy's sources) is also copy-text for the three appendices, all introduced by Mrs Hardy and retained here for the sake of including all those elements which have formed part of the "Life" in its printed forms. For Florence's use of notes and other documents prepared by Hardy before his death, see the "Memoranda II" notebook as transcribed by Richard H. Taylor, *Personal Notebooks*, 43–102; for material which she considered using but ultimately rejected, see *Personal Notebooks*, 276–87.

The substantives of the identified Hardyan "layer" of the copy-texts are followed in all respects, except that:

(a) as indicated above, readings in Hardy's own hand in TS1 are preferred to the readings in his hand in the copy-texts themselves;

(b) as also indicated above, readings in Hardy's own hand in other non-copy-text forms are preferred to readings not in his hand in the copy-texts themselves;

(c) errors in the titles of Hardy's own works have been corrected whenever it seemed appropriate to do so;

(d) abbreviated forms of Hardy's own name are spelled out in full,

"T.H." being given as "Thomas Hardy" and "T.H.2" as Thomas Hardy the Second";

(e) a few textual problems have been resolved by the additional introduction of substantive or accidental readings not available in any form in the copy-texts themselves.

All such departures from the copy-texts are recorded in the list headed "Editorial Emendations in the Copy-texts".

The accidentals of the copy-texts—including the many Hardyan dashes which Barrie persuaded Florence to replace by commas— have also been followed whenever possible. Some corrections of spelling, punctuation, and lay-out have been made, however, as part of the necessary process of preparing for publication texts for whose non-verbal features (in so far as they were typed by Florence) Hardy himself was not directly responsible. Thus:

(a) spelling and punctuation errors have been sparingly but silently corrected;

(b) book and journal titles are always given in italics, those of poems, stories, and essays in roman type within quotation marks;

(c) extracts from letters are indented as set-off quotations in order to permit omission of the quotation marks placed in the typescripts at the beginning of each quoted paragraph, including each line of the address;

(d) dates and times of day are given as numerals, omitting "st", "nd", "rd", and "th" except in quotations or in such constructions as "the 2nd of September"; other numerals lower than 100 are spelled out as words;

(e) standard abbreviations of Latin origin (viz., i.e., e.g.) are left unitalicised as Hardy himself customarily left them, and "&c." is given as "etc.";

(f) periods are supplied following "Rev." (Hardy's usual abbreviation for "Reverend") and "St." but not following "Mr", "Mrs", or "Dr".

Such standardization has to some extent been relaxed in handling quotations from diaries, notebooks, and letters—whether by Hardy himself or by others—for the sake of those features of the originals (for example, the eccentric capitalization found in Mrs Procter's letters) which have survived transcription and seem worth preserving further. Corrections of spelling and punctuation have been kept to a minimum (especially when the passage is inscribed in Hardy's own hand) and titles, quotations, and abbreviations are left precisely as they appear in the copy-texts.

Specification of the year(s) and of Hardy's age at the top of each opening is provided in accordance with Hardy's own directions on fol. 5 of TS2: "every left hand page onward to bear date, right hand age".

The textual apparatus to the edition, placed after the main text and its appendices, comprises the list of editorial emendations in the copy-texts, the list of biographically significant post-Hardyan revisions (that is, those made on Florence Hardy's responsibility after Hardy's death and incorporated into *Early Life* and *Later Years*), and a sequence of textual notes keyed to the main text and cross-referenced, where necessary, to the two preceding lists. The index incorporates brief identifications—so far as has proved possible—of all persons referred to, either directly or indirectly, in the main text and its appendices.

A Note on the Illustrations

When Florence Hardy drew up the lists of illustrations for inclusion in *Early Life* and *Later Years*—assisted on the latter occasion by Harold Macmillan—she did so on the basis of only rather meagre guidance from her late husband. Hardy had indeed left behind a list of possible illustrations (see *The Personal Notebooks of Thomas Hardy*, p. 289) but he seems to have given little thought to their selection, and none at all to the question of where they should be located within the work as published. The present edition follows Hardy's instructions in so far as they are specific, supplementing that small group of illustrations with a selection from among those chosen by Florence.

Hardy's own plan of the gallery of Stinsford Church was bound up with the typescript of the first volume of the "Life" and occurs here (as in *Early Life*) in its original position within the main body of the text. His list further directs that portraits be included of his parents, his first wife (Emma Lavinia Gifford), and his second wife, Florence herself; such portraits all appeared in either *Early Life* or *Later Years* and they reappear here. Florence did not, however, use either of the photographs of herself that Hardy had recommended, substituting instead the crayon sketch drawn by William Strang—and assigning it in the "List of Illustrations" to the year 1918, though in fact it dates from 1910. The present edition therefore supplies, in addition to the Strang portrait, a photograph which seems to be one of those Hardy had in mind: "from coloured photo, by Swaine, showing her seated writing".

All the remaining items in Hardy's list are given as "optional": first, any other portraits of the four people already mentioned or of "other relatives"; second, "any of T. H. himself. (Perhaps the one at 21 would be interesting.)"; and, third, illustrations "of houses &c"., if deemed "desirable". The present edition follows Florence in including the photograph of Hardy at the age of twenty-one; it also selects from among the portraits of Hardy and the illustrations of houses that were used in *Early Life* and *Later Years* but excludes (since Hardy nowhere makes mention of them) the facsimile reproductions of manuscripts.

The Life and Work
of
Thomas Hardy

Compiled largely from contemporary notes, books of memoranda, letters, miscellaneous writings and diaries of a biographical nature written for his private use, together with oral information in conversations extending over many years.

Prefatory Note

Mr Hardy's feeling for a long time was that he would not care to have his life written at all. And though often asked to record his recollections he would say that he "had not sufficient admiration for himself" to do so. But later, having observed many erroneous and grotesque statements advanced as his experiences, and a so-called "Life" published as authoritative, his hand was forced, and he agreed to my strong request that the facts of his career should be set down for use in the event of it proving necessary to print them.

To this end he put on paper headings of chapters, etc., and, in especial, memories of his early days whenever they came into his mind, also communicating many particulars by word of mouth from time to time. In addition a great help has been given by the dated observations which he made in pocket-books, etc., during the years of his novel-writing, apparently with the idea that if one followed the trade of fiction one must take notes, rather than from natural tendency, for when he ceased fiction and resumed the writing of verses he left off note-taking, except to a very limited extent.

The opinions quoted from these pocket-books and fugitive papers are often to be understood as his passing thoughts only, temporarily jotted there for consideration, and not as permanent conclusions—a fact of which we are reminded by his frequent remarks on the tentative character of his theories.

As such memoranda were not written with any view to their being printed, at least as they stood, and hence are often abrupt, a few words of explanation have been given occasionally.

It may be added that in the book generally Mr Hardy's own reminiscent phrases have been used or approximated to whenever they could be remembered or were written down at the time of their expression *viva voce*. On this point great trouble has been taken to secure exactness.

Some incidents of his country experiences herein recorded may be considered as trivial, or as not strictly appertaining to a personal biography, but they have been included from a sense that they embody customs and manners of old West-of-England life that have now entirely passed away.

F. E. H.

PART I

Early Life and Architecture

CHAPTER I

Birth and Boyhood

1840–1855: *Aet.* 1–15

June 2nd, 1840. It was in a lonely and silent spot between woodland and heathland that Thomas Hardy was born, about eight o'clock on Tuesday morning the 2nd of June 1840, the place of his birth being the seven-roomed rambling house that stands easternmost of the few scattered dwellings called Higher Bockhampton, in the parish of Stinsford, Dorset. The domiciles were quaint, brass-knockered, and green-shuttered then, some with green garden-doors and white balls on the posts, and mainly occupied by lifeholders of substantial footing like the Hardys themselves. In the years of his infancy, or shortly preceding it, the personages tenanting these few houses included two retired military officers, one old navy lieutenant, a small farmer and tranter, a relieving officer and registrar, and an old militiaman whose wife was the monthly nurse that assisted Thomas Hardy into the world. These being mostly elderly people the place was at one time nicknamed "Veterans' Valley". It was also dubbed "Cherry Alley", the lane or street leading through it being planted with an avenue of cherry-trees. But the lifeholds fell into hand, and the quaint residences with their trees, clipped hedges, orchards, white gatepost-balls, the naval officer's masts and weather-cocks, have now perished every one, and have been replaced by labourers' brick cottages and other new farm buildings, a convenient pump occupying the site of the mossy well and bucket. The Hardy homestead, too, is much demeaned and reduced, having comprised, in addition to the house, two gardens (one of them part orchard), a

7

horse-paddock, and sand-and-gravel pits, afterwards exhausted and overgrown: also stabling and like buildings since removed; while the leaves and mould washed down by rains from the plantation have risen high against the back wall of the house that was formerly covered with ivy. The wide, brilliantly white chimney-corner, in his child-time such a feature of the sitting-room, is also gone.

Some Wordsworthian lines—the earliest discoverable of young Hardy's attempts in verse—give with obvious and naïve fidelity the appearance of the paternal homestead at a date nearly half a century before the birth of their writer, when his grandparents settled there, after his great-grandfather had built for their residence the first house in the valley.[1]

---

[1] The poem runs as follows:

DOMICILIUM

It faces west, and round the back and sides
High beeches, bending, hang a veil of boughs,
And sweep against the roof. Wild honeysucks
Climb on the walls, and seem to sprout a wish
(If we may fancy wish of trees and plants)
To overtop the apple-trees hard by.

Red roses, lilacs, variegated box
Are there in plenty, and such hardy flowers
As flourish best untrained. Adjoining these
Are herbs and esculents; and farther still
A field; then cottages with trees, and last
The distant hills and sky.

Behind, the scene is wilder. Heath and furze
Are everything that seems to grow and thrive
Upon the uneven ground. A stunted thorn
Stands here and there, indeed; and from a pit
An oak uprises, springing from a seed
Dropped by some bird a hundred years ago.

　　　　In days bygone—
Long gone—my father's mother, who is now
Blest with the blest, would take me out to walk.
At such a time I once inquired of her
How looked the spot when first she settled here.
The answer I remember. "Fifty years

The family, on Hardy's paternal side, like all the Hardys of the south-west, derived from the Jersey le Hardys who had sailed across to Dorset for centuries—the coasts being just opposite. Hardy often thought he would like to restore the "le" to his name, and call himself "Thomas le Hardy"; but he never did so. The Dorset Hardys were traditionally said to descend in particular from a Clement le Hardy, Baily of Jersey, whose son John settled hereabouts in the fifteenth century, having probably landed at Wareham, then a port. They all had the characteristics of an old family of spent social energies, that were revealed even in the Thomas Hardy of this memoir (as in his father and grandfather) who never cared to take advantage of the many worldly opportunities that his popularity and esteem as an author afforded him. They had dwelt for many generations in or near the valley of the River Froom or Frome, which extends inland from Wareham, occupying various properties whose sites lay scattered about from Woolcombe, Toller-Welme, and Up-Sydling (near the higher course of the river), down the stream to Dorchester, Weymouth, and onward to Wareham, where the Froom flows into Poole Harbour. It was a family whose diverse Dorset sections included the Elizabethan Thomas Hardy who endowed the Dorchester Grammar School, the Thomas Hardy captain of the *Victory* at Trafalgar, Thomas Hardy an influential burgess of Wareham, Thomas Hardy of Chaldon, and others of local note, the tablet commemorating the first-mentioned being still in St. Peter's Church, Dorchester, though shifted from its original position in the "Hardy Chapel", the inscription running as follows:

> Have passed since then, my child, and change has marked
> The face of all things. Yonder garden-plots
> And orchards were uncultivated slopes
> O'ergrown with bramble bushes, furze and thorn:
> That road a narrow path shut in by ferns,
> Which, almost trees, obscured the passer-by.
>
> "Our house stood quite alone, and those tall firs
> And beeches were not planted. Snakes and efts
> Swarmed in the summer days, and nightly bats
> Would fly about our bedrooms. Heathcroppers
> Lived on the hills, and were our only friends;
> So wild it was when first we settled here."

TO THE MEMORYE OF
THOMAS HARDY OF MELCOMBE REGIS, IN THE
COUNTY OF DORSETT, ESQUIER, WHOE ENDOWED
THIS BORROUGHE WTH A YEARELY REVENEW OF
50*l*.; AND APPOYNTED OUT OF IT, TO BE EM-
PLOYED FOR Y^E BETTER MAYNTENANCE OF A
PREACHER, 20*l*.; A SCHOOLEMASTER, TWENTY
POUNDES; AN HUISHER, TWENTY NOBLES; THE
ALMES WOMEN FIVE MARKS. THE BAYLIVES
AND BURGISSES OF DORCHESTER, IN TESTIMONY
OF THEIR GRATITUDE, AND TO COMMEND TO
POSTERITY AN EXAMPLE SO WORTHY OF IMITA-
TION, HATH ERECTED THIS MONUMENT.
HE DYED THE 15 OF OCTOBER, ANNO DO: 1599.

But at the birth of the subject of this biography the family had declined, so far as its Dorset representatives were concerned, from whatever importance it once might have been able to claim there; and at his father's death the latter was, it is believed, the only landowner of the name in the county, his property being, besides the acre-and-half lifehold at Bockhampton, a small freehold farm at Talbothays, with some houses there, and about a dozen freehold cottages and a brick-yard and kiln elsewhere. The Talbothays farm was a small outlying property standing detached in a ring fence, its possessors in the reign of Henry VIII having been Talbots, from a seventeenth-century daughter of whom Hardy borrowed the name of Avis or Avice in *The Well-Beloved*.

On the maternal side he was Anglo-Saxon, being descended from the Childs, Chiles, or Childses (who gave their names to the villages of Child-Okeford, Chil-Frome, Childhay, etc.), the Swetmans, and other families of north-west Dorset, who were small proprietors of lands there in the reign of Charles the First (see Hutchins' *History of Dorset*); and also from the Hanns or Hands of the Pidele Valley, Dorset, and earlier of the Vale of Blackmoor. (In the parish register of Affpuddle the spelling is Hann.) The Swetmans and the Childses seem to have been involved in the Monmouth rising and one of the former to have been brought before Jeffreys, "for being absent from home att the tyme of the Rebellion". As his name does not appear in the lists of those executed he was probably transported, and this connection with Monmouth's adventures and misfortunes seems to have helped to becloud the family prospects of the maternal line of Hardy's ancestry, if they had ever been bright.

Several traditions survived in the family concerning the Rebellion. An indubitably true one was that after the Battle of Sedgemoor two of the Swetman daughters—Grace and Leonarde —were beset in their house by some of the victorious soldiery, and only escaped violation by slipping from the upper rooms down the back stairs into the orchard. It is said that Hardy's great-grandmother could remember them as very old women. Part of the house, now in the possession of the Earl of Ilchester, and divided into two cottages, is still standing with its old Elizabethan windows; but the hall and open oak staircase have disappeared, and also the Ham-Hill stone chimneys. The spot is called "Townsend".

Another tradition, of more doubtful authenticity, is that to which the short story by Hardy called "The Duke's Reappearance" approximates. Certainly a mysterious man did come to Swetman after the battle, but it was generally understood that he was one of Monmouth's defeated officers.

Thomas Hardy's maternal grandmother Elizabeth, or Betty, was the daughter of one of those Swetmans by his wife Maria Childs, sister of the Christopher Childs who married into the Cave family, became a mining engineer in Cornwall, and founded the *West Briton* newspaper, his portrait being painted when he was about eighty by Sir Charles Eastlake. The traditions about Betty, Maria's daughter, were that she was tall, handsome, had thirty gowns, was an omnivorous reader, and one who owned a stock of books of exceptional extent for a yeoman's daughter living in a remote place.[1]

She knew the writings of Addison, Steele, and others of the *Spectator* group, almost by heart, was familiar with Richardson and Fielding, and, of course, with such standard works as *Paradise Lost* and *The Pilgrim's Progress*. From the old medical books in her possession she doctored half the village, her sheet-anchor being Culpeper's *Herbal* and *Dispensary*; and if ever there was any doubt

---

[1] A curious reminiscence by her daughter bears testimony to her rather striking features. She was crossing the fields with the latter as a child, a few years after Waterloo, when a gentleman shouted after her: "A relation of Wellington's? You must be! That nose!" He excitedly followed them till they were frightened, jumping over stiles till they reached home. He was found to be an officer who had fought under Wellington, and had been wounded in the head, so that he was at times deranged.

as to the position of particular graves in the churchyard, the parson, sexton, and relatives applied to her as an unerring authority.

But alas for her fortunes! Her bright intelligence in a literary direction did not serve her in domestic life. After her mother's death she clandestinely married a young man of whom her father strongly disapproved. The sturdy yeoman, apparently a severe and unyielding parent, never forgave her, and never would see her again. His unbending temper is illustrated by the only anecdote known of him. A fortune-telling gipsy had encamped on the edge of one of his fields, and on a Sunday morning he went to order her away. Finding her obdurate he said: "If you don't take yourself off I'll have you burnt as a witch!" She pulled his handkerchief from his pocket, and threw it into her fire, saying, "If that burn I burn". The flames curled up round the handkerchief, which was his best, of India silk, but it did not burn, and she handed it back to him intact. The tale goes that he was so impressed by her magic that he left her alone.

Not so long after the death of this stern father of Elizabeth's— Hardy's maternal great-grandfather—her husband also died, leaving her with several children, the youngest only a few months old. Her father, though in comfortable circumstances, had bequeathed her nothing, and she was at her wit's end to maintain herself and her family, if ever widow was. Among Elizabeth's children there was one, a girl, of unusual ability and judgment, and an energy that might have carried her to incalculable issues. This was the child Jemima, the mother of Thomas Hardy. By reason of her parent's bereavement and consequent poverty under the burden of a young family, Jemima saw during girlhood and young womanhood some very stressful experiences of which she could never speak in her maturer years without pain, though she appears to have mollified her troubles by reading every book she could lay hands on. Moreover she turned her manual activities to whatever came in her way; grew to be exceptionally skilled in, among other things, "tambouring" gloves, also was good at mantua-making, and excellent in the oddly dissimilar occupation of cookery. She resolved to be a cook in a London club-house; but her plans in this direction were ended by her meeting her future husband, and being married to him at the age of five-and-twenty.

He carried on an old-established building and master-masoning business (the designation of "builder", denoting a manager of and contractor for all trades, was then unknown in the country districts). It was occasionally extensive, demanding from twelve to fifteen men, but frequently smaller; and the partner with whom she had thrown in her lot, though in substantial circumstances and unexceptionable in every other way, did not possess the art of enriching himself by business. Moreover he was devoted to church music, and secondarily to mundane, of the country-dance, horn-pipe, and early waltz description, as had been his father, and was his brother also. It may be mentioned that an ancestral Thomas Hardy, living in Dorchester in 1724, was a subscriber to "Thirty Select Anthems in Score", by Dr W. Croft, organist of the Chapel Royal and Westminster Abbey, which seems to show that the family were interested in church music at an early date.

Jemima's husband's father, our subject's grandfather, the first Thomas of three in succession, when a young man living at Puddletown before the year 1800, had expressed his strong musical bias by playing the violoncello in the church of that parish. He had somewhat improvidently married at one-and-twenty, whereupon his father John had set him up in business by purchasing a piece of land at Bockhampton in the adjoining parish of Stinsford, and building a house for him there. On removing with his wife in 1801 to this home provided by his father John, Thomas Hardy the First (of these Stinsford Hardys) found the church music there in a deplorable condition, it being conducted from the gallery by a solitary old man with an oboe. He immediately set himself, with the easy-going vicar's hearty concurrence, to improve it, and got together some instrumentalists, himself taking the bass-viol as before, which he played in the gallery of Stinsford Church at two services every Sunday from 1801 or 1802 till his death in 1837, being joined later by his two sons who, with other reinforcement, continued playing till about 1842, the period of performance by the three Hardys thus covering inclusively a little under forty years.

It was, and is, an interesting old church of various styles from Transition-Norman to late Perpendicular. In its vaults lie many members of the Grey and Pitt families, the latter collaterally related to the famous Prime Minister; there also lies the actor and dramatist William O'Brien with his wife Lady Susan, daughter of the first Earl of Ilchester, whose secret marriage in 1764 with the handsome Irish comedian whom Garrick had discovered and brought to Drury Lane caused such scandal in aristocratic circles. "Even a footman were preferable," wrote Walpole. "I could not have believed that Lady Susan would have stooped so low."

Though in these modern days the "stooping" might have been

viewed inversely—for O'Brien, besides being *jeune premier* at Drury, was an accomplished and well-read man, whose presentations of the gay Lothario in Rowe's *Fair Penitent*, Brisk in *The Double Dealer*, Sir Harry Wildair in *The Constant Couple*, Archer in *The Beaux' Stratagem*, Sir Andrew Aguecheek, the Prince in *Henry the Fourth*, and many other leading parts, made him highly popular, and whose own plays were of considerable merit. His marriage annihilated a promising career, for his wife's father would not hear of his remaining on the stage. The coincidence that both young Hardy's grandmothers had seen and admired O'Brien, that he was one of the Stinsford congregation for many years, that young Thomas's great-grandfather and grandfather had known him well, and that the latter as the local builder had constructed the vault for him and his wife (according to the builder's old Day-books still in existence his workmen drank nineteen quarts of beer over the job), had been asked by her to "make it just large enough for our two selves only", had placed them in it, and erected their monument, lent the occupants of the little vault in the chancel a romantic interest in the boy's mind at an early age.

In this church (see the annexed plan, which is reproduced from a drawing made by Hardy many years ago under the supervision of his father) the Hardys became well-known as violinists, Thomas the Second, the poet and novelist's father aforesaid, after his early boyhood as chorister beginning as a youth with the "counter" viol, and later taking on the tenor and treble.

They were considered among the best church-players in the neighbourhood, accident having helped their natural bent. This was the fact that in 1822, shortly after the death of the old vicar Mr Floyer, the Rev. Edward Murray, a connection of the Earl of Ilchester who was the patron of the living, was presented to it. Mr Murray was an ardent musician and performer on the violin himself, and the two younger Hardys and sometimes their father used to practise two or three times a week with him in his study at Stinsford House, where he lived instead of at the Vicarage.

Thus it was that the Hardy instrumentalists, though never more than four, maintained an easy superiority over the larger bodies in parishes near. For while Puddletown west-gallery, for instance, could boast of eight players, and Maiden Newton of nine, these included wood-wind and leather—that is to say, clarinets and serpents—which were apt to be a little too sonorous, even strident, when zealously blown. But the few and well-practised violists of

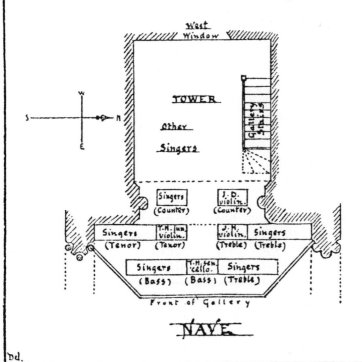

Stinsford were never unduly emphatic, according to tradition.

Elaborate Canticle services—such as the noted "Jackson in F", and in "E flat"—popular in the west of England, possibly because Jackson had been an Exeter man—Pope's Ode, and anthems with portentous repetitions and "mountainous fugues", were carried through by the performers every Sunday, with what real success is not known, but to their own great satisfaction and the hearty approval of the musical vicar.

In their psalmody they adhered strictly to Tate-and-Brady—upon whom, in truth, the modern hymn-book has been no great improvement—such tunes as the "Old Hundredth", "New Sabbath", "Devizes", "Wilton", "Lydia", and "Cambridge New" being their staple ones; while Barthélémon and Tallis were played to Ken's Morning and Evening Hymns respectively every Sunday throughout the year: a practice now obsolete, but a great stimulus to congregational singing.

As if the superintendence of the Stinsford choir were not enough distraction from business for Thomas Hardy the First, he would go whenever opportunity served and assist other choirs by performing with his violoncello in the galleries of their parish churches, mostly to the high contentment of the congregations. Although Thomas the Third had not come into the world soon enough to know his grandfather in person, there is no doubt that the description by Fairway in *The Return of the Native* of the bowing of Thomasin's father, when lending his services to the choir of Kingsbere, is a humorous exaggeration of the traditions concerning Thomas Hardy the First's musical triumphs as locum-tenens.

In addition it may be mentioned that he had been a volunteer till the end of the war, and lay in Weymouth with his company from time to time waiting for Bonaparte who never came.

Conducting the church choir all the year round involved carol-playing and singing at Christmas, which Thomas Hardy the Second loved as much as did his father. In addition to the ordinary practice, the work of preparing and copying carols a month of evenings beforehand was not light, and incidental expenses were appreciable. The parish being a large and scattered one it was the custom of Thomas Hardy the First to assemble the rather perfunctory rank-and-file of the choir at his house; and this necessitated suppers, and suppers demanded (in those days) plenty of liquor. This was especially the case on Christmas Eve itself, when the rule was to go to the northern part of the parish and play at every house before supper; then to return to Bockhampton and sit over the meal till twelve o'clock, during which interval a good deal was consumed at the Hardys' expense, the choir being mainly poor men and hungry. They then started for the other parts of the parish, and did not get home till all was finished at about six in the morning, the performers themselves feeling "no more than malkins"[1] in church next day, as they used to declare. The practice was kept up by Thomas Hardy the Second, much as described in *Under the Greenwood Tree or The Mellstock Quire*, though its author Thomas Hardy the Third invented the personages, incidents, manners, etc., never having seen or heard the choir as such, they ending their office when he was about a year old. He was accustomed to say that on this account he had rather burlesqued them, the story not adequately reflecting as he could have wished in later years the poetry and romance that coloured their time-honoured observances.

This preoccupation of the Hardys with the music of the parish church and less solemn assemblies did not, to say the least, assist their building business, and it was somewhat of a relief to Thomas Hardy the Second's young wife—though musical herself to a degree—when ecclesiastical changes after the death of Thomas Hardy the First, including the cession of the living by Murray, led to her husband's abandoning in 1841 or 1842 all connection with the choir. The First Thomas's death having been quite unexpected— inasmuch as he was playing in the church one Sunday, and brought in for burial on the next—there could be no such quiring over his grave as he had performed over the graves of so many, owing to the remaining players being chief mourners. And thus ended his devoted musical services to Stinsford Church, in which he had occupied the middle seat of the gallery with his bass-viol on Sundays for a period of thirty-five years—to no worldly profit—far the reverse, indeed.

After his death the building and masoning business also saw changes, being carried on by his widow, her sons assisting—an unsatisfactory arrangement which ultimately led to the division of the goodwill between the brothers.

The second Thomas Hardy, the author's father, was a man who in his prime could be, and was, called handsome. To the courtesy of his manners there was much testimony among the local county-ladies with whom he came in contact as a builder. All the Dorset

---

[1] *Malkin*, a damp rag on a stem, for swabbing out ovens.

Hardys have more or less a family likeness (of which the Admiral may be considered the middle type), and the present one was a good specimen. He was about five feet nine in height, of good figure, with dark Vandyke-brown hair, and a beard which he wore cut back all round in the custom of his date; with teeth that were white and regular to nearly the last years of his life, and blue eyes that never faded grey; a quick step, and a habit of bearing his head a little to one side as he walked. He carried no stick or umbrella till past middle-life, and was altogether an open-air liver, and a great walker always. He was good, too, when young, at hornpipes and jigs, and other folk-dances, performing them with all the old movements of leg-crossing and hop, to the delight of the children, till warned by his wife that this fast perishing style might tend to teach them what it was not quite necessary they should be familiar with, the more genteel "country-dance" having superseded the former.

Mrs Hardy once described him to her son as he was when she first set eyes on him in the now removed west-gallery of Stinsford Church, appearing to her more travelled glance (she had lived for a time in London, Weymouth, and other towns) and somewhat satirical vision, "rather amusingly old-fashioned, in spite of being decidedly good-looking—wearing the blue swallow tailed coat with gilt embossed buttons then customary, a red and black flowered waistcoat, Wellington boots, and French-blue trousers". The sonnet which follows expresses her first view of him.

A CHURCH ROMANCE

(Mellstock, circa 1836)

She turned in the high pew, until her sight
Swept the west gallery, and caught its row
Of music-men with viol, book, and bow
Against the sinking, sad tower-window light.

She turned again; and in her pride's despite
One strenuous viol's inspirer seemed to throw
A message from his string to her below,
Which said: "I claim thee as my own forthright!"

Thus their hearts' bond began, in due time signed,
And long years thence, when Age had scared Romance,
At some old attitude of his or glance

> That gallery-scene would break upon her mind,
> With him as minstrel, ardent, young, and trim,
> Bowing "New Sabbath" or "Mount Ephraim".

Mrs Hardy herself was rather below the middle height, with chestnut hair and grey eyes, and a trim and upright figure. Her movement also in walking being buoyant through life, strangers approaching her from behind imagined themselves, even when she was nearly seventy, about to overtake quite a young woman. The Roman nose and countenance inherited from her mother would better have suited a taller build. Like her mother, too, she read omnivorously. She sang songs of the date, such as the then popular Haynes Bayly's "Isle of Beauty", and "Gaily the Troubadour"; also "Why are you wandering here, I pray?" and "Jeannette and Jeannot". The children had a quaint old piano for their practice, over which she would sigh because she could not play it herself.

Thomas Hardy the Third, their eldest child of a family of four (and the only one of the four who married, so that he had no blood nephew or niece) showed not the physique of his father. Of his infancy nothing has been handed down save the curious fact that on his mother returning from out-of-doors one hot afternoon, to him asleep in his cradle, she found a large snake curled up upon his breast, comfortably asleep like himself. It had crept into the house from the heath hard by, where there were many.

Though healthy he was fragile, and precocious to a degree, being able to read almost before he could walk, and to tune a violin when of quite tender years. He was of ecstatic temperament, extraordinarily sensitive to music, and among the endless jigs, hornpipes, reels, waltzes, and country-dances that his father played of an evening in his early married years, and to which the boy danced a *pas seul* in the middle of the room, there were three or four that always moved the child to tears, though he strenuously tried to hide them. Among the airs (though he did not know their names at that time) were, by the way, "Enrico" (popular in the Regency), "The Fairy Dance", "Miss Macleod of Ayr" (an old Scotch tune to which Burns may have danced), and a melody named "My Fancy Lad" or "Johnny's gone to sea". This peculiarity in himself troubled the mind of "Tommy" as he was called, and set him wondering at a phenomenon to which he ventured not to confess. He used to say in later life that, like Calantha in Ford's *Broken Heart*, he danced on at these times to conceal his weeping. He was not over four years of age at this date.

One or two more characteristics of his personality at this childhood-time can be recounted. In those days the staircase at Bockhampton (later removed) had its walls coloured Venetian red by his father, and was so situated that the evening sun shone into it, adding to its colour a great intensity for a quarter of an hour or more. Tommy used to wait for this chromatic effect, and, sitting alone there, would recite to himself "And now another day is gone" from Dr Watts's Hymns with great fervency, though perhaps not for any religious reason, but from a sense that the scene suited the lines.

It is not therefore to be wondered at that a boy of this sort should have a dramatic sense of the church services, and on wet Sunday mornings should wrap himself in a tablecloth, and read the Morning Prayer standing in a chair, his cousin playing the clerk with loud Amens, and his grandmother representing the congregation. The sermon which followed was simply a patchwork of the sentences used by the vicar. Everybody said that Tommy would have to be a parson, being obviously no good for any practical pursuit; which remark caused his mother many misgivings.

One event of this date or a little later stood out, he used to say, more distinctly than any. He was lying on his back in the sun, thinking how useless he was, and covered his face with his straw hat. The sun's rays streamed through the interstices of the straw, the lining having disappeared. Reflecting on his experiences of the world so far as he had got he came to the conclusion that he did not wish to grow up. Other boys were always talking of when they would be men; he did not want at all to be a man, or to possess things, but to remain as he was, in the same spot, and to know no more people than he already knew (about half a dozen). Yet this early evidence of that lack of social ambition which followed him through life was shown when he was in perfect health and happy circumstances.

Afterwards he told his mother of his conclusions on existence, thinking she would enter into his views. But to his great surprise she was very much hurt, which was natural enough considering she had been near death's door in bringing him forth. And she never forgot what he had said, a source of much regret to him in after years.

When but little older he was puzzled at what seemed to him a resemblance between two marches of totally opposite sentiments— "See the conquering hero comes", and "The Dead March in *Saul*". Some dozen years were to pass before he discovered that they were by the same composer.

It may be added here that this sensitiveness to melody which, though he was no skilled musician, remained with him through life, was remarkable as being a characteristic of one whose critics in after years were never tired of repeating of his verses that they revealed an ear deaf to music.

1848. FIRST SCHOOL

Until his fifth or sixth year his parents hardly supposed he would survive to grow up, but at eight he was thought strong enough to go to the village school, to learn the rudiments before being sent further afield; and by a curious coincidence he was the first pupil to enter the new school-building, arriving on the day of opening, and awaiting tremulously and alone, in the empty room, the formal entry of the other scholars two-and-two with the schoolmaster and mistress from the temporary premises near. The school is still standing much in its original condition.

Here he worked at Walkingame's *Arithmetic* and at geography, in both of which he excelled, though his handwriting was indifferent. About this time his mother gave him Dryden's *Virgil*, Johnson's *Rasselas*, and *Paul and Virginia*. He also found in a closet *A History of the Wars*—a periodical in loose numbers of the war with Napoleon, which his grandfather had subscribed to at the time, having been himself a volunteer. The torn pages of these contemporary numbers with their melodramatic prints of serried ranks, crossed bayonets, huge knapsacks, and dead bodies, were the first to set him on the train of ideas that led to *The Trumpet-Major* and *The Dynasts*.

A JOURNEY

The boy Thomas's first experience of travel was when, at eight or nine years old, his mother took him with her—"for protection", as she used to say—being then an attractive and still young woman—on a visit to her sister in Hertfordshire. As the visit lasted three weeks or a month he was sent while there to a private school which appears to have been somewhat on the Squeers model. Since however he was only a day-scholar this did not affect him much, though he was mercilessly tyrannized over by the bigger boys whom he could beat hollow in arithmetic and geography.

Their return from this visit was marked by an experience which became of interest in the light of after events. The Great Northern Railway to London was then only in process of construction, and it was necessary to go thither by coach from Hertfordshire in order to take the train at Waterloo Station for Dorchester. Mrs Hardy had not been to London since she had lived there for some months twelve years earlier. The coaching-inn was The Cross-Keys, St. John Street, Clerkenwell, and here mother and boy put up for the night. It was the inn at which Shelley and Mary Godwin had been accustomed to meet on week-ends not two-score years before, and was at this time unaltered from its state during the lovers' romantic experiences there—the oval stone staircase, the skylight, and the hotel entrance being untouched. As Mrs Hardy and her little boy took a room rather high up the staircase for economy, and the poet had probably done the same from impecuniousness, there is a possibility that this may have been the same as that occupied by our most marvellous lyrist.

They stayed but a short time in London, but long enough for him to see and remember some of the streets, the Pantheon, then a fashionable Pantechnicon, Cumberland Gate into Hyde Park, which then could boast of no Marble Arch, and the pandemonium of Smithfield, with its mud, curses, and cries of ill-treated animals. Also, that when passing through the city on the way up, they stopped at the point now called Swiss Cottage, and looked back at the *outside* of London creeping towards them across green fields.

1849–1850

By another year he was judged to be strong enough to walk further than to the village school, and after some postponements he was sent to a Dorchester day-school, whose headmaster his mother had learnt to be an exceptionally able man, and a good teacher of Latin, which was quite enough to lead her to waive the fact that the school was Nonconformist, though she had no nonconforming tendencies whatever.

It is somewhat curious, and shows the honour with which the school was conducted, that the boy did not know till he had been there several months that it was a Nonconformist school, a large number, probably a majority, of the boys coming like himself from Church-of-England homes, having been attracted thither by the reputation of the said master; though Thomas used to wonder why the familiar but rather boring Church Catechism had vanished—or rather all of it except the Ten Commandments, in which the pupils were made proficient once a week. However, though nominally unorthodox during the week Thomas was kept strictly at church on Sundays as usual, till he knew the Morning and Evening Services by heart including the rubrics, as well as large portions of the New Version of the Psalms. The aspect of that time to him is clearly indicated in the verses "Afternoon Service at Mellstock", included in *Moments of Vision*.

The removal of the boy from Bockhampton school seriously wounded the lady of the manor who had erected it, though she must have guessed that he had only been sent there till sturdy enough to go further. To his mother this came as an unpleasant misunderstanding. While not wishing to be uncivil she had, naturally, not consulted the other at all in taking him away, considering his interests solely, the Hardys being comparatively independent of the manor, as their house and the adjoining land were a family lifehold, and the estate-work forming only part of Mr Hardy's business. That the school to which he was removed was not a Church-of-England one was another rock of offence to this too sensitive lady, though, as has been stated, it was an accident as unwished by the boy's mother as by the Squire's wife. The latter had just built a model school at her own expense and, though it was but small, had provided it with a well-trained master and mistress; had made it her hobby, till it was far superior to an ordinary village school. Moreover under her dignity lay a tender heart, and having no children of her own she had grown passionately fond of Tommy almost from his infancy— said to have been an attractive little fellow at this time—whom she had been accustomed to take into her lap and kiss until he was quite a big child. He quite reciprocated her fondness.

Shortly before or after the boy's removal the estate-building work was taken out of the hands of Tommy's father, who went further afield to replace it, soon obtaining a mansion to enlarge, and other contracts, and thus not suffering much from his loss of business in the immediate vicinity of his home. He would have left the parish altogether, the house his grandfather John had built for his father Thomas the First, as stated, being awkwardly small and ill-arranged (though possessing more outbuildings than now), and the spot inconvenient for a builder. But as the rambling dwelling, field, and sandpits attached were his for life he remained.

Thomas Hardy the youngest, however, secretly mourned the loss of his friend the landowner's wife, to whom he had grown more attached than he cared to own. In fact, though he was only nine or ten and she must have been nearly forty, his feeling for her was almost that of a lover. He had been wont to make drawings of animals in water-colours for her, and to sing to her—one of his songs being "I've journeyed over many lands, I've sailed on every sea", which was comical enough considering the extent of his travels. He so much longed to see her that he jumped at the offer of a young woman of the village to take him to a harvest-supper—as harvest-homes were called here—at which he knew she would be present, one of the farms on the estate being carried on by the landowner himself as a hobby, with the aid of a bailiff—much to his pecuniary loss as it turned out. The young woman, a small farmer's daughter, called for young Thomas on the afternoon of the festivity. Together they went off, his mother being away from home, though they left word where he had gone. The "Supper", an early meal at that date, probably about four o'clock, was over by the time they reached the barn, and tea was going on—after which there was singing and dancing, some non-commissioned officers having been invited from the barracks by the Squire as partners for the girls. The Squire showed himself by no means strait-laced in this respect. What his wife thought is not recorded. It may be remarked in passing that here probably began Thomas's extensive acquaintance with soldiers of the old uniforms and long service, which was to serve him in good stead when he came to write *The Trumpet-Major* and *The Dynasts*.

Presently the manor-lady, her husband, and a house-party arrived to lead off some dances. As soon as she saw little Thomas—who had no business whatever there—she came up to him and said reproachfully: "O Tommy, how is this! I thought you had deserted me!"

Tommy assured her through his tears that he had not deserted her, and never would desert her: and then the dance went on. He being wildly fond of dancing she gave him for a partner a little niece of hers about his own age staying at her house, who had come with her. The manor-house party remained for a few figures and then left, but Tommy perforce stayed on, being afraid to go home without the strapping young woman his companion, who was dancing with the soldiers. There he wearily waited for her till three in the morning, having eaten and drunk nothing since one o'clock on the previous day, through his fear of asking the merry-makers for food. What the estate owner's tender wife would have given him had she but known of his hunger and thirst and how carefully have sent him home had she been aware of his dilemma! A reproof from both his parents when Tommy reached home ended the day's adventure. It was the only harvest-supper and dance that he ever saw, save one that he dropped into by chance years after.

In spite of his lover-like promise of fidelity to her ladyship the two never met again till he was a young man of twenty-two, and she quite an elderly woman; though it was not his fault, her husband selling the estate shortly after and occupying a house in London.

It may be worthy of note that this harvest-home was among the last at which the old traditional ballads were sung, the railway having been extended to Dorchester just then, and the orally transmitted ditties of centuries being slain at a stroke by the London comic songs that were introduced. The particular ballad which he remembered hearing that night from the lips of the farm-women was that one variously called "The Outlandish Knight", "May Colvine", "The Western Tragedy", etc. He could recall to old age the scene of the young women in their light gowns sitting on a bench against the wall in the barn, and leaning against each other as they warbled the Dorset version of the ballad, which differed a little from the northern:

> "Lie there, lie there, thou false-hearted man,
>   Lie there instead o' me;
> For six pretty maidens thou hast a-drown'd here,
>   But the seventh hath drown-ed thee!"
>
>   .   .   .   .   .
>
> "O tell no more, my pretty par-rot,
>   Lay not the blame on me;
> And your cage shall be made o' the glittering gold,
>   Wi' a door o' the white ivo-rie!"

The question of moving from the parish, above alluded to, and taking more commodious premises nearer to or in the town, again arose with the Hardys—was, indeed, always arising. An opportunity to develop her husband's business which a more convenient centre would have afforded him had been long in Mrs Hardy's perception, and she thought he should seek it for the sake of his growing family. It must be admitted that a lonely spot between a heath and a wood, the search for which by messengers and other people of affairs often became wearisomely tedious to them, was almost unreasonable as a place for carrying on the building trade. But Thomas Hardy the Second was in nature the furthest removed from a tradesman that could be conceived. Instead of waylaying possible needers of brick and stone in the market-place or elsewhere, he liked going alone into the woods or on the heath, where, with a telescope inherited from some collateral ancestor who had been captain of a merchant craft, he would stay peering into the distance by the half-hour; or, in the hot weather, lying on a bank of thyme or camomile with the grasshoppers leaping over him. Furthermore the dwelling, with garden, and field attached, was the place of his birth, having, as stated, been built by his grandfather John for his (Thomas the Second's) father on the latter's marriage, as the beginning of a house which was meant to be enlarged but never was. So he remained there even through after-years, when he owned several small freeholds elsewhere. His wife, seeing what his feeling was, acquiesced at last with the cheerfulness natural to her, and made the best of it she could. Before his death he entered on some negotiations to purchase also the freehold of this Bockhampton spot of which he had the lifehold; but, as has been explained, by this time he owned other freeholds, and the place though picturesque, was cramped and inconvenient. The landlord, too, who owned the reversion was obdurate, though it lay on the outside edge of his estate; so Thomas Hardy the Second finally gave up the idea of retaining the Higher Bockhampton house in his family after his death.

To return to their son. Among his other childish memories were those of seeing men in the stocks, corn-law agitations, mail-coaches, road-waggons, tinder-boxes, and candle-snuffing. When still a small boy he was taken by his father to witness the burning in effigy of the Pope and Cardinal Wiseman in the old Roman Amphitheatre at Dorchester during the No-Popery Riots. The sight to young Hardy was most lurid, and he never forgot it; and when the cowl of one of the monks in the ghastly procession blew aside and revealed the features of one of his father's workmen his bewilderment was great.

It was natural that with the imitativeness of a boy he should have at an early age attempted to perform on the violin, and under his father's instruction was soon able to tweedle from notation some hundreds of jigs and country-dances that he found in his father's and grandfather's old books. From tuning fiddles as a boy he went on as a youth in his teens to keep his mother's old table-piano in tune whenever he had the time, and was worried at "the Wolf" in a musical octave, which he thought a defect in his own ear.

One other experience of his boyhood may be mentioned which, though comical in itself, gave him much mental distress. This was at church when listening to the sermon. Some mischievous movement of his mind set him imagining that the vicar was preaching mockingly, and he began trying to trace a humorous twitch in the corners of Mr S——'s mouth, as if he could hardly keep a serious countenance. Once having imagined this the impish boy found to his consternation that he could not dismiss the idea. Like Sterne in the pulpit, the vicar seemed to be "always tottering on the verge of laughter", and hence against his will Thomas could scarcely control his merriment, till it became a positive discomfort to him.

By good fortune the report that the schoolmaster was an able teacher turned out to be true—and finding that he had an apt pupil who galloped unconcernedly over the ordinary school lessons, he either agreed to Thomas Hardy's parents' proposal, or proposed himself, that he should teach the boy Latin immediately, Latin being considered an extra.

1852

So at twelve years of age he was started on the old Eton grammar and readings in Eutropius and Caesar. Though extraordinarily quick in acquisition he was undoubtedly rather an idle schoolboy; and in respect of the grammar having, like so many thousands of schoolboys before him, been worried by the "Propria quae maribus", he devised a plan for saving himself trouble in learning the genders by colouring the nouns in three tints respectively; but whether he profited much by his plan is not known. Once, many years after, he deplored to a friend, a classical scholar and Fellow of his College, that he had been taught from the venerable Etonian *Introduction to the Latin Tongue*, and not from the celebrated new Latin primer which came out later. His friend said grimly: "The old one was just as good as the new."

But despite the classics and his general bookishness he loved adventures with the fiddle, both now and far on towards young manhood, though it was strange that his mother, a "progressive" woman, ambitious on his account though not on her own, did not object to these performances. Possibly it was from a feeling that they would help to teach him what life was. His father however objected to them strongly, though as he himself had not been averse to them when young he could hardly do other than wink at them. So little Thomas Hardy played sometimes at village weddings, at one of which the bride, all in white, kissed him in her intense pleasure at the dance; once at a New Year's Eve party in the house of the tailor who had breeched him; also in farmers' parlours; and on another occasion at a homestead where he was stopped by his hostess clutching his bow-arm at the end of a three-quarter-hour's unbroken footing to his notes by twelve tireless couples in the favourite country-dance of "The New-Rigged Ship". The matron had done it lest he should "burst a bloodvessel", fearing the sustained exertion to be too much for a boy of thirteen or fourteen.

Among the queer occurrences accompanying these merry minstrellings may be described one that happened when he was coming home with his father at three in the morning from a gentleman-farmer's house where he had been second violin to his senior's first for six or seven hours, his father for some reason having had a generous wish to oblige the entertainers to the full. It was bitterly cold, and the moon glistened bright upon the encrusted snow, amid which they saw motionless in the hedge what appeared to be a white human figure without a head. The boy, being very tired, with finger-tips tingling from pressing the strings, was for passing the ghastly sight quickly, but the elder went up to the object, which proved to be a very tall thin man in a long white smock-frock, leaning against the bank in a drunken stupor, his head hanging forward so low that at a distance he had seemed to have no head at all. Hardy senior, seeing the danger of leaving the man where he might be frozen to death, awoke him after much exertion, and they supported him to a cottage near, where he lived, and pushed him in through the door, their ears being greeted as they left with a stream of abuse from the man's wife, which was also vented upon her unfortunate husband, whom she promptly knocked down. Hardy's father grimly remarked that it might have been as well to leave him where he was, to take his chance of being frozen to death.

At this age Thomas also loved reading Dumas *père's* romances, which he did in an English translation, and Shakespeare's tragedies for the plots only, not thinking much of *Hamlet* because the ghost did not play his part up to the end as he ought to have done.

1853–1854

A year or two later his accomplished schoolmaster opened a more advanced school called an Academy, where boarders were taken. His abilities had in fact attracted the notice of parents and guardians, and but for an affection of the chest which compelled him later to give up teaching he would no doubt have been heard of further afield. (His son, it may be observed, became a well-known science-master at South Kensington.) Hardy followed him to the new school—the Grammar-school founded by his namesake being reported to be indifferent just then—and remained there all the rest of his school life—thus continuing his Latin under the same teacher, and winning the prize of Beza's Latin Testament for his progress in the tongue—a little pocket edition which he often carried with him in after years. His course of instruction also included elementary drawing, advanced arithmetic, geometry, and algebra—in which he was fairly good, always saying that he found a certain poetry in the rule for the extraction of the cube-root, owing to its rhythm, and in some of the "Miscellaneous Questions" of Walkingame. In applied mathematics he worked completely through Tate's *Mechanics* and Nesbitt's *Mensuration*.

One day at this time Hardy, then a boy of fourteen, fell madly in love with a pretty girl who passed him on horseback near the South Walk, Dorchester, as he came out of school hard by, and for some unaccountable reason smiled at him. She was a total stranger. Next day he saw her with an old gentleman, probably her father. He wandered about miserably, looking for her through several days, and caught sight of her once again—this time riding with a young man. Then she disappeared for ever. He told other boys in confidence, who sympathized, but could do nothing, though some boarders watched for her on his behalf. He was more than a week getting over this desperate attachment.

At fifteen he was sent to receive French lessons from a lady who was the French governess at the school attended by his sister, and began the study of German from a periodical in which he had become deeply interested, entitled *The Popular Educator*, published by that genius in home-education, John Cassell. Thomas Hardy's mother had begun to buy the publications of that firm for her son, and he himself continued their purchase whenever he had any pocket-money.

And it was about this date that he formed one of a trio of youths who taught in the Sunday School of the parish, the vicar's sons being the other two, where as a pupil in his class he had a dairy-maid four years older than himself, who afterwards appeared in *Tess of the d'Urbervilles* as Marian—one of the few portraits from life in his works. This pink and plump damsel had a marvellous power of memorizing whole chapters in the Bible, and would repeat to him by heart in class, to his boredom, the long gospels before Easter without missing a word, and with evident delight in her facility; though she was by no means a model of virtue in her love-affairs.

Somewhat later, though it may as well be mentioned here among other such trivialities, he lost his heart for a few days to a young girl who had come from Windsor just after he had been reading Ainsworth's *Windsor Castle*. But she disappointed him on his finding that she took no interest in Herne the Hunter or Anne Boleyn. In this kind there was another young girl, a game-keeper's pretty daughter, who won Hardy's boyish admiration because of her beautiful bay-red hair. But she despised him, as being two or three years her junior, and married early. He celebrated her later on as "Lizbie Browne". Yet another attachment, somewhat later, which went deeper, was to a well-to-do farmer's daughter named Louisa. There were more probably. They all appear, however, to have been quite fugitive, except perhaps the one for Louisa, which may have lasted a year or longer, since he used to meet her down to his 23rd or 24th year on his visits to Dorset from London.

CHAPTER II

Student and Architect

1856–1862: *Aet.* 16–21

ARCHITECT'S PUPIL

At sixteen, though he had just begun to be interested in French and the Latin classics, the question arose of a profession or business. His father as a builder had carried out the designs of, and so become associated with, Mr John Hicks, an architect and church-restorer originally in practice in Bristol and now in Dorchester. Having seen Thomas Hardy junior when his father conjointly with another builder was executing Mr Hicks's restoration of, it is believed, Woodsford Castle, and tested him by inviting him to assist at a survey, Hicks wished to have him as a pupil, offering to take him for somewhat less than the usual premium, payable in the middle of a term of three years. As Thomas Hardy's father was a ready-money man, Mrs Hardy suggested to the architect a substantial abatement for paying down the whole premium at the beginning of the term, and to this Mr Hicks, who was not a ready-money man, agreed. Hardy was a born bookworm, that and that alone was unchanging in him; he had sometimes, too, wished to enter the Church; but he cheerfully agreed to go to Mr Hicks's.

JULY 1856

The architect's office was at 39 South Street, Dorchester (now part of a Temperance Hotel, though the room in which Hardy used to draw is unchanged), a house which happened to be next door to that of Barnes the Dorset poet and philologist. On arriving Thomas found there a pupil of twenty-one, who was at the end of his term and was just leaving; also a pupil in the first year of his articles, a year or more older than himself, who had been well educated at a good school in or near London, and who, having a liking for the classical tongues, regretted his recent necessity of breaking off his studies to take up architecture. They began later to read together, and during the ensuing two or three years often gave more time to books than to drawing. Hicks, too, was exceptionally well educated, for an ordinary country architect. The son of a Gloucestershire rector, who had been a good classical scholar, he had read some Greek, and had a smattering of Hebrew (probably taught him by his father); though, rather oddly, he was less at home with Latin. He was a kindly-natured man, almost jovial, and allowed the two youths some leisure for other than architectural study, though much of Hardy's reading in the ensuing years was done between five and eight in the morning before he left home for the office. In the long summer days he would even rise at four and begin. In these circumstances he got through a moderately good number of the usual classical pages—several books of the *Aeneid*, some Horace and Ovid, etc.; and in fact grew so familiar with his authors that in his walks to and from the town he often caught himself soliloquizing in Latin on his various projects. He also took up Greek—which he had not learnt at school—getting on with some books of the *Iliad*. He once said that nearly all his reading in the last-named—such as it was—had been done in the morning before breakfast.

Hicks was ahead of them in Greek, though they could beat him in Latin—and he used to ridicule their construings—often when these were more correct than his own were. When cornered and proved wrong he would take shelter behind the excuse that his school-days were longer ago than theirs.

An unusual incident occurred during his pupillage at Hicks's which, though it had nothing to do with his own life, was dramatic enough to have mention. One summer morning at Bockhampton, just before he sat down to breakfast, he remembered that a man was to be hanged at eight o'clock at Dorchester. He took up the big brass telescope that had been handed on in the family, and hastened to a hill on the heath a quarter of a mile from the house, whence he looked towards the town. The sun behind his back shone straight on the white stone façade of the gaol, the gallows upon it, and the form of the murderer in white fustian, the executioner and officials in dark clothing, and the crowd below, being invisible at this distance of three miles. At the moment of his placing the glass to his eye the white figure dropped downwards, and the faint note of the town clock struck eight.

The whole thing had been so sudden that the glass nearly fell from Hardy's hands. He seemed alone on the heath with the hanged man; and he crept homeward wishing he had not been so curious. It was the second and last execution he witnessed, the first having been that of a woman two or three years earlier, when he stood close to the gallows.

It had so happened that B——, the other pupil (who, strangely enough for an architect mostly occupied with church-work, had been bred a Baptist), became very doctrinal during this time; he said he was going to be baptized, and in fact was baptized shortly after. He so impressed young Hardy with his earnestness and the necessity of doing likewise that, though the junior pupil had been brought up in High Church principles, he almost felt that he ought to be baptized again as an adult. He went to the vicar of his parish and stated the case. The vicar, an Oxford man, seemed bewildered, and said that the only book he possessed that might help Hardy was Hooker's *Ecclesiastical Polity*, which he lent his inquirer. Finding that this learned work did not help much in the peculiar circumstances, Hardy went to the curate of another parish with whom he was acquainted. But all that the curate had was a handbook on the Sacraments of an elementary kind.

However, he got hold of as many books and notes on Paedo-baptism as he could, and though he was appalled at the feebleness of the arguments for infant christening (assuming that New Testament practice must be followed) he incontinently determined to "stick to his own side"—as he considered the Church to be—at some costs of conscience. The clash of polemics between the two pupils in the office sometimes reached such a pitch of clamour that the architect's wife would send down a message from the drawing-room, which was on the first floor over, imploring them not to make so much noise. To add to the heat, two of the Dorchester Baptist minister's sons, friends of B——, hard-headed Scotch youths fresh from Aberdeen University, good classics, who could rattle off at a moment's notice the Greek original of any passage in the New Testament, joined in the controversy. But though Hardy thus found himself in the position of one against three, he fought on with his back to the wall as it were—working at night at the Greek Testament to confute his opponents, and in his purpose getting a new text, Griesbach's, that he had seen advertised as the most correct, instead of his old one, and conceding to his serious-minded disputants as much as he thought a Churchman fairly could concede, namely—that he would limit his Greek reading to the New Testament in future, giving up the heathen authors, and would show his broad-mindedness by attending a prayer-meeting in the chapel-vestry.

At half-past six on a hot August evening he entered the chapel for the meeting. Not a soul was in the building, and he waited in the dreary little vestry till the hour of appointment had passed by nearly half an hour, the yellow sun shining in on the drab paint through the skylight, through which also came the faint notes of a brass band. Just as he was about to leave at a quarter-past-seven, B—— and the minister's sons tumbled breathlessly in, apologizing for their lateness. Cooke's then popular circus had entered the town at the moment of the prayer-meeting, and they had all dismissed the engagement for awhile, and remained for the spectacle. Hardy had known the circus entry was going to take place; but he had kept his appointment faithfully. How the meeting ended Hardy had forgotten when he related the experience.

His convictions on the necessity of adult baptism gradually wore out of him. Though he was younger than his companions he seems to have possessed a breadth of mind which they lacked; and while perceiving that there was not a shred of evidence for infant baptism in the New Testament, he saw that Christianity did not hang on temporary details that expediency might modify, and that the practice of an isolated few in the early ages could not be binding on its multitudes in differing circumstances, when it had grown to be the religion of continents.

Nevertheless it would be unjust to the Baptist minister P—— and his argumentative family to omit from these gleanings out of the past Hardy's remarks on their finer qualities. They formed an austere and frugal household, and won his admiration by their thoroughness and strenuousness. He often visited them, and one of the sons about his own age, not insistent on Baptist doctrines like his two brethren, was a great friend of Hardy's till his death of consumption a year or two after. It was through these Scotch people that Thomas Hardy first became impressed with the necessity for "plain living and high thinking", which stood him in such good stead in later years. Among the few portraits of actual persons in Hardy's novels, that of the Baptist minister in *A Laodicean* is one—being a recognisable drawing of P—— the father as he appeared to Hardy at this time, though the incidents are invented.

To return to the architect's pupils. The Greek Testament had been now taken up by both of them—though it had necessitated the younger's learning a new dialect—and Homer and Virgil were thrown aside (a misfortune to Hardy, who was just getting pleasure from these). In pursuing this study it became an occasional practice for the youths to take out their Testaments into the fields and sit on a gate reading them. The gate of the enclosure in Kingston-Maurward eweleaze, now the cricket-ground, was the scene of some of the readings. They were brought to an end by the expiry of B——'s term of four years as a pupil, and his departure for the office of a London architect, which, it may be mentioned, he shortly afterwards left to start in practice on his own account in Tasmania.

1860–1861

With the departure of B——, Hardy's duties grew more exacting, and though, in consideration of his immaturity, the term of his pupillage had been lengthened by between one and two years, a time had arrived at which it became necessary that he should give more attention to practical architecture than he had hitherto done. Church "restoration" was at this time in full cry in Dorsetshire and the neighbouring counties, and young Hardy found himself making many surveys, measurements, and sketches of old churches with a view to such changes. Much beautiful ancient Gothic, and particularly also Jacobean and Georgian work, he was passively instrumental in destroying or in altering beyond identification—a matter for his deep regret in later years.

Despite the greater demands of architecture upon his attention it appears that Hardy kept up his classics for some time after the departure of his fellow-pupil for Tasmania; since, in an old letter of B——'s, replying to Hardy from Hobart Town in May 1861, the emigrant says:

> Really you are a plodding chap to have got through such a lot of Homer and all the rest. I am not a bit farther than I was in Dorchester; indeed, I think I have scarcely touched a book— Greek, I mean—since. I see you are trying all you can to cut me out!

The allusion to Homer seems to show that after his earnest Baptist-senior's departure and the weakening of his influence, Hardy, like St. Augustine, lapsed from the Greek New Testament back again to pagan writers, though he was rather impulsive than "plodding" in his studies, his strength lying in a power of keeping going in most disheartening circumstances.

Owing to the accident of his being an architect's pupil in a county-town of assizes and aldermen, which had advanced to railways and telegraphs and daily London papers; yet not living there, but walking in every day from a world of shepherds and ploughmen in a hamlet three miles off, where modern improvements were still regarded as wonders, he saw rustic and borough doings in a juxtaposition peculiarly close. To these externals may be added the peculiarities of his inner life, which might almost have been called academic—a triple existence unusual for a young man—what he used to call, in looking back, a life twisted of three strands—the professional life, the scholar's life, and the rustic life, combined in the twenty-four hours of one day, as it was with him through these years. He would be reading the *Iliad*, the *Aeneid*, or the Greek Testament from six to eight in the morning, would work at Gothic architecture all day, and then in the evening rush off with his fiddle under his arm—sometimes in the company of his father as first violin and uncle as 'celloist—to play country-dances, reels, and hornpipes at an agriculturist's wedding, christening, or Christmas party in a remote dwelling among the fallow fields, not returning sometimes till nearly dawn, the Hardys still being traditionally string-bandsmen available on such occasions, and having the added recommendation of charging nothing for their services, which was a firm principle with them, the entertainers being mostly acquaintances; though the tireless zeal of young couples in the dance often rendered the Hardys' act of friendship anything but an enjoyment to themselves. But young Hardy's physical vigour was now much greater than it had been when he was a child, and it enabled him, like a conjuror at a fair, to keep in the air the three balls of architecture, scholarship, and dance-fiddling, without ill effects, the fiddling being of course not daily like the other two.

His immaturity—above alluded to—was greater than is common for his years, and it may be mentioned here that a clue to much of his character and action throughout his life is afforded by his lateness of development in virility, while mentally precocious. He himself said humorously in later times that he was a child till he was sixteen, a youth till he was five-and-twenty, and a young man till he was nearly fifty. Whether this was intrinsic, or owed anything to his having lived in a remote spot in early life, is an open question.

During the years of architectural pupillage Hardy had two other literary friends in Dorchester. One was Hooper Tolbort, orphan-nephew of one of the partners in a firm of mechanical engineers, who had an extraordinary facility in the acquisition of languages. He was a pupil of the Rev. W. Barnes, the Dorset poet and school-master, and was preparing for the Indian Civil Service. The other was Horace Moule of Queens' College, Cambridge—just then beginning practice as author and reviewer. Walks in the fields with each of these by Thomas Hardy biassed him still further in the direction of books, one of which among those he met with impressed him much—the newly published *Essays and Reviews*, by "The Seven against Christ", as the authors were nicknamed; and Walter Bagehot's *Estimates*, afterwards called *Literary Studies*. He began writing verses, and also a few prose articles, which do not appear to have been printed anywhere. The first effusion of his to see the light of print was an anonymous skit in a Dorchester paper on the disappearance of the Alms-House clock, which then as now stood on a bracket in South Street, the paragraph being in the form of a plaintive letter from the ghost of the clock. (It had been taken down to be cleaned, and neglected.) As the author was supposed to be an alderman of influence the clock was immediately replaced. He would never have been known to be Hardy but for the conspiracy of a post-office clerk, who watched the handwriting of letters posted till he had spotted the culprit. After this followed the descriptive verses "Domicilium" given *ante*, page 8, and accounts of church-restoration carried out by Hicks, which Hardy prepared for the grateful reporter of the *Dorset Chronicle*.

It seems he had also set to work on either the *Agamemnon* or the

Oedipus; but on his inquiring of Moule—who was a fine Greek scholar and was always ready to act the tutor in any classical difficulty—if he ought not to go on reading some Greek plays, Moule's reluctant opinion was that if Hardy really had (as his father had insisted, and as indeed was reasonable since he never as yet had earned a farthing in his life) to make an income in some way by architecture in 1862, it would be hardly worth while for him to read Aeschylus or Sophocles in 1859–61. He had secretly wished that Moule would advise him to go on with Greek plays, in spite of the serious damage it might do his architecture; but he felt bound to listen to reason and prudence. So, as much Greek as he had got he had to be content with, the language being almost dropped from that date; for though he did take up one or two of the dramatists again some years later, it was in a fragmentary way only. Nevertheless, his substantial knowledge of them was not small.

It may be permissible to ponder whether Hardy's career might not have been altogether different if Moule's opinion had been the contrary one, and he had advised going on with Greek plays. The younger man would hardly have resisted the suggestion, and might have risked the consequences, so strong was his bias that way. The upshot might have been his abandonment of architecture for a University career, his father never absolutely refusing to advance him money in a good cause. Having every instinct of a scholar he might have ended his life as a Don of whom it could be said that

> He settled *Hoti's* business,
> Properly based *Oun*.

But this was not to be, and it was possibly better so.

One other Dorchester young man, who has been cursorily mentioned—the pupil of Hicks's whose time had expired shortly after Hardy's arrival, and who then departed permanently from the west of England—may be again given a word for the single thing about him that had attracted the fresh-comer—his one or two trips to London during their passing acquaintance, and his return thence whistling quadrilles and other popular music, with accounts of his dancing experiences at the Argyle Rooms and Cremorne—both then in full swing. Hardy would relate that one quadrille in particular his precursor Fippard could whistle faultlessly, and while giving it would caper about the office to an imaginary dance-figure, embracing an imaginary Cremorne or Argyle *danseuse*. The fascinating quadrille remained with Hardy all his life, but he never could identify it. Being some six years the junior of this comet-like young man, Hardy was treated by him with the superciliousness such a boy usually gets from such seniority, and with the other's departure from Dorchester he passed quite out of Hardy's knowledge.

CHAPTER III

London

1862–1867: *Aet.* 21–27

A NEW START

On Thursday, April 17, 1862, Thomas Hardy started alone for London, to pursue the art and science of architecture on more advanced lines. He had for some time left Bockhampton as a permanent resident, living, except at week-ends, in Dorchester, either with Hicks or at lodgings; though he often sojourned at Bockhampton later on.

The Great Exhibition of that year was about to be opened, and this perhaps influenced him in the choice of a date for his migration. His only previous journey to the capital had been made with his mother in 1848 or 1849, when they passed through it on the way to and back from Hertfordshire, on a visit to a relative, as mentioned earlier.

Hardy used to relate humorously that on the afternoon of his arrival he called to inquire for lodgings at a house where was employed a bachelor some ten years older than himself, whose cousin Hardy had known. This acquaintance, looking him up and down, was sceptical about his establishing himself in London. "Wait till you have walked the streets a few weeks", he said satirically, "and your elbows begin to shine, and the hems of your trousers get frayed, as if nibbled by rats! Only practical men are wanted here." Thomas began to wish he had thought less of the Greek Testament and more of iron girders.

However, he had at least two letters of introduction in his pocket—one from a gushing lady to Mr Benjamin Ferrey,

F.R.I.B.A., of Trinity Place, Charing Cross, an architect who had been a pupil of the elder Pugin's, was connected with the West of England, and had designed a Dorset mansion of which Hardy's father had been one of the builders, carrying out the work to that gentleman's complete satisfaction. But, as usually happens, this sheet-anchor was less trustworthy than had been expected. Mr Ferrey was civil to the young man, remembered his father, promised every assistance; and there the matter ended.

The other introduction was to Mr John Norton of Old Bond Street—also an architect in full practice. Mr Norton was a Bristol man, a pupil of Ferrey's, and a friend of Hicks of Dorchester, by reason, it is believed, of their joint association with Bristol. Anyhow, Norton received young Thomas Hardy with great kindness, and his friendship coming at the nick of time when it was needed, he proved himself one of the best helps Hardy ever had. The generous architect told him that he must on no account be doing nothing in London (Hardy looked quite a pink-faced youth even now), and arranged that he should come daily and make drawings in his office for a merely nominal remuneration whilst looking further about town. As Mr Norton was in no real need of assistance the proposal was most considerate of him.

LAST WEEK IN APRIL 1862

Here was indeed as good a thing as could have happened. It was an anchorage, and Hardy never forgot it. Strangely enough, on his arriving on the following Monday to begin, Mr Norton informed him that a friend whom he had met at the Institute of British Architects had asked him if he knew of a young Gothic draughtsman who could restore and design churches and rectory-houses. He had strongly recommended Hardy, and packed him off at once to call on Mr Arthur Blomfield, the friend in question.

Blomfield was a son of the recently deceased Dr Blomfield, Bishop of London; a Rugbeian, a graduate of Trinity College Cambridge, where he had been a great boating man; and a well-known church-designer and restorer, whose architectural pupillage had been under Philip C. Hardwick. Hardy found him in—a lithe, brisk man of thirty-three, with whom Hardy was to keep up a friendship for near on forty years. Arrangements were made, and on the following

Monday, May 5, he began work as an assistant-architect in Mr Blomfield's drawing-office—at that time at 8 St. Martin's Place, in rooms also used by the Alpine Club. This was another linking coincidence with aftertimes, for Leslie Stephen, an ardent climber and a member of the Club, was a visitor to these rooms, though ten years were to elapse before Hardy got to know him, and to be mentally influenced by him so deeply. In the following autumn or winter, however, more commodious and lighter drawing-offices were taken at 8 Adelphi Terrace, first floor; which Blomfield continued to occupy during the remaining five years that Hardy worked with him. Shortly after his entry there Hardy had an experience which might have been serious:

"March 10. Went into the streets in the evening to see the illuminations on the occasion of the P. of Wales's marriage. By the fortunate accident of beginning my walk at the city end of the route I had left the neighbourhood of the Mansion House before the great mass of people got there, but I had enough to do to hold my own at the bottom of Bond Street, where my waistcoat buttons were torn off and my ribs bent in before I could get into a doorway. Molsey and Paris [two pupils of Ferrey's, friends of Hardy's] were in the Mansion House crush, having started from the West End, like most of the spectators. Six people were killed close to them, and they did not expect to get out alive."

In a letter written many years after to an inquirer who was interested in his association with the Terrace, Hardy states:

> I sat there drawing, inside the easternmost window of the front room on the first floor above the ground floor, occasionally varying the experience by idling on the balcony. I saw from there the Embankment and Charing-Cross Bridge built, and of course used to think of Garrick and Johnson. The rooms contained at that date fine Adam mantelpieces in white marble, on which we used to sketch caricatures in pencil.

It may be added that the ground-floor rooms of this 8 Adelphi Terrace were occupied by the Reform League during Hardy's stay overhead, and that Swinburne in one of his letters speaks of a correspondence with the League about this date. "The Reform League," he says, "a body of extreme reformers not now extant I believe, but of some note and power for a time, solicited me to sit in Parliament—as representative of more advanced democratic or republican opinions than were represented there." Swinburne consulted Mazzini, who dissuaded him from consenting. The heads of the League were familiar personages to Blomfield's pupils who, as became Tory and Churchy young men, indulged in satire at the League's expense, letting down ironical bits of paper on the heads of members, and once coming nearly to loggerheads with the worthy resident secretary, Mr George Howell—to whom they had to apologize for their exasperating conduct—all this being unknown to Mr Blomfield himself.

During the first few months of Hardy's life in London he had not forgotten to pay a call on the lady of his earliest passion as a child, who had been so tender towards him in those days, and had used to take him in her arms. She and her husband were now living in Bruton Street. The butler who opened the door was, he recalled, the same one who had been with the family at Kingston-Maurward all those years ago, and looked little altered. But the lady of his dreams—alas! To her, too, the meeting must have been no less painful than pleasant: she was plainly embarrassed at having in her presence a young man of over twenty-one, who was very much of a handful in comparison with the rosy-cheeked, innocent little boy she had almost expected "Tommy" to remain. One interview was not quite sufficient to wear off the stiffness resulting from such changed conditions, though, warming up, she asked him to come again. But getting immersed in London life he did not respond to her invitation, showing that the fickleness was his alone. But they occasionally corresponded, as will be seen.

It may be hardly necessary to record—since he somewhere describes it himself—that the metropolis into which he had plunged at this date differed greatly from the London of even a short time after. It was the London of Dickens and Thackeray, and Evans's supper-rooms were still in existence in an underground hall in Covent Garden, which Hardy once at least visited. The Cider Cellars and the Coal Hole were still flourishing, with "Judge and Jury" mock trials, "Baron Nicholson" or his successor being judge. And Dr Donovan the phrenologist gauged heads in the Strand, informing Hardy that his would lead him to no good.

The ladies talked about by the architect's pupils and other young men into whose society Hardy was thrown were Cora Pearl, "Skittles", Agnes Willoughby, Adah Menken, and others successively, of whom they professed to know many romantic and *risqué* details, but really knew nothing at all. Another of their romantic interests that Hardy recalled being, a little later, the moorhen dive of Lady Florence Paget into Marshall & Snelgrove's shop away from Mr Chaplin, her *fiancé*, and her emergence at the other door into the arms of Lord Hastings, and marriage with him— a sensational piece of news with which they came in breathless the week it happened.

Hungerford Market was still in being where the Charing-Cross Station now stands, and Hardy occasionally lunched at a "coffee house" there. He also lunched or dined at Bertolini's with some pupils of Ferrey's, the architect who had known his father and been the pupil of Pugin. This restaurant in St. Martin's Street, Leicester Square, called Newton House, had been the residence and observatory of Sir Isaac Newton, and later the home of the Burneys, who were visited there by Johnson, Reynolds, etc., and the stone floors were still sanded as in former days. A few years after Hardy frequented it Swinburne used to dine there as a member of the "Cannibal Club". Tennyson is also stated to have often dined at Bertolini's. To Hardy's great regret this building of many associations was pulled down in later years.

On his way to Adelphi Terrace he used to take some short cut near Seven Dials, passing daily the liquor saloons of Alec Keene and Tom King (?) in West Street (now demolished), and Nat Langham at the top of St. Martin's Lane, when he could sometimes discern the forms of those famous prize-fighters behind their respective bars.

There was no Thames Embankment. Temple Bar still stood in its place, and the huge block of buildings known as the Law Courts was not erected. Holborn Hill was still a steep and noisy thoroughfare which almost broke the legs of the slipping horses, and Skinner Street ran close by, with presumably Godwin's house yet standing in it, at which Shelley first set eyes on Mary. No bridge across Ludgate Hill disfigured St. Paul's and the whole neighbourhood. The South Kensington Museum was housed in iron sheds nicknamed the "Brompton Boilers", which Hardy used to frequent this year to obtain materials for an Essay he sent in to the Royal Institute of British Architects; it was awarded the prize in the following spring. There was no underground railway, and omnibus conductors leaving "Kilburn Gate", near which Hardy lived awhile, cried "Any more passengers for London!" The list of such changes might be infinitely extended.

Charles Kean and his wife were still performing Shakespeare at the Princess's Theatre, and Buckstone was at the Haymarket in the new play of *Our American Cousin and Lord Dundreary*. At most of the theatres about nine o'clock there was a noise of trampling feet, and the audience whispered, "Half-price coming in". The play paused for a few moments, and when all was quiet went on again.

Balls were constant at Willis's Rooms—earlier Almack's—and in 1862 Hardy danced at these rooms—or at Almack's as he preferred to call the place, realizing its historic character. He used to recount that in those old days the pretty Lancers and Caledonians were still footed there to the original charming tunes, which brought out the beauty of the figures as no later tunes did, and every movement was a correct quadrille step and gesture. For those dances had not at that date degenerated to a waltzing step, to be followed by galloping romps to uproarious pieces.

Cremorne and the Argyle he also sought, remembering the jaunty senior-pupil at Hicks's who had used to haunt those gallant resorts. But he did not dance there much himself, if at all, and the fascinating quadrille-tune had vanished like a ghost, though he went one day to second-hand music-shops and also to the British Museum, and hunted over a lot of such music in a search for it. Allusions to these experiences occur in more than one of his poems, "Reminiscences of a Dancing Man" in particular; and they were largely drawn upon, so he once remarked, in the destroyed novel *The Poor Man and the Lady*—of which later on.

In a corresponding fit of musical enthusiasm he also bought an old fiddle at this time, with which he practised at his lodgings, with another man there who performed on the piano, pieces from the romantic Italian operas of Covent Garden and Her Majesty's—the latter being then also an opera house—which places they used to frequent two or three times a week; not, except on rare occasions, in the best parts of the houses, as will be well imagined, but in the half-crown amphitheatre.

The foreign operas in vogue were those of Rossini, Donizetti, Verdi, Meyerbeer, Bellini: and thus Hardy became familiar with such singers as Mario (Grisi had just departed), Tietjens, Nilsson, Patti (just come), Giuglini, Parepa, and others of the date. An English Opera Company was also in existence, and Hardy patriotically supported it by going often to operas by Balfe, Wallace, and others. Here he had the painful experience of hearing the gradual breakdown of William Harrison's once fine voice, who, with Miss Louisa Pyne, had established the company and endeavoured to keep such opera going. Hardy was heard to assert that, as it were in defiance of fate, Harrison would sing night after night his favourite songs—such as "Let me like a soldier fall" in *Maritana,* and, particularly, "When other lips" in *The Bohemian Girl,* wherein his complete failure towards the last attempts would move a sensitive listener to tears: he thought Harrison's courage in struggling on, hoping against hope, might probably cause him to be remembered longer than the greatest success would have done.

AT BLOMFIELD'S

Mr Blomfield (afterwards Sir Arthur) being the son of a late Bishop of London, was considered a right and proper man for supervising the removal of human bodies in cases where railways had obtained a faculty for making cuttings through the city churchyards, so that it should be done decently and in order. A case occurred in which this function on the Bishop's behalf was considered to be duly carried out. But afterwards Mr Blomfield came to Hardy and informed him with a look of concern that he had just returned from visiting the site on which all the removed bodies were said by the company to be reinterred; but there appeared to be nothing deposited, the surface of the ground lying quite level as before. Also that there were rumours of mysterious full bags of something that rattled, and cartage to bone-mills. He much feared that he had not exercised a sufficiently sharp supervision, and that the railway company had got over him somehow. "I believe those people are all ground up!" said Blomfield grimly.

Soon there was to occur a similar proceeding on a much larger scale by another company—the carrying of a cutting by the Midland Railway through Old St. Pancras Churchyard, which would necessitate the removal of many hundreds of coffins, and bones in huge quantities. In this business Mr Blomfield was to represent the Bishop as before. The architect said that now there should be no mistake about his thoroughly carrying out the superintendence. Accordingly, he set a clerk-of-works in the churchyard, who was never to leave during working hours; and as the removals were effected by night, and the clerk-of-works might be lax or late, he deputed Hardy to go on evenings at uncertain hours, to see that the clerk-of-works was performing his duties; while Hardy's chief himself was to drop in at unexpected moments during the week, presumably to see that neither his assistant nor the clerk-of-works was a defaulter.

The plan worked excellently, and throughout the late autumn and early winter (of probably the year 1865 or thereabouts) Hardy attended at the churchyard—each evening between five and six, as well as sometimes at other hours. There after nightfall, within a high hoarding that could not be overlooked, and by the light of flare-lamps, the exhumation went on continuously of the coffins that had been uncovered during the day, new coffins being provided for those that came apart in lifting, and for loose skeletons; and those that held together being carried to the new ground on a board merely; Hardy supervising these mournful processions when present—with what thoughts may be imagined, and Blomfield sometimes meeting him there. In one coffin that fell apart was a skeleton and two skulls. He used to tell that when, after some fifteen years of separation, he met Arthur Blomfield again and their friendship was fully renewed, among the latter's first words were: "Do you remember how we found the man with two heads at St. Pancras?"

It may conceivably have been some rumour of the possibility of this lamentable upheaval in the near future of Old St. Pancras Churchyard by the railway company, which had led Sir Percy, the son of Mary Shelley, to remove the bodies of her parents therefrom to St. Peter's, Bournemouth, where she had been buried in 1851, and where they now lie beside her, though few people seem to know that such an illustrious group is in the churchyard.

Hardy used to tell some amusing stories of his chief, a genuine humorist like his father the Bishop. Among other strange ways in which he and his pupils, including Hardy, used to get on with their architecture was by singing glees and catches at intervals during office hours. Having always been musically inclined and, as has been stated, a fiddler of countless jigs and reels in his boyhood, he could sing at sight with moderate accuracy from notation though his voice was not strong. Hence Blomfield welcomed him in the office choir, where he himself took the bass, the rest waiting till he had "got his low E". Hardy also at Blomfield's request sang in the church-choir at the opening of the organ at St. Matthias' Church, Richmond, where Blomfield took a bass part, one of his pupils being organist. But in the office the alto-part was the difficulty, and Blomfield would say: "If you meet an alto anywhere in the Strand, Hardy, ask him to come in and join us."

On an occasion when a builder had called on business, Hardy

being present and some pupils, Blomfield airily said to the builder: "Well Mr T——, what can I do for you? What will you take this morning—sherry or port? " Though it was only between 10 and 11 Mr T—— reflected earnestly and said, "Port, sir, if you please." As they naturally had no wine or any other liquor at the offices, Blomfield was comically disconcerted at the worthy builder's seriousness, but was as good as his word, and the office-boy was secretly dispatched to the Strand to buy a bottle of port, and to the housekeeper to borrow a glass.

Grotesque incidents that seldom happened to other people seemed to happen to Blomfield. One day he and Hardy went together to some slum near Soho to survey the site for a new building. The inspection made their boots muddy, and on the way back Blomfield suggested they should have them cleaned, as two bootblacks had come up pointing significantly. When Hardy and he had placed themselves Blomfield asked the second why he did not proceed with his brushing, like the first. " 'Cause he's got no blacking nor brush," said the first. "What good is he then?" asked Blomfield. "I've cracked my blacking-bottle, and it goes dry; so I pay him a penny a day to spit for me."

However, matters were graver sometimes. Hardy remembered how one morning he arrived at the Terrace to find Blomfield standing with his back to the fireplace, and with a very anxious face. The architect said slowly without any preface, "Hardy, that tower has fallen." His eyes were fixed on the opposite wall where was the drawing of a new church just then finished. It was a serious matter, especially as some years earlier another well-known architect had been sentenced to a year's imprisonment for manslaughter, one of his new erections having fallen and killed some people. Fortunately no one was killed in the present case, and the designer was quite exonerated by having the tower rebuilt stone by stone as it had been before, and so proving the construction to be unimpeachable, for there it has stood ever since without a crack. What had caused the fall was always a mystery.

This used to remind Hardy of another church-tower story. Mr Hicks, with whom he served his pupillage, once told him that at the beginning of his practice he built a church-tower near Bristol, and on a night just after its erection he dreamt that on approaching it he saw a huge crack in its west wall from the parapet downwards. He was so disturbed that next morning he mounted his horse—it was before railways, and architects often rode on horseback to the supervision of their buildings then—and trotting off to the village the tower rose into his view. There was the crack in its face exactly as he had beheld it in his dream.

Having somewhat settled down with Blomfield, and feeling that architectural drawing in which the actual designing had no great part was monotonous and mechanical; having besides neither the inclination nor the keenness for getting into social affairs and influential sets which would help him to start a practice of his own, Hardy's tastes reverted to the literary pursuits that he had been compelled to abandon in 1861, and had not resumed except to write the Prize Architectural Essay beforementioned. By as early as the end of 1863 he had recommenced to read a great deal—with a growing tendency towards poetry. But he was forced to consider ways and means, and it was suggested to him that he might combine literature with architecture by becoming an art-critic for the press—particularly in the province of architectural art. It is probable that he might easily have carried this out, reviewers with a speciality being then, and possibly now, in demand. His preparations for such a course were, however, quickly abandoned, and by 1865 he had begun to write verses, and by 1866 to send his productions to magazines. That these were rejected by editors, and that he paid such respect to their judgment as scarcely ever to send out a MS. twice, was in one feature fortunate for him, since in years long after he was able to examine those poems of which he kept copies, and by the mere change of a few words or the rewriting of a line or two, to make them quite worthy of publication. Such of them as are dated in these years were all written in his lodgings at 16 Westbourne Park Villas. He also began turning the Book of Ecclesiastes into Spenserian stanzas, but finding the original unmatchable abandoned the task.

As another outcome of the same drift of mind he used to deliver short addresses or talks on poets and poetry to Blomfield's pupils and assistants on afternoons when there was not much to be done, or at all events when not much was done. There is no tradition of what Blomfield thought of this method of passing office hours instead of making architectural plans.

The only thing he got published at the time was, so far as is known, a humorous trifle in *Chambers's Journal* in 1865 entitled "How I built myself a house"—written to amuse the pupils of

Blomfield. It may have been the acceptance of this *jeu d'esprit* that turned his mind in the direction of prose; yet he made such notes as the following:

"April, 1865.—The form on the canvas which immortalizes the painter is but the last of a series of tentative & abandoned sketches each of which probably contained some particular feature nearer perfection than any part of the finished product."

"Public opinion is of the nature of a woman."

"There is not that regular gradation among womankind that there is among men. You may meet with 999 exactly alike, and then the thousandth—not a little better, but far above them. Practically therefore it is useless for a man to seek after this thousandth to make her his."

"May.—How often we see a vital truth flung about carelessly wrapt in a commonplace subject, without the slightest conception on the speaker's part that his words contain an unsmelted treasure."

"In architecture, men who are clever in details are bunglers in generalities. So it is in everything whatsoever."

"More conducive to success in life than the desire for much knowledge is the being satisfied with ignorance on irrelevant subjects."

"The world does not despise us; it only neglects us."

Whether or no, he did not seriously take up prose till two or three years later, when he was practically compelled to try his hand on it by finding himself perilously near coming to the ground between the two stools of architecture and literature.

Subsequent historic events brought back to his mind that this year he went with Blomfield to New Windsor, to the laying of the Memorial-stone of a church there by the Crown Princess of Germany (the English Princess Royal). She was accompanied by her husband the Crown Prince, afterwards the Emperor Frederick. "Blomfield handed her the trowel, and during the ceremony she got her glove daubed with the mortar. In her distress she handed the trowel back to him with an impatient whisper of 'Take it, take it!' "

Here is another note of his relating to this time:

"July 2 (1865). Worked at J. H. Newman's *Apologia*, which we have all been talking about lately. A great desire to be convinced by him, because H.M.M. likes him so much. Style charming, and his logic really human, being based not on syllogisms but on converging probabilities. Only—and here comes the fatal catastrophe—there is no first link to his excellent chain of reasoning, and down you come headlong. Poor Newman! His gentle childish faith in revelation and tradition must have made him a very charming character. . . . Read some Horace; also Childe Harold and Lalla Rookh till ½ past 12."

However, as yet he did not by any means abandon verse, which he wrote constantly, but kept private, through the years 1866 and most of 1867—resolving to send no more to magazines whose editors probably did not know good poetry from bad, and forming meanwhile the Quixotic opinion that, as in verse was concentrated the essence of all imaginative and emotional literature, to read verse and nothing else was the shortest way to the fountain-head of such for one who had not a great deal of spare time. And in fact for nearly or quite two years he did not read a word of prose except such as came under his eye in the daily newspapers and weekly reviews. Thus his reading naturally covered a fairly large tract of English poetry, and it may be mentioned, as showing that he had some views of his own, that he preferred Scott the poet to Scott the novelist, and never ceased to regret that the author of the most Homeric poem in the English language—*Marmion*—should later have declined on prose fiction.

It is somewhat unusual that he was not so keenly anxious to get into print as most young men are found to be, in this indifference, as in some qualities of his verse, curiously resembling Donne. The Horatian exhortation that he had come across in his reading—to keep his own compositions back till the ninth year—had made a deep impression on him. *Nescit vox missa reverti*; and by retaining his poems, and destroying those he thought irremediably bad—though he afterwards fancied he had destroyed too many—he may have been saved from the annoyance of seeing his early crude effusions crop up in later life.

At the same time there can be no doubt that some closer association with living poets and the poetry of the moment would have afforded Hardy considerable stimulus and help. But his unfortunate shyness—or rather aloofness, for he was not shy in the ordinary sense—served him badly at this period of his life. During part of his residence at Westbourne Park Villas he was living within half a mile of Swinburne, and hardly more than a stone's throw from Browning, to whom introductions would not have been difficult through literary friends of Blomfield's. He might have obtained at least encouragement from these, and, if he had cared, possibly have floated off some of his poems in a small volume. But such a proceeding as trying to know these contemporaries seems never to have crossed his mind.

During his residence in London he had entered himself at King's College for the French classes, where he studied the tongue through a term or two under Professor Stièvenard, never having taken it up seriously since in his boyhood he had worked at exercises under a governess. He used to say that Stièvenard was the most charming Frenchman he ever met, as well as being a fine teacher. Hardy's mind had, however, become at this date so deeply immersed in the study and practice of English poetry that he gave but a perfunctory attention to his French readings.

"March 11.—The woman at a first interview will know as much of the man as he will know of her on the wedding morning; whilst she will know as little of him then as he knew of her when they first shook hands. Her knowledge will have come upon her like a flood, and have as gradually soaked away."

"June 2.—My 25th birthday. Not very cheerful. Feel as if I had lived a long time, and done very little. Walked about by moonlight in the evening. Wondered what woman, if any, I should be thinking about in five years' time."

"July 9.—The greatest and most majestic being on the face of the earth will accept pleasure from the most insignificant."

"July 19.—Patience is the union of moral courage with physical cowardice."

"End of July.—The dull period in the life of an event is when it ceases to be news & has not begun to be history."

"August.—The anguish of a defeat is most severely felt when we look upon weak ones who have believed us invincible and have made preparations for our victory."

"Aug. 23. The poetry of a scene varies with the minds of the perceivers. Indeed, it does not lie in the scene at all."

About this time Hardy nourished a scheme of a highly visionary character. He perceived from the impossibility of getting his verses accepted by magazines that he could not live by poetry, and (rather strangely) thought that architecture and poetry—particularly architecture in London—would not work well together. So he formed the idea of combining poetry and the Church—towards which he had long had a leaning—and wrote to a friend in Cambridge for particulars as to Matriculation at that University— which with his late Classical reading would have been easy for him, and knowing that what money he could not muster himself for keeping terms his father would lend him for a few years, his idea being that of a curate in a country village. This fell through less because of its difficulty than from a conscientious feeling, after some theological study, that he could hardly take the step with honour while holding the views that on examination he found himself to hold. And so he allowed the curious scheme to drift out of sight, though not till after he had begun to practise orthodoxy; for example:

"July 5. Sunday. To Westminster Abbey morning service. Stayed to the Sacrament. A very odd experience, amid a crowd of strangers."

Among other incidents of his life in London during these years was also one that he used to recall with interest when writing *The Dynasts*—his hearing Palmerston speak in the House of Commons a short time before his death, Palmerston having been War Secretary during the decisive hostilities with Napoleon embodied in the third part of Hardy's Epic-Drama, a personal conjunction which brought its writer face to face not only with actual participants in the great struggle—as was the case with his numerous acquaintance of rank-and-file who had fought in the Peninsula and at Waterloo—but with one who had contributed to direct the affairs of that war. The only note on the fact that can be found is the following:

"Oct 18. [1865]—Wet evening. At Regent Circus coming home saw the announcement of the death of Ld. Palmerston, whom I heard speak in the House of Commons a year or two ago."

"Oct 27.—To Westminster Abbey with Mr Heaton and Lee. Took up a position in the Triforium, from which spot I saw Ld. Palmerston lowered into the grave. Purcell's service. Dead March in Saul."

Through this winter the following note continually occurs: "Read some more Horace."

His interest in painting led him to devote for many months, on every day that the National Gallery was open, twenty minutes after lunch to an inspection of the masters hung there, confining his attention to a single master on each visit, and forbidding his eyes to stray to any other. He went there from sheer liking, and not with any practical object; but he used to recommend the plan to young people, telling them that they would insensibly acquire a greater insight into schools and styles by this means than from any guide books to the painters' works and manners.

During Phelps's series of Shakespeare plays at Drury Lane Hardy followed up every one, his companion being one of Blomfield's pupils. They used to carry a good edition of the play with them, and be among the first of the pit queue, holding the book edgewise on the barrier in front during the performance—a severe enough test for the actors if they noticed the two enthusiasts. He always said that Phelps never received his due as a Shakespearean actor—particularly as Falstaff.

He also frequented the later readings by Charles Dickens at the Hanover Square Rooms, and oratorios at Exeter Hall.

SUMMER 1867

Adelphi Terrace, as everybody knows, faces the river, and in each recurrent summer while Hardy was there the stench from the mud at low water increased, the Metropolitan main-drainage system not having been yet constructed. Whether from the effects of this smell upon a constitution that had grown up in a pure country atmosphere (as he himself supposed), or because he had been accustomed to shut himself up in his rooms at Westbourne Park Villas every evening from six to twelve reading incessantly, instead of getting out for air after the day's confinement, Hardy's health had become much weakened. He used to say that on sitting down to begin drawing in the morning he had scarcely physical power left him to hold the pencil and square. When he visited his friends in Dorset they were shocked at the pallor which sheeted a countenance formerly ruddy with health. His languor increased month by month. Blomfield, who must have been inconvenienced by it, suggested to Hardy that he should go into the country for a time to regain vigour. Hardy was beginning to feel that he would rather go into the country altogether. He constitutionally shrank from the business of social advancement, caring for life as an emotion rather than for life as a science of climbing, in which respect he was quizzed by his acquaintance for his lack of ambition. However, Blomfield thought that to stay permanently in the country would be a mistake, advising him to return to London by the following October at latest.

An opportunity of trying the experiment, at any rate, was afforded by the arrival of a communication from Mr Hicks, his old instructor in architecture, asking if he could recommend him any good assistant accustomed to church-restoration, as he was hampered by frequently suffering from gout. Hardy wrote that he would go himself, and at the latter part of July (1867) went down to Dorchester, leaving most of his books and other belongings behind him at Westbourne Park, which included such of his poems in manuscript as he had thought worth keeping. Of these the only ones not ultimately destroyed were consigned to darkness till between thirty and forty years after, when they were printed—mainly in *Wessex Poems*, though several, that had been overlooked at first, in later volumes. Among the earliest were "Amabel", "Hap", "In Vision I Roamed", "At a Bridal", "Postponement", "A Confession to a Friend", "Neutral Tones", "Her Dilemma", "Revulsion", "Her Reproach", "The Ruined Maid", "Heiress and Architect", and four sonnets called "She, to Him" (part of a much larger number which perished). Some had been sent to magazines, one sonnet that he rather liked, which began "Many a one has loved as much as I", having been lost, the editor never returning it and Hardy having kept no copy. But most had never been sent anywhere.

It should be mentioned that several months before leaving London he had formed an idea of writing plays in blank verse—and had planned to try the stage as a supernumerary for six or twelve months, to acquire technical skill in their construction—going so far as to make use of an introduction to Mark Lemon the then editor of *Punch,* and an ardent amateur-actor, for his opinion on this point. Nothing however came of the idea beyond the call on the genial editor, and on Mr Coe the stage-manager at the Haymarket under Buckstone's lesseeship, with whom he had a conversation. The former rather damped the young man's ardour by reminding him that the elder Mathews had said that he would not let a dog of his go on the stage, and that he himself, much as he personally liked the art of acting, would rather see a daughter of his in her grave than on the boards of a theatre. In fact almost the first moment of his sight of stage realities disinclined him to push further in that direction; and his only actual contact with the stage at this time was his appearance at Covent Garden as a nondescript in the pantomime of "The Forty Thieves", and in a representation of the Oxford and Cambridge boat-race—this having come about through the accident of the smith who did the ironwork for the pantomime being the man who executed some of Blomfield's designs for church metalwork, and who made crucifixes and harlequin-traps with equal imperturbability. More than forty years were to elapse before Hardy trod the same boards again—this time at rehearsals of the Italian Opera by Baron Frédéric d'Erlanger, founded on *Tess of the d'Urbervilles*.

"End of Dec. 1865.—To insects the twelvemonth has been an epoch, to leaves a life, to tweeting birds a generation, to man a year."

NOTES OF 1866–67

"A certain man: He creeps away to a meeting with his own sensations."

"He feels himself shrink into nothing when contemplating other people's *means* of working. When he looks upon their *ends* he expands with triumph."

"There is no more painful lesson to be learnt by a man of capacious mind than that of excluding general knowledge for particular."

"The defects of a class are more perceptible to the class immediately below it than to itself."

"June 6. Went to Hatfield. Changed since my early visit. A youth thought the altered highway had always run as it did. Pied rabbits in the Park, descendants of those I knew. The once children are quite old inhabitants. I regretted that the beautiful sunset did not occur in a place of no reminiscences, that I might have enjoyed it without their tinge."

"June 19. A widely appreciative mind mostly fails to achieve a great work from pure far-sightedness. The very clearness with which he discerns remote possibilities is, from its nature, scarcely ever co-existent with the microscopic vision demanded for tracing the narrow path that leads to them."

"July 13. A man's grief has a touch of the ludicrous unless it is so keen as to be awful."

"Feb. 18. Remember that Evil dies as well as Good."

"April 29. Had the teachings of experience grown cumulatively with the age of the world we should have been ere now as great as God."

CHAPTER IV

Between Architecture and Literature

1867–1870: *Aet.* 27–30

END OF SUMMER 1867

A few weeks in the country—where he returned to his former custom of walking to the Dorchester architect's office from his mother's house every day—completely restored him. He easily fell into the old routes that he had followed before, though, with between five and six years superadded of experience as a young man at large in London, it was with very different ideas of things.

Among the churches for restoration or rebuilding that Hicks had in hand, or in prospect, was one which should be named here—that of the parish of St. Juliot in Cornwall—for which remote spot Mr Hicks set out one day to report upon the said building, shortly after Hardy had gone back to help him. Hardy noticed the romantic name of the church and parish—but had no idea of the meaning it would have for him in aftertime.

An effect among others of his return to the country was to take him out of the fitful yet mechanical and monotonous existence that befalls many a young man in London lodgings. Almost suddenly he became more practical, and queried of himself definitely how to achieve some tangible result from his desultory yet strenuous labours at literature during the previous four years. He considered that he knew fairly well both West-country life in its less explored recesses, and the life of an isolated student cast upon the billows of London with no protection but his brains—the young man of whom it may be said more truly than perhaps of any, that "save his own soul he hath no star". The two contrasting experiences seemed to afford him abundant materials out of which to evolve a striking socialistic novel—not that he mentally defined it as such, for the word had probably never, or scarcely ever, been heard of at that date.

So down he sat in one of the intervals of his attendances at Mr Hicks's drawing-office (which were not regular), and, abandoning verse as a waste of labour—though he had resumed it awhile on arriving in the country—he began the novel the title of which is here written as it was at first intended to be:

The Poor Man and the Lady.
A Story with no plot;
Containing some original verses.

This however he plainly did not like, for it was ultimately abridged to

The Poor Man and the Lady;
By the Poor Man.

And the narrative was proceeded with till, in October of this year (1867), he paid a flying visit to London to fetch his books and other impedimenta.

Thus it happened that under the stress of necessity he had set about a kind of literature in which he had hitherto taken but little interest—prose fiction; so little indeed, that at one of the brief literary lectures, or speeches, he had occasionally delivered to Blomfield's pupils in a spare half-hour of an afternoon, he had expressed to their astonishment an indifference to a popular novelist's fame.

1868. JANUARY 16 AND ONWARDS

We find from an entry in a note-book that on this date he began to make a fair copy of the projected story, so that all of it must have been written out roughly during the five preceding months in the intervals of his architectural work for Hicks. In the February following a memorandum shows that he composed a lyric entitled "A Departure by Train", which has disappeared. In April he was reading Browning and Thackeray; also taking down the exact sound of the song of the nightingale—the latter showing that he must have been living in sylvan shades at his parents', or at least sleeping there, at the time, where nightingales sang within a yard of the bedroom windows in those days, though they do not now.

On June 9 he enters, "Finished copying MS.", and on the 17th is recorded at some length the outline of a narrative poem on the Battle of the Nile. It was never finished, but it shows that the war with Napoleon was even then in his mind as material for poetry of some sort.

On July 1 he writes down—in all likelihood after a time of mental depression over his work and prospects:

"Cures for despair:

    To read Wordsworth's 'Resolution and Independence'.

    „   „   Stuart Mill's 'Individuality' (in *Liberty*).

    „   „   Carlyle's 'Jean Paul Richter'."

On July 17 he writes: "Perhaps I can do a volume of poems consisting of the *other side* of common emotions." What this means is not quite clear.

On July 25 he posted the MS. of *The Poor Man and the Lady* to Mr Alexander Macmillan, and now being free of it lent some more help to Mr Hicks in his drawings for church-restorations, reading the Seventh Book of the *Aeneid* between whiles.

"August 12. A reply from Macmillan on the MS."

The letter was a very long and interesting one, and is printed in full in the *Letters of Alexander Macmillan*. The well-known publisher begins by stating that he had read the novel "with care, and with much interest and admiration, but feeling at the same time that it has what seem to me drawbacks fatal to its success, and what I think, judging the writer from the book itself, you would feel even more strongly, to its truthfulness and justice".

He then went into particulars of criticism. "The utter heartlessness of *all* the conversation you give in drawing-rooms and ballrooms about the working-classes has some ground of truth, I fear, and might justly be scourged as you aim at doing; but your chastisement would fall harmless from its very excess. Will's speech to the working men is full of wisdom. . . .

"Much of the writing seems to me admirable. The scene in Rotten Row is full of power and insight. . . . You see I am writing to you as a writer who seems to me, at least potentially, of considerable mark, of power and purpose. If this is your first book I think you ought to go on. May I ask if it is, and—you are not a lady, so perhaps you will forgive the question—are you young?

"I have shown your MS. to one friend, whose judgment coincides with my own."

The opinion of the friend—who was Mr John Morley—was enclosed. He said that the book was "A very curious and original performance: the opening pictures of the Christmas-Eve in the tranter's house are really of good quality: much of the writing is strong and fresh". But he added as to its faults that "the thing hangs too loosely together", and that some of the scenes were wildly extravagant, "so that they read like some clever lad's dream". He wound up by saying, "If the man is young he has stuff and purpose in him."

It was perhaps not usual for a first haphazard attempt at fiction to receive such close attention from so experienced a publisher as Mr Macmillan, and so real a man of letters as Mr Morley. However, Hardy seems to have done little in the matter during the autumn, beyond rewriting some of the pages; but in December he paid a flying visit to London, and saw Mr Macmillan.

The substance of the interview was that though *The Poor Man and the Lady*, if printed, might create a considerable curiosity, it was a class of book which Macmillan himself could not publish; but if Hardy were bent on issuing it he would probably have no difficulty in doing so through another firm, such as that of Chapman and Hall. The young man, it is assumed, was so bent, for Mr Macmillan gave him an introduction to Mr Frederick Chapman, and Hardy called on the latter with the MS. under his arm. He makes a note on December 8 that he had been to see Chapman, adding: "I fear the interview was an unfortunate one." He returned to Dorchester, leaving the MS. in Mr Chapman's hands, and this brought the year to an unsatisfactory close—so far as it affected Hardy's desire to get into print as the author of a three-volume novel, since he could not do so as a poet without paying for publication.

In the midst of these attempts at authorship, and the intermittent preparation of architectural drawings, Hardy found time to read a good many books. The only reference discoverable includes various plays of Shakespeare, Walpole's *Letters to Sir Horace Mann* in six volumes, Thackeray, Macaulay, Walt Whitman, Virgil's *Aeneid* (of which he never wearied), and other books during his interval of leisure.

The following note, amongst others, occurs in his pocket-book this autumn:

"The village sermon. If it was very bad the parish concluded that he [the vicar] wrote it himself; if very good, that his wife wrote it; if middling, that he bought it, so that they could have a nap without offending him." What parish this refers to is unknown.

There is also another note, some days later:

"How people will laugh in the midst of a misery! Some would soon get to whistle in Hell."

1869

Presumably it was the uncertainty of his position between architecture and literature, and a vague sense of ominousness at getting no reply (so far as can be ascertained) from Messrs Chapman and Hall, that led Hardy to London again during the January of the new year.

Suggestions that he should try his hand at articles in reviews were made to him by Mr Macmillan, and also by the critic of his manuscript, Mr Morley, with whom he got acquainted about this time, Morley offering him an introduction to the editor of the *Saturday Review*. But Hardy was not so much in want of a means of subsistence—having always his father's house to fall back upon in addition to architectural jobs—which were offered him readily by Blomfield and other London architects—as of a clear call to him which course in life to take—the course he loved, and which was his natural instinct, that of letters, or the course all practical wisdom dictated—that of architecture.

He stayed on in London at lodgings, studying pictures at the

South Kensington Museum and other places, and reading desultorily, till at last a letter did arrive from Chapman and Hall. On his calling at their address in Piccadilly Chapman was in the back part of the shop, and on Hardy's joining him said with nonchalance, ignoring Hardy's business, "You see that old man talking to my clerk. He's Thomas Carlyle." Hardy turned and saw leaning on one elbow at the clerk's desk an aged figure in an inverness cape and slouched hat. "Have a good look at him," continued Chapman. "You'll be glad I pointed him out to you some day." Hardy was rather surprised that Chapman did not think enough of Thomas Carlyle to attend to his wants in person; but said nothing.

The publisher stated they could not purchase the MS. outright, but that they would publish it if he would guarantee a small sum against loss—say £20. The offer on the whole was fair and reasonable: Hardy agreed to the guarantee, Chapman promised to put the book in hand and send a memorandum of his undertaking to publish it; and Hardy shortly after left London, expecting proof-sheets soon to be forwarded.

As they did not come he may have written to inquire about them; anyhow Messrs Chapman suddenly asked him in a note if he would call on them and meet "the gentleman who read your manuscript"—whose opinion they would like him to have.

He went in March, by appointment as to the day and hour, it is believed, not knowing that the "gentleman" was Mr George Meredith. He was shown into a back room of the publishing offices (opposite Sackville Street, and where Prince's Restaurant now stands); and before him, in the dusty and untidy apartment, piled with books and papers, was a handsome man in a frock coat— "buttoned at the waist, but loose above"—no other than Meredith in person, his ample dark-brown beard, wavy locks, and somewhat dramatic manner lending him a striking appearance to the younger man's eye, who even then did not know his name.

Meredith had the manuscript in his hand, and began lecturing Hardy upon it in a sonorous voice. No record was kept by the latter of their conversation, but the gist of it he remembered very well. It was that the firm were willing to publish the novel as agreed, but that he, the speaker, strongly advised its author not to "nail his colours to the mast" so definitely in a first book, if he wished to do anything practical at literature; for if he printed so pronounced a thing he would be attacked on all sides by the conventional reviewers, and his future injured. The story was, in fact, a sweeping dramatic satire of the squirearchy and nobility, London society, the vulgarity of the middle class, modern Christianity, church restoration, and political and domestic morals in general, the author's views, in fact, being obviously those of a young man with "a passion for reforming the world"—those of many a young man before and after him, the tendency of the writing being socialistic, not to say revolutionary; yet not argumentatively so, the style having the affected simplicity of De Foe's (which had long attracted Hardy, as it did Stevenson, years later, to imitation of it); this naïve realism in circumstantial details that were pure inventions being so well assumed that both Macmillan and Morley had been perhaps a little, or more than a little, deceived by its seeming actuality; to Hardy's surprise, when he thought the matter over in later years, that his inexperienced imagination should have created figments that could win credence from such experienced heads.

The satire was obviously pushed too far—as sometimes by Swift and De Foe—and portions of the book apparently taken in earnest by Mr Morley and Mr Macmillan had no foundation either in Hardy's beliefs or his experience. One instance he could remember was a chapter in which, with every circumstantial detail, he described in the first person his introduction to the kept mistress of an architect who "took in washing" (as it was called)—that is, worked at his own office for other architects—the said mistress adding to her lover's income by designing for him the pulpits, altars, reredoses, texts, holy vessels, crucifixes, and other ecclesiastical furniture which were handed on to him by the nominal architects who employed her keeper—the lady herself being a dancer at a music-hall when not engaged in designing Christian emblems—all told so plausibly as to seem actual proof of the degeneracy of the age. There is no doubt that this scene, if printed, would have brought down upon his head the cudgels of all the orthodox reviews.

Whatever might have been the case with the other two, Meredith was not taken in by the affected simplicity of the narrative, and that was obviously why he warned his young acquaintance that the press would be about his ears like hornets if he published his manuscript. For though the novel might have been accepted calmly enough by the reviewers and public in these days, in genteel mid-Victorian 1869 it would no doubt have incurred, as Meredith judged, severe strictures which might have handicapped a young writer for a long time. It may be added that the most important scenes were laid in London, of which city Hardy had just had between five and six years' constant and varied experience—as only a young man in the metropolis can get it—knowing every street and alley west of St. Paul's like a born Londoner, which he was often supposed to be; an experience quite ignored by the reviewers of his later books who, if he only touched on London in his pages, promptly reminded him not to write of a place he was unacquainted with, but to get back to his sheepfolds.

The upshot of this interview was that Hardy took away the MS. with him to decide on a course.

Mr Meredith had added that Hardy could rewrite the story, softening it down considerably; or what would be much better, put it away altogether for the present, and attempt a novel with a purely artistic purpose, giving it a more complicated "plot" than was attempted with *The Poor Man and the Lady*.

Thus it happened that a first and probably very crude manuscript by an unknown young man, who had no connection with the press, or with literary circles, was read by a most experienced publisher, and by two authors among the most eminent in letters of their time. Also that they had been interested to more than an average degree in his work, as was shown by their wish to see him, and their voluntary bestowal of good counsel.

Except the writer himself, these three seem to have been the only ones whose eyes ever scanned the MS.

It was surprising enough to Hardy to find that, in the opinion of such experienced critics, he had written so aggressive and even dangerous a work (Mr Macmillan had said it "meant mischief") almost without knowing it, for his mind had been given in the main to poetry and other forms of pure literature. What he did with the MS. is uncertain, and he could not precisely remember in after years, though he found a few unimportant leaves of it—now also gone. He fancied that he may have sent it to some other publisher just as it stood, to get another opinion before finally deciding its fate, which publisher may have thought it too risky also. What happened in respect of new writing was that he took Meredith's advice too literally, and set about constructing the eminently "sensational" plot of *Desperate Remedies*, of which anon.

Meanwhile, during his stay in London in the winter, Hardy heard news of the death at Dorchester of Mr John Hicks whose pupil he had been, and whom he had lately assisted; and at the end of April received a request from Mr G. R. Crickmay, an architect of Weymouth, who had purchased Mr Hicks's practice, to aid him in carrying out the church-restorations that Hicks had begun, or undertaken to begin. Hardy called on Mr Crickmay, who appeared not to have specially studied Gothic architecture, if at all, but was an amiable, straight-dealing man; and Hardy assented to help him finish the churches. Probably thinking of his book, he agreed for a fortnight only in the first place, though Mr Crickmay had asked for a longer time.

During May Hardy continued to prepare for Crickmay, in Hicks's old Dorchester office, the church-drawings he had already made some progress with; and the arrangement proved eminently satisfactory, as is evident, Mr Crickmay proposing to enlist Hardy's services for three months certain at his Weymouth office, the church-work left unfinished by Hicks turning out to be more than had been anticipated. It is to be gathered that Hardy considered this brief occupation would afford, at any rate, breathing-time while he should ruminate on what it was best to do about the novels, and he closed with Crickmay for a term which was afterwards still further lengthened, by unforeseen circumstances.

He used to remember that after coming away from the interview with Crickmay with much lightness of heart at having shelved further thought about himself for at least three months, he stood opposite the Burdon Hotel on the Esplanade, facing the beautiful sun-lit bay, and listened to the Town band's performance of a set of charming new waltzes by Johann Strauss. He inquired their name, and found that it was the "Morgenblätter". The verses "At a Seaside Town" must refer in their background to this place at this time and a little onward, though the gist of them can be fancy only.

He now became regularly resident at Weymouth, and took lodgings there, rowing in the Bay almost every evening of this summer, and bathing at seven in the morning either on the pebble-beach towards Preston, or diving off from a boat. Being—like Swinburne—a swimmer, he would lie a long time on his back on the surface of the waves, rising and falling with the tide in the warmth of the morning sun. He used to tell that, after the enervation of London, this tonic existence by the sea seemed ideal, and that physically he went back ten years in his age almost as by the touch of an enchanter's wand.

In August or September a new assistant came to Mr Crickmay's drawing-offices, who was afterwards sketched in *Desperate Remedies* as "Edward Springrove"—and in November this young man persuaded Hardy to join a quadrille class in the town, which was a source of much amusement to them both. Dancing was still an art in those days, though Hardy remarked once that he found the young ladies of Weymouth heavier on the arm than their London sisters. By the time that winter drew on he had finished all the drawings for church-restoration that had been placed in his hands, but he remained at his Weymouth lodgings working at the MS. of *Desperate Remedies*, the melodramatic novel quite below the level of *The Poor Man and the Lady* which was the unfortunate consequence of Mr Meredith's advice to "write a story with a plot".

A DEVELOPMENT

So 1869 passed, and at the beginning of February in the year following Hardy gave up his rooms at Weymouth and returned to his rural home to be able to concentrate more particularly on the MS. than he could do in a lively town and as a member of a dancing-class where a good deal of flirtation went on, the so-called "class" being, in fact, a gay gathering for dances and love-making by adepts of both sexes. The poem entitled "The Dawn after the Dance", and dated "Weymouth, 1869", is supposed, though without proof, to have some bearing on these dances.

He had not been in the seclusion of his mother's house more than a week when he received the following letter from Mr Crickmay, which, as it led to unexpected emotional developments, it may be worth while to give verbatim:

> Weymouth,
> 11th. February 1870
>
> Dear Sir:
>
> Can you go into Cornwall for me, to take a plan and particulars of a church I am about to rebuild there? It must be done early next week, and I should be glad to see you on Monday morning.
>
> Yours truly,
>
> G. R. Crickmay.

This was the church of St. Juliot, near Boscastle, of which Hardy had vaguely heard in Mr John Hicks's time as being likely to turn up for manipulation, and had been struck by its romantic sound.

Despite the somewhat urgent summons he declined the job, the moment being inconvenient with the new novel in hand. But receiving a more persuasive request from Crickmay later, and having finished the MS. of *Desperate Remedies* (except the three or four final chapters) by the beginning of March, he agreed to go on the errand.

Sending off therefore on the previous Saturday the copy of his second novel to Mr Alexander Macmillan, whom he now regarded as a friend, he set out on Monday, March 7, for the remote parish mentioned, in a county he had never entered, though it was not distant. It was a journey of seeming unimportance, and was reluctantly undertaken, yet it turned out to have life-long consequences for him. The restoration of this church was, moreover, the work which brought to a close Hardy's labours in Gothic architecture, though he did not know it at the time.

Though the distance was not great the way was tedious, there being few railways in Cornwall at this date. Rising at four in the morning, and starting by starlight from his country retreat armed with sketch-book, measuring-tape and rule, he did not reach Launceston till four in the afternoon, where he hired a conveyance for the additional sixteen or seventeen miles' distance by the Boscastle road towards the north coast and the spot with the charming name—the dilapidated church, parish, and residence of the Rev. Caddell Holder, M. A. Oxon.

It was a cloudy evening at the end of a fine day, with a dry breeze blowing, and leaving the Boscastle highway by a bye-road to the left he reached St. Juliot rectory, by which time it was quite dark. His arrival and entry can best be described in the words of the lady whom he met that night for the first time, and who later on became his wife. Long afterwards she wrote down her "Recollections" which are given in the following pages in full so far as they relate to her husband, these making up the whole of the second half of her manuscript, the first half being entirely concerned with other members of her family and herself before she knew him.

She was born at 10 York Street, Plymouth, and baptized at St. Andrew's Church, being the younger daughter of Mr J. Attersoll Gifford, a solicitor. She had grown up in a house close to the Hoe, which she used to call "the playground of her childhood". She would relate how, to her terror at first, she was daily dipped as a little girl in the pools under the Hoe; and on its cliffs—very much more rugged than now—had had her youthful adventures, one of which, leaving her clinging to a crag, would have cost her her life but for the timely aid of a kind boatman. Her education was carried on at a school for young ladies also overlooking the Hoe's green slopes, where, to use her own words, "military drills took place on frequent mornings, and then our dear instructress drew down the blinds". At nineteen she removed from Plymouth with her parents.

CHAPTER V

A Journal, a Supplement, and Literary Vicissitudes

1870: *Aet.* 29–30

The latter part of Mrs (Emma Lavinia) Hardy's MS., found after her death, and entitled "Some Recollections". The words in square brackets are added to make the allusions intelligible.

"My only sister married the Revd. Caddell Holder, son of a Judge of Barbadoes, where he was born: he often spoke of his beautiful home there, with oranges growing by his bedroom window. At Trinity College Oxford he was a 'gentleman-commoner' (this is now abolished), where so far as he could discover his only privilege [from the distinction] was being allowed to walk upon the grass and wear a gold-tasselled cap, he used to say. He was rector of St. Juliot, North Cornwall, where I [first] knew him; and it was there that my husband first made my acquaintance, which afterwards proved a romance in full for us. . . .

"[He was] a man older than herself by many years, and somewhat delicate because of his West Indian birth; he was, however, energetic, and a very Boanerges in his preaching, which style was greatly relished by the simple folk of his scattered parish. In those days clergymen were [often] very lax in their duties, but he was quite exact and faithful, and [after I went to live there with my sister] we were marshalled off in regular staff style to the services. On Sundays they were two only, and the choir *nil*—the whole being carried out by the parson, his wife, myself, and the clerk. The congregation were mostly silent, or merely murmuring occasionally. The duty, however, was only arduous on Sundays.

"They were married from our home, and immediately after went to his—and I went with them—to the said St. Juliot Rectory. My sister required my help, for it was a difficult parish, from neglect by a former incumbent, whose wife, however, had done as much as she could, even to ringing the bell for service.

"At this date [of writing, i.e. 1911] it seems as if all had been arranged in orderly sequence for me, link after link occurring in a chain of movements to bring me to the point where my own fortunes came on.

"St. Juliot is a romantic spot indeed of North Cornwall. It was sixteen miles away from a station then, [and a place] where the belief in witchcraft was carried out in actual practice among the primitive inhabitants. Traditions and strange gossipings [were] the common talk . . . indulged in by those isolated natives [of a parish] where newspapers rarely penetrated, or [were] thrown aside for local news; where new books rarely came, or strangers, and where hard labour upon the stony soil made a cold, often ill-natured, working class; yet with some good traits and fine exceptions. Our neighbours beyond the hamlets were nine miles off, or most of them.

"When we arrived at the Rectory there was a great gathering and welcome from the parishioners, and a tremendous fusilade of salutes, cheering, and bell-ringing—quite a hubbub to welcome the Rector home with his new wife. Then these welcomers (all men and nearly all young) came into the hall to drink the healths of bridegroom and bride, and a speech was made by the foremost young farmer and duly replied to by my brother-in-law. . . . It proved indeed an eventful day for me, for my future was bound up in that day in a way which I could not foresee.

"The whole parish seemed delighted with the event and the prospect of having things in better order after the long neglect. . . . Riding about on my Fanny [her pony] I enjoyed the place immensely, and helped my sister in the house affairs, visiting the parish folk, and playing the harmonium on Sundays. . . .

"It was a very poor parish; the church had been a long while out of repair for want of funds; the Patron lived abroad: in contrast with these days of frequent services [and attendance] it was unfrequented, the Sunday congregation in the morning not large, not much larger in the evenings [afternoons]. No week-day services were held. The tower went on cracking from year to year, and the bells remained in the little north transept [to which they had been removed for safety], their mouths open upward. The carved bench-ends rotted more and more, the ivy hung gaily from the roof timbers, and the birds and the bats had a good time up there unmolested; no one seemed to care. The Architect continued delaying and delaying to come or send his head man to begin operations, though my sister was active in the matter, both Patron and Architect getting urgent appeals from her, till the former decided at last to commence.

"It was the period of Church restoration, most churches being dilapidated more or less. My life now began. . . .

"Scarcely any author and his wife could have had a much more romantic meeting, with its unusual circumstances in bringing them together from two different though neighbouring counties to this one at this very remote spot, with a beautiful sea-coast, and the wild Atlantic Ocean rolling in with its magnificent waves and spray, its white gulls, and black choughs and grey puffins, its cliffs and rocks and gorgeous sunsettings, sparkling redness in a track widening from the horizon to the shore. All this should be seen in the winter to be truly appreciated. No summer visitors can have a true idea of its power to awaken heart and soul. [It was] an unforgettable experience to me, scampering up and down the hills on my beloved mare alone, wanting no protection, the rain going down my back often, and my hair floating in the wind.

"I wore a soft deep dark coloured brown habit longer than to my heels, (as worn then), which had to be caught up to one side when walking, and thrown over the left arm gracefully and carefully, and this to be practised during the riding instruction—all of which my father [had] taught me with great pleasure and pride in my appearance and aptitude. I also wore a brown felt hat turned up at the sides. Fanny and I were one creature, and very happy. She was a lovely brown colour too, stopping where she liked, to drink or munch, I often getting off sketching and gathering flowers. The villagers stopped to gaze when I rushed down the hills, and a butterman laid down his basket once to exclaim loudly. No one except myself dared to ride in such fashion.

"Sometimes I left Fanny, and clambered down to the rocks and seal-caves. Sometimes I visited a favourite in the scattered parish. . . .

"When it was known that the church-restoration was to be gone on with the whole village was alive about it. Mr Crickmay of Weymouth undertook it—Mr Hicks, the first architect consulted, having died in the interval. The [assistant-architect] of his office was to come on a certain day. The letter that brought this intelligence interested the whole house, and afterwards, later in the day, the whole parish too; it seemed almost wonderful that a fixed date should at last be given and the work set in hand, after so many years of waiting, of difficulties, and delays, since back in the time of the previous incumbent. All were delighted. I had myself worked hard for my brother-in-law, collecting small sums from time to time and selling water-colour sketches I had painted, and saving household expenses in order that the historic old church might be rebuilt— there being no landed proprietor, no 'equals' in the parish (as the rector often explained plaintively). So we were all ready to see the fruition of our endeavours, that is, my sister's and mine particularly.

"I must confess to a curiosity started by the coming event as to what the Architect would be like; seeing few strangers we had a vivid interest in every one who came: a strange clergyman, an occasional *locum-tenens*, a school-inspector, a stray missionary, or school-lecturer—all were welcome, including this architect to put us to rights at once.

"It was a lovely Monday evening in March [1870], after a wild winter, that we were on the qui-vive for the stranger,[1] who would have a tedious journey, his home being two counties off by the route necessitated, changing trains many times, and waiting at stations, a sort of cross-jump journey like a chess-knight's move. The only damp to our gladness was the sudden laying up of my brother-in-law by gout, and he who was the chief person could not be present on the arrival of our guest. The dinner cloth was laid; my sister had

---

[1] The verses entitled "A Man was Drawing Near to Me" obviously relate to this arrival. But in them Hardy assumes that she was not thinking about his coming, though from this diary one gathers that she was; which seems to show that when writing them he had either not read her reminiscence of the evening as printed above, or had forgotten it.

gone to her husband who required her constant attention. At that very moment the front-door bell rang, and the architect was ushered in. I had to receive him alone, and felt a curious uneasy embarrassment at receiving anyone, especially so necessary a person as the architect. I was immediately arrested by his familiar appearance, as if I had seen him in a dream—his slightly different accent, his soft voice; also I noticed a blue paper sticking out of his pocket. I was explaining who I was, as I saw that he took me for the parson's daughter or wife, when my sister appeared, to my great relief, and he went up to Mr Holder's room with her.

"So I met my husband. I thought him much older than he was. He had a beard, and a rather shabby great-coat, and had quite a business appearance. Afterwards he seemed younger, and by daylight especially so. . . . The blue paper proved to be the MS. of a poem, and not a plan of the church, he informed me, to my surprise.

"After this our first meeting there had to be many visits to the church, and these visits, of deep interest to both, merged in those of further acquaintance and affection, to end in marriage, but not till after four years.

"At first, though I was interested in him, the church-matters were paramount—and in due time I laid the foundation stone one morning [for the aisle and tower that were to be rebuilt], with a bottle containing a record of the proceedings, the school-children attending. I plastered it well, the foreman said. Mr Holder made a speech to the young ones to remember the event and speak of it to their descendants—just as if it had been a matter of world-wide interest. I wonder if they do remember it, and me.

"The work went rapidly on under the direction of the Architect, who had stayed on his first visit rather longer than intended. We showed him some of the neighbourhood, some clergymen and their wives came to visit us: we were all much pleased at the beginning. Mr Holder got well again. The Patron of the living, who lived in Antigua, wrote to inquire about it, an account was duly sent, and he replied that he was coming to see it if he could, and would certainly be at the opening.

"My Architect came two or three times a year from that time to visit me. I rode my pretty mare Fanny and he walked by my side, and I showed him some [more] of the neighbourhood—the cliffs, along the roads, and through the scattered hamlets, sometimes gazing down at the solemn small shores below, where the seals lived,

coming out of great deep caverns very occasionally. We sketched
and talked of books; often we walked to Boscastle Harbour down the
beautiful Vallency Valley where we had to jump over stones and
climb over a low wall by rough steps, or get through a narrow
pathway, to come out on great wide spaces suddenly, with a
sparkling little brook going the same way, in which we once lost a
tiny picnic-tumbler, and there it is to this day no doubt between two
of the boulders.[1]

"Sometimes we all drove to Tintagel, and Trebarwith Strand
where donkeys [word illegible] employed to carry seaweed to the
farmers; Strangles Beach also, Bossiney, Bude, and other places on
the coast. Lovely drives they were, with sea-views all along at
intervals, and very dawdling enjoyable slow ones; sometimes to visit
a neighbouring clergyman and his family. We grew much interested
in each other. I found him a perfectly new subject of study and
delight and he found a 'mine' in me he said. He was quite unlike any
other person who came to see us, for they were slow of speech and
ideas.

"In the intervals of his visits we corresponded, and I studied, and
sketched, and drove my brother-in-law and sister to the nearest
market-town, Camelford, nine miles off, or to Launceston to see my
cousins. The man-servant taught me to jump hurdles on Fanny, but
Fanny, though not at all objecting, got a little lame, so we stopped
jumping.

"I like to think of those details and small events, and am fancying
some other people may like to have them.

"It was a pleasant time, though there were difficulties in the
parish. I have never liked the Cornish working-orders as I do
Devonshire folk; their so-called admirable independence of character was most disagreeable to live with, and usually amounted to
absence of kindly interest in others, though it was unnoticeable by
casual acquaintance. . . . Nevertheless their nature had a glamour
about it—that of an old-world romantic expression; and then
sometimes there came to one's cognizance in the hamlets a dear
heart-whole person.

"So the days went on between the visits. The church-opening was
somewhat impressive, the element of unusualness being more
conspicuous however by the immense numbers of people outside

[1] This incident was versified by Hardy afterwards and entitled "Under the
Waterfall".

waiting for it to be over and the lunch to begin, than the many attentive and admiring parishioners within, collected imperatively by the rector's wife and himself. Mr Holder was in a good state of health and spirits; my sister was very important. The patron of the living Mr [Bishop?] Rawle, who lived at Antigua, was present; but no architect came on that brilliant occasion.[1] He appeared, however, on the same scene from time to time afterwards.

"I had two pleasant changes—one to stay at Bath with an old friend of the family; and when my chosen came there too, by her kindness, we together had an interesting time. And I went as country cousin to my brother in London, and was duly astonished, which gave him even more pleasure than it did me.

"After a little time I copied a good deal of manuscript, which went to and fro by post, and I was very proud and happy doing this—which I did in the privacy of my own room, where I also read and wrote the letters.

"The rarity of the visits made them highly delightful to both; we talked much of plots, possible scenes, tales and poetry, and of his own work. He came either from Dorset or London, driving from Launceston station eighteen [sixteen and a half] miles off.

"The day we were married was a perfect September day—the 17th. of the month—1874,—not of brilliant sunshine, but wearing a soft sunny luminousness; just as it should be.

"I have had various experiences, interesting some, sad others, since that lovely day, but all showing that an Unseen Power of great benevolence directs my ways; I have some philosophy and mysticism, and an ardent belief in Christianity and the life beyond this present one, all which makes any existence curiously interesting. As one watches *happenings* (and even if should occur unhappy happenings), outward circumstances are of less importance if Christ is our highest ideal. A strange unearthly brilliance shines around our path, penetrating and dispersing difficulties with its warmth and glow.

[signed] "E. L. Hardy,
"Max Gate,
"January 4th. 1911."[2]

This transcript from the first Mrs Hardy's "Recollections" (of the

---

[1] Neither Hardy nor Crickmay was able to attend, for some unknown reason.
[2] It will be seen later that she died the year after this was written.

existence of which he was unaware till after her death) has carried us onward four years further than the date of Thomas Hardy's arrival in Cornwall on that evening of March 1870. He himself entered in a memorandum-book a few rough notes of his visit, and from these we are able to glean vaguely his impressions of the experience.

It is apparent that he was soon, if not immediately, struck by the nature and appearance of the lady who received him. She was so *living*, he used to say. Though her features were not regular her complexion at this date was perfect in hue, her figure and movement graceful, and her corn-coloured hair abundant in its coils. A lock still in existence shows, even after the fading and deterioration of more than half a century, that there was no exaggeration in her friends' admiring memories of it.

It may be mentioned here that the story *A Pair of Blue Eyes* (which Hardy himself classes among his Romances and Fantasies—as if to suggest its visionary nature) has been considered to show a picture of his own personality as the architect on this visit. But in addition to Hardy's own testimony there is proof that this is not the case, he having ever been shy of putting his personal characteristics into his novels. The Adonis depicted was known to be both in appearance and temperament an idealization of a pupil whom Hardy found at Mr John Hicks's on his return there temporarily from London; believed to be a nephew of that architect, and exactly of the age attributed to Stephen Smith. He is represented as altogether more youthful and sanguine in nature than Hardy, a thoughtful man of twenty-nine, with years of London buffeting, and architectural and literary experiences, was at this time. Many of his verses with which readers have since grown familiar in *Wessex Poems* had already been written. Stephen Smith's father was drawn from a mason in Hardy's father's employ, combined with one near Boscastle; while Smith's ingenious mode of being tutored in Latin was based on a story Hardy had from Holder, as that of a man he had known. Its practicability is, however, doubtful. Henry Knight the reviewer, Elfride's second lover, was really much more like Thomas Hardy as described in his future wife's diary just given; while the event of the young man arriving as a town stranger at a village with which he was quite familiar, and the catastrophe that ensued when his familiarity with it was discovered, was an experience of an uncle of his, of which the dramatic possibilities had long arrested him. His own wooing in the "Delectable Duchy" ran, in fact, without a hitch, and with much encouragement from all parties concerned, from beginning to end, any want of smoothness lying on his own side as to the question of ways and means to marriage.

But the whole story, except as to the lonely drive across the hills towards the coast, the architectural detail, and a few other external scenes and incidents, is so at variance with any possible facts as to be quite misleading, Hardy's wilful purpose in his early novels until *Far from the Madding Crowd* appeared, if not later, having been to mystify the reader as to their locality, origin, and authorship by various interchanges and inventions, probably owing at first to his extreme doubt if he would pursue the craft, and his sense of the shadow that would fall on an architect who had failed as a novelist. He even modified the landscape, and called the rectory a vicarage in early editions, showing a church with the sea visible from it, which was not true of St. Juliot. The character and appearance of Elfride have points in common with those of Mrs Hardy in quite young womanhood, a few years before Hardy met her (though her eyes would have been described as deep grey, not as blue); moreover, like Elfride, the moment she was on a horse she was part of the animal. But this is all that can be asserted, the plot of the story being one that he had thought of and written down long before he knew her.

What he says about the visit is laconic and hurried, but interesting enough to be given here:

"March 7. The dreary yet poetical drive over the hills. Arrived at St. Juliot Rectory between 6 and 7 [somewhat later probably]. Received by young lady in brown, (Miss Gifford, the rector's sister-in-law). Mr Holder gout. Saw Mrs Holder. The meal. Talk. To Mr Holder's room. Returned downstairs. Music."

"March 8. Austere grey view of hills from bedroom window. A funeral. Man tolled the bell (which stood inverted on the ground in the neglected transept) by lifting the clapper and letting it fall against the side. Five bells stood thus in a row (having been taken down from the cracked tower for safety). Stayed there drawing and measuring all day, with intervals for meals at rectory."

"March 9. Drove with Mrs Holder and Miss Gifford to Boscastle, and on to Tintagel and Penpethy slate-quarries, with a view to the church roofing. Mr Symons accompanied us to the quarries. Mr Symons did not think himself a native;—he was only born there. Now Mrs Symons *was* a native; her family had been there 500 years.

Talked about Douglas Cook coming home [the first editor of the *Saturday Review*, whom the Holders had known; buried on the hill above Tintagel]. . . . Music in the evening. The two ladies sang duets, including 'The Elfin Call', 'Let us dance on the sands', etc. . . . Miss Gifford said that a man asked her for 'a drop o' that that isn't gin, please, Miss.' He meant hollands, which they kept at the Rectory, as he knew."

"March 10th. Went with E. L. G. to Beeny Cliff. She on horseback—. . . . On the cliff. . . . 'The tender grace of a day', etc. The run down to the edge. The coming home. . . .

"In the afternoon I walked to Boscastle, Mrs H. and E. L. G. accompanying me three-quarters of the way: the overshot mill: E. provokingly reading as she walked; evening in garden; music later in evening."

"March 11. Dawn. Adieu. E. L. G. had struck a light six times in her anxiety to call the servants early enough for me. The journey home. Photo of Bishop of Exeter (for Mrs Holder). . . . "

The poem entitled "At the Word 'Farewell' " seems to refer either to this or the following visit; and the one called "When I set out for Lyonnesse" refers certainly to this first visit, it having been his custom to apply the name "Lyonnesse" to the whole of Cornwall. The latter poem, it may be mentioned, was hailed by a distant voice from the West of America as his sweetest lyric, an opinion from which he himself did not dissent, though in England the lines passed quite without notice.

"March 12th. (Sat.) Went to Weymouth. Mr Crickmay's account £6—10—9."

On April 5, having resumed lodgings at Weymouth, to proceed, probably, with the detailed drawings for the restoration of St. Juliot Church by the light of the survey and measurements he had made, Hardy received a letter from the Messrs Macmillan declining to publish *Desperate Remedies*, the MS. of which they returned, on the ground (it is conjectured) of their disapproval of the incidents. By this time it seemed to have dawned upon him that the Macmillan publishing-house was not in the way of issuing novels of a sensational kind: and accordingly he packed up the MS. again and posted it to the Messrs Tinsley, a firm to which he was a stranger, but which did publish such novels. Why he did not send it to Messrs Chapman and Hall, with whom he had now a slight link, and whose reader, Mr Meredith, had recommended him to write what Hardy understood to be a story of this kind, is inexplicable. Possibly it was from an adventurous feeling that he would like the story to be judged on its own merits by a house which had no knowledge of how it came into existence; possibly from inexperience. Anyhow it was a mistake from which he suffered, for there is no doubt that Meredith would have taken an interest in a book he had, or was supposed to have, instigated; and would have offered some suggestions on how to make a better use of the good material at the back of the book. However, to Tinsley's it had gone, and on May 6 Tinsley wrote, stating the terms on which he would publish it, if Hardy would complete the remaining three or four chapters of which a *précis* only had been sent.

About the second week in May, and possibly as a result of the correspondence, Hardy left Mr Crickmay (whose church-designing he appears to have airily used as something of a stop-gap when his own literary enterprises hung fire) and on the following Monday, the 16th, he started again for London—sadly, as he said, for he had left his heart in Cornwall.

"May 18. Royal Academy. No. 118. 'Death of Ney', by Gérôme. The presence of Death makes the picture great.

"No. 985. 'Jerusalem', by the same. The *shadows only* of the three crucified ones are seen. A fine conception."

He seems to have passed the days in Town desultorily and dreamily—mostly visiting museums and picture-galleries, and it is not clear what he was waiting for there. In his leisure he seems to have written the "Ditty" in *Wessex Poems*, inscribed with Miss Gifford's initials. In May he was reading Comte. Crossing Hyde Park one morning in June he saw the announcement of Dickens's death. He was welcomed by Mr Blomfield, to whom he lent help in finishing some drawings. Being acquainted with another well-known Gothic architect, Mr Raphael Brandon, Hardy assisted him also for a few weeks, though not continuously.

Brandon was a man who interested him much. In collaboration with his brother David he had published, several years before, the *Analysis of Gothic Architecture* in two quarto volumes, and an extra volume on the *Open Timber Roofs of the Middle Ages*. Both these works were familiar to Hardy, having been quite text-books for architects' pupils till latterly, when the absorbing interest given to French Gothic had caused them to be superseded by the works of Norman Shaw, Nesfield, and Viollet-le-Duc. Brandon, however, was convinced that the development of modern English architecture should be based on English Gothic and not on French, as was shown in his well-known design for the Catholic-apostolic Church in Gordon Square; and that his opinion was the true one was proved in the sequel, notwithstanding that the more fashionable architects, including Arthur Blomfield, were heart and soul of the other opinion at this date. It may have been partly on this account, partly because he was a "literary architect"—a person always suspect in the profession in those days, Hardy used to say—that Brandon's practice had latterly declined, and he had drifted into a backwater, spending much time in strange projects and hopes, one of these being a scheme for unifying railway fares on the principle of letter postage. Hardy was in something of a similar backwater himself—so far as there could be similarity in the circumstances of a man of twenty-nine and a man of sixty, and the old-world out-of-the-way corner of Clement's Inn where Brandon's offices were situate made his weeks with Brandon still more attractive to him, Knight's chambers in *A Pair of Blue Eyes* being drawn from Brandon's. Whilst the latter attended to his scheme for railway travel, Hardy attended off and on to Brandon's architecture, which had fallen behindhand. Sometimes Hardy helped him also in the details of his scheme; though, having proved to himself its utter futility, he felt in an awkward dilemma; whether to show Brandon its futility and offend him, or to go against his own conscience by indulging him in the hobby.

However, the summer was passed in this way, and his friend Moule, the reviewer and leader-writer, being also in London, the time was pleasant enough. Nothing seems to have been done about the novel, of which the MS., representing about seven-eighths of the whole, was apparently still lying at Tinsley's. He kept up a regular correspondence with "the young lady in brown" who had attracted him at St. Juliot rectory, and sent books to her, reading himself among other works Shakespeare and general poetry as usual, the Bible, Alison's *Europe*, and *Mohammed and Mohammedanism* by Bosworth Smith, his friend in later years; though it does not appear that he wrote any verses.

"June 30. What the world is saying, and what the world is thinking: It is the man who bases his action upon what the world is thinking, no matter what it may be saying, who rises to the top.

"It is not by rushing straight towards fame that men come up with her, but by so adapting the direction of their path to hers that at some point ahead the two must inevitably intersect."

On July 15 war was declared by France against Prussia—a cause of much excitement to Brandon, who during the early weeks of the struggle would go into the Strand for every edition of the afternoon papers as they came out, and bring them in and read them to Hardy, who grew as excited as he; though probably the younger man did not realize that, should England have become involved in the Continental strife, he might have been among the first to be called upon to serve, outside the regular army. All he seems to have done was to go to a service at Chelsea Hospital and look at the tattered banners mended with netting, and talk to the old asthmatic and crippled men, many of whom in the hospital at that date had fought at Waterloo, and some in the Peninsula.

On August 6 occurred the Battle of Wörth: and on the 8th, in keeping with a promise given when he was previously there, he severed his temporary connection with Brandon and left for Cornwall.

Here, as he said, he found the "young lady in brown" of the previous winter—at that time thickly muffled from the wind—to have become metamorphosed into a young lady in summer blue, which suited her fair complexion far better; and the visit was a most happy one. His hosts drove him to various picturesque points on the wild and rugged coast near the rectory, among others to King Arthur's Castle, Tintagel, which he now saw for the first time; and where, owing to their lingering too long among the ruins, they found themselves locked in, only narrowly escaping being imprisoned there for the night by much signalling with their handkerchiefs to cottagers in the valley. The lingering might have been considered prophetic, seeing that, after smouldering in his mind for between forty and fifty years, he constructed *The Famous Tragedy of The Queen of Cornwall* from the legends connected with that romantic spot. Why he did not do it sooner, while she was still living who knew the scene so well, and had frequently painted it, it is impossible to say.

H. M. Moule, who knew of the vague understanding between the pair, sent them from time to time such of the daily and weekly papers as contained his leading articles on the war. Concerning such wars Hardy entered in his notebook: "Quicquid delirant reges, plectuntur Achivi!" On the day that the bloody battle of Gravelotte was fought they were reading Tennyson in the grounds of the rectory. It was at this time and spot that Hardy was struck by the incident of the old horse harrowing the arable field in the valley below, which, when in far later years it was recalled to him by a still bloodier war, he made into the little poem of three verses entitled "In Time of 'the Breaking of Nations' ". Several of the pieces—as is obvious—grouped as "Poems of 1912–13" in the same volume with "Satires of Circumstance", and three in *Moments of Vision*, namely "The Figure in the Scene", "Why did I sketch", and "It never looks like summer now"—with doubtless many others—are known to be also memories of the present and later sojourns here in this vague romantic land of "Lyonnesse".

It was at this time, too, that he saw the last of St. Juliot Church in its original condition of picturesque neglect, the local builder laying hands on it shortly after, and razing to the ground the tower and the north aisle (which had hitherto been the nave), and the transept. Hardy much regretted the obliteration in this manner of the church's history, and, too, that he should be instrumental in such obliteration, the building as he had first set eyes on it having been so associated with what was romantic in his life. Yet his instrumentality was involuntary, the decision to alter and diminish its area having been come to before he arrived on the scene. What else could be done with the dilapidated structure was difficult to say if it had to be retained for use. The old walls of the former nave, dating from Norman or even earlier times, might possibly have been preserved. A north door, much like a Saxon one, was inadvertently destroyed, but Hardy made a drawing of it which is preserved in the present church, with his drawings of the highly carved seat-ends and other details that have disappeared. Fortunately the old south aisle was kept intact, with its arcade, the aisle now being adapted for a nave.

It was at this church that occurred his humorous experience of the builder's view of the old chancel-screen. Hardy had made a careful drawing of it, with its decayed tracery, posts, and gilding, marking thereon where sundry patchings and scarfings were to be applied. Reaching the building one day he found a new and highly varnished travesty of the old screen standing in its place. "Well, Mr Hardy," replied the builder in answer to his astonished inquiries, "I said to myself, I won't stand on a pound or two while I'm about it, and I'll give 'em a new screen instead of that patched-up old thing."

PART II

Novels—to Illness

CHAPTER VI

A Plot, an Idyll, and a Romance

1870–1873: *Aet.* 30–33

He must when in London have obtained from Tinsley the MS. of *Desperate Remedies*; for during the autumn of this year 1870 there were passing between him and Miss Gifford chapters of the story for her to make a fair copy of, the original MS. having been interlined and altered, so that it may have suffered, he thought, in the eyes of a publisher's reader by being difficult to read. He meanwhile wrote the three or four remaining chapters, and the novel—this time finished—was packed off to Tinsley in December. However, a minute fact seems to suggest that Hardy was far from being in bright spirits about his book, himself, and his future at this time. On the margin of his copy of *Hamlet* the following passage is marked with the date, "December 15. 1870":

"Thou wouldst not think how ill all's here about my heart: but it is no matter!"

Tinsley wrote his terms again, which for some unaccountable reason were worse now than they had been in the first place, an advance of £75 being demanded; and the following is a transcript of Hardy's letter to the publisher on these points, at the end of December:

I believe I am right in understanding your terms thus—that if the gross receipts reach the costs of publishing I shall receive the

85

£75 back again, and if they are more than the costs I shall have
£75, added to half the receipts beyond the costs (i.e., assuming
the expenditure to be £100, and the receipts £200, I should have
returned to me £75 + £50 = £125).

Will you be good enough to say, too, if the sum includes
advertising to the customary extent, and about how long after my
paying the money the book would appear.

This adventurous arrangement by the would-be author, who at
that date had only £123 in the world, beyond what he might have
obtained from his father—which was not much—and who was
virtually if not distinctly engaged to be married to a girl with no
money except in reversion after the death of relatives, was actually
carried out by him in the January following (1871): when, being in
London again, he paid the £75 over to Tinsley in Bank of England
notes (rather, as it seemed, to Tinsley's astonishment, Hardy said)
and retired to Dorset to correct the proofs, filling up leisure
moments not by anything practical, but by writing down such
snatches of the old country ballads as he could hear from aged
people. On the 25th March the book was published anonymously in
three volumes; and on the 30th he again went to his Weymouth
lodgings to lend Mr Crickmay more help in his church-restorations.

On April 1 *Desperate Remedies* received a striking review in the
Athenæum as being a powerful novel, and on April 13 an even better
notice in the *Morning Post* as being an eminent success. But alas, on
the 22nd the *Spectator* brought down its heaviest-leaded pastoral staff
on the prematurely happy volumes, the reason for this violence
being mainly the author's daring to suppose it possible that an
unmarried lady owning an estate could have an illegitimate child.

"This is an absolutely anonymous story," began the review: "no
assumption of a *nom-de-plume* which might, at some future time,
disgrace the family name, and still more the Christian name, of a
repentant and remorseful novelist—and very right too. By all means
let him bury the secret in the profoundest depths of his own heart,
out of reach, if possible, of his own consciousness. The law is hardly
just which prevents Tinsley Brothers from concealing their participation also."

When Moule, whom Hardy had not consulted on the venture,
read the reception of the novel by the *Spectator* he wrote a brief line to
Hardy bidding him not to mind the slating. After its first impact,
which was staggering with good reason, it does not seem to have

worried Hardy much, or at any rate for long (though one of the personalities insinuated by the reviewer, in clumsy humour, that the novel must have been "a desperate remedy for an emaciated purse", may well have been galling enough). And indeed about this time he noted down: "Strictly, we should resent wrongs, be placid at justice, and grateful for favours. But I know one who is placid at a wrong, and would be grateful for simple justice; while a favour, if he ever gained one, would turn his brain."

But that humorous observation was not seriously disturbed in him is shown by what he entered immediately after:

"End of April. At the dairy. The dog looks as if he were glad that he is a dog. The cows look at him with a melancholy expression, as though they were sorry they are cows, and have to be milked, and to show too much dignity to roll in the mulch as he does. . . . The dairymaid flings her feet about the dairy floor in walking, as if they were mops."

Anyhow, in May he enjoyed another visit to Cornwall. But in returning therefrom the day after his birthday in June he received a fresh buffet from circumstance in seeing at Exeter Station *Desperate Remedies* in Messrs Smith and Son's surplus catalogue for sale at 2s. 6d. the three volumes, and thought the *Spectator* had snuffed out the book, as it probably had done.

Although this was a serious matter for a beginner who had ventured on the novel £75 out of the £123 he possessed, one reason for the mitigation of his trouble may well have been that the powerfully not to say wildly melodramatic situations had been concocted in a style which was quite against his natural grain, through too crude an interpretation of Mr Meredith's advice. It was a sort of thing he had never contemplated writing, till, finding himself in a corner, it seemed necessary to attract public attention at all hazards. What Mr Meredith would have thought of the result of his teaching was not ascertained. Yet there was nothing in the book—admittedly an extremely clever novel—to call for such castigation, which, oddly enough, rather stultified itself by certain concessions on the nameless author's ability. Moreover he was surprised some time later by a letter from the reviewer, a stranger— whether dictated by pricks of conscience, an uneasy suspicion that he had mistaken his man, or otherwise, is unknown—showing some regret for his violence. Hardy replied to the letter—tardily and curtly enough at first it is true—but as it dawned upon him that the harm had been done him not through malice but honest wrong-

headedness, he ceased to harbour resentment, and became acquainted with his critic, the *Spectator* reviewing him later with much
generosity.

During June and July he marked time, as it were, by doing some
more Gothic drawings for Crickmay, though in no very grand
spirits, if we may judge from a marginal mark with the date "July
1871" in his Shakespeare, opposite the passage in *Macbeth*:

> Things at their worst will cease, or else climb upward
> To what they were before.

Later in the summer he finished the short and quite rustic story
entitled *Under the Greenwood Tree. A Rural Painting of the Dutch
School*—the execution of which had arisen from a remark of Mr John
Morley's on *The Poor Man and the Lady*, that the country scenes in the
latter were the best in the book, the "tranter" of *The Poor Man and the
Lady* being reintroduced.

The pages of this idyll—at first intended to be called *The Mellstock
Quire* but altered to *Under the Greenwood Tree* because titles from
poetry were in fashion just then—were dispatched to the Messrs
Macmillan some time the same autumn, and in due course Hardy
received from them a letter which, events having rendered him
sensitive, he read to mean that the firm did not wish to have
anything to do with his "Rural Painting of the Dutch School",
although they said that "they felt strongly inclined to avail
themselves of his offer of it"; hence he wrote to them to return the
MS. This was an unfortunate misunderstanding. It was not till its
acceptance and issue by another publishing house the year after that
he discovered they had never declined it, and indeed would have
been quite willing to print it a little later on.

They had taken the trouble to enclose when writing about the
tale the opinion of the "accomplished critic" to whom they had
submitted it, the chief points of which may be quoted here:

> The work in this story is extremely careful, natural, and delicate,
> and the writer deserves more than common credit for the pains
> which he has taken with his style, and with the harmony of his
> construction and treatment. It is a simple and uneventful sketch
> of a rural courtship, with a climax of real delicacy of idea. . . . I
> don't prophesy a large market for it, because the work is so
> delicate as not to hit every taste by any means. But it is good

work, and would please people whose taste was not ruined by
novels of exaggerated action or forced ingenuity. . . . The writer
would do well to shut his ears to the fooleries of critics, which his
letter to you proves that he does not do.

However, deeming their reply on the question of publishing the
tale to be ambiguous at least, he got it back, threw the MS. into a
box with his old poems, being quite sick of all such, and began to
think about other ways and means. He consulted Miss Gifford by
letter, declaring that he had banished novel-writing for ever, and
was going on with architecture henceforward. But she, with no great
opportunity of reasoning on the matter, yet, as Hardy used to think
and say—truly or not—with that rapid instinct which serves women
in such good stead, and may almost be called preternatural vision,
wrote back instantly her desire that he should adhere to authorship,
which she felt sure would be his true vocation. From the very fact
that she wished thus, and set herself aside altogether—architecture
being obviously the quick way to an income for marrying on—he
was impelled to consider her interests more than his own. Unlike the
case of Browning and Elizabeth Barrett no letters between the
couple are extant, to show the fluctuation of their minds on this vital
matter. But what happened was that Hardy applied himself to
architectural work during the winter 1871–72 more steadily than he
had ever done in his life before, and in the spring of the latter year
again set out for London, determined to stifle his constitutional
tendency to care for life only as an emotion and not as a scientific
game, and fully bent on sticking to the profession which had been
the choice of his parents for him rather than his own; but with a faint
dream at the back of his mind that he might perhaps write verses as
an occasional hobby.

The years 1872 and 1873 were pre-eminently years of un-
expectedness. Having engaged to give some help to Mr T. Roger
Smith, a well-known London architect and Professor of Architecture at the Royal Institute of British Architects, he speedily found
himself on his arrival in the first-named year assisting Professor
Smith in designing schools for the London School Board, which had
then lately come into existence, public competition between
architects for such designs being arranged by the Board from time to
time. The proverbial new broom was sweeping large spaces clear in
the city for the purpose of these erections. Hardy had no sooner

settled down to do his best in this business than he met in the middle
of a crossing by Trafalgar Square his friend Moule, whom he had
not seen for a long time. Moule, a scholar and critic of perfect taste,
firmly believed in Hardy's potentialities as a writer, and said he
hoped he still kept a hand on the pen; but Hardy seems to have
declared that he had thrown up authorship at last and for all. Moule
was grieved at this, but merely advised him not to give up writing
altogether, since, supposing anything were to happen to his eyes
from the fine architectural drawing, literature would be a resource
for him; he could dictate a book, article, or poem, but not a
geometrical design. This, Hardy used to say, was essentially all that
passed between them; but by a strange coincidence Moule's words
were brought back to his mind one morning shortly after by his
seeing, for the first time in his life, what seemed like floating specks
on the white drawing-paper before him.

For some reason or other at this date—a year after its publication—he wrote to his publishers to render an account of their
transactions over *Desperate Remedies*, which he had once before
requested, but had not been very curious upon; for though the
Saturday Review had brought the volumes to life after their slaughter
by the *Spectator*, he quite supposed he had lost on the venture both
his time and his money. By the return of post Tinsley Brothers
rendered the account, showing that they had printed 500 copies of
the novel in three volumes, and sold 370, and enclosing a cheque for
£60, as being all that was returnable to him out of the £75 paid as
guarantee—after the costs and the receipts were balanced, no part
of the receipts being due to him.

From these figures Hardy, who did not examine them closely,
found that after all he had only lost his labour and £15 in money—
and was much gratified thereby.

Quite soon after, while reading in the Strand a poster of the
Italian Opera, a heavy hand was laid on his shoulder, and turning
he saw Tinsley himself, who asked when Hardy was going to let him
have another novel.

Hardy, with thoughts of the balance-sheet, drily told him never.

"Wot, now!" said Tinsley. "Haven't you anything written?"

Hardy remarked that he had written a short story some time
before, but didn't know what had become of the MS., and did not
care. He also had outlined one for three volumes; but had
abandoned it. He was now doing better things, and attending to his
profession of architect.

"Damned if that isn't what I thought you wos!" exclaimed

Mr Tinsley. "Well, now, can't you get that story, and show it to me?"

Hardy would not promise, reminding the publisher that the account he had rendered for the other book was not likely to tempt him to publish a second.

"'Pon my soul, Mr Hardy," said Tinsley, "you wouldn't have got another man in London to print it! Oh, be hanged if you would! 'twas a blood-curdling story! Now please try to find that new manuscript and let me see it."

Hardy could not at first recollect what he had done with the MS., but recalling at last he wrote to his parents at home, telling them where to search for it, and to forward it to him.

When, the first week in April, *Under the Greenwood Tree* arrived Hardy sent it on to Tinsley without looking at it, saying he would have nothing to do with any publishing accounts. This probably was the reason why Tinsley offered him £30 for the copyright, which Hardy accepted, caring nothing about the book. It should be added that Tinsley afterwards sent him £10 extra, and quite voluntarily, being, he said, half the amount he had obtained from Tauchnitz for the Continental copyright, of which transaction Hardy had known nothing.

Hardy's indifference in selling *Under the Greenwood Tree* for a trifle could not have been because he still had altogether other aims than the literature of fiction, as had been the case in the previous winter; for he casually mentioned to Tinsley that he thought of going on with the three-volume novel before alluded to. Moule's words on keeping a hand on the pen, and the specks in his eyes while drawing, may have influenced him in this harking back.

In the early part of May he was correcting the proofs of the rural story. It was mostly done late at night, at Westbourne Park, where he was again living, the day being occupied with the competition-drawings for Board schools in the various London districts—and some occasional evenings in preparing drawings for Blomfield, with whom Hardy was in frequent and friendly touch—though he told Blomfield at that time nothing about his adventures as a novel-writer.

Under the Greenwood Tree was published about the last week in May (1872) and met with a very kindly and gentle reception, being reviewed in the *Athenæum* as a book which could induce people "to give up valuable time to see a marriage accomplished in its pages", and in the *Pall Mall Gazette* as a story of much freshness and originality.

As Hardy was at Bedford Chambers in Bedford Street—Professor

Smith's offices—every day, and the office of the publishers was only a street or two further along the Strand, he was not infrequently encountering Tinsley, who one day asked him—the book continuing to receive good notices—for how much he would write a story for *Tinsley's Magazine*, to run a twelvemonth, the question being probably prompted by this tone of the press towards *Under the Greenwood Tree*.

Hardy reflected—on the outlined novel he had abandoned—considered that he could do it in six months—but "to guard against temptation" (as he put it) multiplied by two the utmost he could expect to make at architecture in the time, and told his inquirer the sum.

"All right, all right, Mr Hardy—very reasonable," said the friendly publisher, smacking Hardy's shoulder. "Now come along into the office here, and we'll sign the agreement, and the job will be off our minds."

Hardy, however, for some reason or other was growing wary, and said he would call next day. During the afternoon he went to a law-bookseller, bought *Copinger on Copyright*, the only book on the subject he could meet with, and sat up half the night studying it. Next day he called on Tinsley, and said he would write the story for the sum mentioned, it being understood that the amount paid was for the magazine-issue solely, after which publication all rights were to return to the author.

"Well, I'm damned!" Tinsley said, with a grim laugh. "Who the devil have you been talking to, Mr Hardy, if I may ask, since I saw you yesterday?"

Hardy said "Nobody". (Which was true, though only literally.)

"Well, but—Now, Mr Hardy, you are hard, very hard upon me! However, I do like your writings: and if you'll throw in the three-volume edition of the novel with the magazine rights I'll agree."

Hardy assented to this, having, as he used to say, some liking for Tinsley's keen sense of humour even when it went against himself; and the business was settled shortly after, the author agreeing to be ready with the first monthly part of his story for the magazine soon enough to give the artist time to prepare an illustration for it, and enable it to be printed in the September number, which in the case of this periodical came out on August 15.

It was now the 24th July, and walking back towards Professor

Roger Smith's chambers Hardy began to feel that he had done rather a rash thing. He knew but vaguely the value of a three-volume edition, and as to the story, he had as already mentioned thought of a possible one some time before, roughly noted down the opening chapters and general outline, and then abandoned it with the rest of his literary schemes. He had never written a serial narrative and had no journalistic experience; and he was pledged to the Board-school drawings for at least another week, when they were to be sent in to the Committee. Nevertheless, having promised Tinsley, he resolved to stick to his promise, and on the 27th July agreed by letter.

Apparently without saying anything of his new commitment, he informed the genial Professor of Architecture that he thought he would take a holiday in August, when there would be little more of a pressing nature to do for that year; and going home to Westbourne Park wrote between then and midnight the first chapter or two of *A Pair of Blue Eyes* (not dreaming it was to become the favourite novel of two eminent poets, Tennyson and Coventry Patmore). Even though he may have thought over and roughly set down the beginning of the romance, the writing it out connectedly must have been done very rapidly, despite the physical enervation that London always brought upon him. (It may be noticed that he gave the youth who appears first in the novel the surname of the Professor of Architecture he had been assisting.) At any rate the MS. of the first number, with something over, was ready for the illustrator in an incredibly quick time. Thereupon, though he had shaped nothing of what the later chapters were to be like, he dismissed the subject as Sheridan dismissed a bill he had backed, and on August 7 went on board the *Avoca*, of the Irish Mail Packet Company, at London Bridge, to proceed to Cornwall by water (a boat which, by the way, went to the bottom shortly after).

In Cornwall he paid a visit to some friends—Captain and Mrs Serjeant, of St. Benet's Abbey, who owned valuable china-clay works near, which were just then being developed; drove to St. Juliot, and met there among other visitors Miss d'Arville, a delightful old lady from Bath, who had a canary that fainted and fell to the bottom of the cage whenever a cat came into the room, or the picture of a cat was shown it. He walked to Tintagel Castle and sketched there a stone altar, having an Early-English ornamentation on its edge; which altar in after years he could never find; and in the intervals of this and other excursions went on with his MS., having naturally enough received an urgent letter for more copy from the publisher. He returned to London by way of Bath, where he left Miss d'Arville, who had accompanied him thus far.

He could not, however, get on with his novel in London, and late in September went down to the seclusion of Dorset to set about it more thoroughly. On this day *Under the Greenwood Tree* was reviewed by Moule in the *Saturday*. The *Spectator*, however, which had so mauled *Desperate Remedies*, took little notice of the book.

An entry in the diary at this time was: "Sept. 30. Posted MS. of 'A Pair of Blue Eyes' to Tinsley up to Page 163."

Before the date was reached he had received a letter from Professor Roger Smith, informing him that another of the six Board-school competitions for which Hardy had helped him to prepare designs had been successful, and suggesting that he had "been at grass" long enough, and would be welcomed back on any more liberal terms, if he felt dissatisfied.

This architectural success, for which he would have given much had it come sooner, was now merely provoking. However, Hardy confessed to the surprised and amused Smith what he had been doing, and was still occupied with; and thus was severed to his great regret an extremely pleasant if short professional connection with an able and amiable man; though their friendship was not broken, being renewed from time to time, and continued till the death of the elder of them.

Till the end of the year he was at Bockhampton finishing *A Pair of Blue Eyes*, the action of which, as is known, proceeds on the coast near "Lyonnesse"—not far from King Arthur's Castle at Tintagel. Its scene, he said, would have been clearly indicated by calling the romance *Elfride of Lyonnesse*, but for a wish to avoid drawing attention to the neighbouring St. Juliot while his friends were living there. After a flying visit to the rectory, he remained on through the spring at his mother's; and it may be mentioned here that while staying at this place or at the rectory—or possibly in London— Hardy received an account of the death of "The Tranter", after whom the character in *Under the Greenwood Tree* had been called, though it was not a portrait, nor was the fictitious tranter's kinship to the other musicians based on fact. He had been the many years' neighbour of the Hardys, and did the haulage of building materials for Hardy's father, of whom he also rented a field for his horses. The scene of his last moments was detailed in a letter to Hardy by one present at his death-bedside:

He was quite in his senses, but not able to speak. A dark purple stain began in his leg that was injured many years ago by his waggon going over it; the stain ran up it about as fast as a fly walks. It ran up his body in the same way till, arriving level with his fingers, it began in them, and went on up his arms, up his neck and face, to the top of his head, when he breathed his last. Then a pure white began at his foot, and went upwards at the same rate and in the same way, and he became as white throughout as he had been purple a minute before.

In this connection it may be interesting to add that the actual name of the shoe-maker "Robert Penny" in the same story was Robert Reason. He, like the Tranter and the Tranter's wife, is buried in Stinsford Churchyard near the tombs of the Hardys, though his name is almost illegible. Hardy once said he would much have preferred to use the real name, as being better suited to the character, but thought at the time of writing that there were possible relatives who might be hurt by the use of it, though he afterwards found there were none. The only real name in the story is that of "Voss", who brought the hot mead and viands to the choir on their rounds. It can still be read on a headstone, also quite near to where the Hardys lie. It will be remembered that these headstones are alluded to in the poem entitled "The Dead Quire"—

> Old Dewy lay by the gaunt yew tree,
> And Reuben and Michael a pace behind,
> And Bowman with his family
>   By the wall that the ivies bind.

Old Dewy has been called a portrait of Hardy's grandfather, but this was not the case; he died three years before the birth of the story-teller, almost in his prime, and long ere reaching the supposed age of William Dewy. There was, in fact, no family portrait in the tale.

A Pair of Blue Eyes was published in three volumes the latter part of May.

"May 5. 'Maniel' [Immanuel] Riggs found dead [a shepherd Hardy knew]. A curious man, who used to moisten his lips between every two or three words."

"June 9th. 1873. To London. Went to French Plays. Saw Brasseur etc."

"June 15. Met H. M. Moule at the Golden Cross Hotel. Dined

with him at the British Hotel. Moule then left for Ipswich on his duties as Poor Law Inspector."

"June 16–20. About London with my brother Henry."

"June 20. By evening train to Cambridge. Stayed in College— Queens'—Went out with H.M.M. after dinner. A magnificent evening: sun over 'the Backs'.

"Next morning went with H.M.M. to King's Chapel early. M. opened the great West doors to show the interior vista: we got upon the roof, where we could see Ely Cathedral gleaming in the distant sunlight. A never-to-be-forgotten morning. H. M. M. saw me off for London. His last smile."

From London Hardy travelled on to Bath, arriving late at night and putting up at 8 Great Stanhope Street, where lodgings had been obtained for him by his warm-hearted friend Miss d'Arville, whom Miss Gifford was then visiting. The following dates are from the intermittent diary Hardy kept in these years.

"June 23rd. Excursions about Bath and Bristol with the ladies."

"June 28th. To Clifton with Miss Gifford."—where they were surprised by accidentally seeing in a newsagent's shop a com- mendatory review of *A Pair of Blue Eyes* in the *Spectator*.

"July 30th. About Bath alone. . . . Bath has a rural complexion on an urban substance. . . ."

"June 1st. A day's trip with Miss G. To Chepstow, the Wye, the Wynd Cliff, which we climbed, and Tintern, where we repeated some of Wordsworth's lines thereon.

"At Tintern, silence is part of the pile. Destroy that, and you take a limb from an organism. . . . A wooded slope visible from every unmullioned window. But compare the age of the building with that of the marble hills from which it was drawn! . . ."

Here may be stated, in relation to the above words on the age of the hills, that this shortcoming of the most ancient architecture by comparison with geology was a consideration that frequently worried Hardy when measuring and drawing old Norman and other early buildings, just as he had been troubled by "the Wolf" in his musical tuning, and by the thought that Greek literature had been at the mercy of dialects.

"July 2. Bath to Dorchester."

CHAPTER VII

"Far from the Madding Crowd", Marriage, and Another Novel

1873–1876: *Aet.* 33–36

Some half-year before this, in December 1872, Hardy had received at Bockhampton a letter from Leslie Stephen, the editor of the *Cornhill*—by that time well known as a man of letters, *Saturday* reviewer, and Alpine climber—asking for a serial story for his magazine. He had lately read *Under the Greenwood Tree*, and thought "the descriptions admirable". It was "long since he had received more pleasure from a new writer", and it had occurred to him that such writing would probably please the readers of the *Cornhill Magazine* as much as it had pleased him.

Hardy had replied that he feared the date at which he could write a story for the *Cornhill* would be too late for Mr Stephen's purpose, since he already had on hand a succeeding novel (i.e. *A Pair of Blue Eyes*), which was arranged for; but that the next after should be at Mr Stephen's disposal. He had thought of making it a pastoral tale with the title of *Far from the Madding Crowd*—and that the chief characters would probably be a young woman-farmer, a shepherd, and a sergeant of cavalry. That was all he had done. Mr Stephen had rejoined that he was sorry he could not expect a story from Hardy at an earlier date; that he did not however mean to fix any particular time; that the idea of the story attracted him; also the proposed title; and that he would like Hardy to call and talk it over when he came to Town. There the matter had been left. Now Hardy set about the pastoral tale, the success of *A Pair of Blue Eyes* meanwhile surpassing his expectations, the influential *Saturday Review* pronouncing it to be the most artistically constructed of the novels of its time—a quality which, by the bye, would carry little recommendation in these days of loose construction and indifference to organic homogeneity.

But Hardy did not call on Stephen just then.

It was, indeed, by the merest chance that he had ever got the *Cornhill* letter at all. The postal arrangements in Dorset were still so primitive at this date that the only delivery of letters at Hardy's father's house was by the hands of some friendly neighbour who had come from the next village; and Mr Stephen's request for a story had been picked up in the mud of the lane by a labouring man, the schoolchildren to whom it had been entrusted having dropped it on the way.

While thus in the seclusion of Bockhampton writing *Far from the Madding Crowd* we find him on September 21 walking to Woodbury-Hill Fair, approximately described in the novel as "Greenhill Fair". On the 24th he was shocked at hearing of the death of his friend Moule, from whom he had parted cheerfully at Cambridge in June. The body was brought to be buried at Fordington, Dorchester, and Hardy attended the funeral. It was a matter of keen regret to him now, and for a long time after, that Moule and the woman to whom Hardy was warmly attached had never set eyes on each other; and that she could never make Moule's acquaintance, or be his friend.

On the 30th of September he sent to Leslie Stephen at his request as much of the MS. of *Far from the Madding Crowd* as was written—apparently between two and three monthly parts, though some of it only in rough outline—and a few days after a letter came from Stephen stating that the story suited him admirably as far as it had gone, and that though as a rule it was desirable to see the whole of a novel before definitely accepting it, under the circumstances he decided to accept it at once.

So Hardy went on writing *Far from the Madding Crowd*—sometimes indoors, sometimes out—when he would occasionally find himself without a scrap of paper at the very moment that he felt volumes. In such circumstances he would use large dead leaves, white chips left by the wood-cutters, or pieces of stone or slate that came to hand. He used to say that when he carried a pocket-book his mind was barren as Sahara.

This autumn Hardy assisted at his father's cider-making—a proceeding he had always enjoyed from childhood—the apples being from huge old trees that have now long perished, as well as the old outbuildings. It was the last time he ever took part in a work whose sweet smells and oozings in the crisp autumn air can never be forgotten by those who have had a hand in it.

Memorandum by Thomas Hardy:

"Met J. D. one of the old Mellstock fiddlers—who kept me talking interminably: a man who speaks neither truth nor lies, but a sort of Not Proven compound which is very relishable. Told me of Jack—who spent all the money he had—sixpence—at The Oak inn, took his sixpence out of the till when the landlady's back was turned, and spent it over again: then stole it again, and again spent it, till he had had a real skinful. 'Was too honest to take any money but his own,' said J. D." (Some of J. D.'s characteristics appear in "the Tranter" of *Under the Greenwood Tree.*)

At the end of October an unexpected note from the *Cornhill* editor asked if, supposing he were to start *Far from the Madding Crowd* in the January number (which would be out the third week in December) instead of the spring, as intended, Hardy could keep in front of the printers with his copy. He learnt afterwards that what had happened was that the MS. of a novel which the editor had arranged to begin in his pages in January had been lost in the post, according, at any rate, to its author's account. Hardy thought January not too soon for him, and that he could keep the printers going. Terms were consequently arranged with the publishers and proofs of the first number sent forthwith, Hardy incidentally expressing with regard to any illustrations, in a letter of October 1873, "a hope that the rustics, although *quaint*, may be made to appear intelligent, and not boorish at all"; adding in a later letter: "In reference to the illustrations, I have sketched in my note-book during the past summer a few correct outlines of smockfrocks, gaiters, sheep-crooks, rick-'staddles', a sheep-washing pool, one of the old-fashioned malt-houses, and some other out-of-the-way things that might have to be shown. These I could send you if they would be of any use to the artist, but if he is a sensitive man and you think he would rather not be interfered with, I would not do so."

No response had been made to this, and he was not quite clear whether, after all, Mr Stephen had finally decided to begin so soon when, returning from Cornwall on a fine December noontide (being New Year's Eve 1873–74), he opened on Plymouth Hoe a copy of the *Cornhill* that he had bought at the station, and there to his surprise saw his story placed at the beginning of the magazine, with a striking illustration, the artist being—also to his surprise—not a man but a woman, Miss Helen Paterson. He had only expected from the undistinguished rank of the characters in the tale that it would be put at the end, and possibly without a picture. Why this had come without warning to him was owing to the accident of his being away from his permanent address for several days, and nothing having been forwarded. It can be imagined how delighted Miss Gifford was to receive the first number of the story, whose nature he had kept from her to give her a pleasant surprise, and to find that her desire of a literary course for Hardy was in fair way of being justified.

In the first week of January 1874 the story was noticed in a marked degree by the *Spectator*, and a guess hazarded that it might be from the pen of George Eliot—why, the author could never understand, since, so far as he had read that great thinker—one of the greatest living, he thought, though not a born storyteller by any means—she had never touched the life of the fields: her country-people having seemed to him, too, more like small townsfolk than rustics; and as evidencing a woman's wit cast in country dialogue rather than real country humour, which he regarded as rather of the Shakespeare and Fielding sort. However he conjectured, as a possible reason for the flattering guess, that he had latterly been reading Comte's *Positive Philosophy*, and writings of that school, some of whose expressions had thus passed into his vocabulary, expressions which were also common to George Eliot. Leslie Stephen wrote:

> I am glad to congratulate you on the reception of your first number. Besides the gentle *Spectator*, which thinks that you must be George Eliot because you know the names of the stars, several good judges have spoken to me warmly of the Madding Crowd. Moreover the *Spectator*, though flighty in its head, has really a good deal of critical feeling. I always like to be praised by it—and indeed by other people! . . . The story comes out very well, I think, and I have no criticism to make.

Respecting the public interest in the opening of the story, in later days Miss Thackeray informed him, with some of her father's humour, that to inquiries with which she was besieged on the sex of the author, and requests to be given an introduction to him or her, she would reply: "*It* lives in the country, and I could not very well introduce you to *it* in town."

A passage may be quoted here from Mr F. W. Maitland's *Life of Leslie Stephen* (to which Hardy contributed half a chapter or so, on Stephen as editor) which affords a humorous illustration of the difficulties of "serial" writing in Victorian days. Stephen had written to say that the seduction of Fanny Robin must be treated in "a gingerly fashion", adding that it was owing to an "excessive prudery of which I am ashamed".

"I wondered what had so suddenly caused, in one who had seemed anything but a prude, the 'excessive prudery' alluded to. But I did not learn till I saw him in April. Then he told me that an unexpected Grundian cloud, though no bigger than a man's hand as yet, had appeared on our serene horizon. Three respectable ladies and subscribers, representing he knew not how many more, had written to upbraid him for an improper passage in a page of the story which had already been published.

'I was struck mute, till I said, 'Well, if you value the opinion of such people, why didn't you think of them beforehand, and strike out the passage?'—'I ought to have, since it is their opinion, whether I value it or no,' he said with a half groan. 'But it didn't occur to me that there was anything to object to!' I reminded him that though three objectors who disliked the passage, or pretended to, might write their disapproval, three hundred who possibly approved of it would not take the trouble to write, and hence he might have a false impression of the public as a body. 'Yes; I agree. Still I suppose I ought to have foreseen these gentry, and have omitted it,' he murmured.

"It may be added here, to finish with this detail (though it anticipates dates), that when the novel came out in volume-form *The Times* quoted in a commendatory review the very passage that had offended. As soon as I met him, I said, 'You see what *The Times* says about that paragraph; and you cannot say that *The Times* is not respectable.' He was smoking and answered tardily: 'No, I can't say that *The Times* is not respectable.' I then urged that if he had omitted the sentences, as he had wished he had done, I should never have taken the trouble to restore them in the reprint, and *The Times* could not have quoted them with approbation. I suppose my manner was slightly triumphant; at any rate, he said, 'I spoke as an editor, not as a man. You have no more consciousness of these things than a child.'"

To go back for a moment. Having attracted so much attention he now again withdrew into retreat at Bockhampton to get ahead with the novel, which was in a lamentably unadvanced condition, writing to Stephen, when requesting that the proofs might be sent to that hermitage: "I have decided to finish it here, which is within a walk of the district in which the incidents are supposed to occur. I find it a great advantage to be actually among the people described at the time of describing them."

However, that he did not care much for a reputation as a novelist in lieu of being able to follow the pursuit of poetry—now for ever hindered, as it seemed—becomes obvious from a remark written to Mr Stephen about this time:

> The truth is that I am willing, and indeed anxious, to give up any points which may be desirable in a story when read as a whole, for the sake of others which shall please those who read it in numbers. Perhaps I may have higher aims some day, and be a great stickler for the proper artistic balance of the completed work, but for the present circumstances lead me to wish merely to be considered a good hand at a serial.

The fact was that at this date he was bent on carrying out later in the year an intention beside which a high repute as an artistic novelist loomed even less importantly than in ordinary—an intention to be presently mentioned.

He found he had drifted anew into a position he had vowed after his past experience he would in future keep clear of—that of having unfinished on his hands a novel of which the beginning was already before the public, and so having to write against time. He wrote so rapidly in fact that by February he was able to send the editor an instalment of copy sufficient for two or three months further, and another instalment in April.

On a visit to London in the winter Hardy had made the personal acquaintance of Mr Stephen, the man whose philosophy was to influence his own for many years, indeed, more than that of any other contemporary, and received a welcome in his household, which was renewed from time to time, whereby he became acquainted with Mrs Stephen and her sister Miss Thackeray. He also made acquaintance with Mr G. Murray Smith the publisher and his family in April. At dinner there in May he met his skilful illustrator Miss Helen Paterson, and gave her a few points; Mr Frederick Greenwood; and Mrs Procter, wife and soon after widow of "Barry Cornwall" the poet. She was an interesting and well-known woman, daughter of Basil Montagu, and grand-daughter of the fourth Earl of Sandwich by Miss Martha Ray, who was shot by a jealous lover in 1779. The enormous acquaintance of Mrs Procter with past celebrities was astonishing, and her humour in relating anecdotes of them charmed Hardy. She used to tell him that sometimes after avowing to Americans her acquiantance with a long list of famous bygone people, she had been compelled to deny knowledge of certain others she had equally well known, to re-establish her listener's wavering faith in her veracity.

Back again in Dorsetshire he continued his application to the story, and by July had written it all, the last few chapters having been done at a gallop, for a reason to be told directly. In the middle of the month he resumed residence in London, where he hurriedly corrected the concluding pages and posted the end of the MS. to the editor early in August.

The next month Thomas Hardy and Miss Emma Lavinia Gifford were married at St. Peter's, Elgin Avenue, Paddington, by her uncle Dr E. Hamilton Gifford, Canon of Worcester, and afterwards Archdeacon of London, a relative for whom the bride had a great affection. Dr Gifford himself had married as his second wife a sister of Sir Francis Jeune, afterwards Lord St. Helier, and the family connection thus formed was a source of much social intercourse to the Hardys in after years. In the November following *Far from the Madding Crowd* was published in two volumes, with the illustrations by Miss Helen Paterson, who by an odd coincidence had also thought fit to marry during the progress of the story. It may be said in passing that the development of the chapters month by month had brought these lines from Mrs Procter:

You would be gratified to know what a shock the Marriage of Bathsheba was. I resembled Mr Boldwood—and to deceive such an old novel-reader as myself is a triumph. We are always looking out for traps, and scent a long way off a surprise. . . .

I hear that you are coming to live in stony-hearted London.

Our great fault is that we are all alike. . . . We press so closely against each other that any small shoots are cut off at once, and the young tree grows in shape like the old one.

When the book appeared complete the author and his wife, after a short visit to the Continent—their first Continental days having been spent at Rouen—had temporarily gone to live at Surbiton, and remained there for a considerable time without nearly realizing the full extent of the interest that had been excited among the reading public by the novel, which unsophistication was only partially removed by their seeing with unusual frequency, during their journeys to and from London, ladies carrying about copies of it with Mudie's label on the covers. Its author's unawareness of the extent of its popularity may have been partly owing to the reviews which, in spite of a general approval, were for the most part leavened with minor belittlements in the manner beloved of so many Victorian critics, and possibly later ones, though there were a few generous exceptions.

Meanwhile Mr George Smith, head of the firm of Smith and Elder—a man of wide experience, who had brought Charlotte Brontë before the reading public, and who became a disinterested friend of Hardy's—suggested to him that he should if possible get back the copyright of *Under the Greenwood Tree*—which he had sold to Tinsley Brothers for £30. Tinsley at first replied that he would not return it for any sum: then that he would sell it for £300. Hardy offered half, which offer Tinsley did not respond to, and there the matter dropped.

Among the curious consequences of the popularity of *Far from the Madding Crowd* was a letter from the lady he had so admired as a child, when she was the grand dame of the parish in which he was born. He had seen her only once since—at her town-house in Bruton Street as aforesaid. But it should be stated in justice to her that her writing was not merely a rekindled interest on account of his book's popularity, for she had written to him in his obscurity, before he had published a line, asking him to come and see her, and addressing him as her dear Tommy, as when he was a small boy, apologizing for doing so on the ground that she could not help it. She was now quite an elderly lady, but by signing her letter "Julia Augusta" she revived throbs of tender feeling in him, and brought back to his memory the thrilling "frou-frou" of her four grey silk flounces when she had used to bend over him, and when they brushed against the font as she entered church on Sundays. He replied, but, as it appears, did not go to see her. Thus though their eyes never met again after his call on her in London, nor their lips from the time when she had held him in her arms, who can say that both occurrences might not have been in the order of things, if he had developed their reacquaintance earlier, now that she was in her widowhood, with nothing to hinder her mind from rolling back upon her past.

Meanwhile the more tangible result of the demand for *Far from the Madding Crowd* was an immediate request from the editor and publishers of the *Cornhill* for another story, which should begin as early as possible in 1875.

This was the means of urging Hardy into the unfortunate course of hurrying forward a further production before he was aware of what there had been of value in his previous one: before learning, that is, not only what had attracted the public, but what was of true and genuine substance on which to build a career as a writer with a real literary message. For mere popularity he cared little, as little as he did for large payments; but having now to live by the pen—or, as he would quote, "to keep base life afoot"—he had to consider popularity. This request for more of his writing not only from the *Cornhill* but from other quarters, coincided with quizzing personal gossip, among other paragraphs being one that novel-writing was coming to a pretty pass, the author of *Lorna Doone* having avowed himself a market-gardener, and the author of *Far from the Madding Crowd* having been discovered to be a house-decorator (!); also with cuckoo-cries on his limitations, which were really the irritation of dullards at his freshness. So, forgetting the wise counsel of Mr Macmillan's reader, to take no notice of "the fooleries of critics", the latter cry influenced him to put aside a woodland story he had thought of (which later took shape in *The Woodlanders*), and make a plunge in a new and untried direction. He was aware of the pecuniary value of a reputation for a speciality; and as above stated the acquisition of something like a regular income had become important. Yet he had not the slightest intention of writing for ever about sheepfarming, as the reading public was apparently expecting him to do, and as, in fact, they presently resented his not doing. Hence, to the consternation of his editor and publishers, in March he sent up as a response to their request the beginning of a tale called *The Hand of Ethelberta—A Comedy in Chapters*, which had nothing whatever in common with anything he had written before.

In March he went with his wife to the Oxford and Cambridge Boat-Race, and entered rooms taken in Newton Road, Westbourne Grove, a light being thrown on the domestic and practical side of his life at this time by the following:

> Newton Road, Westbourne Grove
> March 19. 1875.
>
> Messrs Townly and Bonniwell.
> Surbiton.
> Gentlemen: Please to warehouse the cases and boxes sent herewith, and numbered as follows:
> No 1. size 3 ft. 6 ins. × 2 ft. 6 ins × 2 ft. 2 ins, containing linen and books.
> „ 2. size 2 ft. 0 ins. × 1 ft. 9 ins × 1 ft. 7½ ins. containing books.
> „ 3. „ 2 ft. 0 ins. × 1 ft. 4 ins × 1ft. 2 ins. containing books.
> „ 4. „ 1 ft. 5 ins × 1 ft. 0 ins × 1 ft. 0 ins. „ sundries.
> A receipt for same will oblige.

Their entire worldly goods were contained in this small compass.

The next three months were spent at Newton Road, Westbourne Grove, while following an ordinary round of museum, theatre, and concert-going, with some dining-out, in keeping with what he had written earlier to Mr George Smith: "We are coming to Town for three months on account of Ethelberta, some London scenes occurring in her chequered career which I want to do as vigorously as possible—having already visited Rouen and Paris with the same object, other adventures of hers taking place there." He also asked Smith's advice on a German translation of *Far from the Madding Crowd*, which had been asked for.

The *Comedy in Chapters*, despite its departure from a path desired by his new-found readers, and to some extent desired by himself, was accepted for the magazine. The beginning appeared in the *Cornhill* for May, when Hardy had at last the satisfaction of proving, amid the general disappointment at the lack of sheep and shepherds, that he did not mean to imitate anybody, whatever the satisfaction might have been worth. The sub-title did not appear in the magazine, Mr Stephen having written in respect of it:

I am sorry to have to bother you about a trifle! I fully approved of your suggestion for adding to 'Ethelberta's Hand' the descriptive title 'A Comedy in Chapters'. I find however from other people that it gives rather an unfortunate idea. They understand by Comedy something of the farce description, and expect you to be funny after the fashion of Mr——, or some professional joker. This, of course, is stupid; but then, advertisements are meant for stupid people. The question is, unluckily, not what they ought to feel but what they do feel. . . . I think therefore, that if you have no strong reason to the contrary it will be better to drop the second title for the present. When the book is reprinted it can of course appear, because then the illusion would be immediately dispelled.

One reflection about himself at this date sometimes made Hardy uneasy. He perceived that he was "up against" the position of having to carry on his life not as an emotion, but as a scientific game; that he was committed by circumstances to novel-writing as a regular trade, as much as he had formerly been to architecture; and that hence he would, he deemed, have to look for material in manners—in ordinary social and fashionable life as other novelists did. Yet he took no interest in manners, but in the substance of life only. So far what he had written had not been novels at all, as usually understood—that is pictures of modern customs and observances—and might not long sustain the interest of the circulating-library subscriber who cared mainly for those things. On the other hand, to go about to dinners and clubs and crushes as a business was not much to his mind. Yet that was necessary meat and drink to the popular author. Not that he was unsociable, but events and long habit had accustomed him to solitary living. So it was also with his wife, of whom he wrote later, in the poem entitled "A Dream or No":

> Lonely I found her,
> The sea-birds around her,
> And other than nigh things uncaring to know.

He mentioned this doubt of himself one day to Miss Thackeray, who confirmed his gloomy misgivings by saying with surprise: "Certainly; a novelist must necessarily like society!"

Another incident which added to his dubiety was the arrival of a letter from Coventry Patmore, a total stranger to him, expressing the view that *A Pair of Blue Eyes* was in its nature not a conception for prose, and that he "regretted at almost every page that such unequalled beauty and power should not have assured themselves the immortality which would have been impressed upon them by the form of verse". (Strangely enough another poet, Tennyson, years after, told Hardy that he liked *A Pair of Blue Eyes* the best of his novels.) Hardy was much struck by this opinion from Patmore. However, finding himself committed to prose, he renewed his consideration of a prose style, as it is evident from the following note:

"Read again Addison, Macaulay, Newman, Sterne, De Foe, Lamb, Gibbon, Burke, Times Leaders, &c. in a study of style. Am more and more confirmed in an idea I have long held, as a matter of commonsense, long before I thought of any old aphorism bearing on the subject: 'Ars est celare artem'. The whole secret of a living style and the difference between it and a dead style, lies in not having too much style—being—in fact, a little careless, or rather seeming to be, here and there. It brings wonderful life into the writing:—

> A sweet disorder in the dress . . .
> A careless shoe-string, in whose tie
> I see a wild civility,
> Do more bewitch me than when art
> Is too precise in every part.

Otherwise your style is like worn half-pence—all the fresh images rounded off by rubbing, and no crispness or movement at all.

"It is, of course, simply a carrying into prose the knowledge I have acquired in poetry—that inexact rhymes and rhythms now and then are far more pleasing than correct ones."

About the time at which the Hardys were leaving Surbiton for Newton Road occurred an incident, which can best be described by quoting Hardy's own account of it as printed in Mr F. W. Maitland's *Life of Leslie Stephen*:

"One day (March 23, 1875) I received from Stephen a mysterious note asking me to call in the evening, as late as I liked. I went, and found him alone, wandering up and down his library in slippers; his tall thin figure wrapt in a heath-coloured dressing-gown. After a few remarks on our magazine arrangements he said he wanted me to witness his signature to what, for a moment, I thought was his will; but it turned out to be a deed renunciatory of holy-orders under the act of 1870. He said grimly that he was really a reverend gentleman still, little as he might look it, and that he thought it was as well to cut himself adrift of a calling for which, to say the least, he had always been utterly unfit. The deed was executed with due formality. Our conversation then turned upon theologies decayed and defunct, the origin of things, the constitution of matter, the unreality of time, and kindred subjects. He told me that he had 'wasted' much time on systems of religion and metaphysics, and that the new theory of vortex rings had 'a staggering fascination' for him."

On this description the editor of the *Life*, Mr Maitland, remarks: "This scene—I need not say it—is well drawn. A tall thin figure wrapt in a heath-coloured dressing-gown was what one saw if one climbed to that Stylites study at dead of night."

In May Hardy formed one of a deputation to Mr Disraeli in support of a motion for a Select Committee to inquire into the state of Copyright Law; and on Waterloo Day he and his wife went to Chelsea Hospital—it being the 60th anniversary of the Battle—and made acquaintance with the Waterloo men still surviving there. Hardy would tell that one of these—a delightful old campaigner named John Bentley whom he knew to the last—put his arm round Mrs Hardy's waist, and interlarded his discourse with "my dear young woman", while he described to her his experiences of that memorable day, one rather incisive touch in his tale to her being that through the haze of smoke all that could be discerned was "anything that shined", such as bayonets, helmets, and swords. The wet eve of the battle, when they slept in the rain with nothing over them, he spoke of as "last night", as if he were speaking on the actual day. Another experience he related to her was a love-affair. While quartered in Brussels he had a sweetheart. When ordered to advance to Waterloo her friends offered to hide him if he would desert, as the French were sure to win. He refused, urging the oath he had taken, but he felt strongly tempted, as she was very fond of him, and he of her. She begged him to write, if he lived through the campaign, and to be sure to get a Belgian or Frenchman to direct the letter, or it might not find her. After the battle, and when he was in Paris, he did write, and received an answer, saying she would come to Paris and meet him on Christmas Day at 3 o'clock. His regiment had received orders to march before that time, and at Christmas he was—Mrs Hardy forgot where. But he thought of her, and wondered if she came. "Yes, you see, 'twas God's will we should meet no more," said Bentley, speaking of her with peculiar tenderness. In this same month of 1875, it may be interesting to note, occurs the first mention in Hardy's memoranda of the idea of an epic on the war with Napoleon—carried out so many years later in *The Dynasts*. This earliest note runs as follows:

"Mem: A Ballad of The Hundred Days. Then another of Moscow. Others of earlier campaigns—forming altogether an Iliad of Europe from 1789 to 1815."

That Hardy however was endeavouring to live practically at this time as well as imaginatively is shown by an entry immediately following:

"House at Childe-Okeford, Dorset. To be sold by auction June 10."; and by his starting on the 22nd for a day or two in Dorsetshire house-hunting, first visiting Shaftesbury, where he found a cottage for £25 a year, that did not, however, suit; thence to Blandford, and thence to Wimborne, where on arrival he entered the Minster at ten at night, having seen a light within, and sat in a stall listening to the organist practising, while the rays from the musician's solitary candle streamed across the arcades. This incident seems to have inclined him to Wimborne; but he did not go there yet.

In July the couple went to Bournemouth, and thence by steamer to Swanage, where they found lodgings at the house of an invalided captain of smacks and ketches; and Hardy, suspending his house-hunting, settled down there for the autumn and winter to finish *The Hand of Ethelberta*.

While completing it he published in the *Gentleman's Magazine* a ballad he had written nine or ten years earlier during his time with Blomfield, called "The Fire at Tranter Sweatley's" (and in some editions "The Bride-night Fire")—which, as with his other verses, he had been unable to get into print at the date of their composition by the rather perfunctory efforts he made.

"28 Nov. I sit under a tree, and feel alone: I think of certain insects around me as magnified by the microscope: creatures like elephants, flying dragons, etc. And I feel I am by no means alone."

"29. He has read well who has learnt that there is more to read outside books than in them."

Their landlord, the "captain", used to tell them, as sailors will, strange stories of his sea-farings; mostly smuggling stories—one of them Hardy always remembered because of its odd development. The narrator was in a fishing-boat going to meet a French lugger half-Channel-over, to receive spirit-tubs and land them. He and his mates were some nine miles off Portland, which was the limit allowed, when they were sighted by the revenue-cutter. Seeing the cutter coming up they said "We must act as if we were fishing for mackerel". But they had no bait, and the ruse would be discovered. They snapped up the stems of their tobacco-pipes, and unfastening the hook from a line they had with them slipped on the bits of tobacco-pipe above the shank. The officers came—saw them fishing, and merely observing that they were a long way from shore, and dubiously asking why, and being innocently told because the fish were there, left them. Then, as if the bait had been genuine, to their surprise on pulling up the sham line they began to haul in mackerel. The fish had made their deception truth.

Masters also told them that when persons are drowned in a high sea in the West (or Deadman's) Bay "the sea undresses them"— mauling off their clothes and leaving them naked.

While here at Swanage they walked daily on the cliffs and shore, Hardy noting thereon:

"Evening. Just after sunset. Sitting with E. on a stone under the wall before the Refreshment Cottage. The sounds are two, and only two. On the left Durlstone Head roaring high and low, like a giant asleep. On the right a thrush. Above the bird hangs the new moon, and a steady planet."

In the same winter of 1875, an article appeared in the *Revue des Deux Mondes* on *Far from the Madding Crowd* entitled the "Roman pastoral en Angleterre".

Ethelberta was finished in the January of the next year (1876) and the MS. dispatched. Pending the appearance of the story in volumes the twain removed in March to lodgings at Yeovil to facilitate their search for a little dwelling. Here they were living when the novel was published. It was received in a friendly spirit and even with admiration in some quarters—more, indeed, than Hardy had expected—one experienced critic going so far as to write that it was the finest ideal comedy since the days of Shakespeare. "Show me the lady in the flesh", he said in a letter to the author, "and I vow on my honour as a bachelor to become a humble addition to her devoted train." It did not however win the cordiality that had greeted its two forerunners, the chief objection seeming to be that it was "impossible". It was, in fact, thirty years too soon for a Comedy of Society of that kind—just as *The Poor Man and the Lady* had been too soon for a socialist story, and as other of his writings—in prose and verse—were too soon for their date. The most impossible situation in it was said to be that of the heroine sitting at table at a dinner-party of "the best people", at which her father was present by the sideboard as butler. Yet a similar situation has been applauded in a play in recent years by Mr Bernard Shaw, without any sense of improbability.

Had this very clever satire been discovered to come from the hands of a man about town, its author would have been proclaimed as worthy of a place beside Congreve and Sheridan; indeed, such had been hinted before its authorship was well known. But rumours that he had passed all his life in a hermitage smote like an east wind upon all appreciation of the tale. That the stories of his seclusion were untrue, that Hardy had been living in London for many years in the best of all situations for observing manners, was of course unknown.

This ended Hardy's connection with Leslie Stephen as editor, though not as friend; and in the course of a letter expressing a hope that it might be renewed, Stephen wrote (May 16, 1876):

My remark about modern lectures [?] was of course "wrote sarcastic" as Artemus Ward says, and intended for a passing dig in the ribs of some modern critics, who think that they can lay down laws in art like the pope in religion; e.g.,—the whole Rossetti-Swinburne school——I think as a critic that the less authors read of criticism the better. You, e.g., have a perfectly fresh and original vein, and I think the less you bother yourself about critical canons the less chance there is of your becoming self-conscious and cramped. . . . Ste. Beuve, and Mat. Arnold (in a smaller way), are the only modern critics who seem to me worth reading. . . . we are generally a poor lot, horribly afraid of not being in the fashion, and disposed to give ourselves airs on very small grounds.

"May. In an orchard at Closeworth. Cowslips under trees. A light proceeds from them, as from Chinese lanterns or glow-worms."

CHAPTER VIII

Holland, the Rhine, and Sturminster Newton

1876–1878: *Aet.* 36–37

From their lodgings in Yeovil they set out at the end of May for Holland and the Rhine—the first thing that struck them being that "the Dutch seemed like police perpetually keeping back an unruly crowd composed of waves". They visited Rotterdam—"looking over-clean and new, with not enough shadow, and with houses nearly all out of the perpendicular"; then the Hague, Scheveningen, Emmerich, and Cologne, where Hardy was disappointed by the machine-made Gothic of the Cathedral, and whence in a few days they went on "between the banks that bear the vine", to Bonn, Coblentz, Ehrenbreitstein, and Mainz, where they were impressed by a huge confirmation in the cathedral which, by the way, was accompanied by a tune like that of Keble's Evening Hymn. Heidelberg they loved, and looking west one evening from the top of the tower on the Königsstuhl, Hardy remarks on a singular optical effect that was almost tragic. Owing to mist the wide landscape itself was not visible, but "the Rhine glared like a riband of blood, as if it serpentined through the atmosphere above the earth's surface". Thence they went to Carlsruhe, where they attended a fair, and searched for a German lady Hardy had known in England, but were unable to find her. Baden and the

Black Forest followed, and next they proceeded to Strassburg, where Mrs Hardy was laid up (probably by excessive walking). A thick brown mysterious fluid which her husband obtained at an Italian apothecary's and could never afterwards identify, set her right in a day or two, and then they turned back, proceeding by way of Metz to Brussels. Here Hardy—maybe with his mind on *The Dynasts*—explored the field of Waterloo, and a day or two later spent some time in investigating the problem of the actual scene of the Duchess of Richmond's Ball, with no result that satisfied him, writing a letter while here to some London paper to that effect—a letter which has not been traced.

A short stay in Brussels was followed by their homeward course through Antwerp, where they halted awhile, and Harwich, having a miserable passage on a windy night in a small steamer with cattle on board.

In London they were much astonished and amused to see in large letters on the newspaper-posters that there had been riots at Antwerp; and they recalled that they had noticed a brass band parading the streets with about a dozen workmen walking quietly behind.

June (1876). Arriving at Yeovil again after another Waterloo-day visit to Chelsea by Hardy (where, in the private parlour of "The Turk's Head" over glasses of grog, the battle was fought yet again by the dwindling number of pensioners who had taken part in it), his first consideration was the resumed question of a cottage, having ere this received hints from relatives that he and his wife "appeared to be wandering about like two tramps"; and also growing incommoded by an accumulation of luggage in packing cases, mostly books, for of other furniture they had as yet not a stick; till they went out one day to an auction and bought a door-scraper and a book-case, with which two articles they laid the foundation of household goods and effects.

"June 25. The irritating necessity of conforming to rules which in themselves have no virtue."

"June 26. If it be possible to compress into a sentence all that a man learns between 20 & 40, it is that all things merge in one another—good into evil, generosity into justice, religion into politics, the year into the ages, the world into the universe. With this in view the evolution of species seems but a minute process in the same movement."

A pretty cottage overlooking the Dorset Stour—called

"Riverside Villa"—offered itself at Sturminster Newton, and this they took at Midsummer, hastily furnished it in part by going to Bristol and buying £100 worth of mid-Victorian furniture in two hours; entering on July 3. It was their first house and, though small, probably that in which they spent their happiest days. Several poems commemorate their term there of nearly two years. A memorandum dated just after their entry runs as follows:

"Rowed on the Stour in the evening, the sun setting up the river. Just afterwards a faint exhalation visible on surface of water as we stirred it with the oars. A fishy smell from the numerous eels and other fish beneath. Mowers salute us. Rowed among the water-lilies to gather them. Their long ropy stems.

"Passing the island drove out a flock of swallows from the bushes and sedge, which had gone there to roost. Gathered meadow-sweet. Rowed with difficulty through the weeds, the rushes on the border standing like palisades against the bright sky. . . . A Cloud in the sky like a huge quill-pen."

Another entry at this time:

"A story has been told me of a doctor at Maiden Newton, who attended a woman who could not pay him. He said he would take the dead baby in payment. He had it, and it was kept on his mantelpiece in a large glass jar in spirits, which stained the body brown. The doctor, who was a young man, afterwards married and used his wife badly, insisting on keeping the other woman's dead baby on his mantelpiece."

Another:

"Mr Warry says that a farmer who was tenant of a friend of his used to take the heart of every calf that died, and, sticking it full of black thorns, hang it on the cotterel, or cross-bar, of his chimney: this was done to prevent the spread of the disease that had killed the calf. When the next tenant came the chimney smoked very much, and examining it they found it choked with hearts treated in the manner described—by that time dry and parched."

Another:

" 'Toad Fair.' An old man, a wizard, used to bring toads' legs in little bags to Bagber Bridge [close to where Hardy was living], where he was met by crowds of people who came in vehicles and on foot, and bought them as charms to cure scrofula by wearing them round the neck. These legs were supposed to twitch occasionally in the bag, and probably did, when it gave the wearer's blood a 'turn', and changed the course of the disease."

"There are two sorts of church-people; those who go, and those who don't go: there is only one sort of chapel-people; those who go."

" 'All is vanity', saith the Preacher. But if all were only vanity, who would mind? Alas, it is too often worse than vanity; agony, darkness, death also."

"A man would never laugh were he not to forget his situation, or were he not one who never has learnt it. After risibility from comedy how often does the thoughtful mind reproach itself for forgetting the truth! Laughter always means blindness—either from defect, choice, or accident."

During a visit to London in December Hardy attended a conference at St. James's Hall, and heard speak Mr Gladstone, Lord Shaftesbury, Hon. E. Ashley, Anthony Trollope, and the Duke of Westminster. "Trollope outran the five or seven minutes allowed for each speech, and the Duke, who was chairman, after various soundings of the bell, and other hints that he must stop, tugged at Trollope's coat-tails in desperation. Trollope turned round, exclaimed parenthetically, 'Please leave my coat alone,' and went on speaking."

They spent Christmas with Hardy's father and mother; and while there his father told them that when he was a boy the hobby-horse was still a Christmas amusement. On one occasion the village band of West Stafford was at Mr Floyer's (the landowner's) at a party, where among other entertainments was that of the said hobby-horse. One of the servants was terrified death-white at the sight of it running about, and rushed into an adjoining dark room where the band's violoncello was lying, entering with such force as to knock off the neck of the instrument.

A Pair of Blue Eyes was much to the taste of French readers, and was favourably criticized in the *Revue des Deux Mondes* early the next year (1877). It appears to have been also a romance that Hardy himself did not wish to let die, for we find him writing to Mr George Smith in the following April:

> There are circumstances in connection with "A Pair of Blue Eyes" which make me anxious to favour it, even at the expense of profit, if I can possibly do so. . . . I know that you do sometimes, not to say frequently, take an interest in producing a book quite apart from commercial views as a publisher, and I should like to gain such interest for this one of mine. . . . I can get a photograph of the picturesque Cornish coast, the scene of the story, from which a drawing could be made for the frontispiece.

Mr Smith replied that though he had not printed the original edition he would take it up, profit or no profit; but for some unexplained reason the book was published at other hands, the re-issue receiving much commendatory notice.

"May 1. A man comes every evening to the cliff in front of our house to see the sun set, timing himself to arrive a few minutes before the descent. Last night he came, but there was a cloud. His disappointment."

"May 30th. Walking to Marnhull. The prime of bird-singing. The thrushes and blackbirds are the most prominent,—pleading earnestly rather than singing, and with such modulation that you seem to see their little tongues curl inside their bills in their emphasis. A bullfinch sings from a tree with a metallic sweetness piercing as a fife. Further on I come to a hideous carcase of a house in a green landscape, like a skull on a table of dessert."

Same date:

"I sometimes look upon all things in inanimate Nature as pensive mutes."

"June 3. Mr Young says that his grandfather [about 1750–1830] was very much excited, as was everybody in Sturminster, when a mail-coach ran from Poole to Bristol. On the morning it ran for the first time he got up early, swept *the whole street*, and sprinkled sand for the vehicle & horses to pass over."

Same date:

"The world often feels certain works of genius to be great, without knowing why: hence it may be that particular poets and novelists may have had the wrong quality in them noticed and applauded as that which makes them great."

We also find in this June of 1877 an entry that adumbrates *The Dynasts* yet again—showing that the idea by this time has advanced a stage—from that of a ballad, or ballad-sequence, to a "grand drama": viz.:

"Consider a grand drama, based on the wars with Napoleon, or some one campaign (but not as Shakespeare's historical dramas). It might be called 'Napoleon', or 'Josephine', or by some other person's name."

He writes also, in another connection:

"There is enough poetry in what is left [in life], after all the false romance has been abstracted, to make a sweet pattern: e.g., the poem by H. Coleridge:

'She is not fair to outward view'.

So, then, if Nature's defects must be looked in the face and transcribed, whence arises the *art* in poetry and novel-writing? which must certainly show art, or it becomes merely mechanical reporting. I think the art lies in making these defects the basis of a hitherto unperceived beauty, by irradiating them with 'the light that never was' on their surface, but is seen to be latent in them by the spiritual eye."

"June 28. Being Coronation Day there are games and dancing on the green at Sturminster Newton. The stewards with white rosettes. One is very anxious, fearing that while he is attending to the runners the leg of mutton on the pole will go wrong; hence he walks hither and thither with a compressed countenance and eyes far ahead.

"The pretty girls, just before a dance, stand in inviting positions on the grass. As the couples in each figure pass near where their immediate friends loiter, each girl-partner gives a laughing glance at such friends, and whirls on."

"June 29th. Have just passed through a painful night and morning. Our servant, whom we liked very much, was given a holiday yesterday to go to Bournemouth with her young man. Came home last night at ten, seeming oppressed. At about half-past twelve, when we were supposed to be asleep, she crept downstairs, went out, and on looking from the back window of our bedroom I saw her come from the outhouse with a man. She appeared to have only her night-gown on and something round her shoulders. Beside her slight white figure in the moonlight his form looked dark and gigantic. She preceded him to the door. Before I had thought what to do E. had run downstairs, and met her, and ordered her to bed. The man disappeared. Found that the bolts of the back-door had been oiled. He had evidently often stayed in the house.

"She remained quiet till between four and five, when she got out of the dining-room window and vanished."

"June 30. About one o'clock went to her father's cottage in the village, where we thought she had gone. Found them poorer than I expected (for they are said to be an old county family). Her father was in the field haymaking, and a little girl fetched him from the haymakers. He came across to me amid the windrows of hay, and seemed to read bad news in my face. She had not been home. I remembered that she had dressed up in her best clothes, and she probably has gone to Stalbridge to her lover."

The further career of this young woman is not recorded, except as to one trifling detail.

"July 4. Went to Stalbridge. Mrs —— is a charming woman. When we were looking over the church she recommended me to try a curious seat, adding, though we were only talking about the church itself, 'That's where I sat when Jamie was christened, and I could see him very well'. Another seat she pointed out with assumed casualness as being the one where she sat when she was churched; as if it were rather interesting that she did sit in those places, in spite of her not being a romantic person. When we arrived at her house she told us that Jamie really could not be seen—he was in a dreadful state—covered with hay; half laughing and catching our eyes while she spoke, as if we should know at once how intensely humorous he must appear under those circumstances. Jamie was evidently her life, and flesh, and raiment. . . . Her husband is what we call a 'yopping, or yapping man'. He strains his countenance hard in smiling, and keeps it so for a distinct length of time, so that you may on no account whatever miss his smile and the point of the words that gave rise to it. Picks up pictures and china for eighteenpence worth ever so much more. Gives cottagers a new set of tea-cups with handles for old ones without handles—an exchange which they are delighted to make."

"Country life at Sturminster. Vegetables pass from growing to boiling, fruit from the bushes to the pudding, without a moment's halt, and the gooseberries that were ripening on the twigs at noon are in the tart an hour later."

"July 13. The sudden disappointment of a hope leaves a scar which the ultimate fulfilment of that hope never entirely removes."

"July 27. James Bushrod of Broadmayne saw the two German soldiers [of the York Hussars] shot [for desertion] on Bincombe Down in 1801. It was in the path across the down, or near it. James Selby of the same village thinks there is a mark." [The tragedy was used in "The Melancholy Hussar", the real names of the deserters being given.]

"Aug. 13. We hear that Jane, our late servant is soon to have a baby. Yet never a sign of one is there for us."

"Sept. 25. Went to Shroton Fair. In a twopenny show saw a woman beheaded. In another a man whose hair grew on one side of his face. Coming back across Hambledon Hill (where the Club-Men assembled, temp. Cromwell) a fog came on. I nearly got lost in the dark inside the earthworks, the old hump-backed man I had parted from on the other side of the hill, who was going somewhere else before coming across the earth-works in my direction, being at the bottom as soon as I. A man might go round and round all night in such a place."

"September 28. . . . An object or mark raised or made by man on a scene is worth ten times any such formed by unconscious Nature. Hence clouds, mists, and mountains are unimportant beside the wear on a threshold, or the print of a hand."

"October 31. To Bath. Took lodgings for my father near the baths and Abbey. Met him at G. W. Station. Took him to the lodgings. To theatre in the evening. Stayed in Bath. Next day went with father to the baths, to begin the cure."

During this year 1877 Hardy had the sadness of hearing of the death of Raphael Brandon, the literary architect whom he had been thrown with seven years earlier, at a critical stage in his own career. He also at this time entered into an interesting correspondence with Mrs Chatteris, daughter of Admiral Sir Thomas Hardy, upon some facts in the life of the latter. But his main occupation at Riverside Villa (or "Rivercliff" as they sometimes called it) was writing *The Return of the Native*. The only note he makes of its progress is that, on November 8, parts 3, 4, and 5 of the story were posted to Messrs Chatto and Windus for publication in (of all places) *Belgravia*—a monthly magazine then running. Strangely enough, the rich alluvial district of Sturminster Newton in which the author was now living was not used by him at this time as a setting for the story he was constructing there, but the heath country twenty miles off. It may be mentioned here that the name "Eustacia" which he gave to his heroine was that of the wife of the owner of the manor of Ower-Moigne in the reign of Henry IV, which parish includes part of the "Egdon" Heath of the story (vide Hutchins's *Dorset*); and that "Clement", the name of the hero, was suggested by its being borne by one of his supposed ancestors, Clement le Hardy, of Jersey, whose family migrated from that isle to the west of England at the beginning of the sixteenth century.

On the same day he jots down:

"Nov. 8. Mr and Mrs Dashwood came to tea. Mr Dashwood [a local solicitor & landowner] says that poachers elevate a pan of brimstone on a stick under pheasants at roost, and so stupefy them that they fall.

"Sometimes the keepers make dummy pheasants and fix them in places where pheasants are known to roost: then watch by them. The poachers come; shoot and shoot again, when the keepers rush out.

"At a *battue* the other day lots of the birds ran into the keeper's *house* for protection.

"Mr D. says that a poacher he defended at Quarter Sessions asked for time to pay the fine imposed, and they gave him till the next Justice meeting. He said to Mr D., 'I shall be able to get it out of 'em before then'—and in fact he had in a week poached enough birds from the Justices' preserves to pay the five pounds."

"Nov. 12. A flooded river after the incessant rains of yesterday. Lumps of froth float down like swans in front of our house. At the arches of the large stone bridge the froth has accumulated and lies like hillocks of salt against the bridge; then the arch chokes, and after a silence coughs out the air and froth, and gurgles on."

"End of November. This evening the west is like some vast foundry where new worlds are being cast."

"December 22. In the evening I went with Dr Leach the coroner to an inquest which was to be held at Stourton Caundell on the body of a boy. Arrived at the Trooper Inn after a lonely drive through dark and muddy lanes. Met at the door by the Superintendent of Police and a policeman in plain clothes. Also by Mr Long, who had begun the *post-mortem*. We then went to the cottage; a woman or two, and children, were sitting by the fire, who looked at us with a cowed expression. Upstairs the body of the boy lay on a box covered with a sheet. It was uncovered, and Mr Long went on with his autopsy I holding a candle to light him and the policeman another. The body had been opened by a vertical and horizontal cut. Found a clot in the heart, but no irritant poison in the stomach, as had been suspected. The inquest was then held at the inn."

"Dec. 26. In literature young men usually begin their careers by being judges, and as wisdom and old experience arrive they reach the dignity of standing as culprits at the bar before new young bloods who have in their turn sprung up in the judgment-seat."

A correspondence with Baron Tauchnitz in reference to Continental editions of his books was one of the businesses of the year-end.

Despite the pleasure of this life at Sturminster Newton Hardy had decided that the practical side of his vocation of novelist demanded that he should have his head-quarters in or near London. The wisdom of his decision, considering the nature of his writing, he afterwards questioned. So in the first week of February he and Mrs Hardy went up to look for a house, and about the middle of the month he signed an agreement for a three-years' lease of one at Upper Tooting, close to Wandsworth Common.

"March 5. Concert at Sturminster. A Miss Marsh of Sutton [Keinton?] Mandeville sang 'Should he upbraid', to Bishop's old tune. She is the sweetest of singers—thrush-like in the descending scale, and lark-like in the ascending—drawing out the soul of listeners in a gradual thread of excruciating attenuation like silk from a cocoon."

Many years after Hardy was accustomed to say that this was the most marvellous old song in English music in its power of touching an audience. There was no surer card to play as an *encore*, even when it was executed but indifferently well. He wrote some lines thereon entitled "The Maid of Keinton Mandeville".

"March 18. End of the Sturminster Newton idyll. . . ." [The following is written in later] "Our happiest time."

It was also a poetical time. Several poems in *Moments of Vision* contain memories of it, such as "Overlooking the River Stour", "The Musical Box", and "On Sturminster Foot-Bridge".

That evening of March 18 a man came to arrange about packing their furniture, and the next day it was all out of the house. They slept at Mrs Dashwood's, after breakfasting, lunching, and dining there; and in the morning saw their goods off, and left Sturminster for London.

CHAPTER IX

Life and Literature in a London Suburb

1878–1879: *Aet.* 37–39

Two days later they beheld their furniture descending from a pair of vans at 1 Arundel Terrace ("The Larches"), in Trinity Road, just beyond Wandsworth Common. They had stayed at Bolingbroke Grove to be near.

"March 22.—We came from Bolingbroke Grove to Arundel Terrace and slept here for the first time. Our house is the south-east corner one where Brodrick Road crosses Trinity Road down towards Wandsworth Common Station, the side door being in Brodrick Road."

"April—Note. A Plot, or Tragedy, should arise from the gradual closing in of a situation that comes of ordinary human passions, prejudices, and ambitions, by reason of the characters taking no trouble to ward off the disastrous events produced by the said passions, prejudices, and ambitions."

"The advantages of the letter-system of telling a story (passing over the disadvantages) are that, hearing what one side has to say, you are led constantly to the imagination of what the other side must be feeling, and at last are anxious to know if the other side does really feel what you imagine."

"April 22.—The method of Boldini, the painter of 'The Morning Walk' in the French Gallery two or three years ago (a young lady beside an ugly blank wall on an ugly highway)—of Hobbema, in his

123

view of a road with formal lopped trees and flat tame scenery—is that of infusing emotion into the baldest external objects either by the presence of a human figure among them, or by mark of some human connection with them.

"This accords with my feeling about, say, Heidelberg and Baden *versus* Scheveningen—as I wrote at the beginning of 'The Return of the Native'—that the beauty of association is entirely superior to the beauty of aspect, and a beloved relative's old battered tankard to the finest Greek vase. Paradoxically put, it is to see the beauty in ugliness."

"April 29.—Mr George Smith (Smith Elder and Co) informs me that how he first got to know Thackeray was through 'a mutual friend'—to whom Smith said, 'Tell Thackeray that I will publish everything he likes to write'. This was before Thackeray was much known, and when he had only published the Titmarsh and Yellowplush papers. However, Thackeray did not appear. When they at length met, Thackeray said he wished to publish 'Vanity Fair', and Smith undertook it. Thackeray also said he had offered it to three or four publishers who had refused it. 'Why didn't you come to me?' said Smith. 'Why didn't you come to me?' said Thackeray."

"June 8.—To Grosvenor Gallery. Seemed to have left flesh behind, and entered a world of soul. In some of the pictures, e.g. A. Tadema's 'Sculpture' (men at work carving the Sphinx), and 'Ariadne abandoned by Theseus' (an uninteresting dreary shore, little tent one corner, etc.) the principles I have mentioned have been applied to choice of subject."

"June 16. Sunday evening. At Mr Alexander Macmillan's with E. He told me a story the late Mrs Carlyle told him. One day when she was standing alone on Craigenputtock Moor, where she and Mr Carlyle were living, she discerned in the distance a red spot. It proved to be the red cloak of a woman who passed for a witch in those parts. Mrs Carlyle got to know her, and ultimately learnt her history. She was the daughter of a laird owning about eighty acres, and there had come to their house in her young-womanhood a young dealer in cattle. The daughter and he fell in love, and were married, and both lived with their father, whose farm the young man took in hand to manage. But he ran the farmer into debt, and ultimately (I think) house and property had to be sold. The young man vanished. A boy was born to the wife, and after a while she went away to find her husband. She came back in a state of great misery, but would not tell where she had been. It leaked out that the husband was a married man. She was proud and would not complain; but her father died; the boy grew up and was intended for a schoolmaster, but he was crossing the moor one night and lost his way; was buried in the snow, and frozen to death. She lived on in a hut there, and become the red-cloaked old woman who was Mrs Carlyle's witch-neighbour."

In June he was elected a member of the Savile Club, and by degrees fell into line as a London man again. Dining at Mr Kegan Paul's, Kensington Square, the same summer, they met Mr Leighton (Sir F. Leighton's father), his daughter Mrs Sutherland Orr, who had been in India during the Mutiny, and Professor Huxley, whom they had met before at Mr Macmillan's. "We sat down by daylight, and as we dined the moon brightened the trees in the garden and shone under them into the room." For Huxley Hardy had a liking which grew with knowledge of him—though that was never great—speaking of him as a man who united a fearless mind with the warmest of hearts and the most modest of manners.

"July. When a couple are shown to their room at an hotel, before the husband has seen that it is a room at all, the wife has found the looking-glass & is arranging her bonnet."

"August 3. Minto dined with me at the club. Joined at end of dinner by W. H. Pollock, and we all three went to the Lyceum. It was Irving's last night, in which he appeared in a scene from 'Richard III'; then as 'Jingle'; then recited Eugene Aram's 'Dream'—(the only piece of literature outside plays that actors seem to know of). As 'Jingle', forgetting his part, he kept up one shoulder as in 'Richard III'. We went to his dressing-room;—found him naked to the waist:—champagne in tumblers."

"August 31. to Sept. 9.—In Dorset. Called on William Barnes the poet. Went to Kingston Lacy to see the pictures. Dined at West-Stafford Rectory. Went with C. W. Moule [Fellow of Corpus, Cambridge,] to Ford Abbey."

"September 30.—Returned and called on G. Smith. Agreed to his terms for publishing 'The Return of the Native'."

Shortly after he wrote to Messrs Smith and Elder:

I enclose a sketch-map of the supposed scene in which "The Return of the Native" is laid, copied from the one I used in writing the story; and my suggestion is that we place an engraving of it as frontispiece to the first volume. Unity of place is so seldom preserved in novels that a map of the scene of action is as a rule quite impracticable. But since the present story affords an opportunity of doing so I am of opinion that it would be a desirable novelty.

The publishers fell in with the idea and the map was made. It was afterwards adopted by R. L. Stevenson in *Treasure Island*.

A peculiarity in the local descriptions running through all Hardy's writings may be instanced here—that he never uses the word "Dorset", never names the county at all (except possibly in an explanatory footnote), but obliterates the names of the six counties whose area he traverses in his scenes under the general appellation of "Wessex"—an old word that became quite popular after the date of *Far from the Madding Crowd*, where he first introduced it. So far did he carry this idea of the unity of Wessex that he used to say he had grown to forget the crossing of county boundaries within the ancient Kingdom—in this respect being quite unlike the poet Barnes, who was "Dorset" emphatically.

Mrs Hardy used to relate that during this summer, she could not tell exactly when, she looked out of a window at the back of the house, and saw her husband running without a hat down Brodrick Road, and disappearing round a corner into a bye-street. Before she had done wondering what could have happened he returned, and all was explained. While sitting in his writing-room he had heard a street barrel-organ of the kind that used to be called a "harmoni-flute", playing somewhere near at hand the very quadrille over which the jaunty young man who had reached the end of his time at Hicks's had spread such a bewitching halo more than twenty years earlier, by describing the glories of dancing round to its beats on the Cremorne platform or at the Argyle Rooms, and which Hardy had never been able to identify. He had thrown down his pen, and, as she had beheld, flown out and approached the organ-grinder with such speed that the latter, looking frightened, began to shuffle off. Hardy called out, "What's the name of that tune?" The grinder—a young foreigner who could not speak English—exclaimed trembling as he stopped, "Quad-ree-ya! quad-ree-ya!" and pointed to the index in front of the instrument. Hardy looked: "Quadrille" was the only word there. He had till then never heard it since his smart senior had whistled it; he never heard it again, and never ascertained its name. It was possibly one of Jullien's—then gone out of vogue—set off rather by the youthful imagination of Hardy at sixteen than by any virtue in the music itself.

"October 27.—Sunday. To Chelsea Hospital and Ranelagh Gardens: met a palsied pensioner—deaf. He is 88—was in the Seventh (?) Hussars. He enlisted in 1807 or 1808, served under Sir John Moore in the Peninsula, through the Retreat, and was at Waterloo. It was extraordinary to talk and shake hands with a man who had shared in that terrible winter march to Coruna, and had seen Moore face to face.

"Afterwards spoke to two or three others. When an incorrigible was drummed out of barracks to the tune of the Rogue's March—(as my father had told me)—all the facings and the buttons were previously cut from his uniform, and a shilling given him. The fifes and drums accompanied him only just beyond the barrack-gates.

"In those days if you only turned your eye you were punished. My informant had known men receive 600 lashes—300 at a time, or 900, if the doctor said it could be borne. After the punishment salt was rubbed on the victim's back, to harden it. He did not feel the pain of this, his back being numbed by the lashes. The men would hold a bullet between their teeth and chew it during the operation."

The Return of the Native was published by Messrs Smith and Elder in November, *The Times'* remark upon the book being that the reader found himself taken farther from the madding crowd than ever. Old Mrs Procter's amusing criticism in a letter was: "Poor Eustacia. I so fully understand her longing for the Beautiful. *I* love the Common; but still one may wish for something else. I rejoice that Venn [a character] is happy. A man is never cured when he loves a stupid woman [Thomasin]. Beauty fades, and intelligence and wit grow irritating; but your dear Dulness is always the same."

"November 28. Woke before it was light. Felt that I had not enough staying power to hold my own in the world."

On the last day of the year Hardy's father wrote, saying that his mother was unwell, and that he had "drunk both their healths in gin and rhubarb wine, with hopes that they would live to see many and many a New Year's day". He suggested that they should come ere long.

"1879. January 1. New Year's thought. A perception of the FAILURE of THINGS to be what they are meant to be, lends them, in place of the intended interest, a new and greater interest of an unintended kind."

The poem "A January Night—1879" in *Moments of Vision* relates to an incident of this new year (1879) which occurred here at Tooting, where they seemed to begin to feel that "there had past away a glory from the earth". And it was in this house that their troubles began. This however is anticipating unduly.

"January 30. 1879. In Stevens's book-shop, Holywell Street. A bustling vigorous young curate comes in—red-faced and full of life—the warm breath puffing from his mouth in a jet into the frosty air, and religion sitting with an ill grace upon him.

" 'Have you *Able to Save?*'

"Shopman addressed does not know, and passes on the inquiry to the master standing behind with his hat on: '*Able to Save?*'

" 'I don't know—hoi! (to boy at other end) Got *Able to Save?* Why the devil can't you attend!'

" 'What sir?'

" '*Able to Save!*'

"Boy's face a blank. Shopman to curate: 'Get it by to-morrow afternoon, Sir.'

" 'And please get *Words of Comfort.*'

" '*Words of Comfort.* Yes Sir.' Exit curate.

"Master: 'Why the h—— don't anybody here know what's in stock?' Business proceeds in a subdued manner."

"February 1.—To Dorchester. Cold. Rain on snow. Henry seen advancing through it, with Wagonette and Bob [Hardy's father's horse], to the station entrance. Drove me to Bockhampton through the sleet and rain from the East, which shaved us like a razor. Wind on Fordington Moor cut up my sleeves and round my wrists—even up to my elbows. The light of the lamp at the bottom of the town shone on the reins in Henry's hands, and showed them glistening with ice. Bob's behind-part was a mere grey Arabic arch; his foreparts invisible."

"February 4. To Weymouth and Portland. As to the ruined walls in the low part of Chesil, a woman says the house was washed down in the November gale of 1824. The owner never rebuilt it, but emigrated with his family. She says that in her house one person was drowned (they were all in bed except the fishermen) and next door two people. It was about four in the morning that the wave came."

"February 7. Father says that when there was a hanging at Dorchester in his boyhood it was carried out at one o'clock, it being the custom to wait till the mail-coach came in from London in case of a reprieve.

"He says that at Puddletown Church, at the time of the old west-gallery violin, oboe, and clarionet players, Tom Sherren (one of them) used to copy tunes during the sermon. So did my grandfather at Stinsford Church. Old Squibb the parish-clerk used also to stay up late at night helping my grandfather in his 'prick-noting', (as he called it).

"He says that William, son of Mr S—— the Rector of Woodsford-and-Tincleton, became a miller at Owre-Moigne Mill, and married a German woman whom he met at Puddletown Fair playing her tambourine. When her husband was gone to market she used to call in John Porter, who could play the fiddle, and lived near, and give him some gin, when she would beat the tambourine to his playing. She was a good-natured woman with blue eyes, brown hair, and a round face; rather slovenly. Her husband was a hot, hasty fellow, though you could hear by his speech that he was a better educated man than ordinary millers.

"G. R. —— (who is a humorist) showed me his fowl-house, which was built of old church-materials bought at Wellspring the builder's sale. R's chickens roost under the gilt-lettered Lord's Prayer, and Creed, and the cock crows and flaps his wings against the Ten Commandments. It reminded me that I had seen these same Ten Commandments, Lord's Prayer, and Creed, before, forming the sides of the stone-mason's shed in that same builder's yard, and that he had remarked casually that they did not prevent the workmen 'cussing and damning' the same as ever. It also reminded me of seeing the old font of —— Church, Dorchester, in a garden, used as a flower-vase, the initials of ancient godparents and church-wardens still legible upon it. A comic business—church restoration.

"A villager says of the parson, who has been asked to pray for a sick person: 'His prayers wouldn't save a mouse.' "

"February 12. Sketched the English Channel from Mayne Down.

"I am told that when Jack Ketch had done whipping by the Town Pump [Dorchester] the prisoners' coats were thrown over their bleeding backs, and, guarded by the town-constables with their long staves, they were conducted back to prison. Close at their heels came J. K., the cats held erect—there was one cat to each man—the lashes were of knotted whipcord.

"Also that in a village near Yeovil about 100 years ago there lived a dumb woman, well known to my informant's mother. One day the woman suddenly spoke and said:

'A cold winter, a forward spring,
A bloody summer, a dead King.'

She then dropped dead. The French Revolution followed immediately after."

"February 15. Returned to London."

"April 5. Mary writes to tell me that 'there is a very queer quire at Steepleton Church. It consists only of a shoemaker who plays the bass-viol, and his mother who sings the air.' "

"June 9. To the International Literary Congress at the rooms of the Society of Arts. Met M. de Lesseps. A few days afterwards to the Soirée Musicale at the Hanover Square Club, to meet members of the Literary Congress and the Comédie Française: A large gathering. The whole thing a free-and-easy mix-up. I was a total stranger, and wondered why I was there: many others were total strangers to everybody else; sometimes two or three of these total strangers would fraternize from very despair. A little old Frenchman, however, who bustled about in a skull cap and frilled shirt, seemed to know everybody."

"June 21. With E. to Bosworth Smith's, Harrow (for the weekend). In the aviary he has a raven and a barn owl. One ridiculously small boy was in tails—he must have been a bright boy, but I forgot to ask about him. One of the boys in charity-tails could have eaten him.

"Bos's brother Henry the invalid has what I fear to be a churchyard cough [he died not so very long after]. His cough pleases the baby, so he coughs artificially much more than required by his disease, to go on pleasing the baby. Mrs H. S. implores her husband not to do so; but he does, nevertheless, showing the extraordinary nonchalance about death that so many of his family show.

"In chapel—which we attended—the little tablets in memory of the boys who have died at school there were a moving sight.

"Sunday night we went with Bos. to the boys' dormitories. One boy was unwell, and we talked to him as he lay in bed, his arm thrown over his head. Another boy has his room hung with proof engravings after Landseer. In another room were the two K——s of Clyffe. In another a big boy and a little boy—the little boy being very earnest about birds' eggs, and the big boy silently affecting a mind above the subject though covertly interested."

"27. From Tooting to Town again. In railway carriage a *too* statuesque girl; but her features were absolutely perfect. She sat quite still, and her smiles did not extend further than a finger-nail's breadth from the edge of her mouth. The repose of her face was such that when the train shook her it seemed painful. Her mouth was very small, and her face not unlike that of a nymph. In the train coming home there was a contrasting girl of sly humour—the pupil of her eye being mostly half under the outer side of her eyelid."

It was in this year that pourparlers were opened with Leslie Stephen about another story for the *Cornhill*; and Hardy informed him that he was writing a tale of the reign of George III; on which Stephen remarks in respect of historical novels:

> I can only tell you what is my own taste, but I rather think that my taste is in this case the common one. I think that a historical character in a novel is almost always a nuisance; but I like to have a bit of history in the background, so to speak; to feel that George III is just round the corner, though he does not present himself in full front.

Since coming into contact with Leslie Stephen about 1873, as has been shown, Hardy had been much influenced by his philosophy, and also by his criticism. He quotes the following sentence from Stephen in his note-book under the date of July 1, 1879:

"The ultimate aim of the poet should be to touch our hearts by showing his own, and not to exhibit his learning, or his fine taste, or his skill in mimicking the notes of his predecessors." That Hardy adhered pretty closely to this principle when he resumed the writing of poetry can hardly be denied.

"July 8 or 9. With E. to Mrs [Alexander] Macmillan's garden-party at Knapdale, near our house. A great many present. Talked to Mr White of Harvard University, and Mr Henry Holt the New York publisher, who said that American spelling and idiom must prevail over the English, as it was sixty millions against thirty. I forgot for the moment to say that it did not follow, the usage set up by a few people of rank, education, and fashion being the deciding factor. Also to John Morley, whom I had not seen since he read my first manuscript. He remembered it, and said in his level uninterested voice: 'Well, since we met, you have . . .' etc etc. Also met a Mrs H., who pretended to be an admirer of my books, and apparently had never read one. She had with her an American lady, sallow, with black dancing eyes, dangling earrings, yellow costume, and gay laugh." It was at this garden-party at Mrs Macmillan's that the thunderstorm came on which Hardy made use of in a similar scene in *A Laodicean*.

"July 12. To Chislehurst to funeral of young Louis Napoleon. Met

[Sir G.] Greenhill in the crowd. We stood on the common while the procession passed. Was struck by the profile of Prince Napoleon as he walked by bareheaded, a son on each arm: complexion dark, sallow, even sinister: a round projecting chin: countenance altogether extraordinarily remindful of Boney." Hardy said long after that this sight of Napoleon's nephew—"Plon Plon"—had been of enormous use to him, when writing *The Dynasts*, in imagining the Emperor's appearance. And it has been remarked somewhere in print that when the Prince had been met, without warning in Paris at night, crossing one of the bridges over the Seine, the beholder had started back aghast under the impression that he was seeing the spirit of the great Napoleon.

"July 29. Charles Leland—a man of higher literary rank than ever was accorded him [the American author of *Hans Breitmann's Ballads* and translator of Heine]—told some of his gipsy tales at the Savile Club, including one of how he visited at a country mansion, and while there went to see a gipsy-family living in a tent on the squire's land. He talked to them in Romany, and was received by the whole family as a bosom-friend. He was told by the head gipsy that his, the gipsy's, brother would be happy to know him when he came out of gaol, but that at present he was doing six months for a horse. While Leland was sitting by the fire drinking brandy-and-water with this friend, the arrival of some gentlemen and ladies, fellow-guests at the house he was staying at, was announced. They had come to see the gipsies out of curiosity. Leland threw his brandy from his glass into the fire, not to be seen tippling there, but as they entered it blazed up in a blue flare much to their amazement, as if they thought it some unholy libation, which added to their surprise at discovering him. How he explained himself I cannot remember."

In the latter half of August Hardy paid a visit to his parents in Dorset and a week later Mrs Hardy joined him there. They spent a few days in going about the district, and then took lodgings at Weymouth, right over the harbour, his mother coming to see them, and driving to Portland, Upwey, etc., in their company. Their time in the port was mostly wet;—"the [excursion-]steamer-bell ringing persistently, and nobody going on board except an unfortunate boys' school that had come eight miles by train that morning to spend a happy day by the sea. The rain goes into their baskets of provisions, and runs out a strange mixture of cake-juice and mustard-water, but they try to look as if they were enjoying it—all except the pale thin assistant-master who has come with them, and whose face is tragic with his responsibilities. The Quay seems quite deserted till, on going along it, groups of boatmen are discovered behind each projecting angle of wall—martyrs in countenance, talking of what their receipts would have been if the season had turned out fine; and the landladies' faces at every lodging-house window watching the drizzle and the sea it half obscures. Two adventurous visitors have emerged from their lodgings as far as the doorway, where they stand in their waterproof cloaks and goloshes, saying cheerfully, 'the air will do us good, and we can change as soon as we come in'. Young men rush to the bathing machines in ulsters, and the men engaged in loading a long-voyage steamer lose all patience, and say: 'I'm blanked if it goes on much longer like this we shall be rotted alive!' The tradespeople are exceptionally civil, and fancy prices have miraculously disappeared. . . .

"Am told that —— has turned upon her drunken husband at last, and knocks him down without ceremony. In the morning he holds out his trembling hand and says, 'Give me a sixpence for a drop o'brandy—please do ye, my dear!' " This was a woman Hardy had known as a pretty laughing girl, who had been married for the little money she had.

CHAPTER X

London Life, France, and Cambridge

1879–1880: *Aet.* 39–40

After their return to London they visited and dined out here and there, and as Mrs Hardy had never seen the Lord Mayor's Show Hardy took her to view it from the upper windows of *Good Words* in Ludgate Hill. She remarked that the surface of the crowd seemed like a boiling cauldron of porridge. He jots down that "as the crowd grows denser it loses its character of an aggregate of countless units, and becomes an organic whole, a molluscous black creature having nothing in common with humanity, that takes the shape of the streets along which it has lain itself, and throws out horrid excrescences and limbs into neighbouring alleys; a creature whose voice exudes from its scaly coat, and who has an eye in every pore of its body. The balconies, stands, and railway-bridge are occupied by small detached shapes of the same tissue, but of gentler motion, as if they were the spawn of the monster in their midst."

On a Sunday in the same November they met in Mr Frith's studio to which they had been invited, Sir Percy Shelley (the son of Percy Bysshe) and Lady Shelley. Hardy said afterwards that the meeting was as shadowy and remote as were those previous occasions when he had impinged on the penumbra of the poet he loved—that time of

his sleeping at the Cross Keys, St. John Street, and that of the visits 22
he paid to Old St. Pancras Churchyard. He was to enter that faint
penumbra twice more, once when he stood beside Shelley's dust in
the English cemetery at Rome, and last when by Mary Shelley's
grave at Bournemouth.

They also met in the studio a deaf old lady, introduced as "Lady
Bacon" (though she must have been Lady Charlotte Bacon), who
"talked vapidly of novels, saying she never read them—not thinking
them *positively wicked*, but, well . . . ." Mr Frith afterwards explained
that she was Byron's Ianthe, to whom he dedicated the First and
Second Cantos of *Childe Harold*, when she was Lady Charlotte
Harley. That "Peri of the West", with an eye "wild as the
Gazelle's", and a voice that had entered Byron's ear, was now a
feeble beldame muffled up in black and furs. (It may be mentioned
that she died the following year.)

Hardy met there too—a distinctly modern juxtaposition—Miss
Braddon, who "had a broad, thought-creased, world-beaten face—
a most amiable woman", whom he always liked.

In December Hardy attended the inaugural dinner of the
Rabelais Club at the Tavistock Hotel, in a "large, empty, dimly-lit,
cheerless apartment, with a gloomy crimson screen hiding what
remained of the only cheerful object there—the fire. There was a fog
in the room as in the streets, and one man only came in evening
dress, who, Walter Pollock said, looked like the skull at the banquet,
but who really looked like a conjuror dying of the cold among a
common set of thick-jacketed men who could stand it. When I came
in Leland turned his high flat façade to me—like that of a clock-
tower; his face being the clock-face, his coat swaying like a
pendulum; features earnest and energetic, altogether those of a
single-minded man. There were also Fred Pollock, girlish-looking;
and genial Walter Besant, with his West-of-England sailor face and
silent pantomimic laughter. Sir Patrick Colquhoun was as if he
didn't know what he was there for, how he arrived there, or how he
was going to get home again. Two others present—Palmer [after-
wards murdered in the East], and Joe Knight [the dramatic critic],
also seemed puzzled about it.

"When dinner was over and things had got warmer, Leland in his
speech remarked with much emphasis that we were men who ought
to be encouraged, which sentiment was applauded with no misgivings of self-conceit. D——, now as always, made himself the
clown of our court, privileged to say anything by virtue of his office.

Hence when we rose to drink the health of absent members he stayed firmly sitting, saying he would not drink it because they ought to have been there, afterwards lapsing into Spanish on the strength of his being going some day to publish a translation of Don Quixote. Altogether we were as Rabelaisian as it was possible to be in the foggy circumstances, though I succeeded but poorly."

It should be explained that this Rabelais Club, which had a successful existence for many years, had been instituted by Sir Walter Besant—a great lover of clubs and societies—as a declaration for virility in literature. Hardy was pressed to join as being the most virile writer of works of the imagination then in London; while, it may be added, Henry James, after a discussion, was rejected for the lack of that quality, though he was afterwards invited as a guest.

On the first of February 1880 Hardy observed a man skating by himself on the pond by the Trinity-Church Schools at Upper Tooting, near his own house, and was moved to note down:

"It is a warm evening for the date, and there has been a thaw for two or three days, so that the birds sing cheerfully. A buttercup is said to be visible somewhere, and spring has, in short, peeped in upon us. What can the sentiments of that man be, to enjoy *ice* at such a time? The mental jar must overcome physical enjoyment in any well-regulated mind. He skates round the edge, it being unsafe to go into the middle, and he seems to sigh as he puts up with a limitation resulting from blessed promise."

> 1 Arundel Terrace
> Trinity Road,
> Upper Tooting. S.W.
> Feb. 2. 1880.

Dear Mr Locker,

I can hardly express to you how grateful I am to get your letter. When I consider the perfect literary taste that is shown in all your own writings, apart from their other merits, I am not sure that I do not value your expressions of pleasure more highly than all the printed criticisms put together. It is very generous of you to pass over the defects of style in the book which, whenever I look into it, seem blunders that any child ought to have avoided.

In enjoying your poems over again, I felt,—will you mind my saying it?—quite ill-used to find you had altered two of my favourite lines which I had been in the habit of muttering to myself for some years past. I mean

> 'They never do so now—because
> I'm not so handsome as I was.'

I shall stick to the old reading as much the nicest, whatever you may choose to do in new editions.

One other remark of quite a different sort. I unhesitatingly affirm that nothing more beautiful and powerful, for its length, than "the Old Stone-Mason" has been done by any modern poet. The only poem which has affected me at all in the same way is Wordsworth's "Two April Mornings", but this being less condensed than yours does not strike through one with such sudden power as yours in the last verse.

I will not forget to give myself the pleasure of calling some Sunday afternoon. Meanwhile I should hope that you will be so kindly disposed as to give us a few more "old stone-masons" as well as ballads of a lighter kind.

Believe me,

Yours very truly,

Thomas Hardy.

The same week Hardy met Matthew Arnold—probably for the first time—at a dinner given by Mr G. Murray Smith the publisher at the Continental Hotel, where also were present Henry James, and Richard Jefferies—the latter a modest young man then getting into notice, as a writer, through having a year or so earlier published his first book, entitled *The Gamekeeper at Home.*

Arnold, according to Hardy's account of their meeting much later, "had a manner of having made up his mind upon everything years ago, so that it was a pleasing futility for his interlocutor to begin thinking new ideas, different from his own, at that time of day". Yet he was frank and modest enough to assure Hardy deprecatingly that he was only a hard-worked school-inspector.

He seems to have discussed the subject of literary style with the younger writer, but all the latter could recall of his remarks thereon was his saying that "the best man to read for style—narrative style— was Swift"—an opinion that may well be questioned, like many more of Arnold's pronouncements, despite his undoubtedly true ones.

At dinner an incident occurred in which he was charmingly

amusing. Mrs Murray Smith having that afternoon found herself suddenly too unwell to preside, her place had to be taken at the last minute by her daughter, and, it being the latter's first experience of the kind, she was timorous as to the time of withdrawal, murmuring to Arnold, "I—think we must retire now?" Arnold put his hand upon her shoulder and pressed her down into her seat as if she were a child—she was not much more—saying "No, no! What's the use of going into that room. Now I'll pour you out a glass of sherry to keep you here." And kept there she and the other ladies were.

Savile Club,
Savile Row, W.
February 11. 1880.

Dear Mr Handley Moule,

I have just been reading in a Dorset paper a report of your sermon on the death of the Rev. H. Moule, and I cannot refrain from sending you a line to tell you how deeply it has affected me, and—what is more to the point—to express my sense of the singular power with which you have brought Mr Moule's life and innermost heart before all readers of that address.

You will, I am sure, believe me when I say that I have been frequently with you and your brothers in spirit during the last few days. Though not, topographically, a parishioner of your father's I virtually stood in that relation to him, and his home generally, during many years of my life, and I always feel precisely as if I had been one. I had many times resolved during the year or two before his death to try to attend a service in the old church in the old way before he should be gone: but tomorrow, and tomorrow, and tomorrow!—I never did.

A day or two ago Matthew Arnold talked a good deal about him to me: he was greatly struck with an imperfect description I gave him (from what I had heard my father say) of the state of Fordington 50 years ago, and its state after the vicar had brought his energies to bear upon the village for a few years. His words "energy is genius" express your father very happily.

Please give my kind remembrances to Mr Charles Moule and your other brothers who have not forgotten me—if they are with you—and believe me

Sincerely yours,

Thomas Hardy.

The first week in March the Hardys called by arrangement on Mrs Procter—the widow of "Barry Cornwall"—at her flat in Queen Anne's Mansions. Hardy had been asked to her house when he first made her acquaintance before his marriage, and when her husband was living, though bedridden: but being then, as always, backward in seeking new friends Hardy had never gone—to his regret. He was evidently impressed newly by her on this call, as one who was a remarkable link with the literary past, though she herself was not a literary woman; and the visit on this Sunday afternoon was the first one of a long series of such, extending over many years almost to her death, for she showed a great liking for Hardy and his wife, and especially for Mrs Hardy, which she did not show for every woman (far from it!); and she always made them particularly welcome. It was here on these Sunday afternoons that they used frequently to meet Browning.

Hardy said after her death that on such occasions she sat in a fixed attitude, almost as if placed in her seat like an unconscious image or Buddha. Into her eyes and face would come continually an expression from a time fifty or sixty years before, when she was a handsome coquette, a faint tendency to which would show even in old age in the momentary archness of her glance now and then. "You would talk to her", he said, "and believe you were talking to a person of the same date as yourself, with recent emotions and impulses: you would see her sideways when crossing the room to show you something, and realize her, with sudden sadness, to be a withered woman whose interests and emotions must be nearly extinct."

Of the poets she had met she expressed herself to have been unattracted by Wordsworth's personality, but to have had a great liking for Leigh Hunt. She remembered that the latter called one day, bringing with him "a youth whom nobody noticed much", and who remained in the background, Hunt casually introducing him as "Mr Keats".

She would also tell of an experience she and her husband had, shortly after their marriage, when they were living in fashionable lodgings in Southampton Row. They went to see Lamb at Edmonton, and caused him much embarrassment by a hint that she would like to wash her hands, it being a hot day. He seemed bewildered, and asked stammeringly if she would mind washing them in the kitchen, which she did.

A little later she wrote to Hardy concerning his short story

"Fellow-Townsmen" which had lately come out in a periodical:

> You are cruel. Why not let him come home again and marry his first love? But I see you are right. He should not have deserted her. I smiled about the Tombstone. Sir Francis Chantrey told me that he had prepared fine plans—nothing could be too beautiful and too expensive at first, and the end was generally merely a head-stone.

It was in the same month, and in the company of Mrs Procter, that Hardy lunched at Tennyson's at a house Tennyson had temporarily taken in Belgrave Street; Mrs Tennyson, though an invalid, presiding at the table, at the end of which she reclined, and his friends F. Locker, Countess Russell (Lord John's widow), Lady Agatha Russell, and others, being present. "When I arrived Mrs Tennyson was lying as if in a coffin, but she got up to welcome me." Hardy often said that he was surprised to find such an expression of humour in the poet-laureate's face, the corners of his mouth twitching with that mood when he talked; it was a genial human face, which all his portraits belied; and it was enhanced by a beard and hair straggling like briars, a shirt with a large loose collar, and old steel spectacles. He was very sociable that day, asking Mrs Procter absurd riddles, and telling Hardy amusing stories, and about misprints in his books that drove him wild, one in especial of late, where "airy does" had appeared as "hairy does". He said he liked *A Pair of Blue Eyes* the best of Hardy's novels. Tennyson also told him that he and his family were compelled to come to London for a month or two every year, though he hated it, because they all "got so rusty" down in the Isle of Wight if they did not come at all. Hardy often regretted that he never again went to see them, though warmly invited that day both by Tennyson and his wife to pay them a visit at Freshwater.

"March 24. Lunched with Mrs Procter. She showed me one of her late husband's love-letters, date 1824. Also a photo of Henry James. She says he has made her an offer of marriage. Can it be so?"

During the first half of 1880 Hardy also became friendly, in one way and another, with Colonel Chesney, author of *The Battle of Dorking*, with Lord Houghton, a fellow-member of the Rabelais Club, Professor Huxley (met before), Thomas Woolner the sculptor, George du Maurier, and several more.

At this time he writes down, "A Hint for Reviewers—adapted from Carlyle":

"Observe what is true, not what is false; what is to be loved and held fast, and earnestly laid to heart; not what is to be contemned, and derided, and sportfully cast out-of-doors." Through the long years after, when only the bad lines were quoted from his verses by certain critics, and only the careless sentences and doubtful opinions from his prose, he would speak on this point and say, "These people are hopeless! *Why* don't they see that the same treatment of any poet great or small who ever lived would produce the same results, and therefore that they prove nothing by their probings except their own incompetence for their business."

The Hardys' house at Upper Tooting stood in a rather elevated position, and when the air was clear they could see a long way from the top windows. The following note on London at dawn occurs on May 19, a night on which he could not sleep, partly on account of an eerie feeling which sometimes haunted him, a horror at lying down in close proximity to "a monster whose body had four million heads and eight million eyes":

"In upper back bedroom at daybreak: just past three. A golden light behind the horizon; within it are the Four Millions. The roofs are damp gray: the streets are still filled with night as with a dark stagnant flood whose surface brims to the tops of the houses. Above the air is light. A fire or two glares within the mass. Behind are the Highgate Hills. On the Crystal Palace hills in the other direction a lamp is still burning up in the daylight. The lamps are also still flickering in the street, and one policeman walks down it as if it were noon."

Two days later they were sitting in the chairs by Rotten Row and the Park Drive, and the chief thing he noticed against the sun in the west was that "a sparrow descends from the tree amid the stream of vehicles, and drinks from the little pool left by the watering-cart"— the same sunlight causing "a glitter from carriage-lamp glasses, from Coachmen's and footmen's buttons, from silver carriage handles and harness mountings, from a matron's bracelet, from four parasols of four young ladies in a landau, their parasol-hems touching like four mushrooms growing close together."

On the 26th, the Derby Day, Hardy went alone to Epsom. On his way he noticed that "all the people going to the races have a twinkle in their eye, particularly the old men". He lunched there with a friend, and together they proceeded, by permission, through Lord

Rosebery's grounds to the Down. They saw and examined the favourite before he emerged—neither one of the twain knowing anything of race-horses or betting—"the jockeys in their great-coats; little ghastly men looking half putrid, standing silent and apathetic while their horses were rubbed down, and saddles adjusted"; till they passed on into the paddock, and the race was run, and the shouts arose, and they "were greeted by a breeze of tobacco-smoke and orange-smells".

During the summer he dined at clubs, etc., meeting again Lord Houghton, du Maurier, Henry Irving, and Alma-Tadema, among others. Toole, who was at one of these dinners, imitated a number of other actors, Irving included; and though the mimicry was funny and good, "ghostliness arose, in my mind at least, when after a few living ones had been mimicked, each succeeding representation turned out to be that of an actor then in his grave. 'What did they go dying for, stupids!' said somebody, when Toole's face suddenly lost its smiling."

In July he met Lord Houghton again at dinner, and was introduced by him to Lowell the American Minister, who was also present. His opinion of Lowell was that as a man he was charming, as a writer one of extraordinary talent, but of no instinctive and creative genius.

In the same month he arranged with Messrs Smith and Elder for the three-volume publication of *The Trumpet-Major*, which had been coming out in a periodical, and on the 27th started with Mrs Hardy for Boulogne, Amiens—"the misfortune of the Cathedral is that it does not look half so lofty as it really is"—and several other towns in Normandy, including Etretât, where they put up at the Hôtel Blanquet, and stayed some time, bathing every day—a recreation which cost Hardy dear, for being fond of swimming he was apt to stay too long in the water. Anyhow he blamed these frequent immersions for starting the long illness from which he suffered the following autumn and winter.

From Etretât they went to Havre, and here they had half an hour of whimsical uneasiness. The hotel they chose was on the Quay, one that had been recommended to Hardy by a stranger on the coach, and was old and gloomy in the extreme when they got inside. Mrs Hardy fancied that the landlord's look was sinister; also the landlady's; and the waiters' manner seemed queer. Their room was hung with heavy dark velvet, and when the chambermaid came, and they talked to her, she sighed continually and spoke in a foreboding voice; as if she knew what was going to happen to them, and was on their side, but could do nothing. The floor of the bedroom was painted a bloody red, and the wall beside the bed was a little battered, as if struggles had taken place there. When they were left to themselves Hardy suddenly remembered that he had told the friendly stranger with whom he had travelled on the coach from Etretât, and who had recommended the inn, that he carried his money with him in Bank notes to save the trouble of circular notes. He had known it was a thing one never should do; yet he had done it.

They then began to search the room, found a small door behind the curtains of one of their beds, and on opening it there was revealed inside a closet of lumber, which had at its innermost recess another door, leading they did not know whither. With their luggage they barricaded the closet door, so jamming their trunks and portmanteau between the door and the nearest bedstead that it was impossible to open the closet. They lay down and waited, keeping the light burning a long time. Nothing happened, and they slept soundly at last, and awoke to a bright sunny morning.

August 5. They went on to Trouville, to the then fashionable Hôtel Bellevue, and thence to Honfleur, a place more to Hardy's mind, after the fast life of Trouville. On a gloomy gusty afternoon, going up the steep incline through the trees behind the town they came upon a Calvary tottering to its fall; and as it rocked in the wind like a ship's mast Hardy thought that the crudely painted figure of Christ upon it seemed to writhe and cry in the twilight: "Yes, Yes! I agree that this travesty of me and my doctrines should totter and overturn in this modern world!" They hastened on from the strange and ghastly scene.

Thence they went to Lisieux and Caen, where they spent some days, returning to London by the way they had come.

Going down to Dorset in September Hardy was informed of a curious bit of family history; that his mother's grandfather William was a man who worried a good deal about the disposition of his property as he grew old. It was mostly in the form of long leasehold and life-hold houses, and he would call on his lawyer about once a fortnight to make some alteration in his will. The lawyer lived at Bere Regis, and her grandfather used to talk the matter over with the man who was accustomed to drive him there and back—a connection of his by marriage. Gradually this man so influenced the testator on each journey, by artfully playing on his nervous perplexities as they drove along, that he got three-quarters of the property, including the houses, bequeathed to himself.

The same month he replied to a letter from Mr Lowell, then American Minister in London:

Dear Mr Lowell:

I have read with great interest the outline of the proposed Copyright treaty that you have communicated to me in your letter of the 16th.

For my own part I should be quite ready to accept some such treaty—with a modification in detail mentioned below—since whatever may be one's opinion on an author's abstract right to manufacture his property in any country most convenient to him, the treaty would unquestionably remove the heaviest grievances complained of under the existing law.

The modification I mention refers to the three months term of grace to be allowed to foreign authors who do not choose to print in both countries simultaneously.

If I clearly understand the provisions under this head it may happen that in the event of any difficulty about terms between the author and his foreign publishers the author would be bound to give way as the end of the three months approached, or lose all by lapse of copyright. With some provision to meet such a contingency as this the treaty would seem to me satisfactory.

Accompanying Mrs Hardy on a day's shopping in October Hardy makes this remark on the saleswoman at a fashionable dressmaking establishment in Regent Street, from observing her while he sat waiting:

"She is a woman of somewhat striking appearance, tall, thin, decided; one who knows what life is, and human nature, to plenitude. Hence she acts as by clockwork; she puts each cloak on herself, turns round, makes a remark, puts on the next cloak, and the next, and so on, like an automaton. She knows by heart every mood in which a feminine buyer of cloaks can possibly be, and has a machine-made answer promptly ready for each."

On the 16th of October he and his wife paid a visit of a week to Cambridge, in spirits that would have been considerably lower if they had known what was to befall them on their return. They received much hospitality, and were shown the usual buildings and other things worth seeing, though Cambridge was not new to Hardy. After the first day or two he felt an indescribable physical weariness, which was really the beginning of the long illness he was to endure; but he kept going.

Attending the 5 o'clock service at King's Chapel he comments upon the architect "who planned this glorious work of fine intelligence"; also upon Milton's "dim religious light" beheld here, and the scene presented by the growing darkness as viewed from the stalls where they sat. "The reds and the blues of the windows became of one indistinguishable black, the candles guttered in the most fantastic shapes I ever saw,—and while the wicks burnt down these weird shapes changed form; so that you were fascinated into watching them, and wondering what shape those wisps of wax would take next, till they dropped off with a click during a silence. They were stalactites, plumes, laces; or rather they were surplices,— frayed shreds from those of bygone 'white-robed scholars', or from their shrouds—dropping bit by bit in a ghostly decay. Wordsworth's ghost, too, seemed to haunt the place, lingering and wandering on somewhere alone in the fan-traceried vaulting."

PART III

Illness, Novels, and Italy

CHAPTER XI

Writing Under Difficulties; and a Change

1880–1881: *Aet.* 40–41

They returned to London on October the 23rd—the very day *The Trumpet-Major* was published, Hardy feeling by this time very unwell, so unwell that he had to write and postpone an engagement or two, and decline an invitation to Fryston by Lord Houghton. On the Sunday after he was worse, and seeing the name of a surgeon on a brass plate opposite his house, sent for him. The surgeon came at once, and came again on that and the two or three succeeding days; he said that Hardy was bleeding internally. Mrs Hardy, in her distress, called on their neighbours the Macmillans, to ask their opinion, and they immediately sent their own doctor. He agreed about the bleeding, said the case was serious; and that the patient was not to get up on any account.

Later it was supposed that a dangerous operation would be necessary, till the doctor enquired how long Hardy could lie in bed—could he lie there, if necessary, for months?—in which case there possibly need be no operation.

Now he had already written the early chapters of a story for *Harper's Magazine*—A Laodicean, which was to begin in the (nominally) December number, issued in November. This first part was already printed, and du Maurier was illustrating it. The story had to go on somehow, it happening, unfortunately, that the number containing it was the first number also of the publication of *Harper's* as an English and not exclusively American magazine as hitherto, and the success of its launch in London depended largely upon the serial tale. Its writer was, during the first few weeks, in considerable pain, and compelled to lie on an inclined plane with the lower part of his body higher than his head. Yet he felt determined to finish the novel, at whatever stress to himself—so as not to ruin the new venture of the publishers, and also in the interests of his wife, for whom as yet he had made but a poor provision in the event of his own decease. Accordingly from November onwards he began dictating it to her from the awkward position he occupied; and continued to do so—with greater ease as the pain and hæmorrhage went off. She worked bravely both at writing and nursing, till at the beginning of the following May a rough draft was finished by one shift and another.

"Nov. 20—Freiherr von Tauchnitz junior called." This was probably about a Continental edition of *The Trumpet-Major*. But Hardy was still too ill to see him. *The Trumpet-Major* however duly appeared in the Tauchnitz series.

It is somewhat strange that at the end of November he makes a note of an intention to resume poetry as soon as possible. Having plenty of time to think he also projected as he lay what he calls a "Great Modern Drama"—which seems to have been a considerable advance on his first conception, in June 1875, of a Napoleonic chronicle in Ballad form—a sequence of such making a lyrical whole. Yet it does not appear to have been quite the same in detail as that of *The Dynasts* later on. He also made the following irrelative note of rather vague import:

"Discover for how many years, and on how many occasions, the organism, Society, has been standing, lying, etc, in varied positions, as if it were a tree or a man hit by vicissitudes.

"There would be found these periods:—

1. Upright, normal, or healthy periods.
2. Oblique or cramped periods.
3. Prostrate periods (intellect counterpoised by ignorance or narrowness, producing stagnation.)
4. Drooping periods.
5. Inverted periods."

George Eliot died during the winter in which he lay ill, and this set him thinking about Positivism, on which he remarks:

"If Comte had introduced Christ among the worthies in his calendar it would have made Positivism tolerable to thousands who, from position, family connection, or early education, now decry what in their heart of hearts they hold to contain the germs of a true system. It would have enabled them to modulate gently into the new religion by deceiving themselves with the sophistry that they still continued one-quarter Christians, or one-eighth, or one twentieth, as the case might be: This as a matter of *policy*, without which no religion succeeds in making way."

Also, on literary criticism:

"Arnold is wrong about provincialism, if he means anything more than a provincialism of style and manner in exposition. A certain provincialism of feeling is invaluable. It is of the essence of individuality, and is largely made up of that crude enthusiasm without which no great thoughts are thought, no great deeds done."

Some days later he writes:

"Romanticism will exist in human nature as long as human nature itself exists. The point is (in imaginative literature) to adopt that form of romanticism which is the mood of the age."

Also on adversity—no doubt suggested by the distresses he was undergoing:

"There is mercy in troubles coming in battalions—they neutralize each other. Tell a man in prosperity that he must suffer the amputation of a limb, and it is a horror to him; but tell him this the minute after he has been reduced to beggary and his only son has died: it hurts him but feebly."

"January 1881. My third month in bed. Driving snow: fine, and so fast that individual flakes cannot be seen. In sheltered places they occasionally stop, and balance themselves in the air like hawks. . . . It creeps into the house, the window-plants being covered as if out-of-doors. Our passage (downstairs) is sole-deep, Em says, and feet leave tracks on it."

(Same month.) "Style—Consider the Wordsworthian dictum (the more perfectly the natural object is reproduced, the more truly poetic the picture). This reproduction is achieved by seeing into the *heart of a thing* (as rain, wind, for instance,) and is realism, in fact, though through being pursued by means of the imagination it is confounded with invention, which is pursued by the same means. It is, in short, reached by what M. Arnold calls 'the imaginative reason.'"

"January 30. Sunday. Dr S. called as usual. I can by this time see all round his knowledge of my illness. He showed a lost manner on entering as if among his many cases he had forgotten all about my case and me, which has to be revived in his mind by looking hard at me, when it all comes back.

"He told us of having been called in to an accident which, do the best he possibly could, would only end in discredit to him. A lady had fallen down, and so badly broken her wrist that it must always be deformed even after the most careful treatment. But, seeing the result, she would give him a bad name for want of skill in setting it. These cases often occur in a surgeon's practice, he says."

"Jan. 31. Incidents of lying in bed for months. Skin gets fair: corns take their leave: feet and toes grow shapely as those of a Greek statue. Keys get rusty; watch dim, boots mildewed; hat and clothes old-fashioned; umbrella eaten out with rust; children seen through the window are grown taller."

"Feb. 7. Carlyle died last Saturday. Both he & George Eliot have vanished into nescience while I have been lying here."

"February 17. Conservatism is not estimable in itself, nor is change, or Radicalism. To conserve the existing good, to supplant the existing bad by good, is to act on a true political principle, which is neither Conservative nor Radical."

"February 21. A. G. called. Explained to Em about Aerostation, and how long her wings would have to be if she flew,—how light her weight, etc., and the process generally of turning her into a flying person."

"March 22. Maggie Macmillan called. Sat with Em in my room—had tea. She and Em worked, watching the sun set gorgeously. That I should also be able to see it Miss Macmillan conceived the kind idea of reflecting the sun into my face by a looking-glass." [The incident was made use of in *Jude the Obscure* as a plan adopted by Sue when the schoolmaster was ill.]

"March 27. A Homeric Ballad, in which Napoleon is a sort of Achilles, to be written." [This entry, of a kind with earlier ones, is, however, superseded a few days later by the following:] "Mode for a historical Drama. Action mostly automatic, reflex movement, etc. Not the result of what is called *motive*, though always ostensibly so, even to the actors' own consciousness. Apply an enlargement of these theories to, say, 'The Hundred Days'!"

This note is, apparently, Hardy's first written idea of a philosophic scheme or framework as the larger feature of *The Dynasts*, enclosing the historic scenes.

On the 10th of April he went outside the door again for the first time since that October afternoon of the previous year when he returned from Cambridge, driving out with his wife and the doctor. On the 19th occurred the death of Disraeli, whom Hardy had met twice, and found unexpectedly urbane. On Sunday the 1st of May he finished *A Laodicean* in pencil, and on the 3rd went with Mrs Hardy by appointment to call on Sir Henry Thompson for a consultation.

"May 9. After infinite trying to reconcile a scientific view of life with the emotional and spiritual, so that they may not be interdestructive, I come to the following:—

"General Principles. Law has produced in man a child who cannot but constantly reproach its parent for doing much and yet not all, and constantly say to such parent that it would have been better never to have begun doing than to have *over*done so indecisively; that is, than to have created so far beyond all apparent first intention (on the emotional side), without mending matters by a second intent and execution, to eliminate the evils of the blunder of overdoing. The emotions have no place in a world of defect, and it is a cruel injustice that they should have developed in it.

"If Law itself had consciousness, how the aspect of its creatures would terrify it, fill it with remorse!"

Though he had been out in vehicles it was not till a day early in May, more than six months after he had taken to his bed, that he went forth on foot alone; and it being a warm and sunny morning he walked on Wandsworth Common, where, as he used to tell, standing still he repeated out loud to himself:

> "See the wretch that long has tost
>   On the thorny bed of pain,
> At length repair his vigour lost,
>   And breathe and walk again:
>
> The meanest flowret of the vale,
> The simplest note that swells the gale,
> The common sun, the air, the skies,
> To him are opening Paradise."

Immediately on Hardy's recovery the question arose of whereabouts he and his wife should live. The three years' lease of the house at Upper Tooting had run out on the preceding Lady Day, when Hardy was too ill to change, and he had been obliged to apply for a three months' extension, which was granted. During the latter part of May they searched in Dorset, having concluded that it would be better to make London a place of sojourn for a few months only in each year, and establish their home in the country, both for reasons of health and for mental inspiration, Hardy finding, or thinking he found, that residence in or near a city tended to force mechanical and ordinary productions from his pen, concerning ordinary society-life and habits.

They found a little house called "Llanherne", in the Avenue, Wimborne, that would at any rate suit them temporarily, and till they could discover a better, or perhaps build one. Hardy makes a note that on June 25 they slept in Llanherne for the first time, and saw the new comet from the conservatory. "Our garden", he says a few days later, "has all sorts of old-fashioned flowers, in full bloom: Canterbury Bells, blue and white, and Sweet Williams of every variety, strawberries and cherries that are ripe, currants and gooseberries that are almost ripe, peaches that are green, and apples that are decidedly immature."

In July he jots down some notes on fiction, possibly for an article that was never written:

"The real, if unavowed, purpose of fiction is to give pleasure by gratifying the love of the uncommon in human experience mental or corporeal.

"This is done all the more perfectly in proportion as the reader is illuded to believe the personages true and real like himself.

"Solely to this latter end a work of fiction should be a precise transcript of ordinary life: but,

"The uncommon would be absent and the interest lost. Hence,

"The writer's problem is, how to strike the balance between the uncommon and the ordinary so as on the one hand to give interest, on the other to give reality.

"In working out this problem, human nature must never be made abnormal, which is introducing incredibility. The uncommonness must be in the events, not in the characters; and the writer's art lies in shaping that uncommonness while disguising its unlikelihood, if it be unlikely."

On August 23 Hardy and his wife left Wimborne for Scotland. Arriving at Edinburgh on the 24th they discovered to their dismay that Queen Victoria was to review the Volunteers in that city on the very next day, and that they could get no lodging anywhere. They took train to Roslin and put up at the Royal Hotel there. At sight of the crowds in the city Hardy had made the entry: "There are, then, some Scotch people who stay at home."

The next day or two, though wet, they spent in viewing Roslin Castle and Chapel, and Hawthornden, the old man who showed them the castle saying that he remembered Sir Walter Scott. Returning to Edinburgh, now calm and normal, they stayed there a few days, and at the beginning of September went on to Stirling, where they were laid up with colds. They started again for Callander and the Trossachs, where Hardy made a sketch of Ben Venue, and followed the usual route across Loch Katrine, by coach to Inversnaid, down Loch Lomond, and so on to Glasgow. On their way back they visited Windermere and Chester, returning through London to Wimborne.

During some sunny days in September Hardy corrected *A Laodicean* for the issue in volumes, sitting under the vine on their stable-wall, "which for want of training hangs in long arms over my head nearly to the ground. The sun tries to shine through the great leaves, making a green light on the paper, the tendrils twisting in every direction, in gymnastic endeavours to find something to lay hold of."

Though they had expected to feel lonely in Wimborne after London they were visited by many casual friends, were called in to Shakespeare readings, then much in vogue, and had a genial neighbour in the county-court judge, Tindal-Atkinson, one of the last of the serjeants-at-law, who took care they should not mope if dinners and his and his daughter's music could prevent it. They kept in touch with London, however, and were there in the following December, where they met acquaintance, and Hardy did some business in arranging for the publication of a novel in the *Atlantic Monthly* that he was about to begin writing, called off-hand by the title of *Two on a Tower*, a title he afterwards disliked, though it was much imitated. An amusing experience of formality occurred to him in connection with this novel. It was necessary that he should examine an observatory, the story moving in an astronomical medium, and he applied to the Astronomer Royal for permission to see Greenwich. He was requested to state before it could be granted if his application was made for astronomical and scientific reasons or not. He therefore drew up a scientific letter, the gist of which was that he wished to ascertain if it would be possible for him to adapt an old tower, built in a plantation in the West of England for other objects, to the requirements of a telescopic study of the stars by a young man very ardent in that pursuit (this being the imagined situation in the proposed novel). An order to view Greenwich Observatory was promptly sent.

The year was wound up by Hardy and his wife at a ball at Lady Wimborne's, Canford Manor, where he met Sir H. Layard. Lord Wimborne in a conversation about the house complained that it was rendered damp by the miller below penning the water for grinding, and, on Hardy's suggesting the removal of the mill, his host amused him by saying that was out of the question, because the miller paid him £50 a year in rent. However that might have been Hardy felt glad the old mill was to remain, having as great a repugnance to pulling down a mill where (to use his own words) they ground food for the body, as to pulling down a church where they ground food for the soul.

Thus ended 1881—with a much brighter atmosphere for the author and his wife than the opening had shown.

CHAPTER XII

Wimborne and the Astronomical Romance

1882–1883: *Aet.* 41–43

"January 26. Coleridge says, aim at *illusion* in audience or readers—i.e., the mental state when dreaming, intermediate between complete *de*lusion (which the French mistakenly aim at) and a clear perception of falsity."

"February 4th. and 11th. Shakespeare readings at ——'s, 'The Tempest' being the play chosen. The host was omnivorous of parts—absorbing other people's besides his own, and was greedily vexed when I read a line of his part by mistake. When I praise his reading he tells me meditatively, 'Oh, yes; I've given it a deal of study—thrown myself into the life of the character, you know; thought of what my supposed parents were, and my early life.' The firelight shone out as the day diminished, the young girl N.P. crouching on a footstool, the wealthy Mrs B. impassive and grand in her unintelligence, like a Carthaginian statue. . . . The General reads with gingerly caution, telling me privately that he blurted out one of Shakespeare's improprieties last time before he was aware, and is in fear and trembling lest he may do it again."

In this month's entries occurs another note which appears to be related to the philosophic scheme afterwards adopted as a framework for *The Dynasts*:

"February 16. Write a history of human automatism, or impulsion—viz., an account of human action in spite of human knowledge, showing how very far conduct lags behind the knowledge that should really guide it."

A dramatization of *Far from the Madding Crowd*, prepared by Mr J. Comyns Carr some months earlier, was produced during March at the Prince of Wales's Theatre, Liverpool, and Hardy and his wife took the trouble to make a trip to Liverpool to be present. The play, with Miss Marion Terry as the heroine, was not sufficiently near the novel to be to Hardy's liking, but it was well received, and was staged in London at the Globe Theatre in April, where it ran for many nights, but brought Hardy no profit, nor the adapter, as he was informed. During his stay in London he attended, on April 26, the funeral of Darwin in Westminster Abbey. As a young man he had been among the earliest acclaimers of *The Origin of Species*.

"May 13. The slow meditative lives of people who live in habitual solitude. . . . Solitude renders every trivial act of a solitary full of interest, as showing thoughts that cannot be expressed for want of an interlocutor."

"June 3rd. . . . As, in looking at a carpet, by following one colour a certain pattern is suggested, by following another colour, another; so in life the seer should watch that pattern among general things which his idiosyncrasy moves him to observe, and describe that alone. This is, quite accurately, a going to Nature; yet the result is no mere photograph, but purely the product of the writer's own mind."

"June 18th. M.F., son of Parson F. was well-known by sight to my mother in her childhood. He had taken his degree and had been ordained. But he drank. He worked with the labourers and 'yarn-barton-wenches' (as they were called in the village) in the yarn-barton. After a rollick as they worked he would suddenly stop, down his implement, and mounting a log or trestle preach an excellent sermon to them; then go on cursing and swearing as before. He wore faded black clothes, and had an allowance of some small sum from his family, to which he liked to add a little by manual labour. He was a tall, upright, dignified man. She did not know what became of him."

"August.—An ample theme: the intense interests, passions, and strategy that throb through the commonest lives.

"This month blackbirds and thrushes creep about under fruit-bushes and in other shady places in gardens rather like four-legged animals than birds. . . . I notice that a blackbird has eaten nearly a whole pear lying in the garden-path in the course of the day."

"September 9th. Dr and Mrs Brine . . . came to tea. Brine says that Jack White's gibbet (near Wincanton) was standing as late as 1835—i.e. the oak-post with the iron arm sticking out, and a portion of the cage in which the body had formerly hung. It would have been standing now if some young men had not burnt it down by piling faggots round it one fifth of November."

Later in the month he went with Mrs Hardy on a small circular tour in the adjoining counties—taking in Salisbury, Axminster, Lyme Regis, Charmouth, Bridport, Dorchester, and back to Wimborne. From Axminster to Lyme the journey on the coach was spoilt for them by the condition of one of the horses:

"The off-horse was weak and worn. 'O yes, tender on his vore veet,' said the driver with nonchalance. The coach itself weighed a ton. The horse swayed, leant against the pole, then outwards. His head hung like his tail. The straps and brass rings of the harness seemed barbarously harsh on his shrinking skin. E., with her admirable courage, would have interfered, at the cost of walking the rest of the distance: then we felt helpless against the anger of the other passengers who wanted to get on." They were, in fact, on the tableland half-way between the two towns. But they complained when they alighted—with what effect Hardy could not remember.

At Lyme they "met a man who had turned his trousers hind part before, because the knees had worn through".

On The Cobb they encountered an old man who had undergone an operation for cataract:

"It was like a red-hot needle in yer eye whilst he was doing it. But he wasn't long about it. Oh no. If he had been long I couldn't ha' beared it. He wasn't a minute more than three-quarters of an hour at the outside. When he had done one eye, 'a said, 'Now my man, you must make shift with that one, and be thankful you bain't left wi' narn.' So he didn't do the other. And I'm glad 'a didn't. I've saved half-crowns and half-crowns out of number in only wanting one glass to my spectacles. T'other eye would never have paid the expenses of keeping en going."

From Charmouth they came to Bridport on the box of a coach better horsed, and driven by a merry coachman, "who wore a lavish quantity of wool in his ears, and in smiling checked his smile in the centre of his mouth by closing his lips, letting it continue at the corners". (A sketch of the coachman's mouth in the act of smiling was attached to illustrate this.)

Before returning to Wimborne Hardy called on the poet Barnes at Came Rectory. Mr Barnes told him of an old woman who had asked him to explain a picture she possessed. He told her it was the family of Darius at the feet of Alexander. She shook her head, and said: "But that's not in the Bible", looking up and down his clerical attire as if she thought him a wicked old man who disgraced his cloth by speaking of profane history.

This autumn *Two on a Tower*, which was ending its career in the *Atlantic Monthly*, came out in three volumes, and at the beginning of October its author and his wife started for Cherbourg via Weymouth, and onward to Paris, where they took a little *appartement* of two bedrooms and a sitting room, near the left bank of the Seine. Here they stayed for some weeks, away from English and American tourists, roving about the city and to Versailles, studying the pictures at the Louvre and the Luxembourg, practising housekeeping in the Parisian bourgeois manner, buying their own groceries and vegetables, dining at restaurants, and catching bad colds owing to the uncertain weather. He seems to have done little in the French capital besides these things, making only one memorandum beyond personal trifles, expenses, and a few picture-notes:

"Since I discovered, several years ago, that I was living in a world where nothing bears out in practice what it promises incipiently, I have troubled myself very little about theories. . . . Where development according to perfect reason is limited to the narrow region of pure mathematics, I am content with tentativeness from day to day."

At the end of the autumn Mrs Hardy received news at Wimborne of the death of her brother-in-law the Rev. C. Holder at St. Juliot Rectory, Cornwall, of which he had long been the incumbent; and they realized that the scene of the fairest romance of their lives, in the picturesque land of Lyonnesse, would have no more kinship with them. By this loss Hardy was reminded of the genial and genuine humour of his clerical relative and friend despite his fragility and ill-health; of his qualities, among them a mysterious power he had (as it seemed to his brother-in-law) of counting his congregation to a man before he had got half-a-dozen lines down the page in "Dearly beloved brethren"; and of his many strange and amusing stories of his experiences, such as that of the sick man to whose bedside he was called to read a chapter in the Bible, and who said when it was ended that it did him almost as much good as a glass of gin-and-water: or of the astonishing entry in the marriage register of Holder's parish before he was rector, by which the bridegroom and bridesmaid had made themselves husband and wife, and the bride and best man the witnesses. Hardy himself had seen the entry.

Of another cast was the following. Holder as a young man was a curate in Bristol during the terrible cholera visitation. He related that one day at a friend's house he met a charming young widow, who invited him to call on her. With pleasant anticipations he went at tea-time a day or two later, and duly inquired if she was at home. The servant said with a strange face: "Why, Sir, you buried her this morning!" He found that amongst the many funerals of cholera victims he had conducted that day, as on every day, hers had been one.

At another of these funerals the clerk or sexton rushed to him immediately before the procession arrived to ask him to come and look at the just opened grave, which was of brick, with room for two or more, the first place being occupied by the coffin of the deceased person's relative who had died three weeks before. The coffin was overturned into the space beside it. Holder hastily told the sexton to turn it back into its place, and say nothing, to avoid distressing the relatives on the obvious inference.

All the rector's reminiscences, however, were not of this tragic cast. When curate-in-charge of a populous parish in Gloucestershire he had preached the afternoon sermon, and was about to doff his surplice in the vestry when he was called by the clerk. He was tired, but readjusted his robes, and going into the chancel saw that all the congregation had left except a young woman sitting in the front pew. Thinking she had come to be churched, as was often the case, he quickly opened his book and began with some little impatience at the hindrance: "Forasmuch as it hath pleased God to give you safe deliverance, and hath preserved you in the great danger of childbirth—" The young woman thereon sprang up and cried, "O no, Sir, no: I haven't had a baby—I wouldn't do such an undecent thing! I've come to be christened!" He apologized, and they went to the font, where he began the form for adult baptism.

He also remembered a singular alarm to which he had once been subjected. He was roused one night by a voice calling from below, "Holder, Holder! Can you help me!" It was the voice of a neighbouring incumbent named Woodman, and wondering what terrible thing had happened he rushed downstairs as soon as he could, seizing a heavy stick on the way. He found his neighbour in great agitation, who explained that the news had come late the previous evening that a certain noble lord the patron, who was a great critic of sermons, had arrived in the parish, and was going to attend next morning's service. "Have you a sermon that will do? I have nothing—nothing!" The conjuncture had so preyed upon his friend's nerves during the night that he had not been able to resist getting up and coming. Holder found something he thought might suit the noble critic, and Woodman departed with it under his arm, much relieved.

Some of Holder's stories to him were, as Hardy guessed, rather well-found than well-founded, but they were always told with much solemnity. Yet he would sometimes recount one "the truth of which he could not quite guarantee". It was what had been related to him by some of his aged parishioners concerning an incumbent of that or an adjacent living many years before. This worthy ecclesiastic was a bachelor addicted to drinking habits, and one night when riding up Boscastle Hill fell off his horse. He lay a few minutes in the road, when he said "Help me up, Jolly!" and a local man who was returning home behind him saw a dark figure with a cloven foot emerge from the fence, and toss him upon his horse in a jiffy. The end of him was that on one night of terrific lightning and thunder he was missed, and was found to have entirely disappeared.

Holder had kept up a friendly acquaintance with Hawker of Morwenstow, who predeceased him by seven years, though the broad and tolerant views of the rector of St. Juliot did not quite chime in with the poet-vicar's precisianism; and the twenty miles of wild Cornish coast that separated their livings was a heavy bit of road for the rector's stout cob to traverse both ways in a day. Hardy regretted the loss of his relative, and was reminded sadly of the pleasure he used to find in reading the lessons in the ancient church when his brother-in-law was not in vigour. The poem "Quid hic agis?" in *Moments of Vision* is in part apparently a reminiscence of these readings.

In December Hardy was told a story by a Mrs Cross, a very old country-woman he met, of a girl she had known who had been betrayed and deserted by a lover. She kept her child by her own exertions, and lived bravely and throve. After a time the man returned poorer than she, and wanted to marry her; but she refused. He ultimately went into the Union workhouse. The young woman's conduct in not caring to be "made respectable" won the novelist-poet's admiration, and he wished to know her name; but the old narrator said, "Oh, never mind their names: they be dead and rotted by now."

The eminently modern idea embodied in this example—of a woman's not becoming necessarily the chattel and slave of her seducer—impressed Hardy as being one of the first glimmers of woman's enfranchisement; and he made use of it in succeeding years in more than one case in his fiction and verse.

In the same month the Hardys attended Ambulance-Society lectures—First-Aid teaching being in fashion just then. He makes a note concerning a particular lecture:

"A skeleton—the one used in these lectures—is hung up inside the window. We face it as we sit. Outside the band is playing, and the children are dancing. I can see their little figures through the window past the skeleton dangling in front."

Another note—this on the wintry weather:

"Heard of an open cart being driven through the freezing rain. The people in it became literally packed in ice; the men's beards and hair were hung with icicles. Getting one of the men into the house was like bringing in a chandelier of lustres."

In the same month he replied as follows to a question asked him by letter:

To A. A. Reade Esq.
Dear Sir,

I can say that I have never found alcohol helpful to literary production in any degree. My experience goes to prove that the effect of wine, taken as a preliminary to imaginative work, as it is called, is to blind the writer to the quality of what he produces rather than to raise its quality.

When walking much out of doors, and particularly when on Continental rambles, I occasionally drink a glass or two of claret or mild ale. The German beers seem really beneficial at these times of exertion, which (as wine seems otherwise) may be owing to some alimentary qualities they possess apart from their stimulating property. With these rare exceptions I have taken no alcoholic liquor for the last two years.

Yours truly,

T. Hardy.

"February 25th 1883.—Sent a short hastily written novel to the

Graphic for Summer Number." [It was "The Romantic Adventures of a Milkmaid".]

"Feb. 28th. Walked with Walter Fletcher (County Surveyor) to Corfe Mullen. He says that the scene of the auction of turnpike tolls used to be curious. It was held at an inn, and at one end of the room would be the auctioneer and trustees, at the other a crowd of strange beings, looking as not worth sixpence among them. Yet the biddings for the Poole Trust would sometimes reach £1400. Sometimes the bidders would say, 'Beg yer pardon, gentlemen, but will you wait to let us step outside a minute or two?' Perhaps the trustees would say they could not. The men would say, 'Then we'll step out without your letting us'. On their return only one or two would bid, and the peremptory trustees be nettled.

"Passed a lonely old house formerly an inn. The road-contractor now living there showed us into the stable, and drew our attention to the furthest stall. When the place was an inn, he said, it was the haunt of smugglers, and in a quarrel there one night a man was killed in that stall. If a horse is put there on certain nights, at about two in the morning (when the smuggler died) the horse cries like a child, and on entering you find him in a lather of sweat.

"The huge chestnut tree which stood in front of this melancholy house is dead, but the trunk is left standing. In it are still the hooks to which horses were fastened by the reins while their owners were inside."

"March 13th.—M. writes to me that when a farmer at Puddlehinton who did not want rain found that a neighbouring farmer had sent to the parson to pray for it, and it had come, he went and abused the other farmer, and told him 'twas a very dirty trick of his to catch God A'mighty unawares, and he ought to be ashamed of it.

"Our servant Ann brings us a report, which has been verified, that the carpenter who made a coffin for Mr W. who died the other day, made it too short. A bystander said satirically, 'Anybody would think you'd made it for yourself John!' (the carpenter was a short man). The maker said, 'Ah—they would!' and fell dead instantly."

In reply to a letter from Miss Mary Christie:

Wimborne. April 11. 1883.

Dear Madam:

I have read with great interest the account of your scheme for encouraging a feeling for art in National schools, and if my name be of any service in support of the general proposition I willingly consent to your using it. As to the details of such a scheme, my views differ somewhat from your own. For instance, I think that for children between 9 and 12 or 13—the great mass of those in elementary schools—fairly good engravings, such as those in the *Graphic*, *Illustrated News*, &c. (not the coloured pictures) to be as conducive to the end desired as more finished pictures and photographs. A child's imagination is so powerful that it only requires the ideas to set it to work: and hence a dozen suggestions of scenes and persons by as many prints would seem to me to be of more value to him or her than the perfect representation of one,— while the latter would cost as much as the former. This, however, is altogether a secondary point, and I daresay that if we were to talk over the subject we should soon be quite at one about it.

Hardy and his wife were in London off and on during May and June, seeing pictures, plays, and friends. At a lunch at Lord Houghton's, who with his sister Lady Galway had taken a small house off Park Lane for this season, Hardy met Robert Browning again, Rhoda Broughton for the first time, and several others, including Mrs —— from America, "a large-eyed lady-owner of ten serial publications, which, she told me, she called her ten children. Also Lady C. who talked to me about Rabelais—without knowledge obviously—having heard that I belonged to the Rabelais Club. She said she meant to read him through. She had read one chapter, but couldn't get on with the old French, so was looking for a literal translation. Heaven bless her reading!

"Houghton, seeing Browning about to introduce me to Rhoda Broughton, hastened forward before Browning, and emphatically introduced us with the manner of a man who means to see things properly done in his own house; then walked round, pleased with himself as the company dropped in; like one who, having set a machinery in motion, has now only to wait and observe how it goes."

"June 24th. Sunday. Went in the afternoon to see Mrs Procter at Albert Hall Mansions. Found Browning present. He told me that Mrs ——, whom he and I had met at Lord Houghton's, had made £200,000 by publishing pirated works of authors who had made comparatively nothing. Presently Lady Duff-Gordon and another lady arrived—the former emphatically in the family-way. Afterwards Mrs Sutherland Orr and Mrs Frank Hill (Daily News) came in. Also two Jewesses—the Misses Lazarus—from America.

Browning tried the elder with Hebrew, and she appeared to understand so well that he said he perceived she knew the tongue better than he. When some of these had gone George Smith [the publisher] called. He and Mrs Procter declared that there was something tender between Mrs Orr and Browning. 'Why don't they settle it!' said Mrs P.

"In the evening went to the Irving dinner. Sir Frederick Pollock, who took the chair, and made a speech, said that the departure of Irving for America would be a loss that would eclipse the gaiety of nations (!) Irving in his reply said that in the 27 years he had been on the stage he had enacted 650 different characters."

"June 25th. Dined at the Savile with Gosse. Met W. D. Howells of New York there. He told me a story of Emerson's loss of memory. At the funeral of Longfellow he had to make a speech. 'The brightness and beauty of soul', he began, 'of him we have lost, has been acknowledged wherever the English language is spoken. I've known him these forty years; and no American, whatever may be his opinions, will deny that in—in—in—I can't remember the gentleman's name—beat the heart of a true poet.'

"Howells said that Mark Twain usually makes a good speech. But once he heard him fail. In his speech he was telling a story of an occasion when he was in some western city, and found that some impostors personating Longfellow, Emerson, and others had been there. Mark began to describe these impostors, and while doing it found that Longfellow, Emerson, etc. were present, listening, and, from a titter or two, found also that his satirical description of the impostors was becoming regarded as an oblique satirical description of the originals. He was overspread by a sudden cold chill, and struggled to a lame ending. He was so convinced that he had given offence that he wrote to Emerson and Longfellow, apologizing. Emerson could not understand the letter, his memory of the incident having failed him, and wrote to Mark asking what it meant. Then Mark had to tell him what he wished he had never uttered: and altogether the fiasco was complete."

CHAPTER XIII

The County Town

1883–1885: *Aet.* 43–45

In this month of June the Hardys removed from Wimborne to Dorchester, which town and its neighbourhood, though they did not foresee it, was to be their country-quarters for the remainder of their lives. But several months of each spring and summer were to be spent in London during the ensuing twenty years, and occasionally spells abroad. This removal to the county-town, and later to a spot a little outside it, was a step they often regretted having taken; but the bracing air brought them health and renewed vigour, and in the long run it proved not ill-advised.

"July 19th. In future I am not going to praise things because the accumulated remarks of ages say they are great and good, if those accumulated remarks are not based on observation. And I am not going to condemn things because a pile of accepted views raked together from tradition, and acquired by instillation, say antecedently that they are bad."

"July 22nd. To Winterborne Came Church with Gosse, to hear and see the poet Barnes. Stayed for sermon. Barnes, knowing we should be on the watch for a prepared sermon, addressed it entirely to his own flock, almost pointedly excluding us. Afterwards walked to the rectory and looked at his pictures.

"Poetry versus reason: e.g., A band plays 'God save the Queen', and being musical the uncompromising Republican joins in the harmony: a hymn rolls from a church-window, and the uncompromising No-God-ist or Unconscious-God-ist takes up the refrain."

Mr T. W. H. Tolbort, a friend of Hardy's from youth, and a pupil of Barnes's, who years earlier had come out at the top in the India Civil Service examination, died at the beginning of the next month, after a bright and promising career in India, and Hardy wrote an obituary notice of him in the *Dorset Chronicle*. The only note Hardy makes on him in addition to the printed account is as follows:

"August 13th. Tolbort lived and studied as if everything in the world were so very much worth while. But what a bright mind has gone out at one-and-forty!"

He writes elsewhere of an anecdote told him by Barnes touching his tuition of Tolbort. Barnes had relinquished his school and retired to the country rectory in which he ended his days, when Tolbort's name, and Barnes's as his schoolmaster, appeared in *The Times* at the head of the Indian examination list, a wide proportion of marks separating it from the name following. It was in the early days when these lists excited great interest. In a few mornings Mr Barnes was deluged with letters from all parts of the country requesting him at almost any price to take innumerable sons, and produce upon them the same successful effect. "I told them that it took two to do it," he would say, adding sadly that a popularity which would have been invaluable during the hard-working years of his life came at almost the first moment when it was no longer of use to him.

In this month of August he made a memorandum on another matter:

"Write a list of things which everybody thinks and nobody says; and a list of things that everybody says and nobody thinks."

At this time too, Hardy encountered an old man named P——, whose father, or grandfather, had been one of the keepers of the Rainbarrows Beacon, 1800–1815, as described in *The Dynasts*, the remains of whose hut are still to be seen on the spot. It may be interesting to mention that the daughter of a travelling waxwork proprietor had some years before when exhibiting at Puddletown entirely lost her heart to P——'s brother, a handsome young labourer of the village, and he had married her. As her father grew old and infirm the son-in-law and his wife succeeded to the showman's business and carried it on successfully. They were a worthy and happy couple, and whenever in their rounds they came to P——'s native village the husband's old acquaintance were admitted gratis to the exhibition, which was of a highly moral and religious cast, including Solomon's Judgment, and Daniel in the Den of Lions, where the lions moved their heads, tails, eyes, and paws terrifically, while Daniel lifted his hands in prayer. Heads of murderers were ranged on the other side as a wholesome lesson to evil-doers. Hardy duly attended the show because the man's forefather had kept Rainbarrows Beacon (described in *The Dynasts*); and the last he saw of old P—— was in the private tent attached to the exhibition, where he was sitting as a glorified figure drinking gin-and-water with his relatives.

Not having been able when he came to Dorchester to find a house to suit him, Hardy had obtained a plot of land of the Duchy of Cornwall in Fordington Field, about a mile into the country, on which to build one; and at the beginning of October marked out as a preliminary the spot where the well was to be sunk. The only drawback to the site seemed to him to be its newness. But before the well-diggers had got deeper than three feet they came upon Romano-British urns and skeletons. Hardy and his wife found that the spot was steeped in antiquity, and thought the omens gloomy; but they did not prove so, the extreme age of the relics dissipating any sense of gruesomeness. More of the sort were found in digging the house-foundations, and Hardy wrote an account of the remains, which he read at the Dorchester Meeting of the Dorset Field Club, 1884. It was printed in the *Proceedings* of the Club in 1890.

"November 3rd. *The Athenæum* says 'The glass-stainer maintains his existence at the sacrifice of everything the painter holds dear. In place of the freedom and sweet abandonment which is nature's own charm and which the painter can achieve, the glass-stainer gives us splendour as luminous as that of the rainbow . . . in patches, and stripes, and bars.'

"The above canons are interesting in their conveyance of a half truth. All art is only approximative—not exact, as the reviewer thinks; and hence the methods of all art differ from that of the glass-stainer but in degree."

"Nov. 17th. Poem. We [human beings] have reached a degree of intelligence which Nature never contemplated when framing her laws, and for which she consequently has provided no adequate satisfactions." [This, which he had adumbrated before, was clearly the germ of the poem entitled "The Mother Mourns" and others.]

"December 23. There is what we used to call 'The Birds' Bedroom' in the plantation at Bockhampton. Some large hollies grow among leafless ash, oak, birch, etc. At this time of year the birds select the hollies for roosting in, and at dusk noises not unlike the creaking of withy-chairs arise, with a busy rustling as of people going to bed in a lodging-house; accompanied by sundry shakings, adjustings, and pattings, as if they were making their beds vigorously before turning in.

"Death of old Billy C—— at a great age. He used to talk enthusiastically of Lady Susan O'Brien [the daughter of Lord Ilchester, who excited London by eloping with O'Brien the actor, as so inimitably described in Walpole's *Letters*, and afterwards settled in Hardy's parish as beforementioned]. 'She kept a splendid house— a cellarful of home-brewed strong beer that would a'most knock you down; everybody drank as much as he liked. The head-gardener [whom Billy as a youth assisted] was drunk every morning before breakfast. There are no such houses now! On wet days we used to make a point of working opposite the drawing-room window, that she might pity us. She would send out and tell us to go indoors, and not expose ourselves to the weather so reekless.'" [A kind-hearted woman, Lady Susan.]

On the eve of the New Year 1884 Hardy planted some trees on his new property at Max Gate, Dorchester, and passed part of the January following in London, where he saw Henry James, Gosse, and Thornycroft, and talked to Alma-Tadema about the Anglo-Roman remains he was finding on the site of his proposed house, over which discovery Tadema was much excited, as he was painting, or about to paint, a picture expressing the art of that date.

"February. 'Ye shall weep and mourn, and the world shall rejoice.' Such shows the natural limitation of the Christian view when the Christians were a small and despised community. The widened view of nowadays perceives that the world weeps and mourns all round.—Nevertheless, if 'the world' denotes the brutal and thoughtless merely, the text is eternally true."

"James S——, [the quaint old man already mentioned, who worked forty years for Hardy's father, and had been a smuggler], once heard a hurdlemaker bet at the 'Black Dog', Broadmayne, that he would make a hurdle sooner than the other man (not a hurdler) could pull one to pieces. They put it to the test, and the hurdlemaker won the stakes."

"When trees and underwood are cut down, and the ground bared, three crops of flowers follow. First a sheet of yellow; they are primroses. Then a sheet of blue; they are wild hyacinths, or as we call them, graegles. Then a sheet of red; they are ragged robins, or as they are called here, robin-hoods. What have these plants been doing through the scores of years before the trees were felled, and how did they come there?"

"March. Write a novel entitled 'Time against Two', in which the antagonism of the parents of a Romeo and Juliet *does* succeed in separating the couple and stamping out their love,—alas, a more probable development than the other!" [The idea is briefly used in *The Well-Beloved*.]

March or April: "Every error under the sun seems to arise from thinking that you are right yourself because you *are* yourself, and other people wrong because they are not you."

"It is now spring; when, according to the poets, birds pipe, and (the householder adds) day-labourers get independent after their preternatural civility through the frost and snow."

"April 26. Curious scene. A fine poem in it:

"Four girls—itinerant musicians—sisters—have been playing opposite Parmiter's in the High Street. The eldest had a fixed, old, hard face, and wore white roses in her hat. Her eyes remained on one close object, such as the buttons of her sister's dress; she played the violin. The next sister, with red roses in her hat, had rather bold dark eyes, and a coquettish smirk. She too played a violin. The next, with her hair in ringlets, beat the tambourine. The youngest, a mere child, dinged the triangle. She wore a bead necklace. All wore large brass earrings like Jews'-harps, which dangled to the time of the jig.

"I saw them again in the evening, the silvery gleams from Saunders's [silver-smith's] shop shining out upon them. They were now sublimed to a wondrous charm. The hard face of the eldest was flooded with soft solicitous thought; the coquettish one was no longer bold but archly tender; her dirty white roses were pure as snow; her sister's red ones a fine crimson: the brass earrings were golden; the iron triangle silver; the tambourine Miriam's own; the third child's face that of an angel; the fourth that of a cherub. The pretty one smiled on the second, and began to play 'In the gloaming', the little voices singing it. *Now* they were what Nature made them, before the smear of 'civilization' had sullied their existences." [An impression of a somewhat similar scene is given in the poem entitled "Music in a Snowy Street".]

"Rural low life may reveal coarseness of considerable leaven; but that libidinousness which makes the scum of cities so noxious is not usually there."

"June 2. At Bockhampton. My birthday—44. Alone in the

plantation at 9 o'clock. A weird hour: strange faces and figures formed by dying lights. Holm leaves shine like human eyes, and the sky glimpses between the trunks are like white phantoms and cloven tongues. It is so silent and still that a footstep on the dead leaves could be heard a quarter of a mile off. Squirrels run up the trunks in fear, stamping and crying 'chut-chut-chut!' " (There is not a single squirrel in that plantation now.)

The following letter was written to Hardy on his birthday:

> Burford Bridge,
> Box Hill.
> June 2. 1884.

What a good day this was for Anne Benson Procter, when Thomas Hardy was born! She little knew what stores of delightful reading she would owe to the Baby of 1840.

If she could write an Ode—or, even worse, a Sonnet!

He has something to be thankful for. He *must* have read the verses—and he is so good and kind that he would have praised them.

We go home on Wednesday next, having been here for ten days—sitting by the fire, 'for the summer comes slowly up this way'.

> Your old admirer,
>
> Anne B. Procter.

"June 3rd. The leaves are approaching their finished summer shape, the evergreens wear new pale suits over the old deep attire. I watered the thirsty earth at Max Gate, which drank in the liquid with a swallowing noise. In the evening I entered Tayleure's Circus in Fordington Field for a short time during the performance. There is a dim haze in the tent, and the green grass in the middle, within the circular horse-track, looks amazingly fresh in the artificial light. The damp orbits of the spectators' eyes gleam in its rays. The clowns, when 'off', lounge and smoke cigarettes, and chat with serious cynicism, and as if the necessity of their occupation to society at large were not to be questioned, their true domestic expression being visible under the official expression given by the paint. This sub-expression is one of good-humoured pain."

Hardy seems to have had something of a craze for circuses in these years, and went to all that came to Dorchester. In one performance the equestrienne who leapt through hoops on her circuit missed her footing and fell with a thud on the turf. He followed her into the dressing-tent, and became deeply interested in her recovery. The incident seems to have some bearing on the verses of many years after entitled "Circus-Rider to Ringmaster".

They were in London part of June and July, and among other places went to an evening party at Alma-Tadema's, meeting an artistic crowd which included Burne-Jones; and to another at Mrs Murray Smith's with Mrs Procter, where they met again Matthew Arnold, whom Hardy liked better now than he did at their first meeting; also du Maurier; also Henry James "with his nebulous gaze". Mrs Procter, though so old, "swam about through the crowd like a swan".

Of Madame Judic's acting in *Niniche*, Hardy says, "This woman has genius. The picture of the pair of them—Judic and Lassouche— putting their faces side by side and bumping each other in making love, was the most comic phase of real art I ever saw. . . . And yet the world calls —— a great actress."

During this summer they became acquainted with Lord and Lady Portsmouth and their daughters. Lady Portsmouth (Eveline, daughter of the 3rd Earl of Carnarvon), a woman of large social experience who afterwards proved to be the kindest and firmest of friends till her death, told Hardy that Ethelberta in his novel, who had been pronounced an impossible person by the reviewers, and the social manners unreal, had attracted her immensely because of her reality and naturalness, acting precisely as such women did or would act in such circumstances; and that the society scenes were just as society was, which was not the case with other novels.

"July 14. Assizes. Dorchester—The Lord Chief Justice, eminent counsel, etc, reveal more of their weaknesses and vanities here in the country than in London. Their foibles expand, being off their guard. A shabby lad on trial for setting fire to a common, holds an amusingly familiar conversation with the C. J. (Coleridge) when asked if he has anything to say. Witnesses always begin their evidence in sentences containing ornamental words, evidently prepared beforehand, but when they get into the thick of it this breaks down to struggling grammar and lamentably jumbled narrative."

"August 14. Strolling players at Dorchester in the market-field. Went to 'Othello'. A vermilion sunset fell on the West end of the booth, where, while the audience assembled, Cassio, in supposed Venetian costume, was lounging and smoking in the red light at the bottom of the van-steps behind the theatre: Othello also lounging in the same sunlight on the grass by the stage door, and touching up the black of his face.

"The play begins as the dusk comes on, the theatre-lights within throwing the spectators' and the actors' profiles on the canvas, so that they are visible outside, and the immortal words spread through it into the silence around, and to the trees, and stars.

"I enter. A woman plays Montano, and her fencing with Cassio leaves much to the imagination. Desdemona's face still retains its anxiety about the supper that she has been cooking a few minutes earlier in the stove without.

"Othello is played by the proprietor, and his speeches can be heard as far as to the town-pump. Emilia wears the earrings I saw her wearing when buying the family vegetables this morning. The tragedy goes on successfully, till the audience laughs at the beginning of the murder scene. Othello stops, and turning, says sternly to them after an awful pause: 'Is this the Nineteenth Century?' The conscience-stricken audience feel the justice of the reproof, and preserve an abashed silence as he resumes. When he comes to the pillow-scene they applaud with tragic vehemence, to show that their hearts are in the right place after all."

August 16. Hardy took a trip to the Channel Islands from Weymouth with his brother. They went to Guernsey, Jersey, and Sark; and at one of the hotels found that every man there except themselves was a commercial traveller. As they seemed so lonely they were allowed to dine with these gentlemen, and became very friendly with them. Manners at the dinner-table were highly ceremonious: "Can I send you a cut of this boiled mutton, Mr President?"—"No thank you, Mr Vice. May I help you to beef?"—At the end of dinner: "Gentlemen, you can leave the table."—Chorus of diners: "Thank you, Mr President."

Conversation turned on a certain town in England, and it was defined as being "a warm place". Hardy, who had lived there, was puzzled, and said he had not noticed that it was particularly warm. The speaker scarcely condescended to reply that he did not understand the meaning they attached to the word.

On October 18 he dined at the Mansion House with a number of other writers at a banquet given by the Lord Mayor to the Society of Authors. The ex-Lord Mayor, who was Hardy's neighbour at table, told him that during the year of office nothing but the duties of the

Mayoralty could be attended to. This was probably Hardy's first dinner there, though he often dined there afterwards.

Off and on he was now writing *The Mayor of Casterbridge*; but before leaving London he agreed with the Macmillans to take in hand later a story of twelve numbers for their magazine, no time being fixed. It came out two years later under the title of *The Woodlanders*.

"October 20th. Query: Is not the present quasi-scientific system of writing history mere charlatanism? Events and tendencies are traced as if they were rivers of voluntary activity, and courses reasoned out from the circumstances in which natures, religions, or what-not, have found themselves. But are they not in the main the outcome of *passivity*—acted upon by unconscious propensity?"

"November 16th. My sister Mary says that women of the past generation have faces now out of fashion. Face-expressions have their fashions like clothes."

During the general election about this time Mr John Morley wrote to Hardy from Newcastle:

"Your letter recalls literature, art, and sober reason—visitants as welcome as they are rare in the heats of electioneering." And a few days later he heard from Professor Beesly, who had been beaten at the Westminster poll: "I suppose there is not a more hopeless seat in England. We might have made head against its Toryism alone, or the clergy, or the Baroness's legitimate influence from her alms-giving of old date there (it being her special preserve), or the special tap of philanthropy turned on for the occasion. But all united were much too strong for us. . . . I return to my work in much contentment."

Leslie Stephen (like Hardy himself, quite outside politics) wrote the same week: "I am glad to have got that book off my hands, though any vacuum in my occupations is very soon filled up (not that *my* Nature abhors it!) and though in many ways I am very ill-satisfied with the result. However I meant well, and I can now begin to forget it."

"December 4. A gusty wind makes the rain-drops hit the window in stars, and the sunshine flaps open and shut like a fan, flinging into the room a tin-coloured light. . . ."

"Conjuror Mynterne [of whom mention has already been made] when consulted by Pult P—— (a strapping handsome woman), told her that her husband would die on a certain day, and showed her the funeral in a glass of water. She said she could see the legs of the bearers moving along. She made her mourning. She used to impress all this on her inoffensive husband, and assure him that he would go to hell if he made the conjuror a liar. He didn't, but died on the day foretold. Oddly enough she never married again.''

"December 31st. To St. Peter's belfry to the New-Year's-Eve ringing. The night-wind whiffed in through the louvres as the men prepared the mufflers with tar-twine and pieces of horse-cloth. Climbed over the bells to fix the mufflers. I climbed with them and looked into the tenor bell: it is worn into a bright pit where the clapper has struck so many years, and the clapper is battered with its many blows.

"The ringers now put their coats and waistcoats and hats upon the chimes and clock and stand to. Old John is fragile, as if the bell would pull him up rather than he pull the rope down, his neck being withered and white as his white neckcloth. But his manner is severe as he says, 'Tenor out?' One of the two tenor men gently eases the bell forward—that fine old E flat [?] (probably D in modern sharpened pitch), my father's admiration, unsurpassed in metal all the world over—and answers, 'Tenor's out'. Then old John tells them to 'Go!' and they start. Through long practice he rings with the least possible movement of his body, though the youngest ringers— strong, dark-haired men with ruddy faces—soon perspire with their exertions. The red, green and white sallies bolt up through the holes like rats between the huge beams overhead.

"The grey stones of the fifteenth century masonry have many of their joints mortarless, and are carved with many initials and dates. On the sill of one louvred window stands a great pewter pot with a hinged cover and engraved: 'For the use of the ringers 16—.'" [It is now in the County Museum.]

In the early part of the next year (1885) Hardy accepted a long-standing invitation to Eggesford by his friend Lady Portsmouth, whither he was to bring his work and continue it as if at home; but Mrs Hardy was unable to accompany him. He found her there surrounded by her daughters, and their cousin Lady Winifred Herbert, afterwards Lady Burghclere; making altogether a lively house-party, Lady Portsmouth apologizing for it being mostly composed of 'better halves'. Hence, though the library was placed at his disposal, and entry forbidden, that his labours should not be interrupted, very little work indeed was done while he stayed there, most of the time being spent in driving about the villages with his hosts and walking in the Park. Lord Portsmouth he found to be "a farmer-like man with a broad Devon accent. He showed me a bridge over which bastards were thrown and drowned, even down to quite recent times." Lady Dorothea, one of the daughters, told him of some of the escapades of her uncle Auberon Herbert—whom Hardy afterwards got to know very well—one of the most amusing being how he had personated a groom of his father's at a Drawing-room, and by that trick got to see a flame of his who was to be there. Altogether they were an extraordinarily sympathetic group of women, and among other discussions was, of course, one on love, in which Lady Camilla informed him that "a woman is never so near being in love with a man she does not love as immediately he has left her after she has refused him".

"Lady P. tells me she never knew real anxiety till she had a family of daughters. She wants us to come to Devonshire and live near them. She says they would find a house for us. Cannot think why we live in benighted Dorset. Em would go willingly, as it is her native county; but alas, my house at Dorchester is nearly finished."

"Easter Sunday. Evidences of art in Bible narratives. They are written with a watchful attention (though disguised) as to their effect on their reader. Their so-called simplicity is, in fact, the simplicity of the highest cunning. And one is led to inquire, when even in these latter days artistic development and arrangement are the qualities least appreciated by readers, who was there likely to appreciate the art in these chronicles at that day?

"Looking round on a well-selected shelf of fiction or history, how few stories of any length does one recognize as well told from beginning to end! The first half of this story, the last half of that, the middle of another. . . . The modern art of narration is yet in its infancy.

"But in these Bible lives and adventures there is the spherical completeness of perfect art. And our first, and second, feeling that they must be true because they are so impressive, becomes, as a third feeling, modified to, "Are they so very true, after all? Is not the fact of their being so convincing, an argument, not for their actuality, but for the actuality of a consummate artist who was no more content with what Nature offered than Sophocles and Pheidias were content?"

"Friday, April 17. Wrote the last page of 'The Mayor of Casterbridge', begun at least a year ago, and frequently interrupted in the writing of each part."

"April 19th. The business of the poet and novelist is to show the sorriness underlying the grandest things, and the grandeur underlying the sorriest things."

He was in London at the end of April and probably saw Leslie Stephen there, since he makes the following remark: "Leslie Stephen as a critic. His approval is disapproval minimized."

They went to the Academy this year as usual. On the Private View Hardy remarks: "The great difference between a Private View and a public one is the loud chatter that prevails at the former, everybody knowing everybody else." In the evening of the same day they were at a party at Lady Carnarvon's, where Hardy met Lord Salisbury for the first time, and had an interesting talk with him on the art of making speeches—"whether it is best to plunge in medias res, or to adopt a developing method". In the middle of May they were at another of these parties of Lady Carnarvon's, where they met Browning again; also Mrs Jeune (afterwards Lady St. Helier) and the usual friends whom they found there.

"May 28th. Waiting at the Marble Arch while Em called a little way further on to enquire after ——'s children. . . . This hum of the wheel—the roar of London! What is it composed of? Hurry, speech, laughters, moans, cries of little children. The people in this tragedy laugh, sing, smoke, toss off wines, etc, make love to girls in drawing-rooms and areas; and yet are playing their parts in the tragedy just the same. Some wear jewels and feathers, some wear rags. All are caged birds; the only difference lies in the size of the cage. This too is part of the tragedy. . . . At last E. returned, telling me the children were ill—that little L—— looked quite different, and when asked 'Don't you know me?' said, 'Not now; but I used to know you once.' How pathetic it all is!"

"Sunday May 31st. Called on Mrs Procter. Shocked to find her in mourning for Edith. Can't tell why I did not see announcement of her death. Madame M—— and Baroness —— came in while I was there. Browning also present.

"Mrs Procter was vexed with Browning and myself for sending cards to Victor Hugo's funeral to attach to wreaths.

"In the evening met Frederic Harrison, Beesly, and Dr. J. H. Bridges (a Dorset man)."

During the latter half of May and through June, Hardy was reading philosophy at the British Museum, and going with his wife to some parties and dinners in the evenings—among others frequently to Mrs Jeune's, where they always met a good many people they knew, including Mrs Hardy's relations; and once or twice to Lord Houghton's and his sister Lady Galway's combination crushes, where they scarcely knew a single soul except the host and hostess.

At one of these crushes in the early part of 1885, probably Lady Carnarvon's, they found themselves on a particular evening amid a simmer of political excitement. It was supposed to be a non-political "small-and-early", but on their arrival the house was already full to overflowing; and a well-known Conservative peeress of that date, who had lately invited Hardy to her friendship, came up to him as if she must express her feelings to somebody, and said, "I'm ashamed of my party! They are actually all hoping that General Gordon is murdered, in order that it may ruin Gladstone!" It seems to have been this rumour of Gordon's death, which had just been circulated, that had brought so many brilliant and titled people there. Auberon Herbert, who was also there, told Hardy privately that it was true. Presently another and grimmer lady, the Dowager Viscountess Galway, said to him that she half-believed Gordon was still alive, because no relic, bloody rag, or any scrap of him had been produced, which from her experience of those countries she knew to be almost the invariable custom. So the crowd waited, and conjectured, and did not leave till a late hour, the truth as to Gordon's fate not being generally known till some days after.

It must have been his experiences at these nominally social but really political parties that gave rise to the following note at the same date:

"History is rather a stream than a tree. There is nothing organic in its shape, nothing systematic in its development. It flows on like a thunderstorm-rill by a road side; now a straw turns it this way, now a tiny barrier of sand that. The offhand decision of some commonplace mind high in office at a critical moment influences the course of events for a hundred years. Consider the evenings at Lord C——'s, and the intensely average conversation on politics held there by average men who two or three weeks later were members of the Cabinet. A row of shopkeepers in Oxford Street taken just as they came would conduct the affairs of the nation as ably as these.

"Thus, judging by bulk of effect, it becomes impossible to estimate the intrinsic value of ideas, acts, material things: we are forced to appraise them by the curves of their career. There were more beautiful women in Greece than Helen; but what of them?

"What Ruskin says as to the cause of the want of imagination in works of the present age is probably true—that it is the flippant sarcasm of the time. 'Men dare not open their hearts to us if we are to broil them on a thorn fire.' "

At the end of the month of June Hardy was obliged to go down to Dorset to superintend the removal of his furniture from the house he had temporarily taken in Dorchester to the one he had built in the fields at Max Gate, a mile out of the town.

CHAPTER XIV

The New House and "The Woodlanders"

1885–1887: *Aet.* 45–46

On June 29 the Hardys slept at Max Gate for the first time—the house being one they were destined to occupy permanently thence onward, except during the four or five months in each year that were spent in London or abroad. Almost the first visitor at their new house was R. L. Stevenson, till then a stranger to Hardy, who wrote from Bournemouth to announce his coming, adding characteristically: "I could have got an introduction, but my acquaintance with your mind is already of old date. . . . If you should be busy or unwilling, the irregularity of my approach leaves you the safer retreat." He appeared two days afterwards, with his wife, wife's son, and cousin. They were on their way to Dartmoor, the air of which Stevenson had learnt would be good for his complaint. But, alas, he never reached Dartmoor, falling ill at Exeter and being detained there till he was well enough to go home again.

"September 16. Dined with [Hon. Aubrey] Spring Rice [who lived at Dorchester]. Met there his cousin Aubrey de Vere the poet, and Father Poole. De Vere says that his father used to say a Greek drama was the fifth act of an Elizabethan one, which of course it is, when not a sixth."

"October 17th. Called on Barnes [the Dorset poet]. Talked of old families. He told me a story of Louis Napoleon. During his residence in England he was friendly with the Damers, and used to visit at Winterborne-Came House, near Dorchester, where they lived. (It was a current tradition that he wished to marry Miss Damer; also that he would dreamily remark that it was fated he should be the Emperor of the French to avenge the defeat of Waterloo.) It was the fashion then for the Dorchester people to parade in full dress in the South Walk on Sunday afternoons, and on one occasion the Damers with their guest came in from their house a mile off and joined in the promenade. Barnes, who kept a school in the town, had an usher from Blackmore Vale named Hann (whose people seem to have been of my mother's stock), and Barnes and his usher also promenaded. For a freak Louis Napoleon, who was walking with Colonel Damer, slipt his cane between Hann's legs when they brushed past each other in opposite directions, and nearly threw the usher down. Hann was peppery, like all of that pedigree, my maternal line included, and almost before Barnes knew what was happening had pulled off his coat, thrown it on Barnes, and was challenging Louis Napoleon to fight. The latter apologized profusely, said it was quite an accident, and laughed the affair off; so the burghers who had stood round expecting a fight resumed their walk disappointed."

"Nov. 17th–19th. In a fit of depression, as if enveloped in a leaden cloud. Have gone back to my original plot for 'The Woodlanders' after all. Am working from half-past ten a.m. to twelve p.m., to get my mind made up on the details."

"Nov. 21st–22nd. Sick headache."

"Tragedy. It may be put thus in brief: a tragedy exhibits a state of things in the life of an individual which unavoidably causes some natural aim or desire of his to end in a catastrophe when carried out."

"Nov. 25th. Letter from John Morley [probably about *The Woodlanders*, he being then editor of *Macmillan's Magazine* in which it was to appear]; and one from Leslie Stephen, with remarks on books he had read between whiles."

"December 9th. 'Everything looks so little—so ghastly little!' A local exclamation heard."

"Dec. 12. Experience *un*teaches—(what one at first thinks to be the rule in events)."

"Dec. 21st. The Hypocrisy of things. Nature is an arch-dissembler. A child is deceived completely: the older members of society more or less according to their penetration; though even they seldom get to realize that *nothing* is as it appears."

"December 31st. This evening, the end of the old year 1885 finds me sadder than many previous New Year's eves have done. Whether building this house at Max Gate was a wise expenditure of energy is one doubt, which, if resolved in the negative, is depressing enough. And there are others. But:

" 'This is the chief thing: Be not perturbed; for all things are according to the nature of the universal.' " [Marcus Aurelius.]

"1886.—January 2nd. 'The Mayor of Casterbridge' begins today in the *Graphic* newspaper, and *Harper's Weekly*. I fear it will not be so good as I meant, but after all it is not improbabilities of incident but improbabilities of character that matter."

"Cold weather brings out upon the faces of people the written marks of their habits, vices, passions, and memories, as warmth brings out on paper a writing in sympathetic ink. The drunkard looks still more a drunkard when the splotches have their margins made distinct by frost, the hectic blush becomes a stain now, the cadaverous complexion reveals the bone under, the quality of handsomeness is reduced to its lowest terms."

"Jan 3. My art is to intensify the expression of things, as is done by Crivelli, Bellini, &c. so that the heart and inner meaning is made vividly visible."

"Jan. 6. Misapprehension. The shrinking soul thinks its weak place is going to be laid bare, and shows its thought by a suddenly clipped manner. The other shrinking soul thinks the clipped manner of the first to be the result of its own weakness in some way, not of its strength, and shows its fear also by its constrained air! So they withdraw from each other and misunderstand."

"4th, March. Novel-writing as an art cannot go backward. Having reached the analytic stage it must transcend it by going still further in the same direction. Why not by rendering as visible essences, spectres, &c. the abstract thoughts of the analytic school?"

This notion was approximately carried out, not in a novel, but through the much more appropriate medium of poetry, in the supernatural framework of *The Dynasts* as also in smaller poems. And a further note of the same date enlarges the same idea:

"The human race to be shown as one great network or tissue, which quivers in every part when one point is shaken, like a spider's web if touched. Abstract realisms to be in the form of Spirits, Spectral figures, &c.

"The Realities to be the true realities of life, hitherto called abstractions. The old material realities to be placed behind the former, as shadowy accessories."

In the spring and summer they were again in London, staying in Bloomsbury to have the Reading Room of the Museum at hand. It was the spring during which Gladstone brought in his Home Rule Bill for Ireland. The first that Hardy says about it occurs in an entry dated April 8, 9, 10, 11:

"A critical time, politically. I never remember a debate of such absorbing interest as this on Gladstone's Bill for Irish Government. He spoke lucidly: Chamberlain with manly practical earnestness; Hartington fairly forcibly; Morley without much effect (for him). Morley's speech shows that in Parliament a fine intelligence is not appreciated without sword-and-buckler doggedness. Chamberlain impresses me most of all, as combining these qualities."

And on May 10th:

"Saw Gladstone enter the Houses of Parliament. The crowd was very excited, not only waving their hats and shouting and running, but leaping in the air. His head was bare, and his now bald crown showed pale and distinct over the top of Mrs Gladstone's bonnet."

On the 13th Hardy was in the House, the debate on the Government of Ireland still continuing:

"Gladstone was suave in replying to Bradlaugh, almost unctuous. 'Not accustomed to recognize Parliamentary debts after five years', &c. He would shake his head and smile contradictions to his opponents across the table and red box, on which he wrote from time to time. Heard Morley say a few words, also Sir W. Harcourt, and Lord Hartington; a speech from Sir H. James, also from Lord G. Hamilton, Campbell-Bannerman, &c. Saw the dandy party enter in evening-dress, eye-glasses, diamond rings, &c. They were a great contrast to Joseph Arch and the Irish members in their plain, simple, ill-fitting clothes. The House is a motley assembly nowadays. Gladstone's frock-coat dangled and swung as he went in and out with a white flower in his button-hole and open waistcoat. Lord Randolph's manner in turning to Dillon, the Irish member, was almost arrogant. Sir R. Cross was sturdy, like T. B. the Dorchester butcher, when he used to stand at the chopping-block on market-days. The earnestness of the Irish members who spoke was very impressive; Lord G. Hamilton was entirely wanting in earnestness; Sir H. James quite the reverse; E. Clarke direct, firm, and incisive, but inhumane.

"To realize the difficulty of the Irish question it is necessary to *see* the Irish phalanx sitting tight: it then seems as if one must go with Morley, and get rid of them at any cost.

"Morley kept trying to look used to it all, and not as if he were a consummate man of letters there by mistake. Gladstone was quite distinct from all others in the House, though he sits low in his seat from age. When he smiled one could see benevolence on his face. Large-heartedness *versus* small-heartedness is a distinct attitude which the House of Commons takes up to an observer's eye."

Though he did not enter it here Hardy often wrote elsewhere and said of Home Rule that it was a staring dilemma, of which good policy and good philanthropy were the huge horns. Policy for England required that it should not be granted; humanity to Ireland that it should. Neither Liberals nor Conservatives would honestly own up to this opposition between two moralities, but speciously insisted that humanity and policy were both on one side—of course their own.

"May. Reading in the British Museum. Have been thinking over the dictum of Hegel—that the real is the rational and the rational the real—that real pain is compatible with a formal pleasure—that the idea is all, etc. But it doesn't help much. These venerable philosophers seem to start wrong; they cannot get away from a prepossession that the world must somehow have been made to be a comfortable place for man. If I remember it was Comte who said that metaphysics was a mere sorry attempt to reconcile theology and physics."

"May 17th. At a curious soirée in Bond Street. Met a Hindu Buddhist, a remarkably well-educated man who speaks English fluently. He is the coach of the Theosophical Society. Also encountered a Mr E. Maitland, author of a book called—'The Pilgrim and the Shrine', which I remember. He mentioned also another, written, I think he said, by himself and Dr Anna Kingsford in collaboration. If he could not get on with the work on any particular night he would go to her next morning and she would supply him with the sentences, written down by her on waking, as sentences she had dreamt of without knowing why. Met also Dr Anna Kingsford herself, and others; all very strange people."

The Mayor of Casterbridge was issued complete about the end of May. It was a story which Hardy fancied he had damaged more recklessly as an artistic whole, in the interest of the newspaper in which it appeared serially, than perhaps any other of his novels, his aiming to get an incident into almost every week's part causing him in his own judgment to add events to the narrative somewhat too freely. However as at this time he called his novel-writing "mere journeywork", he cared little about it as art, though it must be said in favour of the plot, as he admitted later, that it was quite coherent and organic, in spite of its complication. And others thought better of it than he did himself, as is shown by the letter R. L. Stevenson writes thereon:

Skerryvore, Bournemouth.
[1886]

My dear Hardy:

I have read the Mayor of Casterbridge with sincere admiration: Henchard is a great fellow, and Dorchester is touched in with the hand of a master.

Do you think you would let me try to dramatize it? I keep unusually well, and am

Yours very sincerely,
Robert Louis Stevenson.

What became of this dramatic project there is no evidence to show in the *Life of Stevenson*, so far as is remembered by the present writer. The story in long after years became highly popular; but it is curious to find that Hardy had some difficulty in getting it issued in volume-form, Mr James Payn the publishers' reader having reported to Mr Smith that the lack of gentry among the characters made it uninteresting—a typical estimate of what was, or was supposed to be, mid-Victorian taste.

During the remainder of this month, and through June and July, they were dining and lunching out almost every day. Hardy did not take much account of these functions, though some remarks he makes are interesting. For instance he describes the charming daughter of a then popular peeress with whom he and his wife had been lunching:

"Lady M—— W—— is still as childlike as when I first met her. She has an instinct to *give* something which she cannot resist. Gave me a flower. She expresses, as usual, contrary opinions at different moments. At one time she is going to marry; then she never is: at one moment she has been ill; at another she is always well. Pities the row of poor husbands at Marshall and Snelgrove's. Gave a poor crossing sweeper a shilling; came back and found her drunk. An emotional delicate girl, in spite of what she calls her 'largeness', i.e. her being bigly built."

In these weeks the Hardys met "the Humphry Wards, both amiable people", and Walter Pater, "whose manner is that of one carrying weighty ideas without spilling them". At Mrs Jeune's at different times about now they met Lord Lytton, Mrs Butler (Miss Elizabeth Thompson), J. A. Froude, Lady Pembroke, Sir John and Lady Lubbock, and J. R. Lowell. Also a lot of politicians, on whom Hardy notes:

"Plenty of form in their handling of politics, but no matter, or originality." Either on this occasion or a few days later the hostess drew the attention of Justin McCarthy—also a guest—to the Conservative placard in her window. "I hope you don't mind the blue bill?"—"Not at all," said the amiable McCarthy blandly. "Blue is a colour I have liked from a boy."

At Mr and Mrs Gosse's they met Dr Oliver Wendell Holmes and his daughter:

"His is a little figure, that of an aged boy. He said markedly that he did not read novels; I did not say I had never read his essays, though it would have been true, I am ashamed to think. . . . But authors are not so touchy as they are supposed to be on such matters—at least I am not—and I found him a very bright, pleasant, juvenile old man." At a Rabelais Club dinner a few days later he renewed acquaintance with Dr Holmes, and with Henry James, "who has a ponderously warm manner of saying nothing in infinite sentences; and who left suddenly in the midst of the meal because he was placed low down the table, as I was. Rather comical in Henry." Hardy also talked to George Meredith. This may possibly have been the first time he and Meredith had met since Hardy received Meredith's advice about novel-writing; but it is not clear that it was so. At dinners elsewhere in these weeks he met Whistler and Charles Keene, Bret Harte, Sambourne, and others— most of them for the first and last time; at Mr Sidney Colvin's he renewed acquaintance with R. L. Stevenson, then in London; and at Lord Portsmouth's sat next to a genial old lady, Lady Camperdown, and "could not get rid of the feeling that I was close to a great naval engagement".

On some Wagner-music listened to at a concert at this time when it was less familiar to the public than after, Hardy remarks: "It was *weather-* and ghost-music—whistling of wind and storm, the strumming of a gale on iron railings, the creaking of doors; low screams of entreaty and agony through key-holes, amid which trumpet-voices are heard. Such music, like any other, may be made to express emotion of various kinds; but it cannot express the subject or reason of that emotion."

Apropos of this it may be mentioned here that, many years after, Hardy met Grieg the famous Norwegian composer and rival of Wagner, and in doing his best to talk about music Hardy explained that Wagner's compositions seemed to him like the wind-effects above described. "I would rather have the wind and rain myself," Grieg replied, severely shaking his head.

Mrs Procter, who was still strong enough to go out, came to the Hardys to tea, and among her stores of anecdotes told one that was amusing about Macaulay and Sydney Smith, who had dined at her house in years gone by:

"When Macaulay had gone she said to Sydney Smith: 'You gave him no chance at all to talk.'—'On the contrary,' said Sydney Smith, 'I gave him several opportunities—which you took advantage of'."

It was during this summer that the Hardys either began or renewed their acquaintance with Mrs Henry Reeve and her sister Miss Gollop, whose family was an old Dorset one; and with Reeve himself, the well-known editor of the *Edinburgh Review* and of the famous *Greville Memoirs*. Notwithstanding a slight pompousness of manner he attracted the younger man by his wide experience of Continental men of letters, musicians, and princes, and of English affairs political and journalistic.

"June 29th. Called on Leslie Stephen. He is just the same or worse; as if dying to express sympathy, but suffering under some terrible curse which prevents his saying any but caustic things, and showing antipathy instead." [Hardy was not aware that Stephen was unwell, and growing deaf—or he would not have put in this form his impression of a man he so much liked, and who had been so much to him.]

"Afterwards had a good talk with Auberon Herbert at Lady Portsmouth's. He said that the clue to Gladstone's faults was personal vanity. His niece Lady Winifred Herbert, who was present, said that politics had revealed themselves to her as a horror of late. Nevertheless she insisted that to listen to our conversation on the same horror was not an infliction."

Mr George Gissing, finding that Hardy was in London this summer, had asked if he might call upon him for some advice about novel-writing; which he did. Sending one of his own novels afterwards, Gissing writes at the end of June:

It is possible you will find "The Unclassed" detestable. I myself should not dare to read it now; it is too saturated with bygone miseries of every kind. . . . May I add in one word what very real pleasure it has given me to meet and speak with you? I have not been the least careful of your readers, and in your books I have constantly found refreshment and onward help. That aid is much needed now-a-days by anyone who wishes to pursue literature as distinct from the profession of letters. In literature my interests begin and end; I hope to make my life and all its acquirements subservient to my ideal of artistic creation. The end of it all may prove ineffectual, but as well spend one's strength thus as in another way. The misery of it is that, writing for English people, one may not be thorough: reticences and superficialities have so often to fill places where one is willing to put in honest work.

"July 11. Met and talked to Browning at Mrs Procter's again, and a day or two later at Mrs Skirrow's, where was also Oscar Wilde, etc. Also met on the 16th at Mrs Robinson's (Mary R's mother) my very remote consanguinean Iza Duffus Hardy, with some others with whom we had returned from the Macmillan's garden-party the day before.

"In Rotten Row.—Every now & then each woman, however interesting, puts on her *battle-face*.

"In evening to bookstalls in Holywell Street known to me so many years ago."

Hardy by this time had quite resigned himself to novel-writing as a trade, which he had never wanted to carry on as such. He now went about the business mechanically. He was in court a part of the time during which the Crawford-Dilke case was proceeding. He makes no comment on the case itself, but a general remark on the Court:

"The personality which fills the court is that of *the witness*. The judge's personality during the cross-examination contracts to his corporeal dimensions merely. So do they all save that of the pervasive witness aforesaid. . . . The witness is also the fool of the court. . . . The witness's little peculiarities supersede those of all the other personages together. He is at once king and victim.

"As to the architecture of the courts, there are everywhere religious art-forces masquerading as law symbols! The leaf, flower, fret, suggested by spiritual emotion, are pressed into the service of social strife."

The remainder of his spare time in London this year appears to have been spent in the British Museum Library and elsewhere considering the question of *The Dynasts*.

At the end of July they returned to Max Gate where he went on with *The Woodlanders*; and in October they paid another visit to Lady Portsmouth in Devon, where they had a pleasant week, visiting local scenes and surroundings down to the kennels (Lord Portsmouth being Master of Hounds) and the dogs' cemetery. "Lord Portsmouth made his whipper-in tell Emma the story of the hunted fox that ran up the old woman's clock-case, adding corroborative words with much gravity as the story proceeded, and enjoying it more than she did, though he had heard it 100 times."

In October the Dorset poet William Barnes died. Hardy had known him ever since his schoolmastering time in South Street, Dorchester, next door to the architect under whom Hardy had served his years of pupillage. In 1864 Barnes had retired from school-keeping, and accepted the living of Winterborne Came-cum-Whitcombe, the rectory house being, by chance, not half a mile from the only spot Hardy could find convenient for building a dwelling on. Hardy's walk across the fields to attend the poet's funeral was marked by the singular incident to which he alludes in the poem entitled "The Last Signal". He also wrote an obituary notice of his friend for the *Athenæum*, which was afterwards drawn upon for details of his life in the *Dictionary of National Biography*. It was not till many years after that he made and edited a selection of Barnes's poems.

The beginning of December covers this entry:

"I often view society-gatherings, people in the street, in a room, or elsewhere, as if they were beings in a somnambulistic state, making their motions automatically—not realizing what they mean."

And a few days later another, when going to London:

"December 7th. Winter. The landscape has turned from a painting to an engraving: the birds that love worms fall back upon berries: the back parts of homesteads assume, in the general nakedness of the trees, a humiliating squalidness as to their details that has not been contemplated by their occupiers.

"A man I met in the train says in a tone of bitter regret that he wore out seven sets of horseshoes in riding from Sturminster Newton to Weymouth when courting a young woman at the latter place. He did not say whether he won and married her, or not; but I fancy he did.

"At the Society of British Artists there is good technique in abundance; but ideas for subjects are lacking. The impressionist school is strong. It is even more suggestive in the direction of literature than in that of art. As usual it is pushed to absurdity by some. But their principle is, as I understand it, that what you carry away with you from a scene is the true feature to grasp; or in other words, *what appeals to your own individual eye and heart in particular* amid much that does not so appeal, and which you therefore omit to record.

"Talked to Bob Stevenson—Louis's cousin—at the Savile. A more solid character than Louis.

"Called on Mrs Jeune. She was in a rich pinky-red gown, and looked handsome as we sat by the firelight en tête-á-tête: she was, curiously enough, an example of Whistler's study in red that I had seen in the morning at the Gallery.

"To Lady Carnarvon's 'small and early'. Weather too wretched for Em to go. Snow falling: the cabman drove me furiously—I don't know why. The familiar man with the lantern at the door. Her drawing-room was differently arranged from its method during her summer crushes. They seemed glad to see me. Lady Winifred told me she was going to be married on the 10th of January at the Savoy Chapel, with other details of the wedding. She was serious and thoughtful—I fancied a little careworn. Said she was not going to let her honeymoon interfere with her reading, and means to carry a parcel of books. Spoke of her betrothed as 'He'—as a workman speaks of his employer—never mentioning his name. Wants me to call my heroine 'Winifred', but it is too late to alter it.

"Talked to Lady Carnarvon, who looked remarkably pretty, about the trees at Highclere in relation to my work in hand [*The Woodlanders*]. Lord C. told me he had filled several bookshelves with books all written by members of his own family—from Sir Philip Sidney, who was his mother's mother's mother's, &c. brother, downwards.

"The last time, I suppose, that I shall see friendly Winifred Herbert pouring out tea from the big tea-pot in that house, as I have seen her do so many times. Lady Carnarvon went about the room weaving little webs of sympathy between her guests."

So came the end of 1886.

January 1887 was uneventful at Max Gate, and the only remark its occupier makes during the month is the following:

"After looking at the landscape by Bonington in our drawing room [given to Mrs Hardy by T. Woolner, R. A., the sculptor] I feel that Nature is played out as a Beauty, but not as a Mystery. I don't want to see landscapes, i.e., scenic paintings of them, because I don't want to see the original realities—as optical effects, that is. I want to see the deeper reality underlying the scenic, the expression of what are sometimes called abstract imaginings.

"The 'simply natural' is interesting no longer. The much-decried, mad, late-Turner rendering is now necessary to create my interest. The exact truth as to material fact ceases to be of importance in art—it is a student's style—the style of a period when the mind is serene and unawakened to the tragical mysteries of life; when it does not bring anything to the object that coalesces with and translates the qualities that are already there,—half hidden, it may be—and the two united are depicted as the All."

"Feb. 4th. 8.20 p.m. Finished 'The Woodlanders'. Thought I should feel glad, but I do not particularly,—though relieved."

"February 6th. Sunday. To see my father. It was three men whom he last saw flogged in Dorchester by the Town-pump—about 1830. He happened to go in from Stinsford about mid-day. Some soldiers coming down the street from the Barracks interfered, and swore at Davis [Jack Ketch] because he did not 'flog fair'; that is to say he waited between each lash for the flesh to recover sensation, whereas, as they knew from experience, by striking quickly the flesh remained numb through several strokes."

"February 13th. You may regard a throng of people as containing a certain small minority who have sensitive souls; these, and the aspects of these, being what is worth observing. So you divide them into the mentally unquickened, mechanical, soulless; and the living, throbbing, suffering, vital. In other words into souls and machines, ether and clay.

"I was thinking a night or two ago that people are somnambulists—that the material is not the real—only the visible, the real being invisible optically. That it is because we are in a somnambulistic hallucination that we think the real to be what we see as real."

"Faces. The features to beholders so commonplace are to their possessor lineaments of striking, hopeful, high estimation."

Having now some leisure, and the spring drawing near, Hardy

carried into effect an idea that he had long entertained, and on Monday, March 14, 1887, left Dorchester with Mrs Hardy for London on their way to Italy, the day before *The Woodlanders* was published by the Messrs Macmillan.

CHAPTER XV

Italy

1887: *Aet.* 46

The month had been mild hitherto, but no sooner had they started than the weather turned to snow; and a snow-storm persistently accompanied them across the Channel and southward beyond. They broke the journey at Aix-les-Bains, at which place they arrived past midnight, and the snow being by this time deep a path was cleared with spades for them to the fly in waiting, which two horses, aided by men turning the wheels, dragged with difficulty up the hill to the Hôtel Château Durieux—an old-fashioned place with stone floors and wide fireplaces. They were the only people there—the first visitors of the season—and in spite of a huge fire in their bedroom they found the next morning a cone of snow within each casement, and a snow film on the floor sufficient to show their tracks in moving about. Hardy used to speak of a curious atmospheric effect next morning. He was surprised that the windows of the room they occupied—one of the best—should command the view of a commonplace paddock only, with a few broken rails and sheds. But presently "what had seemed like the sky evolved a scene which uncurtained itself high up in the midst of the aerial expanse, as in a magic lantern, and vast mountains appeared there, tantalizingly withdrawing again as if they had been a mere illusion".

They stayed here a day or two, "the mountains showing again coquettish signs of uncovering themselves, and again coquettishly pulling down their veil".

Leaving for Turin they stayed there awhile, then duly reached Genoa, concerning the first aspect of which from the train Hardy wrote a long time after the lines entitled "Genoa and the Mediterranean", though that city—so pre-eminently the city of marble ("everything marble", he writes, "even little doorways in slums")—nobly redeemed its character when they visited its palaces—notably the Palazzo Doria—during their stay.

At Pisa after visiting the Cathedral and Baptistery they stood at the top of the leaning tower during a peal of the bells, which shook it under their feet, and saw the sun set from one of the bridges over the Arno, as Shelley had probably seen it from the same bridge many a time. Thence by "melancholy olives and cheerful lemons" they proceeded to Florence, where they were met by a long inhabitant of that city, Lucy Baxter, the daughter of the poet Barnes, married and settled there since Hardy had known her in girlhood, and who wrote under the name of "Leader Scott". She had obtained for them lodgings at the Villa Trollope, in the Piazza dell' Indipendenza; and there they remained all the time they were in Florence. Their Florentine experiences onward were much like those of other people visiting for the first time the buildings, pictures, and historic sites of that city. They were fortunately able to see the old Market just before its destruction. Having gone through the galleries and churches of Florence they drove out and visited another English resident in the country near, and also went over the Certosa di Val d'Ema. Then they travelled on to Rome, their first glimpse of it being of the Dome of St. Peter's across the stagnant flats of the Campagna.

They put up at the Hôtel d'Allemagne, in the Via Condotti, a street opposite the Piazza di Spagna and the steps descending from the church of SS. Trinità dei Monti, on the south side of which stands the house where Keats died. Hardy liked to watch of an evening, when the streets below were immersed in shade, the figures ascending and descending these steps in the sunset glow, the front of the church orange in the same light; and also the house hard by, in which no mind could conjecture what had been lost to English literature in the early part of the same century that saw him there.

After some days spent in the Holy City Hardy began to feel, he frequently said, its measureless layers of history to lie upon him like a physical weight. The time of their visit was not so long after the peeling of the Coliseum and other ruins of their vast accumulations of parasitic growths, which, though Hardy as an architect defended the much deplored process on the score of its absolute necessity if the walls were to be preserved, he yet wished had not been taken in hand till after his inspection of them. This made the ruins of the ancient city, the "altae moenia Romae" as he called them from the *Aeneid*, more gaunt to the vision and more depressing to the mind than they had been to visitors when covered with greenery, and accounts for his allusions to the city in the poems on Rome written after his return, as exhibiting "ochreous gauntness", "umbered walls", and so forth.

He mentions in a note the dustiness of the Pincio: "Dust rising in clouds from the windy drive to the top, whitening the leaves of the evergreen oaks, and making the pale splotches on the trunks of the plane trees yet paler. The busts of illustrious Romans seem to require hats and goggles as a protection. But in the sheltered gardens beneath palms spread, and oranges still hang on the trees."

There was a great spurt of building going on at this time, on which he remarks, "I wonder how anybody can have any zest to erect a new building in Rome, in the overpowering presence of decay on the mangy and rotting walls of old erections, originally of fifty times the strength of the new." This sentiment was embodied in the sonnet called "Building a New Street in the Ancient Quarter".

A visit to the graves of Shelley and Keats was also the inspiration of more verses—probably not written till later—his nearly falling asleep in the Sala delle Muse of the Vatican was the source of another poem, the weariness being the effect of the deadly fatiguing size of St. Peter's; and the musical incident which, as he once said, took him by surprise when investigating the remains of Caligula's palace, that of another.

"The quality of the faces in the streets of Rome: Satyrs: Emperors: Faustinas."

Two or three slightly unpleasant occurrences chequered their stay in Rome, but were not of serious moment. One was that when Hardy was descending the Via di Aracoeli, carrying a small old painting he had just bought in a slum at the back of the Capitoline Hill, three men prepared to close on him as if to rob him, apparently mistaking him for a wealthy man owing to his wearing a fur-edged coat. They could see that both his hands were occupied in holding the picture, but what they seemed not to be perceiving was that he was not alone, Mrs Hardy being on the opposite side of the narrow way. She cried out to her husband to be aware, and with her usual courage rushed across at the back of the men, who disappeared as if by magic.

Another risk, of which however they were not conscious at the moment, was one incurred by herself, who in her eagerness for exploration lingered for rather a long time in the underground dens of the Coliseum. An attack of malaria in a mild form followed, which went off in a few days; but with, to them, the singular result that at the same date in spring for three or four years afterwards the same feverishness returned, in decreasing strength, till it finally left off appearing.

The third was nothing more than amusing, it being that the priest who conducted them through the Catacombs of S. Callistus, and had seemed puzzled about the way, was a new man who had himself got lost in them for some hours the day before.

Hardy's notes of Rome were of a very jumbled and confusing kind. But probably from a surviving architectural instinct he made a few measurements in the "Via Appia Antica", where he was obsessed by a vision of a chained file of prisoners plodding wearily along towards Rome, one of the most haggard of whom was to be famous through the ages as the founder of Pauline Christianity. He also noticed that the pavement of the fashionable promenade, the Corso, was two feet six inches wide. Of a different kind was his note that

"The monk who showed us the hole in which stood Saint Peter's Cross in the Church of S. Pietro in Montorio, and fetched up a pinch of clean sand from it, implying it had been there ever since the apostle's crucifixion, was a man of cynical humour, and gave me an indescribably funny glance from the tail of his eye as if to say: 'You see well enough what an imposture it all is!' I have noticed this sly humour in some more of these Roman monks, such as the one who sent me on alone into the vaults of the Cappuccini [among the thousands of skulls there], not knowing that I was aware of them, and therefore not startled at the ghastly scene. Perhaps there is something in my appearance which makes them think me a humourist also."

On the Roman pictures and statuary the only remark he makes except in verse is: "Paintings. In Roman art the kernel of truth has acquired a thick rind of affectation: e.g., I find that pictures by Giotto have been touched up so thoroughly that what you see is not Giotto at all, but the over-lying renovations. A disappointing sight. Alas for this 'wronged great soul of an ancient master'!" (The remark, though written at Rome, seems to refer more particularly to Florence.)

By curious chance Hardy was present at a wedding at the church of S. Lorenzo-in-Lucina, and was vexed with himself that he did not recollect till afterwards that it was the church of Pompilia's marriage in *The Ring and the Book*. But he was on the whole more interested in Pagan than in Christian Rome, of the latter preferring churches in which he could detect columns from ancient temples. Christian Rome, he said, was so rambling and stratified that to comprehend it in a single visit was like trying to read Gibbon through at a sitting. So that, for instance, standing on the meagre remains of the Via Sacra then recently uncovered, he seemed to catch more echoes of the inquisitive bore's conversation there with the poet Horace than of worship from the huge basilicas hard by, which were in point of time many centuries nearer to him. But he was careful to remind one to whom he spoke about this that it was really a question of familiarity, time being nothing beside knowledge, and that he happened to remember the scene in the Satires which he, like so many schoolboys, had read, while his mind was a blank on the most august ceremonial of the Middle-Age Christian services in the Basilica Julia or the Basilica of Constantine.

"April. Our spirits. As we get older they are less subject to steep gradients than in youth. We lower the elevations, and fill the hollows with sustained judgments."

While here he received among other letters one from Mrs Procter containing the following remarks:

It is very kind of you to think of me in Rome, and stretch out a friendly hand. Perhaps, as you are living amidst the Ancient, there is a propriety in thinking of the Oldish, and, I must say, the truest, friend you have.——

We are still in Winter: to-day a bitter East wind, and tiles and chimney pots flying about. Never have we had so long a season of cold weather—all our Money gone in Coals and Gas.

I have been displeased, so much as one ever is by a Man whom you care nothing about, by an Article written by a Dr Wendell Holmes the American. He comes here, and then says, "the most wonderful thing I saw in England were the Old Ladies—they are so active, and tough, like Old Macaws"—Now am I like an Old Macaw?—He might have said Parrots.

Then Mr Thackeray's letters! [to Mrs Brookfield]; so common, so vulgar! You will see them in Scribner's Magazine.—He was never in love with me, but the 200 letters he wrote me were very superior to these.

It was with a sense of having grasped very little of its history that he left the city, though with some relief, which may have been partly physical and partly mental.

Returning to Florence on "a soft green misty evening following rain", he found the scenery soothing after the gauntness of Rome. On a day of warm sun he sat down for a long time, he said, on the steps of the Lanzi, in the Piazza della Signoria, while his wife was sketching, near; and thought of many things:

"It is three in the afternoon, and the faces of the buildings are steeped in afternoon stagnation. The figure of Neptune is looking an intense white against the brown-grey houses behind, and the bronze forms round the basin [of the fountain] are starred with rays on their noses, elbows, knees, bosoms and shoulders. The shade from the Loggia dei Lanzi falls half across the Piazza. Turning my head there rise the three great arches with their sculptures, then those in the middle of the Loggia, then the row of six at the back with their uplifted fingers, as if——" [sentence unfinished].

"In the Caffe near there is a patter of speech, and on the pavement outside a noise of hoofs. The reflection from that statue of Neptune throws a secondary light into the Caffe.

"Everybody is thinking, even amid these art examples from various ages, that this present age is the ultimate climax and upshot of the previous ages, and not a link in a chain of them.

"In a work of art it is the accident which *charms*, not the intention; that we love and admire. Instance the amber tones that pervade the folds of drapery in ancient marbles, the deadened polish of the surfaces, and the cracks and the scratches."

In visiting Fiesole they met with a mishap which might have ended in a serious accident. With Mrs Baxter they had journeyed out from Florence to the foot of the hill on which the little town stands, and were about to walk up the height, when on second thoughts they entered a gimcrack omnibus that plied to the top. The driver went to have a drink before starting, and left the omnibus untended, only one of the two horses being put to. The horse immediately started with the three inside at a furious pace towards Florence. The highway was dotted with heaps of large stones for repair, but he avoided them by a miracle, until the steam-tram from Florence appeared a little way ahead, and a collision seemed inevitable. Two workmen, however, seeing the danger, descended from the roof of a house and stepping in front of the horse stopped it. They again attempted Fiesole, and climbed up—this time on foot despite all invitations from flymen.

In a sonnet on Fiesole called "In the Old Theatre" Hardy makes use of an incident that occurred while he was sitting in the stone Amphitheatre on the summit of the hill.

A few more looks at Florence, including the Easter ceremony of the Scoppio del Carro, a visit to Mrs Browning's tomb, and to the supposed scene in the Piazza dell' Annunziata of one of Browning's finest poems, "The Statue and the Bust", ended their visit to this half-English city, and after seeing Siena they left for Bologna, Ferrara, and Venice by the railway across the Apennines, not forgetting to gaze at the Euganean Hills so inseparable from thoughts of Shelley. It is rather noticeable that two such differing poets as Browning and Shelley, in their writings, their mentality, and their lives, should have so mingled in Hardy's thoughts during this Italian tour, almost to the exclusion of other English poets equally, or nearly so, associated with Italy, with whose works he was just as well acquainted.

Hardy seems to have found more pleasure in Venice than in any Italian city previously visited, in spite of bad weather during a part of his stay there. Byron of course was introduced here among the other phantom-poets marshalled through his brain in front of the sea-queen's historic succession of scenes.

A wet windy morning accompanied their first curious examination of the Ducal Palace, "the shining ferri of the gondolas curtesying down and up against the wharf wall, and the gondoliers standing looking on at us. The wet draught sweeps through the colonnade by Munster's shop, not a soul being within it but Munster, whose face brightens at sight of us like that of a man on a desert island. . . . The dumb boy who showed us the way to the Rialto has haunted us silently ever since.

"The Hall of the Great Council is saturated with Doge-domry. The faces of the Doges pictured on the frieze float out into the air of the room in front of me. 'We know nothing of you', say these spectres. 'Who may you be, pray?' The draught brushing past seems like inquiring touches by their cold hands, feeling, feeling like blind people what you are. Yes: here to this visionary place I solidly bring in my person Dorchester and Wessex life; and they may well ask why do I do it. . . . Yet there is a connection. The bell of the Campanile of S. Marco strikes the hour, and its sound has exactly that tin-tray *timbre* given out by the bells of Longpuddle and Weatherbury, showing that they are of precisely the same-proportioned alloy."

Hardy had been, for many reasons, keen to see St. Mark's; and he formed his own opinion on it:

"Well. There is surely some conventional ecstasy, exaggeration,—shall I say humbug?—in what Ruskin writes about this, if I remember, (though I have not read him lately), when the church is looked at *as a whole*. One architectural defect nothing can get over—its squatness as seen from the natural point of view—the glassy marble pavement of the Grand Piazza. Second, its weak, flexuous, constructional lines. Then, the fantastic Oriental character of its details makes it barbaric in its general impression, in spite of their great beauty.

"Mosaics, mosaics, mosaics, gilding, gilding, everywhere inside and out. The domes like inverted china-bowls within—much gilt also.

"This being said, see what good things are left to say—of its art, of its history! That floor, of every colour and rich device, is worn into undulations by the infinite multitudes of feet that have trodden it, and *what* feet there have been among the rest!

"A commonplace man stoops in a dark corner where he strikes a common match, and shows us—what—a lost article?—a purse, pipe, or tobacco-pouch? no; shows us—drags from the depths of time as by a miracle—wonderful diaphanous alabaster pillars that were once in Solomon's temple."

On Venice generally he makes the following desultory remarks: "When it rains in Italy it makes one shrink and shiver; it is so far more serious a matter than in England. We have our stern gray stone and brick walls, and weathered copings, and buttress-slopes, to fend such. But here there are exposed to the decaying rain, marbles, and frescoes, and tesserae, and gildings, and endless things—driving one to implore mentally that all these treasures may be put under a glass case!"

When the weather was finer:

"Venice is composed of blue and sunlight. Hence I incline, after all, to 'sun-girt' rather than 'sea-girt', which I once upheld." [In Shelley's poem, "Many a green isle needs must be".]

"Venice requires *heat* to complete the picture of her. Heat is an artistic part of the portrait of all southern towns."

They were most kindly received and entertained during their brief stay by friends to whom they had introductions. Browning's friend Mrs Bronson showed them things; and in respect of an evening party given for them by Mrs Daniel Curtis at the Palazzo Barbaro, it could not be said that "silent rows the songless gondolier", several boats lit by lanterns pausing in front of the open windows on the Grand Canal while their rowers and the singers they brought serenaded the guests within. But alas, it was true that "Tasso's echoes were no more", the music being that of the latest popular song of the date:

> "Fu-ni-cu-li-fu-ni-cu-la,
> Fu-ni-cu-li-cu-la!"

However, the scene was picturesque, Hardy used to say—the dark shapes of the gondoliers creeping near to them silently, like cats or other nocturnal animals, the gleam of a ferro here and there: then the lanterns suddenly lighting up over the heads of the singers, throwing a diffused light on their faces and forms; a sky as of black velvet stretching above with its star points, as the notes flapped back from the dilapidated palaces behind with a hollow and almost sepulchral echo, as if from a vault.

Quoting Byron brings to the mind a regret which Hardy sometimes expressed, that though he possibly encountered some old native man or woman of fourscore who could remember Byron's residence at the Spinelli and Mocenigo palaces, he never questioned any likely one among them on the point, though once in especial he stood on the Riva degli Schiavoni beside such an aged personage whose appearance made him feel her to be an instance of such recollection.

He was curious to know if any descendants of the powerful Doges were left in decayed modern Venice. Mr Curtis told him that there were some in Venetian society still—poor, but proud, though not offensively so. The majority were extinct, their palaces being ruinous. Going on to Mrs Bronson's immediately afterwards the Contessa M—— called. She was a great beauty, having the well-defined hues and contours of foreigners in the south; and she turned out to be one of the very descendants Hardy had inquired about. When asked afterwards how she was dressed, he said in a green velvet jacket with fluffy tags, a grey hat and feathers, a white veil with seed pearls, and a light figured skirt of a yellowish colour. She had a charming manner, her mind flying from one subject to another like a child's as she spoke her pretty attempts at English. "But I li—eek moch to do it!" . . . "Si, si!" . . . "Oh noh, noh!"

However, Hardy was not altogether listening, he afterwards recalled. This correct, modest, modern lady, the friend of his English and American acquaintance in Venice, and now his own, was to him primarily the symbol and relic of the bygone ancient families; and the chief effect, he said, of her good looks and pretty voice on him was to carry him at one spring back to those behind the centuries, who here

> took their pleasure when the sea was warm in May,
> Balls and masks begun at midnight, burning ever to midday,
> When they made up fresh adventures for the morrow. . . .

It is not known whether the Italian Contessa in *A Group of Noble Dames* was suggested by her; but there are resemblances.

Then they left Venice. "The Riva degli Schiavoni is interested along its whole length in our departure, just as nautical people at ports always are, and as we left the station we could see the tops of the Alps floating in the sky above the fog." They had been unable to follow Ruskin's excellent advice to approach Venice by water, but they had seen it from the water a good deal while there.

"The Cathedral, Milan,—Yes, perhaps it is architectural filigree: and yet I admire it. The vaulting of the interior is infinite quadrilles in carved-work. A momentary vexation comes when I am reminded that it is not real—even a disgust. And yet I admire. The sense of space alone demands admiration, being beyond that expressed anywhere except at St. Peter's."

The cheerful scenes of life and gaiety here after the poetical decay of Venice came as the greatest possible contrast, and a not unwelcome change. Here Hardy's mind reverted to Napoleon, particularly when he was sitting in the sun with his wife on the roof of the Cathedral, and regarding the city in vistas between the flying buttresses. It was while here on the roof, he thought in after years, though he was not quite sure, that he conceived the Milan Cathedral scene in *The Dynasts*.

Hardy had lately been obsessed by an old French tune of his father's, "The Bridge of Lodi", owing to his having drawn near the spot of that famous Napoleonic struggle; and at a large music-shop in the Gallery of Victor Emmanuel he enquired about it; as may be expected his whimsical questioning met with no success. He felt it could meet with none, and yet went on with his search. At dinner at the Grand Hôtel de Milan that evening, where the Hardys had put up, they became friendly with a young Scotch officer of Foot returning from India, and Hardy told him about Lodi, and how he could not get the old tune.

"The Bridge of Lodi?" said the Scotchman (apparently a sort of Farfrae). "Ay, but I've never heard of it!"

"But you've heard of the battle, anyhow?" says the astonished Hardy.

"Nay, and I never have whatever!" says the young soldier.

Hardy then proceeded to describe the conflict, and by degrees his companion rose to an enthusiasm for Lodi greater than Hardy's own. When the latter said he would like to go and see the spot his friend cried "And I'll go too!"

The next morning they started, leaving Mrs Hardy at the hotel; and passing through levels of fat meads and blooming fruit-trees reached the little town of their quest, and more especially the historic bridge itself—much changed, but at any rate sufficiently well denoting the scene of Napoleon's exploit in the earlier and better days of his career. Over the quiet flowing of the Adda the two re-enacted the fight and the "Little Corporal's" dramatic victory over the Austrians.

The pleasant jingle in *Poems of the Past and the Present* named after the bridge, and written some time after the excursion to the scene, fully enough describes the visit, but the young Scotch lieutenant from India is not mentioned, though his zest by this time had grown more than equal to Hardy's—the latter's becoming somewhat damped at finding that the most persevering inquiries at Lodi failed to elicit any tradition of the event, and the furthest search to furnish any photograph of the town and river.

They returned to England by way of Como and the St. Gothard, one of the remarks Hardy makes on the former place being on the vying of "the young greens with the old greens, the greens of yesterday and the greens of yesteryear". It was too early in the year for Lucerne, and they stayed there only a day. Passing through Paris they went to see the Crown jewels that chanced just then to be on exhibition, previous to their sale.

PART IV

Between Town and Country

CHAPTER XVI

London Friends, Paris, and Short Stories

1887–1888: *Aet.* 47–48

Reaching London Hardy attended the annual dinner of the Royal Academy. He remarks thereon:

"The watching presence of so many portraits gives a distinct character to this dinner. . . . In speaking, the Duke of Cambridge could not decide whether he had ended his speech or not, and so tagged and tagged on a bit more, and a bit more, till the sentences were like acrobats hanging down from a trapeze. Lord Salisbury's satire was rather too serious for after dinner. Huxley began well but ended disastrously; the Archbishop was dreary; Morley tried to look a regular dining-out man-of-the-world, but really looked what he is by nature, the student. Everybody afterwards walked about, the Prince of Wales included, remaining till 12. I spoke to a good many; was apparently unknown to a good many more I knew. At these times men do not want to talk to their equals, but to their superiors."

On the Sunday after the Hardys again met Browning at Mrs Procter's, and being full of Italy Hardy alluded to "The Statue and the Bust" (which he often thought one of the finest of Browning's poems); and observed that, looking at "the empty shrine" opposite the figure of Ferdinand in the Piazza dell' Annunziata, he had wondered where the bust had gone to, and had been informed by an officious waiter standing at a neighbouring door that he remembered seeing it in its place; after which he gave further interesting details about it, for which information he was gratefully rewarded. Browning smiled and said, "I invented it."

Shortly afterwards they settled till the end of July at a house in Campden-Hill Road.

Speaking of this date Hardy said that in looking for a place to stay at for the season he called at a house-agent's as usual, where, not seeing the man at the desk who had been there a day or two before, and who knew his wants in flats and apartments, he inquired for the man and was told he was out. Saying he would call again in an hour, Hardy left. On coming back he was told he was still out. He called a day or two afterwards, and the answer then was that the clerk he wanted was away.

"But you said yesterday he was only out," exclaimed Hardy. His informant looked round him as if not wishing to be overheard, and replied:

"Well, *strictly* he is not *out*, but *in*."

"Why didn't you say so?"

"Because you can't speak to him. He's dead and buried."

"16 May. Met Lowell at Lady Carnarvon's. Also Lady Winifred Byng for the first time since her marriage. Lady Camilla her cousin asked in a roguish whisper if I did not think Winifred looked gloomy. Talked to Lady Rosamond C——. She tells me she is in trouble about the colour of her hair; but it is certainly not red as she says. Lady ——, whose eyes had a wild look, declares she has not slept for *two months*, since she met with an accident out hunting. Lady Marge W—— looked pretty in gauzy muslin—going to a ball, she told me."

"May 29. Instance of a *wrong* (i.e., selfish) philosophy in poetry:
> Thrice happy he who on the sunless side
> Of a romantic mountain . . .
> Sits coolly calm; while all the world without,
> Unsatisfied and sick, tosses at noon.
>
>   Thomson."

"End of May. Read Drummond's 'Natural Law in the Spiritual World'—worthless. Also some of Calderon's Plays—Fitzgerald's translation."

"June 2. The forty-seventh birthday of Thomas the Unworthy."

"June 8. Met at a dinner at the Savile Club: Goschen Chancellor of the Exchequer, Lord Lytton, A. J. Balfour, and others."

"June 9. At dinner at (Juliet) Lady Pollock's, Sir F. told Emma that he had danced in the same quadrille with a gentleman who had danced with Marie Antoinette.

"Sir Patrick Colquhoun said that Lord Strath——(illegible) told him he was once dining with Rogers when Sir Philip Francis was present. The conversation turned on 'Junius'. Rogers said he would ask Sir Philip point-blank if he really were the man, so going to him he said 'Sir Philip, I want to ask you a question.'——Sir P. 'At your peril, Sir!' Rogers retreated saying 'He's not only Junius, but Junius *Brutus!*'

"He also told us that Lord S—— once related to him how George III met him on Richmond Hill, and said to him: 'Eton boy, what are you doing here?'—'Taking a walk, Sir.'—'What form are you in?'—'The sixth.'—'Then you have that which I couldn't give you.'—(Characteristic.)"

"14th. To Lady Carnarvon's with E. The dullest and stupidest of all her parties this season. A Rajah there. Talked to Lady Winifred, Lady Camilla Wallop, &c. Introduced to her sister Lady Kath: Milnes-Gaskell. The latter the prettiest of all Lady Portsmouth's daughters. Round luminous enquiring eyes. Lady Winifred puts on the married woman already."

"Sunday. To Mrs Procter's. Browning there. He was sleepy. In telling a story would break off, forgetting what he was going to say."

"18. To dinner at Mansion House."

On the 21st was Queen Victoria's Jubilee, and Hardy took his wife to see the procession from the Savile Club in Piccadilly.—"The Queen was very jolly-looking. The general opinion is that there will certainly never be another jubilee in England; anyhow, probably never such a gathering of royal personages again."

"25. At a concert at Prince's Hall I saw Souls outside Bodies."

"26. We were at Mrs Procter's when Browning came in as usual. He seemed galled at not having been invited to the Abbey (Jubilee) ceremony. He says that so far from receiving (as stated in the *Pall Mall*) an invitation even so late as 24 hours before, he received absolutely no invitation from the Lord Chamberlain (Lord Lathom) at all. The Dean offered him one of his own family tickets, but B. did not care to go on such terms, so went off to Oxford to stay with Jowett. People who were present say there were crowds of Court-servants and other nobodies there. An eminent actor had 25 tickets sent him . . . Millais, Huxley, Arnold, Spencer, etc. had none. Altogether Literature, Art, and Science had been unmistakeably snubbed, and they should turn republican forthwith."

An interesting comment on the reign of Queen Victoria!

The remainder of this London season in the brilliant Jubilee-year was passed by the Hardys gaily enough. At some houses the scene was made very radiant by the presence of so many Indian princes in their jewelled robes. At a certain reception Hardy was rather struck by one of the Indian dignitaries (who seems to have been the Anniwalia of Kapurthala); remarking of him:

"In his mass of jewels and white turban and tunic he stood and sat apart amid the babble and gaiety, evidently feeling himself *alone*, and having too much character to pretend to belong to and throw himself into a thoughtless world of chit-chat and pleasure which he understood nothing of."

"June 30th. Talked to Matthew Arnold at the Royal Academy *Soirée*. Also to Lang, du Maurier, Thornycrofts, Mrs Jeune &c."

"July 1. Dined at the House of Commons with Justin McCarthy. Met T. P. O'Connor, Dillon, &c. Sat on Terrace after dinner."

"With E. to lunch at Lady Stanley's (of Alderley). Met there Lord Halifax, Lady Airlie, Hon. Maude Stanley, her brother Monsignor Stanley, and others. An exciting family dispute supervened, in which they took no notice of us guests at all."

But Hardy does not comment much on these society-gatherings, his thoughts running upon other subjects, as is shown by the following memorandum made on the same day as the above. (It must always be borne in mind that these memoranda on people and things were made by him only as personal opinions for private consideration, which he meant to destroy, and not for publication; an issue which has come about by his having been asked when old if he would object to their being printed, as there was no harm in them, and his saying passively that he did not mind.)

"July 14. It is the on-going—i.e., the 'becoming'—of the world that produces its sadness. If the world stood still at a felicitous moment there would be no sadness in it. The sun and the moon standing still on Ajalon was not a catastrophe for Israel, but a type of Paradise."

In August he was back again at Max Gate, and there remarks on the difference between children who grow up in solitary country places and those who grow up in towns—the former being imaginative, dreamy, and credulous of vague mysteries; giving as the reason that "The Unknown comes within so short a radius from themselves by comparison with the city-bred".

At the end of the month Mr Edmund Gosse wrote to inform Hardy among other things that R. L. Stevenson was off to Colorado as a last chance, adding in the course of a humorous letter: "I hope your spirits have been pretty good this summer. I have been scarcely fit for human society, I have been so deep in the dumps. I wonder whether climate has anything to do with it? It is the proper thing nowadays to attribute to physical causes all the phenomena which people used to call spiritual. But I am not sure. One may be dyspeptic and yet perfectly cheerful, and one may be quite well and yet no fit company for a churchyard worm. For the last week I should not have ventured to say unto a flea, 'Thou art my sister'."

"Sept. 3. Mother tells me of a woman she knew named Nanny P——, who when she married would never be called by her husband's name 'because she was too proud', she said; and to the end of their lives the couple were spoken of as 'Nanny P—— and John C——'."

"September 25. My grandmother used to say that when sitting at home at Bockhampton she had heard the tranter 'beat out the tune' on the floor with his feet when dancing at a party in his own house, which was a hundred yards or more away from hers."

"Oct. 2. Looked at the thorn bushes by Rushy Pond [on an exposed spot of the heath]. In their wrath with the gales their forms resemble men's in like mood.

"A variant of the superstitions attached to pigeon's hearts is that, when the counteracting process is going on, the person who has bewitched the other *enters*. In the case of a woman in a village near here who was working the spell at midnight a neighbour knocked at the door and said: 'Do ye come in and see my little maid. She is so ill that I don't like to bide with her alone!'"

"October 7. During the funeral of H.S., the rector's son at West Stafford, the cows looked mournfully over the churchyard wall from the adjoining barton, resting their clammy chins on the coping; and clattered their horns in a farewell volley."

Another outline scheme for *The Dynasts* was shaped in November, in which Napoleon was represented as haunted by an Evil Genius or Familiar, whose existence he has to confess to his wives. This was abandoned, and another tried in which Napoleon by means of necromancy becomes possessed of an insight enabling him to see the thoughts of opposing generals. This does not seem to have come to anything either.

But in December he quotes from Addison:

"In the description of Paradise the poet [Milton] has observed Aristotle's rule of lavishing all the ornaments of diction on the weak, inactive parts of the fable." And although Hardy did not slavishly adopt this rule in *The Dynasts*, it is apparent that he had it in mind, in concentrating the "ornaments of diction" in particular places, thus following Coleridge in holding that a long poem should not attempt to be poetical all through.

"December 11. Those who invent vices indulge in them with more judgment and restraint than those who imitate vices invented by others."

"Dec. 31. A silent New Year's Eve—no bell, or band, or voice.

"The year has been a fairly friendly one to me. It showed me and Em the south of Europe—Italy, above all Rome,—and it brought us back unharmed and much illuminated. It has given me some new acquaintances, too, and enabled me to hold my own in fiction, whatever that may be worth, by the completion of 'The Woodlanders'.

"Books read or pieces looked at this year:

Milton, Dante, Calderon, Goethe
Homer, Virgil, Molière, Scott.
The Cid, Nibelungen, Crusoe, Don Quixote
Aristophanes, Theocritus, Boccaccio.
Canty Tales, Sha's Sonnets, Lycidas
Malory. Vic. of W. Ode to West Wind. Ode to Grecian Urn,
Christabel, Wye above Tintern.
Chapman's Iliad, Ld Derby's ditto Worsley's Odyssey."

"Jan. 2. 1888. Different purposes, different men. Those in the city for money-making are not the same men as they were when at home the previous evening. Nor are these the same as they were when lying awake in the small hours."

"Jan. 5. Be rather curious than anxious about your own career; for whatever result may accrue to its intellectual and social value, it will make little difference to your personal well-being. A naturalist's interest in the hatching of a queer egg or germ is the utmost introspective consideration you should allow yourself."

"Jan. 7. On New Year's Eve and day I sent off five copies of the magazine containing a story of mine, and three letters—all eight to friends by way of New Year's greeting and good wishes. *Not a single reply*. Mem.: never send New Year's letters &c. again."

[Two were dying: one ultimately replied. The story was either "The Withered Arm", in *Blackwood*, or "The Waiting Supper" in *Murray's Magazine*, both of which appeared about this time.]

"Apprehension is a great element in imagination. It is a semi-madness, which sees enemies, etc., in inanimate objects."

"Jan. 14. A 'sensation-novel' is possible in which the sensationalism is not casualty but evolution; not physical but psychical. . . . The difference between the latter kind of novel and the novel of physical sensationalism—i.e., personal adventure, etc.,—is this: that whereas in the physical the adventure itself is the subject of interest, the psychical results being passed over as commonplace, in the psychical the casualty or adventure is held to be of no intrinsic interest, but the effect upon the faculties is the important matter to be depicted."

"Jan. 24. I find that my politics really are neither Tory nor Radical. I may be called an Intrinsicalist. I am against privilege derived from accident of any kind, and am therefore equally opposed to aristocratic privilege and democratic privilege. (By the latter I mean the arrogant assumption that the only labour is hand-labour—a worse arrogance than that of the aristocrat, the taxing of the worthy to help those masses of the population who will not help themselves when they might, etc.) Opportunity should be equal for all, but those who will not avail themselves of it should be cared for merely—not be a burden to, nor the rulers over, those who do avail themselves thereof."

"Feb. 5th. Heard a story of a farmer who was 'overlooked' [malignly affected] by *himself*. He used to go and examine his stock every morning before breakfast with anxious scrutiny. The animals pined away. He went to a conjuror or white witch, who told him he had no enemy; that the evil was of his own causing, the eye of a fasting man being very blasting: that he should eat a 'dew-bit' before going to survey any possession about which he had hopes."

In the latter part of this month there arrived the following:

The Rev. Dr A. B. Grosart ventures to address Mr Hardy on a problem that is of life and death; personally, and in relation to young eager intellects for whom he is responsible. . . . Dr Grosart finds abundant evidence that the facts and mysteries of nature and human nature have come urgently before Mr Hardy's penetrative brain.

He enumerated some of the horrors of human and animal life, particularly parasitic, and added:

The problem is how to reconcile these with the absolute goodness and non-limitation of God.

Hardy replied: "Mr Hardy regrets that he is unable to suggest any hypothesis which would reconcile the existence of such evils as Dr Grosart describes with the idea of omnipotent goodness. Perhaps Dr Grosart might be helped to a provisional view of the universe by the recently published Life of Darwin, and the works of Herbert Spencer and other agnostics."

He met Leslie Stephen shortly after, and Stephen told him that he too had received a similar letter from Grosart, to which he had replied that as the reverend doctor was a professor of theology, and he himself only a layman, he should have thought it was the doctor's business to explain the difficulty to his correspondent, and not his to explain it to the doctor.

Two or three days later the Bishop (Wordsworth) of Salisbury wrote to Hardy for his views on the migration of the peasantry, "which is of considerable social importance and has a very distinct bearing on the work of the Church", adding that Hardy with his very accurate knowledge of the custom was well qualified to be the historian of its causes and its results. "Are they good or bad morally and in respect of religion, respectability, etc., to men, women, and children." Hardy's answer cannot be discovered, but he is known to have held that these modern migrations are fatal to local traditions and to cottage horticulture. Labourers formerly, knowing they were permanent residents, would plant apple-trees and fruit-bushes with zealous care, to profit from them: but now they scarce ever plant one, knowing they will be finding a home elsewhere in a year or two; or if they do happen to plant any, digging them up and selling them before leaving! Hence the lack of picturesqueness in modern labourers' dwellings.

"March 1. Youthful recollections of four village beauties:

1. Elizabeth B——, and her red hair [She seems to appear in the poem called 'Lizbie Browne', and was a gamekeeper's daughter, a year or two older than Hardy himself.]

2. Emily D——, and her mere prettiness.

3. Rachel H——, and her rich colour, and vanity, and frailty, and clever artificial dimple-making. [She is probably in some respects the original of Arabella in *Jude the Obscure*.]

4. Alice P—— and her mass of flaxen curls."

"March. At the Temperance Hotel. The people who stay here appear to include religious enthusiasts of all sorts. They talk the old faiths with such new fervours and original aspects that such faiths seem again arresting. They open fresh views of Christianity by turning it in reverse positions, as Gérôme the painter did by painting the *shadow* of the Crucifixion instead of the Crucifixion itself as former painters had done.

"In the street outside I heard a man coaxing money from a prostitute in slang language, his arm round her waist. The outside was a commentary on the inside."

"March 9. British Museum Reading Room. Souls are gliding about here in a sort of dream—screened somewhat by their bodies, but imaginable behind them. Dissolution is gnawing at them all, slightly hampered by renovations. In the great circle of the library Time is looking into Space. Coughs are floating in the same great vault, mixing with the rustle of book-leaves risen from the dead, and the touches of footsteps on the floor."

"March 28. On returning to London after an absence I find the people of my acquaintance abraded, their hair disappearing; also their flesh, by degrees.

"People who to one's-self are transient singularities are to themselves the permanent condition, the inevitable, the normal, the rest of mankind being to them the singularity. Think, that those (to us) strange transitory phenomena, their personalities, are with them always, at their going to bed, at their uprising!

"Footsteps, cabs, &c. are continually passing our lodgings. And every echo, pit-pat, and rumble that makes up the general noise has behind it a motive, a prepossession, a hope, a fear, a fixed thought forward; perhaps more—a joy, a sorrow, a love, a revenge.

"London appears not to *see itself*. Each individual is conscious of *himself*, but nobody conscious of themselves collectively, except perhaps some poor gaper who stares round with a half-idiotic aspect.

"There is no consciousness here of where anything comes from or goes to—only that it is present.

"In the City. The fiendish precision or mechanism of town-life is what makes it so intolerable to the sick and infirm. Like an acrobat performing on a succession of swinging trapezes, as long as you are at particular points at precise instants, everything glides as if afloat; but if you are not up to time——"

"April 16. News of Matthew Arnold's death which occurred yesterday. . . . The *Times* speaks quite truly of his 'enthusiasm for the nobler & detestation of the meaner elements in humanity'."

"April 19. Scenes in ordinary life. What are insipid at 20 become interesting at 30, and tragic at 40."

"April 21. Dr Quain told me some curious medical stories when we were dining at Mary Jeune's. He said it was a mistake for anyone to have so many doctors as the German Emperor has, because neither feels responsible. Gave an account of Queen Adelaide, who died through her physicians' ignorance of her malady, one of them, Dr Chambers, remarking, when asked why he did not investigate her disorder, 'Damn it, I wasn't going to pull about the Queen.'— she being such a prude that she would never have forgiven him for making an examination that as it proved would have saved her life.

"Mary Jeune says that when she tries to convey some sort of moral or religious teaching to the East-end poor, so as to change their views from wrong to right, it ends by their convincing her that their view is the right one—not by her convincing them."

"April 23. To Alma Tadema's musical afternoon. Heckmann Quartett. The architecture of his house is incomplete without sunlight and warmth. Hence the dripping wintry afternoon without mocked his marble basin and brass steps and quilted blinds and silver apse."

"April 26. Thought in bed last night that Byron's 'Childe Harold' will live in the history of English poetry not so much because of the beauty of parts of it, which is great, but because of its good fortune in being an accretion of descriptive poems by the most fascinating personality in the world—for the English—not a common plebeian, but a romantically wicked noble lord. It affects even Arnold's judgment."

"April 28. A short story of a young man—'who could not go to Oxford'—His struggles and ultimate failure. Suicide. [Probably the germ of *Jude the Obscure*.] There is something [in this] the world ought to be shown, and I am the one to show it to them—though I was not altogether hindered going, at least to Cambridge, and could have gone up easily at five-and-twenty.

"In Regent Street, which commemorates the Prince Regent. It is in the fitness of things that The Promenade of Prostitutes should be here. One can imagine *his shade* stalking up and down every night, smiling approvingly."

"May 13. Lord Houghton tells me today at lunch at Lady Catherine Gaskell's of a young lady who gave a full description of a ball to her neighbour during the Chapel Royal service by calling out at each response in the Litany as many details as she could get in. Also of Lord —— who saves all his old tooth-brushes affectionately."

"The Gaskells said that Lord and Lady Lymington and themselves went to the city in an omnibus, and one of them nearly sat on an Irishwoman's baby. G. apologized, when she exclaimed 'Och, 'twas not you: 'twas the ugly one!' (pointing to Lord L.)."

"Lady C. says that the central position of St. James's Square (where their house is) enables her to see so many more people. When she first comes to Town she feels a perfect lump the first fortnight— she knows nothing of the new phrases, and does not understand the social telegraphy and allusions."

May 28. They went to Paris via London and Calais:—and stayed in the Rue du Commandant Rivière several weeks, noticing on their arrival as they always did "the sour smell of a foreign city".

June 4 and 7. At the Salon. "Was arrested by the sensational picture called The Death of Jezebel by Gabriel Guay, a horrible tragedy, and justly so, telling its story in a flash."

"10. To Longchamp and the Grand Prix de Paris. Roar from the course as I got near. It was Pandemonium: not a blade of grass: half overshoe in dust: the ground covered with halves of white, yellow, and blue tickets: bookmakers with staring names and addresses, in the very mockery of honesty. The starter spoke to the jockeys entirely in English, & most of the cursing and swearing was done in English likewise, & done well. The horses passed in a volley, so close together that it seemed they must be striking each other. Excitement. Cries of 'Vive la France' (a French horse having won)."

"11. To the Embassy. Bon Marché with Em. Walked to l'Etoile in twilight. The enormous arch stood up to its knees in lamplight, dark above against the deep blue of the upper sky. Went under and read some names of victories which were never won."

"12. To see the tombs of St. Denis with E. A lantern at the slit on one side of the vault shows the coffins to us at the opposite slit."

"13. Exhibition of Victor Hugo's manuscripts and drawings. Thence to one of the Correctional Courts: heard two or three trivial cases. Afterwards to the Salle des Conférences."

"14. Sunny morning. View from l'Etoile. Fresh, after rain; air clear. Could see distinctly far away along the Avenue de la Grande Armée—down into the hollow and on to rising ground beyond, where the road tapers to an obelisk standing there. Also could see far along the Avenue Wagram. In the afternoon I went to the Archives Nationales. Found them much more interesting than I had expected. As it was not a public day the attendant showed me round alone which, with the gloomy wet afternoon, made the relics more solemn, so that, mentally, I seemed close to those keys from the Bastille, those letters of the Kings of France, those Edicts, and those corridors of white boxes, each containing one year's shady documents of a past monarchy."

Next day, coming out of the Bourse, he learnt of the death of the Emperor of Germany.

On returning to London Hardy had a rheumatic attack which kept him in bed two or three days, after which they entered lodgings at Upper Phillimore Place, Kensington, where they remained till the third week in July. Walter Pater sometimes called on them from over the way and told them the story of George III anent the row of houses they were living in. These, as is well known, have their fronts ornamented with the stone festooning of their date, and the King would exclaim when returning from Weymouth, "Ah—there are the dish-clouts—now I know I shall soon be home." Acquaintance was renewed with various friends, among them, after a dozen years of silence, Mrs Ritchie (Miss Thackeray), later Lady Ritchie. "Talked of the value of life, and its interest. She admits that her interest in the future lies largely in the fact that she has children, and says that when she calls on L. S[tephen] and his wife she feels like a ghost, who arouses sad feelings in the person visited."

As to the above remark on the value of life, Hardy writes whimsically a day or two later:

"I have attempted many modes [of finding it]. For my part, if there is any way of getting a melancholy satisfaction out of life it lies in dying, so to speak, before one is out of the flesh; by which I mean putting on the manners of ghosts, wandering in their haunts, and taking their views of surrounding things. To think of life as passing away is a sadness; to think of it as past is at least tolerable. Hence even when I enter into a room to pay a simple morning call I have unconsciously the habit of regarding the scene as if I were a spectre not solid enough to influence my environment, only fit to behold and say, as another spectre said: 'Peace be unto you'."

"July 3. Called on [Eveline] Lady Portsmouth with Em. Found her alone and stayed to tea. Looked more like a model countess than ever I have seen her do before, her black brocaded silk fitting her well and suiting her eminently. She is not one of those marble people who can be depended upon for their appearance at a particular moment, but like all mobile characters uncertain as to aspect. She is one of the few, very few, women of her own rank for whom I would make a sacrifice: a woman too of talent, part of whose talent consists in concealing that she has any."

"July 5. A letter lies on the red velvet cover of the table; staring up by reason of the contrast. I cover it over, that it may not hit my eyes so hard."

"July 7. One o'clock a.m. I got out of bed, attracted by the never-ending procession [of market-carts to Covent Garden] as seen from our bedroom windows Phillimore Place. Chains rattle, and each cart cracks under its weighty pyramid of vegetables."

"July 8. A service at St Mary Abbots, Kensington. The red plumes and ribbon in two stylish girls' hats in the foreground match the red robes of the persons round Christ on the Cross in the east window. The pale crucified figure rises up from a parterre of London bonnets and artificial hair-coils, as viewed from the back where I am. The sky over Jerusalem seems to have some connection with the corn-flowers in a fashionable hat that bobs about in front of the city of David. . . . When the congregation rises there is a rustling of silks like that of the Devils' wings in Paradise Lost. Every woman then, even if she had forgotten it before, has a single thought to the folds of her clothes. They pray in the litany as if under enchantment. Their real life is spinning on beneath this apparent one of calm, like the District Railway-trains underground just by—throbbing, rushing, hot, concerned with next week, last week. Could these true scenes in which this congregation is living be brought into church bodily with the personages, there would be a churchful of jostling phantasma-gorias crowded like a heap of soap bubbles, infinitely intersecting, but each seeing only his own. That bald-headed man is surrounded by the interior of the Stock Exchange; that girl by the jeweller's shop in which she purchased yesterday. Through this bizarre world of thought circulates the recitative of the parson—a thin solitary note without cadence or change of intensity—and getting lost like a bee in the clerestory."

"July 9. To 'The Taming of the Shrew'. A spirited unconven-tional performance, revitalizing an old subject. The brutal mediaeval view of the sex which animates the comedy does not bore us by its obsoleteness, the Shrew of Miss Ada Rehan being such a real shrew. Her attitude of sad, impotent resignation, when her husband wears out her endurance, in which she stands motionless and almost unconscious of what is going on around her, was well done. At first she hears the cracks of the whip with indifference; at length she begins to shrink at the sound of them, and when he literally whips the domestics out of the room she hides away. At first not looking at him in his tantrums, she gets to steal glances at him, with an awe-struck arrested attention. The scene in which the sun-and-moon argument comes in contained the best of acting. Drew's aspect of inner humorous opinion, lively eye, and made-up mind, is eminently suited to the husband's character.

"Reading H. James's 'Reverberator'. After this kind of work one feels inclined to be purposely careless in detail. The great novels of the future will certainly not concern themselves with the minutiae of manners. . . . James's subjects are those one could be interested in at moments when there is nothing larger to think of."

"11 July. At the Savile. [Sir] Herbert Stephen declares that he met S——r, [another member of the Club] in Pall Mall a few minutes ago, going away from the direction of the club, and that S——r nodded to him; then arriving quickly at the Club he saw S——r seated in the back room. S——r, who is present during the telling, listens to this story of his wraith, and as H. S. repeats it to the other members, becomes quite uncomfortable at the weirdness of it. H. S. adds that he believes S——r is in the back room still, and S——r says he is afraid to go in to himself."

"13 July. After being in the street:—What was it on the faces of those horses?—Resignation. Their eyes looked at me, haunted me. The absoluteness of their resignation was terrible. When afterwards I heard their tramp as I lay in bed, the ghosts of their eyes came in to me, saying, 'Where is your justice, O man and ruler?'

"Lady Portsmouth told me at a dinner party last night that once she sat between Macaulay and Henry Layard in dining at Lord Lansdowne's, and whenever one of them had got the ear of the table the other turned to her and talked, to show that the absolute vacuity of his rival's discourse had to be filled in somehow with any rubbish at hand.

"Lord Portsmouth says that it was his direct ancestor who went down to Devon in the reign of Queen Elizabeth, raised a levy, sailed to Ireland, conquered Desmond King of Munster (?), cut off his head, and sent it to the Queen."

"14 July. Was much struck with Gladstone's appearance at Flinders Petrie's Egyptian Exhibition. The full curves of his Roman face and his cochin-china-egg complexion was not at all like his pallor when I last saw him, and there was an utter absence of any expression of senility or mental weakness.—We dined at Walter Pater's. Met Miss ——, an Amazon; more, an Atalanta; most, a Faustine. Smokes: Handsome girl: cruel small mouth: she's of the class of interesting women one would be afraid to marry."

Here follow long lists of books read, or looked into, or intended to be read, during the year.

CHAPTER XVII

More Town Friends and a Novel's Dismemberment

1888–1889: *Aet.* 48–49

Returning to Dorchester two days later, he notes down: "Thought of the determination to enjoy. We see it in all nature, from the leaf on the tree to the titled lady at the ball. . . . It is achieved, of a sort, under superhuman difficulties. Like pent-up water it will find a chink of possibility somewhere. Even the most oppressed of men and animals find it, so that out of a thousand there is hardly one who has not a sun of some sort for his soul."

"August 5. To find beauty in ugliness is the province of the poet."

"8. The air is close, the sunshine suddenly disappears, and a bad kind of sea-fog comes up, smelling like a laundry or wash-house."

"19. Sent a story to H. Quilter. By request, for his Magazine, entitled 'A Tragedy of Two Ambitions'."

"21. The literary productions of men of rigidly good family and rigidly correct education mostly treat social conventions and contrivances—the artificial forms of living—as if they were cardinal facts of life.

"Society consists of Characters and No-characters—nine at least of the latter to one of the former."

"Sept. 9. My father says that Dick Facey used to rivet on the fetters of criminals when they were going off by coach (Facey was journeyman for Clare the smith). He was always sent for secretly, that people might not know and congregate at the gaol entrance. They were carried away at night, a stage-coach being specially ordered. One K. of Troytown, on the London Road, a poacher in the great fray at Westwood Barn near Lulworth Castle about 1825, was brought past his own door thus, on his way to transportation: he called to his wife and family; they heard his shout and ran out to bid him good-bye as he sat in chains. He was never heard of again by them.

"T. Voss used to take casts of heads of executed convicts. He took those of Preedy and Stone. Dan Pouncy held the heads while it was being done. Voss oiled the faces, and took them in halves, afterwards making casts from the masks. There was a groove where the rope went, and Voss saw a little blood in the case of Stone, where the skin had been broken,—not in Preedy's."

"September 10. Destitution sometimes reaches the point of grandeur in its pathetic grimness: e.g., as shown in the statement of the lodging-house keeper in the Whitechapel murder:—

" 'He had seen her in the lodging-house as late as half-past one o'clock or two that morning. He knew her as an unfortunate, and that she generally frequented Stratford for a living. He asked her for her lodging-money, when she said, "I have not got it. I am weak and ill, and have been in the infirmary." He told her that she knew the rules, whereupon she went out to get some money.' (*Times* report.)

"O richest City in the world! 'She knew the rules.' "

"September 15. Visited the old White Horse Inn, Maiden Newton. Mullioned windows, queer old bedrooms. Fireplace in the late Perpendicular style. The landlady tells me that the attic was closed up for many years, and that on opening it they found a suit of clothes, supposed to be those of a man who was murdered." [This fine old Tudor inn is now pulled down.]

"September 30. 'The Valley of the Great Dairies'—Froom.

" 'The Valley of the Little Dairies.'—Blackmoor.

"In the afternoon by train to Evershot. Walked to Woolcombe, a property once owned by a—I think the senior—branch of the Hardys. Woolcombe House was to the left of where the dairy now is. On by the lane and path to Bubb-Down. Looking east you see High Stoy and the escarpment below it. The Vale of Blackmoor is almost entirely green, every hedge being studded with trees. On the left you see to an immense distance, including Shaftesbury.

"The decline and fall of the Hardys much in evidence hereabout. An instance: Becky S.'s mother's sister married one of the Hardys of this branch, who was considered to have demeaned himself by the marriage. 'All Woolcombe and Froom Quintin belonged to them at one time,' Becky used to say proudly. She might have added Up-Sydling and Toller Welme. This particular couple had an enormous lot of children. I remember when young seeing the man—tall and thin—walking beside a horse and common spring-trap, and my mother pointing him out to me and saying he represented what was once the leading branch of the family. So we go down, down, down."

"October 7. The besetting sin of modern literature is its insincerity. Half its utterances are qualified, even contradicted, by an aside, and this particularly in morals and religion. When dogma has to be balanced on its feet by such hair-splitting as the late Mr M. Arnold's it must be in a very bad way."

"Oct. 15–21. Has the tradition that Cerne-Abbas men have no whiskers any foundation in the fact of their being descendants of a family or tribe or clan who have not intermarried with neighbours on account of their isolation? They are said to be hot-tempered people.

"Stephen B. says that he has 'never had the nerve' to be a bearer at a funeral. Now his brother George, who has plenty of nerve, has borne many neighbours to their graves.

"If you look beneath the surface of any farce you see a tragedy; and, on the contrary, if you blind yourself to the deeper issues of a tragedy you see a farce.

"My mother says that my [paternal] grandmother told her she was ironing her best muslin gown (then worn by young women at any season) when news came that the Queen of France was beheaded. She put down her iron, and stood still, the event so greatly affecting her mind. She remembered the pattern of the gown so well that she would recognize it in a moment." Hardy himself said that one hot and thundery summer in his childhood she remarked to him: "It was like this in the French Revolution, I remember."

"Dec. 10. . . . He, she, had blundered; but not as the Prime Cause had blundered. He, she, had sinned; but not as the Prime Cause had sinned. He, she, was ashamed and sorry; but not as the Prime Cause would be ashamed and sorry if it knew." (The reference is unexplained.)

Among the letters received by Hardy for the New Year (1889) was one from Mr Gosse, who wrote thanking him for "A Tragedy of Two Ambitions", which he thought one of the most thrilling and most complete stories Hardy had written—"I walked under the moral burden of it for the remainder of the day. . . . I am truly happy— being an old faded leaf and disembowelled bloater and wet rag myself—to find your genius ever so fresh and springing."

They were in London the first week of the year, concerning which Hardy remarks:

"On arriving in London I notice more and more that it (viz. London proper—the central parts) is becoming a vast hotel or caravan, having no connection with Middlesex—whole streets which were not so very long ago mostly of private residences consisting entirely of lodging-houses, and having a slatternly look about them.

"Called on Lady ——. She is a slim girl still, and continually tells her age, and speaks practically of 'before I was married'. Tells humorously of how she and Lord —— her father, who is a nervous man, got to the church too soon, and drove drearily up and down the Thames Embankment till the right time. She has just now the fad of adoring art. When she can no longer endure the ugliness of London she goes down to the National Gallery and sits in front of the great Titian.

"Business seems very dull just now in some shops. Em being unwell, I went to a druggist's for a simple remedy. The master-druggist went and poured out the liquid, while the assistant got the bottle, and the shop-boy stood waiting with string and sealing-wax."

"January 8. To the City. Omnibus horses, Ludgate Hill. The greasy state of the streets caused constant slipping. The poor creatures struggled and struggled but could not start the omnibus. A man next me said: 'It must take all heart and hope out of them! I shall get out.' He did; but the whole remaining selfish twenty-five of us sat on. The horses despairingly got us up the hill at last. I *ought* to have taken off my hat to him and said: 'Sir, though I was not stirred by your humane impulse I will profit by your good example'; and have followed him. If Em had been there she would have done it. I should like to know that man; but we shall never meet again!"

"Jan. 9. At the Old Masters, Royal Academy. Turner's water-colours: each is a landscape *plus* a man's soul. . . . What he paints chiefly is *light as modified by objects*. He first recognizes the imposs-ibility of really reproducing on canvas all that is in a landscape; then gives for that which cannot be reproduced a something else which shall have upon the spectator an approximative effect to that of the real. He said, in his maddest and greatest days: 'What pictorial drug can I dose man with, which shall affect his eyes somewhat in the manner of this reality which I cannot carry to him?'—and set to make such strange mixtures as he was tending towards in 'Rain, Steam and Speed', 'The Burial of Wilkie', 'Agrippina landing with the ashes of Germanicus', 'Approach to Venice', 'Snowstorm and a Steamboat', etc. Hence, one may say, Art is the secret of how to produce by a false thing the effect of a true. . . .

"I am struck by the red glow of Romney's backgrounds, and his red flesh shades. . . . Watteau paints claws for hands. They are unnatural—hideous sometimes. . . . Then the pictures of Sir Joshua, in which middle-aged people sit out of doors without hats on damp stone seats under porticoes, and expose themselves imprudently to draughts and chills, as if they had lost their senses. . . . Besides the above there were also the Holls, and the works of other recent English painters, such as Maclise. . . .

"How Time begins to lift the veil and show us by degrees the truly great men among these, as distinct from the vaunted and the fashionable. The false glow thrown on them by their generation dies down, and we see them as they are."

"Jan. 28. A. P. the landscape painter here. He gave as a reason for living in London & mixing a good deal with people (intellectual I presume) that you can let them do your thinking for you. A practice that will be disastrous to A. P.'s brush, I fear!"

"Feb. 6. (After reading Plato's dialogue 'Cratylus'): A very good way of looking at things would be to regard everything as having an actual or false name, and an intrinsic or true name, to ascertain which all endeavour should be made. . . . The fact is that nearly all things are falsely, or rather inadequately, named."

"Feb. 19. The story of a face which goes through three generations or more, would make a fine novel or poem of the passage of Time. The differences in personality to be ignored." [This idea was to some extent carried out in the novel *The Well-Beloved*, the poem entitled "Heredity", etc.]

"Feb. 26. In time one might get to regard every object, and every action, as composed, not of this or that material, this or that movement, but of the qualities pleasure and pain in varying proportions."

"March 1. In a Botticelli the soul is outside the body, permeating its spectator with its emotions. In a Rubens the flesh is without, and the soul (possibly) within. The very odour of the flesh is distinguishable in the latter."

"March 4. A Village story recalled to me yesterday:—

"Mary L., a handsome wench, had come to B., leaving a lover at A., her native parish. W. K. fell in love with her at the new place. The old lover, who was a shoemaker, smelling a rat, came anxiously to see her, with a present of a dainty pair of shoes he had made. He met her by chance at the pathway stile, but alas, on the arm of the other lover. In the rage of love the two men fought for her till they were out of breath, she looking on and holding both their hats the while; till W. K., wiping his face, said: 'Now, Polly, which of we two do you love best? Say it out straight!' She would not state then, but said she would consider (the hussy!). The young man to whom she had been fickle left her indignantly—throwing the shoes at her and her new lover as he went. She never saw or heard of him again, and accepted the other. But *she kept the shoes, and was married in them.* I knew her well as an old woman."

"March 15. What has been written cannot be blotted. Each new style of novel must be the old with added ideas, not an ignoring and avoidance of the old. And so of religion, and a good many other things!"

"April 5. London. Four million forlorn hopes!"

"April 7. A woeful fact—that the human race is too extremely developed for its corporeal conditions, the nerves being evolved to an activity abnormal in such an environment. Even the higher animals are in excess in this respect. It may be questioned if Nature, or what we call Nature, so far back as when she crossed the line from invertebrates to vertebrates, did not exceed her mission. This planet does not supply the materials for happiness to higher existences. Other planets may, though one can hardly see how."

A day or two later brought him a long and interesting letter from J. Addington Symonds at Davos Platz concerning *The Return of the Native*, which he had just met with and read, and dwelling enthusiastically on "its vigour and its freshness and its charm". The last week in April they went off to London again for a few months, staying at the West Central Hotel till they could find something more permanent, which this year chanced to be two furnished floors in Monmouth Road, Bayswater.

"May 5. Morning. Sunday. To Bow Church Cheapside with Em. The classic architecture, especially now that it has been regilt and painted, makes one feel in Rome. About twenty or thirty people present. When you enter, the curate from the reading-desk and the rector from the chancel almost smile a greeting as they look up in their surplices, so glad are they that you have condescended to visit them in their loneliness."

"That which, socially, is a great tragedy, may be in Nature no alarming circumstance."

"May 12. Evening. Sunday. To St. James's, Westmoreland Street, with Em. Heard Haweis—a small lame figure who could with difficulty climb into the pulpit. His black hair, black beard, hollow cheeks and black gown, made him look like one of the skeletons in the church of the Capuchins, Rome. The subject of his discourse was Cain and Abel, his first proposition being that Cain had excellent qualities, and was the larger character of the twain, though Abel might have been the better man in some things. Yet, he reminded us, good people are very irritating sometimes, and the occasion was probably one of agricultural depression like the present, so that Cain said to himself: 'Tis this year as it was last year, and all my labour wasted!' (titter from the congregation). Altogether the effect was comical. But one sympathised with the preacher, he was so weak, and quite in a perspiration when he had finished."

"May 20. Called on the Alma Tademas. Tadema is like a school-boy, with untidy hair, a sturdy inquiring look, and bustling manner. I like this phase of him better than his man-of-the-world phase. He introduced me to M. Taine, a kindly, nicely trimmed old man with a slightly bent head."

Earlier in the year Hardy had asked one of the Miss Sheridans, a daughter of Mr and Mrs A. Brinsley Sheridan, Hardy's neighbours at Frampton Court, Dorset, if she could sing to him "How oft, Louisa!" the once celebrated song in her ancestor's comic opera *The Duenna*. (It was not a woman's song, by the way.) His literary sense was shocked by her telling him that she had never heard of it, since he himself had sung it as a youth, having in fact been in love with a Louisa himself. Now he was in London he remembered that he had promised it to her, and looked for a copy, but, much to his surprise, to find one seemed beyond his power. At last he called at a second-hand music-shop that used to stand where the Oxford Circus Tube-Station now is, and repeated hopelessly, "How oft, Louisa?" The shop was kept by an old man who was sitting on an office stool in a rusty dress-suit and very tall hat, and at the sound of the words he threw himself back in his seat, spread his arms like an opera-singer, and sang in a withered voice by way of answer:

> "How oft, Louisa, hast thou told,
>> (Nor wilt thou the fond boast disown)
> Thou would'st not lose Antonio's love
>> To reign the partner of a throne!

"Ah, that carries me back to times that will never return!" he added. "Yes; when I was a young man it was my favourite song. As to my having it, why, certainly, it is here *somewhere*. But I could not find it in a week." Hardy left him singing it, promising to return again.

When his shop was pulled down the delightful old man disappeared, and though Hardy searched for him afterwards he never saw him any more.

"May 29. That girl in the omnibus had one of those faces of marvellous beauty which are seen casually in the streets, but never among one's friends. It was perfect in its softened classicality:—a Greek face translated into English. Moreover she was fair, and her hair pale chestnut. Where do these women come from? Who marries them? Who knows them?"

They went to picture-galleries, concerts, French plays, and the usual lunches and dinners during the season; and in June Hardy ran down to Dorchester for a day or two, on which occasion, taking a walk in the meadows, he remarks: "The birds are so passionately happy that they introduce variations into their songs to an outrageous degree—which are not always improvements."

In London anew: "One difference between the manners of the intellectual middle class and of the nobility is that the latter have more flexibility, almost a dependence on their encompassment, as if they were waiting upon future events; while the former are direct, and energetic, and crude, as if they were manufacturing a future to please them."

"June 29. Em had an afternoon party. The same evening we dined at Mrs Jeune's, [Lady St. Helier] meeting the Lord Chief Justice and Lady Coleridge, [Hon.] Evelyn Ashley, Sir George Russell and Lady Russell, Mr Long (painter), Mr Nelson Page (American), and others. Lady Coleridge could honestly claim to be a beauty. Responsive and open in manner. Really fine eyes. She told me about going on circuit, and sitting in court half-an-hour to please her husband, who, if she does not, says that she takes no interest in his duties. When Lord Coleridge and she had left the ladies discussed her age. Mr and Mrs Jeune went on to the Duchess of Abercorn's."

"July 9. Love lives on propinquity, but dies of contact."

"July 14. Sunday. Centenary of the fall of the Bastille. Went to Newton Hall to hear Frederic Harrison lecture on the French Revolution. The audience sang 'The Marseillaise'. Very impressive."

"July 17–23. We lunched here and there this week and earlier, meeting a dozen people at Lady Catherine Gaskell's; Mrs Fawcett and Lord Greenock at Lord Portsmouth's; and Lady Metcalfe at Mrs Reeve's, Rutland Gate, (Reeve has a humorous face, as if copied from a print by Rowlandson). Also met Lady Rothschild at Mrs Jeune's; an amply-membered, pleasant woman, unfashionably dressed in brown silk. She and I talked a good deal—about wit, and the nude in art (of all things). H—— with his underground voice was also there. Also Mallock, in a painfully fashionable frock coat, who would keep talking to Lady —— about 'the Duchess's ball last night'. Miss Amélie Rives was the pretty woman of the party—a fair, pink, golden-haired creature, but not quite ethereal enough, suggesting a flesh-surface too palpably. A girlish, almost childish laugh, showing beautiful young teeth.

"In the afternoon at Macmillan's I talked to Mr Craik, who spoke very justly of what he called 'sane criticism'—instancing John Morley's and Leslie Stephen's.

"Of the people I have met this summer, the lady whose mouth recalls more fully than any other beauty's the Elizabethan metaphor 'Her lips are roses full of snow' (or is it Lodge's?) is Mrs H. T—— whom I talked to at Gosse's dinner."

"July 24. B. Museum:

"Εἰ δέ τι πρεσβύτερον, etc. Soph. Oed. Tyr. 1365 ('and if there be a woe surpassing woes it hath become the portion of Oedipus'— Jebb. Cf. Tennyson: 'a deeper deep')."

About this time Hardy was asked by a writer of some experience in adapting novels for the theatre—Mr J. T. Grein—if he would grant permission for *The Woodlanders* to be so adapted. In his reply he says:

You have probably observed that the ending of the story— hinted rather than stated—is that the heroine is doomed to an unhappy life with an inconstant husband. I could not accentuate this strongly in the book, by reason of the conventions of the libraries, etc. Since the story was written, however, truth to character is not considered quite such a crime in literature as it was formerly; and it is therefore a question for you whether you will accent this ending, or prefer to obscure it.

It appears that nothing arose out of the dramatization, it becoming obvious that no English manager at this date would venture to defy the formalities to such an extent as was required by the novel, in which some of the situations were approximately of the kind afterwards introduced to English playgoers by translations from Ibsen. In fact Hardy, foreseeing this difficulty, had taken as in other cases but little interest in the dramatization, though it is believed to have been a good one.

At the end of the month they gave up their rooms in Bayswater and returned to Dorchester; where during August Hardy settled down daily to writing the new story he had conceived, which was *Tess of the d'Urbervilles*, though it had not as yet been christened. During the month he jots down as a casual thought:

"When a married woman who has a lover kills her husband, she does not really wish to kill the husband; she wishes to kill the situation. Of course in Clytaemnestra's case it was not exactly so, since there was the added grievance of Iphigenia, which half-justified her."

"Sept. 21. For carrying out that idea of Napoleon, the Empress, Pitt, Fox, &c., I feel continually that I require a larger canvas. . . . A spectral tone must be adopted. . . . Royal ghosts. . . . Title: 'A Drama of Kings'."[He did not use it, however; preferring *The Dynasts*.]

"Oct. 13. Three wooden-legged men used to dance a three-handed reel at Broadmayne, so my father says."

In November Leslie Stephen wrote concerning a Dorset character for the *Dictionary of National Biography*, then in full progress under his hands:

> I only beg that you will not get into the Dictionary yourself. You can avoid it by living a couple of years—hardly a great price to pay for the exemption. But I will not answer for my grandson, who will probably edit a supplement.

About the same time Hardy answered some questions by Mr Gosse:

> "Oak-apple day" is exotic; "sic-sac day" or "shic-sac day", being what the peasantry call it.

"Ich." This and kindred words, e.g.—"Ich woll", "er woll", etc. are still used by old people in N. W. Dorset and Somerset (*vide* Gammer Oliver's conversation in "The Woodlanders", which is an attempted reproduction). I heard "Ich" only last Sunday; but it is dying rapidly.

However, the business immediately in hand was the new story *Tess of the d'Urbervilles*, for the serial use of which Hardy had three requests, if not more, on his list; and in October as much of it as was written was offered to the first who had asked for it, the editor of *Murray's Magazine*. It was declined and returned to him in the middle of November virtually on the score of its improper explicitness. It was at once sent on to the second, the editor of *Macmillan's Magazine*, and on the 25th was declined by him for practically the same reason. Hardy would now have much preferred to finish the story and bring it out in volume form only, but there were reasons why he could not afford to do this; and he adopted a plan till then, it is believed, unprecedented in the annals of fiction. This was not to offer the novel intact to the third editor on his list (his experience with the first two editors having taught him that it would be useless to send it to the third as it stood), but to send it up with some chapters or parts of chapters cut out, and instead of destroying these to publish them, or much of them, elsewhere, if practicable, as episodic adventures of anonymous personages (which in fact was done, with the omission of a few paragraphs); till they could be put back in their places at the printing of the whole in volume form. In addition several passages were modified. Hardy had never the slightest respect for his own writing, particularly in prose, and he carried out this unceremonious concession to conventionality without compunction and with cynical amusement, knowing the novel was moral enough and to spare. But the work was sheer drudgery, the modified passages having to be written in coloured ink, that the originals might be easily restored, and he frequently asserted that it would have been almost easier for him to write a new story altogether. Hence the labour brought no profit. He resolved to get away from the supply of family fiction to magazines as soon as he conveniently could do so.

However, the treatment was a complete success, and the mutilated novel was accepted by the editor of the *Graphic*, the third editor on Hardy's list, and an arrangement come to for beginning it in the pages of that paper in July 1891. It may be mentioned that no complaint of impropriety in its cut-down form was made by readers, except by one gentleman with a family of daughters, who thought the blood-stain on the ceiling indecent—Hardy could never understand why.

"Dec. 1. It was the custom at Stinsford down to 1820 or so to take a corpse to church on the Sunday of the funeral, and let it remain in the nave through the service, after which the burial took place. The people liked the custom, and always tried to keep a corpse till Sunday. The funeral psalms were used for the psalms of the day, and the funeral chapter for the second lesson."

"Dec. 13. Read in the papers that Browning died at Venice yesterday. Buried in Westminster Abbey Dec. 31.

" 'Incidents in the development of a soul: little else is worth study.'—Browning.

"What the *Athenæum* says is true, though not all the truth, that intellectual subtlety is the disturbing element in his art."

Among other poems written about this time was the one called "At Middle-field Gate in February", describing the field-women of the author's childhood. On the present writer once asking Hardy the names of those he calls the "bevy now underground", he said they were Unity Sargent, Susan Chamberlain, Esther Oliver, Emma Shipton, Anna Barrett, Ann West, Elizabeth Hurden, Eliza Trevis, and others, who had been young women about twenty when he was a child.

CHAPTER XVIII

Observations on People and Things

1890: *Aet.* 49–50

"Jan. 5. Looking over old Punches. Am struck with the frequent wrong direction of satire & of commendation, when seen by the light of later days."

"Jan. 29. I have been looking for God 50 years, and I think that if he had existed I should have discovered him. As an external personality, of course—the only true meaning of the word."

"March—A staid, worn, weak man at the railway station. His back, his legs, his hands, his face, were longing to be out of the world. His brain was not longing to be, because, like the brain of most people, it was the last part of his body to realize a situation.

"In the train on the way to London. Wrote the first four or six lines of 'Not a line of her writing have I'. It was a curious instance of sympathetic telepathy. The woman whom I was thinking of—a cousin—was dying at the time, and I quite in ignorance of it. She died six days later. The remainder of the piece was not written till after her death."

"March 15. With E. to a crush at the Jeunes' to meet the Duke and Duchess of Teck. Young Princess Mary also there. Duchess in black velvet with long black sleeves and a few diamonds. She bears a likeness to the Queen. The daughter is a pretty young woman in skim-milk-blue muslin, [afterwards Queen Mary.] Lady Burdett Coutts was in a head-dress that was a castellated façade of diamonds;

she has strongly marked features. Met Mrs T. and her great eyes in a corner of the rooms, as if washed up by the surging crowd. The most beautiful woman present. . . . But these women! If put into rough wrappers in a turnip-field, where would their beauty be?

"At lunch at Mary Jeune's next day I found she had a cough and feverish flush, though she was as bright as ever. She told me that at the end of her reception it seemed as if she had a red-hot ball in her throat."

He observes later in respect of such scenes as these: "Society, *collectively*, has neither seen what any ordinary person can see, read what every ordinary person has read, nor thought what every ordinary person has thought."

"March–April:—

"Altruism, or The Golden Rule, or whatever 'Love your Neighbour as Yourself' may be called, will ultimately be brought about I think by the pain we see in others reacting on ourselves, as if we and they were a part of one body. Mankind, in fact, may be, and possibly will be, viewed as members of one corporeal frame.

"Tories will often do by way of exception to their principles more extreme acts of democratism or broad-mindedness than Radicals do by rule—such as help on promising plebeians, tolerate wild beliefs, etc.

"Art consists in so depicting the common events of life as to bring out the features which illustrate the author's idiosyncratic mode of regard; making old incidents and things seem as new."

"Easter. Sir George Douglas came. Went to Barnes's grave with him; next day to Portland. Lunched at the Mermaid. Next day Mrs Algernon Sheridan, the Misses Fetherstonhaugh, Mr R. D. Thornton, &c., came to lunch. Douglas left.

"In an article on Ibsen in the *Fortnightly* the writer says that his manner is wrong. That the drama, like the novel, should not be for edification. In this I think the writer errs. It should be so, but the edified should not perceive the edification. Ibsen's edifying is too obvious."

"April 26.—View the Prime Cause or Invariable Antecedent as 'It' and recount Its doings." [This was done in *The Dynasts*.]

In May the Hardys were again resident in London, and went their customary round of picture-viewing, luncheons, calls, dinners, and receptions. At the Academy he reminds himself of old Academy exhibitions, e.g., the years in which there was a rail round Frith's pictures, and of the curious effect upon an observer of the fashionable crowd—seeming like people moving about under enchantment, or as somnambulists. At an evening service at St. George's, Hanover Square, "everything looks the Modern World: the electric light and old theology seem strange companions; and the sermon was as if addressed to native tribes of primitive simplicity, and not to the Nineteenth-Century English." Coming out of church he went into the Criterion for supper, where, first going to the second floor, he stumbled into a room whence proceeded "low laughter and murmurs, the light of lamps with pink shades; where the men were all in evening clothes, ringed and studded, and the women much uncovered in the neck and heavily jewelled, their glazed and lamp-blacked eyes wandering". He descended and had his supper in the grill-room.

"May 9. MS. of 'A Group of Noble Dames' sent to *The Graphic* as promised.

"In the streets I see patient hundreds, labouring on, and boxes on wheels packed with men and women. There are charcoal trees in the squares. A man says: 'When one is half-drunk London seems a wonderfully enjoyable place, with its lamps, and cabs moving like fire-flies.' Yes, man has done more with his materials than God has done with his.

"A physician cannot cure a disease, but he can change its mode of expression."

"May 15. Coming home from seeing Irving in 'The Bells'. Between 11 and 12. The 4,000,000 suggest their existence now, when one sees the brilliancy about Piccadilly Circus and discerns the kiln-dried features around."

At Mr Gosse's this month they met Miss Balestier—an attractive and thoughtful young woman on her first visit to England from America, who remarked to him that it was so reposeful over here: "In America you feel at night, 'I must be quick and sleep; there is not much time to give to it'." She afterwards became Mrs Rudyard Kipling. About the same date Hardy also met—it is probable for the first time—Mr Kipling himself. "He talked about the East, and he well said that the East is the world, both in numbers and in experiences. It has passed through our present bustling stages, and has become quiescent. He told curious details of Indian life."

Hardy remarks that June 2 is his fiftieth birthday: and during the month went frequently to the Savile Club, sometimes dining there with acquaintances, among others J. H. Middleton the friend of William Morris. Hardy used to find fault with Middleton as having no sense of life as such; as one who would talk, for instance, about bishops' copes and mitres with an earnest, serious, anxious manner, as if there were no cakes and ale in the world, or laughter and tears, or human misery beyond tears. His sense of art had caused him to lose all sense of relativity, and of art's subsidiary relation to existence.

This season also Hardy seems to have had a humour for going the round of the music-halls, and pronounces upon the beauties "whose lustrous eyes and pearly countenances show that they owe their attractions to art", that they are seldom well-formed physically; notes the "round-hatted young men gaping at the stage, with receding chins and rudimentary mouths"; and comments upon the odd fact that though there were so many obvious drunkards around him, the character on the stage which always gave the most delight was that of a drunkard imitated. At Bizet's opera of *Carmen* he was struck, as he had been struck before, with the manner in which people conducted themselves on the operatic stage; that of being "possessed, maudlin, distraught, as if they lived on a planet whose atmosphere was intoxicating". At a ballet at the Alhambra he noticed "the air of docile obedience on the faces of some of the dancing women, a passive resignation like that of a plodding horse, as if long accustomed to correction. Also marks of fatigue. The morality of actresses, dancers, &c., cannot be judged by the same standard as that of people who lead slower lives. Living in a throbbing atmosphere they are perforce throbbed by it in spite of themselves. We should either put down these places altogether because of their effect upon the performers, or forgive the performers as irresponsibles. . . . The Première Danseuse strokes each calf with the sole of her other foot like a fly,—on her mouth hanging a perpetual smile."

"June 23. Called on Arthur Locker [editor] at The Graphic office in answer to his letter. He says he does not object to the stories [*A Group of Noble Dames*] but the Directors do. Here's a pretty job! Must smooth down those Directors somehow I suppose."

In the same month he met Mr (afterwards Sir) H. M. Stanley the explorer at a dinner given by the publishers of his travels. Hardy does not seem to have been much attracted by his personality. He observed that Stanley was shorter than himself, "with a disdainful curve on his mouth and look in his eye which would soon become resentment". He made a speech in the worst taste, in Hardy's opinion, being to the effect that everybody who had had to do with producing his book was, rightly, delighted with the honour. At the same dinner Hardy talked to Du Chaillu, who had also spoken a few words. Hardy asked him: "Why didn't you claim more credit for finding those dwarfs?" The good-natured Du Chaillu said with a twinkle: "Noh, noh! It is *his* dinner." Hardy also made the acquaintance of the Bishop of Ripon at that dinner, from what he says: "He [the Bishop] has a nice face—a sort of ingenuous archness in it—as if he would be quite willing to let supernaturalism down easy if he could."

At the police courts, where just at this time he occasionally spent half an hour, being still compelled to get novel-padding, he noticed that "the public" appeared to be mostly represented by grimy gentlemen who had had previous experience of the courts from a position in the dock: that there were people sitting round an anteroom of the courts as if waiting for the doctor; that the character of the witness usually deteriorated under cross-examination; and that the magistrate's spectacles as a rule endeavoured to flash out a strictly just manner combined with as much generosity as justice would allow.

On the last day of the month he wound up his series of visits to London entertainments and law-offices with the remark, "Am getting tired of investigating life at music-halls and police-courts". About the same time he lost his friend Lord Carnarvon, who had written with prophetic insight when proposing him for the Athenæum that it would have been better if his proposer had been a younger man. Before leaving London he met Miss Ada Rehan, for whom he had a great liking, and, in some of her parts, admiration, that of the Shrew being of course one of them. He says of her: "A kindly natured, winning woman with really a heart. Em is quite in love with her. I fear she is wearing herself out with too hard work." Two days later they were present at the Lyceum to see her as Rosalind in *As You Like It*. She was not so real—indeed could not be—in the character as in *The Shrew*. Before starting Hardy wrote: "Am going with E. to see Rosalind, after not seeing her for more than twenty years. This time she is composed of Ada Rehan." After going he added: "At the end of the second act I went round, and found her alone, in a highly strung throbbing state—and rather despondent. 'O yes—it goes smoothly,' she said. 'But I am in a whirlwind. . . . Well, it is an old thing, and Mr Daly liked to produce it!' I endeavoured to assure her that it was going to be satisfactory, and perhaps succeeded, for in the remaining acts she played full of spirit." It is possible that the dramatic poem entitled "The Two Rosalinds" was suggested by this performance combined with some other; but there is no certainty about this, and dates and other characteristics do not quite accord.

Mrs Hardy had to leave London shortly after, on account of the illness and death of her father; but her husband had promised to write an Epilogue to be spoken by Miss Rehan at a performance on behalf of Mrs Jeune's Holiday Fund for Children. So he remained in London till he had written it, and it had been duly delivered. He did not go himself to the performance, but in the evening of the same day was present at a debate at the St. James's Hall between Messrs Hyndman and Bradlaugh, in which he was much struck by the extraordinary force in the features of the latter.

"July 24. Mary Jeune delighted with the verses: says Miss Rehan's hand shook so much when she read them that she seemed scarcely able to follow them."

"August 5.——Reflections on Art. Art is a changing of the actual proportions and order of things, so as to bring out more forcibly than might otherwise be done that feature in them which appeals most strongly to the idiosyncrasy of the artist. The changing, or distortion, may be of two kinds: (1) The kind which increases the sense of vraisemblance: (2) That which diminishes it. (1) is high art: (2) is low art.

"High art may choose to depict evil as well as good, without losing its quality. Its choice of evil, however, must be limited by the sense of worthiness." A continuation of the same note was made a little later, and can be given here:

"Art is a disproportioning—(i.e., distorting, throwing out of proportion)—of realities, to show more clearly the features that matter in those realities, which, if merely copied or reported inventorially, might possibly be observed, but would more probably be overlooked. Hence 'realism' is not Art."

"August 8 to 17. With E. to Weymouth and back. Alfred Parsons, R.A., came. Went to see some Sir Joshuas and Pinturicchios belonging to Pearce-Edgcumbe. Then drove to Weymouth over Ridgeway Hill with Parsons. Lunch at the Royal." This was the Old Royal Hotel, now pulled down, where George III and his daughters had used to dance at the town assemblies, a red cord dividing the royal dancers from the townspeople. The sockets for the standards bearing the cord were still visible in the floor while the building was standing.

Later in this month of August Hardy started with his brother for
Paris by way of Southampton and Havre, leaving the former port at
night, when "the Jersey boat and ours were almost overwhelmed by
the enormous bulk of the 'Magdalena' (Brazil and River Plate.)—
the white figure of her at the ship's head stretching into the blue-
black sky above us". The journey was undertaken by Hardy solely
on his brother's account and they merely went the usual round of
sight-seeing. As was the case with Hardy almost always, a strangely
bizarre effect was noticed by him at the Moulin Rouge—in those
days a very popular place of entertainment. As everybody knows, or
knew, it was close to the cemetery of Montmartre, being, it seems,
only divided therefrom by a wall and erection or two, and as he stood
somewhere in the building looking down at the young women
dancing the *cancan*, and grimacing at the men, it appears that he
could see through some back windows over their heads to the last
resting-place of so many similar gay Parisians silent under the
moonlight, and, as he notes, to near the grave of Heinrich Heine.

Coming back towards Havre he sees "A Cleopatra in the railway
carriage. Her French husband sits opposite, and seems to study her;
to keep wondering why he married her; and why she married him.
She is a good-natured amative creature by her voice, and her heavy
moist lips."

The autumn was passed in the country, visiting and entertaining
neighbours, and attending garden-parties. In September to their
great grief their watch-dog "Moss" died—an affectionate retriever
whose grave can still be seen at Max Gate.

In the latter part of this year, having finished adapting *Tess of the
d'Urbervilles* for the serial issue, he seems to have dipped into a good
many books—mostly the satirists: including Horace, Martial,
Lucian, "the Voltaire of Paganism", Voltaire himself, Cervantes,
Le Sage, Molière, Dryden, Fielding, Smollett, Swift, Byron, Heine,
Carlyle, Thackeray, *Satires and Profanities* by James Thomson, and
Weismann's *Essays on Heredity*.

In December, staying in London, Hardy chanced to find himself
in political circles for a time, though he never sought them. At one
house he was a fellow-guest with Mr (afterwards Lord) Goschen,
then Chancellor of the Exchequer, and the "I forgot Goschen" story
was still going about. At another house just afterwards he chanced to
converse with the then Dowager Duchess of Marlborough, Lord
Randolph Churchill's mother: "She is a nice warm-feeling woman,
and expressed her grief at what had happened to her son, though her

hostess had told her flatly it was his own doing. She deplores that young men like —— should stand in the fore-front of the Tory party, and her son should be nowhere. She says he has learnt by bitter experience, and would take any subordinate position the Government might offer him. Poor woman—I was sorry for her, as she really suffers about it. Parnell, however, was the main thing talked about, and not Randolph.”

“Dec. 4. I am more than ever convinced that persons are successively various persons, according as each special strand in their characters is brought uppermost by circumstances.”

“Dec 8 onwards. Lodging at the Jeunes. Lord Rowton, who is great on lodging-houses, says I am her ‘dosser’.”

“Dec. 18. Mr E. Clodd this morning gives an excellently neat answer to my question why the superstitions of a remote Asiatic and a Dorset labourer are the same;—‘The attitude of man’, he says, ‘at corresponding levels of culture, before like phenomena, is pretty much the same, your Dorset peasants representing the persistence of the barbaric idea which confuses persons and things, and founds wide generalizations on the slenderest analogies.’

“(This ‘barbaric idea which confuses persons and things’ is, by the way, also common to the highest imaginative genius—that of the poet.)”

“Christmas Day.—While thinking of resuming ‘the viewless wings of poesy’ before dawn this morning, new horizons seemed to open, and worrying pettinesses to disappear.

“Heard today an old country tradition; that if a woman goes off her own premises before being churched,—e.g., crosses a road that forms the boundary of her residence—she may be made to do penance, or be excommunicated. I cannot explain this, but it reminds me of what old Mr Hibbs of Bere Regis told me lately; that a native of that place, now ninety, says he remembers a young woman doing penance in Bere Church for singing scandalous songs about ‘a great lady’. The girl stood in a white sheet while she went through ‘the service of penance’, whatever that was.

“Also heard another curious story. Mil [Amelia] C—— had an illegitimate child by the parish doctor. She christened him all the doctor’s names, which happened to be a mouthful—Frederick Washington Ingen—and always called him by the three names complete. Moreover the doctor had a squint, and to identify him still more fully as the father she hung a bobbin from the baby’s cap between his eyes, and so trained him to squint likewise.”

Next day they lunched with a remote cousin of Hardy's on the maternal side—Dr Christopher Childs, M. A., of Weymouth—to meet his brother and sister-in-law Mr and Mrs Borlase Childs on a visit from Cornwall, and heard from Borlase Childs (whose grandfather had married into the Borlase family) some traditions of his and Hardy's common ancestors, on which Hardy remarks: "The Christopher Childs, brother of my great-grandmother, who left Dorset, was a Jacobite, which accounted for the fall in their fortunes. There is also a tradition—that I had heard before from my mother—that one of the family added the 's' to the name, and that it was connected with the Josiah Child who founded Child's Bank, and with the family of Lord Jersey. I doubt the first statement, and have no real evidence of the latter."

"New Year's Eve. Looked out of doors just before twelve, and was confronted by the toneless white of the snow spread in front, against which stood the row of pines breathing out: "Tis no better with us than with the rest of creation, you see!' I could not hear the church bells."

CHAPTER XIX

The Novel "Tess" Restored and Published

1891: *Aet.* 50–51

At the beginning of January he was at home arranging *A Group of Noble Dames* for publication in a volume. He was also in London a part of the month, where he saw "what is called sunshine up here—a red-hot bullet hanging in a livid atmosphere—reflected from window-panes in the form of bleared copper eyes, and inflaming the sheets of plate glass with smears of gory light. A drab snow mingled itself with liquid horsedung, and in the river puddings of ice moved slowly on. The steamers were moored, with snow on their gangways. A captain, in sad solitude, smoked his pipe against the bulk-head of the cabin stairs. The lack of traffic made the water like a stream through a deserted metropolis. In the City George Peabody sat comfortably in his easy chair, with snow on the folds of his ample waistcoat, the top of his bare head, and shoulders, and knees."

After seeing Irving at the Lyceum, and admiring the staging: "But, after all, scenic perfection such as this only banishes one plane further back the jarring point between illusion and disillusion. You must have it *somewhere*, and begin calling in 'make believe' forthwith, and it may as well be soon as late—immediate as postponed —and no elaborate scenery be attempted.

"I don't care about the fashionable first night at a play: it is so insincere, meretricious; the staginess behind the footlights seems to flow over upon the audience."

On the Sunday following a number of people dined at the house where Hardy was staying. "The Marchioness of Tweeddale looked well in geranium red. Presently Ellen Terry arrived—diaphanous—a sort of balsam or sea-anemone, without shadow. Also Irving, Sir Henry Thompson, Evelyn Ashley, Lady Dorothy [Nevill], Justin McCarthy, and many others. Ellen Terry was like a machine in which, if you press a spring, all the works fly open. E. Ashley's laugh is like a clap, or report; it was so loud that it woke the children asleep on the third floor. Lady Dorothy said she collected death's-heads—(what did she mean?). Ashley told me about his electioneering experiences. The spectacle of another guest—a Judge of the Supreme Court—telling broad stories with a broad laugh in a broad accent, after the ladies had gone, reminded one of Baron Nicholson of 'Judge-and-Jury' fame. 'Tom' Hughes and Miss Hughes came in after dinner. Miss Hilda Gorst said that at dinner we made such a noise at our end of the table that at her end they wondered what we had to amuse us so much. (That's how it always seems.) . . . A great crush of people afterwards, till at one o'clock they dwindled away, leaving nothing but us, blank, on the wide polished floor."

At the end of the month he and his wife were at a ball at Mrs Sheridan's at Frampton Court, Dorset, where he saw a friend of his "waltzing round with a face of ambition, not of slightest pleasure, as if he were saying to himself 'this has to be done'. We are all inveterate joy-makers: some do it more successfully than others; and the actual fabrication is hardly pleasure."

"Feb: 10. Newman, & Carlyle. The former's was a feminine nature, which first decides, & then finds reasons for having decided. He was an enthusiast with the absurd reputation of a logician and reasoner. Carlyle was a poet with the reputation of a philosopher. Neither was truly a *thinker*."

On the 21st Hardy notes that Mrs Hardy rode on horse-back for what turned out to be the last time in her life. It was to Mrs Sheridan's, Frampton, and a train crossed a bridge overhead, causing the mare to rear; but happily not throwing her rider. Very few horses could.

In March they were again in London, and attended a party at Mrs Jeune's to meet the Prince and Princess Christian and their two daughters, but do not seem to have done anything beyond this. A deep snow came on shortly after, but they had got home. It was in drifts:

"Sculptured, scooped, gouged, pared, trowelled, moulded, by the wind. Em says it is architectural. . . . A person aged 50 is an old man in winter and a young man in summer. . . . Was told by J. A. of a poor young fellow who is dying of consumption, so that he has to sit up in the night, and to get up because he cannot sleep. Yet he described to my informant that one night he had such a funny dream of pigs knocking down a thatcher's ladder that he lay awake laughing uncontrollably."

In the same month Hardy erected what he called "The Druid Stone" on the lawn at Max Gate. This was a large block they discovered about three feet underground in the garden, and the labour of getting it from the hole where it had lain for perhaps two thousand years was a heavy one even for seven men with levers and other appliances.—"It was a primitive problem in mechanics, and the scene was such a one as may have occurred in building the Tower of Babel." Round the stone, which had been lying flat, they had found a quantity of ashes and half charred bones.

Though Hardy was at this time putting the finishing touches to *Tess* he was thinking of "A Bird's-Eye View of Europe at the beginning of the nineteenth century. . . . It may be called 'A Drama of the Times of the First Napoleon'." He does not appear to have done more than think of it at this date.

In April he was at a morning performance at the old Olympic Theatre of that once popular play *The Stranger* by Kotzebue; and he "thought of the eyes and ears that had followed the acting first and last, including Thackeray's". Miss Winifred Emery was Mrs Haller on this occasion. During his time in London he notes the difference between English and French stage-dancing; "The English girls dance as if they had learned dancing; the French as if dancing had produced them." He also while in Town dined at the Lushingtons' "and looked at the portrait of Lushington's father who had known Lady Byron's secret". He went to hear Spurgeon preach, for the first and last time. As Spurgeon died soon after he was glad he had gone, the preacher having been a great force in his day, though it had been spent for many years. He witnessed the performance of *Hedda Gabler* at the Vaudeville, on which he remarks that it seems to him that the rule for staging nowadays should be to have no scene which would not be physically possible in the time of acting. [An idea carried out years after in *The Queen of Cornwall*.]

The Hardys were now as usual looking for a place in which to spend three or four months in London. Much as they disliked handling other people's furniture, taking on their breakages, cracks, and stains, and paying for them at the end of the season as if they had made them themselves, there was no help for it in their inability to afford a London house or flat all the year round. "The dirty house-fronts, leaning gate-piers, rusty gates, broken bells, Doré monstrosities of womankind who showed us the rooms, left Em nearly fainting, and at one place she could not stay for the drawing-room floor to be exhibited." They found a flat at last in Mandeville Place, just about the time that Hardy learnt of his being elected to the Athenæum Club by the Committee under Rule 2.

"April 28. Talking to Kipling today at the Savile he said that he once as an experiment took the ideas of some mature writer or speaker (on Indian politics, I think,) and translating them into his own language used them as his. They were pronounced to be the crude ideas of an immature boy."

The Royal Academy this year struck Hardy as containing some good colouring but no creative power, and that as visitors went by names only, the new geniuses, even if there were any, were likely to be overlooked. He recalled in respect of the fair spring and summer landscapes that "They were not pictures of *this* spring and summer, although they seem to be so. All this green grass and fresh leafage perished yesterday; after withering and falling it is gone like a dream."

In the Gallery of the English Art Club: "If I were a painter I would paint a picture of a room as viewed by a mouse from a chink under the skirting."

Hardy's friend Dr (afterwards Sir) Joshua Fitch took him over Whitelands Training College for schoolmistresses, where it was the custom in those days, and may be now, to choose a May Queen every year, a custom originated by Ruskin. Hardy did not, however, make any observation on this, but merely: "A community of women, especially young women, inspires not reverence but protective tenderness in the breast of one who views them. Their belief in circumstances, in convention, in the rightness of things which you know to be not only wrong but damnably wrong, makes the heart ache, even when they are waspish and hard. . . . You feel how entirely the difference of their ideas from yours is of the nature of misunderstanding. . . . There is much that is pathetic about these girls, and I wouldn't have missed the visit for anything. How far nobler in its aspirations is the life here than the life of those I met at the crush two nights back!"

Piccadilly at night.—"A girl held a long-stemmed narcissus to my nose as we went by each other. At the Circus among all the wily crew of harlots there was a little innocent family standing waiting, I suppose for an omnibus. How pure they looked! A man on a stretcher, with a bloody bandage round his head, was wheeled past by two policemen, stragglers following. Such is Piccadilly."

He used to see Piccadilly under other aspects however, for the next day, Sunday, he attended the service at St. James's—as he did off and on for many years—because it was the church his mother had been accustomed to go to when as a young woman she was living for some months in London. "The preacher said that only five per cent of the inhabitants entered a church, according to the Bishop of London. On coming out there was a drizzle across the electric lights, and the paper-boys were shouting, not, 'Go to church!' but, 'Weenaw of the French Oaks!'"

Next day—wet—at the British Museum: "Crowds parading and gaily traipsing round the mummies, thinking to-day is for ever, and the girls casting sly glances at young men across the swathed dust of Mycerinus [?]. They pass with flippant comments the illuminated MSS.—the labours of years—and stand under Rameses the Great, joking. Democratic government may be justice to man, but it will probably merge in proletarian, and when these people are our masters it will lead to more of this contempt, and possibly be the utter ruin of art and literature! . . . . Looking, when I came out, at the Oxford Music Hall, an hour before the time of opening, there was already a queue."

"May 3. Sunday. Em & I lunch at the Jeunes' to see the house they have just moved into—79 Harley St. Sun came in hot upon us through back windows, the blinds not being yet up. Frederic Harrison called afterwards. He is leaving London to live in the country."

During this month of May he was much impressed by a visit paid with his friend Dr (later Sir) T. Clifford Allbutt, then a Commissioner in Lunacy, to a large private lunatic asylum, where he had intended to stay only a quarter of an hour, but became so interested in the pathos of the cases that he remained the greater part of the day. He talked to "the gentleman who was staying there of his own will, to expose the devices of the Commissioners; to the old man who offers snuff to everybody; to the scholar of high literary aims, as sane in his conversation as any of us; to the artist whose great trouble was that he could not hear the birds sing; 'which as you will see, Mr Hardy, is hard on a man of my temperament'; and, on the women's side, listened to their stories of their seduction; to the Jewess who sang to us; to the young woman who, with eyes brimming with reproach, said to the doctor, 'When are you going to let me out of this? [Hardy appealed for a re-examination of her, which was done afterwards.] Then came the ladies who thought themselves queens—less touching cases, as they were quite happy,—one of them, who was really a Plantagenet by descent, perversely insisted on being considered a Stuart. All the women seemed prematurely dried, faded, *flétries*."

In June he visited Stockwell Training College. "A pretty custom among the girls here is that of each senior student choosing *a daughter* from the list of junior girls who are coming. The senior is *mother* to the daughter for the whole year, and looks after her. Sometimes the pair get fond of each other; at other times not. I gather that they are chosen blindly before arrival, from the names only. There must be singular expectancies, confrontings, and excitements resulting therefrom."

In July he took Mrs Hardy to the balcony of the Athenæum Club to see the German Emperor William II pass to the City; the next day he met W. E. Henley at the Savile. "He is paler, & his once brown locks are getting iron gray": and the day after they had a surprise visit at their flat from Lady Camilla Gurdon and Sir Brampton, whom they thought in the country. "She came bounding in, in her old spontaneous way. She is still Raffaelesque, but paler." On the 13th, lunching at Lady Wynford's, Grosvenor Square, Hardy discovered, or thought he did, that the ceiling of the drawing-room contained oval paintings by Angelica Kauffmann, and that the house was built by the Adams; "I was amused by Ld. Wynford, who told me he would not live in Dorset for £50,000 a year, and wanted me to smoke cigarettes made of tobacco from Lebanon—'same as smoked by Laurence Oliphant'. Wynford's nose is two sides of a spherical triangle in profile." In the same week, on a visit with his wife to G. F. Watts the painter, he was much struck with his host; "that old small man with a grey coat and black velvet skull-cap, who, when he saw one of his picture-frames pressing against a figure on canvas, moved it away gently, as if the figure could feel."

Dining at the Milnes-Gaskells' in Hereford Gardens Hardy judged that Lady Catherine had at this date "less of Raffaelle, and more of Rubens than her sister Camilla, with a dash of coquetry and pride added; also quite a 'Tess' mouth and eyes: with these two beauties she can afford to be indifferent about the remainder of her face. She told me that the ———s of Newstead have buried the skulls that Byron used to drink from, but that the place seems to throw 'a sort of doom on the family'. I then told her of the tragic Damers of the last century, who owned Abbey property, and thought she rather shrank from what I said; I afterwards remembered to my dismay that her own place was an Abbey." Hardy, however, found later that this was only a moment's mood, she being as free from superstitions as any woman. At Max Gate there are still growing violets sent by her years ago from Wenlock.

"19 July. Note the weight of a landau and pair, the coachman in his grey great-coat, footman ditto. All this mass of matter is moved along with brute force and clatter through a street congested and obstructed, to bear the *petite* figure of the owner's young wife in violet velvet and silver trimming, slim, small; who could be easily carried under a man's arm, and who, if held up by the hair and slipped out of her clothes, carriage, etc. etc., aforesaid, would not be much larger than a skinned rabbit, and of less use.

"At Mary Jeune's lunch to-day sat between a pair of beauties.— Mrs A. G——— with her violet eyes, was the more seductive; Mrs R. C——— the more vivacious. The latter in yellow: the former in pale brown, and more venust and warm-blooded than Mrs C———, who is large-eyed, somewhat slight, with quick impulsive motions, and who neglects the dishes and the coffee because possessed by some idea." At another luncheon or dinner at this time "the talk was entirely political—of when the next election would be—of the probable Prime Minister—of ins and outs—of Lord This and the Duke of That—everything except the people for whose existence alone these politicians exist. Their welfare is never once thought of."

The same week, "After a day of headache, went to I———'s Hotel to supper. This is one of the few old taverns remaining in London, whose frequenters after theatre-closing know each other, and talk across from table to table. The head waiter is called William. There is always something homely when the waiter is called William. He talks of his affairs to the guests, as the guests talk of theirs to him. He has whiskers of the rare old mutton-chop pattern, and a manner of confidence. He has shaved so many years that his face is of a bluish soap-colour, and if wetted and rubbed would raise a lather of itself. . . . Shakespeare is largely quoted at the tables; especially

'How long will a man lie i' the earth ere he rot.' Theatrical affairs are discussed neither from the point of view of the audience, nor of the actors, but from a third point—that of the recaller of past appearances.

"Old-fashioned country couples also come in, their fathers having recommended the tavern from recollections of the early part of the century. They talk on innocently-friendly terms with the theatrical young men, and handsome ladies who enter with them as their 'husbands' after the play."

They annexed to their London campaign this year a visit to Sir Brampton and Lady Camilla Gurdon at Grundesburgh Hall, Suffolk—a house standing amid green slopes timbered with old oaks. The attraction was its possession of the most old-fashioned and delightful—probably Elizabethan—garden with high buttressed walls that Hardy had ever seen, which happily had been left unimproved and unchanged, owing to the Hall having been used merely as a farm-house for a century or two, and hence neglected. The vegetables were planted in the middle of square plots surrounded by broad green alleys, and screened by thickets and palisades of tall flowers, "so that one does not know any vegetables are there".

Hardy spent a good deal of time in August and the autumn correcting *Tess of the d'Urbervilles* for its volume form, which process consisted in restoring to their places the passages and chapters of the original MS. that had been omitted from the serial publication. That Tess should put on the jewels was Mrs Hardy's suggestion. The name "Talbothays", given to the dairy, was based on that of a farm belonging to his father, which, however, had no house on it at that time.

In September he and his wife paid a visit to his friend Sir George Douglas at Springwood Park, in fulfilment of a long promise, passing on their way north by the coastline near Holy Isle or Lindisfarne, at that moment glowing reddish on a deep blue sea under the evening sun, with all the romance of *Marmion* about its aspect. It was the place which he afterwards urged Swinburne to make his headquarters, as being specially suited for him—a Northumbrian—an idea which Swinburne was much attracted by, though he owned that "to his great shame" he had never been on the isle. They had a very charming time in Scotland, visiting many Scott scenes, including Edie Ochiltree's grave, and one that Hardy had always been anxious to see—Smaylho'me Tower—the setting of the "Eve of St. John"—a ballad which was among the verse he liked better than any of Scott's prose. At Springwood they met at dinner one evening old Mr Usher, aged eighty-one, who had known Scott and Lady Scott well, and whose father had sold Scott the land called Huntley Burn. He said that when he was a boy Scott asked him to sing, which he did; and Scott was so pleased that he gave him a pony. When Hardy wondered why Lady Scott should have taken the poet's fancy, Mr Usher replied grimly, "She wadna' ha' taken mine!"

They finished this autumn visit by a little tour to Durham, Whitby, Scarborough, York, and Peterborough. At the last-mentioned place the verger "told us of a lady's body found in excavating, of which the neck and bosoms glistened, being coated with a species of enamel. She had been maid of honour to Catherine of Aragon who lies near. . . . In the train there was a woman of various ages—hands old, frame middle-aged, and face young. What her mean age was I had no conception of."

"October 28. It is the incompleteness that is loved, when love is sterling and true. This is what differentiates the real one from the imaginary, the practicable from the impossible, the Love who returns the kiss from the Vision that melts away. A man sees the Diana or the Venus in his beloved, but what he loves is the difference."

"October 30. Howells and those of his school forget that a story *must* be striking enough to be worth telling. Therein lies the problem—to reconcile the average with that uncommonness which alone makes it natural that a tale or experience would dwell in the memory and induce repetition."

Sir Charles Cave was the judge at the Dorset assizes this autumn, and Hardy dined with him and Mr Frith his marshal while they were in the town. Cave told him, among other things, that when he and Sir J. F. Stephen, also on the bench, were struggling young men the latter came to him and said a man was going to be hanged at the Old Bailey, jocularly remarking as an excuse for proposing to go and see it: "Who knows; we may be judges some day; and it will be well to have learnt how the last sentence of the law is carried out."

During the first week in November the Rev. Dr Robertson Nicoll, editor of the *Bookman*, forwarded particulars of a discussion in the papers on whether national recognition should be given to eminent men of letters. Hardy's reply was:

I daresay it would be very interesting that literature should be honoured by the state. But I don't see how it could be satisfactorily done. The highest flights of the pen are mostly the excursions and revelations of souls unreconciled to life, while the natural tendency of a government would be to encourage acquiescence in life as it is. However, I have not thought much about the matter.

The end of the year was saddened for Hardy and his wife by the deaths of two or three relations in quick succession, one of them being Mrs Hardy's mother. *Tess of the d'Urbervilles: a Pure Woman Faithfully Presented* was published complete about the last day of November, with what results Hardy could scarcely have foreseen, since the book, notwithstanding its exceptional popularity, was the beginning of the end of his career as a novelist.

PART V

"Tess", "Jude", and the End of Prose

CHAPTER XX

The Reception of the Book

1892: *Aet.* 51–52

As *Tess of the d'Urbervilles* got into general circulation it attracted an attention that Hardy had apparently not foreseen, for at the time of its publication he was planning something of quite a different kind, according to an entry he made:

"Title:—'Songs of Five-and-Twenty years'. Arrangement of the songs: Lyric Ecstasy inspired by music to have precedence."

However, reviews, letters, and other intelligence speedily called him from these casual thoughts back to the novel, which the tediousness of the alterations and restorations had made him weary of. From the prefaces to later editions can be gathered more or less clearly what happened to the book as, passing into great popularity, an endeavour was made by some critics to change it to scandalous notoriety—the latter kind of clamour, raised by a certain small section of the public and the press, being quite inexplicable to its just judges, and to the writer himself. The sub-title of the book, added as a casual afterthought, seemed to be especially exasperating. All this would have been amusing if it had not revealed such antagonism at the back of it, bearing evidence, as Hardy used to say, "Of that absolute want of principle in the reviewer which gives one a start of fear as to a possible crime he may commit against one's person, such as a stab or a shot in a dark lane for righteousness' sake." Such critics, however, "who, differing from an author of a work purely artistic, in sociological views, politics, or theology, cunningly disguise that

255

illegitimate reason for antagonism by attacking his work on a point of art itself", were not numerous or effectual in this case. And, as has been implied, they were overpowered by the dumb current of opinion.

Among other curious results from the publication of the book was that it started a rumour of Hardy's theological beliefs which lived, and spread, and grew, so that it was never completely extinguished. Near the end of the story he had used the sentence, "The President of the Immortals had finished his sport with Tess", and the words were, as Hardy often explained to his reviewers, but a literal translation of Aesch: *Prom*: 169: Μακάρων πρύτανις. The classical sense in which he had used them is best shown by quoting a reply he wrote thirty years later to some unknown critic who had said in an article:

"Hardy postulates an all powerful being endowed with the baser human passions, who turns everything to evil and rejoices in the mischief he has wrought," another critic taking up the tale by adding: "To him evil is not so much a mystery, a problem, as the wilful malice of his god."

Hardy's reply was written down but (it is believed), as in so many cases with him, never posted; though I am able to give it from the rough draft:

"As I need hardly inform any thinking reader, I do not hold, and never have held, the ludicrous opinions here assumed to be mine— which are really, or approximately, those of the primitive believer in his man-shaped tribal god. And in seeking to ascertain how any exponent of English literature could have supposed that I held them, I find that the writer of the estimate has harked back to a passage in a novel of mine [*Tess*] printed many years ago, in which the forces opposed to the heroine were allegorized as a personality, (a method not unusual in imaginative prose or poetry) by the use of a well-known trope, explained in that venerable work Campbell's *Philosophy of Rhetoric* as 'one in which life, perception, activity, design, passion, or any property of sentient beings, is attributed to things inanimate'.

"Under this species of criticism if an author were to say 'Aeolus maliciously tugged at her garments, and tore her hair in his wrath', the sapient critic would not doubt announce that author's evil creed to be that the wind is a 'powerful being endowed with the baser human passions', etc. etc.

"However, I must put up with it, and say as Parrhasius of

Ephesus said about his pictures: There is nothing that men will not find fault with."

The deep impression produced on the general and uncritical public by the story was the occasion of Hardy's receiving strange letters—some from husbands whose experiences had borne a resemblance to that of Angel Clare, though more, many more, from wives with a past like that of Tess; but who had *not* told their husbands, and asking for his counsel under the burden of their concealment. Some of these were educated women of good position, and Hardy used to say the singular thing was that they should have put themselves in the power of a stranger by these revelations (their names having often been given, though sometimes initials at a post-office only) when they would not trust persons nearest to them with their secret. However, they did themselves no harm, he would add, for though he was unable to advise them, he carefully destroyed their letters, and never mentioned their names, or suspected names, to a living soul. He owed them that much, he said, for their trust in his good faith. A few, too, begged that he would meet them privately, or call on them, and hear their story instead of their writing it. He talked the matter over with his friend Sir Francis Jeune, who had had abundant experience of the like things in the Divorce Court where he presided, and who recommended him not to meet the writers alone, in case they should not be genuine. He himself, he said, also got such letters, but made it a rule never to notice them. Nor did Hardy, thought he sometimes sadly thought that they came from sincere women in trouble.

Tess of the d'Urbervilles was also the cause of Hardy's meeting a good many people of every rank during that spring, summer, and onwards, and of opportunity for meeting a good many more if he had chosen to avail himself of it. Many of the details that follow concerning his adventures in the world of fashion at dinner-parties, crushes, and other social functions, which Hardy himself did not think worth recording, have been obtained from diaries kept by the late Mrs Hardy.

It must be repeated that his own notes on these meetings were set down by him as private memoranda only; and that they, or some of them, are reproduced here to illustrate what contrasting planes of existence he moved in—vibrating at a swing between the artificial gaieties of a London season and the quaintnesses of a primitive rustic life.

Society remarks on *Tess* were curious and humorous. Strangely enough Lord Salisbury, with whom Hardy had a slight acquaintance, was a supporter of the story. Also: "The Duchess of Abercorn tells me that the novel has saved her all future trouble in the assortment of her friends. They have been almost fighting across her dinner-table over Tess's character. What she now says to them is 'Do you support her or not?' If they say 'No indeed. She deserved hanging: a little harlot!' she puts them in one group. If they say 'Poor wronged innocent!' and pity her, she puts them in the other group where she is herself." Discussing the question thus with another noble dame who sat next him at a large dinner-party, they waxed so contentious that they were startled to find the whole table of two-and-twenty silent, listening to their theories on this vexed question. And a well-known beauty and statesman's wife, also present, snapped out at him: "Hanged? They ought all to have been hanged!"

"Called on 'Lucas Malet'. A striking woman: full, slightly voluptuous mouth, red lips, black hair and eyes: and most likeable. Met her sister Miss Rose Kingsley there.

"At Lady Dorothy Nevill's. She told me about her recent visit to Dorsetshire, and that the only family relic she could find in her girlhood's house at 'Weatherbury' was an old door-trig with her father's coronet upon it. Also an extraordinarily tangled scandal about a Princess—now long deceased.

"Took Arthur Balfour's sister in to dinner at the Jeunes'. Liked her frank sensible womanly way of talking. The reviews have made me shy of presenting copies of 'Tess', and I told her plainly that if I gave her one it might be the means of getting me into hot water with her. She said: 'Now don't I really look old enough to read any novel with safety by this time!' Some of the best women don't marry— perhaps wisely.

"Mrs Joseph Chamberlain seems quite a girl in talking to her. Did not care so much for the appearance and manner of her husband at first, but that may have been superficial only. Lady Hilda Brodrick is also charming in her girlish naiveté. Also talked to Arthur Balfour and Sir Charles Russell."

"April 10. Leslie Ward, in illustration of the calamities of artists, tells me of a lady's portrait life-size he has on his hands: that he was requested by her husband to paint. When he had just completed the picture she eloped with a noble earl, whereupon her husband wrote to say he did not want the painting, and Ward's labour was wasted, there being no contract. The end of the story was that the husband divorced her, and, like Edith in Browning's 'Too Late', she 'married the other', and brought him a son and heir. At a dinner the very same evening the lady who was my neighbour at the table told me that her husband was counsel in the case, which was hurried through, that the decree might be made absolute and the remarriage take place before the baby was born."

"11. In the afternoon called on Lady Hilda Brodrick and had a long and pleasant tête-à-tête with her. She had wept bitterly over 'Tess', she told me, and made me feel a criminal. In the evening with Sir F. and Lady J. to the Gaiety theatre to hear Lottie Collins in her song 'Ta-ra-ra'. A rather striking tune and performance, to foolish words."

"15. Good Friday. Read review of 'Tess' in *The Quarterly*. A smart and amusing article; but it is easy to be smart and amusing if a man will forgo veracity and sincerity. You can see in every line that the reviewer has his tongue in his cheek. The article is, in fact, full of unblushing misstatements: e.g., 'This clumsy sordid tale of boorish brutality and lust.'

"In one place Bludyer says the story is told in a coarse manner; in another that it is not. So you may go on. How strange that one may write a book without knowing what one puts into it—or rather, the reader reads into it! Well, if this sort of thing continues no more novel-writing for me. A man must be a fool to deliberately stand up to be shot at.

"Such reviews as *The Quarterly* are a dilemma for the literary worker. There is the self-reproach on the one hand of being conventional enough to be praised by them, and the possible pecuniary loss of being abused by them on the other."

But this weighed little with Hardy beside the thought that not to be attacked by papers like the *Quarterly* was not to show any literary *ésprit* whatever. Moreover, the repute of the book was spreading, not only through England, and America, and the Colonies, but through the European Continent and Asia; and during this year translations appeared in various languages, its publication in Russia exciting great interest. On the other hand some local libraries in English-speaking countries "suppressed" the novel—with what effect was not ascertained. Hardy's good-natured friends Henry James and R. L. Stevenson (whom he afterwards called the Polonius and the Osric of novelists) corresponded about it in this vein: "Oh, yes, dear Louis: 'Tess of the d'Urbervilles' is vile. The pretence of sexuality is only equalled by the absence of it, [?] and the abomination of the language by the author's reputation for style." (*Letters of Henry James*.) When Hardy read this after James's death he said, "How indecent of those two virtuous females to expose their mental nakedness in such a manner."

"16. Dr Walter Lock, Warden of Keble, Oxford, called. 'Tess', he said, 'is the Agamemnon without the remainder of the Oresteian trilogy.' This is inexact, but suggestive as to how people think.

"Am glad I have got back from London and all those dinners:— London, that *hot-plate* of humanity, on which we first sing, then simmer, then boil, then dry away to dust and ashes!"

"Easter Sunday. Was told a story of a handsome country-girl. Her lover, though on the point of matrimony with her, would not perform it because of the temper shown by her when they went to buy the corner-cupboard and tea-things, her insistence on a different pattern, and so on. Their child was born illegitimate. Leaving the child at home she went to Jersey, for this reason, that a fellow village-girl had gone there, married, and died; and the other thought that by going and introducing herself to the widower as his late wife's playmate and friend from childhood he would be interested in her and marry her too. She carried this out, and he did marry her. But her temper was so bad that he would not live with her; and she went on the streets. On her voyage home she died of disease she had contracted, and was thrown into the sea—some say before she was quite dead. Query: What became of the baby?"

"April 22nd. The tune of many critics of my book:—

" 'First edition. Poor fellow: it is a fair piece of work. We'll give him a little encouragement.

" 'Second edition. H'm. He's making some noise.

" 'Third edition. Why should he be thought of more than we?

" 'Fourth edition. Miserable impostor! We must slaughter a rascal who is lording it over all of us like this!' "

At the beginning of June in reply to an invitation from the South Dorset Liberal Association to nominate their candidate in the forthcoming election Hardy wrote:

I am and always have been compelled to forgo all participation in active politics, by reason of the neutrality of my own pursuits, which would be stultified to a great extent if I could not approach all classes of thinkers from an absolutely unpledged point—the point of "men, not measures",—exactly the converse of a true politician's.

"May 2. Wasted time in the B. Museum in hunting up a book that contains a tragedy, according to Lang in the New Review, of which 'Tess' is a plagiarism. Discovered there was no resemblance, it being about an idiot. Why should one's club-acquaintance bring such charges?"

During May they were again in London, going out a good deal. "Took in to dinner my friend Lady N——, who does not know who her mother was." Among others Hardy met at dinners at this date were Lady Salisbury, who was "at first stiff, but grew very friendly", Lord and Lady Wimborne again, with whom he dined, and the Prince and Princess Christian, "who were by this time most affable".

He notes that on the 27th of the month, when he was dining at Lady Metcalfe's, his father, away in the country, "went upstairs for the last time". On the 31st he received a letter from his sister Mary on their father's illness, saying that it being of a mild lingering kind there was no immediate hurry for his return; and hence he dined with Lady Malmesbury on his birthday, June 2nd, in fulfilment of a three-weeks' engagement, before returning to Dorchester. This however he did the next day, arriving at his house just when his brother had come to fetch him.

He found his father much changed; and yet he rallied for some weeks onward.

In the town one day Hardy passed by chance the tent just erected for Sanger's Circus, when the procession was about to start. "Saw the Queen climb up on her lofty gilt-and-crimson throne by a stepladder. Then the various nations personified climbed up on theirs. They, being men, mounted anyhow, 'no swearin'!' being said to them as a caution. The Queen, seated in her chair on the terrestrial globe, adjusts her crimson and white robes over her soiled satin shoes for the start, and looks around on Hayne's trees, the church-tower, and Egdon Heath in the distance. As she passes along the South-walk Road she is obliged to duck her head to avoid the chestnut boughs tearing off her crown."

"June 26. Considered methods for the Napoleon drama. Forces; emotions; tendencies. The characters do not act under the influence of reason."

"July 1. We don't always remember as we should that in getting at the truth we get only at the true nature of the impression that an object, etc., produces on us, the true thing in itself being still beyond our knowledge, as Kant shows.

"The art of observation (during travel, etc.) consists in this: the seeing of great things in little things, the whole in the part—even the infinitesimal part. For instance, you are abroad: you see an English flag on a ship-mast from the window of your hotel: you realize the English navy. Or, at home, in a soldier you see the British Army, in a bishop at your club, the Church of England; and in a steam hooter you hear Industry."

He was paying almost daily visits to his father at this time. On the 19th his brother told him the patient was no worse, so he did not go that day. But on the 20th Crocker, one of his brother's men, came to say that their father had died quickly that afternoon—in the house in which he was born. Thus, in spite of his endeavours, Hardy had not been present.

Almost the last thing his father had asked for was water fresh drawn from the well—which was brought and given him; he tasted it and said, "Yes—that's our well-water. Now I know I am at home."

Hardy frequently stated in after years that the character of Horatio in *Hamlet* was his father's to a nicety, and in Hardy's copy of that play his father's name and the date of his death are written opposite the following lines:

"Thou hast been
As one in suffering all that suffers nothing;
A man that fortune's buffets and rewards
Hast ta'en with equal thanks."

He was buried close to his father and mother, and near the Knights of various dates in the seventeenth and eighteenth centuries, with whom the Hardys had been connected.

"August 14. Mother described to-day the three Hardys as they used to appear passing over the brow of the hill to Stinsford Church on a Sunday morning, three or four years before my birth. They were always hurrying, being rather late, their fiddles and violoncello in green-baize bags under their left arms. They wore top hats, stick-up shirt-collars, dark blue coats with great collars and gilt buttons, deep cuffs and black silk 'stocks' or neckerchiefs. Had curly hair, and carried their heads to one side as they walked. My grandfather wore drab cloth breeches and buckled shoes, but his sons wore trousers and Wellington boots."

In August they received at Max Gate a long-promised visit from Sir Arthur Blomfield, who had taken a house a few miles off for a month or two. Contrary to Hardy's expectations Blomfield liked the design of the Max Gate house. The visit was a very pleasant one, abounding in reminiscences of 8 Adelphi Terrace, and included a drive to "Weatherbury" Church and an examination of its architecture.

"August 31. My Mother says she looks at the furniture and feels she is nothing to it. All those belonging to it, and the place, are gone, and it is left in her hands, a stranger. (She has, however, lived there these fifty-three years!)"

"August. I hear of a girl of Maiden Newton who was shod by contract like a horse, at so much a year."

"Sept. Mr Shorter, Editor of the *Illustrated News*, called for a story or article. Stayed to lunch."

"Sept. 4. There is a curious Dorset expression—'tankard-legged'. This style of leg seems to have its biggest end downwards, and I have certainly seen legs of that sort. My mother says that my Irish ancestress had them, the accomplished lady who is reputed to have read the Bible through seven times; though how my mother should know what the legs of her husband's great-great-grand-mother were like I cannot tell."

"Among the many stories of spell-working that I have been told the following is one of how it was done by two girls about 1830. They killed a pigeon, stuck its heart full of pins, made a tripod of three knitting-needles, and suspended the heart on them over a lamp, murmuring an incantation while it roasted, and using the name of the young man in whom one or both were interested. The said young man felt racking pains about the region of the heart, and suspecting something went to the constables. The girls were sent to prison."

This month they attended a Field-Club meeting at Swanage, and were introduced to "old Mr B——, 'the King of Swanage'. He had a good profile, but was rougher in speech than I should have expected after his years of London,—being the ordinary type of Dorset man self-made by trade, whenever one of the county does self-make himself, which is not often. . . . Met Dr Yeatman the Bishop of Southwark [after of Worcester]. He says the Endicotts [Mrs J. Chamberlain's ancestors] are a Dorset family."

"Sept. 17. Stinsford House burnt. Discovered it to be on fire when driving home from Dorchester with E. I left the carriage and ran across the meads. She drove on, having promised to dine out at Canon R. Smith's. I could soon see that the old mansion was doomed, though there was not a breath of wind. Coppery flames were visible in the sun through the trees of the park, and a few figures in shirt-sleeves on the roof. Furniture on the lawn: several servants perspiring and crying. Men battering out windows to get out the things—a bruising of tender memories for me. I worked in carrying books and other articles to the vicarage. When it grew dark the flames entered the drawing and dining rooms, lighting up the chambers of so much romance. The delicate tones of the wall-painting seemed pleased at the illumination at first, till the inside of the rooms became one roaring oven; and then the ceiling fell, and then the roof, sending a fountain of sparks from the old oak into the sky.

"Met Mary in the churchyard, who had been laying flowers on Father's grave, on which the firelight now flickered.

"Walked to Canon Smith's dinner-party just as I was, it being too late to change. E. had preceded me there, since I did not arrive until nine. Dinner disorganized and pushed back between one and two hours, they having been to the fire. Met Bosworth Smith [Harrow master] who had taken E. to the fire, though I saw neither of them. Late home.

"I am sorry for the house. It was where Lady Susan Strangways, afterwards Lady Susan O'Brien, lived so many years with her actor-husband, after the famous elopement in 1764, so excellently described in Walpole's Letters, Mary Frampton's Journal, &c. [and already alluded to in the early pages of this book.]

"As stated, she knew my grandfather well, and he carefully heeded her tearful instructions to build the vault for her husband, and later herself, 'just large enough for us two'. Walpole's satire on her romantic choice, that 'a footman were preferable', would have missed fire somewhat if tested by time.

"My father when a boy-chorister in the gallery of the church used to see her, an old and lonely widow, walking in the garden in a red cloak."

"End of September. In London. This is the time to realize London as an old city, all the pulsing excitements of May being absent.

"Drove home from dining with McIlvaine at the Café Royal,

behind a horse who had no interest in me, was going a way he had no interest in going, and was whipped on by a man who had no interest in me, or the horse, or the way. Amid this string of compulsions reached home."

"October. At Great Fawley, Berks. Entered a ploughed vale which might be called the Valley of Brown Melancholy. The silence is remarkable. . . . Though I am alive with the living I can only see the dead here, and am scarcely conscious of the happy children at play."

"October 7. Tennyson died yesterday morning."

"October 12. At Tennyson's funeral in Westminster Abbey. The music was sweet and impressive, but as a funeral the scene was less penetrating than a plain country interment would have been. Lunched afterwards at the National Club with E. Gosse, Austin Dobson, Theodore Watts, and William Watson.

"The *Daily News* of yesterday coins the word 'Tessimism' in the following sentence:— 'At this hour the world is pessimistic, and pessimism (we had almost said Tessimism) is popular and fashionable.' I think I discern in this bit of smart journalism the fine Roman hand of A. Lang."

"18. Hurt my tooth at breakfast-time. I look in the glass. Am conscious of the humiliating sorriness of my earthly tabernacle, and of the sad fact that the best of parents could do no better for me. . . . Why should a man's mind have been thrown into such close, sad, sensational, inexplicable relations with such a precarious object as his own body!"

"Oct. 24. The best tragedy—highest tragedy in short—is that of the WORTHY encompassed by the INEVITABLE. The tragedies of immoral and worthless people are not of the best."

December. "At the 'Empire' [Music-Hall]. The dancing-girls are nearly all skeletons. One can see drawn lines and puckers in their young flesh. They should be penned and fattened for a month to round out their beauty."

"December 17. At an interesting legal dinner at Sir Francis Jeune's. They were all men of law but myself—mostly judges. Their stories, so old and boring to one another, were all new to me, and I was delighted. Hawkins told me his experiences in the Tichborne case, and that it was by a mere chance that he was not on the other side. Lord Coleridge—(the cross-examiner in the same case, with his famous 'Would you be surprised to hear?') was also anecdotic. Afterwards, when Lady J. had a large reception, the Electric-lights all went out, just when the rooms were most crowded, but fortunately there being a shine from the fire we all stood still till candles were brought in old rummaged-up candlesticks."

"Dec. 18. Met at lunch or dinner Col. Mackenzie, Lady Shrewsbury, Hon. Mrs Barrington, Henry Irving, Arnold Morley, Mrs Adair, Hamilton Aidé, Terriss, and Grossmith. Talked a good deal to Lady Sh., Mrs A., and H. Aidé."

CHAPTER XXI

Visits and Intermittent Writing

1893: *Aet.* 52–53

"Jan. 13. 'The Fiddler of the Reels' (Short Story) posted to Messrs Scribner, New York."

"Feb. 16. Heard a curious account of a grave that was ordered (by telegraph?) at West Stafford, and dug. But no funeral ever came, the person who had ordered it being unknown; and the grave had to be filled up." This entry had probably arisen from Hardy's occupation during some days of this winter in designing his father's tombstone, of which he made complete drawings for the stonemason, and it was possibly his contact with the stonemason that made him think of that trade for his next hero, though in designing church stonework as an architect's pupil he had of course met with many."

"Feb. 22. There cannot be equity in one kind. Assuming, e.g., that the possession of £1,000,000 sterling or 10,000 acres of land be the coveted ideal, all cannot possess £1,000,000 or 10,000 acres. But there is a practicable equity possible: that the happiness which one man derives from one thing shall be equalled by what another man derives from another thing. Freedom from worry, for instance, is a counterpoise to the lack of great possessions, though he who enjoys that freedom may not think so."

"Feb. 23. A story must be exceptional enough to justify its telling. We tale-tellers are all Ancient Mariners, and none of us is warranted in stopping Wedding Guests (in other words, the hurrying public) unless he has something more unusual to relate than the ordinary experience of every average man and woman.

"The whole secret of fiction and the drama—in the constructional part—lies in the adjustment of things unusual to things eternal and universal. The writer who knows exactly how exceptional, and how non-exceptional, his events should be made, possesses the key to the art."

"April. I note that a clever thrush, and a stupid nightingale, sing very much alike."

"Am told that Nat C——'s good-for-nothing grandson has 'turned ranter'—i.e. street preacher—and, meeting a girl he used to carry on with, the following dialogue ensued:—

He. 'Do you read your Bible for your spiritual good?'

She. 'Ho-ho! Git along wi' thee!'

He. 'But do you, my dear young woman?'

She. 'Haw-haw! Not this morning!'

He. 'Do you read your Bible, I implore?'

She. (tongue out) 'No, nor you neither. Come, you can't act in that show, Natty! You haven't the guts to carry it off.' The discussion was ended by their going off to Came Plantation."

In London this spring they again met many people, the popularity of Hardy as an author now making him welcome anywhere. For the first time they took a whole house, 70 Hamilton Terrace, and brought up their own servants, and found themselves much more comfortable under this arrangement than they had been before.

While getting into the house, however, Hardy stayed with their friends the Jeunes, and met there among many others "the Bancrofts, Miss Mary Moore, Mr Goschen, Lord and Lady Wimborne, Miss Julia Peel, Lady Louisa Loder, Lady Hilda Brodrick and her husband, Sir Spencer Ponsonby Fane, Lord Sudeley, and Mr Peel". During a large party one evening, "M. J. remembered she had promised some friends to be at theirs early; but three of her men-about-town guests stayed and stayed as if they would never go. At length the last one did leave, and we rushed off to Lord Stanhope's in Grosvenor Place, arrived about half past twelve, had a charming hob-and-nob time, everybody but one or two being gone, and reached bed about two o'clock."

At such crushes, luncheons, and dinners the Hardys made or renewed acquaintance also with Mrs R. Chamberlain, Mr Charles Wyndham, Mr Goschen, and the Duke, Duchess, and Princess May of Teck—afterwards Queen Mary. "Lady Winifred Gardner whispered to me that meeting the Royal Family always reminded her of family prayers. The Duke confused the lady who introduced me to him by saying it was unnecessary, as he had known me for years, adding privately to me when she was gone, 'That's good enough for her: of course I meant I had known you spiritually.' I sat opposite Princess May at table: she is not a bad-looking girl, and a man might marry a worse. She has nice eyes as have so many of the Royal family. The Duke was vexed that he had been put next to the Countess of ——. Lady Dorothy Nevill, Sir H. James, and Mr Justice Hawkins also present."

"13. Whibley dined with me at the Savile, and I afterwards went with him to the Trocadero Music Hall. Saw the great men—the famous performers at the Halls—drinking at the bar in long coats before going on: upon their faces an expression of not wishing in the least to emphasize their importance to the world."

"14. Dined with Charles Whibley at Millbank Street, a quaint place: I wonder how he found it out. Met there W. E. Henley, Bob Stevenson, and Pennell. An enjoyable evening."

"15. Dined with Ray Lankester at the Savile, and met James Knowles, Sir H. Thompson, Dr Lauder Brunton, and others."

"April 19. Thought while dressing, and seeing people go by to their offices, how strange it is that we should talk so glibly of 'this cold world which shows no sympathy', when this is the feeling of so many components of the same world—probably a majority—and nearly everyone's neighbour is waiting to give and receive sympathy."

"25. Courage has been idealized; why not Fear?—which is a higher consciousness, and based on a deeper insight."

"27. A great lack of tact in A. J. B., who was in the chair at the Royal Literary Fund dinner which I attended last night. The purpose of the dinner was of course to raise funds for poor authors, largely from the pockets of the more successful ones who were present with the other guests. Yet he dwelt with much emphasis on the decline of the literary art, and on his opinion that there were no writers of high rank living in these days. We hid our diminished heads, and buttoned our pockets. What he said may have been true enough, but alas for saying it then!"

"28. At Academy Private View. Find that there is a very good painting here of Woolbridge Manor-House under the (erroneous) title of 'Tess of the d'Urbervilles' ancestral home'. Also one entitled 'In Hardy's Country, Egdon Heath'.

"The worst of taking a furnished house is that the articles in the rooms are saturated with the thoughts and glances of others."

"May 10. Spent a scientific evening at the conversazione of the Royal Society, where I talked on the exhibits to Sir R. Quain, Dr Clifford Allbutt, Humphry Ward, Bosworth Smith, Sir J. Crichton Browne, F. and G. Macmillan, Ray Lankester, and others, without (I flatter myself) betraying excessive ignorance in respect of the points in the show."

"May 18. Left Euston by 9 o'clock morning train with E. for Llandudno, *en route* for Dublin. After arrival at Llandudno drove round Great Orme's Head. Magnificent deep purple-grey mountains, the fine colour being on account of an approaching storm."

"19. Went on to Holyhead and Kingstown. Met on board John Morley the Chief Secretary, and Sir John Pender. Were awaited at Dublin by conveyance from Vice-Regal Lodge as promised, this invitation being one renewed from last year, when I was obliged to postpone my visit on account of my father's death. We were received by Mrs Arthur Henniker, the Lord-Lieutenant's sister. A charming, *intuitive* woman apparently. Lord Houghton came in shortly after.

"Our bedroom-windows face the Phoenix Park and the Wicklow Mountains. The Lodge appears to have been built some time in the last century. A roomy building with many corridors."

"20. To Dublin Castle, Christ Church, etc., conducted by Mr Trevelyan, Em having gone with Mrs Henniker, Mrs Greer, and Miss Beresford to a Bazaar. Next day (Sunday) she went to Christ Church with them, and Trevelyan and I, after depositing them at the church door, went on to Bray, where we found the Chief Secretary and the Lord Chancellor at the grey hotel by the shore, 'making magistrates by the dozen' as Morley said."

"22. Whit Monday. Several went to the races. Mr Lucy (who is also here) and I, however, went into Dublin, and viewed the public buildings and some comical drunken women dancing, I suppose because it was Whitsuntide. Afterwards drove with Em to the Castle, which we had a good look over, returning afterwards to Phoenix Park.

"A larger party at dinner, including General Milman and

daughter. Mr Dundas, an A.D.C., played banjo and sang: Mrs Henniker the zithern."

"23. Em went to races with Mrs Greer, Miss Beresford and others. Morley came to lunch. In afternoon I went with H. Lucy to the scene of the Phoenix Park murders."

"24. Queen's birthday review. Troops and carriages at door at ½ past 11. The Aides—of whom there are about a dozen—are transformed by superb accoutrements into warriors—Mr St John Meyrick into a Gordon Highlander [he was killed in the South African War], Mr Dundas into a dashing hussar. Went in one of the carriages of the procession with E. and the rest. A romantic scene, pathetically gay, especially as to the horses in the gallop past. 'Yes: very pretty!' Mr Dundas said, as one who knew the real thing.

"At lunch Lord Wolseley told me interesting things about war. On the other side of me was a young lieutenant, grandson of Lady de Ros, who recalled the Napoleonic wars. By Wolseley's invitation I visited him at the Military Hospital. Thence drove to Mrs Lyttelton's to tea at the Chief Secretary's Lodge (which she rented). She showed me the rooms in which the bodies of Lord F. Cavendish and Mr Burke were placed, and told some gruesome details of the discovery of a roll of bloody clothes under the sofa after the entry of the succeeding Secretary. The room had not been cleaned out since the murders.

"We dined this evening at the Private Secretary's Lodge with Mrs Jekyll. Met Mahaffy there, a rattling, amusing talker, and others. Went back to the Viceregal Lodge soon enough to join the state diners in the drawingroom. Talked to several, and the Viceroy. Very funny altogether, this little Court."

"25. Went over Guinness's Brewery, with Mrs Henniker and several of the Viceregal guests, in the morning. Mr Guinness conducted us. On the miniature railway we all got splashed with porter, or possibly dirty water, spoiling Em's & Mrs Henniker's clothes. E. and I left the Lodge after lunch and proceeded by 3 o'clock train to Killarney, Lord Houghton having given me a copy of his poems. Put up at the Great Southern Railway Hotel."

"26. Drove in car round Middle Lake, first driving to Ross Castle. Walked in afternoon about Killarney town, where the cows stand about the streets like people."

"27. Started in wagonette for the Gap of Dunloe. Just below Kate Kearney's house Em mounted a pony and I proceeded more leisurely on foot by the path. The scenery of the Black Valley is deeply impressive. Here are beauties of Nature to delight man, and to degrade him by attracting all the vagabonds in the country. Boats met us at the head of the Upper Lake, and we were rowed through the three to Ross Castle, whence we drove back to Killarney Town."

On the following Sunday they left and passed through Dublin, sleeping at the Marine Hotel at Kingstown, and early the next morning took the boat to Holyhead. "Found on board General Milman and Miss Milman, Sir Eyre Shaw, Mrs Henniker, and others. Reached London the same evening."

Next day Hardy attended a rehearsal at Terry's Theatre of his one-act play called *The Three Wayfarers*—a dramatization of his story "The Three Strangers". On the 3rd June the play was produced with one equally short by Mr J. M. Barrie, and another or two. The Hardys went with Lady Jeune and some more friends, and found that the little piece was well received.

During the week he saw Ibsen's *Hedda Gabler* and *Rosmersholm*, in which Miss Elizabeth Robins played. The former he had already seen, but was again impressed by it, as well as by the latter. Hardy could not at all understand the attitude of the English press towards these tragic productions—the culminating evidence of our blinkered insular taste being afforded by the nickname of "the Ibscene drama" which they received.

On the eighth he met for the first time (it is believed) that brilliant woman Mrs Craigie; and about this date various other people, including Mr Hamilton Aidé, an old friend of Sir Arthur Blomfield's. In the week he still followed up Ibsen, going to *The Master Builder* with Sir Gerald and Lady Fitzgerald and her sister Mrs Henniker, who said afterwards that she was so excited by the play as not to be able to sleep all night; and on Friday lunched with General Milman at the Tower, inspecting "Little-ease", and other rooms not generally shown at that time. In the evening he went with Mrs Hardy and Miss Milman to Barrie's play, *Walker, London*, going behind the scenes with Barrie, and making the acquaintance of J. L. Toole, who said he could not go on even now on a first night without almost breaking down with nervousness.

Some ten days later Hardy was at Oxford. It was during the Encaenia, with the Christ-church and other college balls, garden parties, and suchlike bright functions, but Hardy did not make himself known, his object being to view the proceedings entirely as a stranger. It may be mentioned that the recipients of Honorary Degrees this year included Lord Rosebery, the Bishop of Oxford, Dr Liddell, and Sir Charles Euan Smith, a friend of his own. It is believed that he viewed the Commemoration proceedings from the undergraduates' gallery of the Sheldonian, his quarters while at Oxford being at the Wilberforce Temperance Hotel.

The remainder of their season in London this year was of the usual sort. A little dinner at Lady Shrewsbury's, a public one at the Mansion House, a memorial service to Admiral Tryon, a view of the marriage procession of the Duke of York and Princess May from the Club window, performances by Eleanora Duse and Ada Rehan in their respective theatres, with various dinners and luncheons, brought on the end of their term in Hamilton Terrace, and they returned to Dorchester. A note he made this month runs as follows:

"I often think that women, even those who consider themselves experienced in sexual strategy, do not know how to manage an *honest* man."

In the latter part of July Hardy had to go up to Town again for a few days, when he took occasion to attend a lecture by Stepniak on Tolstoy, to visit City churches, and to go with Lady Jeune and her daughters to a farewell performance by Irving. At Mrs Arthur Kennard's he met Lady Harcourt and the widowed Lady Mayo, and at Lady Shrewsbury's her bright brisk-thoughted daughter Lady Gwendolen Little—elsewhere becoming acquainted with Lady Powis, Mrs Patrick Campbell, Lady Charles Beresford, Lord Rowton, and renewing acquaintance with Mr J. Chamberlain. His last call this summer was on Lady Londonderry, who remained his friend through the ensuing years. "A beautiful woman still", he says of her; "and very glad to see me, which beautiful women are not always. The Duchess of Manchester [Consuelo] called while I was there, and Lady Jeune. All four of us talked of the marriage-laws, a conversation which they started, not I; also of the difficulties of separation, of terminable marriages where there are children, and of the nervous strain of living with a man when you know he can throw you over at any moment."

It may be mentioned here that after the Duchess of Manchester's death a good many years later Hardy described her as having been when he first knew her "a warm-natured woman, laughing-eyed, and bubbling with impulses, in temperament very much like 'Julie-Jane' in one of my poems".

At Dorchester.—"July 31st. Mrs R. Eliot lunched. Her story of the twins, 'May' and 'June'. May was born between 11 and 12 on the 31st May, and June between 12 and 1 on June the 1st."

"August 4. I feel very guilty this morning. A lady I much respect writes that she wept so much over the last volume of 'Tess' that her husband or brother said with vexation he would leave her to read it by herself. When finished she said to him that a man (meaning me) ought not to give readers so much pain. I have apologized. Truly, whatever romance-writers feel about being *greater*, they may feel that they are *crueller* than they know."

This month, in reply to an enquiry by the editors of the Parisian paper *L'Ermitage*, he wrote:

I consider a social system based on individual spontaneity to promise better for happiness than a curbed and uniform one under which all temperaments are bound to shape themselves to a single pattern of living. To this end I would have society divided into *groups of temperaments*, with a different code of observances, for each group.

It is doubtful if this Utopian scheme possessed Hardy's fancy for any long time.

In the middle of August Hardy and his wife accepted an invitation to visit the Milnes-Gaskells at Wenlock Abbey, on their way thither calling at Hereford to see the Cathedral, Hardy always making a point of not missing such achievements in architecture, even if familiar. Lady Catherine and her daughter met them at the station. "Lady C. is as sweet as ever, and almost as pretty, and occasionally shows a quizzical wit. The pet name 'Catty' which her dearest friends give her has, I fear, a suspicious tremor of malice." They were interested to find their bedroom in the Norman part of the building, Hardy saying he felt quite mouldy at sleeping within walls of such high antiquity.

Their time at the Abbey appears to have been very pleasant. They idled about in the shade of the ruins. Hardy discussed social problems with Lady C., and was her father-confessor on a "wicked, wanton" flirtation she had once indulged in, which had pricked her conscience ever since. Milnes-Gaskell told an amusing story of a congratulatory dinner by fellow-townsmen to a burgher who had just obtained a divorce from his wife, where the mayor made a speech beginning, "On this auspicious occasion". During their stay they went with him to Stokesay Castle and Shrewsbury. Lady Wenlock came one day; and on Sunday Hardy and Lady C. walked till they were tired, when they "sat down on the edge of a lonely sandpit and talked of suicide, pessimism, whether life was worth living, and kindred dismal subjects, till we were quite miserable. After dinner all sat round a lantern in the court under the stars—where Lady C. told stories in the Devonshire dialect, moths flying about the lantern as in *In Memoriam*. She also defined the difference between coquetting and flirting, considering the latter a grosser form of the first, and alluded to Zola's phrase, 'a woman whose presence was like a caress', saying that some women could not help it being so, even if they wished it otherwise. I doubted it, considering it but their excuse for carrying on."

On their way back the Hardys went to Ludlow Castle .and deplored the wanton treatment which had led to the rooflessness of the historic pile where *Comus* was first performed and *Hudibras* partly written. Hardy thought that even now a millionaire might be able to reroof it and make it his residence.

On a flying visit to London at the end of this month, dining at the Conservative Club with Sir George Douglas, he had "an interesting scientific conversation" with Sir James Crichton Browne. "A woman's brain, according to him, is as large in proportion to her body as a man's. The most passionate women are not those selected in civilized society to breed from, as in a state of nature, but the colder; the former going on the streets (I am sceptical about this). The doctrines of Darwin require readjusting largely; for instance, the survival of the fittest in the struggle for life. There is an altruism and coalescence between cells as well as an antagonism. Certain cells destroy certain cells; but others assist and combine.—Well, I can't say."

"September 13. At Max Gate. A striated crimson sunset; opposite it I sit in the study writing by the light of a shaded lamp, which looks primrose against the red." This was Hardy's old study facing west (now altered) in which he wrote *Tess of the d'Urbervilles*, before he removed into his subsequent one looking east, where he wrote *The Dynasts* and all his later poetry, and which is still unchanged.

"Sept. 14. Drove with Em to the Sheridans', Frampton. Tea on lawn. Mrs Mildmay, young Harcourt, Lord Dufferin, &c. On our return all walked with us as far as the first park-gate, May [afterwards Lady Stracey] looked remarkably well, and Sophy [afterwards Lady Wavertree] middling pretty."

"Sept. 17. At Bockhampton heard a story about eels that was almost gruesome—how they jumped out of a bucket at night, crawled all over the house and halfway up the stairs, their tails being heard swishing in the dark, and were ultimately found in the garden; and when water was put to them to wash off the gravel and earth they became lively and leapt about.''

At the end of the month Hardy and his wife went on a visit to Sir Francis and Lady Jeune at Arlington Manor, finding the house when they arrived as cheerful as the Jeunes' house always was in those days, Hardy saying that there was never another house like it for cheerfulness. Among the other house-guests were Mrs Craigie ("John Oliver Hobbes"), Lewis Morris, Mr Stephen (a director of the North-western Railway), Hubert Howard, son of Lord Carlisle, etc.—On Sunday morning Hardy took a two hours' walk with Mrs Craigie on the moor, when she explained to him her reasons for joining the Roman Catholic Church, a step which had vexed him somewhat. Apparently he did not consider her reasons satisfactory, but their friendship remained unbroken. While staying there they went to Shaw House, an intact Elizabethan mansion, and to a picnic in Savernake Forest, "where Lady Jeune cooked luncheon in a great saucepan, with her sleeves rolled up and an apron on".

"Oct. 7–10. Wrote a song." (Which of his songs is not mentioned.)

"Nov. 11. Met Lady Cynthia Graham. In appearance she is something like my idea of 'Tess', though I did not know her when the novel was written."

"Nov. 23. Poem. 'The Glass-stainer'" (published later on).

"Nov. 28. Poem. 'He views himself as an automaton'" (published).

"December. Found and touched up a short story called 'An Imaginative Woman'.

"In London with a slight cold in the head. Dined at the Dss. of Manchester's. Most of the guests had bad colds, and our hostess herself a hacking cough. A lively dinner all the same. As some people had not been able to come I dined with her again a few days later, as did also George [afterwards Lord] Curzon. Lady Londonderry told me that her mother's grand-mother was Spanish, whence the name of Theresa. There were also present the Duke of Devonshire, Arthur Balfour, and Mr and Mrs Lyttelton. When I saw the Duchess again two or three days later she asked me how I liked her relation the Duke. I said not much; he was too heavy for one thing. 'That's because he's so shy!' she urged. 'I assure you he is quite different when it wears off.' I looked as if I did not believe much in the shyness. However I'll assume it was so.''

After looking at a picture of Grindelwald and the Wetterhorn at somebody's house he writes: "I could argue thus: 'There is no real interest or beauty in this mountain, which appeals only to the childish taste for colour or size. The little houses at the foot are the real interest of the scene.'" Hardy never did argue so, nor intend to, nor quite believe the argument; but one understands what he means.

Finishing his London engagements—which included the final revision with the Hon. Florence Henniker of a weird story in which they had collaborated, entitled "The Spectre of the Real"—he spent Christmas at Max Gate as usual, receiving the carol-singers there on Christmas Eve, where "though quite modern, with a harmonium, they made a charming picture with their lanterns under the trees, the rays diminishing away in the winter mist". On New Year's Eve it was calm, and they stood outside the door listening to the muffled peal from the tower of Fordington St. George.

CHAPTER XXII

Another Novel Finished, Mutilated, and Restored

1894–1895: *Aet.* 53–55

"Feb. 4. 1894.—Curious scene encountered this (Sunday) evening as I was walking back to Dorchester from Bockhampton very late—nearly 12 o'clock. A girl almost in white on the top of Stinsford Hill, beating a tambourine and dancing. She looked like one of the 'angelic quire', who had tumbled down out of the sky, and I could hardly believe my eyes. Not a soul there or near but her and myself. Was told she belonged to the Salvation Army, who beat tambourines devotionally." The scene was afterwards put into verse.

One day this month he spent in Stinsford Churchyard with his brother, superintending the erection of their father's tombstone.

Hardy passed the first half of March in London, again seeing a good many people, some of whom were old and some new friends, among them being Lady Pembroke, Sir Edward Lawson, who told Hardy interesting points in his history, Princess Christian and her daughter Victoria, the Duke and Duchess of Teck, Mrs Lyttleton, Lord Rowton, and Lord Herschell the Lord Chancellor, who told Hardy some of his odd legal experiences. At Londonderry House the subject arose of social blunders. The hostess related some amusing ones of hers; but Sir Redvers Buller capped everybody by describing what he called a "double-barrelled" one of his own. He inquired of a lady next him at dinner who a certain gentleman was, "like a hippopotamaus", sitting opposite them. He was the lady's husband; and Sir R—— was so depressed by the disaster that had befallen him that he could not get it off his mind; hence at a dinner the next evening he sought the condolences of an elderly lady, to whom he related his misfortune; and remembered when he had told the story that his listener was the gentleman's mother.

At a very interesting luncheon at the Bachelors' Club given by his friend George Curzon he made the acquaintance of Mr F. C. Selous the mighty hunter, with the nature of whose fame he was not however quite in sympathy, wondering how such a seemingly humane man could live for killing; and also of Lord Roberts and Lord Lansdowne. Elsewhere he met at this time Lord Randolph Churchill and the humorous Lord Morris.

After these cheerful doings he returned to Max Gate for awhile, but when in London again, to look for a house for the spring and summer, he occasionally visited a friend he had earlier known by correspondence, Lord Pembroke, author of "The Earl and the Doctor", a fellow Wessex man as he called himself, for whom Hardy acquired a very warm feeling. He was now ill at a nursing home in London, and an amusing incident occurred while his visitor was sitting by his bedside one afternoon, thinking what havoc of good material it was that such a fine and handsome man should be prostrated. He whispered to Hardy that there was a "Tess" in the establishment, who always came if he rang at that time of the day, and that he would do so then that Hardy might see her. He accordingly rang, whereupon Tess's chronicler was much disappointed at the result; but endeavoured to discern personal beauty in the very indifferent figure who responded, and at last persuaded himself that he could do so. When she had gone the patient apologized, saying that for the first time since he had lain there a stranger had attended to his summons.

On Hardy's next visit to his friend Pembroke said with the faintest reproach: "You go to the fashionable house in front, and you might come round to the back to see me." The nursing home was at the back of Lady Londonderry's. They never met again, and when he heard of Pembroke's unexpected death Hardy remembered the words and grieved.

"April 7. Wrote to Harper's, asking to be allowed to cancel the agreement to supply a serial story to Harpers' Magazine." This agreement was the cause of a good deal of difficulty afterwards (the story being *Jude the Obscure*), as will be seen.

This year they found a house at South Kensington, and moved into it with servants brought from the country, to be surprised a little later by the great attention their house received from butchers' and bakers' young men, postmen, and other passers-by; when they found their innocent country servants to have set up flirtations with all these in a bold style which the London servant was far too cautious to adopt.

At the end of April he paid a visit to George Meredith at his house near Box Hill, and had an interesting and friendly evening there, his son and daughter-in-law being present. "Meredith", he said, "is a shade artificial in manner at first, but not unpleasantly so, and he soon forgets to maintain it, so that it goes off quite."

At a dinner at the Grand Hotel given by Mr Astor to his contributors in May, Hardy had a talk with Lord Roberts, who spoke most modestly of his achievements. It was "an artistic and luxuriant banquet, with beds of roses on the tables, electric lights shining up like glow-worms through their leaves and petals [an arrangement somewhat of a novelty then], and a band playing behind the palms".

This month he spared two or three days from London to go to Aldeburgh in Suffolk, where at the house of Mr Edward Clodd his host he met Grant Allen and Whymper the mountaineer, who told of the tragedy on the Matterhorn in 1865 in which he was the only survivor of the four Englishmen present—a reminiscence which impressed Hardy from the fact that he remembered the particular day, thirty years before, of the arrival of the news in this country. He had walked from his lodgings in Westbourne-Park Villas to Harrow that afternoon, and on entering the place was surprised to notice people standing at the doors discussing something with a serious look. It turned out to be the catastrophe, two of the victims being residents of Harrow. The event lost nothing by Whymper's relation of it. He afterwards marked for Hardy on a sketch of the Matterhorn a red line showing the track of the adventurers to the top—and the spot of the accident—a sketch which is still at Max Gate with his signature.

On a day in the week following he was at the Women Writers' Club—probably its first anniversary meeting—and, knowing what women writers mostly had to put up with, was surprised to find himself in a group of fashionably dressed youngish ladies instead of struggling dowdy females, the Princess Christian being present with other women of rank. "Dear me—are women-writers like this!" he said with changed views.

"May 23. Dined at Mary Jeune's. Talked to people till my throat was tired [his throat was always weak]—namely Lady Brownlow, Mrs Adair, young Harcourt, Lady Charles Beresford, Lady Yarborough, Lady Wantage, Lord C. Beresford, Lord Wantage, Lord Wimborne. Took Lady Wimborne in to dinner. Afterwards went on to Lady Lewis's dinner to pick up Em. Met also a good many people there."

During the same week they fulfilled likewise day or night invitations to Lady Carnarvon's, Mrs Pitt-Rivers's, and other houses. At Lady Malmesbury's one of her green linnets escaped from its cage, and he caught it—reluctantly, but feeling that a green linnet at large in London would be in a worse predicament than as a prisoner. At the Countess of Y——'s, "a woman very rich and very pretty", she [Marcia, Lady Yarborough] informed him mournfully in tête-à-tête that people snubbed her, which so surprised him that he could hardly believe it, and frankly told her it was her own imagination. She was the lady of the "Pretty pink frock" poem, though it should be stated that the deceased was not her husband but an uncle. And at an evening party at her house later he found her in a state of nerves, lest a sudden downpour of rain which had occurred should prevent people coming, and spoil her grand gathering. However, when the worst of the thunderstorm was over they duly streamed in, and she touched him joyfully on the shoulder and said, "You've conjured them!"—"My entertainer's sister Lady P—— was the most beautiful woman there. On coming away there were no cabs to be got [on account of a strike, it seems], and I returned to S.K. on the top of a 'bus. No sooner was I up there than the rain began again. A girl who had scrambled up after me asked for the shelter of my umbrella, and I gave it,—when she startled me by holding on tight to my arm and bestowing on me many kisses for the trivial kindness. She told me she had been to 'The Pav', and was tired, and was going home. She had not been drinking. I descended at the South Kensington Station and watched the 'bus bearing her away. An affectionate nature wasted on the streets! It was a strange contrast to the scene I had just left."

Early in June they were at the first performance of a play by Mrs Craigie at Daly's Theatre, and did some entertaining at their own house, after which Mrs Hardy was unwell, and went to Hastings for a change of air, Hardy going to Dorchester to look at some alterations he was making in his Max Gate house. At the end of a week he fetched his wife from Hastings, and after more dinners and luncheons he went to a melodrama at the Adelphi, which was said to be based without acknowledgement on *Tess of the d'Urbervilles*. He had received many requests for a dramatic version of the novel, but he found that nothing could be done with it among London actor-managers, all of them in their notorious timidity being afraid of the censure from conventional critics that had resisted Ibsen; and he abandoned all idea of producing it, one prominent actor telling him frankly that he could not play such a dubious character as Angel Clare (which would have suited him precisely) "because I have my name to make, and it would risk my reputation with the public if I played anything but a heroic character without spot". Hardy thought of the limited artistic sense of even a leading English actor. Yet before and after this time Hardy received letters or oral messages from almost every actress of note in Europe asking for an opportunity of appearing in the part of "Tess"—among them being Mrs Patrick Campbell, Ellen Terry, Sarah Bernhardt, and Eleanora Duse.

During July Hardy met Mrs Asquith for the first time; and at another house he had an interesting conversation with Dr W. H. Russell on the battles in the Franco-Prussian war, where Russell had been correspondent for *The Times*, and was blamed by some readers for putting too much realism into his accounts. Russell told Hardy a distressing story of a horse with no under jaw, laying its head upon his thigh in a dumb appeal for sympathy, two or three days after the battle of Gravelotte, when he was riding over the field; and other such sickening experiences.

Whether because he was assumed to have written a notorious novel or not Hardy could not say, but he found himself continually invited hither and thither to see famous beauties of the time—some of whom disappointed him; but some he owned to be very beautiful, such as Lady Powis, Lady Yarborough, Lady de Grey—"handsome, tall, glance-giving, arch, friendly"—the Duchess of Montrose, Mrs John Hanbury, Lady Cynthia Graham, Amélie Rives, and many others. A crush at Lady Spencer's at the Admiralty was one of the last of the parties they attended this season. But he mostly was compelled to slip away as soon as he could from these gatherings, finding that they exhausted him both of strength and ideas, few of the latter being given him in return for his own, either because the fashionable throng would not part from those it possessed, or did not possess any.

On the day of their giving up their house at South Kensington a curious mishap befell him. He had dispatched the servants and luggage in the morning; Mrs Hardy also had driven off to the station, leaving him, as they had arranged, to look over the house, see all was right, and await the caretaker, when he and his portmanteau would follow the rest to Dorchester. He was coming down the stairs of the silent house dragging the portmanteau behind him when his back gave way, and there he had to sit till the woman arrived to help him. In the course of the afternoon he was better and managed to get off, the acute pain turning out to be rheumatism aggravated by lifting the portmanteau.

"August 1–7. Dorchester: Seedy: back got better by degrees."

"October 16. To London to meet Henry Harper on business."

"October 20. Dined at the Guards' Mess, St James's, with Major Henniker. After dinner went round with him to the sentries with a lantern."

"October 23. Dining at the Savile last Sunday with Ray Lankester we talked of hypnotism, will, etc. He did not believe in silent influence, such as making a person turn round by force of will without communication. But of willing, for example, certain types of women by speech to do as you desire—such as 'You *shall*, or you *are to*, marry me', he seemed to have not much doubt.—If true it seems to open up unpleasant possibilities."

"November. Painful story. Old P—, who narrowly escaped hanging for arson about 1830, returned after his imprisonment, died at West-Stafford his native village, and was buried there. His widow long after died in Fordington, having saved £5 to be buried with her husband. The rector of the village made no objection, and the grave was dug. Meanwhile the daughter had come home, and said the money was not enough to pay for carrying the body of her mother out there in the country; so the grave was filled in, and the woman buried where she died."

"Nov. 11. Old song heard:—

> 'And then she arose,
> And put on her best clothes,
> And went off to the north with the Blues.'

"Another:

'Come ashore, Jolly Tar, with your trousers on.'

"Another, (sung at J. D.'s wedding):

'Somebody here has been. . .
Or else some charming shepherdess
That wears the gown of green.' "

In December he ran up to London alone on publishing business, and stayed at a temporary room off Piccadilly, to be near his club; when there seems to have occurred, according to remarks of his later, some incident of the kind possibly adumbrated in the verses called "At Mayfair Lodgings", in *Moments of Vision*.

In March of the next year (1895) Hardy was going about the neighbourhood of Dorchester and other places in Wessex with Mr Macbeth Raeburn the well-known etcher, who had been commissioned by the publishers to make sketches on the spot for frontispieces to the Wessex Novels. To those scenes which Hardy could not visit himself he sent the artist alone, one of which places was extremely difficult of access, the owner jealously guarding ingress upon her estate, and particularly to her park and house. Raeburn came back in the evening full of his adventures. Reaching the outer park-gate he found it locked, but the lodge-keeper opened it on his saying he had important business at the house. He then reached the second park-gate, which was unfastened to him on the same representation of urgency, but more dubiously. He then got to the front door of the mansion, rang, and asked permission to sketch the house. "Good God!" said the butler, "you don't know what you are asking. You had better be off before the mis'ess sees you, or the bailiff comes across you!" He started away discomfited, but thought he would make an attempt at a sketch behind the shadow of a tree. Whilst doing this he heard a voice shouting, and beheld a man running up to him—the redoubtable bailiff—who promptly ordered him out of the park. Raeburn as he moved off thought he detected something familiar in the accent of the bailiff, and turning said, "Surely you come from my country?"—"An' faith, man, it may be so!" the bailiff suddenly replied, whereon they compared notes, and found they had grown up in the same Scotch village.

Then matters changed. "Draw where you like and what you like, on'y don't let her see you from the winders at a'. She's a queer auld body, not bad at bottom, though it's rather far down. Draw as ye weel, an' if I see her coming I'll hauld up my hand." Mr Raeburn finished his sketch in peace and comfort, and it stands to this day at the beginning of *Two on a Tower* as evidence of the same.

During the spring they paid a visit of a few days to the Jeunes at Arlington Manor, where they also found Sir H. Drummond Wolff, home from Madrid, Lady Dorothy Nevill, Sir Henry Thompson and other friends; and in May entered a flat at Ashley Gardens, Westminster, for the season. While here a portrait of Hardy was painted by Miss Winifred Thomson. A somewhat new feature in their doings this summer was going to teas on the terrace of the House of Commons—in those days a newly fashionable form of entertainment. Hardy was not a bit of a politician, but he attended several of these, and of course met many Members there.

In the same year at the flat the Hardys themselves entertained more than usual, one of which gatherings, noted in an old diary of Mrs Hardy's, is enough to mention:

"June 25. Had a large lunch-party, including Lord Houghton [Crewe], Lady Jeune and Madeleine [later Countess of Midleton], Lady Lewis, Mr and Lady Margaret Watney, the Hon. Mrs Henniker, General Milman and his daughter Lena, Mrs Craigie and Mr Richards, Mr McIlvaine, Mr and Mrs Maurice Macmillan, Hon. F. Wallop, Mr Forbes Robertson, Mr Julian Sturgis. Several stayed till five o'clock."

On June 29 Hardy attended the laying of the foundation-stone of the Westminster Cathedral, possibly because the site was close to the flat he occupied, for he had no leanings to Roman Catholicism, while his wife was an old-fashioned Evangelical like her mother. However, there he was, and deeply impressed by the scene. In July he visited St. Saviour's, Southwark, by arrangement with Sir Arthur Blomfield, to see how he was getting on with the restoration. Dinners and theatres carried them through the month, in which he also paid a visit to Burford Bridge, to dine at the hotel with the Omar Khayyám Club and meet George Meredith, where the latter made a speech, and Hardy likewise, said to be the first and last ever made by either of them; at any rate it was the first, and last but one or two, by Hardy.

Hardy's entries of his doings were always of a fitful and irregular kind, and now there occurs a hiatus which cannot be filled. But it is clear that at the end of the summer at Max Gate he was "restoring the MS. of 'Jude the Obscure' to its original state"—on which process he sets down an undated remark, probably about the end of August, when he sent off the restored copy to the publishers:

"On account of the labour of altering 'Jude the Obscure' to suit the magazine, and then having to alter it back, I have lost energy for revising and improving the original as I meant to do."

In September they paid a week's visit to General and Mrs Pitt-Rivers at Rushmore, and much enjoyed the time. It was on the occasion of the annual sports at the Larmer Tree, and a full moon and clear sky favouring, the dancing on the green was a great success. The local paper gives more than a readable description of the festivity for this particular year:

"After nightfall the scene was one of extraordinary picturesque-ness and poetry, its great features being the illumination of the grounds by thousands of Vauxhall lamps, and the dancing of hundreds of couples under these lights and the mellow radiance of the full moon. For the dancing a space was especially enclosed, the figures chosen being mostly the polka-mazurka and schottische, though some country-dances were started by the house-party, and led off by the beautiful Mrs Grove, the daughter of General Pitt-Rivers, and her charming sister-in-law Mrs Pitt. Probably at no other spot in England could such a spectacle have been witnessed at any time. One could hardly believe that one was not in a suburb of Paris, instead of a corner in old-fashioned Wiltshire, nearly ten miles from a railway-station in any direction."

It may be worth mentioning that, passionately fond of dancing as Hardy had been from earliest childhood, this was the last occasion on which he ever trod a measure, according to his own recollection; at any rate on the greensward, which is by no means so springy to the foot as it looks, and left him stiff in the knees for some succeeding days. It was he who started the country dances, his partner being the above-mentioned Mrs (afterwards Lady) Grove.

A garden-party of their own at Max Gate finished the summer doings of the Hardys this year; and a very different atmosphere from that of dancing on the green soon succeeded for him, of the coming of which, by a strange divination, he must have had a suspicion, else why should he have made the following note beforehand?—

" 'Never retract. Never explain. Get it done and let them howl.' Words said to Jowett by a very practical friend."

On the 1st November *Jude the Obscure* was published.

A week after, on the 8th, he enters a note: "The Reviews begin to howl at Jude". But other subjects drew off his attention from the book, for on the same day he sets down:

"England seventy years ago.—I have heard of a girl, now a very old woman, who in her youth was seen following a goose about the common all the afternoon to get a quill from the bird, with which the parish-clerk could write for her a letter to her lover. Such a first-hand method of getting a quill-pen for important letters was not infrequent at that date." It may be added that Hardy himself had written such love-letters, and read the answers to them: but this was after the use of the quill had been largely abandoned for that of the steel pen, though old people still stuck to quills, and Hardy himself had to practise his earliest lessons in writing with a quill.

However, the booings at *Jude the Obscure* drew him back again to the subject of that volume, and his notes during the two or three ensuing months have more or less bearing upon it, though in after years he destroyed the great bulk of them, which at first he had intended to embody in an article of reply to the strictures. The clamour is not worth reviving in detail at this distance of time; nevertheless he was called by the most opprobrious names, the criticisms being outrageously personal, unfair, and untrue; for instance, the charge in *Blackwood* brought by a fellow-novelist that Hardy had published the story in a magazine version and in a volume version to make a "shameless" double profit out of it; when the truth was that, having entered into an arrangement with the editor of the magazine before he had written the story, and having found on going thoroughly into the plot that it might not suit a family magazine, he had asked to be allowed to withdraw from the contract; as is proved by the following extract from his letter to the editor some months before the story began in *Harper's Magazine*:

I have some misgivings as to whether my story will suit the magazine. . . . Unfortunately novels will take shapes of their own as the work goes on, almost independently of the writer's wish.

And the following to the publishers:

I am quite unable to assure myself that the novel will be suited to the pages of your magazine. I therefore, to avoid any awkward contingency in respect of the magazine, will ask you to release me from the agreement entered into concerning it.

To which they replied that such a step would seriously embarrass them because there was no time to get a substitute, the serial fiction in the magazine being arranged for long in advance. Hence he had decided to make laborious changes and fulfil his engagement.

The onslaught started by the vituperative section of the press—unequalled in violence since the publication of Swinburne's *Poems and Ballads* thirty years before—was taken up by the anonymous writers of libellous letters and post-cards, and other such gentry. It spread to America and Australia, whence among other appreciations he received a letter containing a packet of ashes, which the virtuous writer stated to be those of his wicked novel.

Thus, though Hardy with his quick sense of humour could not help seeing a ludicrous side to it all, and was well enough aware that the evil complained of was what these "nice minds with nasty ideas" had read into his book, and not what he had put there, he underwent the strange experience of beholding a sinister lay figure of himself constructed by them, which had no sort of resemblance to him as he was, and which he and those who knew him well would not have recognized as being meant for himself if it had not been called by his name. Macaulay's remark in his essay on Byron was well illustrated by Thomas Hardy's experience at this time: "We know of no spectacle so ridiculous as the British public in one of its periodical fits of morality."

In contrast to all this it is worth while to quote what Swinburne wrote to Hardy after reading *Jude the Obscure*:

The tragedy—if I may venture an opinion—is equally beautiful and terrible in its pathos. The beauty, the terror, and the truth, are all yours and yours alone. But (if I may say so) how cruel you are! Only the great and awful father of "Pierrette" and "L'Enfant Maudit" was ever so merciless to his children. I think it would hardly be seemly to enlarge on all that I admire in your work—or on half of it—The man who can do such work can hardly care about criticism or praise, but I will risk saying how thankful we should be (I know that I may speak for other admirers as cordial as myself) for another admission into an English paradise "under the greenwood tree". But if you prefer to be—or to remain—ποιητῶν τραγικώτατος [1] no doubt you may; for Balzac is dead, and there has been no such tragedy in fiction—on anything like the same lines—since he died.

Yours most sincerely

A. C. Swinburne.

Hardy's letter to the editor of *The Animals' Friend* in the middle of this month shows that his mind had been running on quite other subjects than the "obscenity" asserted of him by the reviewers:

Sir,

During the writing of a recent novel of mine it occurred to me that one of the scenes might be made useful in teaching mercy in the slaughtering of animals for the meat-market—the cruelties involved in that business having been a great grief to me for years. The story is now published, and I send herewith a proof of the scene alluded to—which I offer you gratuitously the right of publishing in *The Animals' Friend* or elsewhere.

I am, sir,

Yours faithfully

Thomas Hardy.

In London in December they met some interesting people—Sir Donald M. Wallace, Lady Wynford, T. P. and Mrs O'Connor, Mrs Stratford Dugdale, and others, and went to see Forbes Robertson and Mrs Patrick Campbell as Romeo and Juliet, supping with them afterwards at Willis's Rooms, a building Hardy had known many years earlier, when it was still a ball-room unaltered in appearance from that of its famous days as "Almack's"—indeed, he had himself danced on the old floors shortly after his first arrival in London in 1862, as has been mentioned.

When they got back to Dorchester during December Hardy had plenty of time to read the reviews of *Jude* that continued to pour out. Some paragraphists knowingly assured the public that the book was an honest autobiography, and Hardy did not take the trouble to deny it till more than twenty years later, when he wrote to an inquirer with whom the superstition still lingered that no book he had ever written contained less of his own life—which of course had been known to his friends from the beginning. Some of the incidents

---

[1] The most tragic of authors.

were real in so far as that he had heard of them, or come in contact with them when they were occurring to people he knew; but no more. It is interesting to mention that on his way to school he did once meet with a youth like Jude who drove the bread-cart of a widow, a baker, like Mrs Fawley, and carried on his studies at the same time, to the serious risk of other drivers in the lanes; which youth asked him to lend him his Latin grammar. But Hardy lost sight of this featful student, and never knew if he profited by his plan.

Hardy makes a remark on one or two of the reviews:

"Tragedy may be created by an opposing environment either of things inherent in the universe, or of human institutions. If the former be the means exhibited and deplored, the writer is regarded as impious; if the latter, as subversive and dangerous; when all the while he may never have questioned the necessity or urged the non-necessity of either. . . .

"The dear old marionettes that critics love, and the dear old waxen hero, and the heroine with the glued-on hair! This cowardly time can stand no other. . . .

"It is curious to conjecture what must be the sensations of critics like the writers of these personalities in their times of loneliness, sickness, affliction, and old age, when equally with the criticized they have to pause and ask themselves: What have I been trying to do for so many years? Surely they must say, 'I withered the buds before they were blown, and turned back the feet of the morning'. Pheu, pheu! So it is and will be!"

During this year 1895, and before and after, *Tess of the d'Urbervilles* went through Europe in translations—German, French, Russian, Dutch, Italian, and other tongues, Hardy as a rule stipulating that the translation should be complete and unabridged, on a guarantee of which he would make no charge. Some of the renderings, however, were much hacked about in spite of him. The Russian translation appears to have been read and approved by Tolstoy during its twelvemonth's career in a Moscow monthly periodical.

In December he replied to Mr W. T. Stead, editor of *The Review of Reviews*:

I am unable to answer your inquiry as to "Hymns that have helped me."

But the undermentioned have always been familiar and

favourite hymns of mine as poetry:—

   1. "Thou turnest man, O Lord, to dust." Ps. XC. v. 3, 4, 5, 6 (Tate and Brady.)

   2. "Awake, my soul, and with the sun." (Morning Hymn, Ken.)

   3. "Lead, kindly Light." (Newman.)

So ended the year 1895.

CHAPTER XXIII

More on "Jude", and Issue of "The Well-Beloved"

1896–1897: *Aet.* 55–57

Hardy found that the newspaper comments on *Jude the Obscure* were producing phenomena among his country friends which were extensive and peculiar, they having a pathetic reverence for press opinions. However, on returning to London in the spring he discovered somewhat to his surprise that people there seemed not to be at all concerned at his having been excommunicated by the press, or by at least a noisy section of it, and received him just the same as ever; so that he and his wife passed this season much as usual, going to Lady Malmesbury's wedding and also a little later to the wedding of Sir George Lewis's son at the Jewish Synagogue; renewing acquaintance with the beautiful Duchess of Montrose and Lady Londonderry, also attending a most amusing masked ball at his friends Mr and Mrs Montagu Crackanthorpe's, where he and Henry James were the only two not in dominos, and were recklessly flirted with by the women in consequence; meeting at dinner here and there Mr and Mrs J. Chamberlain, Mr and Mrs Goschen, the Speaker and Mrs Gully, the Russian Ambassador and Mme de Staal, Mr and Mrs Barrie, Lady Henry Somerset, Mr Astor, the Poet-Laureate, and others; being guests, too, at a literary lunch at Mrs Arthur Henniker's, where there gathered William Watson, Mrs

Craigie, "Lucas Malet", Rhoda Broughton, Anstey Guthrie, Mr and Mrs Labouchere, Lord Crewe, Sir Wemyss Reid, and possibly more.

But though the comments on *Jude* had not much effect on "Society", they had an unfortunate result of a practical nature on the dependants of Society—theatre-managers. The popularity of *Tess* had led, as has been mentioned, to Hardy's receiving numerous requests from leading actresses to turn the novel into a play, as they saw great possibilities for themselves in the character. These included, in addition to English tragediennes, Bernhardt and Duse, who had probably read the French and Italian translations of the story. There had also been surreptitious dramatizations; and at last Hardy was led to try his hand on a stage version. He had offered it to Mr Frederick Harrison and Mr Forbes Robertson for the Haymarket Theatre. They now finally refused it, the clamour against *Jude* possibly intimidating them. Hardy was not greatly concerned, and took the play no further, for though he sometimes considered the dramatization of novels to be not much more than "an exercise in ingenious carpentry", he would admit that once in a while a novel might make a good play, just as history might, even if it could not be enough to reckon upon. So the play remained in a drawer till about thirty years later, when at the request of the Dorchester amateurs Hardy hunted it up for them, as will be seen.

This year they took again the house in South Kensington they had occupied two years earlier, and gave some little parties there. But it being a cold damp spring Hardy caught a chill by some means, and was laid up with a rheumatic attack for several days, in May suffering from a relapse. He was advised to go to the seaside for a change of air, and leaving the London house in the charge of the servants went with Mrs Hardy to lodgings at Brighton.

While there he received a request from the members of the Glasgow University Liberal Club to stand as their candidate in the election of a Lord Rector for the University: the objection to Mr Joseph Chamberlain, who had been nominated, being that he was not a man of letters. Hardy's reply to the Honorary Secretary was as under:

Brighton, May 16: 1896.

Dear Sir:

Your letter has just reached me here, where I am staying for a few days for change of air after an illness.

In reply let me assure you that I am deeply sensible of the honour of having been asked by the members of the Glasgow University Liberal Club to stand as their candidate for the Lord Rectorship.

In other circumstances I might have rejoiced at the opportunity. But personal reasons which it would be tedious to detail prevent my entertaining the idea of coming forward for the office, and I can only therefore request you to convey to the Club my regrets that such should be the case; and my sincere thanks for their generous opinion of my worthiness.

I am, dear Sir,

Yours faithfully,

Thomas Hardy.

There they stayed about a week and, finding little improvement effected, returned to South Kensington. By degrees he recovered, and they resumed going out as usual, and doing as much themselves to entertain people as they could accomplish in a house not their own, which mostly took a form then in vogue, one very convenient for literary persons, of having afternoon parties, to the invitations to which their friends of every rank as readily responded as they had done in former years, notwithstanding the fact that at the very height of the season the Bishop of Wakefield announced in a letter to the papers that he had thrown Hardy's novel into the fire. Knowing the difficulty of burning a thick book even in a good fire, and the infrequency of fires of any sort in summer, Hardy was mildly sceptical of the literal truth of the bishop's story; but remembering that Shelley, Milton, and many others of the illustrious, reaching all the way back to the days of Protagoras, had undergone the same sort of indignity at the hands of bigotry and intolerance, he thought it a pity in the interests of his own reputation to disturb the episcopal narrative of adventures with *Jude*. However, it appeared that, further—to quote the testimony in the bishop's *Life*—the scandalized prelate was not ashamed to deal a blow under the belt, but "took an envelope out of his paper-stand and addressed it to W. F. D. Smith, Esq. M.P. The result was the quiet withdrawal of the book from the library, and an assurance that any other books by the same author would be carefully examined before they were allowed to be circulated." Of this precious conspiracy Hardy knew nothing, or it might have moved a mind which the burning could not stir to say a word on literary garrotting. In his ignorance of it he remained silent, being fully aware of one thing, that the ethical teaching of the novel, even if somewhat crudely put, was as high as that of any of the bishop's sermons—(indeed, Hardy was afterwards reproached for its being "too much of a sermon"). And thus feeling quite calm on the ultimate verdict of Time he merely reflected on the shallowness of the episcopal view of the case and of morals generally, which brought to his memory a witty remark he had once read in a *Times* leading article, to the effect that the qualities which enabled a man to become a bishop were often the very reverse of those which made a good bishop when he became one.

The only sad feature in the matter to Hardy was that if the bishop could have known him as he was, he would have found a man whose personal conduct, views of morality, and of the vital facts of religion, hardly differed from his own—that is, to be sure, if he were sincere, which was by no means proven.

The unkindest cut of all, however, seemed to him at the time to come from his acquaintance and fellow-novelist Mrs Oliphant, who after abusing him shamelessly in *Blackwood* as aforesaid, wrote to the bishop commending his action. And yet shortly before this, on hearing that she was ill, Hardy had wasted an afternoon at Windsor in finding her house and seeing her. Now he, no doubt, thought how these novelists love one another!

Possibly soured by all this he wrote a little while after his birthday:

"Every man's birthday is a first of April for him; and he who lives to be fifty and won't own it is a rogue or a fool, hypocrite or simpleton."

At a party at Sir Charles Tennant's to which Hardy and his wife were invited to meet the Eighty Club, Lord Rosebery took occasion in a conversation on the amusing subject of the bishop's doings, to inquire "why Hardy had called Oxford 'Christminster'". Hardy assured him that he had not done anything of the sort, "Christminster" being a city of learning that was certainly suggested by Oxford, but in its entirety existed nowhere else in the world but between the covers of the novel under discussion. The answer was not so flippant as it seemed, for Hardy's idea had been, as he often explained, to use the difficulty of a poor man's acquiring learning at that date merely as the "tragic mischief" (among others) of a dramatic story, for which purpose an old-fashioned university at the very door of the poor man was the most striking method; and though the architecture and scenery of Oxford were the best in England adapted for this, he did not slavishly copy them; indeed in some details he departed considerably from whatever of the city he took as a general model. It is hardly necessary to add that he had no feeling in the matter, and used Jude's difficulties of study as he would have used war, fire, or shipwreck for bringing about a catastrophe.

It has been remarked above that Hardy with his quick sense of humour could not help seeing a ludicrous side to his troubles over *Jude*, and an instance to that effect now occurred. The New York *World* had been among those papers that fell foul of the book in the strongest terms, the critic being a maiden lady who expressed herself thus:

"What has happened to Thomas Hardy? . . . I am shocked, appalled by this story. . . . It is almost the worst book I ever read. . . . I thought that *Tess of the d'Urbervilles* was bad enough, but that is milk for babes compared to this. . . . It is the handling of it that is the horror of it! . . . I do not believe that there is a newspaper in England or America that would print this story of Thomas Hardy's as it stands in the book. Aside from its immorality there is coarseness which is beyond belief. . . . When I finished the story I opened the windows and let in the fresh air, and I turned to my bookshelves and I said: Thank God for Kipling and Stevenson, Barrie and Mrs Humphry Ward. Here are four great writers who have never trailed their talents in the dirt."

It was therefore with some amazement that in the summer after reading the above and other exclamations grossly maligning the book and the character of its author, to show that she would not touch him with a pair of tongs, he received a letter from the writer herself. She was in London, and requested him to let her interview him "to get your side of the argument". He answered:

Savile Club.
July 16. 1896.

My dear Madam:

I have to inform you in answer to your letter that ever since the publication of "Jude the Obscure" I have declined to be interviewed on the subject of that book; and you must make allowance for human nature when I tell you that I do not feel disposed to depart from this rule in favour of the author of the review of the novel in the *New York World*.

I am aware that the outcry against it in America was only an echo of its misrepresentation here by one or two scurrilous papers which got the start of the more sober press, and that dumb public opinion was never with these writers. But the fact remains that such a meeting would be painful to me and, I think, a disappointment to you.

Moreover, my respect for my own writings and reputation is so very slight that I care little about what happens to either, so that the rectification of judgments, &c., and the way in which my books are interpreted, do not much interest me. Those readers who, like yourself, could not see that "Jude" (though a book quite without a "purpose" as it is called) makes for morality more than any other book I have written, are not likely to be made to do so by a newspaper article, even from your attractive pen.

At the same time I cannot but be touched by your kindly wish to set right any misapprehension you may have caused about the story. Such a wish will always be cherished in my recollection, and it removes from my vision of you some obviously unjust characteristics I had given it in my mind. This is, at any rate on my part, a pleasant gain from your letter, whilst I am "never the worse for a touch or two on my speckled hide" as the consequence of your review.

Believe me, dear Madam,

Yours sincerely,

Thomas Hardy.

To Miss Jeannette Gilder.

It may be interesting to give Miss Gilder's reply to this:

Hotel Cecil.
July 17. 96.

Dear Mr Hardy,

I knew that you were a great man, but I did not appreciate your goodness until I received your letter this morning.

Sincerely yours,

Jeannette L. Gilder.

Hardy must indeed have shown some magnanimity in condescending to answer the writer of a review containing such contumelious misrepresentations as hers had contained. But, as he said, she was a woman, after all—one of the sex that makes up for lack of justice by excess of generosity—and she had screamed so grotesquely loud in her article that Hardy's sense of the comicality of it had saved his feelings from being much hurt by the outrageous slurs. She evidently had not perceived the sarcasm that lurked in his letter.

Here, he thought, the matter had ended. But make the doors upon a woman's wit, and it will out at the casement. The amusing sequel to the episode was that the unsuspecting Hardy was invited to an evening party a few days later by an American lady resident in London, and though he knew her but slightly he went, having nothing better to do. While he was talking to his hostess on the sofa a strange lady drew up her chair rather near them, and listened to the conversation, but did not join in it. It was not till afterwards that he discovered that this silent person had been his reviewer, who was an acquaintance of his entertainer, and that the whole thing had been carefully schemed.

More teas on the Terrace at Westminster, dinners, and luncheons took them into and through July; Hardy's chief pleasure however being none of these, but a pretty regular attendance with his wife in this, as in other summers, at the Imperial Institute, not far from their house, where they would sit and listen to the famous bands of Europe that were engaged year after year by the management, but were not, to Hardy's regret, sufficiently appreciated by the London public. Here one evening they met with other of their friends Lady Queensberry and the beautiful Mrs, afterwards Lady, Grove; and the "Blue Danube" Waltz being started, Hardy and the latter lady danced two or three turns to it among the promenaders, who eyed them with a mild surmise as to whether they had been drinking or not. In such wise the London season drew to a close and was wound up, as far as they were concerned, with the wedding of one of Lady Jeune's daughters, Miss Dorothy Stanley, at St. George's, Hanover Square, to Mr Henry Allhusen.

When he reached Dorchester he paid a visit to his mother, on whom he remarks that she was well, but that "her face looked smaller".

On the 12th August they left Dorchester for Malvern, where they put up at the Foley Arms, climbed the Beacon, Hardy on foot, Mrs Hardy on a mule; drove round the hills, visited the Priory Church, and thence went on to Worcester to see the Cathedral and porcelain works; after which they proceeded to Warwick and Kenilworth, stopping to correct proofs at the former place, and to go over the castle and church. A strange reminder of the transitoriness of life was given to Hardy in the church, where, looking through a slit by chance he saw the coffin of the then recent Lord Warwick, who, a most kindly man, some while before, on meeting him in London, had invited him to Warwick Castle, an invitation which he had been unable to accept at the time though he had promised to do so later. "Here I am at last", he said to the coffin as he looked; "and here are you to receive me!" It made an impression on Hardy which he never forgot.

They took lodgings for a week at Stratford-on-Avon, and visited the usual spots associated with Shakespeare's name; going on to Coventry and to Reading, a town which had come into the life of Hardy's paternal grandmother, who had lived here awhile; after which they went to Dover; where Mrs Hardy, having brought her bicycle with her, was knocked off it by a young man learning to ride, and was laid up for some days by the accident. Hardy the while re-read *King Lear*, which was begun at Stratford, and he makes the following observation on the play:

"Sept. 6. Finished reading 'King Lear'. The grand scale of the tragedy, scenically, strikes one, and also the large scheme of the plot. The play rises from and after the beginning of the third act, and Lear's dignity with it. Shakespeare did not quite reach his intention in the King's character, and the splitting of the tragic interest between him and Gloucester does not, to my mind, enhance its intensity, although commentators assert that it does."

"September 8. Why true conclusions are not reached, notwithstanding everlasting palaver. Men endeavour to hold to a mathematical consistency in things, instead of recognizing that certain things may both be good and mutually antagonistic: e.g. patriotism and universal humanity; unbelief and happiness.

"There are certain questions which are made unimportant by their very magnitude. For example the question whether we are moving in Space this way or that; the existence of a God, etc." [The meaning of this does not seem quite clear.]

Having remained at Dover about a fortnight and recovered, Mrs Hardy from her accident, and her husband from a bad cold, they crossed to Ostend in the middle of September and went on to Bruges. He always thought the railway station of this town the only satisfactory one in architectural design that he knew. It was the custom at this date to admire the brick buildings of Flanders, and Hardy himself had written a prize essay as a young man on Brick and Terra-Cotta architecture; but he held then, as always, that nothing can really compensate in architecture for the lack of stone, and would say on this point—with perhaps some intentional exaggeration—that the ashlar back-yards of Bath had more dignity than any brick-front in Europe. From Bruges they went on to Brussels, Namur, and Dinant, through scenes to become synonymous with desolation in the war of after years.

"Sept. 23. At dinner at the public table [of the hotel] met a man possessed of the veritable gambling fever. He has been playing many days at the Casino (Roulette and Trente-et-quarante). He believes thoroughly in his 'system', and yet, inconsistently, believes in luck: e.g., 36 came into his head as he was walking down the street towards the Casino today; and it made him back it, and he won. He plays all the afternoon and all the evening.

"His system appears to be that of watching for numbers which have not turned up for a long time; but I am not sure.

"He is a little man; military looking; large iron-grey moustache standing out detached; iron-grey hair; fresh crimson skin. Produces the book, ruled in vertical columns, in which he records results. Discusses his system incessantly with the big grey-bearded man near. Can talk of nothing else. . . . Has lost today 4,500 francs. Has won back some—is going to play to-night till he has won it all back, and if he can profit enough to pay the expenses of his trip on the Continent he will be satisfied. His friend with the beard, who seems to live in the hotel permanently, commends him by a nod and a word now and then, but not emphatically."

"Sept. 24. After breakfast unexpectedly saw the gambler standing outside the hotel-entrance without a hat, looking wild, and by comparison with the previous night like a tree that has suddenly lost its leaves. He came up to me; said he had had no luck on the previous night; had plunged, and lost heavily. He had not enough money left to take him home third class. Is going to Monte Carlo in November with £2,000 to retrieve his losses. . . .

"We left between 12 and 1. The gambler left at the same time by a train going in the opposite direction, and was carefully put into a third-class carriage by his friend of the hotel, who bought his ticket. He wore a green-grey suit and felt hat, looking bleak-faced and absent, and seemed passive in the other's hands. His friend is apparently a decoy from the Casino."

Mrs Hardy, not being a good walker, had brought her bicycle, as many people did just now, bicycling being wildly popular at the time, and Flanders being level. After they had paid twenty-four francs duty at Ostend for importing it, it had several adventures in its transit from place to place, was always getting lost, and miraculously turned up again when they were just enjoying the relief of finding themselves free of it. At Liège it really did seem gone, Hardy having watched the transfer of all the luggage at a previous junction, and the bicycle not being among it. Having given up thinking of it they were hailed by an official, who took them with a mysterious manner to a store room some way off, unlocked it and with a leer said, to Hardy's dismay: "*Le véloze!*" How it had got there they did not know.

At Spa they drove to the various fountains, examined the old gaming-house in the Rue Vauxhall where those that were now cold skeletons had burnt hot with the excitement of play, thought of the town's associations in fact and fiction, of the crowned heads of all the countries of Europe who had found their pleasure and cure at this Mother of Watering-places—now shrunk small like any other ancient matron.

Getting back to Brussels they put up for association's sake at the same hotel they had patronized twenty years before, but found it had altered for the worse since those bright days. Hardy again went out to Waterloo, which had been his chief reason for stopping at the Belgian capital, and no doubt made some more observations with a view to *The Dynasts*, to which he at this time had given the provisional name of "Europe in Throes". All he writes thereon in his pocket-book while in Brussels is:

> "Europe in Throes.
> Three Parts. Five Acts each.
> Characters: Burke, Pitt, Napoleon, George III, Welling-
> ton . . . and many others."

But he set down more copious notes for the drama elsewhere. It is believed he gave time to further conjectures as to the scene of the Duchess's Ball, which he had considered when here before, and on which it may be remembered there is a note in *The Dynasts*, ending, "The event happened less than a century ago, but the spot is almost as phantasmal in its elusive mystery as towered Camelot, the Palace of Priam, or the Hill of Calvary".

Concerning the scene of the battle itself he writes:

"October 2. To Field of Waterloo. Walked alone from the English line along the Charleroi Road to 'La Belle Alliance'. Struck with the *nearness* of the French and English lines to each other. Shepherds with their flocks and dogs, men ploughing, two cats, and myself, the only living creatures on the field."

Returning homeward through Ostend a little later they found the hotels and shops closed and boarded up, and the Digue empty, Mrs Hardy being the single woman bicyclist where there had been so many.

"Max Gate. October 17. A novel, good, microscopic touch in Crabbe [which would strike one trained in architecture]. He gives surface without outline, describing his church by telling *the colour of the lichens.*"

"Poetry. Perhaps I can express more fully in verse ideas and emotions which run counter to the inert crystallized opinion—hard as a rock—which the vast body of men have vested interests in supporting. To cry out in a passionate poem that (for instance) the Supreme Mover or Movers, the Prime Force or Forces, must be either limited in power, unknowing, or cruel—which is obvious enough, and has been for centuries—will cause them merely a shake of the head; but to put it in argumentative prose will make them sneer, or foam, and set all the literary contortionists jumping upon me, a harmless agnostic, as if I were a clamorous atheist, which in their crass illiteracy they seem to think is the same thing. . . . If Galileo had said in verse that the world moved, the Inquisition might have let him alone."

"1897. January 27. To-day has length, breadth, thickness, colour, smell, voice. As soon as it becomes *yesterday* it is a thin layer among many layers, without substance, colour, or articulate sound."

"Jan. 30. Somebody says that the final dictum of the 'Ion' of Plato is 'inspiration, not art'. The passage is—θεῖον καὶ μὴ τεχνικόν. And what is really meant by it is, I think, more nearly expressed by the words 'inspiration, not technicality'—'art' being too comprehensive in English to use here."

"Feb. 4. Title: 'Wessex Poems: With Sketches of their Scenes by the Author'."

"Feb. 10. In spite of myself I cannot help noticing countenances & tempers in objects of scenery: e.g., trees, hills, houses."

"Feb. 21. My mother's grandfather Swetman—a descendant of the Christopher Swetman of 1631 mentioned in the History of the County as a small landed proprietor in the parish—used to have an old black oak bedstead, with the twelve apostles on it in carved figures—each about one foot six inches high. Some of them got loose, and the children played with them as dolls. What became of that bedstead?"

"March 1. Make a lyric of the speech of Hyllus at the close of the *Trachiniae.*" (It does not appear that this was ever carried out.)

At the beginning of March a dramatization of *Tess of the d'Urbervilles* was produced in America by Mr and Mrs Fiske with much success. About the same date Hardy went with Sir Francis Jeune to a banquet at the Mansion House in honour of Mr Bayard the American Ambassador on his leaving England, which Hardy described as a "brilliant gathering", though the night was so drenching and tempestuous as to blow off house-roofs and flood cellars. In the middle of the month a revised form of a novel of his which had been published serially in 1892 as *The Pursuit of the Well-Beloved: A Sketch of a Temperament*, was issued in volume form as *The Well-Beloved*. The theory on which this fantastic tale of a subjective idea was constructed is explained in the Preface to the novel, and again exemplified in a poem bearing the same name, written about this time and published with *Poems of the Past and the Present* in 1901 — the theory of the transmigration of the ideal beloved one, who only exists in the lover, from material woman to material woman—as exemplified also by Proust many years later. The amazing consequence of the publication of the book was that certain papers affected to find unmentionable moral atrocities in its pages—quite bewildering to the author as to what could be meant by such statements about so fanciful a story, till it was explained to him that some oblique meaning had been ingeniously foisted into the novel as a peg whereon to hang a predetermined attack, which was a purely personal one. It made him say, naturally enough, "What foul cesspits some men's minds must be, and what a Night-cart would be required to empty them!"

Altogether it was a remarkable instance of what intolerance can do when it loses all sense of truth and honour. But being review-proof by this time, and feeling the person deserving "two years hard" (as some print put it) to be a lay figure not himself, also remembering the epithet "swine-born" which Swinburne endured from the press, he was almost if not quite indifferent to these things, and did not answer any of the charges further than by defining in a letter to a literary periodical the scheme of the story somewhat more fully than he had done in the preface:

Not only was it published serially five years ago but it was sketched many years before that date, when I was comparatively a young man, and interested in the Platonic Idea, which, considering its charm and its poetry one could well wish to be interested in always. . . . There is, of course, underlying the fantasy followed by the visionary artist the truth that all men are pursuing a shadow, the Unattainable, and I venture to hope that this may redeem the tragi-comedy from the charge of frivolity. . . . "Avice" is an old name common in the county, and "Caro" (like all the other surnames) is an imitation of a local name . . . this particular modification having been adopted because of its resemblance to the Italian for "dear".

In reply to an inquiry from an editor he wrote:

> No: I do not intend to answer the article on "The Well-Beloved". Personal abuse best answers itself. What struck me, next to its mendacious malice, was its maladroitness, as if the writer were blinded by malignity. . . . Upon those who have read the book the review must have produced the amazed risibility I remember feeling at Wilding's assertions when as a youth I saw Foote's comedy of "The Liar". . . . There is more fleshliness in "The Loves of the Triangles" than in this story—at least to me. To be sure there is one explanation which should not be overlooked: a reviewer *himself* afflicted with "sex-mania" might review so.

Such were the odd effects of Hardy's introduction of the subjective theory of love into modern fiction, and so ended his prose contributions to literature (beyond two or three short sketches to fulfil engagements), his experiences of the few preceding years having killed all his interest in this form of imaginative work, which had ever been secondary to his interest in verse.

A letter from him to Swinburne was written about this time, in which he says:

> I must thank you for your kind note about my fantastic little tale [*The Well-Beloved*] which, if it can make, in its better parts, any faint claim to imaginative feeling, will owe something of such feeling to you, for I often thought of lines of yours during the writing; and indeed, was not able to resist the quotation of your words now and then.

And this reminds me that one day, when examining several English imitations of a well-known fragment of Sappho, I interested myself in trying to strike out a better equivalent for it than the commonplace "Thou, too, shalt die" &c. which all the translators had used during the last hundred years. I then stumbled upon your "Thee, too, the years shall cover", and all my spirit for poetic pains died out of me. Those few words present, I think, the finest *drama* of Death and Oblivion, so to speak, in our tongue.

Believe me to be

Yours very sincerely,

Thomas Hardy.

P.S. I should have added that "The Well Beloved" is a fanciful exhibition of the artistic nature, and has, I think, some little foundation in fact. I have been much surprised, and even grieved, by a ferocious review attributing an immoral quality to the tale. The writer's meaning is beyond me. T.H.

1. Thomas Hardy, aged 16. From a photograph by Pouncy (Dorchester).

2. Thomas Hardy's birthplace, Higher Bockhampton. From a drawing made by Hardy himself.

3. Thomas Hardy, aged 21. From a photograph by Bowen & Carpenter (Kilburn).

4. Emma Lavinia Gifford (afterwards Mrs Thomas Hardy), 1870.

5. Jemima Hardy, 1876. From a photograph by Pouncy.

6. Thomas Hardy, senior, 1877. From a photograph by W. G. Lewis (Bath).

7. Thomas Hardy, *circa* 1880. From a photograph by Frederick Hollyer.

8. Max Gate, when first built.

9. Thomas Hardy's study, about 1900. From a photograph by the Revd Thomas Perkins.

10. Thomas Hardy, *circa* 1908. From a photograph by Walter Barnett.

11. Thomas Hardy, 1913. From a photograph by Olive Edis.

12. Florence Emily Dugdale (afterwards Mrs Thomas Hardy), 1910. From a drawing by William Strang, R.A.

13. Thomas and Florence Hardy at Max Gate, 1914. From a photograph by E. O. Hoppé.

14. Max Gate, from the lawn, 1919.

15. Thomas Hardy, aged 80. From a photograph by Walter Thomas.

16. Florence Hardy, *circa* 1927. From a photograph probably by Swaine.

PART VI

Verse, to the End of "The Dynasts"

CHAPTER XXIV

Collecting Old Poems and Making New

1897–1898: *Aet.* 57–58

The misrepresentations of the last two or three years affected but little, if at all, the informed appreciation of Hardy's writings, being heeded almost entirely by those who had not read him; and turned out ultimately to be the best thing that could have happened; for they well-nigh compelled him, in his own judgment at any rate, if he wished to retain any shadow of self-respect, to abandon at once a form of literary art he had long intended to abandon at some indefinite time, and resume openly that form of it which had always been more instinctive with him, and which he had just been able to keep alive from his early years, half in secrecy, under the pressure of magazine-writing. He abandoned it with all the less reluctance in that the novel was, in his own words, "gradually losing artistic form, with a beginning, middle, and end, and becoming a spasmodic inventory of items, which has nothing to do with art".

The change, after all, was not so great as it seemed. It was not as if he had been a writer of novels proper, and as more specifically understood, that is, stories of modern artificial life and manners showing a certain smartness of treatment. He had mostly aimed, and mostly succeeded, to keep his narratives close to natural life, and as near to poetry in their subject as the conditions would allow, and had often regretted that those conditions would not let him keep them nearer still.

Nevertheless he had not known, whilst a writer of prose, whether he might not be driven to society novels, and hence, as has been seen, he had kept, at casual times, a record of his experiences in upper social life, though doing it had always been a drudgery to him. It was now with a sense of great comfort that he felt he might leave off further chronicles of that sort; and it will be found that from this point the writer of these pages has very little material of the kind available. But his thoughts on literature and life were often written down still, from which much of which follows has been abridged.

He had already for some time been getting together the poems which made up the first volume of verse that he was about to publish. In date they ranged from 1865 intermittently onwards, the middle period of his novel writing producing very few or none, but of late years they had been added to with great rapidity, though at first with some consternation he had found an awkwardness in getting back to an easy expression in numbers after abandoning it for so many years; but that soon wore off.

He and his wife went to London as usual this year (1897) but did not take a house there. After two or three weeks' stay, during which, according to Mrs Hardy's diary, they went to a large dance at Londonderry House, given for Lady Helen Stewart, they adopted the plan of living some way out, and going up and down every few days, the place they made their temporary centre being Basingstoke. In this way they saw London friends, went to concerts at the Imperial Institute (the orchestra this season being the famous Vienna band under Edouard Strauss), saw one or two Ibsen plays, and the year's pictures. Being near they also went over the mournful relics of that city of the past, Silchester; till in the middle of June they started for Switzerland, thus entirely escaping the racket of the coming Diamond Jubilee, and the discomfort it would bring upon people like them who had no residence of their own in London and no invitation to any Jubilee function.

All the world, including the people of fashion habitually abroad, was in London or arriving there, and the charm of a lonely Continent impressed the twain much. The almost empty Channel steamer, the ease with which they crossed France from Havre by Paris, Dijon, and Pontarlier to Neuchâtel, the excellent rooms accorded them by obsequious hosts at the hotels in Switzerland usually frequented by English and American tourists, made them glad they had come. On the actual day, the 20th, they were at Berne, where they celebrated it by attending a Jubilee Concert in the Cathedral, with the few other of their fellow-countryfolk who remained in the town. At Interlaken the comparative solitude was just as refreshing, the rosy glow from the Jungfrau visible at three in the morning from Hardy's bedroom seeming an exhibition got up for themselves alone; and a pathetic procession of empty omnibuses went daily to and from each railway train between shops that looked like a banquet spread for people who delayed to come. They drove up the valley to Grindelwald, and having been conveyed to Scheidegg, walked thence to the Wengern Alp—overlooking the scene of *Manfred*—where a baby had just been born, and where Hardy was more impressed by the thundering rumble of unseen avalanches on the immense Jungfrau immediately facing than by the sight of the visible ones.

The next day, or the next following, *The Times'* account of the celebration in London of Queen Victoria's Diamond Jubilee reached Hardy's hands, and he took it out and read it in the snowy presence of a greater Queen, the maiden-monarch that dominated the whole place.

It was either in the train as it approached Interlaken, or while there looking at the peak, that there passed through his mind the sentiments afterwards expressed in the lines called "The Schreckhorn: with thoughts of Leslie Stephen".

After a look at Lauterbrunnen, the Staubbach, the Lake and Castle of Thun, they stopped at the Hôtel Gibbon, Lausanne, Hardy not having that aversion from the historian of the *Decline and Fall* which Ruskin recommended. He found that, though not much might remain of the original condition of the building or the site, the remoter and sloping part of the garden, with its acacias and irregular contours, could not have been much changed from what it was when Gibbon haunted it, and finished his history. Accordingly his recaller sat out there till midnight on June 27, and imagined the historian closing his last page on the spot, as described in his *Autobiography*:

"It was on the day, or rather the night, of the 27th of June 1787, between the hours of eleven and twelve, that I wrote the last lines of the last page, in a summer house in my garden. After laying down my pen I took several turns in a *berceau*, or covered walk of acacias, which commands a prospect of the country, the lake, and the mountains."

It is uncertain whether Hardy chose that particular evening for sitting out in the garden because he knew that June 27th was Gibbon's date of conclusion, or whether the coincidence of dates was accidental. The later author's imaginings took the form of the lines subjoined, which were printed in *Poems of the Past and the Present.*

LAUSANNE

In Gibbon's old garden: 11–12 p.m.

June 27: 1897.

A spirit seems to pass,
Formal in pose, but grave withal and grand:
He contemplates a volume in his hand,
And far lamps fleck him through the thin acacias.

Anon the book is closed,
With "It is finished!" And at the alley's end
He turns, and when on me his glances bend
As from the Past comes speech—small, muted, yet composed.

"How fares the Truth now?—Ill?
—Do pens but slily further her advance?
May one not speed her but in phrase askance?
Do scribes aver the Comic to be Reverend still?

"Still rule those minds on earth
At whom sage Milton's wormwood words were hurled:
'*Truth like a bastard comes into the world
Never without ill-fame to him who gives her birth*'?"[1]

From Lausanne making excursions to Ouchy, and by steamer to Territet, Chillon, Vevey, and other places on the lake, they afterwards left for Zermatt, going along the valley of the Rhone amid intense heat till they gradually rose out of it beside the roaring torrent of the Visp. That night Hardy looked out of their bedroom window in the Hôtel Mt. Cervin and "Could see where the

---

[1] The quotation is from *The Doctrine and Discipline of Divorce*, the passage running as follows: "Truth is as impossible to be soiled by any outward touch, as the sunbeam; though this ill hap wait on her nativity, that she never comes into the world, but like a bastard, to the ignominy of him that brought her forth; till Time, the midwife rather than the mother of truth, have washed and salted the infant and declared her legitimate."

Matterhorn was by the absence of stars within its outline", it being too dark to see the surface of the mountain itself although it stood facing him. He meant to make a poem of the strange feeling implanted by this black silhouette of the mountain on the pattern of the constellations; but never did so far as is known. However the mountain inspired him to begin one sonnet, finished some time after—that entitled "To the Matterhorn"—the terrible accident on whose summit thirty-two years before this date had so impressed him at the time of its occurrence.

While walking from Zermatt with a Russian gentleman to the Riffel-Alp Hotel, whither Mrs Hardy had preceded him on a pony, he met some English ladies, who informed him of the mysterious disappearance of an Englishman somewhere along the very path he had been following. Having lunched at the hotel and set his wife upon the pony again he sent her on with the guide, and slowly searched all the way down the track for some clue to the missing man, afterwards writing a brief letter to *The Times* to say there was no sign visible of foul play anywhere on the road. The exertion of the search, after walking up the mountain-path in the hot morning sun, so exhausted his strength that on arriving at Geneva, whither they went after leaving Zermatt, he was taken so ill at the Hôtel de la Paix that he had to stay in bed. Here as he lay he listened to the plashing of a fountain night and day just outside his bedroom window, the casements of which were kept widely open on account of the heat. He used to say that he had a curious sense of impending tragedy during these days of illness. It was the fountain beside which the Austrian Empress was murdered shortly after by an Italian anarchist. His accidental nearness in time and place to the spot of her doom moved him much when he heard of it, since thereby hung a tale. She was a woman whose beauty, as shown in her portraits, had attracted him greatly in his youthful years, and had inspired some of his early verses, the same romantic passion having also produced the outline of a novel upon her, which he never developed.

While he was recovering at Geneva Mrs Hardy found by chance the tomb of an ancestor who had died there. But of Geneva, its lake, Diodati, Montalègre, Ferney, and the neighbourhood he merely remarks: "These haunts of the illustrious! Ah, but *they* are gone now, and care for their chosen nooks no more!"

Again in London he went with Lady Jeune to the Jubilee dinner of women, and "talked to Mrs Flora Steel, Elizabeth Robins, Lady

Battersea, and numerous others". He also expressed views on scenery in the following letter:

To the Editor of the *Saturday Review*.

Sir:

I am unable to reply to your inquiry on "The Best Scenery I know". A week or two ago I was looking at the inexorable faces of the Jungfrau and the Matterhorn: a few days later at the Lake of Geneva with all its soft associations. But, which is 'best' of things that do not compare at all, and hence cannot be reduced to a common denominator? At any given moment we like best what meets the mood of that moment.

Not to be entirely negative, however, I may say that, in my own neighbourhood, the following scenes rarely or never fail to delight beholders:

1. View from Castle Hill, Shaftesbury.
2. View from Pilsdon Pen.
3. New Forest vistas near Brockenhurst.
4. The River Dart.
5. The coast from Trebarwith Strand to Beeny Cliff, Cornwall.

From London he returned to Max Gate, and with Mrs Hardy wandered off to Wells Cathedral, and onwards to Frome and Longleat, whence after examining the library and the architecture he proceeded to Salisbury, a place in which he was never tired of sojourning, partly from personal associations and partly because its graceful cathedral pile was the most marked instance in England of an architectural intention carried out to the full.

"August 10. Salisbury: Went into the Close late at night. The moon was visible through both the north and south clerestory windows to me standing on the turf on the north side. . . . Walked to the west front, and watched the moonlight creep round upon the statuary of the facade—stroking tentatively and then more and more firmly the prophets, the martyrs, the bishops, the kings, and the queens. . . . Upon the whole the Close of Salisbury, under the full summer moon on a windless midnight, is as beautiful a scene as any I know in England—or for the matter of that elsewhere.

"Colonel T. W. Higginson of the United States, who is staying at the same hotel as ourselves, introduced himself to us. An amiable well-read man whom I was glad to meet. He fought in the Civil War. Went with him to hunt up the spot of the execution of the Duke of Buckingham, whose spirit is said to haunt King's House still."

After taking Mrs Hardy to Stonehenge, which she had never seen:

"The misfortune of ruins—to be beheld nearly always at noonday by visitors, and not at twilight.

"I see in the papers that Bishop How of Wakefield died yesterday. It is painful to think that people should so recklessly and bitterly attack others who have the same objects in life as themselves, merely because of a difference of method. Apart from theological points I don't know that my ultimate object is far removed from that of the late bishop."

"August 10. Continued—'The day goeth away . . . the shadows of the evening are stretched out . . . I set watchmen over you, saying, Hearken to the sound of the trumpet. But they said, We will not hearken. Therefore hear, ye nations. . . . To what purpose cometh there to me incense from Sheba, and the sweet cane from a far country? Your burnt offerings are not acceptable, nor your sacrifices sweet unto me.' Passages from the first lesson (Jer. VI.) at the Cathedral this afternoon. E. and I present. A beautiful chapter, beautifully read by the old Canon."

"August 13. All tragedy is grotesque—if you allow yourself to see it as such. A risky indulgence for any who have an aspiration towards a little goodness or greatness of heart! Yet there are those who do."

"August 15.—It is so easy nowadays to call any force above or under the sky by the name of 'God'—and so pass as orthodox cheaply, and fill the pocket!"

On August 21 they went to Arlington Manor, Berks, where a lively house-party gathered, including Lord Beauchamp (who walked about hatless), Lady Arthur Butler, Lady Henry Somerset's son and his wife Lady Catherine, Mr and Mrs Henry Allhusen and their baby, Sir Evelyn Wood, and the genial Colonel John Hay the American Ambassador, who appeared in the lightest of summer suits at dinner, his luggage having gone astray, and who reminded Hardy that they were not strangers as he seemed to suppose, but had met at the Rabelais Club years ago.

On August 26 Hardy went to Salisbury again, to meet Mlle Madeleine Rolland of Paris, the charming and accomplished translator of some of his novels, and sister of M. Romain Rolland;

she wished to consult him, and with her mother was passing through the city to Oxford. Hardy used to say drily that Mlle Rolland was the only lady, foreign or British, he ever remembered corresponding with whose letters were written in perfectly correct and graceful English. She afterwards visited at Max Gate.

In September he passed a few pleasant days in bicycling about the neighbourhood with Mr Rudyard Kipling, who had an idea just at that time that he would like to buy a house near Weymouth. They found a suitable house for sale at Rodwell, commanding a full view of Portland Roads; but difficulties arose when inquiries were made, and Mr Kipling abandoned the idea, though Hardy heard afterwards that the house was ultimately sold for the price Mr Kipling had offered.

Bicycling was now in full spirit with the Hardys—and indeed with everybody—and many were the places they visited by that means.

"Oct. 10th. Am told a singularly creepy story—absolutely true, I am assured—of a village girl near here who was about to be married. A watch had been given her by a former lover, his own watch, just before their marriage was prevented by his unexpected death of consumption. She heard it *going* in her box at waking on the morning of the wedding with the second lover, though it had not been touched for years.

"Lizzy D—[the monthly nurse who had attended at Hardy's birth] told my mother that she walked eighteen (?) miles the day after her own baby was born. . . . She was an excellent nurse, much in demand; of infinite kind-heartedness, humour, and quaintness, and as she lived in a cottage quite near our house at Bockhampton, she as it were kept an eye upon the Hardy family always, and being her neighbour gave my mother the preference in clashing cases. She used to tell a story of a woman who came to her to consult her about the ghost of another woman she declared she had seen & who 'troubled her'—the deceased wife of the man who was courting her.

" 'How long hev' the woman been dead?' I said.

" 'Many years!'

" 'Oh, that were no ghost. Now if she'd only been dead a month or two, and you were making her husband your fancy-man, there might have been something in your story. But Lord, much can she care about him after years and years in better company!' "

It may not be inappropriate to mention here that but for this estimable woman's commonsense Thomas Hardy might never have walked the earth. At his birth he was thrown aside as dead till rescued by her as she exclaimed to the surgeon, "Dead! Stop a minute: he's alive enough, sure!"

To return to 1897. Nothing more of much account occurred to Hardy during its lapse, though it may be mentioned that *Jude*, of which only a mutilated version could be printed as a serial in England and America, appeared as a literal translation in Germany, running through several months of a well-known periodical in Berlin and Stuttgart without a word of abridgement.

"1898. Feb. 5.—Write a prayer, or hymn, to One not Omnipotent, but hampered; striving for our good, but unable to achieve it except occasionally." [This idea of a limited God of goodness, often dwelt on by Hardy, was expounded ably and at length in McTaggart's *Some Dogmas of Religion* several years later, and led to a friendship which ended only with the latter's death.]

As the spring drew on they entered upon their yearly residence of a few months in London—this time taking a flat in Wynnstay Gardens, Kensington. Hardy did some reading at the British Museum with a view to *The Dynasts*, and incidentally stumbled upon some details that suggested to him the Waterloo episode embodied in a piece called "The Peasant's Confession". He went to the Conversazione of the Royal Society as in other years, and followed up the concerts at the Imperial Institute, mostly neglected by Londoners. One visit gave him occasion for the following note, the orchestra this year being from the Scala, Milan:

"Scene at the Imperial Institute this afternoon. Rain floating down in wayward drops. Not a soul except myself having tea in the gardens. The west sky begins to brighten. The red, blue, and white fairy lamps are like rubies, sapphires, turquoises, and pearls in the wet. The leaves of the trees, not yet of full size, are dripping, and the waiting-maids stand in a group with nothing to do. Band playing a 'Contemplazione' by Luzzi."

At a dinner at Sir Henry Thompson's he continued his past conversation with Sir W. Russell on his war experiences, and next morning learnt that Mr Gladstone had just died.

Back in Dorset in July he resumed cycling more vigorously than ever, and during the summer went upon that useful wheel to Bristol, Gloucester, Cheltenham, Sherborne, Poole, Weymouth, and many other places—sometimes with Mrs Hardy, sometimes with his brother.

In the middle of December *Wessex Poems* was published; and verse being a new mode of expression with him in print he sent copies to friends, among them one to Leslie Stephen, who said:

> It gave me a real pleasure. I am glad to think that you remember me as a friend. . . . I am always pleased to remember that "Far from the Madding Crowd" came out under my command. I then admired the poetry which was diffused through the prose; and can recognize the same note in the versified form. . . . I will not try to criticise or distinguish, but will simply say that they have pleased me and reminded me vividly of the old time. I have, as you probably know, gone through much since then. . . .

CHAPTER XXV

"Wessex Poems" and Others

1899–1900: *Aet.* 58–60

In the early weeks of this year the poems were reviewed in the customary periodicals—mostly in a friendly tone, even in a tone of respect, and with praise for many pieces in the volume; though by some critics not without umbrage at Hardy's having taken the liberty to adopt another vehicle of expression than prose-fiction without consulting them. It was probably these reviews that suggested to Hardy several reflections on poetry and criticism about this time, and the following gleanings of his opinions are from the rough entries he made thereon. Some no doubt were jotted down hastily, and might have been afterwards revised.

He observes that he had been under no delusion about the coldness and even opposition he would have to encounter—at any rate from some voices—in openly issuing verse after printing nothing (with trifling exceptions) but prose for so many years. That his reviewers should choose not only the subjects but also the methods in which he should exercise his pen; not that he should choose them, their own business being limited to pronouncing if or not he had achieved what he aimed at; was to these, as it still is to such, a canon of criticism. There were, however, many worthy exceptions.

Almost all the fault-finding was, in fact, based on the one great antecedent conclusion that an author who has published prose first and that largely, must necessarily express himself badly in verse, no reservation being added to except cases in which he may have published prose for temporary or compulsory reasons, or prose of a poetical kind, or have written verse first of all, or for a long time intermediately.

But there was really a valid excuse for the short-sighted belittlement of Hardy's art by these minor men wherever it occurred, even had his art been of the best, which perhaps he did not perceive so quickly as he might have perceived. By no fault of their own the power of looking clearly and responsively into his poetry as form and as content—meeting the mood of the poet half-way, as it were—was denied to critics in Hardy's case (except those of distinctly acute vision, few of whom would have been set by editors to waste their powers on a poet's first volume). They *could not* look clearly into it, by reason of the aforesaid obsession of the idea that novel-writing was Hardy's trade, and no other. There were those prose works standing in a row in front, catching the eye at every attempt to see the poetry, and forming an almost impenetrable screen.

Perhaps, had those who were baffled into an antecedent con- clusion by this screen been minds of any great power in judgment, they would have perceived that there might be an obvious trap for their intelligence in his order of publication. Theirs was so cheap a criticism that they might have guarded against it, and have been more inclined to exaggerate the other way, to show their insight.

In criticism generally, the fact that the date of publication is but an accident in the life of a literary creation, that the printing of a book is the least individual occurrence in the history of its contents, is often overlooked. In its visible history the publication is what counts, and that alone. It is then that the contents start into being for the outside public. In the present case, although it was shown that many of the verses had been written before their author dreamt of novels, the critics' view was little affected that he had "at the eleventh hour", as they untruly put it, taken up a hitherto uncared- for art.

It may be observed that in the art-history of the century there was an example staring them in the face of a similar modulation from one style into another by a great artist. Verdi was the instance, "that amazing old man" as he was called. Someone of insight wrote concerning him: "From the ashes of his early popularity, from *Il Trovatore* and its kind, there arose on a sudden a sort of phoenix

Verdi. Had he died at Mozart's death-age he would now be practically unknown." And another: "With long life enough Verdi might have done almost anything; but the trouble with him was that he had only just arrived at maturity at the age of threescore and ten or thereabouts, so that to complete his life he ought to have lived a hundred and fifty years."

But probably few literary critics discern the solidarity of all the arts. Curiously enough Hardy himself dwelt upon it in a poem that seems to have been little understood, though the subject is of such interest. It is called "Rome: The Vatican: Sala delle Muse"; in which a sort of composite Muse addresses him:

> "Be not perturbed", said she. "Though apart in fame,
> I and my sisters are one."

He amused himself by conjecturing that what had probably passed through the adverse section of the Fleet-Street mind—and perhaps did in many cases, not inexcusably, owing to the baffling obstacle mentioned—was reasoning of this sort, which he more than once expressed:

"It must perforce be prosy, for has he not been long a writer of prose?

"It must perforce be harsh and clumsy in form, for how can a writer of prose have any inner acquaintance with the music of verse?"

He would drily go on to trace the logic of those who reasoned thus:

"To prove the truth of my conclusion above stated—that a writer who publishes prose a long while before he publishes verse cannot be a true poet—I will pick out the prosy lines that can be found in his volume, and pillory them in my review, and convince readers by the following syllogism:

"This book of verse contains the above expressions.

"These expressions are not poetry.

"Therefore this book is not poetry."

That this syllogism, Hardy would add, exhibited—designedly or not—the familiar fallacy known as the Undistributed Middle, did not prevent it being employed—usually merrily employed—in dozens of reviews of his poems at this time and for many years later, almost indeed down to the end of his writing. The fact that all the poets of all the ages could be rejected by the same argument did not apparently strike its advancers at all.

Some famous bygone exemplars of this notorious fallacy were of course Gifford, Lockhart, and Macaulay. Looked at dispassionately it seems strange that it still lives on in reviewing practice. "If a valuer should pick out all the blasted and mildewed grains from a sack of a farmer's corn, put them together, and exhibit them as a sample of such corn, we should call him a rascal; but when a reviewer picks out the bad lines from a whole volume and quotes them alone as samples of the poet's work, he is considered a critic of honest insight." Such treatment was dealt out to Hardy by some smart hands—happily not nearly by all.

In short, this was a particular instance of the general and rather appalling conclusion to which he came—had indeed known before—that a volume of poetry, by clever manipulation, can be made to support any *a priori* theory about its quality. Presuppose its outstanding feature to be the defects aforesaid; instances can be found. Presuppose, as here was done, that it is overloaded with derivations from the Latin or Greek when really below the average in such words; they can be found. Presuppose that Wordsworth is unorthodox: instances can be found; that Byron is devout: instances can also be found. [The foregoing paragraphs are abridged from memoranda which Hardy set down apparently for publication; though he never published them.]

A point he realized more fully somewhat later was that he had flown in the face of his chances of a welcome by not being imitative. The only absolutely safe method of winning a hearty reception is that of shadowing and developing the philosophy, manner, and theology of some eminent poet who has lived shortly before the writer's date. There were Wordsworth, Tennyson, Browning: he had only to copy one of them to win commendation—or at any rate toleration, since the fact of having once written prose might prevent more. But no, he did not adopt that royal road.

He wrote somewhere: "There is no new poetry; but the new poet—if he carry the flame on further (and if not he is no new poet)—comes with a new note. And that new note it is that troubles the critical waters."

"Poetry is emotion put into measure. The emotion must come by nature, but the measure can be acquired by art."

One smart paragraphist said that he was nearly deluded into a belief in Hardy's verses after reading them one night; but he saved his critical credit by getting up on a cold wet morning and reading them again on an empty stomach. It happily cured his weakness. It was an apt illustration of the vicious practice of those who, in Henry James's words, prepare beforehand to limit their surrender to the book under review.

In the reception of this and later volumes of Hardy's poems there was, he said, as regards form, the inevitable ascription to ignorance of what was really choice after full knowledge. That the author loved the art of concealing art was undiscerned. For instance, as to rhythm. Years earlier he had decided that too regular a beat was bad art. He had fortified himself in his opinion by thinking of the analogy of architecture, between which art and that of poetry he had discovered, to use his own words, that there existed a close and curious parallel, each art, unlike some others, having to carry a rational content inside its artistic form. He knew that in architecture cunning irregularity is of enormous worth, and it is obvious that he carried on into his verse, perhaps unconsciously, the Gothic art-principle in which he had been trained—the principle of spontaneity, found in mouldings, tracery, and such-like—resulting in the "unforeseen" (as it has been called) character of his metres and stanzas—that of stress rather than of syllable, poetic texture rather than poetic veneer; the latter kind of thing, under the name of "constructed ornament", being what he, in common with every Gothic student, had been taught to avoid as the plague. He shaped his poetry accordingly, introducing metrical pauses, and reversed beats; and found for his trouble that some particular line of a poem exemplifying this principle was greeted by one of those terrible persons, the funny man of the critical press, with a jocular remark that such a line "did not make for immortality", the writer being probably a journalist who had never heard of pauses or beats of any kind. The same critic might have gone to one of our cathedrals (to follow up the analogy of architecture), and on discovering that the carved leafage of some capital or spandrel in the best period of Gothic art strayed freakishly out of its bounds over the moulding, where by rule it had no business to be, or that the enrichments of a string-course were not accurately spaced; or that there was a sudden blank in a wall where a window was to be expected from formal measurement, have declared with equally merry conviction, "This does not make for immortality".

One case of the kind, in which the poem "On Sturminster Foot-Bridge" was quoted with the remark that one could make as good music as that out of a milk-cart, betrayed the reviewer's ignorance of any perception that the metre was intended to be onomatopoeic, resembling the flopping of liquid; and another in the same tone disclosed that the reviewer had tried to scan the author's sapphics as heroics, having probably never heard of the other measure.

If any proof were wanted that Hardy was not at this time and later the apprentice at verse that he was supposed to be, it could be found in an examination of his studies over many years. Among his papers were quantities of notes on rhythm and metre: with outlines and experiments in innumerable original measures, some of which he adopted from time to time. These verse skeletons were mostly blank, and only designated by the usual marks for long and short syllables, accentuations, etc., but they were occasionally made up of "nonsense verses"—such as, he said, were written when he was a boy by students of Latin prosody with the aid of a "Gradus".

He could not discern, he said, in reviewers of the rank and file, that they had any sense of comparative values in literature, though this was of the essence of a good judgment. If a new poet were to arise in the future, to whose personality they had some objection in the role of a poet, they might as above stated devote a whole article to a few awkward phrases or imperfect rhymes picked out here and there from his volume, though it should contain the greatest ideas or strongest emotions of the century, on which endowment—the thing that would chiefly matter—they might say nothing.

Another obvious remark of these judges was: This man was a writer of novels and stories; therefore many of these poems are novels and stories in verse, which sufficiently condemns them. But when some of Browning's best poems, and Wordsworth's, and Chaucer's, and the immortal old balladists', are stories—not to mention all metrical plays—criticism is not helped by the remark.

Lastly, Hardy had a born sense of humour, even a too keen sense occasionally: but his poetry was in general placed by editors in the hands of reviewers well meaning enough, yet who had not a spark of that quality. Even if they were accustomed to Dickensian humour they were not to Swiftian. Hence it unfortunately happened that verses of a satirical, dry, caustic, or farcical cast were regarded by them with the deepest seriousness. In one case the tragic nature of his verse was instanced by the ballad called "The Bride-night Fire", or "The Fire at Tranter Sweatley's", the criticism being by an accomplished old friend of his own, Frederic Harrison, who deplored the painful nature of the bridegroom's end in leaving only a bone behind him. This piece of work Hardy had written and published when quite a young man, and had hesitated to reprint because of its too pronounced obviousness as a jest.

But he had looked the before-mentioned obstacles in the face, and their consideration did not move him much. He had written his poems entirely because he liked doing them, without any ulterior thought; because he wanted to say the things they contained and would contain—mainly the philosophy of life afterwards developed in *The Dynasts*; and so little did he expect from the press after his bitter experience of its caprices, so much less did he expect than he got, that he offered his publishers to take on his own shoulders the risk of producing the volume, so that if nobody bought it they should not be out of pocket. They were kind enough to refuse this offer, and took the risk on themselves; and fortunately they did not suffer.

A more serious meditation of Hardy's at this time than that on critics was the following:

"January (1899)—No man's poetry can be truly judged till its last line is written. What is the last line? The death of the poet. And hence there is this quaint consolation to any writer of verse—that it may be imperishable for all that anybody can tell him to the contrary; and that if worthless he can never know it, unless he be a greater adept at self-criticism than poets usually are."

Writing to Hardy in March about her late husband's tastes in literature Mrs Coventry Patmore observes:

> . . . It shows how constant he was to his *loves*. From 1875 [when he first met with the book—*vide ante*] to 1896 he continually had "A Pair of Blue Eyes" read aloud to him. Each time he felt the same shock of surprise and pleasure at its consummate art and pathos. In illness, when he asked for "A Pair of Blue Eyes" one knew he was able to *enjoy* again.

A correspondence on another matter than literature may be alluded to here. Mr W. T. Stead had asked Hardy to express his opinions on "A Crusade of Peace" in a periodical he was about to publish under the name of *War against War*. In the course of his reply Hardy wrote:

> As a preliminary, all civilized nations might at least show their humanity by covenanting that no horses should be employed in battle except for transport. Soldiers, at worst, know what they are

doing, but these animals are denied even the poor possibilities of glory and reward as a compensation for their sufferings.

His reply brought upon Hardy, naturally, scoffs at his impracticable tenderheartedness from the fire-eating swashbuckler class, and on the other hand, strong expressions of agreement from those who saw eye to eye with him.

In the following April (1899) the Hardys were again in London, where as in the previous year they took a flat in Wynnstay Gardens, though not the same one. They saw their friends as usual, on one of whom Hardy makes this observation after a call from him:

"When a person has gone, though his or her presence was not much desired, we regret the withdrawal of the grain of value in him, and overlook the mass of chaff that spoilt it. We realize that the essence of his personality was a human heart, though the form was uninviting."

"It would be an amusing fact, if it were not one that leads to such bitter strife, that the conception of a First Cause which the theist calls 'God', and the conception of the same that the so-styled atheist calls 'no-God', are nowadays almost exactly identical. So that only a minor literary question of terminology prevents their shaking hands in agreement, and dwelling together in unity ever after."

At the beginning of June Hardy was staying at a country-house not many miles from London, and among the guests was the young Duchess of M——, a lady of great beauty, who asked him if he would conduct her to the grave of the poet Gray, which was within a walk. Hardy did so and, standing half-balanced on one foot by the grave (as is well known, it was also that of Gray's mother), his friend recited in a soft voice the "Elegy" from the first word to the last in leisurely and lengthy clearness—without an error (which Hardy himself could not have done without some hitch in the order of the verses). With startling suddenness while duly commending her performance he seemed to have lived through the experience before. Then he realized what it was that had happened: in love of recitation, attitude, and poise, tone of voice, and readiness of memory, the fair lady had been the duplicate of the handsome dairymaid who had insisted on his listening to her rehearsal of the long and tedious gospels, when he taught in the Sunday school as a youth of fifteen. "What a thin veneer is that of rank and education over the natural woman," he would remark.

On the 18th he met A. E. Housman (the Shropshire Lad) for the first time probably, and on the 20th he visited Swinburne at Putney, of which visit he too briefly speaks; observing, "Again much inclined to his engaging, fresh, frank, almost childlike manner. Showed me his interesting editions, and talked of the play he was writing. Promised to go again." He also went a day or two later, possibly owing to his conversation with Swinburne (though he had been there before), to St. Mildred's, Bread Street, with Sir George Douglas, where Shelley and Mary Godwin were married, and saw the register, with the signatures of Godwin and his wife as witnesses. The church was almost unaltered since the poet and Mary had knelt there, and the vestry absolutely so, not having even received a coat of paint as it seemed. Being probably in the calling mood he visited George Meredith just afterwards, and found him "looking ruddy and well in the upper part; quite cheerful, enthusiastic and warm. Would gladly see him oftener, and must try to do so." At the end of the month he rambled in Westminster Abbey at midnight by the light of a lantern, having with some friends been admitted by Miss Bradley through the Deanery.

The last week or two of their stay in London this year was spent in seeing other friends, amongst them Hamilton Aidé, the earliest of his London acquaintance except Blomfield, and in attending the marriage of Mr (afterwards Lord) Harcourt.

Hardy had suffered from rather bad influenza this summer in town, and it left an affection of the eye behind it which he had never known before; and though he hoped it might leave him on his return to Dorchester it followed him there. He was, indeed, seldom absolutely free from it afterwards.

In July he replied to a communication from the Rationalist Press Association of which his friend Leslie Stephen was an honorary associate:

Though I am interested in the Society I feel it to be one which would naturally compose itself rather of writers on philosophy, science, and history, than of writers of imaginative works, whose effect depends largely on detachment. By belonging to a philosophic association imaginative writers place themselves in this difficulty, that they are misread as propagandist when they mean to be simply artistic and delineative.

The pleasures of bicycling were now at their highest appreciation, and many miles did Hardy and his wife, and other
companions, cover during the latter part of this summer. He was not
a long-distance cyclist, as was natural at fifty-nine, never exceeding
forty to fifty miles a day, but he kept vigorously going within the
limit, this year and for several years after. His wife, though an
indifferent walker, could almost equal him in cycle distances.

In October his sonnet on the departure of the troops for the Boer
War, which he witnessed at Southampton, appeared in the *Daily
Chronicle*, and in November the very popular verses called "The
Going of the Battery" were printed in the *Graphic*, the scene having
been witnessed at Dorchester. In December "The Dead Drummer"
(afterwards called "Drummer Hodge") appeared in *Literature*, and
"A Christmas Ghost Story" in the *Westminster Gazette*.

The latter months of this same year (1899) were saddened for him
by the sudden death of Sir Arthur Blomfield, shortly before the date
which had been fixed for a visit to him at Broadway by Hardy and
his wife. Thus was snapped a friendship which had extended over
thirty-six years.

Hardy's memoranda on his thoughts and movements —particularly the latter—which never reached the regularity of a diary—
had of late grown more and more fitful, and now (1900) that novels
were past and done with, nearly ceased altogether, such notes on
scenes and functions having been dictated by what he had thought
practical necessity; so that it becomes difficult to ascertain what
mainly occupied his mind, or what his social doings were. His
personal ambition in a worldly sense, which had always been weak,
dwindled to nothing, and for some years after 1895 or 1896 he
requested that no record of his life should be made, his verses being
kept going from pleasure in them. However, the poetic fantasy
entitled "The Souls of the Slain" was published in the *Cornhill* in the
April of this year, and he and his wife went to London this month
according to custom, though instead of taking a flat or house as in
former years they stayed on at the West Central Hotel in
Southampton Row, whose proprietor, Mr Frederick Smith, Hardy
had known almost from the time when Mr Smith was the esteemed
secretary to the Band of Hope Temperance Society. Taking no
great interest in fashion and rank as such, of which they had both
seen a good deal during the previous twenty years (though he much
valued the friendships it sometimes brought), he possibly thought it
advisable to economize, seeing that he had sacrificed so much of his

yearly income by not producing more novels. When one considers that he might have made himself a man of affluence in a few years by taking the current of popularity as it served, writing "best sellers", and ringing changes upon the novels he had already written, his bias towards poetry must have been instinctive and disinterested.

In a pocket-book of this date appears a diagram illustrating "the language of verse":

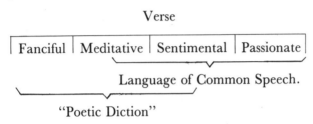

and the following note thereon:

"The confusion of thought to be observed in Wordsworth's teaching in his essay in the Appendix to 'Lyrical Ballads' seems to arise chiefly out of his use of the word 'imagination'. He should have put the matter somewhat like this: In works of *passion and sentiment* (not 'imagination and sentiment') the language of verse is the language of prose. In works of *fancy* (or *imagination*), 'poetic diction' (of the real kind) is proper, and even necessary. The diagram illustrates my meaning."

For some reason he spent time while here in hunting up Latin hymns at the British Museum, and copies that he made of several have been found, of dates ranging from the thirteenth to the seventeenth century, by Thomas of Celano, Adam of St.-Victor, John Mombaer, Jacob Balde, etc. That English prosody might be enriched by adapting some of the verse-forms of these is not unlikely to have been his view.

When they left London this year is uncertain, but we find Hardy at the latter part of July bicycling about Dorset with his friend Mr (later Sir) Hamo Thornycroft, and in August entertaining Mr A. E. Housman, Mr Clodd, and Sir Frederick Pollock, bicycling from Max Gate to Portland Bill and back in one day with the last-named, a performance whose chief onerousness lay in roughness of road-surface and steepness of gradient. Cycling went merrily along through August, September, and into October, mostly with Mrs Hardy and other companions, reaching to the outskirts of the county and into Somerset, Devon, and Hants. In October, declining to be interviewed by the representative of the American National Red Cross Society, he wrote as a substitute:

A society for the relief of suffering is entitled to every man's gratitude; and though, in the past century, material growth has been out of all proportion to moral growth, the existence of your Society leaves one not altogether without hope that during the next hundred years the relations between our inward and our outward progress may become less of a reproach to civilization.

In the same month he replied to the Rev. J. Alexander Smith:

On referring to the incident in "Tess of the d'Urbervilles" to which you draw my attention I do not find there anything more than an opinion, or feeling, on lay baptism by a person who was nettled at having his clerical ministration of the rite repulsed. The truth or error of his opinion is therefore immaterial. Nevertheless if it were worth while it might be plausibly argued that to refuse clerical performance and substitute lay perform-ance not from necessity but from pure obstinacy (as he held), might deprive that particular instance of lay baptism of its validity.

During the latter weeks of the year his wife was called from home to be with her sister, the widow of the Rev. Caddell Holder, the former incumbent of St. Juliot, who was in her last illness, her death occurring in December. At the very close of the year Hardy's much admired poem on the Century's End, entitled "The Darkling Thrush", was published in a periodical.

[End of the Nineteenth Century.]

CHAPTER XXVI

"Poems of the Past and the Present", and Others

1901–1903: *Aet.* 60–63

May found them in London, and hearing music. At an Ysäye Concert at Queen's Hall a passage in the descriptive programme evidently struck him—whether with amusement at the personifications in the rhetoric, or admiration for it, is not mentioned—for he takes the trouble to copy it:

" 'The solo enters at the twelfth bar. . . . Later in the movement a new theme is heard—a brief episode, the thematic material of the opening sufficing the composer's needs. In the Adagio the basses announce and develop a figure. Over this the soloists and first violins enter', &c. (Bach's Concerto in E.) I see them: black headed, larkspurred fellows, marching in on five wires."

"May 11. Leslie Stephen says: 'The old ideals have become obsolete, and the new are not yet constructed. . . . We cannot write living poetry on the ancient model. The gods and heroes are too dead, and we cannot seriously sympathize with . . . the idealized prize-fighter.' "

On May 22 Hardy dined again with Sir Henry Thompson at one of his "octaves" in Wimpole Street, and at the end of the month, while staying at Aldeburgh, visited with others the grave of Fitzgerald the translator of Omar Khayyám, in Boulge Churchyard, whereon was growing the rose-bush that had been raised from hips brought from Omar's grave in Persia.

On his return to London Hardy chronicles a feat of execution by Kubelik at a concert he attended at St. James's Hall—that of playing "pizzicato" on his violin the air of "The Last Rose of Summer" with Ernst's variations, and fingering and bowing a rapid accompaniment at the same time. At Mr Maurice Hewlett's Madame Sarah Bernhardt talked to him pensively on her consciousness that she was getting old, but on his taking his wife a day or two later to see her as the Duc in M. Rostand's *L'Aiglon* she appeared youthful enough, he said, "though unfortunately too melodramatically lime-lighted for naturalness".

At the end of the month the well-known literary and journalistic fraternity called the Whitefriars Club paid Hardy a visit at Max Gate, where they were entertained in a tent on the lawn. To diversify their journey from London they had travelled the last ten miles by road in open carriages, and the beautiful new summer dresses of the ladies were encrusted with dust. But nobody minded—except perhaps some of the ladies themselves—and the visit was a most lively one, though the part of the country they had driven through was not the most picturesque part.

In a letter on Rationalism written about this time, but apparently not sent, he remarks:

> My own interest lies largely in non-rationalistic subjects, since non-rationality seems, so far as one can perceive, to be the principle of the Universe. By which I do not mean foolishness, but rather a principle for which there is no exact name, lying at the indifference-point between rationality and irrationality.

In reply to the letter of an inquirer as to the preservation of the prospect from Richmond Hill, he wrote, 10 June 1901:

> I have always been in love with Richmond Hill—the Lass included—and though I think I could produce a few specimens from this part of the country that would be fairly even with it, or her, in point of beauty, I am grieved to hear that the world-famed view is in danger of disfigurement. I cannot believe that any such foolish local policy will be perservered in.

To Dr Arnaldo Cervesato of Rome

June 20: 1901.

I do not think that there will be any permanent revival of the old transcendental ideals; but I think there may gradually be developed an Idealism of Fancy; that is, an idealism in which fancy is no longer tricked out and made to masquerade as belief, but is frankly and honestly accepted as an imaginative solace in the lack of any substantial solace to be found in life.

"July 8. Pictures. My weakness has always been to prefer the large intention of an unskilful artist to the trivial intention of an accomplished one: in other words I am more interested in the high ideas of a feeble executant than in the high execution of a feeble thinker."

During the seven weeks ensuing he was preparing for the press a number of lyrics and other verses which had accumulated since *Wessex Poems* appeared, and sent off the manuscript to the publishers at the end of August. It was published in the middle of November under the title of *Poems of the Past and the Present*. He seems to have taken no notice of the reception accorded to the book by the press, though it might have flattered him to find that some characteristic ideas in this volume, which he never tried to make consistent—such as in the pieces entitled "The Sleep-worker", "The Lacking Sense", "Doom and She", and others—ideas that were further elaborated in *The Dynasts* and which reviewers in general passed over in silence, found their way into many prose writings after this date.

On the last day of the year he makes the following reflection: "After reading various philosophic systems, and being struck with their contradictions and futilities, I have come to this:—*Let every man make a philosophy for himself out of his own experience.* He will not be able to escape using terms and phraseology from earlier philosophers, but let him avoid adopting their theories if he values his own mental life. Let him remember the fate of Coleridge, and save years of labour by working out his own views as given him by his surroundings."

"Jan. 1 (1902). A Pessimist's apology.—Pessimism (or rather what is called such) is, in brief, playing the sure game. You cannot lose at it; you may gain. It is the only view of life in which you can never be disappointed. Having reckoned what to do in the worst possible circumstances, when better arise, as they may, life becomes child's play."

In reply this month to a writer in the Parisian *Revue Bleue* he gave it as his opinion that the effect of the South African War on English literature had been

> A vast multiplication of books on the war itself, and the issue of large quantities of warlike and patriotic poetry. These works naturally throw into the shade works that breathe a more quiet and philosophic spirit; a curious minor feature in the case among a certain class of writers being the disguise under Christian terminology of principles not necessarily wrong from the point of view of international politics, but obviously anti-Christian, because inexorable and masterful.

In London the same month he attended a meeting at the rooms of the Society of Authors, and with his wife was a guest at the wedding of Lady Helen Stewart and Lord Stavordale, afterwards Lord Ilchester.

In view of the approaching centenary of Victor Hugo's birth, Hardy amongst other European men of letters was asked at this time by a Continental paper for a brief tribute to the genius of the poet; and he sent the following:

> His memory must endure. His works are the cathedrals of literary architecture, his imagination adding greatness to the colossal and charm to the small.

March. "Poetry.—There is a latent music in the sincere utterance of deep emotion, however expressed, which fills the place of the actual word-music in rhythmic phraseology on thinner emotive subjects, or on subjects with next to none at all. And supposing a total poetic effect to be represented by a unit, its component fractions may be either, say:

"Emotion three-quarters, plus Expression one quarter, or

"Emotion one quarter plus Expression three-quarters.

"This suggested conception seems to me to be the only one which explains all cases, including those instances of verse that apparently infringe all rules, and yet bring unreasoned convictions that they are poetry."

In April of this year he was writing "A Trampwoman's Tragedy"—a ballad based on some local story of an event more or less resembling the incidents embodied, which took place between 1820 and 1830.

To Mr (afterwards Sir) Rider Haggard, who was investigating the conditions of agriculture and agricultural labourers, he gave the following information:

March: 1902.

My dear Haggard:

As to your first question, my opinion on the past of the agricultural labourers in this county: I think, indeed know, that down to 1850 or 1855 their condition was in general one of great hardship. I say in general, for there have always been fancy-farms, resembling St Clair's in "Uncle Tom's Cabin", whereon they lived as smiling exceptions to those of their class all around them. I recall one such, the estate-owner being his own farmer, and ultimately ruining himself by his hobby. To go to the other extreme; as a child I knew a sheep-keeping boy who to my horror shortly afterwards died of want—the contents of his stomach at the autopsy being raw turnip only. His father's wages were six shillings a week, with about two pounds at harvest, a cottage rent free, and an allowance of thorn faggots from the hedges as fuel. Between these examples came the great bulk of farms—wages whereon ranged from seven to nine shillings a week, and perquisites being better in proportion.

Secondly: as to the present. Things are of course widely different now. I am told that at the annual hiring-fair just past, the old positions were absolutely reversed, the farmers walking about and importuning the labourers to come and be hired, instead of, as formerly, the labourers anxiously entreating the stolid farmers to take them on at any pittance. Their present life is almost without exception one of comfort, if the most ordinary thrift be observed. I could take you to the cottage of a shepherd not many miles from here that has a carpet and brass-rods to the staircase, and from the open door of which you hear a piano strumming within. Of course bicycles stand by the doorway, while at night a large paraffin lamp throws out a perfect blaze of light upon the passer by.

The son of another labourer I know takes dancing lessons at a quadrille-class in the neighbouring town. Well, why not!

But changes at which we must all rejoice have brought other changes which are not so attractive. The labourers have become more and more migratory—the younger families in especial, who enjoy nothing so much as fresh scenery and new acquaintance. The consequences are curious and unexpected. For one thing, village tradition—a vast mass of unwritten folk-lore, local chronicle, local topography and nomenclature—is absolutely sinking, has nearly sunk, into eternal oblivion. I cannot recall a single instance of a labourer who still lives on the farm where he was born, and I can only recall a few who have been five years on their present farms. Thus you see, there being no continuity of environment in their lives, there is no continuity of information, the names, stories, and relics of one place being speedily forgotten under the incoming facts of the next. For example, if you ask one of the workfolk (they always used to be called "workfolk" hereabout—"labourers" is an imported word) the names of surrounding hills, streams; the character and circumstances of people buried in particular graves; at what spots parish personages lie interred; questions on local fairies, ghosts, herbs, &c, they can give no answer: yet I can recollect the time when the places of burial even of the poor and tombless were all remembered, and the history of the parish and squire's family for 150 years back known. Such and such ballads appertained to such and such a locality, ghost tales were attached to particular sites, and nooks wherein wild herbs grew for the cure of divers maladies were pointed out readily.

On the subject of the migration to the towns I think I have printed my opinions from time to time: so that I will only say a word or two about it here. In this consideration the case of the farm labourers merges itself in that of rural cottagers generally, including jobbing labourers, artisans, and nondescripts of all sorts who go to make up the body of English villagery. That these people have removed to the towns of sheer choice during the last forty years it would be absurd to argue, except as to that percentage of young, adventurous, and ambitious spirits among them which is found in all societies. The prime cause of the removal is, unquestionably, insecurity of tenure. If they do not escape this in the towns it is not fraught with such trying consequences there as in a village whence they may have to travel ten or twenty miles to find another house and other work.

Moreover, if in a town lodging an honest man's daughter should have an illegitimate child, or his wife should take to drinking, he is not compelled by any squire to pack up his furniture and get his living elsewhere, as is, or was lately, too often the case in the country. (I am neither attacking nor defending this order of things; I merely relate it: the landlord sometimes had reason on his side; sometimes not.)

Now why such migrations to cities did not largely take place till within the last forty years or so is, I think (in respect of farm labourers) that they had neither the means nor the knowledge in old times that they have now. And owing to the then stability of villagers of the other class—such as mechanics and small traders, the backbone of village life—they had not the inclination. The tenure of these latter was—down to about fifty years ago, a fairly secure one, even if they were not in the possession of small freeholds. The custom of granting leaseholds for three lives, or other life-holding privileges, obtained largely in our villages, and though tenures by lifehold may not be ideally good or fair they did at least serve the purpose of keeping the native population at home. Villages in which there is not now a single cottager other than a weekly tenant were formerly occupied almost entirely on the lifehold principle, the term extending over seventy or a hundred years; and the young man who knows that he is secure of his father's and grandfather's cottage for his own lifetime thinks twice and three times before he embarks on the uncertainties of a wandering career. Now though, as I have said, these cottagers were not often farm labourers, their permanency reacted on the farm labourers, and made their lives with such comfortable associates better worth living.

Thirdly: as to the future, the evils of instability, and the ultimate results from such a state of things, it hardly becomes me to attempt to prophesy here. That remedies exist for them and are easily applicable you will easily gather from what I have stated above.

"April 20th.—Vagg Hollow, on the way to Load Bridge (Somerset) is a place where 'things' used to be seen—usually taking the form of a wool-pack in the middle of the road. Teams and other horses always stopped on the brow of the hollow, and could only be made to go on by whipping. A waggoner once cut at the pack with his whip: it opened in two, and smoke and a hoofed figure rose out of it."

"May 1st. Life is what we make it as Whist is what we make it; but not as Chess is what we make it; which ranks higher as a purely intellectual game than either Whist or Life."

Letter sent to and printed in the *Academy and Literature*, May 17, 1902, concerning a review of Maeterlinck's *Apology for Nature*:

Sir:

In your review of M. Maeterlinck's book you quote with seeming approval his vindication of Nature's ways which is (as I understand it) to the effect that, though she does not appear to be just from our point of view, she may practise a scheme of morality unknown to us, in which she is just. Now, admit but the bare possibility of such a hidden morality, and she would go out of court without the slightest stain on her character, so certain should we feel that indifference to morality was beneath her greatness.

Far be it from my wish to distrust any comforting fantasy, if it can be barely tenable. But alas, no profound reflection can be needed to detect the sophistry in M. Maeterlinck's argument, and to see that the original difficulty recognized by thinkers like Schopenhauer, Hartmann, Haeckel, etc., and by most of the persons called pessimists, remains unsurmounted.

Pain has been, and pain is: no new sort of morals in Nature can remove pain from the past and make it pleasure for those who are its infallible estimators, the bearers thereof. And no injustice, however slight, can be atoned for by her future generosity, however ample, so long as we consider Nature to be, or to stand for, unlimited power. The exoneration of an omnipotent Mother by her retrospective justice becomes an absurdity when we ask, what made the foregone injustice necessary to her Omnipotence?

So you cannot, I fear, save her good name except by assuming one of two things: that she is blind and not a judge of her actions, or that she is an automaton, and unable to control them: in either of which assumptions, though you have the chivalrous satisfaction of screening one of her sex, you only throw responsibility a stage further back.

But the story is not new. It is true, nevertheless, that, as M. Maeterlinck contends, to dwell too long amid such reflections does no good, and that to model our conduct on Nature's apparent conduct, as Nietzsche would have taught, can only bring disaster to humanity.

> Yours truly,
>
> Thomas Hardy.

Max Gate, Dorchester.

In June Hardy was engaged in a correspondence in the pages of the *Dorset County Chronicle* on Edmund Kean's connection with Dorchester, which town he visited as a player before he became famous, putting up with his wife and child at an inn called "The Little Jockey" on Glyde Path Hill (standing in Hardy's time). His child died whilst here, and was buried in Trinity Churchyard near at hand. The entry in the Register runs as follows:

"Burials in the Parish of Holy Trinity in Dorchester in the County of Dorset in the year 1813:

"Name, Howard son of Edmund and Mary Kean. Abode, Residing at Glyde Path Hill in this Parish. When buried, Nov. 24. Age 4. By whom the Ceremony was performed, Henry John Richman."

Readers of the *Life* of Kean will remember the heaviness of heart with which he noted his experience at Dorchester on this occasion— that it was a very wet night, that there was a small audience, that, unless we are mistaken, the play was *Coriolanus* (fancy playing *Coriolanus* at Dorchester *now!*), that he performed his part badly. Yet he was standing on the very brink of fame, for it was on this very occasion that the emissary from Old Drury—Arnold the stage manager—witnessed his performance, and decided that he was the man for the London boards.

In his letters to the paper under the pseudonym of "History" Hardy observed:

> Your correspondent "Dorset" who proposes to "turn the hose" upon the natural interest of Dorchester people in Edmund Kean, should, I think, first turn the hose upon his own uncharitableness. His contention amounts to this, that because one of the greatest, if not the very greatest, of English tragedians was not without blemish in his morals, no admiration is to be felt for his histrionic achievements or regard for the details of his life. So, then, Lord Nelson should have no place in our sentiment, nor Burns, nor

Byron—not even Shakespeare himself—nor unhappily many another great man whose flesh has been weak. With amusing maladroitness your correspondent calls himself by the name of the county which has lately commemorated King Charles the Second—a worthy who seduced scores of men's wives to Kean's one.

Kean was, in truth, a sorely tried man, and it is no wonder that he may have succumbed. The illegitimate child of a struggling actress, the vicissitudes and hardships of his youth and young manhood left him without moral ballast when the fire of his genius brought him success and adulation. The usual result followed, and owing to the publicity of his life it has been his misfortune ever since to have, like Cassius in "Julius Caesar",

All his faults observed,
Set in a note-book, learn'd and conn'd by rote,

by people who show the Christian feeling of your correspondent.

The following week Hardy sent a supplementary note:

One word as to the building [in Dorchester] in which Kean performed in 1813. There is little doubt that it was in the old theatre yet existing [though not as such], stage and all, at the back of Messrs Godwin's china shop; and for these among other reasons. A new theatre in North Square [Qy. Back West Street?] built by Curme—was opened in February 1828, while there are still dwellers in Dorchester who have heard persons speak of seeing plays in the older theatre about 1821 or 1822, Kean's visit having been only a few years earlier.

During the latter half of this year 1902 Hardy was working more or less on the first part of *The Dynasts*, which was interrupted in August and September by bicycle trips, and in October by a short stay in Bath, where the cycling was continued. On one of these occasions having reached Bristol by road, and suddenly entered on the watered streets, he came off into the mud with a side-slip, and was rubbed down by a kindly coal-heaver with one of his sacks. In this condition he caught sight of some rare old volume in a lumber-shop; and looking him up and down when he asked the price the woman who kept the shop said: "Well, sixpence won't hurt ye, I suppose?" He used to state that if he had proposed threepence he would doubtless have got the volume.

In January (1903) he and his wife were at the wedding of Miss Madeleine Stanley and the Hon. St. John Brodrick, afterwards the Earl of Midleton, at St. George's, Hanover Square, and through May and June in London continuously.

To a correspondent who was preparing a Report on Capital Punishment for the Department of Economics, Stanford University, California, and who asked for the expression of his opinion on the advisability of abolishing it in highly civilized communities, he replied about this time:

> As an acting magistrate I think that Capital Punishment operates as a deterrent from deliberate crimes against life to an extent that no other form of punishment can rival. But the question of the moral right of a community to inflict that punishment is one I cannot enter into in this necessarily brief communication.

It may be observed that the writer describes himself as an "acting magistrate", yet he acted but little at sessions. He was not infrequently, however, on Grand Juries at the Assizes, where he would meet with capital offences.

Returning to the country in July he sat down to finish the first part of *The Dynasts*, the MS. of which was sent to the Messrs Macmillan at the end of September. He then corrected the proofs of "A Trampwoman's Tragedy" for the *North American Review*, in which pages it was published in November. When the ballad was read in England by the few good judges who met with it, they reproached Hardy with sending it out of the country for publication, not knowing that it was first offered to the *Cornhill Magazine*, and declined by the editor on the ground of it not being a poem he could possibly print in a family periodical. That there was any impropriety in the verses had never struck the author at all, nor did it strike any readers, so far as he was aware.

In December he answered an inquiry addressed to him by the editor of *L'Européen*, an international journal published in Paris:

I would say that I am not of opinion that France is in a decadent state. Her history seems to take the form of a serrated line, thus:

and a true judgment of her general tendency cannot be based on a momentary observation, but must extend over whole periods of variation.

What will sustain France as a nation is, I think, her unique accessibility to new ideas, and her ready power of emancipation from those which reveal themselves to be effete.

In the same month of December the first part of *The Dynasts* was published.

It was some time in this year that Hardy, in concurrence with his brother and sisters, erected in Stinsford Church a brass tablet to commemorate the connection of his father, grandfather, and uncle with the musical services there in the early part of the previous century, the west gallery, wherein their ministrations had covered altogether about forty years, having been removed some sixty years before this date. The inscription on the brass runs as follows:

Memoriae · Sacrum · Thomae · Hardy · patris · Jacobi · et · Thomae filiorum · qui · olim · in · hac · Ecclesia · per · annos · quadraginta (MDCCCII—MDCCCXLI) · fidicinis · munere · sunt · perfuncti. Ponendum · curaverunt · Thomae · junioris · filii · et · filiae: Thomas: Henricus: Maria: Catherina. MDCCCCIII.

CHAPTER XXVII

Part First of "The Dynasts"

1904–1905: *Aet.* 63–65

As *The Dynasts* contained ideas of some freshness, and was not a copy of something else, the course of a large number of critics was clear to them—not to consider it on its merits as a dramatic poem, but to save all trouble by treating it facetiously. This facetiousness was, to be sure, one form of censure, and presupposed the application of literary tests; though as a fact these were not applied as they should have been, primarily. The appraisement of the work was in truth, while nominally literary, at the core narrowly Philistine, and even theosophic. Its author had erroneously supposed that by writing a frank preface on his method—that the scheme of the drama was based on a tentative theory of things which seemed to accord with the mind of the age; but that whether such theory did or not so accord, and whether it were true or false, little affected his object, which was a poetical one wherein nothing more was necessary than that the theory should be plausible—a polemic handling of his book would be avoided. Briefly, that the drama being advanced not as a reasoned system of philosophy, nor as a new philosopy, but as a poem, with the discrepancies that are to be expected in an imaginative work, as such it would be read.

However, the latitude claimed was allowed but in few instances, and an invidious reception was pretty general, the substance of which was "On what ground do you arrogate to yourself a right to

343

express in poetry a philosophy which has never been expressed in poetry before?" This, of course, was not said directly, but veiled behind objections to other features of the production, in which the old game was played of describing the worst, and saying no word about the best.

Notwithstanding his hopes, he had a suspicion that such might be the case, as we may gather from a note he had written:

"The old theologies may or may not have worked for good in their time. But they will not bear stretching further in epic or dramatic art. The Greeks used up theirs: the Jews used up theirs; the Christians have used up theirs. So that one must make an independent plunge, embodying the real, if only temporary, thought of the age. But I expect that I shall catch it hot & strong for attempting it!"

Hardy replied to one of these criticisms in *The Times Literary Supplement* (*Times Lit. Sup.* Feb. 5 and Feb. 19, 1904), but did not make many private memoranda on the reviews. One memorandum is as follows:

"I suppose I have handicapped myself by expressing, both in this drama and previous verse, philosophies and feelings as yet not well-established or formally adopted into the general teaching; and by thus over-stepping the standard boundary set up for the thought of the age by the proctors of opinion, I have thrown back my chance of acceptance in poetry by many years. The very fact of my having tried to spread over art the latest illumination of the time has darkened counsel in respect of me.

"What the reviewers really assert is, not 'This is an untrue & inartistic view of life' but 'This is not the view of life that we people who thrive on conventions can permit to be painted.'—If, instead of the machinery I adopted, I had constructed a theory of a world directed by fairies, nobody would have objected, & the critics would probably have said, 'What a charming fancy of Mr Hardy's!' But having chosen a scheme which may or may not be a valid one, but is presumably much nearer reality than the fancy of a world ordered by fairies would be, they straightway lift their brows."

His mind was however drawn away from the perils of attempting to express his age in poetry by a noticeable change in his mother's state of health. She was now in her ninety-first year, and though she had long suffered from deafness was mentally as clear and alert as ever. She sank gradually, but it was not till two days before her death that she failed to comprehend his words to her. She died on

Easter Sunday, April 3, and was buried at Stinsford in the grave of her husband. She had been a woman with an extraordinary store of local memories reaching back to the days when the ancient ballads were everywhere heard at country feasts, in weaving shops, and at spinning-wheels; and her good taste in literature was expressed by the books she selected for her children in circumstances in which opportunities for selection were not numerous. The portraits of her which appeared in the *Sphere*, the *Gentlewoman*, the *Book Monthly* and other papers—the best being from a painting by her daughter Mary—show a face of dignity and judgment.

A month earlier he had sent a reply to the Rev. S. Whittell Key, who had inquired of him concerning "sport":

> I am not sufficiently acquainted with the many varieties of sport to pronounce which is, quantitatively, the most cruel. I can only say generally that the prevalence of those sports which consist in the pleasure of watching a fellow-creature, weaker or less favoured than ourselves, in its struggles by nature's poor resources only to escape the death-agony we mean to inflict by the treacherous contrivances of science, seems one of the many convincing proofs that we have not yet emerged from barbarism.
>
> In the present state of affairs there would appear to be no logical reason why the smaller children, say, of overcrowded families, should not be used for sporting purposes. Darwin has revealed that there would be no difference in principle; moreover, these children would often escape lives intrinsically less happy than those of wild birds and other animals.

During May he was in London reading at the British Museum on various days—probably historic details that bore upon *The Dynasts*—and went to Sunday concerts at the Queen's Hall, and to afternoon services at St. Paul's whenever he happened to be near the Cathedral, a custom of his covering many years before and after. The only large party they attended this summer seems to have been at Stafford House, St. James's; but at teas on the Terrace of the House of Lords and at small parties at Lady Londonderry's, Lady Windsor's, and Mrs Macmillan's they renewed acquaintance with other friends.

On June 28 *The Times* published the following letter:

Sir:

I should like to be allowed space to express in the fewest words a view of Count Tolstoy's philosophic sermon on war, of which you print a translation in your impression of to-day, and a comment in your leading article.

The sermon may show many of the extravagances of detail to which the world has grown accustomed in Count Tolstoy's later writings. It may exhibit, here and there, incoherence as a moral system. Many people may object to the second half of the dissertation—its special application to Russia in the present war (on which I can say nothing). Others may be unable to see advantage in the writer's use of theological terms for describing and illustrating the moral evolutions of past ages. But surely all these objectors should be hushed by his great argument, and every defect in his particular reasonings hidden by the blaze of glory that shines from his masterly general indictment of war as a modern principle, with all its senseless and illogical crimes.

Your obedient servant

Thomas Hardy.

Again in the country in August, Hardy resumed his cycling tours, meeting by accident Mr William Watson, Mr Francis Coutts (Lord Latymer), and Mr John Lane at Glastonbury, and spending a romantic day or two there among the ruins.

In October Hardy learnt by letter from Madras of the death of Mrs Malcolm Nicolson—the gifted and impassioned poetess known as "Laurence Hope", whom he had met in London; and he wrote a brief obituary notice of her in the *Athenæum* at the end of the month. But beyond this, and the aforesaid newspaper-letters, he appears to have printed very little during this year 1904. A German translation of *Life's Little Ironies* was published in *Aus Fremden Zungen*, in Berlin, and a French translation of *The Well-Beloved* undertaken.

His memoranda get more and more meagre as the years go on, until we are almost entirely dependent on letter-references, reviews, and casual remarks of his taken down by the present writer. It is a curious reversal of what is usually found in lives, where notes and diaries grow more elaborate with maturity of years. But it accords with Hardy's frequent saying that he took little interest in himself as a person, and his absolute refusal at all times to write his reminiscences.

In January (1905) he served as Grand Juror at the winter Assizes, and in the latter part of the month met Dr Shipley, Mr Asquith, Lord Monteagle, Sir Edgar Vincent and others at a dinner at the National Club given by Mr Gosse. At this time he was much interested in the paintings of Zurbaran, which he preferred to all others of the old Spanish School, venturing to think that they might some day be held in higher estimation than those of Velasquez, which were just then so much lauded.

About this time the romantic poem entitled "A Noble Lady's Tale" was printed in the *Cornhill Magazine*.

The first week in April Hardy left Dorchester for London *en route* for Aberdeen, the ancient University of which city had offered him the honorary degree of LL.D. and in accepting which he remarked:

> I am impressed by its coming from Aberdeen, for though a stranger to that part of Scotland to a culpable extent I have always observed with admiration the exceptional characteristics of the Northern University, which in its fostering encouragement of mental effort seems to cast an eye over these islands that is unprejudiced, unbiassed and unsleeping.

It was a distance of near 700 miles by the route he would have to take—almost as far as to the Pyrenees—over the northern stage of which winter still lingered, but his journey there and back was an easy one, the section from Euston Square to the north being performed in a train of sleeping-cars which crunched through the snow as if it were January, the occasion coinciding with the opening of the new sculpture-gallery, a function that brought many visitors from London. Hardy was hospitably entertained at the Chanonry Lodge, Old Aberdeen, by Principal and Mrs Marshall Lang, which was the beginning of a friendship that lasted till the death of the former. Among others who received the like honour at the same time were Professor Bury and Lord Reay.

In the evening there was a reception in the Mitchell Hall, Marischal College, made lively by Scotch reels and bag-pipers; and the next day, after attending at the formal opening of the sculpture-gallery, he was a guest at the Corporation Dinner at the Town Hall, where friends were warm, but draughts were keen to one from a southern county, and speeches, though good, so long, that he and the Principal did not get back to Chanonry Lodge till one o'clock.

On Sunday morning Hardy visited spots in and about Aberdeen

associated with Byron and others, and lunched at the Grand Hotel by the invitation of Mr (afterwards Sir) James Murray, dining at the same place with the same host, crossing hands in "Auld Lang Syne" with delightful people whom he had never seen before and, alas, never saw again. This was the "hearty way" (as it would be called in Wessex) in which they did things in the snowy north. To Hardy the whole episode of Aberdeen, he said, was of a most pleasant and unexpected kind, and it remained with him like a romantic dream.

Passing through London on his way south he breakfasted at the Athenæum, where he was shocked to learn of the death of his friend Lord St. Helier (Sir Francis Jeune) who had been ailing more or less since the loss of his only son in the previous August, and whose sister was Mrs Hardy's aunt by marriage. Hardy on his way down to Dorset was led to think of the humorous stories connected with the Divorce Court that the genial judge sometimes had told him when they were walking in the woods of Arlington Manor in the summer holidays; among them the tale of that worthy couple who wished to be divorced but disliked the idea of such an unpleasant person as a co-respondent being concerned in it, and so hit upon the plan of doing without him. The husband, saying he was going to Liverpool for a day or two, got a private detective to watch his house; but, instead of leaving, stayed in London, and at the dead of night went to his own house in disguise, and gave a signal. His wife came down in her dressing-gown and let him in softly, letting him out again before it was light. When the husband enquired of the detective he was informed that there was ample evidence; and the divorce was duly obtained.

Hardy could not remember whether it was a story of the same couple or of another, in which Sir Francis had related that being divorced they grew very fond of each other, the former wife becoming the husband's mistress, and living happily with him ever after.

As they had taken a flat at Hyde Park Mansions for this spring and summer Hardy did not stay long in Dorset, and they entered the flat the week before Easter. During April he followed up Tchaikowsky at the Queen's Hall concerts, saying of the impetuous march-piece in the last part of the Pathetic Symphony that it was the only music he knew that was able to make him feel exactly as if he were in a battle.

"May 5.—To the Lord Mayor's farewell banquet to Mr Choate at the Mansion House. Thought of the continuity of the institution, and the teeming history of the spot. A graceful speech by Arthur Balfour: a less graceful but more humorous one by Mr Choate. Spoke to many whom I knew. Sat between Dr Butler, Master of Trinity, and Sir J. Ramsay. Came home with Sir F. Pollock."

"May 6. On opening *The Times* this morning we found that Emma's uncle [Dr E. H. Gifford, sometime Archdeacon of London, Hon. Canon of Worcester], who married us 30 years ago, died yesterday under an operation." It was just a month after the death of his brother-in-law Lord St. Helier related above, and the two events threw a shadow over the Hardys' London sojourn this year.

"May 10. Lunched at the House of Lords with Gosse. Dined with the Omar Khayyám Club and met Lord Windsor, S. Solomon, Aston Webb, Lord Aberdeen, Sir Brampton Gurdon, &c."

This month he was seeing Ben Jonson's play, *The Silent Woman*, Shaw's *John Bull's Other Island* and *Man and Superman*, and went to the Royal Society's Conversazione; though for some days confined to the house by a sore throat and cough. At a lunch given by Sidney Lee at the Garrick in June he talked about Shakespeare with Sir Henry Irving, and was re-confirmed in his opinion that actors never see a play as a whole and in true perspective, but in a false perspective from the shifting point of their own part in it, Sir Henry having shied at Hardy's suggestion that he should take the part of Jaques.

In this June too, he paid a promised visit to Swinburne, and had a long talk with him; also with Mr Watts-Dunton—"Swinburne's grey eyes are extraordinarily bright still—the brightness of stars that do not twinkle—planets namely. In spite of the nervous twitching of his feet he looked remarkably boyish and well, and rather impish. He told me he could walk twenty miles a day, and was only an old man in his hearing, his sight being as good as ever. He spoke with amusement of a paragraph he had seen in a Scotch paper: 'Swinburne planteth, Hardy watereth, and Satan giveth the increase.' He has had no honours offered him. Said that when he was nearly drowned his thought was, 'My "Bothwell" will never be finished!' That the secret reason for Lady Byron's dismissal of Lord Byron was undoubtedly his *liaison* with Augusta. His (Swinburne's) mother [Lady Jane, *née* Ashburnham] used to say that it was the talk of London at the time. That the last time he visited his friend Landor the latter said plaintively that as he wrote only in a dead language (Latin), and a dying language (English), he would soon

be forgotten. Talking of poets he said that once Mrs Procter told him
that Leigh Hunt on a visit to her father one day brought an
unknown youth in his train and introduced him casually as Mr John
Keats. (I think, by the way, that she also told me of the incident.)
We laughed & condoled with each other on having been the two
most abused of living writers—he for 'Poems & Ballads' & I for
'Jude the Obscure'."

Later on in June he went to Mr Walter Tyndale's Exhibition of
Wessex pictures, some of which Hardy had suggested, and during
the remainder of their stay in London they did little more than
entertain a few friends at Hyde Park Mansions, and dine and lunch
with others.

June 26. 1905. To the Hon. Sec. of the Shakespeare Memorial
Committee:

> I fear that I shall have to leave town before the meeting of the
> Committee takes place.
> All I would say on the form of the Memorial is that one which
> embodies the calling of an important *street* or *square* after
> Shakespeare would seem to be as effectual a means as any of
> keeping his name on the tongues of citizens, and his personality in
> their minds.

In July they went back to Dorset. Here, in the same month, a
Nelson-and-Hardy exhibition was opened in Dorchester, the relics
shown being mainly those of the Captain of the *Victory*, who had
been born and lived near, and belonged to a branch of the Dorset
Hardys, of whom the subject of this memoir belonged to another.

On September 1 Hardy received a visit from 200 members of the
Institute of Journalists at their own suggestion, as they had arranged
a driving tour through his part of the country. There was an
understanding that no interviews should be printed, and to this they
honourably adhered. Their idea had been a call on him only, but
they were entertained at tea, for which purpose a tent 150 feet long
had to be erected on Max Gate lawn. "The interior with the sun
shining through formed a pretty scene when they were sitting down
at the little tables," Mrs Hardy remarks in a diary. "They all drove
off in four-in-hand brakes and other vehicles to Bockhampton,
Puddletown, Bere Regis and Wool." After they had gone it came on
to rain, and Hardy returning from Dorchester at ten o'clock met the
vehicles coming back in a procession, empty; "the horses tired and

steaming after their journey of 30 miles, and their coats and harness shining with rain and perspiration in the light of the lamps".

In pursuance of the above allusion to interviewing it may be stated that there are interviewers and interviewers. It once happened that an interviewer came specially from London to Hardy to get his opinions for the *Daily Mail*. Hardy said positively that he would not be interviewed on any subject. "Very well," said the interviewer, "Then back I go, my day and my expenses all wasted." Hardy felt sorry, his visitor seeming to be a gentlemanly and educated man, and said he did not see why he should hurry off, if he would give his word not to write anything. This was promised, and the interviewer stayed, and had lunch, and a pleasant couple of hours' conversation on all sorts of subjects that would have suited him admirably. Yet he honourably kept his promise, and not a word of his visit appeared anywhere in the pages of the paper.

In the middle of this month the 150th anniversary of the birth of the poet Crabbe at Aldeburgh in Suffolk was celebrated in that town, and Hardy accepted the invitation of Mr Edward Clodd to be present. There were some very good *tableaux vivants* of scenes from the poems exhibited in the Jubilee Hall, some good lectures on the poet, and a sermon also in the parish church on his life and work, all of which Hardy attended, honouring Crabbe as an apostle of realism who practised it in English literature three-quarters of a century before the French realistic school had been heard of.

Returning to Max Gate he finished the second part of *The Dynasts*—that second part which the New York *Tribune* and other papers had been positive would never be heard of, so ridiculous was the first—and sent off the MS. to the Messrs Macmillan in the middle of October.

"First week in November.—The order in which the leaves fall this year is: Chestnuts; Sycamores; Limes; Hornbeams; Elm; Birch; Beech."

A letter written November 5 of this year:

All I know about my family history is that it is indubitably one of the several branches of the Dorset Hardys—having been hereabouts for centuries. But when or how it was connected with the branch to which Nelson's Hardy's people belonged—who have also been hereabouts for centuries—I cannot positively say. The branches are always asserted locally to be connected, and no doubt are, and there is a strong family likeness. I have never investigated the matter, though my great-uncle knew the ramifications. The Admiral left no descendant in the male line, as you may know.

As to your interesting remarks on honours for men of letters, I have always thought that any writer who has expressed unpalatable or possibly subversive views on society, religious dogma, current morals, and any other features of the existing order of things, and who wishes to be free and to express more if they occur to him, must feel hampered by accepting honours from any government,—which are different from academic honours offered for past attainments merely."

To Mr Israel Zangwill on November 10:

It would be altogether presumptuous in me—so entirely outside Jewish life—to express any positive opinion on the scheme embodied in the pamphlet you send to me. I can only say a word or two of the nature of a fancy. To found an autonomous Jewish state or Colony, under British suzerainty or not, wears the look of a good practical idea, and it is possibly all the better for having no retrospective sentiment about it. But I cannot help saying that this retrospective sentiment among Jews is precisely the one I can best enter into.

So that if I were a Jew I should be a rabid Zionist no doubt. I feel that the idea of ultimately getting to Palestine is the particular idea to make the imaginative among your people enthusiastic—"like unto them that dream"—as one of you said in a lyric which is among the finest in any tongue, to judge from its power in a translation. You, I suppose, read it in the original; I wish I could. (This is a digression.)

The only plan that seems to me to reconcile the traditional feeling with the practical is that of regarding the proposed Jewish state on virgin soil as a stepping-stone to Palestine. A Jewish colony united and strong and grown wealthy in, say, East Africa, could make a bid for Palestine (as a sort of annexe)—say 100 years hence—with far greater effect than the race as scattered all over the globe can ever do; and who knows if by that time altruism may not have made such progress that the then ruler or rulers of Palestine, whoever they may be, may even hand it over to the expectant race, and gladly assist them, or part of them, to establish themselves there.

This expectation, nursed throughout the formation and development of the new territory, would at any rate be serviceable as an ultimate ideal to stimulate action. With such an idea lying behind the immediate one, perhaps the Zionists would reunite and co-operate with the New Territorialists.

I have written, as I said, only a fancy. But, as I think you know, nobody outside Jewry can take a deeper interest than I do in a people of such extraordinary character and history; who brought forth, moreover, a young reformer who, though only in the humblest walk of life, became the most famous personage the world has ever known.

At the end of 1905 a letter reached him from a correspondent in the Philippine Islands telling him that to its writer he was "like some terrible old prophet crying in the wilderness".

CHAPTER XXVIII

The Remainder of "The Dynasts"

1906–1908: *Aet.* 65–67

The Dynasts, Part II was not published till the first week in February, 1906, and its reception by the reviews was much more congratulatory than their reception of the first part, an American critical paper going so far as to say, "Who knows that this work may not turn out to be a masterpiece?" Hardy makes no remark, however, upon its reception, unless the following may be considered one:

"Critics.—The business of *knowing* is mostly carried on in the papers by those who don't know—and for the matter of that, everywhere."

This year they re-occupied the flat in Hyde Park Mansions that had been let to them by Lady Thompson the year before, and paid the customary visits to private views, concerts, and plays that are usually paid to such by people full of vigour from the country. Of the Wagner concerts he says:

"I prefer late Wagner, as I prefer late Turner, to early (which I suppose is all wrong in taste), the idiosyncrasies of each master being more strongly shown in these strains. When a man not contented with the grounds of his success goes on and on, and tries to achieve the impossible, then he gets profoundly interesting to me. Today it was early Wagner for the most part: fine music, but not so particularly his—no spectacle of the inside of a brain at work like the inside of a hive."

An attack of influenza, which he usually got while sojourning in London, passed off, and they entertained many friends at the flat as usual—among them, according to Mrs Hardy's diary, being Lady Queensberry, Count and Countess Lützow, Mr and Mrs Crackanthorpe, Lady Burghclere, Mr Owen Wister, Lady Grove, M. and Mme. Jacques Blanche, Miss Tobin of San Francisco, and others whom they were accustomed to see at these times—and went out to various meetings and dinners, though he does not write them down in detail as when he thought he must. They included one at Vernon Lushington's, where Hardy was interested in the portrait of his host's father, the Lushington of the Lady Byron mystery, who kept his secret honourably; also a luncheon in a historic room weighted with its antiquity, the dining-room of the Arch-Deaconry of Westminster, with Dr Wilberforce. It was this year that Hardy met Dr Grieg the composer and his wife, and when, discussing Wagner music, he said to Grieg that the wind and rain through trees, iron railings, and keyholes fairly suggested Wagner music; to which the rival composer responded severely that he himself would sooner have the wind and rain.

On the 21st May the following letter, in which Hardy gives a glimpse of himself as a young man in London, appeared in *The Times*:

Sir,

    This being the 100th anniversary of J. Stuart Mill's birth, and as writers like Carlyle, Leslie Stephen, and others have held that anything, however imperfect, which affords an idea of a human personage in his actual form and flesh, is of value in respect of him, the few following words on how one of the profoundest thinkers of the last century appeared 40 years ago to the man in the street may be worth recording as a footnote to Mr Morley's admirable estimate of Mill's life and philosophy in your impression of Friday.

    It was a day in 1865, about 3 in the afternoon, during Mill's candidature for Westminster. The hustings had been erected in Covent-garden, near the front of St. Paul's Church; and when I—a young man living in London—drew near to the spot, Mill was speaking. The appearance of the author of the treatise "On Liberty" (which we students of that date knew almost by heart) was so different from the look of persons who usually address crowds in the open air that it held the attention of people for whom such a gathering in itself had little interest. Yet it was, primarily, that of a man out of place. The religious sincerity of his speech was jarred on by his environment—a group on the hustings who, with few exceptions, did not care to understand him fully, and a crowd below who could not. He stood bareheaded, and his vast pale brow, so thin-skinned as to show the blue veins, sloped back like a stretching upland, and conveyed to the observer a curious sense of perilous exposure. The picture of him as personified earnestness surrounded for the most part by careless curiosity derived an added piquancy—if it can be called such—from the fact that the cameo clearness of his face chanced to be in relief against the blue shadow of a church which, on its transcendental side, his doctrines antagonized. But it would not be right to say that the throng was absolutely unimpressed by his words; it felt that they were weighty, though it did not quite know why.

Your obedient servant,

Thomas Hardy.

Hyde Park Mansions, May 20.

The same month Mrs Hardy makes the following note: "May 30. Returned to Max Gate for a day or two. I gardened a little, and had the first strange fainting-fit [I had known]. My heart seemed to stop; I fell, and after a while a servant came to me." (Mrs Hardy died of heart-failure six years after.)

During this summer in London M. Jacques Blanche, the well-known French painter, who had a studio in Knightsbridge, painted Hardy's portrait in oils. And a paper called "Memories of Church Restoration", which he had written, was read in his enforced absence by Colonel Eustace Balfour at the annual meeting of the Society for the Protection of Ancient Buildings.

At the end of the lecture great satisfaction was expressed by speakers that Hardy had laid special emphasis on the value of the human associations of ancient buildings—for instance, in the pews of churches—since they were generally slighted in paying regard to artistic and architectural points only.

As the June month drew on Hardy seems to have been at the British Museum Library verifying some remaining details for *The Dynasts*, Part Third; also incidentally going to see the *Daily Telegraph* printed, and to meet a group of German editors on a visit to

England. He returned with his wife to Dorset towards the latter part of July.

At the end of July he wrote to Pittsburgh, U.S.A.—

The handsome invitation of the Trustees of the Pittsburgh Institute that I should attend the dedication with wife or daughter, free of expense to us from the time we leave home till we return again, is a highly honouring and tempting one. But I am compelled to think of many contingent matters that would stand in the way of my paying such a visit, and have concluded that I cannot undertake it.

Please convey my thanks to Mr Carnegie and the trustees.

"August 15. Have just read of the death of Mrs Craigie in the papers. . . . Her description of the artistic temperament is clever; as being that which 'thinks more than there is to think, feels more than there is to feel, sees more than there is to see'. It reveals a bitterness of heart that was not shown on the surface by that brilliant woman."

On August 17 he started on a tour to some English cathedrals with his brother, which included Lincoln, Ely, the Cambridge colleges, and Canterbury; and finished out the summer with bicycling in Dorset and Somerset. He must have been working at the third part of *The Dynasts* at intervals this year, though there is apparently no record of his doing so.

1907

The poem entitled "New Year's Eve", written in 1906, was issued in the·January number of the *Fortnightly Review*, 1907 (afterwards reprinted in the volume called *Time's Laughingstocks*). Some time in the same month he made the following notes on kindred subjects:

"An ephemeral article which might be written:

'The Hard Case of the Would-be-Religious.'
'By Sinceritas.'

"Synopsis.—Many millions of the most thoughtful people in

England are prevented entering any church or chapel from year's end to year's end.

"The days of creeds are as dead and done with as the days of Pterodactyls.

"Required: services at which there are no affirmations and no supplications.

"Rationalists err as far in one direction as Revelationists or Mystics in the other; as far in the direction of logicality as their opponents away from it.

"*Religions, religion,* is to be used in the article in its modern sense entirely, as being expressive of nobler feelings towards humanity and emotional goodness and greatness, the old meaning of the word—ceremony, or ritual—having perished or nearly.

"We enter church, and we have to say, 'We have erred and strayed from thy ways like lost sheep', when what we want to say is, 'Why are we made to err and stray like lost sheep?' Then we have to sing, 'My soul doth magnify the Lord', when what we want to sing is, 'O that my soul could find some Lord that it could magnify! Till it can, let us magnify good works, and develop all means of easing mortals' progress through a world not worthy of them.'

"Still, being present, we say the established words full of the historic sentiment only, mentally adding, 'How happy our ancestors were in repeating in all sincerity these articles of faith!' But we perceive that none of the congregation recognizes that we repeat the words from an antiquarian interest in them, and in a historic sense, and solely in order to keep a church of some sort afoot—a thing indispensable; so that we are pretending what is not true; that we are believers. This must not be; we must leave. And if we do, we reluctantly go to the door, and creep out as it creaks complainingly behind us."

Hardy, however, was not a controversialist in religion or anything else, and it should be added here that he sometimes took a more nebulous view, that may be called transmutative, as in a passage that he wrote some time later:

"Christianity nowadays as expounded by Christian apologists has an entirely different meaning from that which it bore when I was a boy. If I understand, it now limits itself to the religion of emotional morality and altruism that was taught by Jesus Christ, or nearly so limits itself. But this teaching does not appertain especially to Christianity: other moral religions within whose sphere the name of Christ has never been heard, teach the same thing. Perhaps this is a mere question of terminology, and does not much matter. That the dogmatic superstitions read every Sunday are merely a commemorative recitation of old articles of faith held by our grandfathers, may not much matter either, as long as this is well understood. Still it would be more honest to make these points clearer by re-casting the Liturgy, for their real meaning is often misapprehended. But there seems to be no sign of such a clearing up, and I fear that since the 'Apology' [in *Late Lyrics*], in which I expressed as much some years ago, no advance whatever has been shown: rather indeed a childish back-current towards a belief in magic rites."

"February 8th.—E. goes to London to walk in the suffragist procession tomorrow."

In March occurred the death of a friend—the Rev. T. Perkins, rector of Turnworth, Dorset—with whom Hardy was in sympathy for his humane and disinterested views, and staunch support of the principle of justice for animals, in whose cause he made noble sacrifices, and spent time and money that he could ill afford. On the 29th of the month Hardy enters a memorandum:

"Eve of Good Friday. 11.30 p.m. Finished draft of Part III of 'The Dynasts'." He had probably been so far embittered by the supercilious reception of the first part, and the doubtful reception of the second part, as not to expect the change of view which was about to give to the third part, and the whole production, a warm verdict of success, or he would not have followed the entry by the addendum:

"Critics can never be made to understand that the failure may be greater than the success. It is their particular duty to point this out; but the public points it out to them. To have strength to roll a stone weighing a hundredweight to the top of the Mount is a success, and to have the strength to roll a stone of ten hundredweight only half-way up that mount, is a failure. But the latter is two or three times as strong a deed."

They again took the flat in Hyde Park Mansions for the spring and summer, and moved thither the third week in April, whence they made their usual descent on friends and acquaintances, picture-galleries, and concert-rooms. It was this year that they met Mr and Mrs Bernard Shaw—it is belived for the first time. They also received at the flat their customary old friends, including Mr and Mrs J. M. Barrie, Lady Strachey and daughters, Colonel and Mrs Mount-Batten, Sir Walter and Lady Grove, M. and Mme Jacques Blanche, Mrs Saxton Noble, and many others.

In May he was present at an informal but most interesting dinner at the house of his friend Dr Hagberg Wright, where he met M. and Mme Maxim Gorky, Mr H. G. Wells, Mr Bernard Shaw, Mr Conrad, Mr Richard Whiteing, and others. A disconcerting but amusing accident was the difficulty of finding Mr Wright's flat, on account of which the guests arrived at intervals, and had their dinners in succession, the Gorkys coming last after driving two hours about London, including the purlieus of Whitechapel, which he had mistaken for "Westminster". Naturally it was a late hour when the party broke up.

June 2. Hardy's birthday, which he kept by dining at Lady St. Helier's.

Hyde Park Mansions.
June 2nd. 1907.

To Edward Wright Esq.

Dear Sir:

Your interesting letter on the philosophy of "The Dynasts" has reached me here. I will try to answer some of your inquiries.

I quite agree with you in holding that the word "Will" does not perfectly fit the idea to be conveyed—a vague thrusting or urging internal force in no predetermined direction. But it has become accepted in philosophy for want of a better, and is hardly likely to be supplanted by another, unless a highly appropriate one could be found, which I doubt. The word that you suggest—Impulse— seems to me to imply a driving power behind it; also a spasmodic movement unlike that of, say, the tendency of an ape to become a man and other such processes.

In a dramatic epic—which I may perhaps assume "The Dynasts" to be—some philosophy of life was necessary, and I went on using that which I had denoted in my previous volumes of verse (and to some extent prose) as being a generalized form of what the thinking world had gradually come to adopt, myself included. That the Unconscious Will of the Universe is growing aware of Itself I believe I may claim as my own idea solely—at which I arrived by reflecting that what has already taken place in a fraction of the whole (i.e. so much of the world as has become conscious) is likely to take place in the mass;—and there being no Will outside the mass—that is, the Universe—the whole Will becomes conscious thereby: and ultimately, it is to be hoped, sympathetic.

I believe too, that the Prime Cause, this Will, has never before been called "It", in any poetical literature, English or foreign.

This theory, too, seems to me to settle the question of Free-will v. Necessity. The will of a man is, according to it, neither wholly free not wholly unfree. When swayed by the Universal Will (which he mostly must be as a subservient part of it) he is not individually free; but whenever it happens that all the rest of the Great Will is in equilibrium the minute portion called one person's will is free, just as a performer's fingers are free to go on playing the pianoforte of themselves when he talks or thinks of something else and the head does not rule them.

In the first edition of a drama of the extent of "The Dynasts" there may be, of course, accidental discrepancies and oversights which seem not quite to harmonize with these principles; but I hope they are not many.

The third part will probably not be ready till the end of this or the beginning of next year; so that I have no proofs as yet. I do not think, however, that they would help you much in your proposed article. The First and Second Parts already published, and some of the Poems in "Poems of the Past and the Present" exhibit fairly enough the whole philosophy.

Concerning Hardy's remark in this letter on the Unconscious Will being an idea already current, though that its growing aware of Itself might be newer, and that there might be discrepancies in the Spirits' philosophy, it may be stated that he had felt such questions of priority and discrepancy to be immaterial where the work was offered as a poem and not as a system of thought.

On the 22nd of June they were guests at King Edward's Garden-Party at Windsor Castle, and a few days later at Mr Reginald Smith's met Sir Theodore Martin, then nearly ninety-one, Hardy remembering when as a young man he had frequented the pit of Drury Lane to see Lady Martin—then Miss Helen Faucit—in Shakespeare characters. His term at Hyde-Park Mansions came to an end in the latter part of July, and they returned to Max Gate, though Hardy attended as the guest of Dr Macdonald a dinner a week later given by the Medico-Psychological Society, where he had scientific discussions with Sir James Crichton Browne and Sir Clifford Allbutt, and where one of the speakers interested Hardy by saying that all great things were done by men "who were not at ease".

To a Japanese correspondent.

Mr K. Minoura, Vice-President, House of Representatives, Tokio.

August 13. 1907.

Dear Sir:

I am unable to express well-defined opinions on Japan and her people. I can only express a hope, which is that your nation may not become absorbed in material ambitions masked by thread-bare conventions, like the European nations and America, but that it may develop to an enlightened spirituality that shall become a shining example.

That autumn Sir Frederick and Lady Treves took a house near Max Gate, and Hardy frequently discussed with the Serjeant-surgeon a question which had drawn their attention for a long time, both being Dorset men; that of the "poor whites" in Barbadoes—where a connection of Hardy's had been a judge—a degenerate, decadent race, descendants of the Dorset and Somerset "rebels" who were banished there by Judge Jeffreys, and one of whom had been a collateral ancestor of Hardy's on the maternal side.

He was now reaching a time of life when shadows were continually falling. His friend Pretor, Fellow of St. Catharine's College, Cambridge, wrote to tell him he was dying, and asked him for an epitaph. Hardy thought of an old one:

> If a madness 'tis to weepe
> For a man that's fall'n asleepe,
> How much more for that we call
> Death—the sweetest sleepe of all!

They still kept up a little bicycling this autumn, but he did some writing, finishing the third part of *The Dynasts* in September, and posting the MS. to the publishers shortly after.

In November he sent to the Dorsetshire Regiment in India, by request, an old tune of his grandfather's called "The Dorchester Hornpipe", for the fifes-and-drums, as a marching tune with the required local affinity, which he himself had fiddled at dances as a boy. He wound up the year by sending to the Wessex Society of Manchester, also at their request, a motto for the Society:

> While new tongues call, and novel scenes unfold,
> Meet may it be to bear in mind the old. . . .
> Vain dreams, indeed, are thoughts of heretofore;
> What then? Your instant lives are nothing more.

About the same time he forwarded "A Sunday Morning Tragedy" to the *English Review* as wished, where it appeared shortly after; and also in fulfilment of a promise, sent the following old-fashioned psalm-tunes associated with Dorsetshire to the Society of Dorset Men in London, of which he was President elect for the ensuing year:

Frome: Wareham: Blandford: New Poole: Bridport: Lulworth: Rockborne: Mercy: Bridehead: Charmouth.

The concluding part of *The Dynasts* was published about six weeks later and was the cause of his receiving many enthusiastic letters from friends and strangers, among which the following from the far west of Australia may be given as a specimen:

> My thanks for your tremendous new statement in "The Dynasts" of the world-old problem of Freewill versus Necessity. You have carried me on to the mountain with Jesus of Nazareth, and, viewing with him the great conflict below, one chooses with him to side with the Spirit of the Pities, in the belief that they will ultimately triumph; and even if they do not we at least will do our little to add to the joy rather than to the woe of the world. . . . The Spirit of the Pities is indeed young in comparison with The Years, and so we must be patient. . . . Your conception of the Immanent Will—irresponsible, blind, but possibly growing into self-consciousness, was of great significance to me, from my knowledge of Dr Bucke's theory of the Cosmic Consciousness.

In connection with this subject it may be here recalled in answer to writers who now and later were fond of charging Hardy with postulating a malignant and fiendish God, that he never held any views of the sort, merely surmising an indifferent and unconscious force at the back of things, "that neither good nor evil knows". His view is shown, in fact, to approximate to Spinoza's, and later Einstein's—that neither chance nor purpose governs the universe, but necessity.

PART VII

"Time's Laughingstocks", "Satires of Circumstance", and "Moments of Vision"

CHAPTER XXIX

Deaths of Swinburne and Meredith

1908–1909: *Aet.* 67–69

In March he finished preparing a book of selections from the poems of William Barnes, for the Clarendon Press, Oxford, with a critical preface and glossary.

In April Lady St. Helier and a party motored from beyond Newbury to Max Gate and back, arriving within five minutes of the time specified, although the distance each way was seventy-five miles. It was considered a good performance in those days. At the end of the month he dined at the Royal Academy, but was in Dorchester at a performance by the local Dramatic Society of some scenes from *The Dynasts*—the first attempt to put on the stage a dramatic epic that was not intended for staging at all. In May he sent his Presidential Address to the Society of Dorset Men in London, to be read by the Secretary, as he was always a victim to influenza and throat trouble if he read or spoke in London himself, and afterwards on request sent the original manuscript. (By the way, the address never was read, so he might have saved himself the trouble of writing it. What became of the manuscript is unknown.)

The following letter to Mr Robert Donald in May explains itself:

If I felt at all strongly, or indeed weakly, on the desirability of a memorial to Shakespeare in the shape of a theatre, I would join the Committee. But I do not think that Shakespeare appertains particularly to the theatrical world nowadays, if ever he did. His distinction as a minister to the theatre is infinitesimal beside his distinction as a poet, man of letters, and seer of life, and that his expression of himself was cast in the form of words for actors and not in the form of books to be read was an accident of his social circumstances that he himself despised. I would, besides, hazard the guess that he, of all poets of high rank whose works have taken a stage direction, will some day cease altogether to be acted, and be simply studied.

I therefore do not see the good of a memorial theatre, or for that matter any other material monument to him, and prefer not to join the Committee.

Nevertheless I sincerely thank you for letting me know how the movement is progressing, and for your appreciative thought that my joining the promoters would be an advantage.

Hardy afterwards modified the latter part of the above opinion in favour of a colossal statue in some public place.

It appears that the Hardys did not take any house or flat in London this year, contenting themselves with short visits and hotel quarters, so that there is not much to mention. From letters it can be gathered that at a dinner his historic sense was keenly appealed to by the Duchess of St. Albans taking a diamond pin from her neck and casually telling him it had been worn by Nell Gwynne; and that in May or June he paid a few days' visit to Lord Curzon at Hackwood Park, where many of the house-party, which included Lady Elcho, Mr and Mrs Charteris, Sir J. and Lady Poynder, Lord Robert Cecil, Mr Haldane, Alfred and Mrs Alfred Lyttleton, Mr and Mrs Rochfort Maguire, Lord and Lady Cromer, Arthur Balfour, and Professor Walter Raleigh, went into the wood by moonlight to listen to the nightingale, but made such a babble of conversation that no nightingale ventured to open his bill.

In July Hardy was again in London with Mrs Hardy, and was present at the unveiling by Lord Curzon of the memorial to his friend "John Oliver Hobbes" (Mrs Craigie) at University College, where he had the pleasure of hearing his writings cried down by a speaker, nobody knowing him to be present. During some of these days he sat to Sir Hubert Herkomer for his portrait, kindly presented to him by the painter. He went on to Cambridge to the Milton Celebration, where at the house of his friend Sir Clifford Allbutt he met Mr Robert Bridges the poet-laureate for the first time, and made the acquaintance of Dr Peile the Master of Christ's College, Sir James ("Dictionary") Murray, and others. *Comus* was played at the theatre, in which performance young Rupert Brooke appeared as the attendant Spirit, but Hardy did not speak to him, to his after-regret.

This month he lunched at the House of Commons with Sir Benjamin Stone, renewing acquaintance with Arthur Balfour, T. P. O'Connor, Sir E. Poynter, Sir E. Maunde Thompson, and the Japanese Ambassador, afterwards going over Westminster School with Dr Gow.

The remainder of the month was spent in Dorset, where he took his wife as usual to local garden-parties, at one of which he met for the last time his friend Bosworth Smith, the long House-master at Harrow, who told him he was soon to undergo a severe surgical operation—under which operation he sank and died three months after. This was the fourth of his friends and relations that had sunk under the surgeon's knife in four years—leaving a blank that nothing could fill.

"August 18. The Poet takes note of nothing that he cannot feel emotively.

"If all hearts were open and all desires known—as they would be if people showed their souls—how many gapings, sighings, clenched fists, knotted brows, broad grins, and red eyes should we see in the market-place!"

The autumn was filled by little journeys to cathedrals, Mrs Hardy having gone across the Channel with her niece for a few weeks, a visit to his sister at Swanage, whither she had gone for change of air, a visit from Francis Coutts [afterwards Lord Latymer] and Mr Ernest Coleridge, and in December by attending a dinner at the Mansion House to commemorate Milton, from which he returned in company with his friend Mr S. Butcher, walking up and down with him late that night in Russell Square, conversing on many matters as if they knew they would never meet again. Hardy had a great liking for him, and was drawn to him for the added reason that he and his family had been warm friends of Hardy's dead friend Horace Moule.

In the following January (1909) the University of Virginia

invited him to attend the commemoration of the 100th anniversary
of the birth of Edgar Allan Poe, and in writing his thanks for the
invitation Hardy adds these remarks:

> The University of Virginia does well to commemorate the
> birthday of this poet. Now that lapse of time has reduced the
> insignificant and petty details of his life to their true proportion
> beside the measure of his poetry, and softened the horror of the
> correct classes at his lack of respectability, that fantastic and
> romantic genius shows himself in all his rarity. His qualities,
> which would have been extraordinary anywhere, are much more
> extraordinary for the America of his date.
>
> Why one who was in many ways disadvantageously circum-
> stanced for the development of the art of poetry should have been
> the first to realize to the full the possibilities of the English
> language in rhyme and alliteration is not easily explicable.
>
> It is a matter for curious conjecture whether his achievements
> in verse would have been the same if the five years of childhood
> spent in England had been extended to adult life. That
> "unmerciful disaster" hindered those achievements from being
> carried further must be an endless regret to lovers of poetry.

At the beginning of this year Hardy was appointed by the Dorset
Court of Quarter Sessions a Representative Governor of the
Dorchester Grammar School, a position he filled till the end of 1925.
He said he was not practical enough to make a good governor, but
was influenced to accept the office by the fact that his namesake
Thomas Hardy of Melcombe Regis who died in 1599 was the
founder of the school. The latter has a monument in St. Peter's
Church, Dorchester (*vide ante*), and is believed to have been of the
same stock as the Thomas Hardy of this memoir.

In March came the last letter he was ever to receive from George
Meredith, in which the elder writes:

> The French review herewith comes to my address and is, as
> you see by the superscription, intended for you.
>
> I am reminded that you are among the kind souls who thought
> of me on my 80th [birthday] and have not been thanked for their
> testimony of it. . . . The book [*The Dynasts*] was welcome all the
> more as being a sign that this big work was off your mind. How it
> may have been received I cannot say, but any book on so large a
> scale has to suffer the fate of a Panorama, and must be visited

again and again for a just impression of it to be taken. I saw that somewhere in your neighbourhood it was represented in action. That is the way to bring it more rapidly home to the mind. But the speaker of Josephine's last words would have to be a choice one.

The representation had been in Dorchester, and was limited to a few of the country scenes.

On the 10th April he heard of the death of Swinburne, which was the occasion of his writing the following letter:

Max Gate, April 12. 1909

Dear ——

For several reasons I could not bring myself to write on Swinburne immediately I heard that, to use his own words, "Fate had undone the bondage of the gods" for him. . . .

No doubt the press will say some good words about him now he is dead and does not care whether it says them or no. Well, I remember what it said in 1866, when he did care, though you do not remember it, and how it made the blood of some of us young men boil.

Was there ever such a country—looking back at the life, work, and death of Swinburne—is there any other country in Europe whose attitude towards a deceased poet of his rank would have been so ignoring and almost contemptuous? I except *The Times*, which has the fairest estimate I have yet seen. But read *The Academy* and *The Nation*.

The kindly cowardice of many papers is overwhelming him with such toleration, such theological judgments, hypocritical sympathy, and misdirected eulogy that, to use his own words again, "it makes one sick in a corner"—or as we say down here in Wessex, "it is enough to make every little dog run to mixen".

However, we are getting on in our appreciativeness of poets. One thinks of those other two lyricists, Burns and Shelley at this time, for obvious reasons, and of how much harder it was with them. We know how Burns was treated at Dumfries, but by the time that Swinburne was a young man Burns had advanced so far as to be regarded as no worse than "the glory and the shame of literature", (in the words of a critic of that date). As for Shelley, he was not tolerated at all in his lifetime. But Swinburne has been tolerated—at any rate since he has not written anything to speak of. And a few months ago, when old and enfeebled, he was honoured by a rumour that he had been offered a complimentary degree at Oxford. And Shelley too, in these latter days of our memory, has been favoured so far as to be considered no lower than an ineffectual angel beating his luminous wings in vain. . . .

I was so late in getting my poetical barge under way, and he was so early with his flotilla—besides my being between 3 and 4 years younger, and being nominally an architect (an awful impostor at that, really)—that though I read him as he came out I did not personally know him till many years after the "Poems and Ballads" year. . . .

Sincerely yours

T. H.

"April 13. A genius for repartee is a gift for saying what a wise man thinks only."

"April 15. Day of Swinburne's funeral. Find I cannot go with this rheumatism, though it is but slight, the journey being so roundabout.

"Thought of some of Swinburne's lines: e.g.—

"On Shelley: 'O sole thing sweeter than thine own songs were'.

"On Newman and Carlyle: 'With all our hearts we praise you whom ye hate'.

"On Time: 'For time is as wind and as waves are we'.

"On Man: 'Save his own soul he hath no star'."[1]

In May Hardy was in London, and walking along Dover Street on his way to the Academy saw on a poster the announcement of the death of Meredith. After the shock he was reminded of the odd verdict of the *Spectator* many years before—"Mr George Meredith is a clever man, without literary genius, taste, or judgment." He went on to the Athenæum and wrote some memorial lines on his friend, which were published a day or two later in *The Times*, and reprinted in *Time's Laughingstocks*.

On the 22nd he attended a memorial service to Meredith in Westminster Abbey—meeting there Maurice Hewlett, Henry James, Max Beerbohm, Alfred Austin, and other acquaintance; and returned to Dorchester the same afternoon.

---

[1] But Isaiah had said before him: "Mine own arm brought salvation unto me".

In June he was asked to succeed Meredith as President of the Society of Authors; and wrote to Mr Maurice Hewlett, who had brought the proposal before him:

> I am moved more than I can say by learning that in the view of the council I should be offered the succession to the Presidentship. But I must nevertheless perform the disagreeable duty of acting upon my own conviction of what is for the Society's good, and tell you that I feel compelled to decline the honour. I have long had an opinion that although in the early years of the Society it may perhaps have been not unwise to have at its head men who took no part in its management—indeed the mere names of Tennyson and Meredith were in themselves of use to the institution—the time has now come when the President should be one who takes an active part in the Council's deliberations, and if possible one who lives in or near London,—briefly, that he should preside over its affairs. Now this I could never do. I will not go into the reasons why, as they are personal and unavoidable. . . .
>
> I may perhaps add that if there should still be a preponderating opinion in the Council that an inactive President of the old kind is still desirable, the eminent name of Lord Morley suggests itself.

However the matter ended by the acceptance of the Presidency by Hardy on further representations by the Council. His first diffidence had, in fact, arisen, as he stated, out of consideration for the Society's interests, for he remembered that the Society included people of all sorts of views, and that since Swinburne's death there was no living English writer who had been so abused by sections of the press as he himself had been in previous years; "and who knows", he would drily add, "that I may not be again?"

But, as said above, his objections were overruled.

As usual his stay in London had given him influenza, and he could not go to Aldeburgh as he had intended. About this time he wrote to a lady of New York in answer to an inquiry she made:

> The discovery of the law of evolution, which revealed that all organic creatures are of one family, shifted the centre of altruism from humanity to the whole conscious world collectively. Therefore the practice of vivisection, which might have been

defended while the belief ruled that men and animals are essentially different, has been left by that discovery without any logical argument in its favour. And if the practice, to the extent merely of inflicting slight discomfort now and then, be defended [as I sometimes hold it may] on grounds of it being good policy for animals as well as men, it is nevertheless in strictness a wrong, and stands precisely in the same category as would stand its practice on men themselves.

In July the influenza had nearly passed off, and he fulfilled his engagement to go to Aldeburgh—the air of which he always sought if possible after that malady, having found it a quicker restorative than that of any other place he knew.

In the second week of this month he was at rehearsals of Baron F. d'Erlanger's opera *Tess* at Covent Garden, and on the 14th was present with Mrs Hardy at the first performance. Though Italianized to such an extent that Hardy scarcely recognized it as his novel, it was a great success in a crowded house, Queen Alexandra being among the distinguished audience. Destinn's voice suited the title-character admirably; her appearance less so. But the fact that d'Erlanger the composer was also a Director of the Company went rather against his opera: critics wished to show their independence.

In response to an invitation by Dr Max Dessoir, a professor at the University of Berlin, who wished to have an epitome of the culture and thought of the time—the "Weltanschauung" of a few representative men in England and Germany—Hardy wrote the following during August this year:

We call our age an age of Freedom. Yet Freedom, under her incubus of armaments, territorial ambitions smugly disguised as patriotism, superstitions, conventions of every sort, is of such stunted proportions in this her so-called time, that the human race is likely to be extinct before Freedom arrives at maturity.

In the meantime he had been putting together poems written between whiles, some of them already printed in periodicals—and in addition hunting up quite old ones dating from 1865, and overlooked in his earlier volumes, out of which he made a volume called *Time's Laughingstocks*, and sent off the MS. to his publishers the first week in September.

In continuance of the visits to cathedrals he went this autumn to

Chichester, York, Edinburgh, and Durham; and on returning to Dorchester was at a rehearsal of a play by the dramatist of the local Debating and Dramatic Society, based on *Far from the Madding Crowd*, which was performed there in the Corn Exchange. Hardy had nothing to do with the adaptation, but thought it a neater achievement than the London version of 1882 by Mr Comyns Carr.

In December *Time's Laughingstocks* was published, and Hardy was in London, coming back as usual with a choking sore throat which confined him to his bed till the New Year, on the eve of which at twelve o'clock he crouched by the fire and heard in the silence of the night the ringing of the muffled peal down the chimney of his bedroom from the neighbouring church of St. George.

CHAPTER XXX

The Freedom of the Borough

1910: *Aet.* 69–70

In March, being at Ventnor, Hardy visited Swinburne's grave at Bonchurch, and composed the poem entitled "A Singer Asleep". He must have seen some paragraph about the poet's life and ways to make him write the following, either now or a little later:

519add

"What a wretched spectacle the scribblers present who cringed for admission to Swinburne's house, and then went off to write satirical details about his appearance, manners, dinner, and beer-bottle! Surely the most contemptible of all trades is that of the common informer who eats a meal at a man's table, and then betrays his weaknesses to the highest bidder."

To the Secretary of the Humanitarian League.

The Athenæum, Pall Mall. S.W.
10th. April 1910

Sir:

I am glad to think that the Humanitarian League has attained the handsome age of twenty years—the Animals Defence Department particularly.

Few people seem to perceive fully as yet that the most far-reaching consequence of the establishment of the common origin of all species is ethical; that it logically involved a re-adjustment of altruistic morals by enlarging as a *necessity of rightness* the application of what has been called "The Golden Rule" beyond the area of mere mankind to that of the whole animal kingdom. Possibly Darwin himself did not wholly perceive it, though he alluded to it. While man was deemed to be a creation apart from all other creations, a secondary or tertiary morality was considered good enough towards the "inferior" races; but no person who reasons nowadays can escape the trying conclusion that this is not maintainable. And though I myself do not at present see how the principle of equal justice all round is to be carried out in its entirety, I recognize that the League is grappling with the question.

It will be seen that in substance this agrees with a letter written earlier, and no doubt the subject was much in his mind just now.

About this time Hardy was asked by Mr H. Alden, the editor of *Harper's Magazine*, to publish his Reminiscences in the pages of that periodical month by month. Hardy replied:

> I could not appear in a better place. But it is absolutely unlikely that I shall ever change my present intention not to produce my reminiscences to the world.

In this same month of April he was looking for a flat again in London, and found one at Blomfield Court, Maida Vale, which he and his wife and servants entered in May. Looking out of the window while at breakfast on the morning after their arrival they beheld placarded in the street an announcement of the death of King Edward.

Hardy saw from the Athenæum Club the procession of the removal of the King's body to Westminster, and the procession of the funeral from Westminster three days later. On account of the suggestiveness of such events it must have been in these days that he wrote "A King's Soliloquy on the Night of his Funeral". His own seventieth birthday a fortnight later reminded him that he was a year older than the monarch who had just died.

At the flat—the last one they were to take, as it happened—they received their usual friends as in previous years, and there were more performances of the *Tess* opera; but in the middle of June they were compelled to cancel all engagements suddenly owing to Hardy's illness, including five dinner-parties for the immediate week. The illness was happily but brief, and in July he was able to go out again, and on the 19th went to Marlborough House to be invested with the Order of Merit. The King received him pleasantly: "but afterwards I felt that I had failed in the accustomed formalities".

Back in the country at the end of the month they entertained some visitors at Max Gate during the autumn, among others Mrs Hardy's cousin Charles Gifford, Paymaster-in-Chief to the Royal Navy, Mr Stephen Coleridge, Mr William Strang, R. A., and Miss Dugdale, a literary friend of Mrs Hardy's at the Lyceum Club, whose paternal ancestors were Dorset people dwelling near the Hardys, and had intermarried with them some 130 years earlier. A brief visit to Aldeburgh, where he met Professor Bury and Dr (afterwards Sir James) Frazer, and a few cycle rides, diversified the close of this summer.

In September he sat to Mr William Strang for a sketch-portrait which was required for hanging at Windsor Castle among those of other recipients of the Order of Merit; and on November 16 came the interesting occasion of the presentation of the freedom of Dorchester to Hardy, which appealed to his sentiment more perhaps than did many of those recognitions of his literary achievements that had come from the uttermost parts of the earth at a much earlier time. Among the very few speeches or lectures that he ever delivered, the one he made on this occasion was perhaps the most felicitous and personal:

"Mr Mayor and Gentlemen of the Corporation:—This is an occasion that speaks for itself, and so, happily, does not demand many remarks from me. In simply expressing my sincere thanks for the high compliment paid me by having my name enrolled with those of the Honorary Freemen of this historic town, I may be allowed to confess that the freedom of the Borough of Dorchester did seem to me at first something that I had possessed a long while, had helped myself to, (to speak plainly), for when I consider the liberties I have taken with its ancient walls, streets, and precincts through the medium of the printing-press, I feel that I have treated its external features with the hand of freedom indeed. True, it might be urged that my Casterbridge (if I may mention seriously a name coined off-hand in a moment with no thought of its becoming established and localized) is not Dorchester—not even the Dorchester as it existed 60 years ago, but a dream-place that never was outside an irresponsible book. Nevertheless, when somebody said to me that 'Casterbridge' is a sort of essence of the town as it used to be, 'a place more Dorchester than Dorchester itself', I could not absolutely contradict him, though I could not quite perceive it. At any rate, it is not a photograph in words, that inartisitic species of literary produce, particularly in respect of personages. But let me say no more about my own doings. The chronicle of the town has vivid marks on it. Not to go back to events of National importance, lurid scenes have been enacted here within living memory, or not so many years beyond it, whippings in front of the town pump, hangings on the gaol roof. I myself saw a woman hanged not 100 yards from where we now stand, and I saw, too, a man in the stocks in the back part of this very building. Then, if one were to recount the election excitements, Free Trade riots, scenes of soldiers marching down the town to war, the proclamation of Sovereigns now crumbled to dust, it would be an interesting local story.

"Miss Burney, in her diary, speaks of its aspect when she drove through with the rest of King George's Court on her way to Weymouth. She says:—'The houses have the most ancient appearance of any that are inhabited that I have happened to see.' This is not quite the case now, and though we may regret the disappearance of these old buildings, I cannot be blind to the difficulty of keeping a town in what may be called working order while retaining all its ancient features. Yet it must not be forgotten that these are its chief attractions for visitors, particularly American visitors. Old houses, in short, have a far larger commercial value than their owners always remember, and it is only when they have been destroyed, and tourists who have come to see them vow in their disappointment that they will never visit the spot again, that this is realized. An American gentleman came to me the other day in quite a bad temper, saying that he had diverged from his direct route from London to Liverpool to see ancient Dorchester, only to discover that he knew a hundred towns in the United States more ancient-looking than this (*laughter*). Well, we may be older than we look, like some ladies; but if, for instance, the original All-Saints and Trinity Churches, with their square towers, the castle, the fine mansion of the Trenchards at the corner of Shirehall Lane, the old Three-Mariners Inn, the old Greyhound, the old Antelope, Lady Abingdon's house at the corner of Durngate Street, and other mediaeval buildings were still in their places, more visitors of antiquarian tastes would probably haunt the town than haunt it now. Old All-Saints was, I believe, demolished because its buttresses projected too far into the pavement. What a reason for destroying a record of 500 years in stone! I knew the architect who did it; a milder-mannered man never scuttled a sacred edifice. Milton's well-known observation in his 'Areopagitica'—'Almost as well kill a man as kill a good book'—applies not a little to a good old building, which is not only a book but a unique manuscript that has no fellow. But corporations as such cannot help these removals; they can only be prevented by the education of their owners or temporary trustees, or, in the case of churches, by Government guardianship.

"And when all has been said on the desirability of preserving as much as can be preserved, our power to preserve is largely an illusion. Where is the Dorchester of my early recollection—I mean the human Dorchester—the kernel—of which the houses were but the shell? Of the shops as I first recall them not a single owner remains; only in two or three instances does even the name remain. As a German author has said, 'Nothing is permanent but change'. Here in Dorchester, as elsewhere, I see the streets and the turnings not far different from those of my schoolboy time; but the faces that used to be seen at the doors, the inhabitants, where are they? I turn up the Weymouth Road, cross the railway-bridge, enter an iron gate to 'a slope of green access', and there they are! There is the Dorchester that I knew best; there are names on white stones one after the other, names that recall the voices, cheerful and sad, anxious and indifferent, that are missing from the dwellings and pavements. Those who are old enough to have had that experience may feel that after all the permanence or otherwise of inanimate Dorchester concerns but the permanence of what is minor and accessory.

"As to the future of the town, my impression is that its tendency is to become more and more a residential spot, and that the nature of its business will be mainly that of administering to the wants of 'private residents' as they are called. There are several reasons for supposing this. The dryness of its atmosphere and subsoil is unexcelled. It has the great advantage of standing near the coast without being on it, thus escaping the objections some people make to a winter residence close to the sea; while the marine tincture in its breezes tempers the keenness which is felt in those of high and dry chalk slopes further inland. Dorchester's future will not be like its past; we may be sure of that. Like all other provincial towns, it will lose its individuality—has lost much of it already. We have become almost a London suburb owing to the quickened locomotion, and, though some of us may regret this, it has to be.

"I will detain you no longer from Mr Evans's comedy that is about to be played downstairs. Ruskin somewhere says that comedy is tragedy if you only look deep enough. Well, that is a thought to remember; but tonight, at any rate, we will all be young and not look too deeply."

After the presentation—which was witnessed by Mrs Hardy, by Mr (afterwards Sir Henry) Newbolt, by the writer of this memoir, and by other friends, the Dorchester Dramatic Society gave for the first time, at the hands of their own dramatist, an adaptation of *Under the Greenwood Tree* entitled *The Mellstock Quire*—the second title of the novel—Hardy himself doing no more than supply the original carols formerly sung by the Quire of the parish out-shadowed by the name "Mellstock"—the village of Stinsford a mile from the town.

In December the American fleet paid a visit to Portland Roads, and though the weather was bad while they were lying there Hardy went on board the battleship *Connecticut*, where he met the captain, commander, and others; who with several more officers afterwards visited him and Mrs Hardy at Max Gate. On the 29th they went on board the English *Dreadnought*—which was also lying there—and thence to a dance on board the United States flagship *Louisiana*, to which they were welcomed by Admiral Vreeland.

It seems to have been at the end of this year that Hardy published in a well-known review some verses entitled "God's Funeral". The alternative title he had submitted for the poem was "The Funeral of Jahveh"—the subject being the gradual decline and extinction in the human race of a belief in an anthropomorphic god of the King-of-Dahomey type—a fact recognized by all bodies of theologians for many years. But the editor, thinking the longer title clumsy and obscure, as in fact it was, chose the other, to which Hardy made no objection, supposing the meaning of his poem would be clear enough to readers. However what happened was that nobody seemed to read more of the poem than the title, the result of this and kindred lines of his being that the poet was grotesquely denounced as a blaspheming atheist by a "phrasemongering literary con-tortionist" (as Hardy used to call him), and rebuked by dogmatists, because he had turned into verse the views of the age.

CHAPTER XXXI

Bereavement

1911–1912: *Aet.* 70–72

In March (1911) Hardy received a letter from M. Emile Bergerat of Paris asking him to let his name appear as one of the Committee for honouring Théophile Gautier on his approaching centenary, to which Hardy readily agreed. In the same month he visited Bristol Cathedral and Bath Abbey, and in April attended the funeral of the Mayor of Dorchester who had presented him with the freedom of the borough but a few months earlier. A sequence of verses by Hardy entitled "Satires of Circumstance", which were published in the *Fortnightly Review* at this juncture, met with much attention both here and in America, and the curiously blundering reception of the verses here was an amusing instance of English criticism. Unhappily for himself, Hardy was, in fact, like the "stretch-mouth'd rascal" in *The Winter's Tale*, always supposed to "mean mischief" against Church, State, or morals when he was not understood. The verses were imitated in *Punch* for two weeks in succession by its accomplished editor, and people supposed that these mere imitations were clever satires of the poems; not perceiving, even with the title before their eyes, that the originals themselves were satires, which indeed the writer of the imitations had apparently not perceived himself.

In April he and his brother, in pursuance of a plan of seeing or re-seeing all the English cathedrals, visited Lichfield, Worcester and, Hereford; he also looked at London flats, but did not take one; though he was in town at the dinner of the Royal Academy.

He makes only one note this spring, which is not very intelligible: "View the matrices rather than the moulds."

Hardy had been compelled to decline in February an invitation by the Earl Marshal to the Coronation in Westminster Abbey in the coming June, which found him on a tour in the Lake Country, including Carlisle Cathedral and Castle, where the dungeons were another reminder to him of how "evil men out of the evil treasure of their hearts have brought forth evil things". However the tour was pleasant enough despite the wet weather, and probably Hardy got more pleasure out of Coronation Day by spending it on Windermere than he would have done by spending it in a seat at the Abbey.

Of Grasmere Churchyard he says: "Wordsworth's headstone and grave are looking very trim and new. A group of tourists who have never read a line of him sit near, addressing and sending off picture-postcards. . . . Wrote some verses." He visited Chester Cathedral coming homeward, called at Rugby, and went over the school and chapel; and returned to Dorchester through London.

After his return he signed with many other well-known people a protest against the use of aerial vessels in war; appealing to all governments "to foster by any means in their power an international understanding which shall preserve the world from warfare in the air". A futile protest indeed!

In July Mrs Hardy accompanied by her friend Miss Florence Dugdale went to stay at Worthing, and on her return Hardy took his sister Katherine on an excursion to North Somerset, stopping at Minehead, and going on by coach to Porlock and Lynmouth. Thence they went by steamer to Ilfracombe, intending to proceed through Exeter to South Devon. But the heat was so great that further travelling was abandoned, and after going over the Cathedral they returned home. A garden-party at Max Gate the first week in September wound up the summer weather, and about this time he became a life-member of the Council of Justice to Animals, and later one of the Vice-Presidents.

In the preceding month, it may be remarked, had died Mr W. J. Last, A.M.I.C.E., Director of the Science Museum, South Kensington, who was a son of Hardy's old Dorchester schoolmaster, Isaac Glandfield Last. The obituary notices that appeared in *The Times* and other papers gave details of a life more successful than his father's—though not of higher intellectual ability than that by which it had been Hardy's good fortune to profit.

At the end of the month Mr Sydney Cockerell, director of the Fitzwilliam Museum, Cambridge, called, mainly to enquire about Hardy's old manuscripts, which was the occasion of his looking up those that he could find and handing them over to Mr Cockerell to distribute as he thought fit among any museums that would care to possess one, Hardy himself preferring to have no voice in the matter. In the course of October this was done by Mr Cockerell, the MSS. of *The Dynasts* and *Tess of the d'Urbervilles* being accepted by the British Museum, of *Time's Laughingstocks* and *Jude the Obscure* by the Fitzwilliam, and of *Wessex Poems*, with illustrations by the author himself (the only volume he ever largely illustrated), by Birmingham. Others were distributed from time to time by Mr Cockerell, to whom Hardy had sent all the MSS. for him to do what he liked with, having insisted that "it would not be becoming for a writer to send his own MSS. to a museum on his own judgment".

It may be mentioned in passing that in these months Mr F. Saxelby of Birmingham, having been attracted to Hardy's works by finding in them a name which resembled his own, published *A Hardy Dictionary*—containing the names of persons and places in the author's novels and poems. Hardy had offered no objection to its being issued, but accepted no responsibility for its accuracy.

In November the Dorchester Debating and Dramatic Society gave another performance of plays from the Wessex novels. This time the selection was the short one-act piece that Hardy had dramatized himself many years before, from the story called "The Three Strangers", entitled *The Three Wayfarers*; and a rendering by Mr A. H. Evans of the tale of "The Distracted Preacher". The Hardys' friend, Mrs Arthur Henniker, came all the way from London to see it, and went with his wife and himself.

The curator of the Dorset County Museum having expressed a wish for a MS. of Hardy's, he sent this month the holograph of *The Mayor of Casterbridge*.

Being interested at this time in the only Gothic style of architecture that can be called especially and exclusively English—the perpendicular style of the fifteenth century—Hardy made a journey to Gloucester to investigate its origin in that cathedral, which he ascertained to be in the screen between the south aisle and the transept—a fact long known probably to other investigators, but only recently to him. He was so much impressed by the thought that the inventor's name, like the names of the authors of so many noble songs and ballads, was unknown, that on his return he composed a poem thereon, called "The Abbey Mason", which was published a little later in *Harper's Magazine*, and later still was included in a volume with other poems.

The illness of his elder sister Mary saddened the close of 1911; and it was during this year that his wife wrote the Reminiscences printed in the earlier pages of this book, as if she had premonitions that her end was not far off, though nobody else suspected it.

The year 1912, which was to advance and end in such gloom for Hardy, began serenely. In January he went to London for a day or two and witnessed the performance of *Oedipus* at Covent Garden. But in February he learnt of the death of his friend General Henniker, in March that of his neighbour Mrs Caledon Egerton, whom he had known from girlhood; and in April occurred the disaster to the *Titanic* steam-ship, upon which he wrote the poem called "The Convergence of the Twain", in aid of the Fund for the sufferers.

They dined with a few friends in London this season, but did not take a house, putting up at a hotel with which Hardy had long been familiar, the "West Central" in Southampton Row.

On June 1 at Max Gate they had a pleasant week-end visit from Henry Newbolt and W. B. Yeats, who had been deputed by the Royal Society of Literature to present Hardy with the Society's gold medal, on his seventy-second birthday. These two eminent men of letters were the only individuals entertained at Max Gate for the occasion; but everything was done as methodically as if there had been a large audience. Hardy says: "Newbolt wasted on the nearly empty room the best speech he ever made in his life, and Yeats wasted a very good one: mine in returning thanks was as usual a bad one, and the audience was quite properly limited."

In the middle of June he was in London at Lady St. Helier's, and went to the play of *Bunty Pulls the Strings* with her and Prince Albert of Schleswig-Holstein, meeting the heroine, Miss Moffat, at dinner next day; also his old friend Mrs Stuart-Wortley (afterwards Lady Stuart). An amusing anticlimax to a story of the three-crow type occurred in connection with this or some other popular play of the date. It was currently reported and credited that Mr Asquith had gone to see it eight times, and Mr Balfour sixteen. Taking Miss Balfour in to dinner and discussing the play, Hardy told her of the report, and she informed him that her brother had been only once.

How few the visits of Mr Asquith were could not be ascertained. Probably he had not gone at all.

He was occasionally in Town during the remainder of the summer season, meeting Mr Gosse, Sir Edward Poynter, Sir J. Crichton Browne, Professor Herkomer, Sir George Frampton, and general friends; and coming to arrangements with his American publishers. Later on in the autumn a letter was addressed to him on a gross abuse which was said to have occurred—that of publishing details of a lately deceased man's life under the guise of a novel, with assurances of truth scattered in the newspapers. In the course of his reply he said:

What should certainly be protested against, in cases where there is no authorization, is the mixing of fact and fiction in unknown proportions. Infinite mischief would lie in that. If any statements in the dress of fiction are covertly hinted to be fact, all must be fact, and nothing else but fact, for obvious reasons. The power of getting lies believed about people through that channel after they are dead, by stirring in a few truths, is a horror to contemplate.

"June. Here is a sentence from the Edinburgh Review of a short time back which I might have written myself. 'The division [of poems] into separate groups [ballad, lyrical, narrative, &c.] is frequently a question of the preponderance, not of the exclusive possession, of certain aesthetic elements.'"

Meanwhile in July he had returned to Max Gate just in time to be at a garden party on July 16—the last his wife ever gave—which it would have much grieved him afterwards to have missed. The afternoon was sunny and the guests numerous on this final one of many occasions of such a gathering on the lawn there, nobody foreseeing the shadow that was so soon to fall on the house, Mrs Hardy being then, apparently, in her customary health and vigour. In the following month, August, she was at Weymouth for the last time; and Hardy took her and her niece to see the performance of *Bunty* at the Pavilion Theatre. It was her last play.

However, she was noticed to be weaker later on in the autumn, though not ill, and complained of her heart at times. Strangely enough, she one day suddenly sat down to the piano and played a long series of her favourite old tunes, saying at the end she would never play any more. The poem called "The Last Performance" approximately describes this incident.

She went out up to the 22nd November, when, though it was a damp, dark afternoon she motored to pay a visit six miles off. The next day she was distinctly unwell, and the day after that was her birthday, when she seemed depressed. On the 25th two ladies called; and though she consulted with her husband whether or not to go downstairs to see them, and he suggested that she should not in her weak state, not to offend them she did go down. Unfortunately they stayed a very long time, and the strain obliged her to retire immediately they had left. She never went downstairs again.

The next day she agreed to see a doctor, who did not think her seriously ill, but weak from want of nourishment through indigestion. In the evening she assented quite willingly to Hardy's suggestion that he should go to a dramatic rehearsal in Dorchester of a play made by the local company, that he had promised to attend. When he got back at eleven o'clock all the house was in bed and he did not disturb her.

The next morning the maid told him in answer to his inquiry that when she had as usual entered Mrs Hardy's room a little earlier she had said she was better, and would probably get up later on; but that she now seemed worse. Hastening to her he was shocked to find her much worse, lying with her eyes closed and unconscious. The doctor came quite quickly, but before he arrived her breathing softened and ceased.

It was the day fixed for the performance of *The Trumpet-Major* in Dorchester, and it being found impossible to put off the play at such short notice, so many people having come from a distance for it, it was produced, an announcement of Mrs Hardy's unexpected death being made from the stage.

Many years earlier she had fancied that she would like to be buried at Plymouth, her native place; but on going there to the funeral of her father she found that during a "restoration" the family vault in Charles Churchyard, though it was not full, had been broken into, if not removed altogether, either to alter the entrance to the church, or to erect steps; and on coming back she told her husband that this had quite destroyed her wish to be taken there, since she could not lie near her parents.

There was one nook, indeed, which in some respects was pre-eminently the place where she might have lain—the graveyard of St.

Juliot, Cornwall—whose dilapidated old church had been the cause of their meeting, and in whose precincts the early scenes of their romance had a brief being. But circumstances ordered otherwise. Hardy did not favour the thought of her being carried to that lonely coast unless he could be carried thither likewise in due time; and on this point all was uncertain. The funeral was accordingly at Stinsford, a mile from Dorchester and Max Gate, where the Hardys had buried for many years.

She had not mentioned to her husband, or to anybody else so far as he could discover, that she had any anticipations of death before it occurred so suddenly. Yet on his discovery of the manuscript of her "Recollections", written only a year earlier, it seemed as if some kind of presentiment must have crossed her mind—perhaps dictated by the heart-pains to which she was subject—that she was not to be much longer in the world, and that if her brief memories were to be written it were best to write them quickly. This is, however, but conjecture.

CHAPTER XXXII

Revisitings, Second Marriage, and War-Writings

1913–1914: *Aet.* 72–74

Many poems were written by Hardy at the end of the previous year and the early part of this—more than he had ever written before in the same space of time—as can be seen by referring to their subjects, as well as to the dates attached to them. To adopt Walpole's words concerning Gray, Hardy was "in flower" in these days, and, like Gray's, his flower was sad-coloured.

On March 6—almost to a day forty-three years after his first journey to Cornwall—he started for St. Juliot, putting up at Boscastle; and visiting Pentargan Bay and Beeny Cliff, which he had not once set foot on in the long interval. It very unhappily chanced that his wife and he had arranged to go there this very year together, after postponing their intention for several years.

He found the rectory and other scenes with which he had been so familiar changed a little, but not greatly, and returning by way of Plymouth arranged for a memorial tablet to Mrs Hardy in the church with which she had been so closely associated as organist before her marriage, and in other ways. The tablet was afterwards erected to his own design, as was also the tomb in Stinsford Churchyard—in the preparation of which memorials he had to revive a species of work that he had been unaccustomed to since the years of his architectural pupillage.

In June he left for Cambridge to receive the honorary degree of Litt.D., and lunched with the Master of Magdalene (also Vice-Chancellor) Dr Donaldson, and Lady Albinia Donaldson, meeting—some for the first and last time—the Master of Trinity and Mrs Butler, John Sargent, Arthur Benson, Henry Jackson, Vice-Master of Trinity and the Regius Professor of Greek, Sir James Murray, and many others. The visit was full of interest for Hardy as being the sequel to his long indirect connection with the University in several ways, partly through the many graduates who were his friends, his frequent visits to the place, and his intention in the eighteen-sixties to go up himself for a pass-degree, which was abandoned mainly owing to his discovery that he could not conscientiously carry out his idea of entering the church. A few weeks later he was elected an Honorary Fellow of Magdalene, as will be seen.

In July he was in London once or twice, meeting Dr Page the American Ambassador, Mr and Mrs Asquith, and others here and there. A German translation of *The Mayor of Casterbridge* under the title of *Der Bürgermeister* was begun as a serial in Germany at this time, and in the same month the gift of the MS. of his poem on Swinburne's death was acknowledged by the Newnes Librarian at Putney, an offer which had originated with Mr Sydney Cockerell. In response to a request from the Secretary of the General Blind Association he gave his permission to put some of his books in prose and verse into Braille type for the use of the blind, adding:

> I cannot very well suggest which, as I do not know the length you require. . . . If a full-length novel, I would suggest "The Trumpet-Major". If verse, The Battle of Trafalgar Scenes or the Battle of Waterloo scenes, from "The Dynasts", or a selection from the Poems. . . . I am assuming that you require scenes of action rather than those of reflection or analysis.

In August he was at Blandford with Mr John Lane searching about for facts and scenes that might illustrate the life of Alfred Stevens, the sculptor whose best known work is the Wellington monument in St. Paul's, and who was born and grew up in this town. Hardy had suggested that it ought to be written before it was too late, and Mr Lane had taken up the idea. The house of his birth was discovered, but not much material seems to have been gained.

It was not till a year or two later that Hardy discovered that Stevens's father painted the Ten Commandments in the church of Blandford St. Mary, his name being in the corner: "G. Stevens, Blandford, 1825".

"Sept. 15. Thoughts on the recent school of novel-writers. They forget in their insistence on life, and nothing but life, in a plain slice, that a story *must be worth the telling*, that a good deal of life is not worth any such thing, and that they must not occupy a reader's time with what he can get at first hand anywhere around him."

The autumn glided on with its trifling incidents. In the muddle of Hardy's unmistressed housekeeping animal pets of his late wife died, strayed, or were killed, much to Hardy's regret; short visits were paid by friends, including Mr Frederic Harrison: and in November while staying with the Master of his College Hardy was admitted in chapel as Honorary Fellow. "The Ceremony, which consists of a Latin formula of admission before the Altar, and the handing-in of the new Fellow into his stall, was not unimpressive," said the *Cambridge Review*. Hardy had read the lessons in church in his young-manhood, besides having had much to do with churches in other ways, and the experience may have recalled the old ecclesiastical times. In the evening he dined in Hall, where "the Master proposed the health of him who was no longer a guest, but one of the Society, and the day's proceedings terminated happily", continued the *Cambridge Review*. It was an agreeable evening for Hardy, Mr A. E. Housman and Sir Clifford Allbutt being present as guests among other of his friends.

A good sketch-painting of him was made this autumn by Mr Fuller Maitland for his friend Arthur Benson, to be hung with the other portraits in the hall of Magdalene College; and in the middle of November the Dorchester amateurs' version of *The Woodlanders*, adapted by themselves, was performed on the Dorchester stage; but Hardy was not present on the occasion.

In the December of this year M. Anatole France was entertained at a dinner in London by a committee of men of letters and of affairs. Hardy was much disappointed at being unable to attend; and he wrote to express his regret, adding:

> In these days when the literature of narrative and verse seems to be losing its qualities as an art, and to be assuming a structureless and conglomerate character, it is a privilege that we should have come into our midst a writer who is faithful to the

principles that make for permanence, who never forgets the value of organic form and symmetry, the force of reserve, and the emphasis of understatement, even in his lighter works.

In February of the year following (1914) the subject of this memoir married the present writer, who had been for several years the friend of the first Mrs Hardy, and had accompanied her on the little excursions she had liked to make when her husband could not go. As previously stated there had been a marriage between the Hardy and Dugdale families in 177–, and very possibly earlier, seeing that for centuries they had lived within a few miles of each other in Dorset. The wedding was of the quietest kind, at Enfield, the then residence of this branch of the Dugdales, taking place at eight o'clock in the old parish church; and though the morning was exceptionally bright and sunny for February, and the church-door stood wide open to the street, not a soul among the passers-by entered the building.

In April died at Stoke, Plymouth, his late wife's cousin Florence Yolland, daughter of Lieutenant Yolland, R.N.

Hardy was at the dinner of the Royal Academy this spring—the last given before the war; and at sundry hospitalities he and his wife saw several friends in London, including Sir Frederick and Lady Macmillan, Mr and Mrs Edmund Gosse, Mr and Mrs G. and M. Macmillan, and Lady St. Helier. They went on to Cambridge, where they spent a pleasant week in visiting and meeting Mr Arthur Benson, Professor and Mrs Bury, Mr and Mrs Cockerell, Professor Quiller-Couch, the Master of Jesus, Dr James, Provost of King's, Dr and Mrs McTaggart, and the oldest friend of Hardy's in Cambridge, or for that matter anywhere, Mr Charles Moule, President and formerly Tutor of Corpus, who had known him as a boy. A dinner at St. John's—the "Porte-Latin Feast"—with the mellow radiance of the dark mahogany tables, curling tobacco-smoke, and old red wine, charmed Hardy in spite of his drinking very little and not smoking at all. A visit to Girton and tea with Miss Jones and members of her staff ended the Cambridge week for them.

Although Hardy had no sort of anticipation of the restrictions that the war was so soon to bring on motoring, he went about in a car this early summer almost as if he foresaw what was coming, taking his wife to Exeter, Plymouth, and back across Dartmoor—all of them old scenes familiar to him, and interesting to her, as having been so often mentioned to her by her late friend and himself.

After serving as a Grand Juror at the Assizes he dined during June with the Royal Institute of British Architects, a body of which he had never lost sight on account of his early associations with the profession, though nearly all the members he had known—except his old acquaintance the Vice-President, John Slater, and the Blomfields—had passed away. His wife and he put up in London at Lady St. Helier's and were often at Lady Macmillan's and elsewhere, renewing friendships with Mr and Mrs Humphry Ward, Mr and Mrs Winston Churchill, Mr and Mrs Stuart-Wortley, Lady Lewis, and others before the war cloud burst and brought pleasure-visits to an end.

A communication from men of letters and art in Germany who thought of honouring the memory of Friedrich Nietzsche on the seventieth anniversary of his birth, was the occasion of Hardy's writing at this date:

"It is a question whether Nietzsche's philosophy is sufficiently coherent to be of great ultimate value, and whether those views of his which seem so novel and striking appear thus only because they have been rejected for so many centuries as inadmissible under humane rule.

"A continuity of consciousness through the human race would be the only justification of his proposed measures.

"He assumes throughout the great worth intrinsically of human masterfulness. The universe is to him a perfect machine which only requires thorough handling to work wonders. He forgets that the universe is an imperfect machine, and that to do good with an ill-working instrument requires endless adjustments and compromises."

There was nothing to tell of the convulsion of nations that was now imminent, and in Dorset they visited their friends the Lord Lieutenant and Mrs Mount-Batten, and stayed a week-end with Sir Henry and Lady Hoare at Stourhead (where they met as their fellow guests Mr and Mrs Charles Whibley, the latter of whom Hardy had long known, though they had not met for years). To Hardy as to ordinary civilians the murder at Serajevo was a lurid and striking tragedy, but carried no indication that it would much affect English life. On July 28 they were at a quiet little garden party near Dorchester, and still there was no sign of the coming storm: the next day they lunched about five miles off with their friends the Brymers at Ilsington, and paid a call or two—this being the day on which war was declared by Austria on Serbia. Hardy made a few entries just after this date:

"August 4. 11 p.m.—War declared with Germany."

On this day they were lunching with Mr de Lafontaine at Athelhampton Hall six miles off, where a telegram came announcing the rumour to be fact. A discussion arose about food, and there was almost a panic at the table, nobody having any stock. But the full dimensions of what the English declaration meant were not quite realized at once. Their host disappeared to inquire into his stock of flour. The whole news and what it involved burst upon Hardy's mind next morning, for though most people were saying the war would be over by Christmas he felt it might be a matter of years and untold disaster.

"August 9–15. English Expeditionary Force crosses the Channel to assist France and Belgium."

"August onwards. War excitement. 'Quicquid delirant reges, plectuntur Achivi!'" It was the quotation Hardy had made at the outbreak of the Franco-Prussian war forty-four years earlier, when he was quite a young man.

He had been completely at fault, as he often owned, on the coming so soon of such a convulsion as the war, though only three or four months before it broke out he had printed a prophetic poem in the *Fortnightly* entitled "Channel Firing", whereof the theme,

> All nations striving strong to make
> Red war yet redder,

was, to say the least, a perception singularly coincident. However, as stated, that it would really burst he doubted. When the noisy crew of music-hall Jingoes said exultingly, years earlier, that Germany was as anxious for war as they were themselves, he had felt convinced that they were wrong. He had thought that the play *An Englishman's Home*, which he witnessed by chance when it was produced, ought to have been suppressed as provocative, since it gave Germany, even if pacific in intention beforehand, a reason, or excuse, for directing her mind on a war with England. A long study of the European wars of a century earlier had made it appear to him that common-sense had taken the place of bluster in men's minds; and he felt this so strongly that in the very year before war burst on Europe he wrote some verses called "His Country", bearing on the decline of antagonism between peoples; and as long before as 1901 he composed a poem called "The Sick Battle-God", which assumed that zest for slaughter was dying out. It was seldom he had felt so heavy at heart as in seeing his old view of the gradual bettering of human nature, as expressed in these verses of 1901, completely shattered by the events of 1914 and onwards. War, he had supposed, had grown too coldly scientific to kindle again for long all the ardent romance which had characterized it down to Napoleonic times, when the most intense battles were over in a day, and the most exciting tactics and strategy led to the death of comparatively few combatants. Hence nobody was more amazed than he at the German incursion into Belgium, and the contemplation of it led him to despair of the world's history thenceforward. He had not reckoned on the power still retained there by the governing castes whose interests were not the people's. It was, however, no use to despair, and since Germany had not shown the rationality he had expected of her he presently began to consider if there was anything he—an old man of seventy-four—could do in the critical circumstances. A slight opening seemed to offer when he received a letter from the Government asking his attendance at a private Conference in which eminent literary men and women who commanded confidence abroad "should take steps to place the strength of the British case and the principles for which the British troops and their allies are fighting before the populations of neutral countries". He went to London expressly to attend, as explained in the following memorandum:

"September 2. To London in obedience to a summons by Mr Masterman, Chancellor of the Duchy of Lancaster, at the instance of the Cabinet, for the organization of public statements of the strength of the British case and principles in the war by well-known men of letters."

This meeting was at Wellington House, Buckingham Gate, and in view of what the country was entering on has a historic significance. There was a medley of writers present, including, in addition to the Chairman Mr Masterman, among Hardy's friends and acquaintance, Sir James Barrie, Sir Henry Newbolt, J. W. Mackail, Arthur and Monsignor Benson, John Galsworthy, Sir Owen Seaman, G. M. Trevelyan, H. G. Wells, Arnold Bennett, Masefield, Robert Bridges, Anthony Hawkins, Gilbert Murray, and many others. Whatever the effect of the discussion the scene was impressive to more than one of them there. In recalling it Hardy said that the yellow September sun shone in from the dusty street with a tragic cast upon them as they sat round the large blue table, full of misgivings, yet unforeseeing in all their completeness the tremendous events that were to follow. The same evening Hardy left London—"the streets hot and sad, and bustling with soldiers and recruits"—to set about some contribution to the various forms of manifesto that had been discussed.

In Dorset the Hardys kept up between whiles their motoring through September, visiting Broadwindsor, Axminster, the summit called "Cross-in-hand", from which both the Bristol and English Channels are visible, and on which many years earlier Hardy had written a traditional poem, "The Lost Pyx"; also Bridport, Abbotsbury, Portisham, including the old residence of Admiral Hardy's father, still intact with its dial in the garden, dated 1767.

In the same month he published in *The Times* the soldiers' war-song called "Men who March Away", which won an enormous popularity; and in October wrote "England to Germany", a sonnet "On the Belgian Expatriation" for *King Albert's Book*, and in the papers a letter on the destruction of Reims Cathedral. This month too, he brought out another volume of verses entitled *Satires of Circumstance, Lyrics and Reveries*—the book being made up of the "Satires in Fifteen Glimpses", published in a periodical in 1911, and other poems of a very different kind with which the satires ill harmonized—the latter filling but fifteen pages in a volume of 230 pages. But the reviewers, perhaps because the satires were named first in the title, went for them almost entirely, and with a few exceptions passed over the bulk of the book. Through a lack of apprehension, or wilful guile in these judges, the pieces though they had been imitated all the world over were solemnly pronounced to be "mistakes"—just as they had been when they were printed in the *Fortnightly* years earlier—the critics apparently not perceiving that they were caustically humorous productions, and issued with a light heart before the war. Nevertheless, even though only of this character—or perhaps in consequence of being so—they had somewhat embarrassed their author, though not for the reasons on which the critical head-shakes were founded. So much shadow domestic and public had passed over his head since he had written the Satires that he was in no mood now to publish humour or irony, and would readily have suppressed them if they had not already gained such currency from magazine publication that he could not do it. So, by their being put into the book, and by their receiving almost exclusive notice, they were made to give a false tone to the whole volume, and stifled the "Lyrics and Reveries" which filled its far greater part, and contained some of the tenderest and least satirical verse that ever came from his pen. The effect of this misrepresentation upon the poems he most cared for grieved him much; but it could not be helped. It was another instance of the inability of so many critics to catch any but shrill notes, remaining oblivious to deeper tones.

In November he and his wife went to London to a rehearsal of a portion of *The Dynasts*, which the enterprise of Mr Granville-Barker was preparing for the stage at the Kingsway Theatre, and which was produced there on the 25th November, though the author had never dreamt of a single scene of it being staged. Owing to a cold Hardy was unable to be present on the first representation, but he went up two or three weeks later.

Hardy's idea had been that the performance should be called what it really was, namely, "Scenes from *The Dynasts*"—as being less liable to misconception than the book-title unmodified, since people might suppose the whole epic-drama was to be presented, which was quite an impossibility. However, as the scheme of putting any part of it on the boards had originated entirely with Mr Granville-Barker, who himself selected all the scenes, Hardy did not interfere, either with this or any other detail. The one feature he could particularly have wished altered was that of retaining indoor architecture for outdoor scenes, it being difficult for the spectator to realize—say in the Battle of Waterloo—that an open field was represented when pillars and architraves hemmed it in. He thought that for the open scenes a perfectly plain green floorcloth and blue backcloth would have suited better.

However the production was artistically successful. The critics, as is always the case when art takes a step onward, were bewildered, and, as Hardy said, looked at the performance much as a bull looks at a land surveyor's flag in the middle of a meadow, not knowing whether to toss the strange object or walk respectfully round it. One trembles to think what would have occurred had the whole philosophy of the play been put in; but Mr Barker, remembering what happened to Ibsen in this country, was too wise to represent the thought of the age in an English theatre at the beginning of the twentieth century and during a war.

More verses on the war were written by Hardy in December, including "An Appeal to America". A sad vigil during which no bells were heard at Max Gate brought in the first New Year of this unprecedented "breaking of nations".

It may be added here that so mad and brutal a war destroyed all Hardy's belief in the gradual ennoblement of man, a belief he had held for many years, as is shown by poems like "The Sick Battle-God", and others. He said he would probably not have ended *The Dynasts* as he did end it if he could have foreseen what was going to happen within a few years.

Moreover the war gave the *coup de grâce* to any conception he may have nourished of a fundamental ultimate Wisdom at the back of things. With his views on necessitation, or at most a very limited free-will, events seemed to show him that a fancy he had often held and expressed, that the never-ending push of the Universe was an unpurposive and irresponsible groping in the direction of the least resistance, might possibly be the real truth. "Whether or no", he would say,

"Desine fata Deûm flecti sperare precando."

CHAPTER XXXIII

War Efforts, Deaths of Relatives, and "Moments of Vision"

1915–1917: *Aet.* 74–77

He seems to have been studying the *Principia Ethica* of Dr G. E. Moore early this year; and also the philosophy of Bergson. Writing on the latter in answer to a letter from Dr C. W. Saleeby on the subject he states:

I suppose I may think that you are more or less a disciple of his, or fellow-philosopher with him. Therefore you may be rather shocked at some views I hold about his teaching—or did hold, anyhow. His theories are much pleasanter ones than those they contest, and I for one would gladly believe them; but I cannot help feeling all the time that his is rather an imaginative and poetical mind than a reasoner's, and that for his charming and attractive assertions he does not adduce any proofs whatever. His use of the word "creation" seems to me loose and vague. Then as to conduct: I fail to see how, if it is not mechanism, it can be other than caprice, though he denies it. Yet I quite agree with him in regarding finalism as an erroneous doctrine. He says however that Mechanism and Finalism are only external views of our conduct—"Our conduct extends between them, and slips much further". Well it may, but he nowhere shows that it does.

Then again: "A mechanic conception . . . treats the living as the inert. . . . Let us, on the contrary, trace a line of demarcation between the inert and the living." Well, let us, to our great pleasure, if we can see why we should introduce an inconsistent rupture of Order into a uniform and consistent Law of the same.

You will see how much I want to have the pleasure of being a Bergsonian. But I fear his theory is, in the bulk, only our old friend Dualism in a new suit of clothes,—an ingenious fancy without real foundation, and more complicated than the fancies he endeavours to overthrow.

You must not think me a hard-headed rationalist for all this. Half my time—particularly when writing verse—I "believe" (in the modern sense of the word) not only in the things Bergson believes in, but in spectres, mysterious voices, intuitions, omens, dreams, haunted places, etc, etc. But I do not believe in them in the old sense of the word any more for that. . . .

By the way, how do you explain the following from the Cambridge Magazine, by a writer who I imagine to be of a school of thinkers akin to your own, concerning Herbert Spencer's doctrine of the Unknowable:

"We doubt if there is a single philosopher alive today who would subscribe to it. Even men of science are gradually discarding it in favour of Realism and Pragmatism"?

I am utterly bewildered to understand how the doctrine that, beyond the knowable, there must always be an unknown, can be displaced.

In April a distant cousin, of promising ability—a lieutenant in the 5th Batt. Dorset Regiment—came to see him before going abroad, never to be seen by him again; and in the following month he sat to Mr [Sir Hamo] Thornycroft for a model of a head which the sculptor wished to make. At home he heard that two single-page songs in manuscript which he had sent to the Red Cross Sale at Christie's had fetched £48—"Men who March Away", and "The Night of Trafalgar".

"May 14. Have been reading a review of Henry James. It is remarkable that a writer who has no grain of poetry, or humour, or spontaneity in his productions, can yet be a good novelist. Meredith has some poetry, and yet I can read James when I cannot look at Meredith."

"May 27. 'Georgian Poets'.—It is a pity that these promising young writers adopted such a title. The use of it lacks the modesty of true genius, as it confuses the poetic chronology, and implies that the hitherto recognized original Georgians—Shelley, Keats, Wordsworth, Byron, etc., are negligible; or at any rate says that they do not care whether it implies such or no."

"June 10. Motored with F. to Bridport, Lyme, Exeter, and Torquay. Called on Mr and Mrs Eden Phillpotts. Saw their garden and beautiful flowers. Then back to Teignmouth, Dawlish, and Exeter, putting up at the 'Clarence' opposite the Cathedral."

"June 11. To Cathedral.—then home *via* Honiton, Chard, Crewkerne."

In July they were in London on a visit to Lady St. Helier, and paid a long promised call on Sir Frederick and Lady Treves in Richmond Park. Later on in the month he was at the funeral at Stinsford of a suddenly lost friend, Mr Douglas Thornton the banker, and received visits from Sir Henry Hoare, who motored over from Stourhead, and Professor Flinders Petrie, whom he had known but not seen for many years.

In August he learnt of the loss of his second cousin's son Lieutenant George, who had been killed that month in Gallipoli during a brave advance. Hardy makes this note of him:

"Frank George, though so remotely related, is the first one of my family to be killed in battle for the last hundred years, so far as I know. He might say Militavi non sine gloria,—short as his career has been."

Their neighbour Mrs Brinsley Sheridan's son Wilfred was killed a little later. In the autumn Hardy sometimes, and his wife continually, assisted in the evenings at the soldiers' tea-room established in the Dorchester Corn-Exchange; they visited the Australian Camp near Weymouth, and spent two or three days at Melbury House. On returning he learnt that his elder sister was again seriously ill. She died the same week, at his brother's house at Talbothays. The two poems "Logs on the Hearth" and "In the Garden", in *Moments of Vision*, evidently refer to her, as also the Fourth person in "Looking Across", in the same volume.

The hobby of her life had been portrait-painting, and she had shown great aptitude in catching a likeness, particularly of her relations, her picture of her mother in oils bearing a striking resemblance to the striking original. But she had been doomed to school-teaching, and organ-playing in this or that village church, during all her active years, and hence was unable to devote sufficient time to pictorial art till leisure was too late to be effective. Her character was a somewhat unusual one, being remarkably unassertive, even when she was in the right, and could easily have proved it; so that the point of the following remark about her is manifest:

"Nov. 29. Buried her under the yew-tree where the rest of us lie. As Mr Cowley read the words of the psalm 'Dixi Custodiam' they reminded me strongly of her nature, particularly when she was young: 'I held my tongue and spake nothing: I kept silence; yea, even from good words.' That was my poor Mary exactly. She never defended herself, and that not from timidity, but indifference to opinion."

The funeral day had been cold and wet, and Hardy was laid up till the end of the year with a violent bronchitis and racking cough. Nevertheless, during December in response to a request from Winchester House for a contribution to a "Pro-Ally Film" of paragraphs in facsimile from authors' writings, which was "to be exhibited throughout the world and make its appeal particularly to the neutral nations", he was able to send the following passages from Pitt's actual speech in the House of Commons a hundred years earlier, as closely paraphrased in *The Dynasts*:

ENGLAND AT BAY

"The strange fatality that haunts the times
Wherein our lot is cast, has no example;
Times are they fraught with peril, trouble, gloom;
We have to mark their lourings and to face them."

ENGLAND RESOLUTE

"Unprecedented and magnificent
As were our strivings in the previous wars,
Our efforts in the present shall transcend them,
As men will learn."

In January of the next year (1916) a war-ballad of some weirdness, called "The Dead and the Living One", which had been written several months before, was published in the *Sphere* and the New York *World*, and later reprinted in *Moments of Vision*.

In February he was again confined to his room with a cold, the previous one never having quite gone off. But he managed to send to the Red Cross Sale for this year, not any work of his own, but "A Sheaf of Victorian Letters" written to Thomas Hardy by many other writers, nearly all deceased, and of a very interesting kind. Mrs Hardy also sent to the same sale three short MSS. of his, "The Oxen", "The Breaking of Nations", and a fragment of a story—the whole fetching £72 : 10s.

A *Book of Homage* to Shakespeare was printed in April, for which Hardy had written a piece entitled "To Shakespeare after Three Hundred Years", afterwards included in the volume called *Moments of Vision*.

In June he served again as Grand Juror at the Assizes, and was at a rehearsal in Dorchester of *Wessex Scenes from The Dynasts*. This, made by "The Hardy Players", was quite a different selection from that of Mr Granville-Barker, embracing scenes of a local character only, from which could be gathered in echoes of drum and trumpet, and alarming rumours, the great events going on elsewhere. Though more limited in scope than the former it was picturesque and effective as performed by the local actors at the Weymouth Pavilion a fortnight later, and was well appreciated by the London press.

In the same month of June he paid a visit with his wife and remaining sister to a house he had never entered for forty years. This was Riverside Villa, Sturminster Newton, the first he had furnished after his first marriage, and in which he had written *The Return of the Native*. He found it much as it had been in the former years; and it was possibly this visit which suggested the poems about Sturminster that were published in *Moments of Vision*. Motorings to Melbury again, to Swanage, and again to Bridport, passed the midsummer days.

"July 27. *Times* Literary Supplement on 'What is Militarism?' The article suggests a term to express the cause of the present war: 'hypochondria' (in the Prussians). I should rather have said '*apprehensiveness*'. The term would fit some of the facts like a glove."

In September they set out by train for Cornwall, breaking the journey at Launceston to visit Kate Gifford and her sister, relatives of the first Mrs Hardy. Thence they went on to Camelford, Boscastle, and St. Juliot, to see if Hardy's design and inscription for the tablet to her memory in the church had been properly carried out and erected. At Tintagel they met quite by accident Hardy's friends the Stuart-Wortleys, which made their sojourn at that romantic spot a very pleasant one.

"September 10th. Sunday. To Tintagel Church. We sat down in a seat bordering the passage to the transept, but the vicar appalled us by coming to us in his surplice and saying we were in the way of the choir who would have to pass there. He banished us to the back of the transept. However, when he began his sermon we walked out. He thought it was done to be even with him, and looked his indignation; but it was really because we could not see the nave lengthwise, which my wife Emma had sketched in watercolours when she was a young woman before it was 'restored', so that I was interested in noting the changes, as also was F., who was familiar with the sketch. It was saddening enough, though doubtless only a chance, that we were inhospitably received in a church so much visited and appreciated by one we both had known so well. The matter was somewhat mended, however, by their singing the beautiful 34th. Psalm to Smart's fine tune 'Wiltshire'. By the by, that the most poetical verse of that psalm is omitted from it in *Hymns Ancient and Modern* shows the usual ineptness of hymn-selectors. We always sang it at Stinsford. But then, we sang there in the good old High-&-Dry-Church way—straight from the New Version."

Multifarious matters filled up the autumn—among others a visit to the large camp of some 5,000 German prisoners in Dorchester; also visits to the English wounded in hospital, which conjunction led him to say:

"At the German prisoners' camp, including the hospital, operating-room, etc. There were many sufferers. One Prussian, in much pain, died whilst I was with him—to my great relief, and his own.— Men lie helpless here from wounds: in the hospital a hundred yards off other men, English, lie helpless from wounds—each scene of suffering caused by the other!

"These German prisoners seem to think that we are fighting to exterminate Germany, and though it has been said that, so far from it, we are fighting to save what is best in Germany, Cabinet ministers do not in my opinion speak this out clearly enough."

In October the *Selected Poems of Thomas Hardy* were published in Macmillan's Golden Treasury Series, a little book that received some very good reviews; and in December the *Wessex Scenes from The Dynasts*, which had been produced earlier at Weymouth, were performed at Dorchester. Some of Hardy's friends, including J. M. Barrie and Sydney Cockerell, came to see the piece, but Hardy could not accompany them, being kept in bed by another cold. The performances were for Red Cross Societies, and he had suggested introducing speeches to that effect, which were delivered by Mrs Cecil Hanbury and Lady Mary Fox-Strangways.

"January 1. 1917. Am scarcely conscious of New Year's day."

"January 6. I find I wrote in 1888 that 'Art is concerned with seemings only', which is true."

To the Secretary of the Royal Society of Literature.

February 8. 1917.

Dear Sir:

I regret that as I live in a remote part of the country I cannot attend the meeting of the Entente Committee.

In respect of the Memorandum proposing certain basic principles of International education for promoting ethical ideals that shall conduce to a League of Peace, I am in hearty agreement with the proposition.

I would say in considering a *modus operandi*:

That nothing effectual will be accomplished in the cause of *Peace* till the sentiment of *Patriotism* be freed from the narrow meaning attaching to it in the past (still upheld by Junkers and Jingoists) and be extended to the whole globe.

On the other hand that the sentiment of *Foreignness*—if the sense of a contrast be really rhetorically necessary—attach only to other planets and their inhabitants, if any.

I may add that I have been writing in advocacy of those views for the last twenty years.

To Dr L. Litwinski.

March 7: 1917.

Dear Sir:

I feel much honoured by your request that I should be a member of the Committee for commemorating two such writers of distinction as Verhaeren and Sienkiewich. But for reasons of increasing years and my living so far from London I have latterly been compelled to give up membership with several associations;

and I am therefore sorry to say that I must refrain from joining any new committee in which I should be unable actively to support the cause, even when so worthy as the present one.

In this March also a sonnet by him named "A Call to National Service" was printed in the newspapers. An article in the April *Fortnightly* by Dr Courtney the editor on Hardy's writings, especially *The Dynasts*, interested him not only by its appreciativeness, but by the aspect some features of the drama assumed in the reviewer's mind:

"Like so many critics Mr Courtney treats my works of art as if they were a scientific system of philosophy, although I have repeatedly stated in prefaces and elsewhere that the views in them are *seemings*, provisional impressions only, used for artistic purposes because they represent approximately the impressions of the age, and are plausible, till somebody produces better theories of the universe.

"As to his winding up about a God of Mercy, etc.,—if I wished to make a smart retort, which I really should hate doing, I might say that the Good-God theory having, after some thousands of years of trial, produced the present infamous and disgraceful state of Europe—that most Christian Continent!—a theory of a Goodless-and-Badless God (as in 'The Dynasts') might perhaps be given a trial with advantage.

"Much confusion has arisen and much nonsense has been talked latterly in connection with the word 'atheist'. One writer's almost whole stock-in-trade consists of that word and 'blaspheme'. I believe I have been called one by a journalist who has never read a line of my writings. I have never understood how anybody can be one except in the sense of disbelieving in a tribal god, man-shaped, fiery-faced and tyrannous, who flies into a rage on the slightest provocation; or as (according to Horace Walpole) Sir Francis Dashwood defined the Providence believed in by the Lord Shrewsbury of that date to be—a figure like an old angry man in a blue cloak. . . . Fifty meanings attach to the word 'God' nowadays, the only reasonable meaning being the *Cause of Things*, whatever that cause may be.[1] Thus no modern thinker can be an atheist in the modern sense, while all modern thinkers are atheists in the ancient and exploded sense."

[1] In another place he says "Cause" means really but the "invariable antecedent".

In this connection he said once—perhaps oftener—that although invidious critics had cast slurs upon him as Nonconformist, Agnostic, Atheist, Infidel, Immoralist, Heretic, Pessimist or something else equally opprobrious in their eyes, they had never thought of calling him what they might have called him much more plausibly—churchy; not in an intellectual sense, but in so far as instincts and emotions ruled. As a child, to be a parson had been his dream;—moreover, he had had several clerical relatives who held livings; while his grandfather, father, uncle, brother, wife, cousin, and two sisters had been musicians in various churches over a period covering altogether more than a hundred years. He himself had frequently read the church-lessons, and had at one time as a young man begun reading for Cambridge with a view to taking Orders.

His vision had often been that of so many people brought up under Church-of-England influences, a giving of liturgical form to modern ideas, and expressing them in the same old buildings that had already seen previous reforms successfully carried out. He would say to his wife's uncle Archdeacon Gifford, his brother-in-law the Rev. C. Holder, his friends the Warden of Keble, Arthur Benson, and others, that if the bishops only had a little courage, and would modify the liturgy by dropping preternatural assumptions out of it, few churchgoers would object to the change for long, and congregations would be trebled in a brief time. The idea was clearly expressed in the "Apology" prefixed to *Late Lyrics and Earlier*.

"June 9. It is now the time of long days, when the sun seems reluctant to take leave of the trees at evening—the shine climbing up the trunks, reappearing higher, and still fondly grasping the tree-tops till long after."

In July his poem "Then and Now" was printed in *The Times*, and in the latter half of the month he and his wife paid a visit of two days to J. M. Barrie at Adelphi Terrace—a spot with which Hardy had had years of familiarity when their entertainer was still a child, and which was attractive to him on that account. Here they had some interesting meetings with other writers. He came back to pack up in August his MS. of *Moments of Vision* and send to the Messrs Macmillan.

In October he went with Mrs Hardy to Plymouth, calling for a day or two upon Mr and Mrs Eden Phillpotts at Torquay on their way. But the weather being wet at Plymouth they abandoned their stay there and came home.

"I hold that the mission of poetry is to record impressions, not convictions. Wordsworth in his later writings fell into the error of recording the latter. So also did Tennyson, and so do many other poets when they grow old. Absit omen!

"I fear I have always been considered the Dark Horse of contemporary English literature.

"I was quick to bloom; late to ripen.

"I believe it would be said by people who knew me well that I have a faculty (possibly not uncommon) for burying an emotion in my heart or brain for forty years, and exhuming it at the end of that time as fresh as when interred. For instance, the poem entitled 'The Breaking of Nations' contains a feeling that moved me in 1870, during the Franco-Prussian war, when I chanced to be looking at such an agricultural incident in Cornwall. But I did not write the verses till during the war with Germany of 1914, and onwards. Query: where was that sentiment hiding itself during more than 40 years?"

Hardy's mind seems to have been running on himself at this time to a degree quite unusual with him, who often said—and his actions showed it—that he took no interest in himself as a personage.

"November 13. I was a child till I was 16; a youth till I was 25; a young man till I was 40 or 50."

The above note on his being considered a Dark Horse was apt enough, when it is known that none of the society-men who met him suspected from his simple manner the potentialities of observation that were in him. This unassertive air, unconsciously worn, served him as an invisible coat almost to uncanniness. At houses and clubs where he encountered other writers and critics and world-practised readers of character, whose bearing towards him was often as towards one who did not reach their altitudes, he was seeing through them as though they were glass. He set down some cutting and satirical notes on their qualities and compass, but destroyed all of them, not wishing to leave behind him anything which could be deemed a gratuitous belittling of others.

This month *Moments of Vision and Miscellaneous Verses* was published, and it may have been his occupation with the proofs that had set him thinking of himself; and also caused him to make the following entry: "I do not expect much notice will be taken of these poems: they mortify the human sense of self-importance by showing, or suggesting, that human beings are of no matter or appreciable value in this nonchalant universe." He subjoined the Dedication of *Sordello*, where the author remarks: "My own faults of expression are many; but with care for a man or book such would be surmounted, and without it what avails the faultlessness of either?"

It was in this mood that he read such reviews of the book as were sent him.

"December 31. New Year's Eve. Went to bed at eleven. East wind. No bells heard. Slept in the New Year, as did also those 'out there'."

This refers to the poem called "Looking Across" published in the new volume, Stinsford Churchyard lying across the mead from Max Gate.

PART VIII

Life's Decline

CHAPTER XXXIV

Reflections on Poetry

1918: *Aet.* 77–78

On January 2 Mrs Hardy and himself attended a performance of the women-land-workers in the Corn Exchange.—"Met there Mrs Alfred Lyttelton, Lady Shaftesbury, and other supporters of the movement. The girls looked most picturesque in their raiment of emancipation, which they evidently enjoyed wearing."

Meanwhile the shadows lengthened. In the second week of the month he lost his old warm-hearted neighbour Mrs A. Brinsley Sheridan, *née* Motley, of Frampton Court.—"An old friend of 32 years standing. She was, I believe, the first to call when we entered this house at Max Gate, and was warmly attached to both Emma and Florence."

"January 16. As to reviewing: Apart from a few brilliant exceptions, poetry is not at bottom criticized as such, that is, as a particular man's artistic interpretation of life, but with a secret eye on its theological and political propriety. Swinburne used to say to me that so it would be two thousand years hence; but I doubt it.

"As to pessimism. My motto is, first correctly diagnose the complaint—in this case human ills—and ascertain the cause: then set about finding a remedy if one exists. The motto or practice of the optimists is: Blind the eyes to the real malady, and use empirical panaceas to suppress the symptoms.

"Browning said (in a line cited against me so often):—
Never dreamed though right were worsted wrong would triumph.

"Well, that was a lucky dreamlessness for Browning. It kept him comfortably unaware of those millions who cry with the Chorus in *Hellas*: 'Victorious Wrong, with vulture scream, Salutes the risen sun!'[1], or with Hyllus in the *Trachiniae*: 'The vast injustice of the gods is borne in upon me!' "[2]

"January 24. It is *the unwilling mind* that stultifies the contemporary criticism of poetry."

"January 25. The reviewer so often supposes that where Art is not visible it is unknown to the poet under criticism. Why does he not think of the art of concealing art? There is a good reason why."

Probably the reviews of his last book set him thinking of these things. But he does not comment on the reviews themselves, though there were some comicalities in them, like those of the reviewer who supposed that because Browning invented the name "Dramatic Lyrics" he also invented the thing, or those of the fair critic who pretended to be a man, but alas, betrayed her sex at the last moment by condemning a poem because its heroine was dressed in a tasteless Victorian skirt!

"Jan. 30. English writers who endeavour to appraise poets, and discriminate the sheep from the goats, are apt to consider that all true poets must be of one pattern in their lives and developments. But the glory of poetry lies in its largeness, admitting among its creators men of infinite variety. They must all be impractical in the conduct of their affairs; nay, they must almost, like Shelley or Marlowe, be drowned or done to death, or like Keats, die of consumption. They forget that in the ancient world no such necessity was recognized; that Homer sang as a blind old man, that Aeschylus wrote his best up to his death at nearly seventy, that the best of Sophocles appeared between his 55th. and 90th. years, that Euripides wrote up to 70.

"Among those who accomplished late, the poetic spark must always have been latent; but its outspringing may have been frozen and delayed for half a lifetime."

"Jan. 31. Performance of 'The Mellstock Quire' at the Corn Exchange, Dorchester, by the local Company for Hospital pur-

---

[1] Shelley's *Hellas*, line 940.
[2] Soph. *Trach.* 1265.

poses. Paid for the admission of the present 'Mellstock' Quire to see the resuscitated ghosts of their predecessors."

The romantic name of "Little Hintock" in *The Woodlanders* was advanced to a practical application in the February of this year by a request from Mr Dampier Whetham, once Fellow and Tutor of Trinity College, Cambridge, whose hobby when in his Dorset home was dairy farming, to be allowed to define as the "Hintock" herd the fine breed of pedigree cattle he was establishing in the district which Hardy had described under that fictitious name.

In a United States periodical for March it was amusingly stated that "Thomas Hardy is a realistic novelist who . . . has a grim determination to go down to posterity wearing the laurels of a poet". This writer was a glaring illustration of the danger of reading motives into actions. Of course there was no "grim determination", no thought of "laurels". Thomas Hardy was always a person with an unconscious, or rather unreasoning, *tendency*, and the poetic tendency had been his from the earliest. He would tell that it used to be said to him at Sir Arthur Blomfield's: "Hardy, there can hardly have been anybody in the world with less ambition than you." At this time the real state of his mind was, in his own words, that "A sense of the truth of poetry, of its supreme place in literature, had awakened itself in me. At the risk of ruining all my worldly prospects I dabbled in it . . . was forced out of it. . . . It came back upon me. . . . All was of the nature of being led by a mood, without foresight, or regard to whither it led."

It may be added that the same kind of thing had been written about *The Dynasts*. The author, they announced, determined to write the biggest drama in existence. The facts were, as he often said, that he was absorbed by the subject, and sat down to write it in the *smallest* possible compass, compressing as he went on till he could get it no smaller at all. Pitfalls surround those who attribute motives.

To Professor D. A. Robertson, University of Chicago.

February 7th. 1918.
In reply to your inquiry if I am likely to visit the United States after the war I am sorry to say that such an event is highly improbable. . . .

The opinion you quote from Lord Bryce to the effect that Americans do not think internationally, leads one to ask, Does any country think internationally? I should say, none. But there can be no doubt that some countries think thus more nearly than others; and in my opinion the people of America far more than the people of England.

In April there appeared in the *Edinburgh Review* an excellent article on Hardy's lyrics from the experienced pen of Mr Edmund Gosse; and in the same month there was sold at Christie's Red Cross Sale the manuscript of *Far from the Madding Crowd*. The interest of the latter—at least to Hardy himself—lay in the fact of it being a *revenant*—that for forty years he had had no other idea but that the manuscript had been "pulped" after its use in the *Cornhill Magazine* in 1874, since it had completely disappeared, not having been sent back with the proofs. Hardy's rather whimsical regret was that he had not written it on better paper, unforeseeing the preservation. It afterwards came to his knowledge that after the sale it went to America, and ultimately was bought of a New York dealer for the collection of Mr A. E. Newton of Pennsylvania.

"April 30. By the will of God some men are born poetical. Of these some make themselves practical poets, others are made poets by lapse of time who were hardly recognized as such. Particularly has this been the case with the translators of the Bible. They translated into the language of their age; then the years began to corrupt that language as spoken, and to add grey lichen to the translation; until the moderns who use the corrupted tongue marvel at the poetry of the old words. When new they were not more than half so poetical. So that Coverdale, Tyndale, and the rest of them are as ghosts what they never were in the flesh."

"May 8. A letter from Sir George Douglas carries me back to Wimborne and the time when his brother Frank lived opposite us there in The Avenue:

> They are great trees, no doubt, by now,
>   That were so thin in bough—
>   That row of limes—
> When we housed there; I'm loth to reckon when;
>   The world has turned so many times,
>   So many, since then!"

Whether any more of this poem was written is not known.

Two days later Hardy was seized with a violent cough and cold which confined him for a week, and was followed by "a bilious attack". However he was well enough by the 23rd to adjudicate at the Police Court on several food-profiteering cases, undertaken as being "the only War-work I was capable of", and to receive some old friends, including Sydney Cockerell, John Powys, Lady Ilchester, and her mother Lady Londonderry, of whom he says: "Never saw her again: I had known her for more than twenty-five years." A little later came Mrs Henry Allhusen, whom he had known from her childhood, Sir Frederick Treves, and Mr and Mrs Rosalind Hyndman (a charming woman), who were staying at Dorchester for the benefit of the air.

Some sense of the neglect of poetry by the modern English may have led him to write at this time:

"The poet is like one who enters and mounts a platform to give an address as announced. He opens his page, looks around, and finds the hall—*empty*."

A little later he says:

"It bridges over the years to think that Gray might have seen Wordsworth in his cradle, and Wordsworth might have seen me in mine."

Some days later:

"The people in Shakespeare act as if they were not quite closely thinking of what they are doing, but were great philosophers giving the main of their mind to the general human situation.

"I agree with Tennyson, who said he could form no idea how Shakespeare came to write his plays.

"My opinion is that a poet should express the emotion of all the ages and the thought of his own."

CHAPTER XXXV

Letters, Visits, Poetical Questions, and Mellstock Club-Room

1918–1919: *Aet.* 78–79

To Rendel Harris, Esq. Manchester.

May 20: 1918.

Your letter on the proposals you are bringing forward, in conjunction with Lord Bryce and Professor Gilbert Murray, for an Anglo-American University at Plymouth, is of much interest to me, both for general reasons and from my having had a domestic connection with the town for many years.

It appears to me that if the scheme as outlined could be carried into effect the results would be far-reaching and admirable. And as to situation, the large population of Plymouth, the close relation of that port with American history, and the beauty of the town and neighbourhood, point to it as an ideal site for such a University. Curiously enough I was quite lately standing on the stone at the Barbican that marks the spot where the Pilgrim Fathers embarked.

I quite understand that it would offer no rivalry to the

418

proposed English University at Exeter and the Southampton University College.

The idea being but in embryo, as I gather, I am unable to offer any criticisms as you suggest, which would depend largely on details. However, if any remarks upon the proposal should occur to me I will send them. Meanwhile I can only express my hope that the idea may mature.

"Sunday June 2. Seventy-eighth birthday. Several letters." Among others was an interesting one from a lady who informed him that some years earlier she had been made the happiest woman in the world by accidentally meeting for the first time, by the "Druid Stone" on his lawn, at the late Mrs Hardy's last garden-party, the man who was now her husband. And a little later came one he much valued, from a man he long had known—Mr Charles Moule, Senior Fellow and President of Corpus, Cambridge, enclosing a charming poem to Hardy as his "almost lifelong friend. . . . Too seldom seen since far-off times"—times when the two had visited mediaeval buildings together, and dived from a boat on summer mornings into the green water of Weymouth Bay.

To W. M. Stone, Esq. Blind Asylum. Edinburgh.

June 10. 1918.
You have my permission to print "The Woodlanders" and "The Return of the Native" in Braille type for the use of the blind, and I hope the books may be of interest to them.

In the same summer Mrs Champ Clark of Washington, who had sometimes visited him and his wife in London, wrote to tell him of her husband's political adventures. He had been elected Speaker of the House, and would have been elected President of the United States, she said, if the majority had ruled in the Democratic National Convention as it did in the Republican. However, Mr Champ Clark died within about two years.

In September 1918 he received a circular letter asking him to assist in bringing home to people certain facts relating to the future with a view to finding a remedy, and stating that

It is agreed by all students of modern military methods that this war, horrible as it seems to us, is merciful in comparison with what future wars must be. Scientific munition-making is only in its infancy. The next world-war, if there is another, will find the nations provided not with thousands, but with hundreds of thousands of aeroplanes, not with hundreds but with thousands of submarines, and all these as far surpassing the present types in power and destructiveness as they surpass the feeble beginnings of ten years ago. . . .

In his reply he remarked:

If it be all true that the letter prophecies, I do not think a world in which such fiendishness is possible to be worth the saving. Better let Western "civilization" perish, and the black and yellow races have a chance.

However, as a meliorist (not a pessimist as they say) I think better of the world.

Hardy also heard from the Chief Rabbi, who sent him his book of *Jewish Thought*; and towards the end of the year received from Athens a poem in modern Greek on *Tess of the d'Urbervilles*, and Mr Charles A. Speyer's music to the lyric "When I set out for Lyonnesse".

"Dec. 31. New Year's Eve. Did not sit up."

1919

At the beginning of the year Hardy received a letter and volume of verses from Miss Amy Lowell the American poetess, who reminded him of her call at the beginning of the war—"two bedraggled ladies", herself and her friend. Hardy did remember, and their consternation lest they should not be able to get back to their own country. She wrote to him again a few months later, explaining her "polyphonic prose", which had appeared in the volume she had sent him:

I do not think that polyphonic prose is a very good name for it. It is not intended to be prose at all, but poetry. . . . Of course the way to read it is just to take it the way it comes without accentuating either the rhythm or the rhyme, since they are only used to enrich the form, and are not supposed to produce the same effects that they produce in metrical verse. ... . Perhaps it is an impossible form, but when I read it aloud to my audiences (for I have been acting the part of John the Baptist, going all over the country and giving readings and talks to stimulate interest in poetry) I have no difficulty in making them apprehend it.

In February he signed a declaration of sympathy with the Jews in support of a movement for "the reconstitution of Palestine as a National Home for the Jewish People", and during the spring received letters from Quiller-Couch, Crichton Browne, and other friends on near and dear relatives they had lost in the war; about the same time appearing a relevant poem by Hardy in the *Athenæum* which was much liked, entitled, in words from the Burial Service, "According to the Mighty Working".

In May Mr Edmund Gosse wrote that he was very curious to know who drew the rather unusual illustration on the cover of the first edition of *The Trumpet-Major*. Hardy was blank on the matter for a time, until, finding a copy, he remembered that he drew it himself.

Being in London for a few days the same month he went to the dinner of the Royal Academy—the first held since the war—and was saddened to find how many of the guests and Academicians that he had been formerly accustomed to meet there had disappeared from the scene. He felt that he did not wish to go again. Among the incidents of this visit was a meeting at Lady St. Helier's with Dr Bernard, Archbishop of Dublin, and a discussion with him on Coverdale's translation of the Psalms, and the inferiority of the Latin Vulgate in certain passages of them—with which Dr Bernard agreed, sending him afterwards the two versions in parallel readings.

On his birthday in June he did what he had long intended to do— took his wife and sister to Salisbury by the old road which had been travelled by his and their forefathers in their journeys to London— via Blandford, Woodyates Inn, and Harnham Hill, whence Constable had painted his famous view of the cathedral and where the track was still accessible to wheels. Woodyates Inn—now no longer such, to the surprise of everybody since the revival of road traffic—still retained its genial hostelry appearance—and reminded Hardy of the entry in the diary of one of the daughters of George the Third after she and the rest of the family had halted there: "At Woodyates Inn . . . had a beastly breakfast". It is said that Browning's great-grandfather was once the landlord of this famous inn.

In a reply to a letter of this date concerning a new literary periodical started in Canada, he adds, after some commendatory remarks:

> But why does the paper stultify its earlier articles by advertising "The Best Sellers"? Of all marks of the *un*literary journal this is the clearest. If the "Canadian Bookman" were to take a new line and advertise eulogistically the *worst* sellers it might do something towards its object.

Shortly after his birthday he received a charming volume of holograph poems, beautifully bound, from some forty or fifty living poets. The mark of recognition so appealed to him that he determined to answer every one of the contributors by letter, and ultimately did so, though it took him a long while; saying that if they could take the trouble to write the poems he could certainly take the trouble to write the letters. It was almost his first awakening to the consciousness that an opinion had silently grown up, as it were in the night, that he was no mean power in the contemporary world of poetry.

It had impressed him all the more as coming just after his reading quite by chance in an Australian paper a quotation from a recent English review of Hardy's verse—belittling one of the poems—that called "On Sturminster Foot-Bridge"—in a manner that showed the said critic to be quite unaware of what was called "onomatopoeia" in poetry, the principle on which the lines had been composed, which were intended to convey by their rhythm the impression of a clucking of ripples into riverside holes when blown upon by an up-stream wind; so that when his reviewer jested on the syllables of the verse sounding like milk in a cart he was simply stating that the author had succeeded in doing what he had tried to do—the sounds being similar. As the jest by the English review had come back to England from Australia, where it had been quoted to Hardy's damage without the context, he took the trouble to explain the matter to the writer of the article, which he would probably have left undone if it had not so frequently happened that his intentions were shown up as his blunders. But he did not get a more satisfactory reply than that critics like the writer were sheep in wolves' clothing, and meant no harm.

29 June 1919.

My dear Bishop of Durham:

You may agree with me in thinking it a curious coincidence that the evening before your letter arrived, and when it probably was just posted, we were reading a chapter in Job, and on coming to the verse: "All the days of my appointed time will I wait, till my change come", I interrupted and said: "That was the text of the Vicar of Fordington one Sunday evening about 1860". And I can hear his voice repeating the text as the sermon went on—in the way they used to repeat it in those days—just as if it were yesterday. I wonder if you have ever preached from that text; I daresay you have. I should add that he delivered his discourse without note of any kind.

My warm thanks for your good feeling about my birthday. The thoughts of friends about one at these times take off some of the sadness they bring as one gets old.

The study of your father's life (too short, really) has interested me much. I well remember the cholera-years in Fordington: you might have added many details. For instance, every morning a man used to wheel the clothing and bed-linen of those who had died in the night out into the mead, where the Vicar had a large copper set. Some was boiled there, and some burnt. He also had large fires kindled in Mill-Street to carry off infection. An excellent plan I should think.

Many thanks too for the volume of poems which duly came. "Apollo at Pherae" seems to me remarkably well constructed in "plot", and the verse facile: I don't quite know how you could have acquired such readiness at such an early date, and the influence of Milton is not excessive—at least I think not.

I hope you will let us know when you come this way again.

To W. J. Malden—Chairman of the Wessex Saddleback Pig Society.

August 23. 1919.

I must thank you for your attention in sending me particulars of the Wessex Saddleback Pig Society and the Herd Book. I do not know much about breeding such stock, and am more bent on humane methods of slaughtering than on anything else in relation to it. So that in accepting with appreciation Honorary Membership of the Society I add a suggestion that the question of slaughtering, and transit before slaughtering, should be among the matters that the Society takes up, with a view to causing as little suffering as possible to an animal so intelligent. This worthy object would, I think, add distinction to the Society.

I am not aware if the stupid custom still prevails of having pork "well bled". This impoverishment of the meat for the sake of a temporary appearance should, I feel, be discouraged by the Society.

It is satisfactory to know that Hardy's suggestions were acted upon by the Society.

August. The Collected edition of Hardy's poems was published about this time in two volumes, the first containing the shorter poems, and the second *The Dynasts*.

October 1919. A curious question arose in Hardy's mind at this date on whether a romancer was morally justified in going to extreme lengths of assurance—after the manner of De Foe—in respect of a tale he knew to be absolutely false. Thirty-seven years earlier, when much pressed to produce something of the nature of a fireside yarn, he had invented a picturesque account of a stealthy nocturnal visit to England by Napoleon in 1804, during the war, to spy out a good spot for invasion. Being struck with the extreme improbability of such a story he added a circumstantial framework describing it as an old local tradition to blind the reader to the hoax. When it was published he was much surprised at people remarking to him: "I see you have made use of that well-known tradition of Napoleon's landing." He then supposed that, strange as it seemed, such a story must have been in existence without his knowledge, and that perhaps the event had happened. So the matter rested till the time at which we have arrived, when a friend who was interested made inquiries, and was assured by historians and annalists whom he consulted, that such a visit would have been fatuous, and well-nigh impossible. Moreover, that there had never existed any such improbable tradition. Hence arose Hardy's aforesaid case of conscience as to being too natural in the art he could practise so well. Had he not long discontinued the writing of romances he would, he said, have put at the beginning of each new one: "Understand that however true this book may be in essence, in fact it is utterly untrue."

Being interested in a dramatic case of piracy on the high seas, which might have happened a hundred or two hundred years before, Hardy and his wife went to the October Assizes, on the invitation of Mr Justice Darling, and sat through the case. Such sensational trials came to quiet Dorset whenever the port of landing was in the county, even if they happened a thousand miles off.

To Mr ——, Exeter College, Oxford.

October 30th. 1919.

Dear Sir:

In reply to your letter I write for Mr Hardy who is in bed with a chill to say that he cannot furnish you with any biographical details. . . . To your inquiry if "Jude the Obscure" is auto-biographical I have to answer that there is not a scrap of personal detail in it, it having the least to do with his own life of all his books. The rumour, if it still persists, was started by idle pressmen some years ago. Speaking generally, there is more autobiography in a hundred lines of Mr Hardy's poetry than in all the novels.

It is a tribute to Hardy's powers of presentation that readers would not for many years believe that such incidents as Jude's being smacked when birdkeeping, his driving a baker's cart, his working as a journeyman mason, as also many situations described in verse, were not actual transcripts of the writer's personal experience, although the briefest reference to biographical date-books would have shown the impossibility of anything of the sort.

On the last day of October he assisted the Bishop of Salisbury at the opening of a Children's Hospital at Swanage. The wind was very cold, and the Bishop looked so ill that Hardy, who had known him some while, apologized in the name of the Committee for dragging him out on such a day. "Oh, never mind", said Dr Ridgeway drily: "if it hadn't been here it would have been somewhere else!" He was genuinely sorry when he heard of the overworked and worthy Bishop's death shortly after.

Hardy had been asked this autumn if he would object to a

representation of some of the scenes in *The Dynasts* by the Oxford University Dramatic Society in the following year, and on his making no objection, some correspondence ensued with the President and Manager on certain details.

To Mr Maurice Colbourne.

November 11. 1919.
Your plan for showing the out-of-doors scenes is very ingenious and attractive—and more elaborate than I imagined, my idea having been just a backcloth coloured greyish-blue, and a floorcloth coloured greenish-grey—a purely conventional representation for all open-air scenes. . . . My feeling was the same as yours about the Strophe and Antistrophe—that they should be unseen, and as it were speaking from the sky. But it is, as you hint, doubtful if the two ladies will like to have their charms hidden. Would boys do instead, or ugly ladies with good voices? But I do not wish to influence largely your methods of presentation. It will be of the greatest interest to me, whether I can get to Oxford for the performance or not, to see how the questions that arise in doing the thing have been grappled with by younger brains than mine.

"November 18. To my father's grave [he was born Nov. 18. 1811] with F. [Mrs Hardy]. The funeral psalm formerly sung at the graveside to the tune of 'St. Stephen' was the XC, in Tate and Brady's version. Whether Dr Watts's version, beginning 'O God our help in ages past'—said to be a favourite with Gladstone—was written before or after T. & B.'s (from Coverdale's prose of the same psalm) I don't know, but I think it inferior to the other, which contains some good and concise verse, e.g.,

"T. & B.:

> For in thy sight a thousand years
>   Are like a day that's past,
> Or like a watch at dead of night
>   Whose hours unnumbered waste,
> Thou sweep'st us off as with a flood,
>   We vanish hence like dreams. . . .

"Watts (more diffusely):

> A thousand ages in thy sight
>   Are like an evening gone;
> Short as the watch that ends the night
>   Before the rising sun.
> Time like an ever rolling stream
>   Bears all its sons away;
> They fly forgotten, as a dream
>   Dies at the opening day.''

In December Sir George Douglas writes concerning a lecture he is going to give in Edinburgh on Hardy's poems, and incidentally remarks: "Those Aeschylean poems in 'The Past and Present' . . . how would Wordsworth have regarded them, I wonder, differing so markedly as they do from his view of Nature?'' His friend Sir Frederick Pollock also sent a letter containing an impromptu scene of a humorous kind: "Overheard at the sign of the Mermaid in Elysium'', purporting to be a conversation between the shades of Shakespeare, Campion, and Heine, "on a book newly received''—(i.e., Hardy's *Collected Poems*), in which Shakespeare says:

> 'Twas pretty wit, friend Thomas, that you spoke;
> You take the measure of my Stratford folk.

The lines referring to Hardy's poem "To Shakespeare after Three Hundred Years''.

In the same month he opened a village war-memorial in the form of a club-room in Bockhampton. It was close to his first school— erected, as has been told, by the manor-lady of his early affections— and here he danced—probably the last time in his life—with the then lady of the manor, Mrs Cecil Hanbury. The room was erected almost on the very spot where had stood Robert Reason's shoe-making shop when Hardy was a boy, described in *Under the Greenwood Tree* as "Mr Robert Penny's''.

The short speech made by Hardy at this opening, being amongst the very few he ever made in his life, is here given, as it was not reported in any newspaper:

"I feel it an honour—and an honour of a very interesting kind— to have been asked by your President to open this Club as a memorial to the gallant men of this parish who fought in the last great war—a parish I know so well, and which is only about a mile from my own door.

"It is, it seems, to be called 'The Mellstock Club'. I fancy I have heard that name of 'Mellstock' before. But we will let that pass.

"Before I proceed to the formal function of starting the pendulum of the Club, so to speak, I may be allowed to say a word or two about the bygone times of this Parish and Village, and the changes which led on to the present happy stage in the history of the place. There would be many things to interest us in the past of Bockhampton if we could only know them, but we know only a few.

"It has had various owners. In the time of the Conqueror it belonged to a Norman Countess; later to a French Priory; and in the time of Queen Elizabeth to the Dean and Chapter of Exeter, who at the beginning of the last century sold it to Mr Morton Pitt, a cousin of Pitt the Premier, who came, as we all know, of a Dorset family. What a series of scenes does this bare list of owners bring back!

"At one time Bockhampton had a water-mill. Where was that mill, I wonder? It had a wood. Where was that wood?

"However, to come to my own recollections. From times immemorial the village contained several old Elizabethan houses, with mullioned windows and doors, of Ham-hill stone. They stood between General Balguy's house and the withy bed. I remember seeing some of them in process of being pulled down, but some were pulled down before I was born. To this attaches a story. Mr Pitt, by whose orders it was done, came to look on, and asked one of the men several questions as to why he was doing it in such and such a way. Mr Pitt was notorious for his shabby clothes, and the labourer, who did not know him, said at last, 'Look here old chap, don't you ask so many questions, and just go on. Anybody would think the house was yours!' Mr Pitt obeyed orders, and meekly went on, murmuring, 'Well, 'tis mine, after all!'

"Then there were the Poor-houses, I remember—just at the corner turning down to the dairy. These were the homes of the parish paupers before workhouses were built. In one of them lived an old man who was found one day rolling on the floor, with a lot of pence and half-pence scattered round him. They asked him what was the matter, and he said he had heard of people rolling in money, and he thought that for once in his life he would do it, to see what it was like.

"Then there used to be dancing parties at Christmas, and some weeks after. This kind of party was called a Jacob's Join, in which every guest contributed a certain sum to pay the expenses of the entertainment—it was mostly half-a-crown in this village. They were very lively parties I believe. The curious thing is that the man who used to give the house-room for the dances lived in a cottage which stood exactly where this Club house stands now—so that when you dance here you will be simply carrying on the tradition of the spot.

"But though Bockhampton has had all these interesting features in the past it has never till now had a War Memorial—never had a Club-room for social intercourse and reading. That had to wait till your kind-hearted friend and President Mr Hanbury, and no less kind-hearted Mrs Hanbury, came along, and in consultation with your valued friend Mr Cowley, set it going; and here the thing is.

"In conclusion I have now merely to say I declare the Mellstock Club and reading room to be open."

December 26. 1919.

Dear Professor Phelps:

I am much honoured by the request of the Governing Body of Yale University and yourself that I should deliver the first of the lectures instituted as a memorial to Francis Bergen. It is, however, quite out of my power to entertain the notion of such an undertaking; and this for more than one reason. I have never practised lecturing, or had any inclination to do so, and the time of life is now come to me at which, even if I had practised it, I should be compelled to leave off for physical reasons. All the same I thank the University for sending the suggestion to me, and including my wife in the welcome that is offered.

To Mrs Ambrose Dudley.

December 30. 1919.

I am sorry to say that your appeal for a poem that should be worthy of the event of the 8th. August 1918 reaches me at too late a time of life to attempt it. . . . The outline of such a poem, which you very cleverly sketch, is striking, and ought to result, at the hands of somebody or other who may undertake it, in a literary parallel to the Battle of Prague—a piece of music which ceased to be known long before your time, but was extraordinarily popular in its day—reproducing the crashing of guns nearer and nearer, the groans of the wounded, and the final fulfilment, with great fidelity.

The length of the late war exhausted me of all my impromptu poems dealing with that tragedy. . . . I quite think that one of our young poets would rise to the occasion if you were to give him the opportunity.

To an unnamed young poet—

(about December 1919.)

The only practical advice I can give, and I give that with great diffidence, is to begin with *imitative* poetry, adopting the manner and views of any recent poet—say Wordsworth or Tennyson. You will thus attract the praises of the critical papers, and escape the satire and censure which they are sure to bestow on anything that strikes them as unfamiliar. Having won them by good imitations you can introduce your originalities by degrees. For if you want your book to sell it is fatal to begin with any original vein you may be blest with—the hearing of "some new thing", which so fascinated the Athenians, being to the English reviewer as a red rag to a bull.

Be also very careful about the mechanical part of your verse— rhythms, rhymes, &c. They do not know that dissonances, and other irregularities, can be produced advisedly, as art, and so worked as to give more charm than strict conformities, to the mind and ear of those trained and steeped in poetry; but they assume that a poet who commits one of these irregularities does so because of his ignorance, and the inferiority of his ear to that of the critic himself. *Ars est celare artem* they have never heard of, or forget it.

This year went out quietly with Hardy as is shown by the brief entry: "New Year's Eve. Did not sit up."

CHAPTER XXXVI

"The Dynasts" at Oxford; Hon. Degree; a Deputation; a Controversy

1920: *Aet.* 79–80

"January 19. Coming back from Talbothays by West Stafford-Cross I saw Orion upside down in a pool of water under an oak."

To the Secretary of the Navy League.

Jan. 24. 1920

I am sorry to say that I do not belong to a Naval family, though I have many friends both in the English and American navies. All that I can state with certainty is that both Admiral Sir Thomas Hardy's family and my own have been Dorset for centuries, dwelling within a few miles of each other, and that they are reputed to come from the same ancestry, as is antecedently probable for several reasons. But they branched apart before the Admiral's time.

He had no direct descendant in the male line, having left two daughters only.

On February 2 Hardy was invited to receive the Honorary Degree of Doctor of Letters during the time he was to be in Oxford at the performance of *The Dynasts* at the theatre, which he had promised to attend; and on the 9th he set out by train for Oxford with Mrs Hardy, though the members of the O.U.D.S. had offered to send a car for him all the way. The day was unusually fine for February and they were met at the station by enthusiastic representatives of the society, driven round Oxford, and conducted to the house of Sir Walter and Lady Raleigh who were their hosts.

The next day, after lunching with the Giffords at Arlington House, they went to the Sheldonian, and the degree was received, his wife, Evelyn Gifford, and her sister Daisy being present among other friends. Evelyn, daughter of the late Archdeacon Gifford, was his bright and affectionate cousin by marriage, whom Hardy was never to see again. Had he known it when he was parting from her outside the Sheldonian in the rain that afternoon his heart would have been heavier than it was.

In the afternoon he met the Poet-Laureate, Mr Masefield, and many more friends at the Raleighs', and also at the theatre in the evening, from which they did not return till one o'clock—the whole day having been of a most romantic kind, and the performance of *The Dynasts* by the O.U.D.S. everything that could be desired. It was said that the bookings applied for would have filled the theatre for three weeks, had it been available.

To Mr Joseph McCabe, who wrote proposing to include Hardy in a Biographical Dictionary of Modern Rationalists.

February 18. 1920.

Dear Sir:

As Mr Hardy has a cold which makes writing trying to his eyes, I answer your letter for him. He says he thinks he is rather an irrationalist than a rationalist, on account of his inconsistencies. He has, in fact, declared as much in prefaces to some of his poems where he explains his views as being mere impressions that frequently change. Moreover, he thinks he could show that no man is a rationalist, and that human actions are not ruled by reason at all in the last resort. But this, of course, is outside the question. So that he cannot honestly claim to belong to the honourable body you are including in your dictionary, whom he admires for their straightforward sincerity and permanent convictions, though he does not quite think they can claim their title.

Yours very truly,

F. E. Hardy.

To Mr John Slater, F.R.I.B.A.

March 7. 1920.

My dear Slater:

It is very curious that yesterday at lunch I said apropos of nothing: "I never hear or see anything of John Slater nowadays." And lo, here is a letter from you!

As to your question whether I should like to be nominated as an Hon. Fellow of the R.I.B.A. I really don't know what to say. Age has naturally made me, like Gallio, care for none of these things, at any rate very much, especially as I am hardly ever in London. But at the same time I am very conscious of the honour of such a proposition, and like to be reminded in such a way that I once knew what a T square was. So, shall I leave the decision to your judgment? But if you think there would be any doubt in the mind of any member of the Council, please don't propose it.

Your letter recalls those times we had in Bedford Street together. Are there any such amiable architects now as Roger Smith was? Not many. Also, what became of Conder?—the one who had such a keen sense of humour. [Conder, strangely enough, died in Japan that very year.]

Hardy was duly nominated and elected, and it was a matter of regret with him that he could not attend the meetings of the Institute, held still in the same old room in Conduit Street in which he had received the prize medal for his essay in 1863 from the hands of Sir Gilbert Scott. Mr John Slater was almost the only surviving friend of Hardy's architectural years in London since the death of Arthur Blomfield.

"March 25. Joined National Committee for acquiring Wentworth Place—the house once occupied by John Keats."

"April 7. A would-be author, not without humour, writing from S. Africa for a 'foreword' from me, adds: 'Mr Balfour when writing asked me not to use his remarks, mentioning the number of books sent him from all parts of the world (for forewords). But mental dexterity greatly inferior to yours, Sir, could contrive to do somewhat, and yet avoid the consequences contemplated'—i.e., multitudes of other would-be novelists asking the same favour."

"April 21. Went with F. to St. Margaret's, Westminster to the wedding of Harold Macmillan and Lady Dorothy Cavendish. Sat with Lord Morley, and signed as one of the witnesses. Morley, seeing Bryce close by us, and the Duke of Devonshire near, whispered to F.: 'Which weigh most, three O.M.'s or one Duke?'"

"May 14. Motored with F. and K. to Exeter. Called on the Granville-Barkers at Sidmouth. Cathedral service: the beautiful anthem, 'God is gone up' (Croft). Well sung. Psalms to Walker in E-flat. Felt I should prefer to be a cathedral organist to anything in the world. 'Bidding my organ obey, calling its keys to their work, claiming each slave of the sound.' A fine May day."

At the end of May a letter came from C. W. Moule in reply to Hardy's note of sympathy on his loss of his only remaining brother Handley the Bishop of Durham, with whom Hardy had had occasion to correspond the year before. As it was the last letter Hardy received from his correspondent, who himself passed away within the next year, the following passages are quoted:

> In condolence "the half is more than the whole", as the wise Greek paradox saith ($\pi\lambda\acute{\epsilon}ov$ $\mathring{\eta}\mu\iota\sigma\upsilon$ $\pi\alpha\nu\tau\acute{o}\varsigma$). . . . Your friendly acceptance of those stanzas was answered by me, but that in which you told me that dear Horace was one of "The Five Students" in "Moments of Vision" I fear was never answered. . . . I did not know of Handley's nearness in age to your sister Mary [they were only two days apart] nor did I know that your mother and mine knew each other well enough to compare notes on the point. . . . I am glad you saw him at Max Gate. We wish that we could see you here. I may try to send you some book in memoriam H. C. G. M. . . . "Not one is there among us that understandeth any more", as a snapshot of the current generation, is worthy of you. [Hardy had quoted the words from the 74th Psalm in the letter to which this was an answer, alluding probably to the memories familiar to all three.]

On June 2nd of this year came Hardy's eightieth birthday, and he received a deputation from the Society of Authors, consisting of Mr Augustine Birrell, Mr Anthony Hawkins, and Mr John Galsworthy. The occasion was a pleasant one, and the lunch lively. Many messages were received during the day, including one from the King, the Lord Mayor of London, the Cambridge Vice-Chancellor, and the Prime Minister.

Hardy pencilled down the following as "Birthday notes":

"When, like the Psalmist, 'I call mine own ways to remembrance', I find nothing in them that quite justifies this celebration.

"The value of old age depends upon the person who reaches it. To some men of early performance it is useless. To others, who are late to develop, it just enables them to complete their job.

"We have visited two cathedrals during the last month, and I could not help feeling that if men could get a little more of the reposefulness and peace of those buildings into their lives how much better it would be for them.

"Nature's indifference to the advance of her species along what we are accustomed to call civilized lines makes the late war of no importance to her, except as a sort of geological fault in her continuity.

"Though my life, like the lives of my contemporaries, covers a period of more material advance in the world than any of the same length can have done in other centuries, I do not find that real civilization has advanced equally. People are not more humane, so far as I can see, than they were in the year of my birth. Disinterested kindness is less. The spontaneous goodwill that used to characterize manual workers seems to have departed. One day of late a railway porter said to a feeble old lady, a friend of ours, 'See to your luggage yourself'. Human nature had not sunk so low as that in 1840.

"If, as has been lately asserted, only the young and feeble League of Nations stands between us and the *utter destruction of Civilization*, it makes one feel he would rather be old than young. For a person whose chief interest in life has been the literary art—poetry in particular—the thought is depressing that, should such an overturn arrive, poetry will be the first thing to go, probably not to revive again for many centuries. Anyhow, it behoves young poets and other writers to endeavour to stave off such a catastrophe."

The aforesaid somewhat unexpected celebration of his eightieth birthday seems to have set Hardy's mind running on his ancestry and connections: for later in June he made inquiries as to the descendants of the Rev. C. Holder, his deceased brother-in-law, formerly rector of St. Juliot, and about the same time he inquired of a Cornish friend as to the welfare of the newspaper *The West Briton*, which had been founded by his great-great uncle on the maternal side in 17—, and the reply was:

How interesting, your family connection with the birth of "The West Briton"—which still lives. It has circulated mainly in the mining districts, and is now the property of a Company at Truro, where it is published.

Among others who remembered his birthday Mr John Lane sent a glass goblet which had come into his possession many years before, remarking, . . . "no doubt it was intended as a gift for you from some fair but probably shy admirer"; to which Hardy replied:

Alas, for the mysterious goblet inscribed to the mysterious namesake of mine. He must, or may, have been a jockey from the diagrams. . . . Anyhow, no woman ever took the trouble to inscribe her love for me on a cup of crystal—of that you may be sure; and it is best on the whole to leave the history of the glass in vague uncertainty.

The next week Sir J. M. Barrie came to Max Gate on a visit, and in July Hardy and his wife were motoring about Dorset, showing some features of the county to their friend Mrs Arthur Henniker, who was staying at Weymouth, and at that time had ideas of buying a house in the neighbourhood. He was also engaged in further correspondence on the scheme of establishing a South-western University at Exeter.

July 28. Hardy sent the poem on Keats at Hampstead as a contribution to the book proposed to be published on the Centenary of Keats's death, saying, "I wish I could have let you have something more worthy of the occasion and the man; but worthy writing does not come at call at my age."

To Mr G. Herbert Thring.

August 23. 1920

The address from the Members of the Council, representing the Society of Authors all, has reached me safely, and though I knew its contents—its spiritual part—on my actual birthday when the deputation came here, I did not realize its bodily beauty till now—

As to the address itself I can only confirm by this letter what I told the deputation by word of mouth—how much I have been moved by such a mark of good-feeling—affection as I may truly call it—in the body of writers whose President I have had the distinction of being for many years—a do-nothing President, a roi-fainéant, I very greatly fear, in spite of their assurances! However, the Society has been good enough to take me as worth this tribute, and I thank them heartily for it and what it expresses. It will be a cheering reminder of bright things whenever I see it or think of it, which will be often and often.

From Mr A—— M—— of Letchworth.

August 1920.

Dear Sir:

I am driven to wonder why the devil you don't answer letters that are written to you!

Very truly,

A—— M——

"September 6. Death of Evelyn Gifford daughter of Em's uncle, at Arlington House, Oxford. Dear Evelyn! whom I last parted from in apparently perfect health." She was the daughter of Dr Gifford who married Margaret Jeune, and the poem "Evelyn G. of Christminster" was written on this occasion.

Nov. 11. Hardy's poem "And there was a great calm", appeared in *The Times* Armistice Supplement, and on the 13th, the Dorchester amateurs performed *The Return of the Native* in Dorchester, as dramatized by Mr Tilley.

"A much better play than I expected. The dancing was just as it used to be at Bockhampton in my childhood, and Gertrude Bugler as Eustacia looked the part to a T., enacting the hand-kissing scene with Charley excellently."

To Howard Ruff Esq.

December 8. 1920

I have to acknowledge the receipt of your letter of the 4th. informing me of the gratifying suggestion of your Committee that

I should become an Honorary Vice-President of your now well-known and popular Society.

I am sorry to answer that I have been compelled of late, for reasons I need not trouble you with, to forgo such distinctions. . . . All the same I may be allowed to congratulate its members upon their wise insistence on the word "English" as the name of this country's people, and in not giving way to a few short-sighted clamourers for the vague, unhistoric, and pinchbeck title of "British" by which they would fain see it supplanted.

To Mr Alfred Noyes.

Dorchester.
13th. December. 1920.

Dear Mr Noyes:

Somebody has sent me an article from The Morning Post of Dec. 9. entitled "Poetry and Religion", which reports you as saying, in a lecture, that mine is "a philosophy which told them (readers) that the Power behind the Universe was an imbecile jester".

As I hold no such "philosophy", and, to the best of my recollection, never could have done so, I should be glad if you would inform me whereabouts I have seriously asserted such to be my opinion.

Yours truly,

Th. Hardy.

It should be stated that Mr Noyes had always been a friendly critic of Hardy's writings, and one with whom he was on good terms, which was probably Hardy's reason for writing to him, who would be aware there was no personal antagonism in his letter.

Mr Noyes replied that he was sorry the abbreviated report of his address did not contain the tribute he had paid Hardy as a writer with artistic mastery and at the head of living authors, although he did disagree with his pessimistic philosophy; a philosophy which, in his opinion, led logically to the conclusion that the Power behind the Universe was malign; and he referred to various passages in Hardy's poems that seemed to bear out his belief that their writer held the views attributed to him in the lecture; offering however to revise it when reprinted if he had misinterpreted the aforesaid passages.

To Mr Alfred Noyes.

December 19th. 1920.

I am much obliged for your reply, which I really ought not to have troubled you to write. I may say for myself that I very seldom do give critics such trouble, usually letting things drift, though there have been many occasions when a writer who has been so much abused for his opinions as I have been would perhaps have done well not to hold his peace.

I do not know that there can be much use in my saying more than I did say. It seems strange that I should have to remind a man of letters of what, I should have supposed, he would have known as well as I—of the very elementary rule of criticism that a writer's opinions should be judged as a whole, and not from picked passages that contradict them as a whole—and this especially when they are scattered over a period of 50 years.

Also that I should have to remind him of the vast difference between the expression of fancy and the expression of belief. My imagination may have often run away with me; but all the same, my sober opinion—so far as I have any definite one—of the Cause of Things, has been defined in scores of places, and is that of a great many ordinary thinkers:—that the said Cause is neither moral nor immoral, but *un*moral:—"loveless and hateless" I have called it; "which neither good nor evil knows"—etc, etc—(you will find plenty of these definitions in "The Dynasts" as well as in short poems, and I am surprised that you have not taken them in). This view is quite in keeping with what you call a Pessimistic philosophy (a mere nickname with no sense in it), which I am quite unable to see as "leading logically to the conclusion that the Power behind the universe is malign".

In my fancies, or poems of the imagination, I have of course called this Power all sorts of names—never supposing they would be taken for more than fancies. I have even in prefaces warned readers to take them only as such—as mere impressions of the moment, exclamations, in fact. But it has always been my misfortune to presuppose a too intelligent reading public, and no doubt people will go on thinking that I really believe the Prime Mover to be a malignant old gentleman, a sort of King of Dahomey—an idea which, so far from my holding it, is to me irresistibly comic. "What a fool one must have been to write for such a public!" is the inevitable reflection at the end of one's life.

The lines you allude to, "A young man's epigram" dated 1866, I remember finding in a drawer, and printed them merely as an amusing instance of early cynicism. The words "Time's Laughingstocks" are legitimate imagery all of a piece with such expressions as "Life, Time's fool", and thousands in poetry and I am amazed that you should see any *belief* in them. The other verses you mention, "New Year's Eve", "His Education", are the same fanciful impressions of the moment. The poem called "He abjures Love" ending with "and then the curtain", is a love-poem, and lovers are chartered irresponsibles. A poem often quoted against me, and apparently in your mind in the lecture, is the one called "Nature's Questioning", containing the words, "some Vast Imbecility", &c.—as if these definitions were my creed. But they are merely enumerated in the poem as fanciful alternatives to several others, having nothing to do with my own opinion. As for "The Unborn" to which you allude, though the form of it is imaginary, the sentiment is one which I should think, especially since the war, is not uncommon or unreasonable.

This week I have had sent me a review which quotes a poem entitled "To my father's violin" containing a Virgilian reminiscence of mine of Acheron and the Shades. The pennyaliner who writes it comments: "Truly this pessimism is insupportable. . . . One marvels that Hardy is not in a madhouse." Such is English criticism, and I repeat, Why did I ever write a line! And perhaps if the young ladies to whom you lectured really knew that, so far from being the wicked personage they doubtless think me at present to be, I am a harmless old character much like their own grandfathers, they would consider me far less romantic and attractive.

Mr Noyes in a further interesting letter, after reassuring Hardy that he would correct any errors, gave his own views, one of which was that he had "never been able to conceive a Cause of Things that could be less in any respect than the things caused". To which Hardy replied:

Many thanks for your letter. The Scheme of Things is, indeed, incomprehensible; and there I suppose we must leave it—perhaps for the best. Knowledge might be terrible.

It may be added that, as has been stated before, the above

mentioned view that the Cause of things, so far from being malignant, was indifferent and unconscious had long been Hardy's. Mr Noyes' conception that a Cause—which, as Hardy somewhere says, "is but the Invariable Antecedent", in philosophy—could not be less than the thing caused, required no refutation, the opposite being evidenced everywhere.

To the New York *World.*

December 23. 1920.
Yes: I approve of international disarmament, on the lines indicated by the New York World.

The following letter, written to someone about December 1920, obviously refers to his correspondence with Mr Noyes:

A friend of mine writes objecting to what he calls my "philosophy" (though I have no philosophy—merely what I have often explained to be only a confused heap of impressions, like those of a bewildered child at a conjuring show). He says he has never been able to conceive a Cause of Things that could be less in any respect than the thing caused. This apparent impossibility to him, and to so many, has been long ago proved non-existent by philosophers, and is very likely owing to his running his head against a *Single* Cause, and perceiving no possible other. But if he would discern that what we call the First Cause should be called First Causes, his difficulty would be lessened. Assume a thousand unconscious causes—lumped together in poetry as one Cause, or God—and bear in mind that a coloured liquid can be produced by the mixture of colourless ones, a noise by the juxtaposition of silences, etc., etc., and you see that the assumption that intelligent beings arise from the combined action of unintelligent forces is sufficiently probable for imaginative writing, and I have never attempted scientific. It is my misfortune that people *will* treat all my mood-dictated writing as a single scientific theory.

About Christmas the song entitled "When I set out for Lyonnesse" was published as set to music by Mr Charles A. Speyer. It was one of his own poems that Hardy happened to like, and he was agreeably surprised that it should be liked by anybody else, his experience being that an author's preference for particular verses of his own was usually based on the circumstances that gave rise to them, and not on their success as art.

On Christmas night the carol-singers and mummers came to Max Gate as they had promised, the latter performing the *Play of Saint George*, just as he had seen it performed in his childhood. On the last day of the old year a poem by Hardy called "At the Entering of the New Year" appeared in the *Athenæum*.

Conclusion
by
Florence Emily Hardy

Comprising Chapters XXXVII and XXXVIII,
originally published as Chapters XVIII and XIX of
The Later Years of Thomas Hardy

CHAPTER XXXVII

Some Farewells

1921–1925: *Aet.* 80–85

The New Year found Hardy sitting up to hear the bells, which he had not done for some time.

Early in January he was searching through registers of Stinsford for records of a family named Knight, connected with his own. Many generations of this family are buried in nameless graves in Stinsford Churchyard.

J. M. Barrie paid him a brief visit on May 11, staying at Max Gate for one night, and visiting Hardy's birthplace at Bockhampton on the morning of May 12. The same day Hardy learned of the death of a friend, an elder brother of the confidant and guide of his youth and early manhood. In his note-book he writes:

"May 11. Charles Moule died. He is the last of 'the seven brethren'."

On June 2 he notes that his birthday was remembered by the newspapers, and that he received an address from younger writers. Accompanying this was a fine copy of the first edition of *Lamia, Isabella, The Eve of St. Agnes and Other Poems* by John Keats, in the original boards with the half-title and eight pages of advertisements.

The idea had originated with Mr St. John Ervine, who summoned a committee to consider the nature of the Tribute. The address was signed by a hundred and six younger writers, and ran as follows:

Dear Mr Hardy,

We, who are your younger comrades in the craft of letters, wish on this your eighty-first birthday to do honour to ourselves by praising your work, and to thank you for the example of high endeavour and achievement which you have set before us. In your novels and poems you have given us a tragic vision of life which is informed by your knowledge of character and relieved by the charity of your humour, and sweetened by your sympathy with human suffering and endurance. We have learned from you that the proud heart can subdue the hardest fate, even in submitting to it. . . . In all that you have written you have shown the spirit of man, nourished by tradition and sustained by pride, persisting through defeat.

You have inspired us both by your work and by the manner in which it was done. The craftsman in you calls for our admiration as surely as the artist, and few writers have observed so closely as you have the Host's instruction in the *Canterbury Tales*:

> Your tarmes, your colours, and your figures,
> Keep them in store, till so be ye indite
> High style, as when that men to kinges write.

From your first book to your last, you have written in the "high style, as when that men to kinges write", and you have crowned a great prose with a noble poetry.

We thank you, Sir, for all that you have written . . . but most of all, perhaps, for *The Dynasts*.

We beg that you will accept the copy of the first edition of *Lamia* by John Keats which accompanies this letter, and with it, accept also our grateful homage.

A few days later, on June 9, he motored to Sturminster Newton with his wife and Mr Cecil Hanbury to see a performance of *The Mellstock Quire* by the Hardy Players in the Castle ruins. Afterwards he went to Riverside, the house where he had written *The Return of the Native*, and where the Players were then having tea.

On June 16 Mr de la Mare arrived for a visit of two nights. The following day he walked to Stinsford with Hardy and was much interested in hearing about the various graves, and in reading a poem that Hardy had just lately written, "Voices from Things growing in a Country Churchyard". The first verse of the poem runs thus:

These flowers are I, poor Fanny Hurd,
    Sir or Madam,
A little girl here sepultured.
Once I flit-fluttered like a bird
Above the grass, as now I wave
In daisy shapes above my grave,
    All day cheerily,
    All night eerily!

Fanny Hurd's real name was Fanny Hurden, and Hardy remembered her as a delicate child who went to school with him. She
died when she was about eighteen, and her grave and a head-stone
with her name are to be seen in Stinsford Churchyard. The others
mentioned in this poem were known to him by name and repute.

Early in July a company of film actors arrived in Dorchester for
the purpose of preparing a film of *The Mayor of Casterbridge*. Hardy
met them outside The King's Arms, the hotel associated with the
novel. Although the actors had their faces coloured yellow and were
dressed in the fashion of some eighty years earlier, Hardy observed,
to his surprise, that the townsfolk passed by on their ordinary affairs
and seemed not to notice the strange spectacle, nor did any interest
seem aroused when Hardy drove through the town with the actors to
Maiden Castle, that ancient earthwork which formed the background to one part of the film.

About this time he went to St. Peter's Church, to a morning
service, for the purpose of hearing sung by the choir the morning
hymn, "Awake my Soul", to Barthélémon's setting. This had been
arranged for him by Dr Niven, the Rector of St. Peter's. Church
music, as has been shown, had appealed strongly to Hardy from his
earliest years. On July 23 a sonnet, "Barthélémon at Vauxhall",
appeared in *The Times*. He had often imagined the weary musician,
returning from his nightly occupation of making music for a riotous
throng, lingering on Westminster Bridge to see the rising sun and
being thence inspired to the composition of music to be heard
hereafter in places very different from Vauxhall.

In the same month he opened a bazaar in aid of the Dorset
County Hospital, and in the evening of that day he was driven into
Dorchester again to see some dancing in the Borough Gardens. Of
this he writes:

"Saw 'The Lancers' danced (for probably the last time) at my request. Home at 10: outside our gate full moon over cottage: band still heard playing."

At the beginning of September Hardy stood sponsor at the christening of the infant daughter of Mr and Mrs Cecil Hanbury of Kingston Maurward. His gift to his little godchild was the manuscript of a short poem contained in a silver box. This appeared afterwards in *Human Shows* under the title "To C. F. H.". Three days later he was again at Stinsford Church, attending the evening service. In his note-book he records: "A beautiful evening. Evening Hymn Tallis."

During the latter half of September Hardy was sitting to his friend Mr Ouless for his portrait, which now hangs in the National Portrait Gallery. On October 14 he received a visit from Mr and Mrs John Masefield, who brought with them a gift: a full-rigged ship made by John Masefield himself. This ship had been named by its maker *The Triumph*, and was much valued by Hardy, who showed it with pride to callers at Max Gate, with the story of how it arrived. Four days later Hardy writes:

"October 18. In afternoon to Stinsford with F. A matchless October: sunshine, mist and turning leaves."

The first month of 1922 found him writing an energetic preface to a volume of poems entitled *Late Lyrics and Earlier*, the MS. of which he forwarded to the publishers on January 23. Some of his friends regretted this preface, thinking that it betrayed an oversensitiveness to criticism which it were better the world should not know. But sensitiveness was one of Hardy's chief characteristics, and without it his poems would never have been written, nor indeed, the greatest of his novels. He used to say that it was not so much the force of the blow that counted, as the nature of the material that received the blow.

An interesting point in this preface was his attitude towards religion. Through the years 1920 to 1925 Hardy was interested in conjectures on rationalizing the English Church. There had been rumours for some years of a revised Liturgy, and his hopes were accordingly raised by the thought of making the Established Church comprehensive enough to include the majority of thinkers of the previous hundred years who had lost all belief in the supernatural.

When the new Prayer Book appeared, however, his hopes were doomed to disappointment, and he found that the revision had not been in a rationalistic direction, and from that time he lost all expectation of seeing the Church representative of modern thinking minds.

In April J. M. Barrie stayed at Max Gate for one night. The 23rd May saw the publication of *Late Lyrics and Earlier*, and on the following day Hardy motored to Sturminster Newton to call at the house where he had spent some of the early years of his first marriage, and where he wrote *The Return of the Native*. Two days later he notes: "Visited Stinsford and Higher Bockhampton. House at the latter shabby, and garden. Just went through into heath, and up plantation to top of garden." It was becoming increasingly painful to Hardy to visit this old home of his, and often when he left he said that he would go there no more.

On May 29 he copied some old notes made before he had contemplated writing *The Dynasts*.

"We—the people—Humanity, a collective personality—(Thus 'we' could be engaged in the battle of Hohenlinden, say, and in the battle of Waterloo)—dwell with genial humour on 'our' getting into a rage for we knew not what.

"The intelligence of this collective personality Humanity is pervasive, ubiquitous, like that of God. Hence e.g. on the one hand we could hear the roar of the cannon, discern the rush of the battalions, on the other hear the voice of a man protesting, etc.

"Title 'self-slaughter'; 'divided against ourselves'.

"Now these 3 (or 3000) whirling through space at the rate of 40 miles a second—(God's view). 'Some of our family who' (the we of one nation speaking of the 'we' of another).

"A battle. Army as somnambulists—not knowing what it is for.

"We were called 'Artillery' etc. 'We were so under the spell of habit that' (drill).

"It is now necessary to call the reader's attention to those of us who were harnessed and collared in blue and brass. . . .

"*Poem*—the difference between what things are and what they ought to be. (Stated as by a god to the gods—i.e. as God's story.)

"*Poem*—I—First Cause, omniscient, not omnipotent— limitations, difficulties, etc., from being only able to work by Law (His only failing is lack of foresight).

"We will now ask the reader to look eastward with us . . . at what the contingent of us out that way were doing.

"*Poem*. A spectral force seen acting in a man (e.g. Napoleon) and he acting under it—a pathetic sight—this compulsion.

"Patriotism, if aggressive and at the expense of other countries, is a vice; if in sympathy with them, a virtue."

From these notes it will be seen how *The Dynasts* had been slowly developing in his mind. Unfortunately they are not dated, but there is in existence a note-book filled with details of the Napoleonic wars, and reflection upon them, having been written at the time he was gathering material for *The Trumpet-Major*, which was first published in 1880.

During July Hardy had visits from many friends. Florence Henniker came early in the month, and went for a delightful drive with him and his wife in Blackmore Vale, and to Sherborne, the scene of *The Woodlanders*. Later Siegfried Sassoon arrived with Edmund Blunden, and then E. M. Forster, who accompanied him to an amateur performance of *A Midsummer Night's Dream* on the lawn of Trinity Rectory.

In August he was well enough to cycle (no small feat for a man of eighty-two) with his wife to Talbothays to visit his brother and his sister.

On August 11 he writes in his note-book:

"Motored to Sturminster Newton, and back by Dogbury Gate. Walked to top of High Stoy with Flower (probably for the last time), thence back home. A beautiful drive."

"October 12. Walked across Boucher's Close to Eweleaze Stile." (Boucher's Close is a green-wooded meadow next to Stinsford Vicarage, and the Eweleaze Stile is the one whereon, more than fifty years before this date, he had sat and read the review of *Desperate Remedies* in the *Spectator*.)

On the same day Hardy wrote to J. H. Morgan as follows:

Dear General Morgan,

I had already begun a reply to your interesting letter from Berlin, which opened up so many points that had engaged me 20 years ago, but had rather faded in my memory. Now that you are at home I will write it in a more succinct form, for it is not likely that amid the many details you have to attend to after your absence you will want to think much about Napoleonic times.

I cannot for my life recall where I obtained the idea of N's entry into Berlin by the Potsdamer-strasse, though I don't think I should have written it without authority. However, you have to remember that the events generally in *The Dynasts* had to be pulled together into dramatic scenes, to show themselves to the mental eye of the reader as a picture viewed from one point; and hence it was sometimes necessary to see round corners, down crooked streets, and to shift buildings nearer each other than in reality (as Turner did in his landscapes); and it may possibly happen that I gave "A Public Place" in Berlin these convenient facilities without much ceremony.

You allude to Leipzig. That battle bothered me much more than Jena or Ulm (to which you also allude)—in fact more than any other battle I had to handle. I defy any human being to synchronize with any certainty its episodes from descriptions by historians. My time-table was, I believe, as probable a one as can be drawn up at this date. But I will go no further with these stale conjectures, now you are in London.

I have quite recently been reading a yellow old letter written from Berlin in June, 1815, by a Dorset man whose daughter is a friend of ours, and who lately sent it to me. The writer says what is oddly in keeping with your remarks on the annoyance of Prussian officers. "Buonaparte has rendered Germany completely military; at the inns and post-houses a private Gentleman exacts not half the respect exacted by a soldier. This contempt for those who wear no swords displays itself in no very pleasant shape to travellers. About 3 weeks ago I might have died of damp sheets if my German servant had not taken upon him to assure a brute of a Post-master that I was an English General travelling for my health. . . . I have since girded on a sabre, got a military cap, and let my moustache grow: soldiers now present arms as we pass."

It would be strange to find that Napoleon was really the prime cause of German militarism! What a Nemesis for the French nation!

Well, I have gone back to Boney again after all: but no more of him. I hope you find the change to London agreeable, and keep well in your vicissitudes.

Sincerely yours,

Thomas Hardy.

Early in November he was visited by Mrs Henry Allhusen, his friend from her girlhood, when she was Miss Dorothy Stanley, daughter of Lady Jeune, afterwards Lady St. Helier. With Mrs Allhusen and her daughter Elizabeth he motored to Dogbury Gate and other beautiful parts of Dorset. Elizabeth Allhusen, a charming girl, died soon after, to Hardy's grief.

A few days later came a letter from the Pro-Provost of Queen's College, Oxford, to say that it had been decided to elect him to an Honorary Fellowship, which he accepted, an announcement to that effect being made in *The Times* on the 20th of the month.

Another entry in his note-book:

"November 27. E's death-day, ten years ago. Went with F. and tidied her tomb and carried flowers for her and the other two tombs."

"New Year's Eve. Henry and Kate came to 1 o'clock dinner, stayed to tea, left 5.30. Did not sit up."

Early in January 1923 Hardy was appointed Governor of the Dorchester Grammar School for three years.

"February 26. A story (rather than a poem) might be written in the first person, in which 'I' am supposed to live through the centuries in my ancestors, in one person, the particular line of descent chosen being that in which *qualities* are most continuous." (From an old note.)

A few days after this entry is the following:

"April 5. In to-day's *Times*:

"'Henniker.—on the 4th April 1923, of heart failure, the Honourable Mrs. Arthur Henniker. R.I.P.'

"After a friendship of 30 years!"

"April 10. F. Henniker buried to-day at 1 o'clock at Thornham Magna, Eye, Suffolk."

During the month of April Hardy finished the rough draft of his poetical play *The Queen of Cornwall*, and in May he made, with infinite care, his last drawing, an imaginary view of Tintagel Castle. This is delicately drawn, an amazing feat for a man in his eighty-third year, and it indicates his architectural tastes and early training. It was used as an illustration when *The Queen of Cornwall* was published.

In April, replying to a letter from Mr John Galsworthy, he writes:

. . . The exchange of international thought is the only possible salvation for the world: and though I was decidedly premature when I wrote at the beginning of the South African War that I hoped to see patriotism not confined to realms, but circling the earth, I still maintain that such sentiments ought to prevail.

Whether they will do so before the year 10,000 is of course what sceptics may doubt.

Towards the end of May Mr and Mrs Walter de la Mare stayed at Max Gate for two nights, and early in June, the day after Hardy's birthday, Mr and Mrs Granville-Barker came to see him, bringing with them friends he had not seen for many years, Mr and Mrs Max Beerbohm.

"June 10. Relativity. That things and events always were, are, and will be (e.g. Emma, Mother and Father are living still in the past)."

"June 21. Went with F. on board the *Queen Elizabeth* on a visit to Sir John de Robeck, Lady de Robeck, and Admiral W. W. Fisher." More than once, upon the invitation of Admiral Fisher, he had had a pleasant time on board a battleship off Portland.

On June 25 Hardy and his wife went to Oxford by road to stay at Queen's College for two nights. This was the last long journey that Hardy was to make, and the last time that he was to sleep away from Max Gate. It was a delightful drive, by way of Salisbury, Hungerford, and Wantage. At Salisbury they stopped for a little while to look at the Cathedral, as Hardy always loved doing, and at various old buildings, including the Training College which he had visited more than fifty years before when his two sisters were students there, and which is faithfully described in *Jude the Obscure*.

They paused also at Fawley, that pleasant Berkshire village described in the same novel under the name of Marygreen. Here some of Hardy's ancestors were buried, and he searched fruitlessly for their graves in the little churchyard. His father's mother, the gentle, kindly grandmother who lived with the family at Bockhampton during Hardy's childhood, had spent the first thirteen years of her life here as an orphan child, named Mary Head, and her memories of Fawley were so poignant that she never cared to return to the place after she had left it as a young girl. The surname of Jude was taken from this place.

So well had their journey been timed that on their arrival at Oxford they found awaiting them under the entrance gateway of Queen's Mr Godfrey Elton, who was to be their cicerone, and whose impressions of their visit are given herewith.

"Having been elected an Honorary Fellow Mr Hardy paid Queen's College a visit on June 25th and 26th, just after the end of the summer term of 1923. With a colleague, Dr Chattaway, I was deputed to meet him at the College gate—he was to come by road with Mrs Hardy from Dorchester. Neither Chattaway nor I had met Hardy before, but I felt confident that we should recognise the now legendary figure from his portraits. It was almost like awaiting a visit from Thackeray or Dickens. . . . The car arrived punctually, and a smallish, fragile, bright-eyed man, elderly certainly but as certainly not old, climbed out of it. An elderly gentleman, one would have said, who had always lived in the country and knew much of the ways of wild creatures and crops. . . .

"We left Mr and Mrs Hardy at tea in the Provost's Lodgings. The Provost was only one year Mr Hardy's senior, but with his patriarchal white beard appeared a great deal older, and as we left the party—Hardy sitting bright-eyed and upright on the edge of his chair—it seemed almost like leaving a new boy in charge of his headmaster. . . . Next day there was a lunch in Common-room, at which the Fellows and their wives met Mr and Mrs Hardy, and a photograph in the Fellows' garden in which Hardy appeared in his Doctor's gown with his new colleagues. In the morning he was shown the sights of the College. He was obviously happy to be in Oxford and happy, I think, too to be of it, and I wished that it had been term-time and that he could have seen the younger life of the place which one felt in some ways he would have preferred to Tutors and Professors. We took him round College a trifle too fast. He would pause reflectively before Garrick's copy of the First Folio or the contemporary portrait of Henry V and seem about to make some comment when his conductors would be passing on again and some new historical information would be being offered him. It was characteristic of him that in some pause on this perambulation he found occasion to say some kind words to me of some youthful verse of mine he had chanced to see. . . . Afterwards he asked me to take him into the High Street to see the famous curve and we spent some minutes searching for the precise spot from which it can best be viewed, while in my mind memories of *Jude the Obscure* and an earlier Oxford conflicted with anxieties as to the traffic of the existing town—to which he seemed quite indifferent. Then, apparently unwearied, he asked for the Shelley Memorial. . . .

"After this came the Common-room lunch and afterwards Mrs Hardy invited me to accompany them on a visit to the Masefields. We drove to Boar's Hill, paying a visit in Christ Church on the way. Had it not been for my constant consciousness that I was sitting beside a Classic, I should not have guessed that I was with a man who wrote; rather an elderly country gentleman with a bird-like alertness and a rare and charming youthfulness—interested in everything he saw, and cultured, but surely not much occupied with books: indeed almost all of us, his new colleagues, would have struck an impartial observer as far more *bookish* than the author of the Wessex novels. . . .

"At the Masefields' Hardy was asked a question or two about Jude's village, which it was thought he might have passed on the road from Dorchester, and he spoke briefly and depreciatingly of 'that fictitious person'. 'If there ever was such a person. . . .' When we left, Hardy holding a rose which Mr Masefield had cut from his garden, there was still time to see more. I had expected that he would wish to rest but, no; he wanted to see the Martyrs' Memorial and New College Cloisters. Obviously there were certain of the Oxford sights which he had resolved to see again. I am ashamed to remember that, by some error which I cannot now explain, I conducted our guests to the Chapel, instead of the Cloisters, at New College. But perhaps it was a fortunate error, for the choir were about to sing the evening service and at Hardy's wish we sat for about twenty minutes in the ante-chapel listening in silence to the soaring of boys' voices. . . .

"Next morning Mr and Mrs Hardy left. He spoke often afterwards of his pleasure at having seen his College, and he contemplated another visit. His too brief membership and his one visit remain a very happy memory to his colleagues."

The Hardys motored back to Max Gate by way of Newbury, Winchester, and Ringwood, having lunch in a grassy glade in the New Forest in the simple way that Hardy so much preferred.

This occasion was an outstanding one during the last years of his life.

On July 20 the Prince of Wales paid a visit to Dorchester, to open the new Drill Hall for the Dorset Territorials, and Hardy was invited to meet him there, and to drive back to Max Gate where the Prince and the party accompanying him were to lunch. It was a hot day, and the whole episode might well have proved fatiguing and irksome to a man of Hardy's years and retiring nature, but owing to the thoughtfulness of the Prince and his simple and friendly manner, all passed off pleasantly.

At lunch, beside the Prince and the Hardys there were present Lord Shaftesbury, Admiral Sir Lionel Halsey, Sir Godfrey Thomas,

Mr (afterwards Sir) Walter Peacock, and Messrs Proudfoot and Wilson, the Duchy Stewards. The Prince had a friendly talk with Hardy in the garden, before leaving to visit certain Duchy farms in Dorchester: the main characteristic of the visit was its easy informality.

The next few months saw a certain activity on Hardy's part. He visited several friends either for lunch or tea, as he did not go out in the evening except for a short walk, nor did he again sleep away from Max Gate. Many from a distance also called upon him, including his ever faithful friend Lady St. Helier, who travelled from Newbury to Max Gate on October 3, this being their last meeting.

On November 15 the poetic drama *The Famous Tragedy of the Queen of Cornwall* was published. Hardy's plan in writing this is clearly given in a letter to Mr Harold Child:

> The unities are strictly preserved, whatever virtue there may be in that. (I, myself, am old-fashioned enough to think there *is* a virtue in it, if it can be done without artificiality. The only other case I remember attempting it in was *The Return of the Native*.) The original events could have been enacted in the time taken up by the performance, and they continue unbroken throughout. The change of persons on the stage is called a change of scene, there being no change of background.
>
> My temerity in pulling together into the space of an hour events that in the traditional stories covered a long time will doubtless be criticized, if it is noticed. But there are so many versions of the famous romance that I felt free to adapt it to my purpose in any way—as, in fact, the Greek dramatists did in their plays—notably Euripides.
>
> Wishing it to be thoroughly English I have dropped the name of Chorus for the conventional onlookers, and called them Chanters, though they play the part of a Greek Chorus to some extent. I have also called them Ghosts (I don't for the moment recall an instance of this in a Greek play). . . . Whether the lady ghosts in our performance will submit to have their faces whitened I don't know! . . .
>
> I have tried to avoid turning the rude personages of, say, the fifth century into respectable Victorians, as was done by Tennyson, Swinburne, Arnold, etc. On the other hand it would have been impossible to present them as they really were, with their barbaric manners and surroundings.

On the 28th of the same month the play was produced by the Hardy Players at the Corn Exchange at Dorchester. The great difficulties which the play presented to amateur actors, unaccustomed to reciting blank verse, who were at their best in rustic comedy, were more or less overcome, but naturally a poetic drama did not make a wide appeal. However the performance, and particularly the rehearsals, gave Hardy considerable pleasure.

On December 10 the death was announced of Sir Frederick Treves, Hardy's fellow-townsman, the eminent surgeon. Frederick Treves as a child had attended the same school as Hardy's elder sister Mary, and it was from the shop of Treves's father that Hardy as a boy purchased his first writing-desk. The care which he took of all his possessions during his whole life is shown by the fact that this desk was in his study without a mark or scratch upon it at the time of his death. Because of the early association and the love which they both bore to the county there was a strong link between these two Dorset men.

On the last day but one of the year Mr and Mrs G. Bernard Shaw and Colonel T. E. Lawrence lunched with the Hardys and spent several hours with them. The following entry in his note-book ends his brief chronicle of the year's doings:

"31. New Year's Eve. Did not sit up. Heard the bells in the evening."

1924

"January 2. Attended Frederick Treves's funeral at St. Peter's. Very wet day. Sad procession to the cemetery. Casket in a little white grave.

"Lord Dawson of Penn and Mr Newman Flower came out to tea afterwards."

On January 5 a poem by Hardy, "In Memoriam, F.T.", appeared in *The Times*, a last tribute to an old friend.

During February *The Queen of Cornwall* was performed in London by the Hardy Players of Dorchester, but it was not altogether a success, partly owing to the only building available having no stage suitable for the performance, a rather small concert platform having to be used.

On March 7 Hardy notes:

"To Stinsford with F. (E. first met 54 years ago)."

And later, on April 3:

"Mother died 20 years ago today."

Among the many letters which arrived on June 2, the 84th anniversary of his birth, was one from a son of the Baptist minister, Mr Perkins, whom, in his youth, Hardy had so respected. This correspondent was one of the young men who had met him at the Baptist Chapel at the eastern end of the town for a prayer-meeting which was hindered by the arrival of a circus. More than sixty years had elapsed since Hardy had had any contact with this friend of his youth, and for a little while he was strongly tempted to get into touch with him again. However, too wide a gulf lay between and, as might have been told in one of his poems, the gesture was never made and the days slipped on into oblivion.

On June 11 Mr Rutland Boughton arrived at Max Gate for a visit of two days, the purpose of which was to consult Hardy about a plan he had for setting *The Queen of Cornwall* to music. Hardy was greatly interested, though he had heard no modern compositions, not even the immensely popular "Faerie Song" from *The Immortal Hour*. "The Blue Danube", "The Morgenblätter Waltz", and the "Overture to *William Tell*" interested him more strongly, and also church music, mainly on account of the association with his early days.

But he found Mr Boughton a stimulating companion, and was interested in his political views, though he could not share them. After Mr Boughton's departure he said with conviction, "If I had talked to him for a few hours I would soon have converted him".

One feature of this visit was a drive the Hardys took with their guests across parts of Egdon Heath which were then one blaze of purple with rhododendrons in full bloom.

On June 16 a poem by Hardy entitled "Compassion" appeared in *The Times*. It was written in answer to a request, and was intended to celebrate the Centenary of the Royal Society for the Prevention of Cruelty to Animals.

Although not one of his most successful efforts, as he was never happy when writing to order, it served to demonstrate the poet's passionate hatred of injustice and barbarity.

> Much has been won—more, maybe, than we know—
>   And on we labour hopeful. "Ailinon!"
> A mighty voice calls: "But may the good prevail!"
>   And "Blessed are the Merciful!"
>   Calls a yet mightier one.

On July 1 the Balliol Players, a party of undergraduates from Oxford, visited Max Gate, during the course of a tour in the west of England, to perform on the lawn *The Oresteia* as *The Curse of the House of Atreus*. This was a pleasant and informal occasion which gave delight to Hardy. Always sympathetic to youth, and a lifelong admirer of Greek tragedy, he fully appreciated this mark of affection and respect. The performance was not without an amusing side. The day was a windy one, and cold for July, hence the players with their bare arms and legs and scanty costumes must have been none too comfortable. However they ran about the lawn and pranced into the flower-beds with apparent enjoyment. Finding that the carrying of lighted torches in the sunlight was ineffective, they carried instead tall spikes of a giant flowering spiræa which they plucked from a border. While having tea after the play they gathered round Hardy, who talked to them with a sincerity and simplicity that few but he could have shown. Among the names of the players that he jotted down in his note-book were those of Mr A. L. Cliffe—Clytemnestra; Mr Anthony Asquith—Cassandra; Mr Walter Oakeshott—Orestes; Mr H. T. Wade-Gery—Agamemnon; Mr A. M. Farrer—Electra; and he also notes, "The Balliol Players had come on bicycles, sending on their theatrical properties in a lorry that sometimes broke down". Mr and Mrs Granville-Barker were present as spectators on this occasion.

A day or two later, with reference to what is not clear, Hardy copies a quotation from Emerson:

"The foolish man wonders at the unusual, but the wise man at the usual."

On August 4, noted by Hardy as being the day on which war was declared ten years before, he and Mrs Hardy motored to Netherton Hall in Devon to lunch with Mr and Mrs Granville-Barker. Two days later he received a visit from Siegfried Sassoon and Colonel T. E. Lawrence.

About this time Rutland Boughton's music version of *The Queen of Cornwall* was produced at Glastonbury, and on August 28 Hardy with his wife went to see and hear it, making the journey to Glastonbury by car.

From the 25th to the 30th Hardy was sitting to the Russian sculptor Serge Youriévitch for his bust. This was made in Hardy's study at Max Gate, and though he enjoyed conversation with the sculptor he was tired by the sittings, probably on account of his age, and definitely announced that he would not sit again for anything of the kind.

For several years some of the members of the Dorchester Debating and Dramatic Society had wished to perform a dramatization of *Tess of the d'Urbervilles*. After much hesitation Hardy handed over his own dramatization, although, as he notes in his diary, he had come to the conclusion that to dramatize a novel was a mistake in art; moreover, that the play ruined the novel and the novel the play. However, the result was that the company, self-styled "The Hardy Players", produced *Tess* with such unexpected success at Dorchester and Weymouth that it was asked for in London and the following year produced there by professional actors for over a hundred nights, Miss Gwen Ffrangçon-Davies taking the part of "Tess".

On the 22nd of October Hardy with his wife visited for the first time since his childhood the old barn at the back of Kingston Maurward. Here, as a small boy, he had listened to village girls singing old ballads. He pointed out to his wife the corner where they had sat. He looked around at the dusty rafters and the débris, considering possibly the difference that seventy years had made, and his manner as he left the barn was that of one who wished he had not endeavoured to revive a scene from a distant past. Almost certainly he was the only human being left of that once gay party.

A characteristic note ends Hardy's diary for 1924:

"Dec. 31. New Year's Eve. Sat up and heard Big Ben and the London church bells by wireless ring in the New Year."

On this day also he copied a quotation from an essay by L. Pearsall Smith:

"In every representation of Nature which is a work of art there is to be found, as Professor Courthope said, something which is not to be found in the aspect of Nature which it represents; and what that something is has been a matter of dispute from the earliest days of criticism."

"The same writer adds", notes Hardy, "'Better use the word "inspiration" than "genius" for inborn daemonic genius as distinct from conscious artistry.'

"(It seems to me it might be called 'temperamental impulse', which, of course, must be inborn.)"

Early in January 1925 Hardy sent to the *Nineteenth Century Magazine* a poem entitled "The Absolute Explains".

In the spring of this year, in connection with Hardy's dog "Wessex", an incident occurred which was impossible to explain. This dog, a wire-haired terrier, was of great intelligence and very friendly to many who visited Max Gate, though he had defects of temper, due perhaps to a want of thorough training. Among those to whom he showed a partiality was Mr William Watkins, the honorary secretary to the Society of Dorset Men in London.

About nine o'clock on the evening of April 18, Mr Watkins called at Max Gate to discuss with Hardy certain matters connected with his Society. The dog, as was his wont, rushed into the hall and greeted his friend with vociferous barks. Suddenly these gave way to a piteous whine, and the change was so startling that Wessex's mistress went to see what had happened.

Nothing, however, seemed amiss, and the dog returned into the room where Hardy was sitting and where he was joined by Mr Watkins. But even here Wessex seemed ill at ease, and from time to time went to the visitor and touched his coat solicitously with his paw, which he always withdrew giving a sharp cry of distress.

Mr Watkins left a little after ten o'clock, apparently in very good spirits. Early the next morning there came a telephone message from his son to say that the father, Hardy's guest of the night before, had died quite suddenly about an hour after his return to the hotel from Max Gate. As a rule the dog barked furiously when he heard the telephone ring, but on this occasion he remained silent, his nose between his paws.

On May 26 a letter and a leading article appeared in *The Times* on the subject of a Thomas Hardy Chair of Literature and a Wessex University. The letter was signed by many eminent writers and educationalists. At the date of writing, however, the Chair has not been endowed.

Later in the summer, on July 15, a deputation from Bristol University arrived at Max Gate to confer on Hardy the honorary degree of Doctor of Literature. This was the fifth degree he had received from English and Scottish Universities, the others being, in the order in which the degrees were bestowed—Aberdeen, Cambridge, Oxford, and St. Andrews.

At the end of July Hardy sent off the manuscript of his volume of poems, *Human Shows*, to the publishers, and a month later he made arrangements for the performance of his dramatization of *Tess* at the Barnes Theatre. About this time he enters in his note-book:

" 'Truth is what will work,' said William James (Harpers). A worse corruption of language was never perpetrated."

Few other events were of interest to him during the year. *Tess of the d'Urbervilles* was produced in London, but he felt he had not sufficient strength to go up to see it. After nearly two months at Barnes Theatre the play was removed on November 2 to the Garrick Theatre, where the hundredth performance took place.

The many pilgrimages Hardy made with his wife to Stinsford Church took place usually in the evening during the summer, and in the afternoon during the winter. On October 9, however, contrary to his usual custom, he walked to Stinsford in the morning. The bright sunlight shone across the face of a worn tomb whose lettering Hardy had often endeavoured to decipher, so that he might re-carve the letters with his penknife. This day, owing to the sunlight, they were able to read:

SACRED
to the memory of
ROBERT REASON
who departed this life
December 26th 1819
Aged 56 years.

Dear friend should you mourn for me
I am where you soon must be.

Although Robert Reason had died twenty-one years before the birth of the author of *Under the Greenwood Tree*, he was faithfully described in that novel as Mr Penny, the shoemaker, Hardy having heard so much of him from old inhabitants of Bockhampton. He used to regret that he had not used the real name, that being much better for his purpose than the one he had invented.

On December 6 the company of players from the Garrick Theatre arrived at Max Gate in the evening for the purpose of giving a performance of *Tess* in the drawing-room. The following description of this incident is taken from a letter written by one of the company to a correspondent in America who had particularly desired her impression of the visit:

Mr and Mrs Hardy behaved as if it were a most usual occurrence for a party of West-End actors to arrive laden with huge theatrical baskets of clothes and props. They met us in the hall and entertained us with tea, cakes and sandwiches, and Mr Hardy made a point of chatting with everyone. . . .

The drawing-room was rather a fortunate shape—the door

facing an alcove at one end of the room, and we used these to make our exits and entrances, either exiting into the hall or sitting quietly in the alcove.

Mr and Mrs Hardy, a friend of the Hardys, and two maids who, in cap and apron, sat on the floor—made up our audience. I think I am correct in saying there was no-one else. The room was shaded—lamps and firelight throwing the necessary light on our faces.

We played the scenes of Tess's home with chairs and a tiny drawing-room table to represent farm furniture—tea-cups for drinking mugs—when the chairs and tables were removed the corner of the drawing-room became Stonehenge, and yet in some strange way those present said the play gained from the simplicity.

It had seemed as if it would be a paralysingly difficult thing to do, to get the atmosphere at all within a few feet of the author himself and without any of the usual theatrical illusion, but speaking for myself—after the first few seconds it was perfectly easy, and Miss Ffrangçon-Davies's beautiful voice and exquisite playing of the Stonehenge scene in the shadows thrown by the firelight was a thing that I shall never forget. It was beautiful.

Mr Hardy insisted on talking to us until the last minute. He talked of Tess as if she was someone real whom he had known and liked tremendously. I think he enjoyed the evening. I may be quite wrong but I got the impression that to him it seemed quite a proper and usual way to give a play—probably as good if not better than any other—and he seemed to have very little conception of the unusualness and difficulties it might present to us.

The gossip of the village has it that his house was designed and the garden laid out with the idea of being entirely excluded from the gaze of the curious. Of course it was dark when we arrived, but personally I should say he had succeeded.

On December 20 he heard with regret of the death of his friend Sir Hamo Thornycroft, the sculptor, whose bronze head of Hardy was presented later to the National Portrait Gallery by Lady Thornycroft.

Siegfried Sassoon, a nephew of Sir Hamo's, happened to be paying Hardy a visit at the time. He left to go to the funeral of his uncle at Oxford, carrying with him a laurel wreath which Hardy had sent to be placed on the grave. Hardy had a warm regard for the sculptor, whose fine upstanding mien spoke truly of his nobility of character. The hours Hardy had spent in Sir Hamo's London studio and at his home were pleasant ones, and they had cycled together in Dorset while Sir Hamo was staying at Max Gate.

"December 23. Mary's birthday. She came into the world . . . and went out . . . and the world is just same . . . not a ripple on the surface left."

"Dec. 31. New Year's Eve. F. and I sat up. Heard on the wireless various features of New Year's Eve in London: dancing at the Albert Hall, Big Ben striking twelve, singing Auld Lang Syne, God Save the King, Marseillaise, hurrahing."

CHAPTER XXXVIII

The Last Scene

1926–January 11, 1928: *Aet.* 86–87

Early in January 1926, feeling that his age compelled him to such a step, Hardy resigned the Governorship of the Dorchester Grammar School. He had always been reluctant to hold any public offices, knowing that he was by temperament unfitted to sit on committees that controlled or ordained the activities of others. He preferred to be "the man with the watching eye".

On April 27, replying to a letter from an Oxford correspondent, who was one of four who had signed a letter to the *Manchester Guardian* upon the necessity of the reformation of the Prayer Book Services, Hardy writes from Max Gate:

> I have read your letter with interest: also the enclosure that you and your friends sent to the *Manchester Guardian*, particularly because, when I was young, I had a wish to enter the Church.
>
> I am now too old to take up the questions you lay open, but I may say that it has seemed to me that a simpler plan than that of mental reservation in passages no longer literally accepted (which is puzzling to ordinary congregations) would be just to abridge the creeds and other primitive parts of the Liturgy, leaving only the essentials. Unfortunately there appears to be a narrowing instead of a broadening tendency among the clergy of late, which if persisted in will exclude still more people from Church. But if a strong body of young reformers were to make a bold stand, in a sort of New Oxford Movement, they would have a tremendous

backing from the thoughtful laity, and might overcome the retrogressive section of the clergy.

Please don't attach much importance to these casual thoughts, and believe me,

Very truly yours,

T. H.

In May he received from Mr Arthur M. Hind a water-colour sketch of an attractive corner in the village of Minterne, which the artist thought might be the original of "Little Hintock" in *The Woodlanders*. In thanking Mr Hind, Hardy writes:

The drawing of the barn that you have been so kind as to send me has arrived uninjured, and I thank you much for the gift. I think it a charming picture, and a characteristic reproduction of that part of Dorset.

As to the spot being the "Little Hintock" of *The Woodlanders*—that is another question. You will be surprised and shocked at my saying that I myself do not know where "Little Hintock" is! Several tourists have told me that they have found it, in every detail, and have offered to take me to it, but I have never gone.

However, to be more definite, it has features which were to be found fifty years ago in the hamlets of Hermitage, Middlemarsh, Lyons-Gate, Revels Inn, Holnest, Melbury Bubb, etc.—all lying more or less under the eminence called High Stoy, just beyond Minterne and Dogbury Gate, where the country descends into the Vale of Blackmore.

The topographers you mention as identifying the scene are merely guessers and are wrong. . . .

On June 29 he again welcomed the Balliol Players, whose chosen play this summer, the *Hippolytus* of Euripides, was performed on the lawn of Max Gate. About the same time he sent by request a message of congratulation and friendship to Weymouth, Massachusetts, by a deputation which was then leaving England to visit that town.

"July 1926. Note.—It appears that the theory exhibited in *The Well-Beloved* in 1892 has been since developed by Proust still further:

"Peu de personnes comprennent le caractère purement subjectif du phénomène qu'est l'amour, et la sorte de création que c'est d'une personne supplémentaire, distincte de celle qui porte le même nom dans le monde, et dont la plupart des éléments sont tirés de nous-mêmes." (*Ombre,* i. 40.)

"Le désir s'élève, se satisfait, disparaît—et c'est tout. Ainsi, la jeune fille qu'on épouse n'est pas celle dont on est tombé amoureux." (*Ombre,* ii. 158, 159.)

On September 8 a dramatization of *The Mayor of Casterbridge* by Mr John Drinkwater was produced at the Barnes Theatre, and on the 20th the play was brought to Weymouth, where Hardy went to see it. He received a great ovation in the theatre, and also, on his return to Max Gate, from an enthusiastic crowd that collected round the Pavilion Theatre on the pier. From balconies and windows people were seen waving handkerchiefs as he drove past. In his diary he notes:

"20 September. Performance of *Mayor of Casterbridge* at Weymouth by London Company, a 'flying matinée'. Beautiful afternoon, scene outside the theatre finer than within."

Writing to a friend about a proposed dramatization of *Jude the Obscure,* he observes:

> I may say that I am not keen on the new mode (as I suppose it is regarded, though really Elizabethan) of giving a series of episodes in the film manner instead of set scenes. Of the outlines I sent you which suggested themselves to me many years ago, I thought the one I called (I think) "4th Scheme" most feasible.
>
> Would not Arabella be the villain of the piece?—or Jude's personal constitution?—so far as there is any villain more than blind Chance. Christminster is of course the tragic influence of Jude's drama in one sense, but innocently so, and merely as crass obstruction. By the way it is not meant to be exclusively Oxford, but any old-fashioned University about the date of the story, 1860–70, before there were such chances for poor men as there are now. I have somewhere printed that I had no feeling against Oxford in particular.

A few days later he visited Mrs Bankes at Kingston Lacy in Dorset, and was greatly interested in the priceless collection of pictures shown him. Of this occasion he writes:

"End of September. With F. on a visit to Mrs Bankes at Kingston Lacy. She told me an amusing story when showing me a letter to Sir John Bankes from Charles the First, acknowledging that he had borrowed £500 from Sir John. Many years ago when she was showing the same letter to King Edward, who was much interested in it, she said, 'Perhaps, Sir, that's a little matter which could now be set right'. He replied quickly, 'Statute of Limitations, Statute of Limitations'."

Another note:

"1 November. Went with Mr Hanbury to Bockhampton and looked at fencing, trees, etc., with a view to tidying and secluding the Hardy house."

That was his last visit to the place of his birth. It was always a matter of regret to him if he saw this abode in a state of neglect, or the garden uncherished.

During this month, November, his friend Colonel T. E. Lawrence called to say good-bye, before starting for India. Hardy was much affected by this parting, as T. E. Lawrence was one of his most valued friends. He went into the little porch and stood at the front door to see the departure of Lawrence on his motor-bicycle. This machine was difficult to start, and, thinking he might have to wait some time, Hardy turned into the house to fetch a shawl to wrap round him. In the meantime, fearing that Hardy might take a chill, Lawrence started the motor-bicycle and hurried away. Returning a few moments after, Hardy was grieved that he had not seen the actual departure, and said that he had particularly wished to see Lawrence go.

The sight of animals being taken to market or driven to slaughter always aroused in Hardy feelings of intense pity, as he well knew, as must anyone living in or near a market-town, how much needless suffering is inflicted. In his note-book at this time he writes:

"Dec. (1st Week). Walking with F. by railway, saw bullocks and cows going to Islington (?) for slaughter." Under this he drew a little pencil sketch of the rows of trucks as they were seen by him, with animals' heads at every opening, looking out at the green country-side they were leaving for scenes of horror in a far-off city. Hardy thought of this sight for long after. It was found in his will that he had left a sum of money to each of two societies "to be applied so far as practicable to the investigation of the means by which animals are conveyed from their houses to the slaughter-houses with a view to the lessening of their sufferings in such transit".

The year drew quietly to an end. On the 23rd of December a band of carol-singers from St. Peter's, Dorchester, came to Max Gate and sang to Hardy "While Shepherds Watched" to the tune which used to be played by his father and grandfather, a copy of which he had given to the Rector.

A sadness fell upon the household, for Hardy's dog, Wessex, now thirteen years old, was ill and obviously near his end.

Two days after Christmas day Hardy makes this entry:

"27th December. Our famous dog 'Wessex' died at ½ past 6 in the evening, thirteen years of age."

"28. Wessex buried."

"28. Night. Wessex sleeps outside the house the first time for thirteen years."

The dog lies in a small turfed grave in the shrubbery on the west side of Max Gate, where also were buried several pet cats and one other dog, Moss. On the headstone is this incription drawn up by Hardy, and carved from his design:

THE
FAMOUS DOG
WESSEX.

August 1913–27 Dec. 1926
Faithful. Unflinching.

There were those among Hardy's friends who thought that his life was definitely saddened by the loss of Wessex, the dog having been the companion of himself and his wife during twelve years of married life. Upon summer evenings or winter afternoons Wessex would walk with them up the grassy slope in the field in front of their house, to the stile that led into Came Plantation, and while Hardy rested on the stile the dog would sit on the ground and survey the view as his master was doing. On Frome Hill when his companions sat on the green bank by the roadside, or on the barrow that crowns the hill, he would lie in the grass at their feet and gaze at the landscape, "as if", to quote Hardy's oft-repeated comment on this, "it were the right thing to do".

Those were happy innocent hours. A poem written after the dog's death, "Dead Wessex, the dog to the household", well illustrates Hardy's sense of loss. Two of its verses are:

> Do you look for me at times,
>   Wistful ones?
> Do you look for me at times
>   Strained and still?

> Do you look for me at times,
> When the hour for walking chimes,
> On that grassy path that climbs
>   Up the hill?
>
> You may hear a jump or trot,
>   Wistful ones,
> You may hear a jump or trot—
>   Mine, as 'twere—
> You may hear a jump or trot
> On the stair or path or plot;
> But I shall cause it not,
>   Be not there.

On December 29 Hardy wrote to his friends Mr and Mrs Granville-Barker from Max Gate:

> . . . This is intended to be a New Year's letter, but I don't know if I have made a good shot at it. How kind of you to think of sending me Raymond Guyot's *Napoleon*. I have only glanced at it, at the text that is, as yet, but what an interesting collection of records bearing on the life of the man who finished the Revolution with "a whiff of grapeshot", and so crushed not only its final horrors but all the worthy aspirations of its earlier time, made them as if they had never been, and threw back human altruism scores, perhaps hundreds of years.

"31 Dec. New Year's Eve. Did not sit up."

In January 1927 "A Philosophical Fantasy" appeared in the *Fortnightly Review*. Hardy liked the year to open with a poem of this type from him in some leading review or newspaper. The quotation at the heading, "Milton . . . made God argue", gives the keynote, and the philosophy is much as he had set forth before, but still a ray of hope is shown for the future of mankind.

> Aye, to human tribes nor kindlessness
> Nor love I've given, but mindlessness,
> Which state, though far from ending,
> May nevertheless be mending.

Weeks passed through a cold spring and Hardy's eighty-seventh birthday was reached. This year, instead of remaining at Max Gate, he motored with his wife to Netherton Hall in Devonshire, to spend a part of the day with friends, Helen and Harley Granville-Barker. In a letter written some months later, Mrs Granville-Barker describes this visit.

. . . There were no guests, just the peaceful routine of everyday life, for that last birthday here. Mr Hardy said to you afterwards, you told me, that he thought it might be the last, but at the time he was not in any way sad or unlike himself. He noticed, as always, and unlike most old people, the smallest things. At luncheon, I remember, one of the lace doilies at his place got awry in an ugly way, showing the mat underneath, and I saw him, quietly and with the most delicate accuracy, setting it straight again—all the time taking his part in the talk.

Wasn't it that day he said, speaking of Augustus John's portrait of him:

"I don't know whether that is how I look or not—but that is how I *feel*"?

In the afternoon we left him alone in the library because we thought he wanted to rest a little. It was cold, for June, and a wood fire was lighted.

Once we peeped in at him through the garden window. He was not asleep but sitting, walled in with books, staring into the fire with that deep look of his. The cat had established itself on his knees and he was stroking it gently, but half-unconsciously.

It was a wonderful picture of him. I shall not forget it. Nor shall I forget the gay and startlingly youthful gesture with which he flourished his hat towards us as, once in the motor-car, later that afternoon, he drove away from us.

At the end of the day he seemed in a sad mood, and his wife sought to amuse him by a forecast of small festivities she had planned for his ninetieth birthday, which she assured him would be a great occasion. With a flash of gaiety he replied that he intended to spend that day in bed.

Once again the Balliol Players appeared at Max Gate, this year on July 6. As before, their visit gave Hardy considerable pleasure, and after their performance on the lawn of *Iphigenia in Aulis* he talked with them freely, appreciating their boyish ardour and their modesty.

A few days later he received visits from his friends Siegfried

Sassoon and Mr and Mrs John Masefield, and on July 21 he laid the foundation-stone of the new building of the Dorchester Grammar School, which was to be seen clearly from the front gate of his house, looking towards the Hardy Monument, a noticeable object on the sky-line, to the south-west. It was Hardy's custom nearly every fine morning after breakfast in the summer to walk down to the gate to see what the weather was likely to be by observing this tower in the distance.

The day chosen for the stone-laying was cold and windy, by no means a suitable day for a man of Hardy's advanced years to stand in the open air bareheaded. Nevertheless he performed his task with great vigour, and gave the following address in a clear resonant voice that could be heard on the outskirts of the crowd that collected to hear him:

"I have been asked to execute the formal part of today's function which has now been done, and it is not really necessary that I should add anything to the few words that are accustomed to be used at the laying of foundation or dedication stones. But as the circumstances of the present case are somewhat peculiar, I will just enlarge upon them for a minute or two. What I have to say is mainly concerning the Elizabethan philanthropist, Thomas Hardy, who, with some encouragement from the burgesses, endowed and rebuilt this ancient school after its first humble shape—him whose namesake I have the honour to be, and whose monument stands in the church of St. Peter, visible from this spot. The well-known epitaph inscribed upon his tablet, unlike many epitaphs, does not, I am inclined to think, exaggerate his virtues, since it was written, not by his relatives or dependents, but by the free burgesses of Dorchester in gratitude for his good action towards the town. This good deed was accomplished in the latter part of the sixteenth century, and the substantial stone building in which it merged eventually still stands to dignify South Street, as we all know, and hope it may remain there.

"But what we know very little about is the personality of this first recorded Thomas Hardy of the Frome Valley here at our back, though his work abides. He was without doubt of the family of the Hardys who landed in this county from Jersey in the fifteenth century, acquired small estates along the river upwards towards its source, and whose descendants have mostly remained hereabouts ever since, the Christian name of Thomas having been especially affected by them. He died in 1599, and it is curious to think that though he must have had a modern love of learning not common in a remote county in those days, Shakespeare's name could hardly have been known to him, or at the most vaguely as that of a certain ingenious Mr Shakespeare who amused the London playgoers; and that he died before Milton was born.

"In Carlylean phraseology, what manner of man he was when he walked this earth, we can but guess, or what he looked like, what he said and did in his lighter moments, and at what age he died. But we may shrewdly conceive that he was a far-sighted man, and would not be much surprised, if he were to revisit the daylight, to find that his building had been outgrown, and no longer supplied the needs of the present inhabitants for the due education of their sons. His next feeling might be to rejoice in the development of what was possibly an original design of his own, and to wish the reconstruction every success.

"We living ones all do that, and nobody more than I, my retirement from the Governing body having been necessitated by old age only. Certainly everything promises well. The site can hardly be surpassed in England for health, with its open surroundings, elevated and bracing situation, and dry subsoil, while it is near enough to the sea to get very distinct whiffs of marine air. Moreover, it is not so far from the centre of the borough as to be beyond the walking powers of the smallest boy. It has a capable headmaster, holding every modern idea on education within the limits of good judgment, and assistant masters well equipped for their labours, which are not sinecures in these days.

"I will conclude by thanking the Governors and other friends for their kind thought in asking me to undertake this formal initiation of the new building, which marks such an interesting stage in the history of the Dorchester Grammar School."

After the ceremony, having spoken to a few friends, Hardy went away without waiting for the social gathering that followed. He was very tired, and when he reached home he said that he had made his last public appearance.

There seemed no ill after-effects, however, and on August 9 Hardy drove with Gustav Holst to "Egdon Heath", just then purple with heather. They then went on to Puddletown and entered the fine old church, and both climbed up into the gallery, where probably some of Hardy's ancestors had sat in the choir, more than a century earlier.

On August 8 he wrote to Mr J. B. Priestley:

. . . I send my sincere thanks for your kind gift of the "George Meredith" book, and should have done so before if I had not fallen into the sere, and weak eyesight did not trouble me. I have read your essay, or rather have had it read to me, and have been much interested in the bright writing of one in whom I had already fancied I discerned a coming force in letters.

I am not at all a critic, especially *of* a critic, and when the author he reviews is a man who was, off and on, a friend of mine for forty years; but it seems to me that you hold the scales very fairly. Meredith was, as you recognize, and might have insisted on even more strongly, and I always felt, in the direct succession of Congreve and the artificial comedians of the Restoration, and in getting his brilliancy we must put up with the fact that he would not, or could not—at any rate did not—when aiming to represent the "Comic Spirit", let himself discover the tragedy that always underlies Comedy if you only scratch it deeply enough.

During the same month Hardy and his wife motored to Bath and back. On the way they had lunch sitting on a grassy bank, as they had done in former years, to Hardy's pleasure. But now a curious sadness brooded over them; lunching in the open air had lost its charm, and they did not attempt another picnic of this kind.

In Bath Hardy walked about and looked long and silently at various places that seemed to have an interest for him. He seemed like a ghost revisiting scenes of a long-dead past. After a considerable rest in the Pump Room they returned home. Hardy did not seem tired by this drive.

Some weeks later they motored to Ilminster, a little country town that Hardy had long desired to visit. He was interested in the church, and also in the tomb of the founder of Wadham College therein. By his wish, on their return, they drove past the quarries where Ham Hill stone was cut.

Stopping at Yeovil they had tea in a restaurant, where a band of some three musicians were playing. One of Hardy's most attractive characteristics was his ability to be interested in simple things, and before leaving he stood and listened appreciatively to the music, saying afterwards what a delightful episode that had been.

On September 6, an exceedingly wet day, Mr and Mrs John Galsworthy called on their way to London. During the visit Hardy told them the story of a murder that had happened eighty years before. Mr Galsworthy seemed struck by these memories of Hardy's early childhood, and asked whether he had always remembered those days so vividly, or only lately. Hardy replied that he had always remembered clearly. He could recall what his mother had said about the Rush murder when he was about the age of six: "The governess hanged him". He was puzzled, and wondered how a governess could hang a man. Mr and Mrs Galsworthy thought that Hardy seemed better than when they saw him last, better, in fact, than they had ever seen him.

September 7 being a gloriously fine day, Hardy with his wife walked across the fields opposite Max Gate to see the building of the new Grammar School, then in progress.

During September Hardy was revising and rearranging the *Selected Poems* in the Golden Treasury Series in readiness for a new edition. The last entry but one in his note-book refers to the sending of the copy to the publishers, and finally, on the 19th of September, he notes that Mr Weld of Lulworth Castle called with some friends. After this no more is written, but a few notes were made by his wife for the remaining weeks of 1927.

About the 21st of September they drove to Lulworth Castle to lunch with Mr and Mrs Weld and a house-party, and Hardy was much interested in all that he was shown in the Castle and in the adjoining church. A few weeks later he and his wife lunched at Charborough Park, the scene of *Two on a Tower*, the first time he had entered this house.

NOTES BY F. E. H.

"October 24. A glorious day. T. and I walked across the field in front of Max Gate towards Came. We both stood on a little flat stone sunk in the path that we call our wishing stone, and I wished. T. may have done so, but he did not say.

"On the way he gathered up some waste paper that was blowing about the lane at the side of our house and buried it in the hedge with his stick, and going up the path to Came he stopped for quite a long time to pull off the branches of a tree a heap of dead weeds that had been thrown there by some untidy labourer who had been cleaning the field. He says that a man has no public spirit who passes by any untidiness out of doors, litter of paper or similar rubbish."

"October 27. During the evening he spoke of an experience he had a few years ago. There were four or five people to tea at Max Gate, and he noticed a stranger standing by me most of the time.

Afterwards he asked who that dark man was who stood by me. I told him that there was no stranger present, and I gave him the names of the three men who were there, all personal friends. He said that it was not one of these, and seemed to think that another person had actually been there. This afternoon he said: 'I can see his face now'.

"Later in the evening, during a terrific gale, I said that I did not wonder that some people disliked going along the dark road outside our house at night.

"T. replied that for twelve years he walked backwards and forwards from Bockhampton to Dorchester often in the dark, 'and he was only frightened twice. Once was when he was going up Stinsford Hill, no habitation of any sort being in sight, and he came upon two men sitting on chairs, one on either side of the road. By the moonlight he saw that they were strangers to him; terrified, he took to his heels; he never heard who they were or anything to explain the incident.

"The other time was when, as a small boy walking home from school, reading *Pilgrim's Progress*, he was so alarmed by the description of Apollyon that he hastily closed his book and went on his way trembling, thinking that Apollyon was going to spring out of a tree whose dark branches overhung the road. He remembered his terror, he said, that evening, seventy-five years afterwards."

"October 30. At lunch T. H. talked about Severn, speaking with admiration of his friendship towards Keats. He said that it must have been quite disinterested, as Keats was then comparatively obscure."

"October 31. Henry Williamson, the author of *Tarka the Otter*, called."

"November 3. While he was having tea to-day, T. H. said that whenever he heard any music from *Il Trovatore*, it carried him back to the first year when he was in London and when he was strong and vigorous and enjoyed his life immensely. He thought that *Il Trovatore* was good music."

"Nov. 4. We drove in the afternoon to Stinsford, to put flowers on the family graves. The tombs are very green, being covered with moss because they are under a yew-tree. T. H. scraped off most of the moss with a little wooden implement like a toy spade, six inches in length, which he made with his own hands and which he carries in his pocket when he goes to Stinsford. He remarked that Walter de la Mare had told him that he preferred to see the gravestones green.

"Then we drove to Talbothays (his brother's house). As we turned up Dark Hill, T. H. pointed out the place where, as a small boy, he had left an umbrella in the hedge, having put it down while he cut a stick. He did not remember it until he reached home and his mother asked him where was his umbrella. As he went to school next morning he looked in the hedge and found it where he had left it.

"After having been with H. H. and K. H. (the brother and sister) for half an hour we returned home."

Thus ended a series of visits paid regularly to his family extending over forty years. While his parents were alive, Hardy went to see them at Bockhampton nearly every Sunday afternoon when he was in Dorchester, walking at first, then cycling. After his mother's death he visited his two sisters and his brother at Bockhampton, and later at Talbothays, to which house they moved in 1912. These visits continued until the last year or two of his life, when he was unable to go very often. He cycled there in fine weather until he was over eighty, and then he walked, until the distance seemed beyond his powers. Stinsford was a favourite haunt until the last few months of his life, the walk there from Max Gate, across the water-meadows, being a particularly beautiful one; and the churchyard, to him, the most hallowed spot on earth.

"Nov. 4, continued. At tea T. H. said that he had been pleased to read that day an article by the composer Miss Ethel Smyth, saying that *Il Trovatore* was good music. He reminded me of what he said yesterday."

"November 11. Armistice Day. T. came downstairs from his study and listened to the broadcasting of a service at Canterbury Cathedral. We stood there for the two minutes' silence. He said afterwards that he had been thinking of Frank George, his cousin, who was killed at Gallipoli.

"In the afternoon we took one of our usual little walks, around 'the triangle' as we call it, that is down the lane by the side of our house, and along the cinder-path beside the railway line. We stood and watched a goods train carrying away huge blocks of Portland stone as we have done so many times. He seems never tired of watching these stone-laden trucks. He said he thought that the shape of Portland would be changed in the course of years by the continual cutting away of its surface.

"Sitting by the fire after tea he told me about various families of poachers he had known as a boy, and how, when a thatched house at Bockhampton was pulled down, a pair of swingels was found under the thatch. This was an instrument of defence used by poachers, and capable of killing a man.[1]

"He said that if he had his life over again he would prefer to be a small architect in a country town, like Mr Hicks at Dorchester, to whom he was articled."

"November 17. Today T.H. was speaking, and evidently thinking a great deal, about a friend, a year or two older than himself, who was a fellow-pupil at Mr Hicks's office. I felt, as he talked, that he would like to meet this man again more than anyone in the world. He is in Australia now, if alive, and must be nearly ninety. His name is Henry Robert Bastow; he was a Baptist and evidently a very religious youth, and T. H. was devoted to him. I suggested that we might find out something about him by sending an advertisement to Australian newspapers, but T. H. thought that would not be wise."

"Sunday, November 27. The fifteenth anniversary of the death of Emma Lavinia Hardy; Thursday was the anniversary of the death of Mary, his elder sister. For two or three days he has been wearing a black hat as a token of mourning, and carries a black walking-stick that belonged to his first wife, all strangely moving.

"T. H. has been writing almost all the day, revising poems. When he came down to tea he brought one to show me, about a desolate spring morning, and a shepherd counting his sheep and not noticing the weather." This is the poem in *Winter Words* called "An Unkindly May".

"Nov. 28. Speaking about ambition T. said today that he had done all that he meant to do, but he did not know whether it had been worth doing.

"His only ambition, so far as he could remember, was to have some poem or poems in a good anthology like the *Golden Treasury*.

"The model he had set before him was 'Drink to me only', by Ben Jonson."

The earliest recollection of his childhood (as he had told me before) was that when he was four years old his father gave him a small toy concertina and wrote on it, "Thomas Hardy, 1844". By

[1] Poachers' iron swingels. A strip of iron ran down three or four sides of the flail part, and the two flails were united by three or four links of chain, the keepers carrying cutlasses which would cut off the ordinary eel-skin hinge of a flail.—*From T. H.'s notebook, Dec. 1884.*

this inscription he knew, in after years, his age when that happened.

Also he remembered, perhaps a little later than this, being in the garden at Bockhampton with his father on a bitterly cold winter day. They noticed a fieldfare, half-frozen, and the father took up a stone idly and threw it at the bird, possibly not meaning to hit it. The fieldfare fell dead, and the child Thomas picked it up and it was as light as a feather, all skin and bone, practically starved. He said he had never forgotten how the body of the fieldfare felt in his hand: the memory had always haunted him.

He recalled how, crossing the ewe-leaze when a child, he went on hands and knees and pretended to eat grass in order to see what the sheep would do. Presently he looked up and found them gathered around in a close ring, gazing at him with astonished faces.

An illness, which at the commencement did not seem to be serious, began on December 11. On the morning of that day he sat at the writing-table in his study, and felt totally unable to work. This, he said, was the first time that such a thing had happened to him.

From then his strength waned daily. He was anxious that a poem he had written, "Christmas in the Elgin Room", should be copied and sent to *The Times*. This was done, and he asked his wife anxiously whether she had posted it with her own hands. When she assured him that she had done so he seemed content, and said he was glad that he had cleared everything up. Two days later he received a personal letter of thanks, with a warm appreciation of his work, from the editor of *The Times*. This gave him pleasure, and he asked that a reply should be sent.

He continued to come downstairs to sit for a few hours daily, until Christmas-day. After that he came downstairs no more.

On December 26 he said that he had been thinking of the Nativity and of the Massacre of the Innocents, and his wife read to him the gospel accounts, and also articles in the *Encyclopædia Biblica*. He remarked that there was not a grain of evidence that the gospel story was true in any detail.

As the year ended a window in the dressing-room adjoining his bedroom was opened that he might hear the bells, as that had always pleased him. But now he said that he could not hear them, and did not seem interested.

His strength still failed. The weather was bitterly cold, and snow had fallen heavily, being twelve inches deep in parts of the garden. In the road outside there were snowdrifts that in places would reach a man's waist.

By desire of the local practitioner additional advice was called in, and Hardy's friend Sir Henry Head, who was living in the neighbourhood, made invaluable suggestions and kept a watchful eye upon the case. But the weakness increased daily.

He could no longer listen to the reading of prose, though a short poem now and again interested him. In the middle of one night he asked his wife to read aloud to him "The Listeners", by Walter de la Mare.

On January 10 he made a strong rally, and although he was implored not to do so he insisted upon writing a cheque for his subscription to the Pension Fund of the Society of Authors. For the first time in his life he made a slightly feeble signature, unlike his usual beautiful firm handwriting, and then he laid down his pen.

Later he was interested to learn that J. M. Barrie, his friend of many years, had arrived from London to assist in any way that might be possible. He was amused when told that this visitor had gone to the kitchen door to avoid any disturbance by ringing the front-door bell.

In the evening he asked that Robert Browning's poem "Rabbi Ben Ezra" should be read aloud to him. While reading it his wife glanced at his face to see whether he were tired, the poem being a long one of thirty-two stanzas, and she was struck by the look of wistful intentness with which Hardy was listening. He indicated that he wished to hear the poem to the end.

He had a better night, and in the morning of January 11 seemed so much stronger that one at least of those who watched beside him had confident hopes of his recovery, and an atmosphere of joy prevailed in the sickroom. An immense bunch of grapes arrived from London, sent by a friend, and this aroused in Hardy great interest. As a rule he disliked receiving gifts, but on this occasion he showed an almost childlike pleasure, and insisted upon the grapes being held up for the inspection of the doctor, and whoever came into the room. He ate some, and said quite gaily, "I'm going on with these". Everything he had that day in the way of food or drink he seemed to appreciate keenly, though naturally he took but little. As it grew dusk, after a long musing silence, he asked his wife to repeat to him a verse from the *Rubáiyát of Omar Khayyám*, beginning

Oh, Thou, who Man of baser Earth—

She took his copy of this work from his bedside and read to him:

Oh, Thou, who Man of baser Earth didst make,
And ev'n with Paradise devise the Snake:
   For all the Sin wherewith the Face of Man
Is blacken'd—Man's forgiveness give—and take!

He indicated that he wished no more to be read.

In the evening he had a sharp heart attack of a kind he had never had before. The doctor was summoned and came quickly, joining Mrs Hardy at the bedside. Hardy remained conscious until a few minutes before the end. Shortly after nine he died.

An hour later one, going to his bedside yet again, saw on the death-face an expression such as she had never seen before on any being, or indeed on any presentment of the human countenance. It was a look of radiant triumph such as imagination could never have conceived. Later the first radiance passed away, but dignity and peace remained as long as eyes could see the mortal features of Thomas Hardy.

The dawn of the following day rose in almost unparalleled splendour. Flaming and magnificent the sky stretched its banners over the dark pines that stood sentinel around.

Appendices

As included by Florence Emily Hardy in

The Later Years of Thomas Hardy

Appendix I

On the morning of Thursday, January 12, the Dean of Westminster readily gave his consent to a proposal that Hardy should be buried in Westminster Abbey; and news of this proposal and of its acceptance was sent to Max Gate. There it was well known that Hardy's own wish was to be buried at Stinsford, amid the graves of his ancestors and of his first wife. After much consideration a compromise was found between this definite personal wish and the nation's claim to the ashes of the great poet. On Friday, January 13, his heart was taken out of his body and placed by itself in a casket. On Saturday, January 14, the body was sent to Woking for cremation, and thence the ashes were taken the same day to Westminster Abbey and placed in the Chapel of St. Faith to await interment. On Sunday, January 15, the casket containing the heart was taken to the church at Stinsford, where it was laid on the altar steps.

At two o'clock on Monday, January 16, there were three services in three different churches. In Westminster Abbey the poet's wife and sister were the chief mourners, while in the presence of a great crowd, which included representatives of the King and other members of the Royal Family and of many learned and other societies, the ashes of Thomas Hardy were buried with stately ceremonial in Poet's Corner. The pall-bearers were the Prime Minister (Mr Stanley Baldwin) and Mr Ramsay MacDonald, representing the Government and Parliament; Sir James Barrie, Mr John Galsworthy, Sir Edmund Gosse, Professor A. E. Housman, Mr Rudyard Kipling, and Mr Bernard Shaw, representing literature; and the Master of Magdalene College, Cambridge (Mr A. S. Ramsey), and the Pro-Provost of Queen's College, Oxford (Dr E. M. Walker), representing the Colleges of which Hardy was an honorary Fellow. A spadeful of Dorset earth, sent by a Dorset farm labourer, Mr Christopher Corbin, was sprinkled on the casket. In spite of the cold and the wet the streets about the Abbey were full of people who had been unable to obtain admission to the service, but came as near as they might to taking part in it. At the same hour at Stinsford, where Hardy was baptized, and where as boy and man he had often worshipped, his brother, Mr Henry Hardy, was the chief mourner, while, in the presence of a rural population, the heart of this lover of rural Wessex was buried in the grave of his first wife among the Hardy tombs under the great yew-tree in the corner of the churchyard. And in Dorchester all business was suspended for an hour, while at St. Peter's Church the Mayor and Corporation and many other dignitaries and societies attended a memorial service in which the whole neighbourhood joined.

H. C.

Appendix II

I

Max Gate, Dorchester,
Dec 21, 1914.

Dear Sir,

I have read with much interest the lecture on *The Longest Price of War* that you kindly send: and its perusal does not diminish the gloom with which this ghastly business on the Continent fills me, as it fills so many. The argument would seem to favour Conscription, since the inert, if not the unhealthy, would be taken, I imagine.

Your visits to *The Dynasts* show that, as Granville-Barker foretold, thoughtful people would care about it. My own opinion when I saw it was that it was the only sort of thing likely to take persons of a musing turn into a theatre at this time.

I have not read M. Bergson's book, and if you should not find it troublesome to send your copy as you suggest, please do.

The theory of the Prime Force that I used in *The Dynasts* was published in Jan. 1904. The nature of the determinism embraced in the theory is that of a collective will; so that there is a proportion of the total will in each part of the whole, and each part has therefore, in strictness, *some* freedom, which would, in fact, be operative as such whenever the remaining great mass of will in the universe should happen to be in equilibrium.

However, as the work is intended to be a poetic drama and not a philosophic treatise I did not feel bound to develop this.

The assumption of unconsciousness in the driving force is, of course, not new. But I think the view of the unconscious force as gradually *becoming* conscious: i.e. that consciousness is creeping further and further back towards the origin of force, had never (so

487

far as I know) been advanced before *The Dynasts* appeared. But being only a mere impressionist I must not pretend to be a philosopher in a letter, and ask you to believe me,

Sincerely yours,

Thomas Hardy.

Dr. Saleeby.

2

Max Gate, Dorchester,
Feb. 2, 1915.

Dear Dr. Saleeby,

Your activities are unlimited. I should like to hear your address on "Our War for International Law". Personally I feel rather disheartened when I think it probable that the war will end by sheer exhaustion of the combatants, and that things will be left much as they were before. But I hope not.

I have been now and then dipping into your Bergson, and shall be returning the volume soon. I suppose I may assume that you are more or less a disciple, or fellow-philosopher, of his. Therefore you may be rather shocked by some views I hold about his teachings—if I may say I hold any views about anything whatever, which I hardly do.

His theories are certainly much more delightful than those they contest, and I for one would gladly believe them, but I cannot help feeling all the time that he is rather an imaginative and poetical writer than a reasoner, and that for his attractive assertions he does not adduce any proofs whatever. His use of the word "creation" seems loose to me. Then, as to "conduct". I fail to see how, if it is not mechanism, it can be other than Caprice, though he denies it (p. 50). And he says that Mechanism and Finalism (I agree with him as to Finalism) are only external views of our conduct.

"Our conduct extends between them, and slips much further." Well, I hope it may, but he nowhere shows that it does. And again: "a mechanistic conception . . . treats the living as the inert. . . . Let us on the contrary, trace a line of demarcation between the inert and the living (208)." Well, let us, to our great pleasure, if we can see why we should introduce an inconsistent rupture of order into uniform and consistent laws of the same.

You will see how much I want to be a Bergsonian (indeed I have for many years). But I fear that his philosophy is, in the bulk, only our old friend Dualism in a new suit of clothes—an ingenious fancy without real foundation, and more complicated, and therefore less likely, than the determinist fancy and others that he endeavours to overthrow.

You must not think me a hard-headed rationalist for all this. Half my time (particularly when I write verse) I believe—in the modern use of the word—not only in things that Bergson does, but in spectres, mysterious voices, intuitions, omens, dreams, haunted places, etc., etc.

But then, I do not believe in these in the old sense of belief any more for that; and in arguing against Bergsonism I have, of course, meant belief in its old sense when I aver myself incredulous.

Sincerely yours,

Thomas Hardy.[1]

3

Max Gate, Dorchester,
16.3.1915.

Dear Dr. Saleeby,

My thanks for the revised form of *The Longest Price of War*, which I am reading.

.   .   .   .   .   .

I am returning, or shall be in a day or two, your volume of Bergson. It is most interesting reading, and one likes to give way to its views and assurances without criticizing them.

If, however, we ask for reasons and proofs (which I don't care to do) I am afraid we do not get them.

An *élan vital*—by which I understand him to mean a sort of additional and spiritual force, beyond the merely unconscious push of life—the "will" of other philosophers that propels growth and development—seems much less probable than single and simple determinism, or what he calls mechanism, because it is more

---

[1] A great part of this letter will be found in a slightly different form on pp. 399–400 of this volume. Both versions are printed in order to illustrate Hardy's artistic inability to rest content with anything that he wrote until he had brought the expression as near to his thought as language would allow. He would, for instance, often go on revising his poems for his own satisfaction after their publication in book form.—F. E. H.

complex: and where proof is impossible probability must be our guide. His partly mechanistic and partly creative theory seems to me clumsy and confused.

He speaks of "the enormous gap that separates even the lowest form of life from the inorganic world". Here again it is more probable that organic and inorganic modulate into each other, one nature and law operating throughout. But the most fatal objection to his view of creation *plus* propulsion seems to me to lie in the existence of pain. If nature were creative she would have created painlessness, or be in process of creating it—pain being the first thing we instinctively fly from. If on the other hand we cannot introduce into life what is not already there, and are bound to mere recombination of old materials, the persistence of pain is intelligible.

Sincerely yours,

Thomas Hardy.

Appendix III

Max Gate, Dorchester,
New Year's Eve, 1907.

My dear Clodd,

I write a line to thank you for that nice little copy of Munro's Lucretius, and to wish you a happy New Year. I am familiar with two translations of the poet, but not with this one, so the book is not wasted.

I have been thinking what a happy man you must be at this time of the year, in having to write your name 8000 times. Nobody wants me to write mine once!

In two or three days I shall have done with the proofs of *Dynasts* III. It is well that the business should be over, for I have been living in Wellington's campaigns so much lately that, like George IV, I am almost positive that I took part in the battle of Waterloo, and have written of it from memory.

What new side of science are you writing about at present?

Yours sincerely,
Thomas Hardy.

Max Gate,
20:2:1908.

My dear Clodd,

I must send a line or two in answer to your letter. What you remind me of—the lyrical account of the fauna of Waterloo field on the eve of the battle is, curiously enough, the page (p. 282) that struck me, in looking back over the book, as being the most original in it. Though, of course, a thing may be original without being good. However, it does happen that (so far as I know) in the many treatments of Waterloo in literature, those particular personages who were present have never been alluded to before.

Yes: I left off on a note of hope. It was just as well that the Pities should have the last word, since, like *Paradise Lost*, *The Dynasts* proves nothing.

Always yours sincerely,

Thomas Hardy.

P.S.—The idea of the Unconscious Will becoming conscious with flux of time, is also new, I think, whatever it may be worth. At any rate I have never met with it anywhere.—T. H.

Max Gate, Dorchester,
28:8:1914.

My dear Clodd,

I fear we cannot take advantage of your kind invitation, and pay you a visit just now—much as in some respects we should like to. With the Germans (apparently) only a week from Paris, the native hue of resolution is sicklied o'er with the pale cast of thought. We shall hope to come when things look brighter.

Trifling incidents here bring home to us the condition of affairs not far off—as I daresay they do to you still more—sentries with gleaming bayonets at unexpected places as we motor along, the steady flow of soldiers through here to Weymouth, and their disappearance across the Channel in the silence of night, and the 1000 prisoners whom we get glimpses of through chinks, mark these fine days. The prisoners, they say, have already mustered enough broken English to say "Shoot Kaiser!" and oblige us by playing "God Save the King" on their concertinas and fiddles. Whether this is "meant sarcastic", as Artemus Ward used to say, I cannot tell.

I was pleased to know that you were so comfortable, when I was picturing you in your shirt sleeves with a lot of other robust Aldeburghers digging a huge trench from Aldeburgh church to the top of those steps we go down to your house, streaming with sweat, and drinking pots of beer between the shovellings (English beer of course).

Sincerely yours,

Thomas Hardy.

P.S.—Yes: everybody seems to be reading *The Dynasts* just now—at least, so a writer in the *Daily News* who called here this morning tells me.—T. H.

Textual Apparatus

The three following tables are keyed to the text of the present edition by a system of page- and line-numbers. In calculating line-numbers, count downwards from the top of each page (ignoring the running heads) and reckon one line for each full or partial line of type (i.e. words and numerals); spaces, illustrations, and type ornaments should be excluded from such calculations. Thus on p. 69 the first line of the chapter, beginning "The latter part", would be given as 69 : 7 and the first line of Emma Hardy's "Some Recollections" as 69 : 10, while the first line of the next page, beginning "energetic, and", would appear as 70 : 1.

493

Abbreviations Used in the Textual Apparatus

ELH	Emma Lavinia Hardy
FEH	Florence Emily Hardy
JMB	James Matthew Barrie
SCC	Sydney Carlyle Cockerell
TH	Thomas Hardy

DCM	Dorset County Museum
EL	*The Early Life of Thomas Hardy* (London, 1928).
LY	*The Later Years of Thomas Hardy* (London, 1930).
PN	*The Personal Notebooks of Thomas Hardy*, ed. Richard H. Taylor (London, 1978).

TS1	Typescript 1 of "Life": "top" or ribbon copy, sent to printer.
TS2	Typescript 2 of "Life": first carbon copy, used by TH and FEH as a record of approved alterations.
TS3	Typescript 3 of "Life": second carbon, used by TH as his "rough" or working copy.

MN1	Ribbon copy of typescript headed "Memoranda & Notes towards completing the remainder of Vol. II".
MN3	Second carbon copy of "Memoranda & Notes" typescript.
MNR	New typescript of "Memoranda & Notes" material, prepared after TH's death.

[For a fuller account of these typescripts and of the relationships between them, see Introduction and Editorial Procedures, especially pp. xiii–xiv and xxxii–xxxiii.]

Editorial Emendations in the Copy-texts

As indicated in "Editorial Procedures", pp. xxxiii–xxxiv, the following table is devoted to a listing of those points at which the wording of the present edition departs from that of the identified Hardyan "layer" of the copy-texts. Editorial modifications of the punctuation and spelling of the copy-texts are not normally recorded, apart from significant corrections to passages inscribed in Hardy's own hand.

The first citation in each entry is always from the text of the present edition, the second from the copy-text being emended (i.e. TS2, unless otherwise specified). Entries marked † are discussed in the Textual Notes. All emendations recorded here are made on the judgment of the editor, but the symbol ED (= editor) is reserved for those instances when the adopted reading has not been anticipated in one of the other pre-publication forms of the text (e.g. TS1) or in *Early Life* or *Later Years*.

1 : [8]	*absent* ED] By Florence Emily Hardy.
7 : 1	CHAPTER I *EL*] Chapter First.
10 : 22	and a brick-yard *EL*] and brick-yard
13 : 34	lies *EL*] lie
16 : 18	Thomas Hardy *EL*] T.H.
16 : 26	Thomas Hardy *EL*] T.H.
16 : 32	Thomas Hardy *EL*] T.H.
16 : 37	Thomas Hardy *EL*] T.H.
17 : 18–19	Thomas Hardy *EL*; T.H.
26 : 28	Thomas Hardy the Second ED] T.H.2
27 : 21	Thomas Hardy's ED] T.H's
28 : 9	Thomas Hardy ED] T.H.
28 : 15	by *EL*] of
30 : 1	Thomas Hardy's ED] T.H's
†32 : 13–14	educated, for an *EL*] educated, and for an
33 : 2	family, and hastened *EL*] family, hastened

†37:33   cleaned, and ED]   cleaned and
37:38   page 8 ED]   page . . .
44:2   Florence *EL*]   Flora
45:21   "Reminiscences *EL*]   "The Reminiscences
50:5   abandoned TS1]   rejected
50:5–6   sketches each TS1]   sketches, each
50:9   womankind TS1]   women
50:11   thousandth—not TS1]   thousandth, not
50:29   Memorial-stone TS1]   Memorial Stone
51:10   opinion that TS1]   opinion on that
53:11   experience, amid TS1]   experience amid
61:6   includes *EL*]   include
62:33   in *EL*]   on
†63:8   Hardy, as *EL*]   Hardy); as
†63:9   of it); this ED]   of it: this
65:26   Seaside Town" *EL*]   sea-side town"
78:18   Word 'Farewell' " *EL*]   word Farewell"
79:19   Gérôme *EL*]   Gerôme
79:20   Death TS1]   death
82:2   "In Time of 'the Breaking of Nations' " *EL*]   "At the
                Breaking of Nations"
82:3   1912–13" *EL*]   1912–1913"
83:2   novels—to *EL*]   Novels; to
91:25   -volume *EL*]   -volumed
†96:34   he ED]   it
97:6   33– *EL*]   32–
99:11   Thomas Hardy: ED]   T.H.
†105:18–19   as little as he TS1]   as he
†105:19–20   as he TS1]   as little as he
116:12   conference at ED]   conference [what conference?] at
120:29–30   being borne by one TS1]   being that of one
123:4   –1879 ED]   –1880
124:12   me *EL*]   the
126:29   and which Hardy *EL*]   and Hardy
130:1   followed TS1]   came
135:1   John *EL*]   John's
135:30   Pollock, girlish-looking; *EL*]   Pollock; girlish-looking,
139:12–13   woman (far from it!); and ED]   woman; far from it! and
143:17   They lay *EL*]   They they lay
†158:13–14   During . . . Abbey. TS1]   *absent*
†158:14–15   As a young . . . *Species.* TS1]   *absent*
†160:34   them a ED]   them; of a
173:4   "Circus-Rider to *EL*]   "Circus Rider and
179:17   Viscountess *EL*]   Countess
185:20   prepossession *EL*]   preposession
195:26   Via Condotti *EL*]   Via de Condotti
195:28   dei Monti *EL*]   de' Monti
198:17   Basilica of Constantine *EL*]   Basilica Constantine

203:9	begun *EL*] began
†204:21	*Poems of the Past and the Present EL*] *Wessex Poems*
207:24	dell' Annunziata *EL*] SS. Annunziata
†210:8	At a certain reception Hardy TS2 (retyped page)]
	At the last mentioned reception he
215:10	Gérôme *EL*] Gerôme
238:1	was *EL*] were
239:36	Ridgeway *EL*] Ridgway
†240:16	many similar *EL*] many of similar
240:40–1	"She is a nice warm-feeling woman, and expressed TS1]
	"She expressed
245:33–4	known Lady Byron's TS1] known Byron's
245:34	He went *EL*] He and went
†246:39	entirely the *EL*] entirely—the
†251:24–8	"October 30 . . . repetition." *EL*] *absent*

[End of *Early Life*; *Later Years* begins]

258:18	voluptuous mouth TS3] voluptuous, mouth
259:32	book was spreading TS3] book spread
259:39	he afterwards called TS3] he called afterwards
264:33	choice, that TS3] choice that
265:27	highest tragedy TS3] high tragedy
265:40	famous 'Would TS3] famous, 'would
266:6	Terriss TS3] Terris
266:7	Lady Sh. TS3] Lady S.
269:18	upon TS3] on
272:10	others. Reached TS3] others, reaching
†274:12	This month TS3] The following month
†289:6–19	Hardy's letter . . . Thomas Hardy. TS3] *absent*
290:23	themselves: What TS3] themselves: 'what
290:24	say, 'I TS3] say: "I
290:25	and TS3] &
298:8	While he was talking *LY*] While talking
298:16–17	in this, as in other summers, at *LY*] on this (as in other
	summers) at
†299:1	some while before TS3] a few years before
303:7–8	in America by Mr and Mrs Fiske with much success. TS3] in
	America with much success by Mr Fiske.
310:22	dance TS3] party
312:fn (4)	midwife TS3] mid-wife
†313:25–6	He used . . . of illness. TS3] *absent*
313:33–4	which he never TS3] which never
316:41	Thomas Hardy ED] T.H.
†324:2–3	onomatopoeic, resembling the flopping of liquid; and TS3]
	onomatopoeic, plainly as it was shown; and
324:38–9	Fire", or "The Fire *LY*] fire, or the fire

328:13   "Drummer Hodge" *LY*] "Hodge the Drummer"
328:14   Ghost Story" in *LY*] Ghost" in
329:25   Mombaer *LY*] Mauburn
331:3   and the Present" *LY*] *and Present*
331:6   an *LY*] a
332:10   on his taking *LY*] on taking
340:18   [in Dorchester] TS3] in Dorchester
340:25   1822 TS3] 1823
†345:38   June 28 *LY*] June 27
347:36–7   from a southern TS3] from Southern
349:24   Jaques *LY*] Jacques
355:6   Blanche, Miss TS3] Blanche of Paris, Miss
†364:[6]   *absent* ED] *End of Part VI.*
377:17   Hardy ED] H.
381:29–30   King-of-Dahomey TS3] King of Dahomey
381:31   the longer title *LY*] the title
382:15   stretch-mouth'd TS3] stretch-mouthed
383:9   pleasant TS3] agreeable
387:1   "The Last Performance" *LY*] "Her last performance"
389:23   in TS3] for
390:3   honorary degree *LY*] Hon. Degree
391:11   housekeeping animal TS3] housekeeping. Animal
394:39   Battle-God" *LY*] War God"
398:3–4   Battle-God" *LY*] War-God"
398:8   of *LY*] on
400:31   lieutenant *LY*] Lieut
400:32   Regiment *LY*] Regt.
403:6   Thomas Hardy ED] T.H.
403:12   "To Shakespeare *LY*] "Shakespeare
403:12–13   Three Hundred Years ED] 300 years
404:23   a visit TS1] visits
408:30   world-practised *LY*] world-practiced
†409:[15]   *absent LY*] END OF 1917
426:24   Watts's *LY*] Watt's MN3
427:1   Watts *LY*] Watt's MN3
427:30   Hardy *LY*] H. MN3
433:31   1863 *LY*] 1862 MN3
436:35   its *LY*] it MN3
†442:[8]   *absent LY*] End of 1920.
450:23   Eweleaze ED] Ewelease *LY*
450:25   Eweleaze ED] Ewelease *LY*
†453:38   Mr Hardy ED] Hardy *LY*
†454:2   deputed ED] delighted *LY*
†455:1   beside ED] before *LY*
†455:25   His ED] This *LY*
†463:30   village ED] country *LY*
472:35   Frome ED] Froome *LY*
†485:4   and of its ED] and its *LY*
†487:14–15   of a musing ED] of musing *LY*

†487 : 19	determinism ED] determination *LY*
†488 : 17	less a disciple ED] less disciple *LY*
†489 : 7	hard-headed ED] hard-hearted *LY*
†489 : 26	proofs ED] proof *LY*
489 : fn (1)	pp. 399–400 ED] 167–168 *LY*

Selected Post-Hardyan Revisions in *Early Life* and *Later Years*

Given that the aim of the present edition is to recover the text of the "Life" as Hardy left it, little textual importance attaches to most of the changes subsequently made or sanctioned by his widow. The following table lists, therefore, only the biographically significant changes—chiefly additions and deletions—that occurred, at whatever time and in whatever circumstances, between Hardy's death and the first publication of *Early Life* and *Later Years*. The numerous stylistic and "copy-editing" changes are thus left unrecorded, but the list does include *Early life* and *Later Years* readings that correct factual errors in the copy-texts, supply the full names of persons identified in the copy-texts only by initials, or appear to possess any other biographical interest.

The first citation in each entry is from the present edition, the second from *Early Life* or *Later Years*—though many of the published readings were of course anticipated by non-Hardyan interventions in the surviving typescripts. The system adopted allows Florence Hardy's additions to appear in full—always, of course, as part of a second citation, after the square bracket. Deletions of only a few words in length are given in full (always as part of a first citation, before the square bracket); the full texts of longer deletions, represented here only by their opening and closing words or phrases (e.g. "Poor . . . character."), can be found by referring back within this edition to the indicated page, line number(s) and cue words. Asterisked entries are discussed in the Textual Notes; editorial procedures are described above, pp. xxx–xxxv.

1 : 1–7	The Life . . . many years.] THE EARLY LIFE OF/ THOMAS HARDY/ 1840–1891/ COMPILED LARGELY FROM/ CONTEMPORARY NOTES, LETTERS, DIARIES, AND/ BIOGRAPHICAL MEMORANDA, AS WELL AS FROM/ ORAL INFORMATION IN

CONVERSATIONS EXTENDING/ OVER MANY YEARS/ BY/ FLORENCE EMILY HARDY

[* Dedication] *absent*] To/ THE DEAR MEMORY

7 : 26 is much demeaned and] is weather-worn and

* 8 : fn The poem runs] The poem, written between 1857 and 1860, runs

* 19 : 18 father. Of] father. Had it not been for the common sense of the estimable woman who attended as monthly nurse, he might never have walked the earth. At his birth he was thrown aside as dead till rescued by her as she exclaimed to the surgeon, "Dead! Stop a minute: he's alive enough, sure!" ¶ Of

21 : 2–5 life, was . . . music.] life.

21 : 20 periodical in loose numbers of the war] periodical dealing with the war

* 22 : 17 done the same from impecuniousness] done so for the same reason

23 : 41–24 : 1 ill-arranged . . . and] ill-arranged, and

24 : 13–14 harvest-supper—as harvest-homes were called here— at] harvest-supper at

24 : 34 how is this!] how is this?

* 26 : 7–8 Second . . . conceived. Instead] Second had not the tradesman's soul. Instead

26 : 14–31 Furthermore . . . death. ¶ To return to their son.] *absent*

* 26 : 39–40 great. ¶ It was] great. ¶ His earliest recollection was of receiving from his father the gift of a small accordion. He knew that he was but four years old at this time, as his name and the date were written by his father upon the toy: Thomas Hardy. 1844. ¶ Another memory, some two or three years later, is connected with the Corn Law Agitation. The boy had a little wooden sword, which his father had made for him, and this he dipped into the blood of a pig which had just been killed, and brandished it as he walked about the garden exclaiming: "Free Trade or blood!" ¶ A member of his family recalled, even after an interval of sixty years, the innocent glee with which the young Thomas and his mother would set off on various expeditions. They were excellent companions, having each a keen sense of humour and a love of adventure. Hardy would tell of one prank when he and his mother put on fantastic garb, pulling cabbage-nets over their faces to disguise themselves. Thus oddly dressed they walked across the heath to visit a sister of Mrs. Hardy, living at Puddletown, whose amazement was great when she set eyes upon these strange visitors at her door. ¶ It was

* 28 : 18–19 fourteen. ¶ Among] fourteen. ¶ He had always been told by his mother that he must on no account take any payment for these services as fiddler, but on one occasion temptation was too strong. A hatful of pennies was collected, amounting to four or five shillings; and Thomas had that morning seen in a shop in Dorchester a copy of *The Boys' Own Book* which could be

bought with about this sum. He accepted the money and soon
owned the coveted volume. His mother shook her head over the
transaction, and refused to see any merit in a book which was
chiefly about games. This volume was carefully kept, and
remained in his library to the end of his life. ¶ Among

*29 : 23–4   *Mensuration*. ¶ One day]   *Mensuration*. ¶ Hardy was popular
—too popular almost—with his school-fellows, for their friendship at times became burdensome. He loved being alone, but
often, to his concealed discomfort, some of the other boys would
volunteer to accompany him on his homeward journey to
Bockhampton. How much this irked him he recalled long years
after. He tried also to avoid being touched by his playmates.
One lad, with more insight than the rest, discovered the fact:
"Hardy, how is it that you do not like us to touch you?" This
peculiarity never left him, and to the end of his life he disliked
even the most friendly hand being laid on his arm or his
shoulder. Probably no one else ever observed this. ¶ One day

30 : 25   a well-to-do farmer's]   a farmer's
*30 : 27–9   Louisa, which . . . London.]   Louisa. ¶ He believed that his
attachment to this damsel was reciprocated, for on one
occasion when he was walking home from Dorchester he
beheld her sauntering down the lane as if to meet him. He
longed to speak to her, but bashfulness overcame him, and he
passed on with a murmured "Good evening", while poor
Louisa had no word to say. ¶ Later he heard that she had gone
to Weymouth to a boarding school for young ladies, and
thither he went, Sunday after Sunday, until he discovered the
church which the maiden of his affections attended with her
fellow-scholars. But, alas, all that resulted from these efforts was
a shy smile from Louisa. ¶ That the vision remained may be
gathered from a poem "Louisa in the Lane" written not many
months before his death. Louisa lies under a nameless mound
in "Mellstock" churchyard. That "Good evening" was the
only word that passed between them.

32 : 4–5   unchanged), . . . On]   unchanged. On
32 : 29–30   last-named—such as it was—had]   last-named work had
*32 : 35–6   theirs. ¶ An unusual]   theirs. ¶ At this time the Rev. William
Barnes, the Dorset poet and philologist, was keeping school
next door. Knowing him to be an authority upon grammar
Hardy would often run in to ask Barnes to decide some knotty
point in dispute between him and his fellow-pupil. Hardy used
to assert in later years that upon almost every occasion the
verdict was given in his favour. ¶ An unusual

33 : 17   B——]   Bastow
34 : 2   B——]   Bastow
34 : 21   B——]   Bastow
34 : 38   P——]   Perkins
35 : 9   P——]   Perkins
35 : 20   B——'s]   Bastow's

35:24   B——] Bastow
36:2   B——'s] Bastow's
40:2   London] WORK IN LONDON
40:16–17 earlier. ¶ Hardy] earlier. With prudent forethought he
bought a return ticket for the journey, so that he might be able
to travel back to Dorchester did he reach the end of his
resources. After six months he threw away the unused half. ¶
Hardy

*43:9–10 Blomfield himself. ¶ During the] Blomfield himself. ¶ The
following letters were written to his sister, Miss Mary Hardy,
during 1862 and 1863, the first year that Hardy was at St.
Martin's Place and Adelphi Terrace. ¶ KILBURN, 17 *August*
1862. ¶ 9. P.M. ¶ MY DEAR MARY ¶ "After the fire a still
small voice"—I have just come from the evening service at St.
Mary's Kilburn and this verse, which I always notice, was in
the 1st Lesson. ¶ This Ch. of St. Mary is rather to my taste and
they sing most of the tunes in the Salisbury hymn book there. ¶
H. M. M. was up the week before last. We went to a Roman
Catholic Chapel on the Thursday evening. It was a very
impressive service. The Chapel was built by Pugin. Afterwards
we took a cab to the old Hummums, an hotel near Covent
Garden where we had supper. He may come and settle
permanently in London in a few months, but is not certain yet.
¶ E— was up last week. I had half a day at Exhibition with
him. He is now living at home, looking out for a situation. I do
not think he will get into anything yet. ¶ I have not been to a
theatre since you were here. I generally run down to the
Exhibition for an hour in the evening two or three times a week;
after I come out I go to the reading room of the Kensington
Museum. ¶ It has been pouring with rain all the day and last
night, such a disappointment for thousands of Londoners,
whose only holiday is Sunday. ¶ I should like to have a look at
the old Cathedral, etc., in about a month or so. The autumn
seems the proper season for seeing Salisbury. Do you ever go to
St. Thomas's? Be careful about getting cold again and do not
go out in evenings. ¶ P. S. is reading extracts from Ruskin's
"Modern Painters" to me which accounts for the wretched
composition of this epistle as I am obliged to make comments
etc. on what he reads. ¶ Ever yours, ¶ T. H. ¶ KILBURN, 19*th*
February. ¶ MY DEAR MARY: ¶ I don't fancy that 'tis so very
long since I wrote and the Saturdays [*Saturday Reviews*] have
been sent regularly but I really intended to write this week. ¶
You see that we have moved, so for the future my address will
be as on the other side. We have not recovered from the
confusion yet, and our drawings and papers are nohow. ¶The
new office is a capital place. It is on the first floor and on a
terrace that overlooks the river. We can see from our window
right across the Thames, and on a clear day every bridge is
visible. Everybody says that we have a beautiful place. ¶ To-

day has been wretched. It was almost pitch dark in the middle of the day, and everything visible appeared of the colour of brown paper or pea-soup. ¶ There is a great deal of preparation for the approaching wedding. The Princess is to arrive on the 7th March and the wedding will be on the 10th. On her landing at Gravesend she will be received by the Prince, the Mayor, Mayoress, etc. They will then go by train to the Bricklayers' Arms station, and then in procession over London Bridge, along Fleet Street, Strand, Charing Cross, Pall Mall, Piccadilly, through Hyde Park, and up the Edgware Road to Paddington Station—thence to Windsor. The windows along the route are full of notices that seats to view the procession are to be let. There will be an illumination the evening of the 10th. ¶ I went to Richmond yesterday to see Lee. He is better but is going to Kent for a short time before coming back to the office. ¶ I have not heard anything about the Essay yet. The name of the successful competitor will be known in about a fortnight. I am now very busy getting up a design for a country mansion for which a small prize is offered—£3 the best and £2 the second best. It has to be sent in by the 27th March. ¶ I am glad you have got a drawing prize, but you don't say what. I think you have done very well altogether. Tell me about the organ and how the Sundays go off—I am uncommonly interested. How is your friend the blind man etc., School, clergyman etc. *Say how you are*, don't forget. I am quite well. Horace Moule has been ill. So has H. A. as I daresay you know. Has she written yet? I sent a valentine to Harry and Kate to please them. Harry wrote me a letter, and Kate printed one and sent—rather a curiosity in its way. ¶ I sent Mrs. Rolls photographs and she sent me a paper and letter. She says that Parsons is postmaster in place of Lock who has resigned. ¶ I tried the Underground Railway one day— Everything is excellently arranged. ¶ Do you think to run up Easter? If so, you must not mind being left alone all day—but you know your way about. ¶ T. S. has commenced the sketch of our house for you. He says it will soon be finished. ¶ Is Katie coming up to live with you and when is Mother coming? ¶ Ever your affectionate ¶Tom ¶ 8 Adelphi Terrace, ¶19 *Dec*. 1863. ¶ My dear Mary, ¶I was beginning to think you had given up writing altogether, when your letter came. Certainly try to get as long a time as you can Christmas. ¶ I am glad you have been to Oxford again. It must be a jolly place. I shall try to get down there some time or other. You have no right to say you are not connected with art. Everybody is to a certain extent; the only difference between a professor and an amateur being that the former has the (often disgreeable) necessity of making it his means of earning bread and cheese—and thus often rendering what is a pleasure to other people a "bore" to himself. ¶ About Thackeray. You must read something of his.

He is considered to be the greatest novelist of the day—looking at novel writing of the highest kind as a perfect and truthful representation of actual life—which is no doubt the proper view to take. Hence, because his novels stand so high as works of Art or Truth, they often have anything but an elevating tendency, and on that account are particularly unfitted for young people—from their very truthfulness. People say that it is beyond Mr. Thackeray to paint a perfect man or woman—a great fault if novels are intended to instruct, but just the opposite if they are to be considered merely as Pictures. *Vanity Fair* is considered one of his best. ¶ I expect to go home about Tuesday or Wednesday after Xmas and then shall find you there of course—We must have a "bit of a lark". ¶ Ever affectionately ¶Tom. ¶ I am able to write 40 words a minute. The average rate of a speaker is from 100, to 120 and occasionally 140; so I have much more to do yet. ¶ During the

44 : 1–2	the moorhen] the legend of the moorhen
*44 : 36	There was no underground railway, and] The Underground Railway was just in its infancy, and
*45 : 1	play of *Our American Cousin and Lord Dundreary*. At] play of *The American Cousin*, in which he played the name part. At
*46 : 7	than the greatest success would have done.] than his greatest success.
*47 : 40–1	join us." ¶ On an] join us." ¶ Among other things, the architect related that one day before he (Hardy) came, a Punch-and-Judy show performed outside the office in St. Martin's Place. Presently the housekeeper, a woman London-bred, came running upstairs exclaiming, "Why, Mr. Arthur, I declare there's a man inside! And I never knew it before!" ¶ On an
49 : 7–9	besides neither . . . influential] besides little inclination for pushing his way into influential
50 : 38	H.M.M.] Moule
51 : 2–3	Poor . . . character.] *absent*
*51 : 19	of the] of "the
*51 : 20	*Marmion*] *Marmion*"
*53 : 30–1	in Saul." ¶ Through] in *Saul*." ¶ The following letter to his sister describes the ceremony: ¶ *Saturday, Oct.* 28, 1865. ¶ MY DEAR MARY ¶ I sent *Barchester Towers* by B.P., and you are probably by this time acquainted with Eleanor Bold, etc. This novel is considered the best of Trollope's. ¶ Yesterday Lord Palmerston was buried—the Prime Minister. I and the Lees got tickets through a friend of a friend of Mr. B's, and we went of course. Our tickets admitted to the triforium, or monks' walk, of Westminster Abbey, and we got from there a complete view of the ceremony. You will know wh. part of the Abbey I mean if you think of Salisbury Cathedral and of the row of small arches over the large arches, wh. throw open the space between the roof of the aisles and the vaulting. ¶ Where I have

put the × in the Section is where I stood; over the ✖ on the Plan. The mark ⚏ shows where the grave is, between Pitt's and Fox's and close by Canning's. All the Cabinet Ministers were there as pall bearers. The burial service was Purcell's. The opening sentences "I am the resurrection, etc" were sung to Croft's music. Beethoven's Funeral March was played as they went from the choir to the vault, and the Dead March in *Saul*

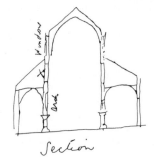
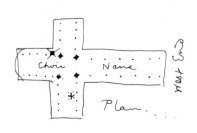

was played at the close. I think I was never so much impressed with a ceremony in my life before, and I wd. not have missed it for anything. The Prince of Wales and Duke of Cambridge were present. ¶ Ld. John Russell, or Earl Russell as he is now, is to be Prime Minister in Pam's place. Only fancy, Ld. P. has been connected with the govt. off and on for the last 60 years, and that he was contemporaneous with Pitt, Fox, Sheridan, Burke, etc. I mean to say his life overlapped theirs so to speak. I sent father a newspaper containing an account of his life, and today one with an account of the funeral. As you are not a politician I didn't send you one, but these things interest him. ¶ If you can get *Pelham*, read it when you want something. Do not hurry over *Barchester*, for I have enough to do. I think Wells is the place intended. Will it be a good thing or will it be awkward for you if H. A. and I come down for Xmas day and the next? ¶ I am rather glad that hot close weather is gone and the bracing air come again. I think I told you I had joined the French class at King's College. ¶ Ever sincerely. ¶ T. H. ¶ A tall man went to see Chang the Chinese Giant, and on his offering to pay, the doorkeeper said "Not at all Sir, we don't take money from the *profession*!" at least so *Punch* says. ¶ Through

54:5	front during] front (which in those days was close to the orchestra) during
63:22	called)—that] called in the profession)—that
*63:27	keeper] protector
63:30–1	There . . . reviews.] *absent*
64:1–2	man in] man at large in

69 : 2–5	A Journal, a Supplement, and Literary Vicissitudes] ST. JULIOT
75 : 5	living Mr [Bishop?] Rawle, who lived at Antigua, was present] living, the Rev. Richard Rawle, [who owned land in the parish, and was about this time consecrated as Bishop of Trinidad] was present
*76 : 12–14	A lock . . . of it.] *absent*
76 : 23–4	London; believed to be a nephew] London; a nephew
76 : 30	was drawn from a mason] was a mason
*77 : 1–4	hitch, and . . . marriage. ¶ But] hitch from beginning to end, and with encouragement from all parties concerned. ¶ But
78 : 24–5	dissent, though in England the lines passed quite without notice.] dissent.
81 : 33	who knew] who by this date knew
85 : 2–3	A Plot, an Idyll, and a Romance] FIRST THREE BOOKS
*87 : 8–9	brain." ¶ But] brain." He remembered, for long years after, how he had read this review as he sat on a stile leading to the eweleaze he had to cross on his way home to Bockhampton. The bitterness of that moment was never forgotten; at the time he wished that he were dead. ¶ But
89 : 38–9	The proverbial . . . erections.] *absent*
91 : 16	accepted, caring nothing about the book. It] accepted. It
93 : 17–18	*Eyes . . . Even*] *Eyes.* Even
99 : 7–8	perished, as well as the old outbuildings. It] perished. It
*103 : 7–10	She was . . . in 1779.] *absent*
103 : 26–30	a relative . . . after years.] *absent*
103 : 33	marry during] marry William Allingham during
104 : 12–17	Its . . . exceptions.] *absent*
105 : 2–8	Thus . . . past.] *absent*
105 : 26–30	house-decorator (!); . . . influenced] house-decorator (!). Criticism like this influenced
106 : 1	went with his wife to] went to
108 : 3–5	(Strangely . . . novels.)] *absent*
111 : 21–2	the "Roman pastoral] "Le roman pastoral
112 : 3–11	Had . . . unknown.] *absent*
114 : 1–5	Strassburg, . . . two, and] Strassburg, and
114 : 39	minute process] minute and obvious process
116 : 12	conference at] Conference on the Eastern Question at
121 : 24–5	The body . . . cut.] *absent*
125 : 34	September 30.] *September 20.*
126 : 5–6	It was . . . *Island*.] *absent*
*129 : 5–6	Woodsford-and-Tincleton] W——
*129 : 6	Owre-Moigne] O——
131 : 3	under the outer side of her eyelid."] under the eyelid."
134 : 2–3	London Life, France, and] LONDON, NORMANDY, AND
137 : 25	first book] first successful book
139 : 11–13	and especially . . . she always] and she always

140 : 33	so?"] so?" Mrs. Procter was born in 1800.
140 : 34–8	During . . . more.] *absent*
141 : 5–12	Through . . . business."] *absent*
149 : 2–3	Writing Under Difficulties; and] A DIFFICULT PERIOD; AND
157 : 2–4	and the Astronomical Romance] AND "TWO ON A TOWER"
159 : 23	a man] a cheerful man
*161 : 17	relative] husband
161 : 21–34	All the rector's . . . baptism.] *absent*
*164 : 18	a horse] an old horse
165 : 37–9	Presently . . . Mrs Sutherland] Presently Mrs. Sutherland
173 : 18–27	During this summer . . . novels.] *absent*
174 : 37–175 : 2	On October . . . afterwards.] *absent*
*175 : 39	Pult P——] Patt P——
178 : 19	on to enquire after ——'s children. . . .] on . . . .
178 : 26–9	At last E . . . all is!] *absent*
178 : 32–3	Madame . . . there.] *absent*
178 : 36–179 : 4	"In the evening . . . hostess.] *absent*
179 : 5–6	1885, probably Lady Carnarvon's, they] 1885 they
179 : 33	C——'s] Carnarvon's
*180 : 7–181 : 1	out of the town. ¶ CHAPTER XIV] out of the town. ¶ This house, one mile east of Dorchester, had been about eighteen months in building, commencing November 26, 1883, during which time Hardy was constantly overlooking operations. The plot of ground, which he bought from the Duchy of Cornwall, was 1½ acres in extent, and nearly forty years later another half-acre was added to the garden. ¶ A visitor to Max Gate in 1886 gives the following description: ¶ "The house that is, from its position, almost the first object in the neighbourhood to catch the sun's morning rays, and the last to relinquish the evening glow, is approached . . . along the Wareham road across an open down. From this side the building appears as an unpretending red-brick structure of moderate size, somewhat quaintly built, and standing in a garden which is divided from the upland without by an enclosing wall. . . . The place is as lonely as it is elevated; and it is evident that from the narrow windows of a turret which rises at the salient angle an extensive view of the surrounding country may be obtained. ¶ "From the white entrance gate in the wall a short drive, planted on the windward side with beech and sycamore, leads up to the house, arrivals being notified to the inmates by the voice of a glossy black setter [Moss], who comes into view from the stable at the back as far as his chain will allow him. Within, we find ourselves in a small square hall, floored with dark polished wood, and resembling rather a cosy sitting-room with a staircase in it than a hall as commonly understood. It is lighted by a window of leaded panes, through which may be seen Conygar Hill, Came Plantation, and the elevated seamark of

Culliford Tree." ¶ Some two or three thousand small trees, mostly Austrian pines, were planted around the house by Hardy himself, and in later years these grew so thickly that the house was almost entirely screened from the road, and finally appeared, in summer, as if at the bottom of a dark green well of trees. ¶ To the right of the front door upon entering is the drawing-room, and to the left the dining-room. Above the drawing-room is the room which Hardy used as his first study at Max Gate, and in this room *The Woodlanders* was written. Later he moved his study to the back of the house with a window facing west, where *Tess of the d'Urbervilles* took shape. In after years another study was built over a new kitchen, and here *The Dynasts* and all the later poems were written, with the remaining literary work of Hardy's life. The rather large window of this, the last of all his workrooms, faced east, and the full moon rising over the tops of the dark pines was a familiar sight. ¶ When Max Gate was built Hardy intended to have a sundial affixed to the easternmost turret, as shown in an illustration drawn by himself for *Wessex Poems*. This design, constantly in his mind, never matured during his life, though at the time of his death the sundial was actually being made in Dorchester, from a model prepared by himself, more than forty years after it was first planned. ¶ A description of his personal appearance at this time, by a careful observer, is as follows: ¶ "A somewhat fair-complexioned man, a trifle below the middle-height [he was actually 5 ft. 6½ ins.] of slight build, with a pleasant thoughtful face, exceptionally broad at the temples, and fringed by a beard trimmed after the Elizabethan manner [this beard was shaved off about 1890, and he never grew another, but had always a moustache]; a man readily sociable and genial, but one whose mien conveys the impression that the world in his eyes has rather more of the tragedy than the comedy about it." ¶ His smile was of exceptional sweetness, and his eyes were a clear blue-grey. His whole aspect was almost childlike in its sincerity and simplicity, the features being strongly marked, and his nose, as he himself once described it, more Roman than aquiline. The nobility of his brow was striking. When young he had abundant hair of a deep chestnut colour, which later became a dark brown, almost black, until it turned grey. His hands were well shaped, with long deft fingers; his shoulders particularly neat, and his gait light and easy. He walked very rapidly. He was always a spare man, though not actually thin, and he never in his life allowed himself to be weighed, as he said he considered that to be unlucky. ¶ CHAPTER XIV

181 : 2	The New House and] MAX GATE AND
186 : 20–1	to Mr Smith that] to Smith, Elder and Co. that
187 : 1–2	weeks the Hardys . . . Walter] weeks Hardy met Walter
187 : 3–6	At Mrs Jeune's . . . Lowell.] *absent*

187 : 9–10	hostess drew] hostess, Mrs. Jeune, drew
187 : 24–6	sentences; . . . also] sentences"; and also
187 : 32–3	at Lord Portsmouth's sat] at another house sat
187 : 36	Wagner-music] some music of Wagner's
188 : 4–5	Grieg . . . Wagner, and] Grieg, and
189 : 17–20	Also met . . . before.] *absent*
191 : 19–20	Weather too wretched for Em to go.] *absent*
191 : 31–2	Carnarvon, who looked remarkably pretty, about] Carnarvon about
192 : 3	landscape by Bonington] landscape ascribed to Bonington
192 : 4	[given . . . sculptor]] *absent*
192 : 19	relieved."] relieved." In after years he often said that in some respects *The Woodlanders* was his best novel.
194 : 2	Italy] ITALIAN JOURNEY
195 : 5	palaces—notably the Palazzo Doria—during] palaces during
196 : 29–197 : 10	Two or . . . day before.] *absent*
199 : 6–7	Signoria, while his wife was sketching, near; and] Signoria, and
*199 : 24	that we love and admire] *that* we only like and admire
*202 : 20	of fourscore who] of fourscore or over who
204 : 13–14	started, leaving Mrs Hardy at the hotel; and] started and
207 : 6	London Hardy] London in April 1887, Hardy
208 : 22–30	Also Lady . . . told me."] *absent*
208 : 37–9	"End of . . . translation."] *absent*
209 : 18–23	"14th. To . . . already."] *absent*
*209 : 26	"18. To . . . House."] *absent*
210 : 18–19	"July 1 . . . dinner."] *absent*
211 : 16	P——] Priddle
211 : 18	P——] Priddle
211 : 19	C——] Cogan
211 : 33	H. S.] Henry Smith
211 : 35	barton, resting] barton at the grave, resting
211 : 35–6	and clattered] and at the end clattered
212 : 16–17	me and Em the] me the
217 : 27	staring names] staring brass-lettered names
219 : 1	Portsmouth with Em. Found] Portsmouth. Found
*220 : 20	Pall Mall] Piccadilly
*220 : 21	club, and] club house door, and
220 : 39–221 : 2	"Lord Portsmouth . . . Queen."] *absent*
222 : 13	August 5. To] *August* 5, 1888. To
*223 : 5	poacher in] poacher, who was in
225 : 23–6	"Business . . . sealing-wax."] *absent*
225 : 35	If Em . . . done it.] *absent*
226 : 22	A. P.] Alfred Parsons
227 : 4	B.] Bockhampton
227 : 5	A.] Askerswell
227 : 5	W. K.] William K.
229 : 32–230 : 1	"June 29 . . . Abercorn's."] *absent*

230:7–24   "July 17–23. . . . Stephen's. ¶ "Of the people]   "*July* 23. Of
               the people
230:26   Mrs H. T——]   Mrs. Hamo Thornycroft—
231:8–10   In fact . . . one.]   *absent*
232:26–7   Hardy had . . . carried]   Hardy carried
232:28–9   conventionality without compunction and with]   convention-
               ality with
*234:11   March — A]   March 5. A
234:21–235:1   Jeunes' to . . . features. Met]   Jeunes'. Met
235:5–8   "At lunch . . . throat."]   *absent*
235:27–9   Next day . . . left.]   *absent*
*236:26   Circus and discerns the]   Circus at this hour, and notices the
236:40–1   Middleton   the   friend   of   William   Morris.   Hardy]
               Middleton, Slade Professor of Fine Art at Cambridge. Hardy
238:29–30   Em is quite in love with her.]   *absent*
*242:2   Childs, M.A., of]   Childs of
244:5–6   "The Marchioness . . . red.]   *absent*
244:39–41   in London, . . . this.]   in London.
247:4–5   crew of harlots there]   crew, there
248:24–7   iron gray": and . . . paler." On]   iron-grey." On
248:40–249:   Milnes-Gaskells' . . . She   told]   Milnes-Gaskells',   Lady
               Catherine told
*249:4   the —s]   the Webbs
249:11–12   At Max . . . Wenlock.]   *absent*
*250:26   That Tess . . . suggestion.]   *absent*
*252:7–10   matter. ¶The end . . . mother. *Tess*]   matter." ¶As the year
               drew to a close an incident that took place during the
               publication of *Tess of the d'Urbervilles* as a serial in the *Graphic*
               might have prepared him for certain events that were to follow.
               The editor objected to the description of Angel Clare carrying
               in his arms, across a flooded lane, Tess and her three dairymaid
               companions. He suggested that it would be more decorous and
               suitable for the pages of a periodical intended for family
               reading if the damsels were wheeled across the lane in a
               wheelbarrow. This was accordingly done. ¶ Also the *Graphic*
               refused to print the chapter describing the christening of the
               infant child of Tess. This appeared in Henley's *Scots Observer*,
               and was afterwards restored to the novel, where it was
               considered one of the finest passages. ¶ *Tess*

[End of *Early Life*; *Later Life* begins]

*255:1   XX]   I
255:18–19   inexplicable to its just judges, and to the]   inexplicable to the
255:19–256:4   The sub-title . . . of opinion.]   *absent*
256:9   the words]   the first five words
258:17–24   "Called on . . . deceased.]   *absent*
258:32–6   "Mrs Joseph . . . Russell."]   *absent*
259:8–10   In . . . criminal.]   *absent*

259:16–21	You can . . . go on.]　*absent*
259:26–32	"Such reviews . . . whatever.]　*absent*
260:3–5	When Hardy . . . a manner."]　*absent*
260:26–261:13	"April 22nd. . . . most affable".]　*absent*
261:14–15	month, when he was dining at Lady Metcalfe's, his]　month his
*262:13	died quickly that]　died quietly that
*262:28	Knights]　knights
263:8	"Weatherbury" Church]　"Weatherbury" (Puddletown) Church
263:16–17	"Sept. Mr . . . lunch."]　*absent*
264:28–29	[and already . . . book.]]　*absent*
265:16–20	"The *Daily* . . . A. Lang."]　*absent*
266:4–7	"Dec. 18. . . . H. Aidé."]　*absent*
268:30–41	While getting . . . o'clock."]　*absent*
269:2	Mrs R.]　Mrs. Richard
269:9–14	I sat . . . also present.]　*absent*
269:20–4	"14. Dined . . . and others."]　*absent*
270:23	Houghton came]　Houghton (the Lord-Lieutenant) came
270:38–40	Afterwards . . . Park.]　*absent*
270:41–271:1	dinner, including General Milman and daughter. Mr Dundas]　dinner. Mr.
271:3	Em went . . . others.]　*absent*
272:8–10	"Found . . . others.]　*absent*
272:11	¶Next day Hardy]　¶Early in June Hardy
*272:13	Strangers".]　*Strangers*, made at the suggestion of J. M. Barrie.
*272:14	by Mr J. M. Barrie, and]　by his friend, and
*272:36	nervousness. ¶ Some ten]　nervousness. In a letter to Mrs. Henniker Hardy describes this experience: "The evening of yesterday I spent in what I fear you will call a frivolous manner—indeed, during the time, my mind reverted to our Ibsen experience; and I could not help being regretfully struck by the contrast—although I honestly was amused. Barrie had arranged to take us and Maarten Maartens to see B.'s play of *Walker, London*, and lunching yesterday with the Milmans at the Tower we asked Miss Milman to be of the party. Mr. Toole heard we had come and invited us behind the scenes. We accordingly went and sat with him in his dressing-room, where he entertained us with hock and champagne, he meanwhile in his paint, wig, and blazer, as he had come off the stage, amusing us with the drollest of stories about a visit he and a friend paid to the Tower some years ago: how he amazed the custodian by entreating the loan of the crown jewels for an amateur dramatic performance for a charitable purpose, offering to deposit 30s. as a guarantee that he would return them, etc., etc., etc. We were rather late home as you may suppose." ¶ Some ten
273:3–4	It is believed that he viewed]　He viewed
273:8–9	sort. A . . . memorial]　sort. A memorial

273:21-6   At Mrs . . . Chamberlain.] *absent*
274:5-11   "August 4. . . . they know."] *absent*
*274:12   This month]   The following month
274:34-7   ruins . . . Milnes-Gaskell]   ruins, and Milnes-Gaskell
275:38-9   well, . . . pretty."]   well."
278:16-22   Hardy passed . . . experiences.] *absent*
279:4   R——]   Redvers
279:14-15   Elsewhere . . . Morris.] *absent*
*279:19-20   "The Earl and the Doctor"]   *South Sea Bubbles*
280:41-281:1   ladies instead of struggling dowdy females, the]   ladies, the
281:4-10   "May 23. Dined . . . there."] *absent*
284:11-12   *of Vision.* ¶ In March]   *of Vision.* He watched during a
                 sleepless night a lighted window close by, wondering who
                 might be lying there ill. Afterwards he discovered that a
                 woman had lain there dying, and that she was one whom he
                 had cared for in his youth, when she was a girl in a
                 neighbouring village. ¶ In March
*284:17-18   places was]   places, Charborough Park, the scene of *Two on a
                 Tower*, was
285:17-26   In the same . . . o'clock."] *absent*
285:29-30   Catholicism, while . . . mother.]   Catholicism.
287:1-3   he enters . . . sets down:]   he sets down:
287:15-288:6   However, . . . his engagement.] *absent*
*289:6-19   A. C. Swinburne. ¶ Hardy's letter . . . Hardy. In
                 London]   A. C. SWINBURNE." ¶ Three letters upon this
                 same subject, written by Hardy himself to a close friend, may
                 appropriately be given here. ¶LETTER 1. ¶ "MAX GATE,
                 ¶ "DORCHESTER, ¶"*November* 10*th*, 1895. ¶". . . Your
                 review (of *Jude the Obscure*) is the most discriminating that has yet
                 appeared. It required an artist to see that the plot is almost
                 geometrically constructed—I ought not to say *constructed*, for,
                 beyond a certain point, the characters necessitated it, and I
                 simply let it come. As for the story itself, it is really sent out to
                 those into whose souls the iron has entered, and has entered
                 deeply at some time of their lives. But one cannot choose one's
                 readers. ¶ "It is curious that some of the papers should look upon
                 the novel as a manifesto on "the marriage question" (although,
                 of course, it involves it), seeing that it is concerned first with the
                 labours of a poor student to get a University degree, and
                 secondly with the tragic issues of two bad marriages, owing in
                 the main to a doom or curse of hereditary temperament
                 peculiar to the family of the parties. The only remarks which
                 can be said to bear on the *general* marriage question occur in
                 dialogue, and comprise no more than half a dozen pages in a
                 book of five hundred. And of these remarks I state (p. 362) that
                 my own views are not expressed therein. I suppose the attitude
                 of these critics is to be accounted for by the accident that,
                 during the serial publication of my story, a sheaf of 'purpose'
                 novels on the matter appeared. ¶ "You have hardly an idea

how poor and feeble the book seems to me, as executed, beside the idea of it that I had formed in prospect. ¶ "I have received some interesting letters about it already—yours not the least so. Swinburne writes, too enthusiastically for me to quote with modesty. ¶ "Believe me, with sincere thanks for your review, ¶ "Ever yours, ¶ "Thomas Hardy. ¶ "*P. S.* One thing I did not answer. The 'grimy' features of the story go to show the contrast between the ideal life a man wished to lead, and the squalid real life he was fated to lead. The throwing of the pizzle, at the supreme moment of his young dream, is to sharply initiate this contrast. But I must have lamentably failed, as I feel I have, if this requires explanation and is not self-evident. The idea was meant to run all through the novel. It is, in fact, to be discovered in *everybody's* life, though it lies less on the surface perhaps than it does in my poor puppet's. ¶ "T. H." ¶LETTER II. ¶ "Max Gate, ¶"Dorchester, ¶ "*November 20th,* 1895. ¶ "I am keen about the new magazine. How interesting that you should be writing this review for it! I wish the book were more worthy of such notice and place. ¶ "You are quite right; there is nothing perverted or depraved in Sue's nature. The abnormalism consists in disproportion, not in inversion, her sexual instinct being healthy as far as it goes, but unusually weak and fastidious. Her sensibilities remain painfully alert notwithstanding, as they do in nature with such women. One point illustrating this I could not dwell upon: that, though she has children, her intimacies with Jude have never been more than occasional, even when they were living together (I mention that they occupy separate rooms, except towards the end), and one of her reasons for fearing the marriage ceremony is that she fears it would be breaking faith with Jude to withhold herself at pleasure, or altogether, after it; though while uncontracted she feels at liberty to yield herself as seldom as she chooses. This has tended to keep his passion as hot at the end as at the beginning, and helps to break his heart. He has never really possessed her as freely as he desired. ¶ "Sue is a type of woman which has always had an attraction for me, but the difficulty of drawing the type has kept me from attempting it till now. ¶ "Of course the book is all contrasts—or was meant to be in its original conception. Alas, what a miserable accomplishment it is, when I compare it with what I meant to make it!—*e.g.* Sue and her heathen gods set against Jude's reading the Greek testament; Christminster academical, Christminster in the slums; Jude the saint, Jude the sinner; Sue the Pagan, Sue the saint; marriage, no marriage; &c., &c. ¶ "As to the 'coarse' scenes with Arabella, the battle in the schoolroom, etc., the newspaper critics might, I thought, have sneered at them for their Fieldingism rather than for their Zolaism. But your everyday critic knows nothing of Fielding. I am read in Zola very little, but have felt akin locally to

Fielding, so many of his scenes having been laid down this way, and his home near. ¶ "Did I tell you I feared I should seem too High-Churchy at the end of the book where Sue recants? You can imagine my surprise at some of the reviews. ¶ "What a self-occupied letter! ¶ "Ever sincerely, ¶ "T.H." ¶ LETTER III. ¶ "Max Gate, ¶ "Dorchester, ¶ "*January* 4, 1896. ¶ "For the last three days I have been tantalized by a difficulty in getting *Cosmopolis*, and had only just read your review when I received your note. My sincere thanks for the generous view you take of the book, which to me is a mass of imperfections. We have both been amused—or rather delighted—by the sub-humour (is there such a word?) of your writing. I think it a rare quality in living essayists, and that you ought to make more of it—I mean write more in that vein than you do. ¶ "But this is apart from the review itself, of which I will talk to you when we meet. The rectangular lines of the story were not premeditated, but came by chance: except, of course, that the involutions of four lives must necessarily be a sort of quadrille. The only point in the novel on which I feel sure is that it makes for morality; and that delicacy or indelicacy in a writer is according to his object. If I say to a lady 'I met a naked woman', it is indelicate. If I go on to say 'I found she was mad with sorrow', it ceases to be indelicate. And in writing Jude my mind was fixed on the ending. ¶ "Sincerely yours, ¶ "T.H." ¶ In London

289:20–2	they met . . . and went] they went
290:17–26	"The dear . . . will be!"] *absent*
292:20–293:23	consequence; meeting . . . be seen.] consequence.
295:14–23	own—that . . . another! ¶ Possibly] own.[1] ¶ Possibly
295:29	conversation on the amusing subject of the bishop's doings, to] conversation to
[295:fn]	*absent*] [1] That the opinions thus expressed by Bishop How in 1895 are not now shared by all the clergy may be gathered from the following extract from an article in *Theology*, August 1928: ¶ "If I were asked to advise a priest preparing to become a *village* rector I would suggest first that he should make a good retreat . . . and then that he should make a careful study of Thomas Hardy's novels. . . . From Thomas Hardy he would learn the essential dignity of country people and what deep and often passionate interest belongs to every individual life. You cannot treat them in the mass: each single soul is to be the object of your special and peculiar prayer." ¶ The author of this article is an eminent clergyman of the Church of England.
298:1–2	She evidently . . . letter.] *absent*
*298:14–15	More teas . . . took] Various social events took
298:21–2	friends Lady Queensberry and the] friends, the
299:11–14	where Mrs Hardy, . . . *King*] where Hardy read *King*
299:30–1	[The meaning of this does not seem quite clear.]] *absent*
299:32–3	fortnight . . . cold, they] fortnight they
303:22–38	later. The amazing . . . not answer] later. Certain critics

affected to find unmentionable moral atrocities in its pages, but
Hardy did not answer

*304 : 23   review so.]   review so—a thing terrible to think of."
310 : 8–10   sort; and . . . available. But]   sort. But
310 : 21–3   stay, during . . . Stewart, they]   stay they
310 : 33–4   London and no invitation to any Jubilee function.]   London.
311 : 19   of a greater Queen, the]   of the
*313 : 25–6   He used . . . illness.]   *absent*
313 : 40–314 : 1   Again in . . . expressed]   Again in London in July he
                   expressed
*315 : 5–7   After . . . seen: ¶ "The]   After revisiting Stonehenge he
                   remarks: ¶"The
315 : 9–14   "I see . . . bishop."]   *absent*
315 : 31–316 : 5   On August 21 . . . Gate.]   *absent*
316 : 11–13   idea, . . . offered.]   idea.
*316 : 40–317 : 3 It may . . . sure!"]   *absent*
317 : 21–3   He went . . . and followed]   He also followed
*317 : 32–6   Luzzi." ¶ At . . . died. ¶ Back]   Luzzi." ¶ On June 24th,
                   declining to write an Introduction to a proposed Library
                   Edition of Fielding's novels, he remarks: ¶ "Fielding as a local
                   novelist has never been clearly regarded, to my mind: and his
                   aristocratic, even feudal, attitude towards the peasantry (*e.g.*
                   his view of Molly as a 'slut' to be ridiculed, not as a simple girl,
                   as worthy a creation of Nature as the lovely Sophia) should be
                   exhibited strongly. But the writer could not well be a working
                   novelist without his bringing upon himself a charge of
                   invidiousness." ¶ Back
317 : 37   went upon that useful wheel to Bristol]   went to Bristol
319 : 18–24   That his reviewers . . . exceptions.]   *absent*
320 : 6–25   But there . . . their insight.]   *absent*
321 : 14–322 : 12 He amused . . . nearly by all.]   *absent*
322 : 25–33   A point . . . royal road.]   *absent*
322 : 40–323 : 5   One smart . . . under review.]   *absent*
323 : 27–8   greeted by . . . a jocular]   greeted with a would-be jocular
323 : 29–31   immortality", . . . kind. The same]   immortality". The same
324 : 5   heroics, having probably never heard of the other
                   measure.]   heroics.
324 : 16–30   He could . . . the remark.]   *absent*
*324 : 32   was in general placed]   was sometimes placed
*324 : 33–4   reviewers . . . that]   reviewers deficient in that
*325 : 8–11   contain—mainly . . . offered]   contain. He offered
326 : 3–5   his impracticable . . . and on]   his unpractical tender-
                   heartedness, and on
326 : 5–6   agreement from those who saw eye to eye with him.]
                   agreement.
327 : 22–5   The last . . . Harcourt.]   *absent*
328 : 35–40   Row, whose . . . he possibly]   Row. He possibly
328 : 41–329 : 1   sacrificed so much of his yearly income]   sacrificed the chance
                   of making a much larger income

330:21-4   During the . . . December.] *absent*
331:22-332:3   On May 22 . . . in Persia.] *absent*
332:4   On his return to London Hardy]   A few days later Hardy
*332:22-3   picturesque part. ¶ In a letter]   picturesque part. ¶Thomas
                Hardy's mother, now in her eighty-eighth year, was greatly
                interested to hear of this visit of the Club to the home of her son.
                Her devoted daughters, Mary and Katherine, promised to take
                her in her wheeled chair, for she was no longer able to walk
                abroad as formerly, to see the carriages drive past the end of a
                lane leading from Higher Bockhampton to the foot of
                Yellowham Hill, some three miles from Max Gate. ¶On the
                day appointed, the chair, its two attendants, and its occupant,
                a little bright-eyed lady in a shady hat, waited under some trees
                bordering the roadside for the members of the Whitefriars Club
                to pass. ¶Mrs. Hardy had announced gaily that she intended
                to wave her handkerchief to the travellers, but her more sedate
                daughters urged that this was not to be done. However, as soon
                as the dusty vehicles had whirled past the old lady pulled out a
                handkerchief which she had concealed under the rug covering
                her knees, and waved it triumphantly at the disappearing
                party. So unquenchable was her gay and youthful spirit even
                when approaching her ninetieth year. ¶Long afterwards one
                member of the visiting party said to the present writer: "If we
                had known who that was, what cheers there would have been,
                what waving of handkerchiefs, what a greeting for Thomas
                Hardy's mother!" ¶ In a letter
333:24   *Dynasts* and which reviewers in general passed over in silence,
                found] *Dynasts* found
334:14-17   In London . . . Ilchester.] *absent*
335:4-5   1830. ¶To]   1830. Hardy considered this, upon the whole, his
                most successful poem. ¶ To
341:3-6   In January . . . continuously.] *absent*
*342:23   MDCCCIII.]   MDCCCIII. ¶In drawing up this inscription
                Hardy was guided by his belief that the English language was
                liable to undergo great alterations in the future, whereas Latin
                would remain unchanged.
343:6-11   else, the . . . The appraisement]   else, a large number of
                critics were too puzzled by it to be unprejudiced. The
                appraisement
343:25   an invidious reception]   an unfavourable reception
344:2-5   This, . . . the best.] *absent*
*344:35-6   brows." His mind]   brows." ¶Writing to his friend Edward
                Clodd on March 22, he says: ¶ "I did not quite think that the
                Dynasts would suit your scientific mind, or shall I say the
                scientific side of your mind, so that I am much pleased to hear
                that you have got pleasure out of it. ¶ "As to my having said
                nothing or little (I think I did just allude to it a long while ago)
                about having it in hand, the explanation is simple enough—I
                did not mean to publish Part I. by itself until after a quite few

days before I sent it up to the publishers: and to be engaged in a desultory way on a MS. which may be finished in five years (the date at which I thought I might print it, complete) does not lead one to say much about it. On my return here from London I had a sudden feeling that I should never carry the thing any further, so off it went. But now I am better inclined to go on with it. Though I rather wish I had kept back the parts till the whole could be launched, as I at first intended. ¶ "What you say about the 'Will' is true enough, if you take the word in its ordinary sense. But in the lack of another word to express precisely what is meant, a secondary sense has gradually arisen, that of effort exercised in a reflex or unconscious manner. Another word would have been better if one could have had it, though 'Power' would not do, as power can be suspended or withheld, and the forces of Nature cannot: However, there are inconsistences in the Phantoms, no doubt. But that was a point to which I was somewhat indifferent, since they are not supposed to be more than the best human intelligences of their time in a sort of quint-essential form. I speak of the 'Years'. The 'Pities' are, of course, merely Humanity, with all its weaknesses. ¶ "You speak of Meredith. I am sorry to learn that he has been so seriously ill. Leslie Stephen gone too. They are thinning out ahead of us. I have just lost an old friend down here, of forty-seven years' standing. A man whose opinions differed almost entirely from my own on most subjects, and yet he was a good and sincere friend—the brother of the present Bishop of Durham, and like him in old-fashioned views of the Evangelical school." ¶His mind

345:33–7	The only . . . other friends.] *absent*
347:7–8	Velasquez, which were just then so much lauded.] Velasquez.
348:13–14	August, and whose sister was Mrs Hardy's aunt by marriage.] August
* 348:38	the last part of] the third movement of
349:7–15	"May 6. . . . Gurdon, &c."] *absent*
350:4	incident.)] incident.[1])
[* 350:fn]	*absent*] [1]See *The Early Life of Thomas Hardy*, p. 177.
351:6	for the *Daily Mail*.] for a popular morning paper.
351:38	say.] say.[1]
[351:fn]	*absent*] [1]Since writing the above I have received from a correspondent what seems to me indubitable proof of the connection of these two branches of the Hardy family.— F.E.H.
354:9–13	Hardy makes . . . everywhere."] *absent*
355:3–7	usual—among . . . times—and went] usual, and went
355:13–14	the dining-room of the Arch-Deaconry of Westminster, with Dr Wilberforce. It] the vaulted dining-room of the house in Dean's Yard then occupied by Dr. Wilberforce as Archdeacon of Westminster. It

359 : 21–3   far embittered . . . as not] far influenced by the reception of the first two parts as not

360 : 1–3   Barrie, . . . Noble, and] Barrie, M. and Madame Jacques Blanche, and

361 : 39   attended as the guest of Dr Macdonald a dinner] attended a dinner

362 : 6–16   To a Japanese . . . shining example.] *absent*

362 : 20–1   Barbadoes—where a connection of Hardy's had been a judge—a degenerate] Barbados, a degenerate

368 : 28–32   house-party, . . . Raleigh, went] house-party went

369 : 9–13   This month . . . Dr Gow.] *absent*.

369 : 14–15   where he . . . he met] where he met

369 : 16   Smith, the long House-master] Smith, long a house-master

369 : 28–30   cathedrals, . . . weeks, a visit] cathedrals and a visit

369 : 31–2   air, . . . Coleridge, and] air; and

369 : 34   Mr S. Butcher] Mr. S. H. Butcher

370 : 28   Dorchester (*vide ante*), and] Dorchester,[1] and

[* 370 : fn]   *absent*] [1] See *The Early Life of Thomas Hardy*, p. 6.

372 : 28–30   After . . . judgment."] *absent*

374 : 19–21   But the fact . . . independence.] *absent*

* 375 : 2   by the dramatist] by Mr. A. H. Evans the dramatist

* 375 : 4   Exchange.] Exchange, and a few days later before the Society of Dorset Men in London.

* 376 : 6–14   Asleep". He . . . bidder." ¶To] Asleep". It is remembered by a friend who accompanied him on this expedition how that windy March day had a poetry of its own, how primroses clustered in the hedges, and noisy rooks wheeled in the air over the little churchyard. Hardy gathered a spray of ivy and laid it on the grave of that brother-poet of whom he never spoke save in words of admiration and affection. ¶"*To*

* 377 : 33–4   just died. ¶At the] just died. ¶There was general satisfaction when Hardy's name appeared as a recipient of the Order of Merit in the Birthday List of Honours in June 1910. He received numerous and gratifying telegrams and letters of congratulation from both friends and strangers, and, though he accepted the award with characteristic quietude, it was evident that this sign of official approval of his work brought him pleasure. . ¶At the

377 : 38–378 : 1   illness, including . . . was] illness, which was

378 : 7–12   Gate during . . . earlier.] Gate.

381 : 26   in a well-known review] in the *Fortnightly Review*

381 : 34–9   However . . . the age.] *absent*

382 : 13–23   America, and . . . himself.] America.

382 : 26–7   Hereford; he . . . Academy.] Hereford.

383 : 1–2   spring, which is not very intelligible: "View] spring: "View

* 383 : 5   tour in the] tour with his brother in the

383 : 24–5   In July Mrs . . . took] In July Hardy took

383 : 31–4   A garden-party . . . Vice-Presidents.] *absent*

385 : 13–14   Henniker, . . . girlhood; and] Henniker, and

*385:17–18   sufferers. ¶They dined] sufferers. ¶On the 22nd April Hardy was correcting proofs for a new edition of his works, the Wessex Edition, concerning which he wrote to a friend: ¶" . . . I am now on to p. 140 of *The Woodlanders* (in *copy* I mean, not in proofs, of course). That is vol. vi. Some of the later ones will be shorter. I read ten hours yesterday—finishing the *proofs* of the *Native* (wh. I have thus got rid of). I got to like the character of Clym before I had done with him. I think he is the nicest of all my heroes, and *not a bit* like me. On taking up *The Woodlanders* and reading it after many years I think I like it, *as a story*, the best of all. Perhaps that is owing to the locality and scenery of the action, a part I am very fond of. It seems a more quaint and fresh story than the *Native*, and the characters are very distinctly drawn. . . . Seven o'clock P.M. It has come on to rain a little: a blackbird is singing outside. I have read on to p. 185 of *The Woodlanders* since the early part of my letter." ¶The Hardys dined

385:32–5   with her and . . . Stuart).] with her.
386:3–7   He was . . . publishers.] *absent*
387:9–10   state, . . . the strain] state, she did go down. The strain
388:13–14   mind—perhaps dictated by the heart-pains to which she was subject—that] mind that
389:15–17   It very . . . years.] *absent*
390:15   of entering the church.] of taking Orders.
*392:5–18   present writer, who . . . Yolland, R. N.] present writer.
*392:19–23   Hardy was . . . to Cambridge,] In the spring of the same year Hardy was at the dinner of the Royal Academy, and he and his wife saw several friends in London, afterwards proceeding to Cambridge,
392:38–40   Dartmoor—all . . . himself.] Dartmoor.
393:6–11   His wife . . . to an end.] *absent*
393:30–1   visited their friends the Lord Lieutenant and Mrs Mount-Batten, and] visited various friends and
393:33   the latter] the former
393:39–40   with their friends the Brymers at] with friends at
394:3–4   Hall with Mr de Lafontaine six] Hall, six
396:23–30   pages. But . . . were caustically] pages. These were caustically
396:31–4   Nevertheless, . . . founded.] *absent*
396:39–397:1   do it. So, . . . contained] do it. The "Lyrics and Reveries", which filled the far greater part of the volume, contained
397:2–6   The effect . . . deeper tones.] *absent*
397:27–8   better. ¶However] better. But the theatre's resources of space were very limited. However,
397:28–37   The critics, . . . a war.] *absent*
398:1   that so mad and brutal a war] that the war
401:30–1   Their . . . later.] *absent*
403:38–9   Launceston to . . . Mrs Hardy.] Launceston.

403 : 41   tablet to her memory in]   tablet in
405 : 4–6   Societies, . . . Fox-Strangways.]   Societies.
405 : 34   Sienkiewich]   Sienkiewicz
406 : 25–8   One writer's . . . writings.]   *absent*
407 : 18–19   his wife's . . . his friends]   his friends
407 : 28–9   long after." ¶ In July]   long after."   ¶ Later in the month
                his friend J. M. Barrie suggested that Hardy should go with
                him to France, to which proposal Hardy replied: ¶ "MAX
                GATE, DORCHESTER, ¶ "23 *June* 1917. ¶ "MY DEAR BARRIE, ¶
                "It was so kind of you to concoct that scheme for my
                accompanying you to the Front—or Back—in France. I
                thought it over carefully, as it was an attractive idea. But I have
                had to come to the conclusion that old men cannot be young
                men, and that I must content myself with the past battles of our
                country if I want to feel military. If I had been ten years
                younger I would have gone. ¶ "I hope you will have a
                pleasant, or rather, impressive, time, and the good company
                you will be in will be helpful all round. I am living in hope of
                seeing you on the date my wife has fixed and of renewing
                acquaintance with my old friend Adelphi Terrace. ¶ "Always
                sincerely yours, ¶ "THOMAS HARDY." ¶ In July
* 407 : 34   other writers. He came]   other writers. Upon one memorable
                evening they sat in a large empty room, which was afterwards
                to be Sir James's study but was then being altered and
                decorated. From the windows they had a fine view over the
                Thames, and searchlights wheeled across the sky. The only
                illumination within the room was from candles placed on the
                floor to avoid breaking war regulations, which forbade too
                bright lighting. ¶ He came
413 : 5   January 2 Mrs Hardy and himself attended]   January 2
                Hardy attended
* 413 : 14–15   Gate, and was warmly attached to both Emma and
                Florence."]   Gate, and she remained staunch to the end of her
                days."
414 : 6–7   *Trachiniae*: 'The Vast injustice of the gods is borne in upon
                me!'"]   *Trachiniae*: 'Mark the vast injustice of the gods!' "
414 : 13–20   Probably . . . Victorian skirt!]   *absent*
414 : fn2   Soph. *Trach.* 1265.]   Sophocles' *Trachiniae*, 1266.
415 : 1   Paid for]   Arranged for
415 : 26–31   It may . . . motives.]   *absent*
416 : 5–7   In April . . . month there]   In April there
417 : 2–3   week, and was followed by "a bilious attack".]   week.
417 : 10   Mr and Mrs]   Mr. H. M. and Mrs.
418 : 2–3   Letters, Visits, Poetical Questions,]   POETICAL
                QUESTIONS:
418 : 7–419 : 7 To Rendel . . . may mature.]   *absent*
419 : 20–31   To W.M. . . . two years.]   *absent*
* 420 : 4–6   hundreds of thousands of aeroplanes, not with hundreds but

with thousands of submarines] hundreds of thousands of submarines

420 : 16–20 Hardy also . . . Lyonnesse".] *absent*

420 : 28–421 : 7 She wrote . . . apprehend it.] *absent*

* 421 : 22–3 the war—and was] the war—with his friend J. M. Barrie, with whom he was then staying, and was

* 421 : 25 again.] again, and, indeed, he never did.

* 422 : 13–14 its object. ¶ Shortly after] its object." ¶ Replying to a birthday letter from Mrs. Arthur Henniker, Hardy writes: ¶ "Max Gate, 5 *June* 1919. ¶ "Sincere thanks for your good wishes, my dear friend, which I echo back towards you. I should care more for my birthdays if at each succeeding one I could see any sign of real improvement in the world—as at one time I fondly hoped there was; but I fear that what appears much more evident is that it is getting worse and worse. All development is of a material and scientific kind—and scarcely any addition to our knowledge is applied to objects philanthropic and ameliorative. I almost think that people were less pitiless towards their fellow-creatures—human and animal—under the Roman Empire than they are now; so why does not Christianity throw up the sponge and say, I am beaten, and let another religion take its place? ¶ "I suddenly remember that we had a call from our Bishop and his wife two or three days ago, so that perhaps it is rather shabby of me to write as above. By a curious coincidence we had motored to Salisbury that very day, and were in his cathedral when he was at our house. ¶ "Do you mean to go to London for any length of time this summer? We are not going again till I don't know when. We squeezed a good deal into the four days we were there, and I got a bad throat as usual, but it has gone off. At Lady St. Helier's we met the Archbishop of Dublin (English Church), and found him a pleasant man. We also met several young poets at Barrie's, where we were staying. ¶ "We do hope you are well—in 'rude health' as they call it. Florence sends her love, and I am, ¶ "Ever affectionately, ¶ "Th. H." ¶ Shortly after

* 422 : 23–4 of poetry. ¶ It had] of poetry. ¶ This "Poets' Tribute" had been arranged by his friend Siegfried Sassoon, who brought the gift and placed it in Hardy's hand. ¶ It had

* 423 : 3–4 no harm ¶ 29 June 1919.] no harm. ¶ Hardy's loyalty to his friends was shown by his devotion to the Moule family, members of which he had known intimately when he was a young man. The following is probably the last letter he wrote to one whom he could remember as a small boy: ¶ "29 *June* 1919.

423 : 34–424 : 14 To W. J. Malden . . . by the Society.] *absent*

425 : 19–20 started by idle pressmen some] started some

* 425 : 29–36 On the . . . shortly after.] *absent*

427 : 27 danced—probably the] danced, for the

427 : 28	manor, Mrs Cecil Hanbury.] manor.
427 : 31–5	Penny's". ¶ The short . . . newspaper: ¶ "I feel] Penny's".
	¶ A speech made by Hardy at the opening of the Bockhampton Reading-room and Club on the 2nd December 1919 was not reported in any newspaper, but the following extracts from it may be of interest: ¶ "I feel
428 : 15	the Premier, who came, as we all know, of a Dorset family.] the Premier.
428 : 22	stood between General Balguy's house and the withy] stood by the withy
429 : 8–13	"But though . . . thing is.] *absent*
429 : 16–27	December 26. . . . is offered.] *absent*
* 430 : 7–28	To an unnamed . . . forget it.] *absent*
431 : 10–432 : 2	To the Secretary . . . daughters only.] *absent*
432 : 12–13	with the Giffords at Arlington House, they] with friends, they
* 432 : 13–14	received, his wife] received. ¶ In presenting Hardy, the Public Orator, Mr. A. D. Godley, made one of the most felicitous of his many excellent speeches. He said: "Scilicet ut Virgilio nostro sic huic quoque 'molle atque facetum adnuerunt gaudentes rure Camenae'. Hic est, qui divini gloriam ruris sicut nemo alius nostrorum idylliis suis intertexuit: hic est, qui agricolarum sensus et colloquia ita vivide verbis effinxit ut videre rusticos consessus, ut ipsos inter se sermocinantes, cum legimus, audire videamur. Obruit multos cita oblivio qui in rebus transitoriis versantur: qui insitos animorum sensus et naturae humanae immutabilitatem exprimit, cuius scripta aeternam silvarum et camporum amoenitatem spirant, hunc diu vivum per ora virum volitaturum esse praedicimus. Quid quod idem in poesi quoque eo evasit ut hoc solo scribendi genere, nisi fabularum narratio vel magis suum aliquid et proprium habeat, immortalem famam assequi possit?"[1] ¶ And then, after a reference to the production that evening by the O.U.D.S. of *The Dynasts*—"opus eius tam scriptoris facundia quam rerum quae tractantur magnitudine insignitum"[2]—he concluded: ¶ "Nunc ut homini si quis alius Musis et dis agrestibus amico titulum debitum dando, non tantum illi quantum nobis ipsis decus addatis, duco ad vos senem illustrem Thomam Hardy. . . . "[3] ¶ His wife,
[432:fn]	*absent*] [1] "Surely as with Virgil, so with him, have the Muses that rejoice in the countryside approved his smoothness and elegance. This is he who has interwoven in his (pastoral) poems, as no other has done, the (heavenly) glory of the (heavenly) countryside: this is he who has portrayed in words the feelings and conversations of rustics so clearly that when we read of them we seem to picture their meetings and hear them discoursing one with another. Speedy forgetfulness overwhelms many who treat of life's fleeting things, but of him who unfolds the inborn feelings of man's soul and the unchangeableness of his nature, whose writings breathe the eternal charm

of (the) woods and fields, we foretell that his living fame shall long hover on the lips of men. ¶ "Why now, is not the excellence of his poems such that, by this type of writing alone, he can achieve immortal fame, even if the narration of his stories has not something about them more peculiarly his own?" ¶² "His work marked not only by the eloquence of the author, but by the magnitude of the events which he describes." ¶³ "Now that you may confer distinction, not so much on him as on our own selves, by granting a deserved title to one who is a friend of the Muses and pastoral gods, I present to you the revered and renowned Thomas Hardy."

432:23–7   kind, and . . . available. ¶ To Mr Joseph] kind. ¶ AN ACCOUNT OF THOMAS HARDY'S COMING TO OXFORD in 1920 to witness a performance of *The Dynasts* by the Oxford University Dramatic Society, and of a later meeting with him in Dorchester when *A Desperate Remedy* was produced there: written in 1929, at Mrs. Hardy's request, by Charles Morgan, who in 1920 was Manager for the O.U.D.S., in 1921 its President, and afterwards dramatic critic of *The Times*. ¶ When the University reassembled after the war, the Oxford University Dramatic Society was in low water. The tradition was broken, the surviving membership was not more than half a dozen, and the treasury was empty. During 1919 new members joined and life began to flicker in the Society, but its future largely depended upon the success or failure of the first annual play in the new series. ¶ An undergraduate was instructed to consider, during the long vacation of 1919, what play should be performed and to report to the Committee. His choice was *The Dynasts*, and he had to defend it against those who objected that it was not Shakespearian and that Shakespeare was a tradition of the Society: and against those more dangerous critics who said that *The Dynasts* would be costly, and, pointing to the balance-sheet, asked whence the money would come. The financial objection was at last overcome by personal guarantees. ¶ The Committee endorsed the choice, and the Vice-Chancellor, whose special consent was needed for the performance of so modern a work, allowed it. The arguments in its favour were, indeed, unanswerable. ¶ *The Dynasts* was unique in literature, an epic-drama without predecessor in its own kind. Its writer was a living Englishman: its subject was closely linked with the tragedy in which nearly all the players had lately participated: and, except for those who had seen Granville-Barker's production, it would be a new theatrical experience. ¶ One difficulty remained: the play was copyright, and it seemed to us very probable that Hardy would refuse permission to perform it. He is an old man, we said, and set fast in Dorset; he will not give a fig for what he will call amateur theatricals, nor will he be troubled with our affairs. It was the impression of us all that he would be forbidding and formidable, and he was approached with misgiving. He gave his play to us, not grudgingly nor with any air of patronage, but with so gracious a courtesy that we were made to feel that he was genuinely pleased to find young men eager to perform his work. I do not remember the text of his reply to the original request, but I remember well the impression made by it—an impression increased by his later correspondence. Long before he came to Oxford his individuality had become established among us. Without whittling away his legend by any of the affectations of modesty, he had, by his gentle plainness, banished our fear of it. ¶ Even so, when we invited him and Mrs. Hardy to come to Oxford to see the play, we had little hope that he would accept, for our ideas had overestimated his age—or, rather, underestimated the vigour of it—and his withdrawal into Wessex was believed to be permanent. But he said he would come, and Sir Walter Raleigh invited him to be his guest. So soon as it was known that he would visit Oxford, everyone perceived what hitherto few had been able to perceive—that, in withholding her highest honour from the author of *The Dynasts* and *The Return of the Native* (perhaps, whispered Cambridge and the world, because he was also the author of *Jude the Obscure*), Christminster was making herself ridiculous. A D.C.L. was offered him. Authority must have sighed with relief when he did not refuse. ¶ It fell to me to meet him at the station. I give my impression of him then and afterwards, not because it is of value as being mine, but for two reasons—first, that Mrs. Hardy has asked it; secondly, that I should dearly love to see some great writer of the past as a contemporary undergraduate saw him. In days to come, even so slight a record as this may have an interest that it cannot now possess. ¶ Hardy made it easy for a young man to be his host— made it easy, not by any loose affability of manner or by a parade of that heartiness which, in too many celebrated men, is a form of patronage, but simply by making no attempt whatever to impress or to startle me. I had not expected cleverness or volubility in him; and his speech was, at first, slight and pleasantly conventional. He introduced me to Mrs. Hardy, asked how long the drive would be to Sir Walter's, used, in brief, the small talk of encounter, giving me time to become accustomed to his presence and to break free of the thought: I must remember this; I shall remember and tell of it when I am an old man. He himself seemed to me prodigiously old, not because there was any failure in his powers—he was, on the contrary, sprightly, alert, bird-like—but because his head had an appearance of being much older than his body, his neck having the thinness and his brow the tightness of great age, and his eyes—so old that age itself seemed to have swung full circle within them—being the eyes of some still young man who had been keeping watch at sea since the beginning of time. I remember that, sitting opposite him in the cab, I began to think of the sea and to imagine his head appearing above the bridge-ladder of a warship. Then I thought of a bird again, a small bird with a great head. And I made another discovery that pleased me: in external things he was deeply old-fashioned, and, fearing perhaps some assertive, new-fangled conduct in an undergraduate, timid and a little suspicious. I knew at once that I had nothing to fear from an old gentleman who by no means wished to pretend that he was young, and would never embarrass me by forsaking those little formalities of ordinary behaviour to which I myself had been trained. ¶ Thus, because he made no attempt to break it, the ice melted easily and naturally. He asked of the play, saying that it had not been intended for the stage and that he wondered at our having chosen it. ¶ Then, breaking off from this and reminded, I think by Mrs. Hardy, he said: "We thought we should like to make a little tour of Oxford before going out to the Raleighs'. I don't know it well as it is to-day, and Mrs. Hardy knows it less." He knew it, however, well enough to have planned a route with precision. We drove slowly, stopping now and then when he commanded it, and of each place he spoke in a different tone as if some mood were connected with it. *Jude* was, of course, the inevitable thought of one who had read that book in a midshipman's hammock when to him also Oxford was a beckoning dream. It seemed very strange to be driving solemnly down the High and up the Broad with the author of *Jude*. It seemed strange because, after all, it was so natural. Here was an old man taking a normal and reasonable interest in the place where he was—quietly "seeing the sights" in the fashion of his own time and without the self-consciousness of ours. ¶ But when we are undergraduates we expect writers to be literary men in all things; we cannot easily dissociate them from their works; and it seemed to me very odd that Thomas Hardy should bother about the Martyrs' Memorial. ¶ When the tour was over, we went forward towards our destination. Hardy began to ask me about the age of undergraduates, and what effect the war had had upon us. I told him that my own war service delivered me from one examination and from compulsory chapels. "Compulsory chapels . . . " said Hardy, and no more; then, opening a little case on the seat beside him and producing from it a handful of small volumes, he asked me if I knew what they were. "Poems", he said, "written by young men. They very kindly send them to me." Very kindly—was there irony in that? But Hardy, reading my thought, dismissed it. He left no doubt that he was glad to have these volumes sent to him, seeing in them a tribute to himself as a poet, not a novelist—and he cared deeply for that. And from this there came to me an opportunity to ask a question that I had been afraid to ask: whether he would ever write another tale? "No," he answered, "I gave it up long ago. I wanted to write poetry in the beginning; now I can. Besides, it is so long since I wrote a novel that novel readers must have forgotten me." And, when I had said something, he added: "No. Much depends on the public expectation. If I wrote a story now, they would want it to be what the old ones were. Besides, my stories are written."

¶ I have no recollection of any conversation after that, nor any picture of Hardy in my mind until, going to Dorchester in 1922 to see the Hardy Players perform a dramatization of *Desperate Remedies*, I was invited by him to Max Gate, where we sat round the fire after tea and he told me of his early days in London, and how he would go to Shakespearian plays with the text in his hands and, seated in the front row, follow the dialogue by the stage light. He told me, too, that he had written a stage version of *Tess*, and something of its early history; how, after the success of the novel, the great ones of the earth had pressed him to dramatize it; how he had done so, and the play had been prepared for the stage; by what mischance the performance of it had been prevented. Where was it now? ¶ In a drawer. Would he allow it to be performed? He smiled, gave no answer, and began at once to talk of criticism—first of dramatic criticism which, he said, in the few newspapers that took it seriously was better than literary criticism, the dramatic critics having less time "to rehearse their prejudices"; then of literary criticism itself—a subject on which he spoke with a bitterness that surprised me. The origin of this bitterness was in the past where, I believe, there was indeed good reason for it, but it was directed now against contemporary critics of his own work, and I could not understand what general reason he had to complain of them. He used no names; he spoke with studied reserve, sadly rather than querulously; but he was persuaded—and there is evidence of this persuasion in the preface to the posthumous volume of his verse—that critics approached his work with an ignorant prejudice against his "pessimism" which they allowed to stand in the way of fair reading and fair judgement. ¶ This was a distortion of facts as I knew them. It was hard to believe that Hardy honestly thought that his genius was not recognized; harder to believe that he thought his work was not read. Such a belief indicated the only failure of balance, the only refusal to seek the truth, which I perceived in Hardy, and I was glad when the coming of a visitor, who was, I think, secretary of the Society of Dorset Men, led him away from criticism to plainer subjects. When the time came for me to go, seeing that he proposed to come out with me, I tried to restrain him, for the night was cold; but he was determined, and Mrs. Hardy followed her own wise course of matching her judgement with his vitality. So he came down among the trees to the dark road, and I saw the last of him standing outside his gate with a lantern swaying in his hand. I shall not know a

greater man, nor have I ever known one who had, in the same
degree, Hardy's power of drawing reverence towards affection.
¶ He was not simple; he had the formal subtlety peculiar to his
own generation; there was something deliberately "ordinary"
in his demeanour which was a concealment of extraordinary
fires—a method of self-protection common enough in my
grandfather's generation, though rare now. ¶ There are many
who might have thought him unimpressive because he was
content to be serious and determined to be unspectacular. But
his was the kind of character to which I lay open. He was an
artist, proud of his art, who yet made no parade of it; he was a
traditionalist and, therefore, suspicious of fashion; he had that
sort of melancholy, the absence of which in any man has always
seemed to me to be a proclamation of blindness. ¶ There was
in him something timid as well as something fierce, as if the
world had hurt him and he expected it to hurt him again. But
what fascinated me above all was the contrast between the
plainness, the quiet rigidity of his behaviour, and the
passionate boldness of his mind, for this I had always believed
to be the tradition of English genius, too often and too
extravagantly denied. ¶ *To Mr. Joseph*

433:7–14   F. E. Hardy. ¶ To Mr John . . . you! ¶ As to] "F. E.
HARDY." ¶ On March 7, 1920, Hardy writes to an old friend
of nearly fifty years' standing, Mr. John Slater, F.R.I.B.A.: ¶
" . . . As to

433:21–7   But if you . . . very year.]]   *absent*
*434:10–11   Duke?' " ¶ "May 14.]   Duke?' ¶ This was Hardy's last visit
to London. He, with his wife, stayed for two nights only at J. M.
Barrie's flat, so near the house in Adelphi Terrace where he had
worked as an architect's assistant nearly sixty years before. ¶
"*May* 14.

435:38–436:8   The aforesaid . . . published.]   *absent*
436:26–30   July 28 . . . my age."]   *absent*
*437:13–19   From Mr A— . . . A—M—]   *absent*
437:20–1   Gifford daughter of Em's uncle, at]   Gifford at
*437:26   Supplement, and on the 13th]   Supplement. ¶ The request to
write this poem had been brought to him from London by one
of the editorial staff. At first Hardy was disinclined, and all but
refused, being generally unable to write to order. In the middle
of the night, however, an idea seized him, and he was heard
moving about the house looking things up. The poem was duly
written and proved worthy of the occasion. ¶ On the 13th

437:29   "A much better play than I expected.]   "More interested
than I expected to be.

437:30   at Bockhampton]   at Higher Bockhampton
437:30–438:5   childhood, and . . . may be]   childhood." ¶ In declining to
become a Vice-President of a well-known Society, Hardy
writes: ¶ "I may be

438:9–10   supplanted. ¶ To Mr Alfred]   supplanted." ¶ Towards the end of the year Hardy was occupied with the following interesting correspondence: ¶ *To Mr. Alfred*

* 440 : 21–2   The pennyaliner who writes it comments] The writer comments

440 : 38–441 : 6   It may be . . . everywhere.]   *absent*

441 : 19–20   so many, . . . and is very]   so many, is very

[For the two concluding chapters, written by Florence Hardy, *Later Years* is itself copy-text]

Textual Notes

Entries marked †offer further discussion of changes already recorded in the table of Editorial Emendations; those marked * refer back to changes listed in the table of Selected Post-Hardyan Revisions. Other entries refer directly to the text of this edition and are specified not just by page and line-number(s) but also by cue-words. When there is genuine uncertainty as to whether a passage excluded from this edition was in fact cancelled during TH's lifetime the note will quote the doubtful passage in its entirety.

[* Dedication] The dedication to *EL* (not repeated in *LY*) was supplied in FEH's letter of 16 August 1928 to George Augustin Macmillan (British Library).

3 : 1–4 : 5 *Prefatory Note.* Bound into TS2 and clearly TH's work; there is one correction in TH's hand—the substitution of "record his recollections" (3 : 3–4) for "write his autobiographical recollections"—and he seems also to have inscribed his wife's initials at the end.

*8 : fn–9 : fn This footnote, inserted into TS2 on typed pages separately numbered, is obviously a late addition, and possibly post-Hardyan. The dates of the poem's composition were supplied by FEH in response to a query in JMB's letter of 21 June 1928 (typed transcript, DCM).

9 : 6 *said to descend.* Cancelled in TS2, almost certainly in TH's lifetime, is the reading, "said to be from that branch of these le Hardys who claimed to descend".

10 : 22–3 *Talbothays farm was a.* Cancelled in TS2, almost certainly in TH's lifetime, is the reading, "Talbothays farm had been sold to his father owing to its being, as it always had been, a".

10 : 23–4 *fence, its.* Cancelled in TS2, almost certainly in TH's lifetime, is the reading, "fence, awkwardly situated for its then owner, its".

17 : 31 *reverse, indeed.* Cancelled in TS2 at this point (clearly by TH) is a brief passage about the cost of entertaining the choir (see *PN*, 215).

* 19 : 18 JMB's letter of 26 March 1928 (DCM) urged FEH to transfer this passage from later in the book (see pp. 316–7) to the opening paragraph. This was attempted but abandoned, as red ink markings on the first page show, and the passage inserted

530

	here instead on a typed (double-spaced) slip affixed to the existing page.
20:23	*having disappeared.* Cancelled in TS2 at this point, almost certainly at TH's instigation, are the two additional words "catching butterflies".
20:37	*puzzled at.* Alteration to *EL* reading "puzzled by" suggested by JMB, letter of 24 June 1928 (typed transcript, DCM).
*22:17	Alteration suggested by JMB, letter of 24 June 1928.
22:28	*1849–1850.* ¶ *By.* Substituted in FEH's hand, and perhaps after TH's death, for the original TS2 reading "September 30th. 1850. ¶ After".
23:36	*further.* Alteration to *EL* reading "farther" suggested by JMB, letter of 24 June 1928.
*26:7–8	Alteration suggested by JMB, letter of 24 June 1928.
26:9	*needers.* JMB's objection to this word in his letter of 24 June 1928 was evidently overruled by FEH.
*26:39–40	The added passage, inserted on a typed (double-spaced) slip, incorporates the anecdote of TH and his mother in disguise mentioned in JMB's letter to FEH of 26 March 1928; also the detail of the accordion, noted (as a "concertina") in FEH's diary shortly before TH's death and in fact repeated by her in the final chapter of *LY* (see pp. 478–9).
27:5	*worried at.* Alteration to *EL* reading "worried by" suggested by JMB, letter of 24 June 1928.
*28:18–19	Passage inserted on typed (double-spaced) slip; JMB owned TH's copy of (correctly) *The Boy's Own Book* and mentioned the anecdote in his letter of 26 March 1928.
*29:23–4	Paragraph omitted on the grounds of its being typed (double-spaced) on a separate slip and affixed to TS2 in the same fashion as other changes (see notes to 26:39–40 and 28:18–19) made in response to JMB's letter of 26 March 1928. Since, however, that letter did not in fact mention TH's dislike of being touched, the evidence is not conclusive and the passage could have been inserted on TH's own authority—although it is perhaps significant that JMB referred particularly to this anecdote in a speech delivered shortly after the publication of *EL*: Barrie, *M'Connachie and J. M. B.* (London, 1938) 158.
*30:27–9	Additional paragraphs typed (double-spaced) on separate slip affixed to TS2; JMB mentioned Louisa Harding in his letter of 26 March 1928 and supplied a revised wording for the last two sentences in his letter of 24 June 1928. Prior to JMB's revision the penultimate paragraph ended, "from Louisa, and a wildly beating heart on his part", and the final paragraph ended, "death, and a nameless green mound in the corner of Mellstock Churchyard was visited more than once by one to whom a boyish dream had never lost its radiance".
†32:13–14	First word of earlier reading ("and somewhat above the level of the ordinary country architect") left uncancelled.
*32:35–6	Paragraph omitted on the grounds of its being typed (double-

spaced) on a separate slip affixed to TS2 in the same manner as changes made subsequently to JMB's letter of 26 March 1928—although JMB himself does not mention Barnes. Cf. entry at 29:23–4.

†37:33 Editorial emendation for sake of clarification; *EL* chooses a more elaborate solution.

38:15 *not small*. Cancelled in TS2 (clearly by TH) is a brief remark about TH's use of translations (see *PN*, 218).

*43:9–10 In his letter of 26 March 1928 JMB asked if there were any surviving letters of TH's written from London between 1862 and 1867. FEH subsequently found that Kate Hardy had five such letters, and four of these were included in *EL*. Those dated 19 February [1863] and 19 December 1863 are typed on four separately numbered pages inserted (not bound) into TS2; those dated 17 August 1862 and (see 53:30–1 below) 28 October 1865 must have been added to the proofs.

*44:36 JMB, in his letter of 24 June 1928, pointed out that in the newly-added letter of 19 February [1863] TH spoke of his having travelled on the Underground Railway; JMB also suggested the new wording incorporated into *EL*.

*45:1 Another correction prompted by a suggestion of JMB's in his 24 June 1928 letter.

*46:7 Revised wording supplied by JMB, 24 June 1928.

*47:40–1 Cancelled in TS2, presumably at TH's instigation, this passage was restored following JMB's reference to the episode in his letter of 26 March 1928.

49:21 *by 1866 to send*. The first surviving leaf of TS1 begins with these words.

*51:19 Quotation marks inserted in TS1, but not certainly by TH.

*51:20 As preceding note.

53:6 *views that*. Although TS1 (like *EL*) reads "views which" the alteration appears to be in SCC's hand.

*53:30–1 See note at 43:9–10 above and JMB's letter to FEH of 17 May 1928 in Viola Meynell (ed.) *Letters of J. M. Barrie* (London, 1942) 152.

54:26 *inconvenienced by it*. Struck through in TS2 at this point, probably but not certainly in TH's lifetime, are the words "through his plans and elevations not getting finished as promptly as before".

†63:8 Caret for insertion wrongly placed in TS2.

†63:9 As preceding note.

*63:27 This revision is made in TS1, but almost certainly in SCC's hand.

65:2 *undertaken to begin*. Cancelled at this point in TS2 by a single straight line, possibly not reflecting a decision of TH's, are the words "since Hardy had already had a hand in them while Hicks was living".

72:fn [1] *The verses . . . forgotten it*. Though typed on a separate slip, this footnote is unlike the additions prompted by JMB in being

(a) single-spaced and (b) affixed to the TS2 page not at the outer edge but at the gutter. It has been accepted as probably Hardyan.

74 : 10   *donkeys [word illegible] employed.* ELH's MS (in DCM) appears in fact to read "donkeys were numerously employed".

* 76 : 12–14   Sentence cancelled in TS1, apparently by FEH.

* 77 : 1–4   Though the *EL* reading appears in TS1 it is not a clearly Hardyan revision; indeed, the entire sentence, beginning at "His own wooing", may have been inserted after TH's death.

81 : 21–32   *His hosts . . . impossible to say.* Although this passage is typed (double-spaced) on a separate slip and affixed to the outer edge of the TS2 page in the same fashion as the insertions recommended by JMB, it is on different paper and uses a different coloured carbon. It has therefore been accepted as probably Hardyan—as, indeed, its style and content strongly suggest.

* 87 : 8–9   Though this passage is not typed on a separate slip but inscribed (apparently by FEH) on both TS2 and TS1, it has been omitted from this edition on the basis of Barrie's recommendation (26 March 1928) that reference be made to the "gate in the field" where TH was "sad about his prospects". See also p. 450.

†96 : 34   Editorial solution to the problem created by the lack of an antecedent for TS2's "it".

* 103 : 7–10   TH's erroneous account of Mrs Procter's background was struck through in TS1, evidently in response to a pencilled note (by E. M. Forster?) which pointed out that she was in fact the daughter by a previous marriage of Basil Montagu's third wife.

†105 : 18–19   TS1 reading editorially adopted; in TS2 these same words have been wrongly inserted within a similar construction one line lower down.

†105 : 19–20   See preceding note.

106 : 17   *Their . . . compass.* Inserted in TS2 in FEH's hand, quite possibly after TH's death. The goods sent to the warehouse must, in fact, have been those the Hardys did not need, or for which they did not have room, at Newton Road.

108 : 6–25   *However, . . . ones."* This entire passage is typed (double-spaced) on a separate sheet and tipped in at the gutter of the bound TS2 (cf. foregoing note at 72 : fn); that it is TH's is confirmed by the presence of an annotation in his hand at the foot of the inserted sheet.

109 : 21–40   *one rather . . . tenderness.* Though typed on a separate slip and fixed to the outer edge of the TS2 page in much the same manner as the insertions prompted by JMB, this passage is single-spaced and contains a small holograph correction almost certainly in TH's hand; its style and content, in any case, point almost irresistibly to its being TH's work.

* 129 : 5–6   Substitution of initial and dash for the full place-name in both TS2 and TS1 seems to have been made by someone other than

TH and perhaps not upon his instructions; the cancelled words have been reinstated as certainly authorial and as possibly reflecting TH's final intentions.

* 129 : 6   As preceding note.

142 : 8   *orange-smells*. The revision to "orange-peel" in TS2 seems to have been made in a hand other than TH's or FEH's.

151 : 6   *be : This as a matter*. It is possible that the original beginning of this sentence ("be: John the Baptist, Paul and others might also have been introduced, to the exclusion of greater men, as a matter") was cancelled after TH's death.

154 : 8   "*Llanherne*". TS2 originally read "Lanherne", which seems to have been correct; it is unclear whether it was TH or FEH who inserted the second "l" here and in the following sentence.

† 158 : 13–14   Inserted into TS1 in TH's hand.

† 158 : 14–15   Inserted into TS1 in a hand that is almost certainly TH's.

† 160 : 34   Editorial solution to confusion in the copy-text apparently caused by an uncompleted revision.

* 161 : 17   Revision made in TS2 but almost certainly after TH's death.

* 164 : 18   The words "an old" were cancelled in TS2, probably during TH's lifetime; their reappearance in *EL* presumably resulted from a failure to transfer the alteration from TS2 to the corresponding (and now missing) page of TS1.

165 : 14   *about it*. Cancelled in TS2, almost certainly at TH's instigation, are the words " 'Yours truly,/ 'Thomas Hardy.' "

175 : 13   *unconscious propensity?"* These two words represent a condensation, clearly at TH's instigation, of what was originally a much longer conclusion to the note being transcribed; see *PN*, 224 and n.

* 175 : 39   Though *EL* offers a possible emendation, the reading of TS2, an insertion in TH's own hand, has been retained.

* 180 : 7–181 : 1   The *EL* passage is in fact present in TS2—but on three (typed) leaves which are not bound in with the remainder of the TS but attached by a paper-clip and which bear no holograph markings of any kind. This physical evidence that the entire passage must have been inserted after TH's death is strongly reinforced by the nature of the contents.

187 : 30–1   *Bret . . . them for*. So TS2, written in by FEH above the uncancelled reading "H. Reeve, Editor of the Edinburgh, all these for"; the inserted references to Reeve at 188 : 18–23 make it clear that his name was meant to be removed at this point.

190 : 27–8   *Barnes's poems*. Cancelled in TS2 at this point, probably but not certainly by TH, is the following paragraph: "At the beginning of December he attended a meeting in Dorchester for considering a memorial to the poet. Various ideas were broached—a middle-Gothic cross, a Runic cross, to stand at the branching roads near his residence,—but ultimately other counsel prevailed, and a bronze statue was selected, and executed by Mr Roscoe Mullins."

* 199 : 24   TH's meaning in this passage was perhaps best expressed by

	the original TS2 reading, "that we only admire", which he himself seems to have revised.
* 202 : 20	The inserted "or over" in TS2 appears to be in SCC's hand.
† 204 : 21	As *EL* correctly asserts, "The Bridge of Lodi" appeared in *Poems of the Past and the Present*, not with the other "Napoleonic" pieces in *Wessex Poems*.
208 : 31–210 : 37	*May 29. Instance . . . of Paradise."* Two versions of this material, each occupying four pages, are bound into TS2, the second incorporating revisions made in the first; the retyped pages probably date from after TH's death and since, in any case, only the first version carries markings in TH's hand it has been chosen as copy-text at this point.
* 209 : 26	This cancellation was perhaps made during TH's lifetime.
210 : 6	*gaily enough. At some houses the scene.* Cancelled—probably but not certainly by TH—in the first TS2 version (see note at 208 : 31, absent from the second, is the following passage: "gaily enough at dinners, crushes, luncheons and other functions, where they encountered a great many people of every sort, title, and fame. At one dinner, Lord Lytton's, he entered the adjoining house by mistake, the door standing open and the hall being brilliantly lighted, and did not discover his error till he got upstairs. At some houses such as Lady Halifax's, and the Hon. Meynell Ingram's, the scene".
† 210 : 8	This revision, effected in the second TS2 version (see note at 208 : 31), was necessitated by the cancellation noted at 210 : 6.
* 220 : 20	Alteration made in TS2, but apparently in JMB's hand.
* 220 : 21	Another TS2 alteration apparently by JMB.
* 223 : 5	TS2 insertion of "who was" apparently in a hand other than TH's or FEH's (JMB's?).
223 : 25	*"O richest.* Cancelled in TS2, almost certainly in TH's lifetime, is the reading, " 'Think of that, O richest'."
228 : 29	*at Frampton.* The abandoned reading "of Frampton" stands uncancelled in TS2.
230 : 31	*deeper deep')."* Cancelled at this point in TS2, probably though not certainly during TH's lifetime, is the following paragraph: "There does not appear to be any possible personal reason for his quoting this at this moment."
* 234 : 11	It is not clear whether the specific date given in *EL* was derived from a consultation of TH's original notebook entry or from a calculation based on knowledge of the date of Tryphena Gale's death.
* 236 : 26	TS1 has the *EL* reading, but not in TH's hand.
237 : 5–6	*relation to existence.* TH's responsibility for the TS2 cancellation at this point of a paragraph quoting a letter from Edmund Gosse (see *PN*, 233) seems confirmed by the heavy over-scoring of the same passage in TS1.
239 : 16	*able to follow them.* Cancelled in TS2 at this point, probably though not certainly by TH, is the following paragraph: "After meeting a few more people, including Sir Henry Thompson,

Lord Pembroke, Lady Waterlow, and Mr Nelson Page, he returned to Dorset, having the day before been to a military exhibition where he mused over Colonel Champion's sword, which had never been unsheathed since the Battle of Inkermann when, wounded, he sheathed it and it had stuck to the scabbard immoveable afterwards."

† 240:16   TS2 originally read, "so many of such gay Parisians"; when "such" was changed to "similar" the "of" was left uncancelled.

241:21–2   *of the poet.)"* As at 237:5–6 (above) TS1 clearly confirms TH's responsibility for the deletion at this point in TS2 of a note about ELH as the object of another woman's envy (see *PN*, 233).

* 242:2   TS2 cancellation of "M.A." (present, uncancelled, in TS1) almost certainly post-Hardyan

† 246:39   The correction is in fact made in TS1, possibly by TH; some confusion seems to remain in the sentence, however.

* 249:4   The "W" cancelled in TS2, perhaps not by TH.

* 250:26   This is evidently the correct location for this sentence, which has in fact been inserted at a point between "original" and "MS." in the previous line of TS2—where it stands uncancelled.

† 251:24–8   Although this note is entirely absent from TS2 it is so clearly Hardyan that it seems reasonable to speculate that TH may have transcribed it from a notebook into TS1 (of which the relevant page is missing) without also transcribing it into TS2. For a Hardyan passage present in TS1 but not in TS2, see note at 158:13–14.

* 252:7–10   The original reading of TS2 has been cancelled (not by TH) and the first part of the substituted passage (to "a wheelbarrow") typed on a separate slip in the same manner as the earlier responses to suggestions by JMB, whose letter of 26 March 1928 specifically recommended inclusion of this episode. The remaining three sentences were evidently added to the proofs of *EL* following JMB's recommendation, 24 June 1928, that reference also be made to the *Graphic*'s refusal to print the christening episode.

[End of *Early Life*; *Later Years* begins]

253:1   *PART V.* At the top of the first text page of the second bound volume of the typescript TH has written (in TS3): "*Mem:/Vol. II. might begin here—if 2 vols./* [Number of typoscript pages in the whole, probably about 650, or under, when/ finished, which at 230 words each page makes 150,000—(a fair length for a biography.)]" The same notation, slightly differently phrased, appears in TS2 in FEH's hand.

* 255:1   The original chapter numbers were, of course, changed for *LY*, sometimes in TS2 itself; subsequent changes in chapter numbers will not be recorded.

255 : 12	*of it, bearing.* Cancelled in TS2, probably but not certainly at TH's instigation, is the reading, "of it, such distortion of the truth bearing".
256 : 23–257 : 2	"*As I . . . fault with.*" These paragraphs seem to have been neither conceived nor sent as part of a letter, and they have not been treated as such.
*262 : 13	The "quickly" inserted in TH's hand into both TS2 and TS3 presumably represented, at least in part, a justification for his not being present at his father's death.
* 262 : 28	TH refers not to any knightly forbears but to members of the Knight family; his great-grandfather, John Hardy, married Jane Knight in 1777 (and see *PN*, 43–5).
263 : 41	*Dorset family.*" Deleted in TS2 and TS3 at this point, clearly by TH, is a paragraph about sending "A Tryst at an Ancient Earthwork" to Clement Shorter (see *PN*, 237–8).
264 : 36	*an old and lonely widow.* As originally typed, this read "an old woman"; in TS2 TH inserted "and lonely widow" but failed to delete "woman", as he had done in TS3, leaving the TS2 deletion to be made subsequently in red ink.
271 : 22–3	*since the murders.* Alongside this passage in TS3 has been affixed a cutting from the *Sunday Times* of 18 July 1926, celebrating the 88th birthday of Sir George Otto Trevelyan and recalling his discovery of Lord Frederick Cavendish's blood-stained coat upon arriving to assume the dead Secretary's office.
271 : 27–8	*Talked to . . . Court.*" TH's substitution in TS2 for a brief cancelled passage about the Viceroy's ordering "The Queen" to be played as a signal that people might leave (see *PN*, 239).
272 : 10	*same evening.*" The following paragraph—inserted into TS2 at this point by FEH, absent from TS3, and never incorporated into *LY*—seems certainly post-Hardyan, but of sufficient interest (not least for its remark on TH's writing in collaboration) to be recorded here: "The chief significance of Hardy's visit to Dublin was his meeting there with Mrs Arthur Henniker (Florence Henniker) who became afterwards one of his closest and most valued friends, remaining so until her death many years after. As befitted the daughter of Monkton Milnes (Lord Houghton) she had a love of the best in literature, and was herself a writer of novels and short stories, none of which, unfortunately, ever received the recognition which, in Hardy's opinion, they undoubtedly deserved. Some of his best short poems were inspired by her, and the only time he ever wrote in collaboration was with her in a short story, 'The Spectre of the Real'."
* 272 : 13	Although the *LY* reading is present in TS2 it appears to be a post-Hardyan insertion; it is not found in TS3.
* 272 : 14	As preceding note.
* 272 : 36	The passage from Mrs Henniker's letter has been inscribed by FEH on a separate leaf of lined paper and slipped, not bound, into TS2; it is absent from TS3. The inclusion of this material in

LY probably dates from FEH's March 1928 consultation of Barrie as to the feasibility of inserting some of Mrs Henniker's letters: see Viola Meynell (ed.) *Letters of J. M. Barrie* (London, 1942) 153–4.

†* 274 : 12　　The original reading, "This month", was changed in TS2 by FEH to accommodate the deletion of 274 : 5–11; TH wrote to *L'Ermitage* 14 August 1893.

* 279 : 19–20　　*LY* here corrects a TS2 error: the book was called *South Sea Bubbles*; its authors were named on the title-page as "The Earl and the Doctor", viz., Lord Pembroke, the 13th Earl, and Dr George Henry Kingsley.

* 284 : 17–18　　*LY* reading present in TS2 but in a hand other than TH's (and apparently not FEH's); absent from TS3.

285 : 6　　*Two on a Tower*. Perhaps a post-Hardyan intervention by the same hand as noted at 284 : 17–18; TS3 still reads "one of the novels".

288 : 26　　*all this*. The TS2 revision "much adverse criticism"— evidently made in light of the proposed, and eventually effected, post-Hardyan cancellation of 287 : 15–288 : 6—was not in the end transferred to *LY*.

†* 289 : 6–19　　TS2 (only) carries in FEH's hand the instruction "Insert 3 letters Defence of 'Jude the Obscure.'", a reference to T. J. Wise's privately printed pamphlet, *A Defence of Jude the Obscure . . . In Three Letters to Sir Edmund Gosse, C.B.* (Edinburgh, 1928), the source of the three letters incorporated into *LY* at this point. The letter to the *Animals' Friend* is present only in TS3, having been excised from TS2 at the same time (after TH's death) as it was decided to insert the three letters to Gosse; the truncated leaf remains bound in with the remainder of TS2.

290 : 16　　*of either*. . . TS2, fol. 383, bears at this point a marginal note in FEH's hand, "[Insert typed pages of letters—383a—etc]"; no fol. 383a now survives, but it appears that letters additional to the three addressed to Gosse were to have been introduced.

293 : 23　　*as will be seen*. The page of TS2 on which this paragraph appears cannot have been typed earlier than November 1924, the date of the first performance of TH's stage-version of *Tess*; the two corrections on the page appear to be in TH's hand, however.

293 : 35–7　　*was as . . . 1896*. The reordering of this information in TS2 (only) is clearly post-Hardyan.

* 298 : 14–15　　This post-Hardyan revision appears in TS2 (only) as "Certain unimportant social events".

† 299 : 1　　This Hardyan revision reappears in TS1, although it was never transferred to TS2.

303 : 20–1　　*the theory . . . woman—as*. So TS2, as revised in TH's hand; TS3, also revised by TH, reads, "the theory that the real is not the ideal beloved one, who only exists in the lover—as".

* 304 : 23　　The additional phrase in *LY*, "—a thing terrible to think of", was part of the text of TH's actual letter, but it has been erased from TS3 and is present in TS2 only in FEH's hand.

305:9	*our tongue.* TH himself deleted from both TS2 and TS3 at this point an additional sentence from the letter to Swinburne (see *P.N.,* 247).
†* 313:25–6	Inserted into TS3 by TH in green crayon; evidently a late addition never transferred to TS2 or TS1.
314:21	*with Mrs Hardy.* In TS2 these words were replaced by "then" in FEH's hand—evidently after Hardy's death—but the change was apparently not transferred to TS1.
* 315:5–7	The *LY* reading, omitting any reference to ELH, was substituted in TS2 in FEH's hand.
316:2	*drily.* Cancelled in TS2 but not, apparently, by TH.
* 316:40–317:3	See note at 19:18.
317:21	*He went.* The "also" in the TS2 reading "He also went" appears to have been inserted simultaneously with the cancellation, almost certainly post-Hardyan, of the words "went . . . years, and".
* 317:32–6	The paragraph about Thompson's dinner was cancelled at the same time (after TH's death) as the 24 June letter was inserted, in FEH's hand, in TS2 only.
321:13	*I and my sisters.* So TS2 and TS3; evidently TH's adaptation of the correct reading, "As I and my sisters".
† 324:2–3	TH insertion in green crayon in TS3, not transferred to TS2 or (presumably) TS1.
* 324:32	Although the *LY* reading is present in TS2 (only), the revision, in FEH's hand, is almost certainly post-Hardyan.
* 324:33–4	As preceding note.
* 325:8–11	The first ten words are not cancelled in TS2; the remainder could conceivably have been cancelled by TH, but they remain uncancelled in TS3 and have therefore been included in this edition.
328:32	*April of this year.* On the verso of fol. 432 of both TS2 and TS3 there is a note, cancelled by TH, about watching a nesting blackbird on Easter Sunday, 15 April 1900; cf. the poem "I Watched a Blackbird".
329:6–20	*In a pocket-book . . . my meaning."* Although typed (double-spaced) on a separate slip affixed to TS2, this passage appears in TS3 as a separate slip in TH's holograph and must therefore have been inserted at his instigation.
* 332:22–3	These added paragraphs appear in neither TS2 nor TS3; the episode was one of those mentioned by JMB in his 26 March 1928 letter to FEH.
342:12–23	*It was . . . MDCCCCIII.* This passage was perhaps a post-Hardyan addition: although present in TS3, the hand in which it has been inscribed does not appear to be TH's, and in TS2 it has been inserted in FEH's hand.
* 342:23	Added sentence present in neither TS2 nor TS3.
* 344:35–6	Letter present in neither TS2 nor TS3; in the American edition of *LY* it appears a second time as the first item in Appendix III (274–5).
† 345:38	The letter was dated 27 June, published 28 June.

*348:38   *LY* reading present in TS2 (only) in FEH's hand, but almost certainly post-Hardyan.

[*350:fn]   The reference is to p. 139 of this edition.

†364:[6]   Excluded, despite its presence in TS2 in TH's hand, in view of the absence of corresponding notations elsewhere in the text. *LY* reads, "END OF PART II".

[*370:fn]   The reference is to p. 10 of this edition.

372:37–373:1   *same afternoon.* TS2 has at this point the (clearly post-Hardyan) insertion in FEH's hand, "Two days later the following letter was written to his friend Mrs Arthur Henniker". The letter in view—though not in fact transcribed—was presumably that of 24 May 1909, which contains several observations on the death of Meredith.

*375:2   Not an *LY* addition but a TH cancellation, in both TS2 and TS3, which appears not to have been transferred to the corresponding (now missing) leaf of TS1.

*375:4   As preceding note.

*376:6–14   The cancellation and insertion (in FEH's hand) seem to have been made simultaneously, in TS2 only; the second sentence of the insertion originally began, "With a touching simplicity Hardy".

*377:33–4   Present in neither TS2 nor TS3.

*383:5   The heavy TS2 and TS3 over-scoring (almost certainly in TH's lifetime) of "with his brother" seems not to have been transferred to TS1.

384:15   *his own judgment".* Cancelled in TS3 at this point, erased in TS2, are the words, "The allocation of the others may be mentioned here; if desirable."

385:4   *with other poems.* Inserted into TS2 (only) at this point in FEH's hand but for some reason not incorporated into *LY* is an additional sentence about Gloucester Cathedral (see *PN*, 260).

*385:17–18   Letter not present in either TS2 or TS3; the "friend" was evidently FEH (or Florence Dugdale, as she then was).

389:24   *in the preparation.* The first surviving leaf of the printer's copy for *LY* (TS1, fol. 512) begins with these words; fols. 512–14 of TS1 and TS2 have been retyped but carry subsequent revisions in TH's hand.

390:13–14   *pass-degree, which . . . discovery.* Recoverable from TS3 is the discarded original reading, "pass-degree, which was only frustrated by an accident, added to the discovery".

391:4   *Blandford, 1825".* Cancelled by TH in TS3 at this point (and absent altogether from the corresponding, retyped, page of TS2) is a sentence referring to a picnic on Egdon Heath and the submission of copy for *A Changed Man* (see *PN*, 262).

391:13   *Mr Frederic Harrison.* Cancelled by TH in TS3 at this point (and absent altogether from the corresponding, retyped, page of TS2) is a reference to the film of *Tess* by the Famous Players Film Company (see *PN*, 262).

391:32   *on the occasion.* Cancelled by TH in TS3 at this point (and absent altogether from the corresponding, retyped, page of TS2) is a reference to TH's having seen the Weymouth performance of *The Woodlanders* play (see *PN*, 262, where "for weeks" should read "a few weeks").

*392 : 5–18 JMB, writing to FEH 4 April 1928 (typed transcript, DCM), suggested that she should keep her marriage "as a sacred thing" to herself and mention only the fact of its occurrence.

*392 : 19–23 *LY* reading present in TS2 as a clearly post-Hardyan revision in FEH's hand.

393 : 14–15 *Hardy's writing at this date.* It is not clear whether TH wrote these remarks as a letter or, as here assumed, as a series of notes.

*396 : 23–30 Although the *LY* reading is present, in FEH's hand, in both TS2 and TS1, no such revision has been made in TS3.

396 : 24 *title, went for them.* The last surviving leaf of TS3 ends with these words.

396 : 29 *critics.* A possibly post-Hardyan revision for "reviewers".

396 : 37 *and would.* This apparently Hardyan revision for "and hence he would" was not transferred to TS1.

403 : 9–10 *of a story–the whole.* In TS2 "were also sent" has been inserted after "story—the remnant of an abandoned post-Hardyan revision.

403 : 27 *his first marriage.* FEH's (post-Hardyan?) alteration of "first" to "earlier" in TS2 was not transferred to TS1.

404 : 19 *from it in Hymns.* So TS2 (and TS1), though the words "it in" may well constitute a post-Hardyan insertion.

404 : 39 *some very good reviews.* Cancelled in TS2 and blanked over by a piece of paper in TS1—evidently by TH or upon his instructions—are some adverse comments upon even these favourable responses to *Selected Poems* (see *PN*, 265).

*407 : 34 Inscribed in FEH's hand in both TS2 and TS1; *LY* omits the additional sentence, "On that occasion beside the host there were present Mr Arnold Bennett, Mr G. B. Shaw, Mr & Mrs H. G. Wells and the Hardys".

408 : 2 *and came home.* Heavily overscored (clearly by TH) at this point in both TS2 and TS1 is a note about falling leaves (see *PN*, 266).

408 : 33–4 *cutting and critical.* FEH's (post-Hardyan) substitution, "outspoken", was not transferred to TS1 or *LY*.

409 : 9 *Went to bed at eleven.* The original reading "to bed ill" has been changed in FEH's hand in both TS2 and TS1; TH seems to have been perfectly well at this date, and "ill" was perhaps a typing error for "at 11" or "11" in TH's MS.

†409 : [15] Neither in TS2 nor in TS1—of which the last surviving leaf concludes at this point—is this clearly a Hardyan reading. See also note at 364 : [6].

411 : 1–2 *PART VIII./Life's Decline.* This was perhaps a division (and title) created by FEH when preparing *LY* for publication; there is some indication that TH thought of Part VIII as beginning with Chapter XXXV; see note at 418 : 1.

*413:14-15 *LY* reading present as a (clearly post-Hardyan) revision by FEH in TS2.

417:29 *of his own."* TS2 concludes at this point (apart from three separately paginated leaves headed "Synopsis of Remainder of Book.") with the typed note, "(From hereabout the writing is mostly in the form of Memoranda only. F.E.H.)" A note by TH on stiff brown paper, slipped into TS2 between fols. 544 and 545, reads, "The MS. is in approximately printable condition to here (p. 545)".

418:1 *CHAPTER XXXV.* MN1 and MN3 ("Memoranda & Notes towards completing the remainder of Vol. II") begin at this point. A slip in TH's hand inserted between the cover and the first page of MN1 reads, "From this point (Part VIII. Chap XXXV. p. 546) to the end, the compilation is mostly in the form of undigested Memoranda, requiring critical consideration as to what biographical particulars should be retained, differently expressed or omitted." A similar slip, written by TH in pencil, appears at the beginning of MN3; the accompanying initials "F.E.H." seem also to be in TH's hand.

*420:4-6 This discrepancy seems to have been the result of a setting error in *LY.*

*421:22-3 Additional words inserted in both MN3 (in red ink) and MN1 in FEH's hand, evidently after TH's death.

*421:25 As preceding note.

*422:13-14 Letter present in neither MN3 nor MN1, although the former has a note in FEH's hand, "[Insert letter to Mrs Arthur Henniker]".

*422:23-4 Addition inserted in FEH's hand into MN1 only, hence very probably post-Hardyan.

*423:3-4 FEH insertion into MN3 only; probably but not certainly post-Hardyan.

*425:29-36 The wording of this passage in MN1 is slightly different.

428:33-4 *These were . . . built.* The longest of several late TH additions to this speech in MN3; not present in MN1.

*430:7-28 It seems possible that no letter was in fact sent and that TH adopted the form in order to justify inclusion of these observations—to which he made a number of late changes (in red crayon) in MN3. Cf. the similar comments on p. 322 of this edition.

430:29-30 *the brief entry.* MN3 adds, in FEH's hand, "repeated so often in his diaries".

*432:13-14 Speech of Public Orator not present in any of the three typescripts.

*432:23-7 Charles Morgan's contribution is present only in MNR.

434:10 *'Which . . . one Duke?"* So MN1; MN3 has been revised (not by TH) to read, "'Three O. M.'s equal one Duke?'"

*434:10-11 Not present in MN1; inserted into MN3 in FEH's hand, almost certainly after TH's death.

*437:13-19 Letter present in MN3 and MN1; also in MNR, where an introductory sentence is supplied: "Like many other literary men Hardy constantly received letters from unknown correspondents, and as years advanced he was quite unable to reply to these. The following letter from an irate stranger caused him genuine amusement:".

*437 : 26   Not present in any of the three typescripts.

437 : 32   *Charley excellently.*" It was apparently TH himself who cancelled at this point in MN3 the sentence, "The dramatic company were entertained at Max Gate later in the month".

439 : 10   *It seems strange that.* The last surviving leaf of MNR breaks off at this point.

*440 : 21–2   TH's holograph revision (for "reviewer") in both MN3 and MN1, altered to "writer" in FEH's hand—probably after his death.

†442 : [8]   For the omission of this reading—present, typed, in both MN3 and MN1, see note at 364 : [6]. Both MN3 and MN1 conclude here. In the former TH has written in pencil, "[The rest is in small Note books of Memoranda beginning 1921]'. The corresponding note in MN1, "[Refer to Note-Book of Memoranda beginning 1921, for continuation.]", is in TH's hand, in ink, but has been cancelled. Loosely inserted in MN3 at this point is a slip of exercise-book paper on which TH has written, in green crayon: "Last words of book:—Hardy often said that a poet's writings could not be judged till the last line had been written, which was the death of the author. The opinion was particularly true of his own poetry, and indeed of all his productions." See p. 325 of this edition.

†453 : 38   Reading of Elton's MS. (DCM) editorially adopted.

†454 : 2   As preceding note.

†455 : 1   As preceding note.

†455 : 25   As preceding note. *LY* omits Elton's previous sentence, "As well as many generous things, there are one or two hard things said, deservedly enough, of Oxford in *Jude the Obscure*, but it was clear that it was a great pleasure to Hardy to be a member of one of its Colleges."

463 : 4   *Mr and Mrs Hardy, a friend.* A separately typed copy of this letter (DCM) reads at this point, "Mr and Mrs Hardy, a press representative (more or less) smuggled in as a 'critic', a friend".

†463 : 30   Reading of separate copy of letter (see preceding note) editorially adopted.

480 : 4   *increased daily.* The typed drafts of Chapter XXXVIII have at this point the reading, "increased daily, and there was slight bladder trouble, from which Hardy had suffered more or less ever since his serious illness in 1880."

481 : 9   *before the end.* The drafts of Chapter XXXVIII have at this point the reading, "before the end, when a few broken sentences, one of these heartrending in its poignancy, showed that his mind had reverted to a sorrow of the past."

†485:4	Reading of Harold Child's own MS. of this Appendix (DCM) editorially adopted.
486:12	*H.C.* Initials of Harold Child.
†487:14–15	Reading of Saleeby's transcription of this letter (DCM) editorially adopted.
†487:19	As preceding note.
†488:17	As preceding note.
†489:7	As preceding note.
†489:26	As preceding note.

Biographical Index

A., J. *See* Antell, John.
"Abbey Mason, The" (poem), 385
Abbotsbury, 396
à Beckett, Gilbert Arthur (1837–91, comic writer, author of *Ali-Baba and the Forty Thieves*; *D.N.B.*), 55
Abercorn, Mary Anna Hamilton, Duchess of (d. 1929, dau. of 1st Earl of Howe, w. of 2nd Duke of Abercorn), 230, 258
Aberdeen, 347–8, 461
Aberdeen, John Campbell Gordon, 7th Earl of (1847–1934, statesman; *D.N.B.*), 349
Abingdon, Mary Bertie, Dowager Countess of (d. 1757, dau. of James Gould of Dorchester, m. 1st General Charles Churchill and 2nd Montagu Bertie, 2nd Earl of Abingdon), 379
"Absolute Explains, The" (poem), 460
Academy, ["periodical"] 303, 371
Academy and Literature, 338
"According to the Mighty Working" (poem), 421
Acland, John Edward (1848–1932, curator of Dorset County Museum 1904–32), 384
Adair, Cornelia (d. 1922, widow of John George Adair of Rathdaire), 266, 281
Adam of St.-Victor (d. between 1177 and 1192, author of Latin sequences), 329
Adam, Robert (1728–92, architect, with his brothers built the Adelphi, London, 1769–71; *D.N.B.*), 42, 248

Adams, William Henry (aged 29 in 1851, butler to Francis P. B. Martin, q.v.), 43
Addison, Joseph (1672–1719, essayist, poet, and statesman; *D.N.B.*), 11, 108, 212
Adelaide (1792–1849, queen of William IV; *D.N.B.*), 216
Aeschylus (525–456 B.C., Greek tragic poet and dramatist), 37, 38, 256, 260, 414, 427, 459
Affpuddle, 10
"Afternoon Service at Mellstock" (poem), 23
Aide, Charles Hamilton (1826–1906, author and musician; *D.N.B.*), 266, 272, 327
Ainsworth, William Harrison (1805–82, novelist; *D.N.B.*), 30
Airlie, Henrietta Blanche Ogilvy, Countess of (d. 1921, dau. of 2nd Baron Stanley of Alderley, w. of 5th Earl of Airlie), 210
Aix-les-Bains, 194
Albert, Prince (1869–1931, 2nd s. of Prince and Princess Christian of Schleswig-Holstein, grandson of Queen Victoria), 385
Aldeburgh, 280, 331, 351, 373, 374, 378, 492
Alden, Henry Mills (1836–1919, American author and editor, edited *Harper's Magazine* 1869–1919), 287, 377
Alexander the Great (356–323 B.C., king of Macedonia), 160
Alexandra (1844–1925, eldest dau. of Prince and Princess Christian of Schleswig-Holstein, queen-